Lecture Notes in Artificial Intelligence   3528

Edited by J. G. Carbonell and J. Siekmann

Subseries of Lecture Notes in Computer Science

T0122452

Piotr S. Szczepaniak   Janusz Kacprzyk
Adam Niewiadomski (Eds.)

Advances in
Web Intelligence

Third International Atlantic Web Intelligence Conference
AWIC 2005
Lodz, Poland, June 6-9, 2005
Proceedings

Series Editors

Jaime G. Carbonell, Carnegie Mellon University, Pittsburgh, PA, USA
Jörg Siekmann, University of Saarland, Saarbrücken, Germany

Volume Editors

Piotr S. Szczepaniak
Adam Niewiadomski
Technical University of Lodz, Institute of Computer Science
ul. Wólczańska 215, 93-005 Lodz, Poland
E-mail: {office, aniewiadomski}@ics.p.lodz.pl

Janusz Kacprzyk
Polish Academy of Sciences, Systems Research Institute
ul. Newelska 6, 01-447 Warsaw, Poland
E-mail: kacprzyk@ibspan.waw.pl

Library of Congress Control Number: 2005926883

CR Subject Classification (1998): I.2, H.3-5, C.2, J.1, J.2

ISSN   0302-9743
ISBN-10   3-540-26219-9 Springer Berlin Heidelberg New York
ISBN-13   978-3-540-26219-0 Springer Berlin Heidelberg New York

Springer is a part of Springer Science+Business Media

springeronline.com

© Springer-Verlag Berlin Heidelberg 2005
Printed in Germany

Typesetting: Camera-ready by author, data conversion by Scientific Publishing Services, Chennai, India
Printed on acid-free paper   SPIN: 11495772   06/3142   5 4 3 2 1 0

Preface

In recent years the Internet has become a source of data and information of indisputable importance and has immensely gained in acceptance and popularity. The World Wide Web (WWW or Web, for short), frequently named "the nervous system of the information society," offers numerous valuable services leaving no doubt about the significance of the Web in our daily activities at work and at home. Consequently, we have a clear aspiration to meet the obvious need for effective use of its potential by making improvements in both the methods and the technology applied. Among the new research directions observable in Web-related applications, intelligent methods from within the broadly perceived topic of soft computing occupy an important place.

AWIC, the "Atlantic Web Intelligence Conferences" are intended to be a forum for exchange of new ideas and novel practical solutions in this new and exciting field. The conference was born as an initiative of the WIC-Poland and the WIC-Spain Research Centres, both belonging to the Web Intelligence Consortium – WIC (http://wi-consortium.org/). So far, three AWIC conferences have been held: in Madrid, Spain (2003), in Cancun, Mexico (2004), and in Łódź, Poland (2005).

The book covers current noteworthy developments in the field of intelligent methods applied to various aspects and ways of Web exploration. However, a few contributions go beyond this frame, providing a wider and more comprehensive view on the subject matter. Originally, about 140 interesting papers were submitted, out of which only 74 contributions, selected in a peer-review process, are presented in this volume. Unfortunately, not all high-quality papers could be included in this volume due to space constraints. The material published in the book is divided into three main parts: papers presented by keynote speakers, contributions of conference participants, and workshop materials. Case studies and workshop materials are arranged in alphabetical order according to the name of the first author.

We deeply appreciate the efforts of the plenary speakers and thank them for their presentations. They are Profs. Witold Abramowicz (Poznań University of Economics, Poland), Jiming Liu (Hong Kong Baptist University, China), Roman Słowiński (Poznań University of Technology, Poland), and Ning Zhong (Maebashi Institute of Technology, Japan; President of the WIC). We are indebted to the reviewers for their reliability and hard work done in a short time. High appreciation is due to the Organizing Committee of the conference, with particular recognition of Mr. Wiktor Wandachowicz's (Technical University of Łódź, Poland) contribution to its accomplishments. Profs. Pilar Herrero, Maria S. Pérez-Hernández and Victor Robles from the Technical University of Madrid, Spain deserve special thanks for their excellent organization of the workshop that enriched the program of the conference. True thanks are also given to the series editor and to the Springer team for their friendly help. The invaluable patronage of Prof. Jan Krysiński, President of the Technical University of Łódź is gratefully acknowledged. The technical cooperation of the IEEE Computational Intelligence Society and the Berkeley Initiative in Soft Computing (BISC), USA is highly appreciated. Our hope is that each reader may find many motivating ideas in this volume.

April 2005

Piotr S. Szczepaniak
Janusz Kacprzyk
Adam Niewiadomski

Organization

Organizers

Institute of Computer Science, Technical University of Łódź, Poland
Systems Research Institute, Polish Academy of Sciences, Warsaw, Poland
Polish Cybernetic Society, Łódź Division
Polish Neural Networks Society

Technical Co-operation

IEEE Computational Intelligence Society
Web Intelligence Consortium (WIC)

Honorary Chair

Lotfi A. Zadeh, University of California, Berkeley, USA

Patron

Jan Krysiński—Rector, Technical University of Łódź, Poland

Chairmen

Piotr S. Szczepaniak, Technical University of Łódź, Poland
  and Systems Research Institute, Polish Academy of Sciences, Warsaw, Poland
Janusz Kacprzyk, Systems Research Institute, Polish Academy of Sciences, Warsaw,
  Poland

Steering Committee

Jesus Favela, CICESE, Mexico
Jiming Liu, Hong Kong Baptist University, Hong Kong, China
Masoud Nikravesh, University of California, Berkeley, USA
Javier Segovia, UPM, Madrid, Spain
Ning Zhong, Maebashi Institute of Technology, Maebashi-City, Japan

Advisory Committee

Lesław Gajek—Dean, Faculty of Technical Physics, Computer Science and Applied
    Mathematics, Technical University of Łódź, Poland
Liliana Byczkowska-Lipińska — Director, Institute of Computer Science, Technical
    University of Łódź, Poland
Leszek Rutkowski — President, Polish Neural Networks Society,
    and Technical University of Częstochowa, Poland
Jacek Zurada — President, IEEE Computational Intelligence Society

Scientific Secretary

Adam Niewiadomski, Institute of Computer Science, Technical University of Łódź,
    Poland

Program Committee

Witold Abramowicz	Poznań University of Economics, Poznań, Poland
Ricardo Baeza-Yates	University of Chile, Chile
Patrick Brezillon	Université Paris 6, Paris, France
Alex Buchner	University of Ulster, UK
Edgar Chávez	Universidad Michoacana, Mexico
Pedro A. da Costa Sousa	Uninova, Portugal
Lipika Dey	Indian Institute of Technology, New Delhi, India
Santiago Eibe	UPM, Madrid, Spain
Jesus Favela	CICESE, Mexico
Michael Hadjimichael	Naval Resarch Laboratory, USA
Enrique Herrera Viedma	Universidad de Granada, Spain
Pilar Herrero	UPM, Madrid, Spain
Esther Hochsztain	ORT, Uruguay
Andreas Hotho	University of Karlsruhe, Germany
Janusz Kacprzyk	Systems Research Institute, Polish Academy of Sciences, Warsaw, Poland
Samuel Kaski	Helsinki University of Technology, Helsinki, Finland
Józef Korbicz	Technical University of Zielona Góra, Poland
Jacek Koronacki	Institute of Computer Science, Polish Academy of Sciences, Warsaw, Poland
Rudolf Kruse	Otto von Guericke University of Magdeburg, Magdeburg, Germany
Liliana Byczkowska-Lipińska	Technical University of Łódź, Poland
Jiming Liu	Hong Kong Baptist University, Hong Kong, China
Vincenzo Loia	University of Salerno, Salerno, Italy
Aurelio Lopez	INAOE, Mexico

Oscar Marban	UPM, Madrid, Spain
Oscar Mayora	ITESM-Morelos, Mexico
Ernestina Menasalvas	Technical University of Madrid, Spain
Socorro Millan	Universidad del Valle de Cali, Colombia
Bamshad Mobasher	DePaul University, Chicago, USA
Manuel Montes-y-Gomez	INAOE, Mexico
Alex Nanolopoulos	Aristotle University, Thessaloniki, Greece
Marian Niedźwiedziński	University of Łódź, Poland
Masoud Nikravesh	University of California, Berkeley, USA
Witold Pedrycz	University of Alberta, Canada
Maria S. Pérez-Hernández	UPM, Madrid, Spain
Mario Piattini	Universidad Castilla-La Mancha, Spain
Paulo Quaresma	Universidade de Evora, Portugal
Victor Robles	UPM, Madrid, Spain
Danuta Rutkowska	Technical University of Częstochowa, Poland
Leszek Rutkowski	Technical University of Częstochowa, Poland
Eugenio Santos	UPM, Madrid, Spain
Javier Segovia	UPM, Madrid, Spain
Andrzej Skowron	University of Warsaw, Poland
Roman Słowiński	Poznań University of Technology, Poznań, Poland
Myra Spiliopoulou	University of Magdeburg, Magdeburg, Germany
Ryszard Tadeusiewicz	AGH University of Science and Technology, Cracow, Poland
Kathryn Thornton	University of Durham, UK
Maria Amparo Vila	University of Granada, Spain
Anita Wasilewska	Stony Brook New York University, USA
Jan Węglarz	Poznań University of Technology, Poznań, Poland
Ronald Yager	Iona College, USA
Yiyu Yao	University of Regina, Canada
Sławomir Zadrożny	Systems Research Institute, Polish Academy of Sciences, Warsaw, Poland
Ning Zhong	Maebashi Institute of Technology, Japan
Wojciech Ziarko	University of Regina, Canada

Keynote Speakers

Witold Abramowicz	Poznań University of Economics, Poland
Jiming Liu	Hong Kong Baptist University, Hong Kong, China
Roman Słowiński	Poznań University of Technology, Poland
Ning Zhong	Maebashi Institute of Technology, Japan

Workshop Organizers

Pilar Herrero, Maria S. Pérez-Hernández, Victor Robles
    Universidad Politécnica de Madrid, Spain

Workshop Program Committee

José María Peña, UPM, Madrid, Spain
Mario Cannataro, University Magna Grécia, Catanzaro, Italy
Steve Chiu, Northwestern University, Chicago, USA
Eduardo Huedo, Centro de Astrobiologia CSIC-INTA, Madrid, Spain
José Luis Bosque, URJC, Madrid, Spain
Jemal Abawajy, Faculty of Science and Technology, Deakin University, Victoria,
    Australia
Ignacio M. Llorente, Universidad Complutense de Madrid, Spain
Alberto Sánchez, UPM, Madrid, Spain
Carole Goble, University of Manchester, UK
Chris Greenhalgh, University of Nottingham, UK
Steve Benford, University of Nottingham, UK
Djamila Ouelhadj, University of Nottingham, UK
Domenico Laforenza, Institute of Science and Information Technology, Pisa, Italy
Jan Humble, University of Nottingham, UK

Local Organizing Committee

Radoslaw Bednarski, Anna Czerkawska-Jasińska, Wiesława Józwa,
    Adam Niewiadomski,
Arkadiusz Tomczyk, Wiktor Wandachowicz
    Institute of Computer Science, Technical University of Łódź, Poland

Table of Contents

III   Workshop: Knowledge and Data Mining Grid

How Much Intelligence in the Semantic Web?

Witold Abramowicz, Tomasz Kaczmarek, and Krzysztof Węcel

The Poznań University of Economics,
Al. Niepodległości 10, 60-967 Poznań, Poland
{W.Abramowicz, T.Kaczmarek, K.Wecel}@kie.ae.poznan.pl

Abstract. The paper discusses the Semantic Web Information Retrieval from the perspective of classical Information Retrieval paradigms and new research carried out with the Semantic Web. It is focused on the impact of new Web incarnation on document indexing, query languages and query resolution, retrieval models and retrieval performance evaluation. Emerging issues are also mentioned: the role of semantic information in classical and SW enabled IR, reasoning and ontology operations necessary for Semantic Web Information Retrieval to function. The challenges of integration of a distributed knowledge base approach with classical document indexing techniques as a general framework for tackling Information Retrieval in new environment are discussed.

1   Background

The article has been written to raise some fundamental questions regarding new approach towards Information Retrieval in the Semantic Web, and give our outlook for the potential answers. The Semantic Web is a hot research topic nowadays. Many researches claim that Semantic Web will finally become more intelligent incarnation of what we know as WWW.

So far, information systems are not able to fully interpret peculiarities of the language that we use in a day-to-day life, nor can they transform it into logical structure with the same meaning. This basic flaw, among the others, makes it impossible to automatically process vast resources of textual information and use knowledge that lies in it. However, growing corpus and knowledge resources in a digital form demands automatic searching and retrieval. Not being able, at this time, to process textual information into artificial knowledge structures, we devise information retrieval to assist us in searching. The classical information retrieval is based on the idea that words reflect information concepts. Therefore it is assumed that the number of particular words that occur in a document reflect its informational content. Based on this the document index is constructed, which may be used in various information retrieval models [2, 12]. These models along with the documents' representations, user's queries, and ranking function, allow for presenting potentially relevant document to the user. However, none of these models goes beyond the idea of counting word occurrences.

There are other approaches that drop word-concept dependence, which leads to Latent Semantic Indexing model. It assumes that concepts are broader than words and therefore concepts should be indexed, which is argued to improve performance. The

P.S. Szczepaniak et al. (Eds.): AWIC 2005, LNAI 3528, pp. 1–6, 2005.

concept space obtained by singular value decomposition has significantly fewer dimensions than the space of terms in vector space model. LSI actually has not been widely accepted due to its impreciseness. Another approach that also is not based on words but is expected to improve precision is employment of the Semantic Web. This concept is developed in the remainder of the paper.

2   Semantic Web

The simplest understanding of the term Semantic Web is the following: a web where information can be 'understood' by machines. But in fact, as with every new topic, there is no common understanding about what SW is or what it should be. To be more precise, there are few notions among researchers that pursue this topic: starting from the vision introduced by Tim Berners-Lee in [4] and [3] up to current works on ontologies and web services. These views are accurately analysed in [14]. As authors point out, the expectations on what the SW should be can be divided into three main areas:

- SW viewed as an enormous digital library - the emphasis is on categorization and uniform access to resources,
- SW as an ultimate tool for dealing with information overload with agent technology - this is called "Knowledge Navigator" approach,
- SW as a distributed knowledge base or database - this approach has been recently chosen by W3C [18]; according to their activity statement "Semantic Web provides a common framework that allows data to be shared and reused".

The last approach - distributed knowledge base - is the only approach achievable with current advances in IT. The idea here is to make a first step, namely represent the data properly. Tim Berners-Lee envisioned early the description of information in the machine processable manner. His initial idea of utilizing knowledge embedded in vast Web resources, expressed in [4], is not denied with the current view on the Semantic Web issues. However putting this idea to life will not be painless. Numerous questions arise regarding the implementation. Just to name some of them:

- how to deal with inconsistencies in the knowledge base (or database) built upon the documents (information) from varying sources that use different approaches (ontologies). First, the issue of trust for a given source arises. Then there is a problem of merging numerous ontologies which is widely addressed in current research on ontologies (for various approaches see: [13], [7], [8], [6]). The outcome of this research is, that so far ontology merging can not be performed without knowledge engineer assistance.
- there may exist inconsistencies in the information arising from its time aspect. Numerous questions have different answers depending on time when they are asked (e.g. who is the president of US?) - these can be solved by incorporating time dimension into knowledge / data / retrieval models as it happened in data warehouses,
- similar problems to those encountered when trying to use metadata may occur. Current searching engines mostly ignore metadata as they were misused for commercial or other purposes. The same may happen with semantic information in

the Semantic Web. Misuse of semantic tags is potentially even more dangerous, as computer programs are even less capable of assessing the information truthfulness and information source reliability, than most of the human users. This problem can be dealt with certain constraints imposed on semantic tagging yet to be devised.

This means that the Semantic Web should be designed for programs to process information easier but still with human needs in mind.

3   Introducing Semantics

Knowledge resources volume grows faster than knowledge quantity so we should ask ourselves whether IR for SW should provide answers, like knowledge base systems, or documents potentially containing the answer, like information retrieval systems? The problems with obtaining single unified answer from the distributed and heterogeneous knowledge base were already mentioned, so our idea is that the system should return document set as an answer, leaving the unavoidable inconsistencies for human user to deal with.

Some steps have been made in IR for dealing with hidden semantics of phrases - these approaches used thesauri and clustering techniques. Introduction of ontologies at least partially solves the semantics issue and addresses three problems that IR had to face from its very beginning. The first one is the problem of synonyms - usually the IR system did not return pages that included synonyms for a query term (without the query term itself). This lowered *recall* and could be solved by query expansion using thesauri. The second typical problem is that of homonyms that impaired retrieval results by lowering *precision*. The famous problem of 'Jaguar' (car) versus 'jaguar' (cat) - can be solved using ontologies (that impose single meaning on concepts appearing within the document) and earlier IR systems tried to solve it by using clustering i.e. splitting the results into clusters with different semantics. [10] gives a brief overview of the concept-based techniques used in information retrieval. These techniques relate to the third problem of the classical IR systems, which is that the same term (with given meaning - lets assume that we are able to deal with homonyms) may occur in different contexts, from which only few were relevant for a given query.

Introduction of semantic tagging and, in particular, relationships between concepts, classes and objects in the SW could partially solve this problem There is ongoing research on the methods for automatic or semi-automatic semantic annotation of web pages (see for example [5]). Yet, giving promising results, those tools are far from maturity. Assuming that such tools will be available, and the web pages will be annotated, the introduction of such semantic tagging will have serious impact on the other information retrieval system components.

4   Taking Advantages of Semantics

4.1   Reasoning

We propose to explore the hypothesis, which says that search index for Semantic Web is a specific knowledge base. The Semantic Web requires operations on concepts and relations among them and logical reasoning. Such functionality is inherent to knowledge bases. However, such an approach faces some limitations. Documents may contain many facts and some of them may be contradictory. This can be usually resolved by a human, but poses problems for machines. Information retrieval systems for the Semantic Web become more like knowledge bases. The Semantic Web documents contain facts, the index of documents in IR system reflects them, the human user understands them, but numerous inconsistencies may arise in the index, which is not acceptable for traditional knowledge base. Moreover, such 'knowledge base' would not answer the queries, but return the documents, that potentially enclose the answer (the opposite approach is taken for example in [17] - given the unified ontology and a controlled environment it is possible to return consistent answers instead of documents).

It is important to notice here that with ontological queries any agent (or user) could use its own ontology for querying as long as the IR system is capable of translating it into the document index ontology. It would be unreasonable to demand from the users or agents that they know the ontology of an IR system.

The use of ontologies as a knowledge representation in SW results in the necessity for reasoning in the information retrieval for Semantic Web. This was obvious from the very beginning since Berners-Lee mentioned it in the Semantic Web roadmap in 1998 [4].

One may think that building single knowledge base is contradictory to the paradigm of Internet, which is decentralized in its nature. However, we do not intend to introduce one knowledge base for all documents and therefore it does not mean centralization. The idea is to reflect the contents of distributed knowledge bases in one index as Internet cataloguing and search engines do nowadays.

4.2   Query Resolution

The document indices build up a kind of knowledge base, and the query resolution mechanism should adopt reasoning techniques to fully utilize semantic tagging.

One may be tempted to create a single, unified ontology to index all documents stored in the repository in order to ease document management and query resolution. However, this is subject to serious obstacles and will be probably impossible in reality:

– the resulting universal ontology would be very complex and hard to manage; therefore there are many initiatives/societies that build domain ontologies (see [8] for problems with ontology management),
– imported documents usually are already annotated with other ontologies and re-indexing them with own ontology will result in knowledge loss; moreover it requires additional computation time,
– it is impossible to execute distributed search nor linking to external documents,
– every change in universal ontology may result in a need for re-indexing of all documents stored in the repository.

The IR system would have to deal with all the ontologies used in the indexed documents. Therefore, we need tools for dynamic merging of ontologies. *Dynamic* means that user can freely select ontologies that are most appropriate for the given searching task. Usually they are small, specialized and fine-grained ontologies.

The query resolution subsystem itself could receive query expressed in one of the known ontologies. For both, indexing and query resolution mechanisms it is essential to gather all the ontologies that are used in the documents and user queries. Since the ontologies are likely to overlap or mismatch it is necessary to perform ontology mapping that would allow matching the documents against queries within the single, unified framework. Therefore we suggest mapping during query resolution instead of mapping during document indexing, which leads to loss of felxibility.

5   Conclusions and Further Work

In this paper we presented a vision, what advantages for information retrieval may be expected by introduction of semantics, and what are possible problems to be dealt with. The semantics is assured by ontologies, which find their application in the Semantic Web.

We argue that the IR system for the SW should be able to:

– deal with large volumes of semantically tagged documents,
– cope with possible inconsistencies in the knowledge represented and in the ontologies used by various authors,
– address the issue of multiple (possibly overlapping) ontologies,
– adopt knowledge base techniques and reasoning to utilize the semantic tagging to the largest extent possible.

What we really expect from the IR systems for SW, is the improvement of the precision, one of classical measures for effectiveness of information retrieval or filtering. Since in the Semantic Web a lot of effort will be devoted to proper data and information description it is assumed that the precision of such result should be better than in the current IR systems. Such claims are supported by an early research described in [1], where it was found that the semantics-based search is superior to the keyword-based search in terms of both precision and recall.

The traditional recall is somewhat of less importance, if we are looking for an answer for certain questions. Retrieving 1000 documents stating the same as 10 documents would not improve the user's knowledge. However the IR for SW system could potentially have high recall, since it is capable to logically reason about the relevance of each of the indexed documents and therefore it does not miss any relevant document.

References

1. Aitken, S.; Reid, S.: Evaluation of an Ontology-Based Information Retrieval Tool. ECAI'00, Applications of Ontologies and Problem-Solving Methods, 2000
2. Bayeza-Yates, R.; Ribeiro-Neto, B.: Modern Information Retrieval. ACM Press, 1999
3. Berners-Lee, T.; Hendler, J.; Lassila, O.: The Semantic Web. Scientific American, May 2001, pp. 34-43.
4. Berners-Lee, T.; A roadmap to the Semantic Web. http://www.w3c.org/2001/sw/, Download 2004-06-23
5. Cimiano, P.; Handschuh, S.; Staab, S.: Towards self-annotating web. In: Proceedings of the 13th international conference on World Wide Web, New York, NY, USA, May 17-20, 2004
6. Das, S.; Shuster, K.; Wu, C.: Ontologies for Agent-Based Information Retrieval and Sequence Mining. In: Proceedings of the Workshop on Ontologies in Agent Systems (OAS02), held at the 1st International Joint Conference on Autonomous Agents and Multi-Agent Systems Bologna, Italy, July 15-19, 2002.

7. Ding, Y.; Fensel, D.; Klein, M.; Omelayenko, B.: Ontology Management: Storing, Aligning and Maintaining Ontologies. In: Davids, J.; Fensel, D.; van Harmelen, F. (Eds.): Towards the Semantic Web: Ontology-Driven Knowledge Management. Wiley, 2002, p. 47-69

8. Dou, D.; McDermott, D.; Qi, P.: Ontology translation by ontology merging and automated reasoning. In: Proceedings of EKAW Workshop on Ontologies for Multi-Agent Systems. Siguenza, Spain, 2002.

9. Guha, R.; McCool, R.; Miller, E.: Semantic Search. Proceedings of the Twelfth International Conference on World Wide Web. ACM Press, May 2003

10. Haav, H-M.;. Lubi, T.-L.: A Survey of Concept-based Information Retrieval Tools on the Web. In: Caplinkas, A.; Eder, J. (Eds), Advances in Databases and Information Systems, Proc. of 5th East-European Conference ADBIS*2001, Vol 2., Vilnius "Technika" 2001, pp 29-41.

11. Wu, Ch.; Jiao, W.; Shi, Z.: Ontology-based Information Retrieval. 16th IFIP World Computer Congress (WCC2000:IIP2000), Beijing, China, August 2000.

12. Kobayashi, M.; Takeda, K.: Information Retrieval on the Web. ACM Computing Surveys. ACM Press, Vol. 32, No. 2, June 2000

13. Maedche, A.: Ontology Learning for the Semantic Web. Kluwer Academic Publishers, 2002

14. Marshall, C.; Shipman, F.: Which Semantic Web?. Proceedings of the fourteenth ACM Conference on Hypertext and Hypermedia. ACM Press: Nottingham, UK, 2003, pp. 57 - 66

15. Mayfield, J. ; Finin, T.: Information Retrieval on the Semantic Web: Integrating Inference and Retrieval. SIGIR 2003 Semantic Web Workshop, Toronto, Canada, August 2003, ACM

16. Quaresma, P.; Rodrigues, I. P.: A natural language interface for information retrieval on Semantic Web documents. In: Menasalvas, E.; Segovia, J.; Szczepaniak, P.: AWIC'2003 - Atlantic Web Intelligence Conference, Lecture Notes in Artificial Intelligence, LNCS/LNAI 2663, Springer-Verlag: Madrid, Spain, May 2003 pp. 142-154.

17. Shah, U.; Finin, T.; Joshi, A.; Scott Cost, R.; Mayfield, J.: Information Retrieval on The Semantic Web. Proceedings of the eleventh international conference on Information and knowledge management, ACM Press, 2002, pp. 461 - 468.

18. Semantic Web Activity Statement. http://www.w3.org/2001/sw/, Download 2004-06-23.

The *Wisdom Web* – A Grand Intellectual Undertaking
(An Extended Abstract)

Jiming Liu

Department of Computer Science,
Hong Kong Baptist University,
Kowloon Tong, Hong Kong
jiming@comp.hkbu.edu.hk

As proposed and advocated in [1, 8, 9], the next generation Web Intelligence (WI) will aim at enabling users to go beyond the existing online information search and knowledge queries functionalities and to gain, from the Web,[1] *practical wisdoms* of living, working, and playing. The paradigm of *Wisdom Web* based computing will provide not only a medium for seamless knowledge and experience sharing but also a supply of self-organized resources for driving sustainable knowledge creation and scientific or social development/evolution [1].

The Wisdom Web encompasses the systems, environments, and activities (1) that are empowered through the global or regional connectivity of computing resources as well as distribution of data, knowledge, and contextual presence, and (2) that are specifically dedicated to enable human beings to gain practical wisdoms throughout their professional and personal activities, such as running a business and living with a certain lifestyle. It will be able to operationally perform and demonstrate in the following three aspects:

1. **Discovering the best means and the best ends:** The Wisdom Web needs to discover: What are the goals and sub-goals that a user is trying to attain? What will be the best strategy? What will be the course of actions for implementation?
2. **Mobilizing distributed resources:** The Wisdom Web needs to determine: What resources are relevant? How can distributed resources be coordinated and streamlined? What are the cost-effective ways to optimally utilize them? What are the dynamics of resource utilization?
3. **Enriching social interaction:** The Wisdom Web need to understand: What is the new form of social interaction to emerge in work, life, and play? How are certain forms of social norms, values, beliefs, as well as common-sense knowledge to be promoted and shared? How can a social community be sustained?

The Wisdom Web can be conceptually regarded as an *ecology of world knowledge resources*. It contains a vast collection of factual and procedural knowledge resources. These resources, although maybe represented via the same or similar

---

[1] Here the notion of **Web** should be taken in a broader sense.

P.S. Szczepaniak et al. (Eds.): AWIC 2005, LNAI 3528, pp. 7–10, 2005.
© Springer-Verlag Berlin Heidelberg 2005

media, utilize different domain ontologies and/or granularities. The collective world knowledge on the Wisdom Web may be comparable to the objective and subjective knowledge that humans use in their real-life communications and problem solving. Through integrating, interpreting, orchestrating various distributed knowledge resources [3, 4], practical wisdoms of living, working, and playing can be generated and communicated.

The Wisdom Web can also be conceived as communities of *intelligent entities* [7] (e.g., Wisdom agents) that establish and maintain a vast collection of socially or scientifically functional/behavioral networks. The dynamic flows of services, such as information and knowledge exchanges following some predefined protocols, will allow for the dynamic formation, reformation, and consolidation of such networks. As a result, networks of common practice or shared markets will emerge. The process of the dynamic interactions among the agents is a complex one, in which many types of interesting complex emergent behaviors can be induced and observed.

The Wisdom Web will operate in the realm of the above new conceptual forms, where Wisdom agents readily perform distributed, networked reasoning. For instance, through such a functional/behavioral network, new organizations, opinions, consensus, ontologies, services, and even markets (e.g., supplies and demands) can be formed.

In a distributed, networked computing environment, services (e.g., contents) may be found either in a designated registry or via an online process of discovery and matching. In order to make the latter option possible, individual contents or services should be developed and written following the syntax and semantics of a pre-defined Problem Solver Markup Language (PSML). As part of the PSML representation, a set of domains is also specified as the possible contexts (or worlds), in which a content/service is supposed to be used. The distributed services coded in PSML may be regarded as partial solutions (e.g., answers) to certain specific problems (e.g., queries).

In a PSML document, it should consist of the following components:

1. **Properties:** A set of properties for describing the identities and contents of a service (e.g., for semantic query and matching);
2. **Contexts:** A set of contexts or domains in which a service can be activated (note: the provision of another service can also become a context);
3. **Partners:** A set of sub-services, constituting a service, or jointly activated service(s), which may be updated and partially ordered according to the constraints given in (5); A set of locations for partner service(s), if they are known, or alternatively a set of descriptions on the requirements of partner service(s) (e.g., their properties);
4. **Constraints/Conditions:** A set of private or publicly known constraints/conditions on accessing (before), launching (during), and closing (after) a service;
5. **Constraints/Relationships:** A set of private or publicly known constraints/relationships among partner service(s);

6. **Metrics:** A set of evaluations (e.g., performance rating, relevance rank, frequency, lifespan, and cost) for describing the usage and quality of a service and/or their respective criteria (e.g., how the evaluations are calculated and updated, in relation to components (1)-(5) over time upon invocation).

The Wisdom Web will enable us to readily exploit and explore the new paradigm of *Autonomy Oriented Computing (AOC)* [2, 5]. With the Wisdom Web, it becomes possible for market researchers to predict the potential market share of a product on-the-fly by performing large-scale simulations of consumer behavior in real time. The tasks of computing are seamlessly carried out through a variety of agent embodiments. There is no single multi-purpose or dedicated machine that can manage to accomplish a job of this nature. The key to success in such an application lies in a large-scale deployment of Wisdom agents capable of autonomously performing localized interactions and making rational decisions in order to achieve their collective goals [6].

In this talk, we will outline a blueprint for the Wisdom Web research and present some specific research problems as well as challenges. We will elaborate their interrelationships and the necessity of their solutions in bringing about several characteristics and requirements of the Wisdom Web. Equally significant are the discussions on the new paradigm of Autonomy Oriented Computing (AOC) that can be utilized and exhibited on the Wisdom Web. Throughout our discussions, we will provide case studies that help illustrate some of our ongoing research efforts in addressing the Wisdom Web research challenges.

Acknowledgements

I am grateful to all my research collaborators, assistants, and students who have, over the years, together contributed to the development of Web Intelligence (WI), Wisdom Web (WW), and Autonomy Oriented Computing (AOC). I would like to express my gratitude to Ning Zhong, Yiyu Yao, and Jinglong Wu for our joint projects and discussions. I want to specially thank AWIC 2005 Chair, Piotr Szczepaniak, as well as other organizers for their kind invitation and great efforts. Finally, I would like to acknowledge the support of the following research grants: (1) Hong Kong Research Grant Council (RGC) Central Allocation Grant (HKBU 2/03/C) and Earmarked Research Grants (HKBU 2121/03E)(HKBU 2040/02E), (2) Major State Basic Research Development Program of China (973 Program) (2003CB317001), (3) Open Foundation of Beijing Municipal Key Laboratory for Multimedia and Intelligent Software Technology (KP0705200379), and (4) Hong Kong Baptist University Faculty Research Grants (FRG).

References

1. Liu, J. (2003). Web Intelligence (WI): What makes Wisdom Web? *Proceedings of the Eighteenth International Joint Conference on Artificial Intelligence (IJCAI-03)*, Acapulco, Mexico, Aug. 9-15, 2003, Morgan Kaufmann Publishers, pp. 1596-1601 (invited talk).

2. Liu, J. (2001). *Autonomous Agents and Multi-Agent Systems: Explorations in Learning, Self-Organization and Adaptive Computation*, World Scientific.
3. Liu, J., Han, J., and Tang, Y. Y. (2002). Multi-agent oriented constraint satisfaction, *Artificial Intelligence*, **136**, 1, pp. 101-144.
4. Liu, J., Jin, X., and Tang, Y. (2004). Multi-agent collaborative service and distributed problem solving, *Cognitive Systems Research*, **5**, 3, pp. 191-206.
5. Liu, J., Jin, X., and Tsui, K.C. (2005). *Autonomy Oriented Computing (AOC): From Problem Solving to Complex Systems Modeling*, Springer.
6. Liu, J., Jin, X., and Wang, S. (2005). Agent-based load balancing on homogeneous minigrids: Macroscopic modeling and characterization, *IEEE Transactions on Parallel and Distributed Systems*, **16**, 6.
7. Liu, J. and Yao, C. (2004). Rational competition and cooperation in ubiquitous agent communities, *Knowledge-Based Systems*, **17**, 5-6, pp. 189-200.
8. Liu, J., Zhong, N., Yao, Y., and Ras, Z. W. (2003). The Wisdom Web: New challenges for Web Intelligence (WI), *Journal of Intelligent Information Systems*, Kluwer Academic Publishers, **20**, 1.
9. Zhong, N., Liu, J., and Yao, Y. (2003). *Web Intelligence*, Springer.

Measuring Attractiveness of Rules from the Viewpoint of Knowledge Representation, Prediction and Efficiency of Intervention

Roman Słowiński[1,2] and Salvatore Greco[3]

[1] Institute of Computing Science, Poznań University of Technology,
60-965 Poznań, Poland
[2] Institute for Systems Research, Polish Academy of Sciences,
Newelska 6, 01-447 Warsaw, Poland
`Roman.Slowinski@cs.put.poznan.pl`
[3] Faculty of Economics, University of Catania,
Corso Italia 55, 95129 Catania, Italy
`salgreco@unict.it`

Abstract. Rules mined from a data set represent knowledge patterns relating premises and decisions in '*if ..., then ...*' statements. Premise is a conjunction of elementary conditions relative to independent variables and decision is a conclusion relative to dependent variables. Given a set of rules, it is interesting to rank them with respect to some attractiveness measures. In this paper, we are considering rule attractiveness measures related to three semantics: knowledge representation, prediction and efficiency of intervention based on a rule. Analysis of existing measures leads us to a conclusion that the best suited measures for the above semantics are: support and certainty, a Bayesian confirmation measure, and two measures related to efficiency of intervention, respectively. These five measures induce a partial order in the set of rules. For building a strategy of intervention, we propose rules discovered using the Dominance-based Rough Set Approach – the "at least" type rules indicate opportunities for improving assignment of objects, and the "at most" type rules indicate threats for deteriorating assignment of objects.

Keywords: Knowledge discovery, Rules, Attractiveness measures, Efficiency of intervention, Dominance-based Rough Set Approach.

1 Introduction

Knowledge patterns discovered from data are usually represented in a form of '*if ..., then ...*' rules, being consequence relations between premise built of independent variables and decision expressed in terms of dependent variables. In data mining and knowledge discovery such rules are induced from data sets concerning a finite set of objects described by a finite set of condition and decision attributes, corresponding to dependent and independent variables, respectively. The rules mined from data may be either decision rules or association rules,

P.S. Szczepaniak et al. (Eds.): AWIC 2005, LNAI 3528, pp. 11–22, 2005.

depending if the division into condition and decision attributes has been fixed or not. Association rules and decision rules have a double utility:

- they **represent knowledge** about relationships between dependent and independent variables existing in data,
- they can be used for **prospective decisions**.

The use of rules for prospective decisions can be understood, however, in two ways:

- **matching up the rules to new objects** with given values of independent variables, in view of **predicting** possible values of dependent variables,
- **building a strategy of intervention** based on discovered rules, in view of transforming a universe in a desired way.

For example, rules mined from data concerning medical diagnosis are useful to represent relationships between symptoms and diseases. Moreover, from one side, the rules can be used to diagnose new patients, assuming that a patient with particular symptoms will probably be sick of a disease suggested by a rule showing a strong relationship between the disease and these symptoms. From the other side, such rules can be seen as general laws and can be considered for application in course of an intervention which consists in modifying some symptoms strongly related with a disease, in order to get out from this disease.

While the first kind of prospective use of rules is rather usual, building a strategy of intervention is relatively new.

Problems related to mining rules from data in view of knowledge representation and building a strategy of intervention can be encountered in many fields, like medical practice, market basket analysis, customer satisfaction and risk analysis. In all practical applications, it is crucial to know how good the rules are for both knowledge representation and efficient intervention. "How good" is a question about attractiveness measures of discovered rules. A review of literature on this subject shows that there is no single measure which would be the best for applications in all possible perspectives (see e.g. [1], [6], [7], [12]).

We claim that the adequacy of interestingness measures to different application perspectives of discovered rules is dependent on **semantics** of these measures. In this paper, we will distinguish three main semantics and for each of them we propose some adequate measures:

- knowledge representation semantics, characterized by the strength and by the certainty degree of discovered rules,
- prediction semantics, underlining the strength of support that a premise gives to a conclusion of a particular rule, known as confirmation degree,
- efficiency of intervention semantics, referring to efficiency of an action based on a rule discovered in one universe and performed in another universe.

The differences between these semantics make impossible any compensatory aggregation of the corresponding measures for ranking the discovered rules according to a comprehensive value. Thus, we postulate to use them all in view of establishing a partial order in the set of discovered rules. While this leaves some rules incomparable, it permits to identify a set of most attractive rules with respect to preferred application perspective.

Considerations of the present article are valid for both association rules and for decision rules; however, for the sake of brevity, we speak about decision rules only.

The paper is organized as follows. In the preliminaries, we introduce some notation and basic definitions concerning rules. Then, we characterize attractiveness measures corresponding to the three semantics mentioned above and, finally, we give an interpretation of the intervention based on monotonic rules coming from Dominance-based Rough Set Approach (DRSA).

2   Preliminaries

Discovering rules from data is the domain of inductive reasoning. Contrary to deductive reasoning, where axioms expressing some universal truths constitute a starting point of reasoning, inductive reasoning uses data about a sample of larger reality to start inference.

Let $S = (U, A)$ be a *data table*, where U and A are finite, non-empty sets called the *universe* and the set of *attributes*, respectively. If in the set A two disjoint subsets of attributes, called *condition* and *decision attributes*, are distinguished, then the system is called a *decision table* and is denoted by $S = (U, C, D)$, where C and D are sets of condition and decision attributes, respectively. With every subset of attributes, one can associate a formal language of logical formulas L defined in a standard way and called the *decision language*. Formulas for a subset $B \subseteq A$ are build up from attribute-value pairs (a, v), where $a \in B$ and $v \in V_a$ (set V_a is a domain of a), by means of logical connectives $\wedge$ (*and*), $\vee$ (*or*), $\neg$ (*not*). We assume that the set of all formula sets in L is partitioned into two classes, called *condition* and *decision formulas*, respectively.

A *decision rule* induced from S and expressed in L is presented as $\Phi \rightarrow \Psi$, and read as "*if Φ, then Ψ*", where Φ and Ψ are condition and decision formulas in L, called *premise* and *decision*, respectively. A decision rule $\Phi \rightarrow \Psi$ is also seen as a binary relation between premise and decision, called *consequence relation* (see a critical discussion about interpretation of decision rules as logical implications in [6]).

Let $||\Phi||_S$ denote the set of all objects from universe U, having property Φ in S. If $\Phi \rightarrow \Psi$ is a decision rule, then $supp_S(\Phi, \Psi) = card(||\Phi \wedge \Psi||_S)$ is the *support* of the decision rule and

$$str_S(\Phi, \Psi) = \frac{supp_S(\Phi, \Psi)}{card(U)} \tag{1}$$

is the *strength* of the decision rule.

With every decision rule $\Phi \rightarrow \Psi$ we associate a *certainty* factor, called also *confidence*,

$$cer_S(\Phi, \Psi) = \frac{supp_S(\Phi, \Psi)}{card(||\Phi||_S)}, \tag{2}$$

and a coverage factor

$$cov_S(\Phi, \Psi) = \frac{supp_S(\Phi, \Psi)}{card(||\Psi||_S)}. \tag{3}$$

Certainty and coverage factors refer to Bayes' theorem:

$$cer_S(\Phi, \Psi) = Pr(\Psi|\Phi) = \frac{Pr(\Psi \wedge \Phi)}{Pr(\Phi)}, \ cov_S(\Phi, \Psi) = Pr(\Phi|\Psi) = \frac{Pr(\Phi \wedge \Psi)}{Pr(\Psi)}$$

Taking into account that given decision table S, the probability (frequency) is calculated as:

$$Pr(\Phi) = \frac{card(||\Phi||_S)}{card(U)}, \ Pr(\Psi) = \frac{card(||\Psi||_S)}{card(U)}, \ Pr(\Phi \wedge \Psi) = \frac{card(||\Phi \wedge \Psi||_S)}{card(U)}$$

one can observe the following relationship between certainty and coverage factors, without referring to prior and posterior probability:

$$cer_S(\Phi, \Psi) = \frac{cov_S(\Phi, \Psi)card(||\Psi||_S)}{card(||\Phi||_S)} \tag{4}$$

Indeed, what is certainty factor for rule $\Phi \rightarrow \Psi$ is a coverage factor for inverse rule $\Psi \rightarrow \Phi$, and vice versa. This result underlines a directional character of the statement '*if Φ, then Ψ*'.

If $cer_S(\Phi, \Psi) = 1$, then the decision rule $\Phi \rightarrow \Psi$ is *certain*, otherwise the decision rule is *uncertain*. A set of decision rules supported in total by the universe U creates a *decision algorithm* in S.

3   Attractiveness Measures with Different Semantics

3.1   Knowledge Representation Semantics

Decision rules $\Phi \rightarrow \Psi$ induced from some universe U represent knowledge about this universe in terms of laws relating some properties Φ with properties Ψ. These laws are naturally characterized by a number of cases from U supporting them, and by a probability of obtaining a particular decision Ψ considering a condition Φ. These correspond precisely to the *strength* form one side, and to the *certainty* or *coverage* factor from the other side. With respect to the latter side, we saw in the previous section that due to (4), in order to characterize the truth of the relationship between Φ and Ψ, it is enough to use one of these factors only; moreover, for the directional character of the statement '*if Φ, then Ψ*', it is natural to choose the certainty factor.

In consequence, we propose to use **strength** $str_S(\Phi, \Psi)$ and **certainty** $cer_S(\Phi, \Psi)$ as attractiveness measures of rules, adequate to the semantics of knowledge representation.

For example, in a data table with medical information on a sample of patients, we can consider as condition attributes a set of symptoms $C = \{c_1, \ldots, c_n\}$, and as decision attributes, a set of diseases $D = \{d_1, \ldots, d_m\}$. In the decision table so obtained we can induce decision rules of the type: "*if* symptoms $c_{i1}, c_{i2}, \ldots, c_{ih}$ appear, *then* there is disease d_j", with $c_{i1}, c_{i2}, \ldots, c_{ih} \in C$ and $d_j \in D$. Such a rule has interpretation of a law characterized as follows (the % is calculated from a hypothetical data table):

- the patients having symptoms $c_{i1}, c_{i2}, \ldots, c_{ih}$ and disease d_j constitute 15% of all the patients in the sample, i.e. 15% is the *strength* of the rule,
- 91% of the patients having symptoms $c_{i1}, c_{i2}, \ldots, c_{ih}$ have also disease d_j, i.e. 91% is the *certainty factor* of the rule.

It is worth noting that strength $str_S(\Phi, \Psi)$ and certainty $cer_S(\Phi, \Psi)$ are more general than a large variety of statistical interestingness measures, like entropy gain, gini, laplace, lift, conviction, chi-squared value and the measure proposed by Piatetsky-Shapiro. Bayardo and Agrawal [1] demonstrated that, for given data table S, the set of Pareto-optimal rules with respect to strength and certainty includes all rules that are best according to any of the above measures.

3.2   Prediction Semantics

The use of rule $\Phi \rightarrow \Psi$ for prediction is based on reasoning by analogy: an object having property Φ will have property Ψ. The truth value of this analogy has the semantics of a degree to which a piece of evidence Φ supports the hypothesis Ψ. As shown in [6], this corresponds to a Bayesian confirmation measure (see e.g. [3] and [8] for surveys). While the confirmation measure is certainly related to the strength of relationship between Φ and Ψ, its meaning is different from a simple statistics of co-occurrence of properties Φ and Ψ in universe U, as shown by the following example borrowed from Popper [9].

Consider a possible result of rolling a die: 1,2,3,4,5,6. We can built a decision table, presented in Table 1, where the fact that the result is even or odd is the condition attribute, while the result itself is the decision attribute.

Table 1. Decision Table

Condition attribute (result odd or even)	Decision attribute (result of rolling the die)
odd	1
even	2
odd	3
even	4
odd	5
even	6

Now, consider the case Ψ = "the result is 6" and the case $\neg\Psi$ = "the result is not 6". Let us also take into account the information Φ = "the result is an even number (i.e. 2 or 4 or 6)". Therefore, we can consider the following two decision rules:

- $\Phi \rightarrow \Psi$ = "if the result is even, then the result is 6", with certainty $cer_S(\Phi, \Psi) = 1/3$,
- $\Phi \rightarrow \neg\Psi$ = "if the result is even, then the result is 6", with certainty $cer_S(\Phi, \neg\Psi) = 2/3$.

Remark that rule $\Phi \rightarrow \Psi$ has a smaller certainty than rule $\Phi \rightarrow \neg\Psi$. However, the probability that the result is 6 is 1/6, while the probability that the result is different from 6 is 5/6. Thus, the information Φ raises the probability of Ψ from 1/6 to 1/3, and decreases the probability of $\neg\Psi$ from 5/6 to 2/3. In conclusion, we can say that Φ confirms Ψ and disconfirms $\neg\Psi$, independently of the fact that the certainty of $\Phi \rightarrow \Psi$ is smaller than the certainty of $\Phi \rightarrow \neg\Psi$.

From this simple example, one can see that certainty and confirmation are two completely different concepts.

Bayesian confirmation measure, denoted by $c(\Phi, \Psi)$, exhibits the impact of evidence Φ on hypothesis Ψ by comparing probability $Pr(\Psi|\Phi)$ with probability $Pr(\Psi)$ as follows:

$$c(\Phi, \Psi) \begin{cases} > 0 \text{ if } Pr(\Psi|\Phi) > Pr(\Psi) \\ = 0 \text{ if } Pr(\Psi|\Phi) = Pr(\Psi) \\ < 0 \text{ if } Pr(\Psi|\Phi) < Pr(\Psi) \end{cases} \tag{5}$$

In data mining, the probability Pr of Ψ is substituted by the relative frequency Fr in the considered data table S, i.e.

$$Fr_S(\Psi) = \frac{card(||\Phi||)}{card(U)}.$$

Analogously, given Φ and Ψ, $Pr(\Psi|\Phi)$ is substituted by the certainty factor $cer_S(\Phi, \Psi)$ of the decision rule $\Phi \rightarrow \Psi$, therefore, a measure of confirmation of property Ψ by property Φ can be rewritten as:

$$c(\Phi, \Psi) \begin{cases} > 0 \text{ if } cer_S(\Phi, \Psi) > Fr_S(\Psi) \\ = 0 \text{ if } cer_S(\Phi, \Psi) = Fr_S(\Psi) \\ < 0 \text{ if } cer_S(\Phi, \Psi) < Fr_S(\Psi) \end{cases} \tag{6}$$

(6) can be interpreted as follows:

- $c(\Phi, \Psi) > 0$ means that property Ψ is satisfied more frequently when Φ is satisfied (then, this frequency is $cer_S(\Phi, \Psi)$), rather than generically in the whole decision table (where this frequency is $Fr_S(\Psi)$),
- $c(\Phi, \Psi) = 0$ means that property Ψ is satisfied with the same frequency when Φ is satisfied and generically in the whole decision table,
- $c(\Phi, \Psi) < 0$ means that property Ψ is satisfied less frequently when Φ is satisfied, rather than generically in the whole decision table.

In other words, the confirmation measure for rule $\Phi \rightarrow \Psi$ is the credibility of the following proposition: Ψ **is satisfied more frequently when** Φ **is satisfied rather than when** Φ **is not satisfied**.

Apart from property (5), many authors have considered other properties of confirmation measures (see [3] for a survey). Among the desirable properties there is a kind of symmetry called *hypothesis symmetry* [2]:

$$c(\Phi, \Psi) = -c(\Phi, \neg\Psi) \tag{7}$$

Greco, Pawlak and Słowiński [6] have formulated yet another desirable property for confirmation measures of rules mined from data tables – this property is called *monotonicity*. It underlines an important difference existing between rules considered as consequence relations and rules considered as logical (material) implications.

Using the denotation: $a = supp_S(\Phi, \Psi)$, $b = supp_S(\neg\Phi, \Psi)$, $c = supp_S(\Phi, \neg\Psi)$, $d = supp_S(\neg\Phi, \neg\Psi)$, the monotonicity property says that $c(\Phi, \Psi) = F(a, b, c, d)$, where F is a function non-decreasing with respect to a and d and non-increasing with respect to b and c.

While monotonicity of the confirmation measure with respect to a and c makes no doubt, the monotonicity with respect to b and d needs a comment. Remembering that $c(\Phi, \Psi)$ is the credibility of the proposition: Ψ is satisfied more frequently when Φ is satisfied rather than when Φ is not satisfied, we can state the following. An evidence in which Φ is not satisfied and Ψ is satisfied (objects $||\neg\Phi \wedge \Psi||$) increases the frequency of Ψ in situations where Φ is not satisfied, so it should decrease the value of $c(\Phi, \Psi)$. Analogously, an evidence in which both Φ and Ψ are not satisfied (objects $||\neg\Phi \wedge \neg\Psi||$) decreases the frequency of Ψ in situations where Φ is not satisfied, so it should increase the value of $c(\Phi, \Psi)$.

In [6], six confirmation measures well known from the literature have been analyzed from the viewpoint of the desirable monotonicity property. It has been proved that only three of them satisfy this property. Moreover, among these three confirmation measures, only two satisfy the hypothesis symmetry (7); these are:

$$l(\Phi, \Psi) = \log\left[\frac{cer_S(\Psi, \Phi)}{cer_S(\neg\Psi, \Phi)}\right] = \log\left[\frac{a/(a+b)}{c/(c+d)}\right] \text{ and}$$

$$f(\Phi, \Psi) = \frac{cer_S(\Psi, \Phi) - cer_S(\neg\Psi, \Phi)}{cer_S(\Psi, \Phi) + cer_S(\neg\Psi, \Phi)} = \frac{ad - bc}{ad + bc + 2ac}. \tag{8}$$

As proved by Fitelson [3], these measures are ordinally equivalent, i.e. for all rules $\Phi \rightarrow \Psi$ and $\Phi' \rightarrow \Psi'$, $l(\Phi, \Psi) \geq l(\Phi', \Psi')$ if and only if $f(\Phi, \Psi) \geq f(\Phi', \Psi')$. Thus, it is sufficient to use one of them, e.g. $f(\Phi, \Psi)$.

In consequence, we propose to use **confirmation measure** $f(\Phi, \Psi)$ as attractiveness measure of rules, adequate to the semantics of reasoning by analogy for prediction.

3.3   Efficiency of Intervention Semantics

The attractiveness measures considered above can be interpreted as characteristics of the universe U where the rules come from, and do not measure the future effects of a possible intervention based on these rules. In [5], we considered expected effects of an intervention which is a three-stage process:

1. Mining rules in universe U.
2. Modification (manipulation) of universe U', based on a rule mined from U, with the aim of getting a desired result.
3. Transition from universe U' to universe U'' due to the modification made in stage 2.

For example, let us suppose a medical rule has been induced from universe U: $r \equiv$ 'if absence of symptom Φ, then no disease Ψ' whose certainty is 90% (i.e. in 90% of cases where symptom Φ is absent there is no disease Ψ). On the basis of r, an intervention may be undertaken in universe U' consisting in eliminating symptom Φ to get out from disease Ψ in universe U''. This intervention is based on a hypothesis of *homogeneity* of universes U and U'. This homogeneity means that r is valid also in U' in the sense that one can expect that 90% of sick patients with symptom Φ will get out from the sickness due to the intervention.

In another application concerning customer satisfaction analysis, the universe is a set of customers and the intervention is a strategy (promotion campaign) modifying perception of a product so as to increase customer satisfaction.

Measures of efficiency of intervention depend not only on characteristics of rules in universe U, but also on characteristics of universe U' where the intervention takes place.

Let $S = (U, A)$, $S' = (U', A)$ and $S'' = (U'', A)$ denote three data tables referring to universes U, U' and U'', respectively.

In [5], the following reasoning has been applied to measure the effect of an intervention based on rule $\Phi \to \Psi$: if we modify property $\neg\Phi$ to property Φ in the set $||\neg\Phi \wedge \neg\Psi||_{S'}$, we may reasonably expect that $cer_S(\Phi, \Psi) \times supp_{S'}(\neg\Phi, \neg\Psi)$ objects from set $||\neg\Phi \wedge \neg\Psi||_{S'}$ in universe U' will enter decision class Ψ in universe U''. In consequence, the expected **relative increment** of objects from U' entering decision class Ψ in universe U'' is:

$$incr_{SS'}(\Psi) = cer_S(\Phi, \Psi) \times \frac{card(||\neg\Phi \wedge \neg\Psi||_{S'})}{card(U')} \tag{9}$$

The relative increment (9) can be rewritten as:

$$incr_{SS'}(\Psi) = cer_S(\Phi, \Psi) \times \frac{card(||\neg\Phi \wedge \neg\Psi||_{S'})}{card(||\neg\Psi||_{S'})} \times \frac{card(||\neg\Psi||_{S'})}{card(U')} =$$
$$= cer_S(\Phi, \Psi) \times cer_{S'}(\neg\Psi, \neg\Phi) \times \frac{card(||\neg\Psi||_{S'})}{card(U')} \tag{10}$$

where $cer_{S'}(\neg\psi, \neg\phi)$ is a certainty factor of the contrapositive rule $s \equiv \neg\Psi \to \neg\Phi$ in U'. Taking into account that $card(||\neg\Psi||_{S'})/card(U')$ is a fraction of all objects having not property Ψ in universe U', the remaining part of (10) is just expressing the **efficiency of the intervention**:

$$\mathit{eff}_{SS'}(\Phi, \Psi) = cer_S(\Phi, \Psi) \times cer_{S'}(\neg\Psi, \neg\Phi). \tag{11}$$

Assuming that the condition formula Φ is composed of n elementary conditions $\Phi_1 \wedge \Phi_2 \wedge \ldots \wedge \Phi_n$, we consider rule $r \equiv \Phi_1 \wedge \Phi_2 \wedge \ldots \wedge \Phi_n \to \Psi$, with certainty $cer_S(\Phi, \Psi)$. Using this rule, one can perform a multi-attribute intervention which consists in modification of attributes with indices from each subset $P \subseteq N = \{1, \ldots, n\}$ on all objects from U' having none of properties Φ_i, $i \in P$, while having all properties Φ_j, $j \notin P$, and having not property Ψ. In this case, the **relative increment** (10) takes the form:

$$incr_{SS'}(\Psi) = \tag{12}$$

$$= \sum_{\emptyset \subset P \subset N} \left[cer_S(\Phi, \Psi) \times cer_{S'} \left(\neg\Psi, \bigwedge_{i \in P} \neg\Phi_i \wedge \bigwedge_{j \notin P} \Phi_j \right) \right] \times \frac{card(||\neg\Psi||_{S'})}{card(U')}$$

where $cer_{S'} \left(\neg\Psi, \bigwedge_{i \in P} \neg\Phi_i \wedge \bigwedge_{j \notin P} \Phi_j \right)$ is a certainty factor of the contrapositive rule $s_P \equiv \neg\Psi \rightarrow \bigwedge_{i \in P} \neg\Phi_i \wedge \bigwedge_{j \notin P} \Phi_j$ in U', for $P \subseteq N$. From (12) it follows that the **efficiency of the multi-attribute intervention** is equal to:

$$eff_{SS'}(\Phi, \Psi) = cer_S(\Phi, \Psi) \times \sum_{\emptyset \subset P \subset N} cer_{S'} \left(\neg\Psi, \bigwedge_{i \in P} \neg\Phi_i \wedge \bigwedge_{j \notin P} \Phi_j \right). \tag{13}$$

Using calculations analogous to calculation of the Shapley value in terms of the Möbius transform of the Choquet capacity, one can assess a contribution of each particular elementary condition Φ_i, $i \in N$, in the efficiency of the whole intervention [5].

Remark that relative increment $incr_{SS'}(\Psi)$ and efficiency of intervention $eff_{SS'}(\Phi, \Psi)$ have a meaning analogical to knowledge representation measures, i.e. strength $str_S(\Phi, \Psi)$ and certainty factor $cer_S(\Phi, \Psi)$, respectively; they refer, however, to intervention in another universe than that of the knowledge representation.

3.4   Partial Order of Rules with Respect to the Five Measures of Attractiveness

A set of rules can be partially ordered using the five attractive measures proposed in this section. These are:

- rule strength $str_S(\Phi, \Psi)$ (1),
- certainty factor $cer_S(\Phi, \Psi)$ (2),
- confirmation measure $f(\Phi, \Psi)$ (8),
- relative increment due to intervention $incr_{SS'}(\Psi)$ (12),
- efficiency of intervention $eff_{SS'}(\Phi, \Psi)$ (13).

Such a partial ranking supports an interactive search in which the user can browse the best rule according to preferences related to a specific application: representation, prediction or intervention. Remark that it also makes sense to use these measures in a lexicographic procedure, ordering first the rules with respect to the most important measure, then, ordering a subset of best rules using the second-most important measure, and so on.

4 Interpretation of the Intervention Based on Monotonic Rules

Let us complete our considerations by interpretation of the intervention based on monotonic rules coming from the Dominance-based Rough Set Approach (DRSA) [4], [10].

Considering decision table $S = (U, C, D)$, where C is a finite set of attributes with preference-ordered domains X_q ($q \in C$), and D is a finite set of decision attributes partitioning U into a finite set of preference-ordered decision classes $Cl_1, Cl_2, \ldots, Cl_k$ (the higher the index the better the class), DRSA permits to mine two kinds of decision rules:

- **"at least" rules**
  if $x_{q1} \succeq_{q1} r_{q1}$ and $x_{q2} \succeq_{q2} r_{q2}$ and $\ldots$ $x_{qp} \succeq_{qp} r_{qp}$, then $x \in Cl_t^{\geq}$,
  where for each $w_q, z_q \in X_q$, "$w_q \succeq_q z_q$" means "w_q is <u>at least</u> as good as z_q", and $x \in Cl_t^{\geq}$ means "x belongs to class Cl_t or better",
- **"at most" rules**
  if $x_{q1} \preceq_{q1} r_{q1}$ and $x_{q2} \preceq_{q2} r_{q2}$ and $\ldots$ $x_{qp} \preceq_{qp} r_{qp}$, then $x \in Cl_t^{\leq}$,
  where for each $w_q, z_q \in X_q$, "$w_q \preceq_q z_q$" means "w_q is <u>at most</u> as good as z_q", and $x \in Cl_t^{\leq}$ means "x belongs to class Cl_t or worse".

The rules "at least" indicate **opportunities for improving** the assignment of object x to class Cl_t or better, if it was not assigned as high and its evaluation on $q1, q2, \ldots, qp$ would grow to $r_{q1}, r_{q2}, \ldots, r_{qp}$ or better.

The rules "at most" indicate **threats for deteriorating** the assignment of object x to class Cl_t or worse, if it was not assigned as low and its evaluation on $q1, q2, \ldots, qp$ would drop to $r_{q1}, r_{q2}, \ldots, r_{qp}$ or worse.

In the context of these two kinds of rules, an **intervention** means either an action of **taking the opportunity** of improving the assignment of a subset of objects, or an action of **protecting against threats** of deteriorating the assignment of a subset of objects.

For example, consider the following "at least" rule mined from a hypothetical data set of customer satisfaction questionnaires:

$$\text{'}if\,(q1 \geq 5) \wedge (q5 \geq 4), then \text{ Satisfaction} \succeq \text{High'}$$

Suppose that an intervention based on this rule is characterized by $incr_{SS'}(\text{High}) = 77\%$; this means that increasing $q1$ above 4 and increasing $q5$ above 3 will result in improvement of customer satisfaction from Medium or Low to High for 77% of customers with Medium or Low satisfaction.

Now, consider the following "at most" rule:

$$\text{'}if\,(q2 \leq 4) \wedge (q4 \leq 4) \wedge (q6 \leq 4), then \text{ Satisfaction} \preceq \text{Medium'}$$

In this case, $incr_{SS'}(\text{Medium}) = 89\%$ means that dropping $q2, q4$ and $q6$ below 5 will result in deterioration of customer satisfaction from High to Medium or Low for 89% of customers with High satisfaction.

In practical applications, the choice of rules used for intervention can also be supported by some additional measures, like:

- length of the rule chosen for intervention (the shorter the better),
- cost of intervention on attributes present in the rule,
- priority of intervention on some types of attributes, like short-term attributes or attributes on which competing firms perform better.

Remark that intervention based on rules shows some similarity with an interesting concept of **action rules** considered by Tsay and Raś [11], however, action rules are pairs of rules representing two scenarios for assignment of an object: one desired and another unsatisfactory, and the action consists in passing from the undesired scenario to desired one, by changing values of so-called flexible attributes. Action rules are characterized by support and confidence only.

5   Conclusions

In this paper, we considered attractiveness measures of rules mined from data, taking into account three application perspectives: knowledge representation, prediction of new classifications and interventions based on discovered rules in some other universe. In order to choose attractiveness measures concordant with the above perspectives we analyzed semantics of particular measures which lead us to a conclusion that the best suited measures for the above applications are: support and certainty, a Bayesian confirmation measure, and two measures related to efficiency of intervention, respectively. These five measures induce a partial order in the set of rules, giving a starting point for an interactive browsing procedure. For building a strategy of intervention, we proposed rules discovered using the Dominance-based Rough Set Approach – the "at least" type rules indicate opportunities for improving assignment of objects, and the "at most" type rules indicate threats for deteriorating assignment of objects.

Acknowledgements

The first author wishes to acknowledge financial support from the State Committee for Scientific Research (KBN). The research of the second author was supported by the Italian Ministry for Education, University and Research (MIUR).

References

1. Bayardo, R.J., Agrawal, R.: Mining the most interesting rules. [In]: Proc. of the Fifth ACM SIGKDD Intl Conf. on Knowledge Discovery and Data Mining, (1999) 145–154
2. Eells, E., Fitelson, B.: Symmetries and asymmetries in evidential support. Philosophical Studies, **107** (2) (2002) 129–142

3. Fitelson, B.: Studies in Bayesian Confirmation Theory. Ph.D. thesis, University of Wisconsin – Madison (2001)
4. Greco, S., Matarazzo, B., Słowiński, R.: Dominance-Based Rough Set Approach to Knowledge Discovery – (I) General Perspective; (II) Extensions and Applications. Chapters 20 and 21 [in]: N.Zhong and J.Liu, Intelligent Technologies for Information Analysis. Springer-Verlag, New York, (2004) 513–612
5. Greco, S., Matarazzo, B., Pappalardo, N., Słowiński, R.: Measuring expected effects of interventions based on decision rules. Journal of Experimental and Applied Artificial Intelligence, **17** (1-2) (2005) 103–118
6. Greco, S., Pawlak, Z., Słowiński, R.: Can Bayesian confirmation measures be useful for rough set decision rules? Engineering Applications of Artificial Intelligence, **17** (4) (2004) 345–361
7. Hilderman, R.J., Hamilton, H.J.: Knowledge Discovery and Measures of Interest. Kluwer Academic Publishers, Boston (2001)
8. Kyburg, H.: Recent work in inductive logic. [In]: K.G. Lucey and T.R. Machan (eds.), Recent Work in Philosophy. Rowman and Allanheld, Totowa, N.J., (1983) 89–150
9. Popper, K. R.: The Logic of Scientific Discovery. Hutchinson, London (1959)
10. Słowiński, R., Greco, S., Matarazzo, B.: Rough Set Based Decision Support. Chapter 15 [in]: E. Burke and G. Kendall (eds.), Introductory Tutorials on Optimization, Search and Decision Support Methodologies, Springer-Verlag, New York (2005)
11. Tsay, L.-S., Raś, Z.: Action rule discovery: system DEAR2, method and experiments. Journal of Experimental and Applied Artificial Intelligence **17** (1-2) (2005) 119–128
12. Yao, Y.Y., Zhong, N.: An analysis of quantitative measures associated with rules. [In]: Proceedings of the Third Pacific-Asia Conference on Knowledge Discovery and Data Mining, LNAI **1574**, Springer-Verlag, Berlin, (1999) 479–488

Web Intelligence Meets Brain Informatics: An Impending Revolution in WI and Brain Sciences (An Extended Abstract)

Ning Zhong

The International WIC Institute &
Department of Information Engineering,
Maebashi Institute of Technology,
460-1 Kamisadori-Cho, Maebashi-City 371-0816, Japan
zhong@maebashi-it.ac.jp

Web Intelligence (WI) is a new direction for scientific research and development that explores the fundamental roles as well as practical impacts of Artificial Intelligence (AI)[1] and advanced Information Technology (IT) on the next generation of Web-empowered systems, services, and environments [1, 8, 9]. In our previous paper [6], we gave perspectives of WI research:

> WI may be reviewed as applying results from existing disciplines (AI and IT) to a totally new domain; WI introduces new problems and challenges to the established disciplines; WI may be considered as an enhancement or an extension of AI and IT.

In this paper, we give a new perspective of WI research: *Web Intelligence meets Brain Informatics.*

Brain Informatics (BI) is a new interdisciplinary field to study human information processing mechanism systematically from both macro and micro points of view by cooperatively using experimental brain/cognitive technology and WI centric advanced information technology. In particular, it attempts to understand human intelligence in depth, towards a holistic view at a long-term, global field of vision, to understand the principle, models and mechanisms of human multi-perception, language, memory, reasoning and inference, learning, problem-solving, discovery and creativity [12].

New instrumentation (fMRI etc) and advanced IT are causing an impending revolution in WI and Brain Sciences. This revolution is bi-directional:

- The WI based portal techniques will provide a new powerful platform for Brain Sciences.
- The new understanding and discovery of the human intelligence models in Brain Sciences will yield a new generation of WI research and development.

The first aspect means that WI techniques provide an agent based multi-database mining grid architecture on the Wisdom Web for building a brain-informatics

---

[1] Here the term of AI includes classical AI, computational intelligence, and soft computing etc.

P.S. Szczepaniak et al. (Eds.): AWIC 2005, LNAI 3528, pp. 23–25, 2005.

portal [10, 12]. A conceptual model with three levels of workflows, corresponding to the grid with three-layers, namely data-grid, mining-grid, and knowledge-grid, respectively, is utilized to manage, represent, integrate, analyze, and utilize the information coming from multiple, huge data sources. Furthermore, the Wisdom Web based computing will provide not only a medium for seamless information exchange and knowledge sharing, but also a type of man-made resources for sustainable knowledge creation, and scientific and social evolution. The Wisdom Web will rely on *grid-like agencies* that self-organize, learn, and evolve their courses of actions in order to perform service tasks as well as their identities and interrelationships in communities [1, 8]. The proposed methodology attempts to change the perspective of brain/cognitive scientists from a single type of experimental data analysis towards a holistic view at a long-term, global field of vision.

The second aspect of the new perspective on WI means that the new generation of WI research and development needs to understand multiple natures of intelligence in depth by studying integrately the three intelligence research related areas: machine intelligence, human intelligence and social intelligence. A good example is the development and use of a Web-based problem-solving system for portal-centralized, adaptable Web services [1, 5, 8, 9]. The core of such a system is the Problem Solver Markup Language (PSML) and PSML-based distributed Web inference engines, in which the following support functions should be provided since this is a must for developing intelligent portals based on WI technologies.

- The expressive power and functional support in PSML for complex adaptive, distributed problem solving;
- Performing automatic reasoning on the Web by incorporating globally distributed contents and meta-knowledge automatically collected and transformed from the Semantic Web and social networks with locally operational knowledge-data bases;
- Representing and organizing multiple, huge knowledge-data sources for distributed Web inference and reasoning.

In order to develop such a Web based problem-solving system, we need to better understand how human being does complex adaptive (distributed) problem solving and reasoning, as well as how intelligence evolves for individuals and societies, over time and place [4, 5, 7].

More specifically, we will investigate ways by discussing the following issues:

- How to design fMRI/EEG experiments to understand the principle of human inference/reasoning and problem solving in depth?
- How to implement human-level inference/reasoning and problem solving on the Web based portals that can serve users wisely?

We will describe our endeavor in this direction, in particular, we will show that grid-based multi-aspect analysis in multiple knowledge and data sources on the Wisdom Web is an important way to investigate human intelligence mechanism, systematically.

Acknowledgments

I would like to thank Jiming Liu, Yiyu Yao, and Jinglong Wu who are my colleagues introduced Web Intelligence (WI) and Brain Informatics (BI) with me together. The contents of this paper include their contributions. We are very grateful to people who have joined or supported the WI community, members of the WIC advisory board, WIC technical committee, and WIC research centres, as well as keynote/invited speakers of WI-IAT conferences, in particular, N. Cercone, J. Bradshaw, B.B. Faltings, E.A. Feigenbaum, G. Gottlob, J. Hendler, W.L. Johnson, C. Kesselman, V. Lesser, J. McCarthy, T.M. Mitchell, S. Ohsuga, P. Raghavan, Z.W. Ras, J. Segovia, A. Skowron, K. Sycara, B. Wah, P.S.P. Wang, M. Wooldridge, X. Wu, P.S. Yu, and L.A. Zadeh. We thank them for their strong support. Special thanks to Piotr S. Szczepaniak (director of the WIC Poland centre) and the organizers of AWIC 2005 for the kind invitation and the excellent organization.

References

1. Liu, J. "Web Intelligence (WI): What Makes Wisdom Web?", *Proc. Eighteenth International Joint Conference on Artificial Intelligence (IJCAI'03)* (2003) 1596-1601.
2. Liu, J., Jin, X., and Tang, Y. "Multi-agent Collaborative Service and Distributed Problem Solving", *Cognitive Systems Research*, 5(3): 191-206, Elsevier, 2004.
3. Mitchell, T.M., Hutchinson, R., Just, M., Niculescu, R.S., Pereira, F., and Wang, X. "Classifying Instantaneous Cognitive States from fMRI Data", *Proc. American Medical Informatics Association Annual Symposium* (2003) 465-469.
4. Sternberg, R.J., Lautrey, J., and Lubart, T.I. *Models of Intelligence*, American Psychological Association (2003).
5. Su, Y., Zheng, L., Zhong, N., Liu, C., and Liu, J. "Distributed Reasoning Based on Problem Solver Markup Language (PSML): A Demonstration through Extended OWL", *Proc. 2005 IEEE International Conference on e-Technology, e-Commerce and e-Service (EEE'05)*, IEEE-CS Press (2005) (in press).
6. Yao, Y.Y., Zhong, N., Liu, J., Ohsuga, S. "Web Intelligence (WI): Research Challenges and Trends in the New Information Age", N. Zhong, Y.Y. Yao, J. Liu, S. Ohsuga (eds.) *Web Intelligence: Research and Development*, LNAI 2198, Springer (2001) 1-17.
7. Zadeh, L.A. "Precisiated Natural Language (PNL)", *AI Magazine*, 25(3) (Fall 2004) 74-91.
8. Zhong, N., Liu, J., and Yao, Y.Y. "In Search of the Wisdom Web", *IEEE Computer*, 35(11) (2002) 27-31.
9. Zhong, N., Liu, J., and Yao. Y.Y. (eds.) *Web Intelligence*, Springer, 2003.
10. Zhong, N. "Developing Intelligent Portals by Using WI Technologies", J.P. Li et al. (eds.) *Wavelet Analysis and Its Applications, and Active Media Technology*, Vol. 2, World Scientific (2004) 555-567.
11. Zhong, N., Wu, J., Nakamaru, A., Ohshima, M., and Mizuhara, H. "Peculiarity Oriented fMRI Brain Data Analysis for Studying Human Multi-Perception Mechanism", *Cognitive Systems Research*, 5(3), Elsevier (2004) 241-256.
12. Zhong, N., Hu, J., Motomura, S., Wu, J., and Liu, C. "Building a Data Mining Grid for Multiple Human Brain Data Analysis", *Computational Intelligence*, 21(2), Blackwell Publishing (2005) 177-196.

Hybrid Computational Intelligence for Ambient Intelligent Environments

Giovanni Acampora, Vincenzo Loia, Michele Nappi, and Stefano Ricciardi

Dipartimento di Matematica e Informatica,
Università degli Studi di Salerno,
via Ponte don Melillo, Fisciano(Salerno), Italy

Abstract. This paper describes an agent-based ambient intelligence architecture able to deliver personalized services on the basis of physical and emotional user status captured from a set of biometric features. Abstract representation and management is achieved thanks to two markup languages, H2ML and FML, able to model behavioral as well as fuzzy control activities and to exploit distribution and concurrent computation in order to gain real-time performances.

1 Introduction

Computational Intelligence (CI) represents the effort in achieving "smart" solutions, by using hardware and software conceived to work in imperfect domains too complex to be solved effectively. CI differs from traditional Artificial Intelligence (AI) approaches by using successful methodologies and techniques, such as Fuzzy Logic, Artificial Neural Network, Genetic Computation, and Machine Learning. Often, the combination of the above-mentioned approaches, results in framework particularly suitable for extracting generalized expert knowledge necessary to automate decision-making tasks for problems difficult to model, ill-defined, with large solution space (see [1] and [2] for CI impact in several domains of applications). This "hybrid" paradigm, based on merging different theories and techniques are often the winning strategy to develop efficient Intelligent Systems. There are many practical situation where this appears evident, one of this is the Ambient Intelligence (AmI) scenarios [6]. AmI provides a wide-ranging vision on how the Information Society will evolve, since the goal is to conceive platforms for seamless delivery of services and applications making them effectively invisible to the user. This is possible by gathering best practices from Ubiquitous Computing, Ubiquitous Communication, and Intelligent User Friendly Interfaces areas. This convergence will lead to smart environments that surround people in pro-active way: the environment reacts autonomously to people by using intelligent intuitive interfaces (often invisible) that are embedded in all kinds of chip-enriched objects (furniture, clothes, vehicles, roads and other smart materials). This means that computing and networking technology is everywhere, embedded in everyday objects in order to automate tasks or enhance the environment for its occupants [4]. This objective is achievable if the

P.S. Szczepaniak et al. (Eds.): AWIC 2005, LNAI 3528, pp. 26–31, 2005.

environment is capable to learn, build and manipulate user profiles considering from a side the need to clearly identify the human attitude (AmI is known to work for people not for users) and from the other the ubiquity of the possible services. Of course, this involves several research trends:

- new generation of devices, sensors, and interfaces;
- new generation of processors and communication infrastructures;
- new intelligence empowerment, provided by software agents embedded in the devices [3].

This paper proposes an ambient intelligence architecture able to distribute domotic services personalized on the basis of physical and emotional user status captured from a set of biometric features, and modelled by means of a web oriented language based on XML. Our AmI architecture integrates different approaches, such as mark-up languages, fuzzy control, distributed and mobile computation and biometric techniques, into a multi-layer framework. Each layer serves to accomplish specific tasks by satisfying the needs of abstraction and flexibility thanks a fuzzy control markup language, namely FML [7]. FML allows designer to achieve transparency and efficiency in customizing the fuzzy control implementation on specific devices plugged in web-level architecture [8].

2   The System Architecture

The proposed system architecure is organized in several layers, as depicted in figure 1. In the first layer from top, **Ambient Intelligence Environment**, a set of sensors and actuator wired via a domotic protocol is used to gather data about current user status (temperature, gait, position, facial expression, etc.). Part of information gathered at this stage are handled by **Morphological Recognition Subsystems** (i.e.: Facial Recognition Subsystem) resulting in a semantic description. These information, together with the remaining information retrieved in the environment, are organized in a web oriented hierarchical structure based on XML technology in order to create a new markup language, called **H2ML** (Human to Markup Language). H2ML is a new approach to model human information allowing a transparent use in different intelligent frameworks. The next layer, **Multilayer controller**, based on hierarchical fuzzy control, represents the core designed to distribute appropriate services related to the information contained in H2ML representation. Each fuzzy controller used in our architecture is coded in FML in order to achieve hardware transparency and to minimize the fuzzy inference time.

2.1   Ambient Intelligence Environment

The Ambient Intelligence Environment can be defined as the set of actuators and sensors composing the system together with the domotic interconnection protocol (Lontalk+IP in our case). The AmI environment is based on the following sensors and actuators: *internal* and *external temperature* sensors and *internal temperature* actuator, *internal* and *external luminosity* sensor and *internal luminosity* actuator, *indoor presence sensor*. Moreover, the system relies on a set of color cameras to capture information about gait and facial expression, and a infrared camera to capture thermal images of user.

2.2   H2ML - Human to Markup Language

In last years, different languanges have been developed to model the human aspect. Virtual Human Markup Language(VHML) [11], Avatar Markup Language [12] and Multi-Modal Presentation Markup Language [10] are examples of languages proposed to simplify the human-computer interaction through a virtual *Web Assistant*. While the above mentioned languages are based on a *high level* description of human status (i.e. happy and fear face concepts) H2ML is focused on detailed, *low level* description of physical human features (i.e. closed and opened eyes or mouth). In order to define language lexicon we have to describe a human in terms of morphological features. The H2ML implementation is based on tags referring to different nodes of human representation tree. Each tag can use two different attributes: *value* and *status*. The value attribute is used to represent human feature by a numeric continuous range, while, status attribute is used to model information through a discrete set of labels. Starting from the root, the <**INDIVIDUAL**> tag corresponding to the root tag of a H2ML program, is created. Each child of this tag represents a specific structured biometric descriptor. In particular, the following set of tags are introduced: <**PHYSICAL**>, <**FACE**>, <**THERMAL**>, <**SPEECH**> and <**GAIT**>.

The <**PHYSICAL**> tag refers to the height, weight and build features of represented individual through corresponding tags <**HEIGHT**>, <**WEIGHT**>, <**BUILD**> and the related attributes *value* and *status*. Similarly, it is possible to model face, thermal, speech and gait features.

2.3   Multiple Hierarchical Fuzzy Control

The system uses a hybrid configuration composed by a hierarchical fuzzy controller and mobile agent technology based on FML language. The transparency and abstraction provided by H2ML allow to use different intelligent hybrid configurations (Neural Networks, Genetic Algorithms, etc.) to control the domotic environment.

The hierarchical structure of the proposed fuzzy controller is suited to apply a divide et impera strategy to the controlled system. Main goals are decomposed into sub-goals by partitioning the input space into a finite number of regions each ones featuring a specific sub-controller.

The divide et impera strategy leads to two different kinds of fuzzy rulebase distribution: *vertical* and *horizontal* distribution.

2.4   Vertical and Horizontal Fuzzy Distribution

By "vertical fuzzy distribution" we mean a collection of dependent *control blocks* each ones represented by a single fuzzy controller or a set of horizontally distributed fuzzy controllers. The *dependency* relationship between control blocks is

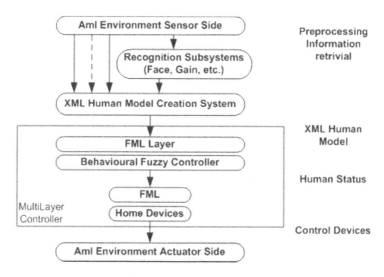

Fig. 1. Ambient Intelligence Architecture

defined as follows: given a finite set of control block CB_1, CB_2,...,CB_i,...,CB_n the output returned from the CB_i control block depends from the output computed from CB_{i-1} control block and so on. The aim of proposed vertical fuzzy distribution scheme is to separate fuzzy concepts not semantically related emphasizing the fuzzy reasoning properties.

Through the "horizontal fuzzy distribution" we can parallelize inferences on different hosts, splitting a large semantically related rulebase by mobile agent technology, thus minimizing the fuzzy inference time.

3   Experimental Results

Our scheme of fuzzy distribution allows to separate the fuzzy variables related to human behavior from those related to domotic devices (vertical distribution). This distinction is thus used to parallelize the fuzzy inference applied to domotic controllers (horizontal distribution). More precisely, the first control block (vertical wise), named *Behavioral Fuzzy Controller*, is a Mamdani controller [5] (implemented in FML) which, basically, (1) operates on H2ML program, (2)parses it, and (3) infers information about human status. The system adopts *singleton* fuzzy variables to model the behavioral concepts in fuzzy terms. *Sleeping, Working* and *Relaxing* are only some examples of singleton behavioral fuzzy variables, the following rules are examples of behavioral rules.

IF velocity is LOW **AND** leftEye is CLOSED **AND** RightEye is CLOSED **AND** Speech is LOW **AND** Position is BED **THEN** SLEEPING is ON

IF velocity is LOW **AND** leftEye is OPENED **AND** RightEye is OPENED **AND** Speech is LOW **AND** Position is Desk **AND** Acceleration is HIGH **THEN** UserStatus is WORKING is ON

IF Velocity is LOW **AND** leftEye is OPENED **AND** rightEye is OPENED **AND** Speech is LOW **AND** Position is not BED **THEN** RELAXING is ON

The information inferred at this stage will be used in the next level to control the actuator devices.

The second control block (vertical wise) is a set of semantically related controllers distributed using horizontal scheme. At this hierarchical level the system uses classic Mamdani fuzzy controllers coded in FML. In particular, we code a whole fuzzy Ambient Intelligence controller distributing the related rules (for instance: HVAC rules or lighting system rules) on different hosts by means of mobile agent technology. In this way we achieve high parallelism and a remarkable minimization for inference time [9].

Some examples of devices control distributed fuzzy rules are shown below:

IF Temperature is LOW **AND** Sleeping is ON **THEN** MotorHVACspeed is High

IF inLuminosity is LOW **AND** Working is ON **THEN** actLuminosity is High

It is simple to note that information related to behavior, inferred from root layer of hierarchic intelligence scheme, is used merely to cut the fuzzy set composing the consequent part of rules in order to influence the devices operation. An example of H2ML representation used to control services distribution is showed in figure 2.

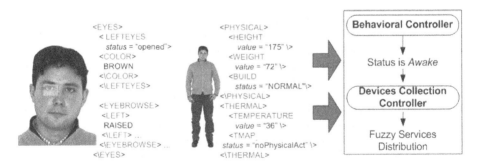

Fig. 2. H2ML-based Fuzzy Services Distribution

4   Conclusion

The combination of FML and H2ML in a multi-layered architecture represents a strong improvement for abstraction representation and efficient control management for real hardware AmI implementation (Echelon Lonworks, X10, Konnex, etc.) . Moreover, the FML layer allows to distribute fuzzy controller components on different hosts thus providing a simple platform for real ubiquitous computing system.

References

1. Z. Chen.: Computational Intelligence for decision support. Florida: CRC Press, 2000.
2. Zimmermann, H-J., Tselentis, G., van Someren M., Dounias M. (Eds.): Advances in computation intelligence and learning: methods and applications Massachusetts: Kluwer Academic Publishers, 2002.
3. Chatterjee S., Sani.: A seamless and non intrusive framework and agent for creating intelligent interactive homes. In Proceedings of the 2nd Int. Conference on Autonomous Agents, pp.436-440, 1998.
4. Mozer M.: The neural network house: An environment that adapts to its Inhabitants. In Proceedings of the 1998 AAAI Spring Symposium on Intelligent Environments, pp. 110-114, 1998.
5. Ying H.: Fuzzy system technology: a brief overview. IEEE Circuits and Systems Society, CAS Magazines, pp. 28-37, 2000.
6. Basten T., Geilen M.: Ambient Intelligence: Impact on Embedded System Design, H. de Groot (Eds.), Kluwer Academic Pub., 2003.
7. Acampora G., Ippolito L., Loia V., Siano P.: Achieving transparency and Adaptivity in Fuzzy Control Framework: an application to Power Transformers Predictive Overload System. In Proceedings of FUZZ-IEEE 2004, vol. 1, 2004.
8. Acampora G., Loia V.: Fuzzy Control Interoperability for Adaptive Domotic Framework. In Proceedings of IEEE International Conference on Industrial Informatics, pp. 184-189, 2004.
9. Acampora G., Loia V.: Fuzzy Control Interoperability for Adaptive Domotic Framework. To be published in Proceedings of FUZZ-IEEE 2005, 2005.
10. Prendinger H., Descamps S., Ishizuka M.: MPML:a markup language for controlling the behavior of life-like characters Journal of Visual Languages and Computing 15 (2004) 183-203
11. Marriott A., Stallo J.: VHML-Uncertainties and problems, A discussion. In Proceedings AAMAS-02 Workshop on EmbodiedConversational Agents-Let's Specify and Evaluate Them! 2002.
12. Arafa Y., Kamyab K., Kshirsagar S., Magnenat-Thalmann N., Guye-Vuilleme A., Thalmann D.: Two approaches to scripting character animation. In Proceedings AAMAS-02 Workshop on Embodied Conversational Agents-Let's Specify and Evaluate Them! 2002.

Towards a Multilingual QA System Based on the Web Data Redundancy[*]

Rita Aceves-Pérez[1], Luis Villaseñor-Pineda[1], and Manuel Montes-y-Gomez[2]

[1] Language Technologies Group, Computer Science Department,
National Institute of Astrophysics, Optics and Electronics (INAOE), Mexico
{rmaceves, villasen, mmontesg}@inaoep.mx
[2] Polytechnic University of Valencia, Spain
mmontes@dsic.upv.es

Abstract. This paper explores the feasibility of a multilingual question answering approach based on the Web redundancy. The paper introduces a system prototype that combines a translation machine with a statistical QA method. The main advantage of this proposal is its small dependence to a given language. The experimental results, obtained from a test set of 165 factual questions, demonstrated the great potential of the approach, and gave interesting insights about the redundancy of the web and the online translators.

1   Introduction

The documents accessible from the Web may satisfy almost every information need. However, without the appropriate access mechanisms all these documents are practically useless. In order to solve this dilemma several text processing approaches have emerged. For instance: information retrieval and question answering (QA). The goal of a QA system is to retrieve answers to questions rather than full documents to general queries [4]. For example, given a question like: "where is the Amparo Museum located?", a QA system must respond "Puebla" instead of just returning a list of documents related to the Amparo Museum. In recent years, due to the Web growth, there has been an explosive demand for better multilingual information access approaches. Multilingual QA systems are one example [3]. These systems allow answering a question based on a set of documents from several languages. In this paper we present our first experiment on multilingual question answering on the Web. This experiment considers answering English questions using Spanish Web documents and vice versa. The system architecture that we propose is different from the traditional approaches [4]. It is based on the use of online translation machines and simple pattern matching methods, rather than on sophisticated linguistic analyzes of both questions

---

[*] The present work was partially financed by the CONACYT (Project 43990A-1 and the scholarship No. 184663) third author thanks to the Secretara de Estado de Educacin y Universidades, España.

P.S. Szczepaniak et al. (Eds.): AWIC 2005, LNAI 3528, pp. 32–37, 2005.

and documents. In some degree, the purpose of this paper is to analyze the performance of automatic online translators, as well as, to study the impact of the incomplete and wrong translations over the answer precision. The rest of the paper is organized as follows. Section 2 introduces a statistical QA system for the Web. Section 3 proposes a general architecture for a multilingual QA system. Sections 4 show the experimental results. Finally, section 5 draws our conclusions and future work.

2   Statistical QA on the Web

This section describes the general architecture of a statistical QA system that allows finding answers to factual questions from the Web. It consists of three major modules: (i) query reformulation, (ii) snippets recollection, and (iii) answer extraction. The architecture is supported on the idea that the questions and their answers are commonly expressed using the same words, and that the probability of finding a simple (lexical) matching between them increases with the redundancy of the target collection [1]. It was originally adapted to Spanish [2], however it is general enough to work with questions in other languages that share some morpho-syntactic characteristics of the Spanish, such as: English, Italian, French, Portuguese and Catalan.

2.1   Query Reformulation

Given a question, this module generates a set of query reformulations. These reformulations are expressions that were probably used to write down the expected answer. We performed several experiments in order to determine the most general and useful reformulations. The following paragraphs present those with the best results. All the cases are illustrated for the question: "Who received the Nobel Peace Prize in 1992?".

First Reformulation: "Bag of Words" This reformulation is the set of non stop-words of the question. For instance, "received Nobel Peace Prize 1992".

Second Reformulation:"Verb Movement" One of our first observations after checking a list of factual questions was that the verb is frequently right after the wh-word. We also know that in order to transform an interrogative sentence into a declarative one is necessary to eliminate the verb or to move it to the final position of the sentence. The resultant sentence is expected to be more abundant in the Web that the original one. In order to take advantage of this phenomenon, but without using any kind of linguistic resource, we propose to build a set of query reformulations eliminating or moving to the end of the sentence the first and second words of the question. Two examples of these kinds of reformulations are:"the Nobel Peace Prize in 1992 received" and "Nobel Peace Prize in 1992".

Third Reformulation: "Components" In this case the question will be divided in components. A component is an expression delimited by prepositions.

Therefore, a question Q having m prepositions will be represented by a set of components $C = \{c_1, c_2, , c_{m+1}\}$. Each component ci is a sub string of the original query. New reformulations will be defined combining them. Some examples of this kind of query reformulations are: "received the Nobel Prize" "of Peace" "in 1992", and "in 1992 received the Nobel Peace Prize".

2.2 Snippets Recollection

Once the set of reformulations has been generated, this module sends them to a search engine (currently we are using Google), and then it collects the returned snippets.

2.3 Answer Extraction

From the snippets collected from the Web we compute all the n-grams (from unigrams to pentagrams) as possible answers to the given question. Then, using some statistical criteria the n-grams are ranked by decreasing likelihood of being the correct answer. The top five are presented to the user. The method for the n-gram extraction and ranking is as follows:

1. Extract the twenty most frequent unigrams satisfying predefined typographic criterion. Currently we are selecting only the words starting with an uppercase letter, the numbers and the names of the months.
2. Determine all the n-grams, from bi-grams to pentagrams, exclusively containing the frequent unigrams.
3. Rank the n-grams based on their compensated relative frequency. The relative frequency of a n-gram $g(n) = (w_1 w_n)$ is computed as follows[1]: P

$$P_{x(n)} = \frac{1}{n} \sum_{i=1}^{n} \sum_{j=1}^{n-i+1} \frac{f_{\hat{x}_j(i)}}{\sum_{y \in G_i} f_{y(i)}} \tag{1}$$

4. Show to the user the top five n-grams as possible answers.

Applying this method we obtained these answers to the example question: Rigoberta Menchu, Rigoberta Menchu Tum, Menchu, Rigoberta Menchu Recibio, Rigoberta.

3   Multilingual QA Prototype

A multilingual QA system enables the users to formulate a question in a language different from the reference corpus. Most common multilingual systems work with two languages, one for the question and another for the target collection. However, a full multilingual QA system would allow searching for answers

---

[1] We introduce the notation x(i) for the sake of simplicity. In this case x(i) indicates the i-gram x, G_i is the set of all i-grams, and j(k) represents the k-gram x contained in n-gram x(i) at the position j.

on documents from several languages. Our proposal for a multilingual QA system for the Web consists of two main modules: (i) a translation machine, and (ii) a language-independent statistical QA system. The main advantage of this prototype is it small dependence to the target language, which allows using the system in a full multilingual scenario. On the other hand, one of the main disadvantages of this architecture is it high dependence to the quality of question translations, and also to the Web redundancy in the target language.

4   Experiments

The experimental evaluation considered a set of 165 factual questions. These questions were taken from the English training corpus of CLEF 2003[2] . The answers for these questions were of four types: names of persons, organizations, locations and dates. We probed with 3 different online translators: Google, Freetranslation and Webtranslation[3]. Tables 1-3 compare the results using the different translation machines and applying the different reformulations techniques (refer to section 2.1). The mean reciprocal rank (MRR)[4] and the precision[5] are indicated for each experiment.

Table 1. MRR/Precision using the "bag of words" reformulation

Query	Translator		
	Webtranslation	Freetranslation	Google
Date	0.086/0.389	0.003/0.111	0.006/0.138
Location	0.330/0.461	0.275/0.442	0.085/0.134
Organization	0.167/0.185	0.106/0.185	0.012/0.037
Person	0.152/0.372	0.126/0.353	0.030/0.196

4.1   The Influence of Data Redundancy

It is well known that English is the most representative language on the Web (68% in accordance with the last report of Global Reach[6]). In order to analyze the effect of data redundancy on our multilingual QA approach, we made an experiment with Spanish questions using English Web documents as data repository. In this experiment we considered the same set of questions that in the

---

[2] The Cross-Language Evaluation Forum (CLEF) http://clef-campaign.org/

[3] www.google.com, www.freetranslation.com and www.imtranslator_webtranslation. paralink.com respectively.

[4] An individual question received a score equal to the reciprocal of the rank at which the first correct response was returned, or 0 if none of the responses contained a correct answer. The score for a sequence of queries is the mean of the individual query's reciprocal ranks.

[5] precision = number of found answers / number of total questions.

[6] http://www.glreach.com

Table 2. MRR/Precision using the "verb movement" reformulation

Query	Translator		
	Webtranslation	Freetranslation	Google
Date	0.120/0.25	0.037/0.055	0.037/0.055
Location	0.183/0.307	0.061/0.096	0.077/0.096
Organization	0.104/0.259	0/0	0/0
Person	0.149/0.352	0.27/0.137	0.076/0.137

Table 3. MRR/Precision using the "bag of words" reformulation

Query	Translator		
	Webtranslation	Freetranslation	Google
Date	0.071/0.111	0.004/0.056	0.048/0.086
Location	0.138/0.154	0.023/0.057	0.019/0.019
Organization	0.015/0.074	0.003/0.037	0/0
Person	0.016/0.137	0.004/0.019	0.009/0.039

previous case, and we employed the Google search engine. We used the Web-translation machine to translate the questions from Spanish to English. The answer extraction process was leaded by the "bag of words" reformulation. Table 4 shows the results.

Table 4. Spanish-English experiment

Question	MRR	Precision
Date	0.091	0.444
Location	0.264	0.596
Organization	0.148	0.444
Person	0.169	0.314

4.2   Results Discussion

The best results were obtained using Webtranslation, which produced the best question translations. This situation is clear enough when we analyzed the results from the tables 2 and 3, where a syntactically well-formed question is required. As we expected, the best results were obtained using the "bag of words" reformulation. This fact indicates that online translators tend to produce accurate word-by-word translations (using the frequent senses of the words), but they tend to generate syntactically incorrect questions. An interesting observation from the experiment was that sometimes the translation machines produce better translations that those manually constructed. This is because they use common words. For instance, the question "Which is the name of John Lennons wife?" was manually translated to Spanish into "Cuál es el nombre de la mujer the John Lennon?", while the automatic translation by Webtranslation was "Cmo se llama la esposa de John Lennon?". The noun "mujer" (woman), used in this context, is less frequent than "esposa" (wife). Another relevant fact is that sometimes the wrong translations facilitate the QA process (i.e., they favor some kind of reformulations). For instance, the question "Who is the President of the Roma football team?" was manually translated to "Cómo se llama el presidente del equipo de fétbol de Roma?", and automatically translated to "Cómo se llama el presidente de la Roma de Fútbol?". Although incorrect, the automatic translation preserves the main concepts of the question, and allows to the system easily find the answer. In addition, our results indicate that the Web redundancy has great influence on the system response. The precision for the Spanish-English experiment was 8(compare table 4 with the second column of the table 1). However, we notice that the MRR was greater on the initial experiment. This indicates that correct answers in Spanish are easily identified. We believe this is because there is less noisy information on Spanish than in English.

References

1. Brill E., Lin J., Banko M., Dumais S. and Ng A.: Data-intensive question answering. In Proceedings of the Tenth Text REtrieval Conference (TREC 2001).
2. Castillo A. del, Montes-y-Gmez M. and Villaseor-Pineda L.: QA on the Web: A preliminary study for Spanish Language. Fifth Mexican International Conference on Computer Science. (ENC04). pp. 322-328. IEEE Computer Society, ISBN 0-7695-2160-6.
3. Perret L.: Question answering system for the French language. Working Notes for the CLEF 2004 Workshop, 2004.
4. Vicedo J. L.: La Bsqueda de Respuestas: Estado Actual y Perspectivas de Futuro. Revista Iberoamericana de Inteligencia Artificial. Nmero 22, Volumen 8, Primavera 2004.

An Intelligent Information System for Detecting Web Commerce Transactions

Ioannis Anagnostopoulos[1], George Kouzas[2], and Christos Anagnostopoulos[3]

[1] Dpt of Information and Communication Systems Engineering,
University of the Aegean,
Karlovassi 83200, Samos Greece
janag@aegean.gr
[2] School of Electrical and Computer Engineering,
National Technical University of Athens,
Zographou 15773, Athens, Greece
[3] Department of Cultural Technology and Communication,
University of the Aegean,
Mytiline 81100, Lesvos Greece

Abstract. This paper proposes an algorithm for detecting web transactions through web page classification. The algorithm is implemented over a generalised regression neural network and detects e-commerce pages classifying them to the respective transaction phase according to a framework, which describes the fundamental phases of commercial transactions in the web. Many types of web pages were used in order to evaluate the robustness of the method, since no restrictions were imposed except for the language of the content, which is English. Except from revealing the accomplished sequences in a web commerce transaction, the system can be used as an assistant and consultative tool for classification purposes.

1   Introduction

The techniques most usually employed in the classification of web pages use concepts from the field of information filtering and retrieval [1] and [2]. Neural networks are chosen mainly for computational reasons, since once trained, they operate very fast and the creation of thesauri and indices is avoided [3],[4]. In addition, the use of evolution-based genetic algorithms, and the utilization of fuzzy function approximation have also been presented as possible solutions for the classification problem [5]. Finally, many experimental investigations on the use of neural networks for implementing relevance feedback in an interactive information retrieval system have been proposed [6].

2   The Web Transactions Framework

This paper describes a system that classifies e-commerce web pages under the concepts of Business Media Framework-BMF [7]. According to this framework,

P.S. Szczepaniak et al. (Eds.): AWIC 2005, LNAI 3528, pp. 38–43, 2005.

an e-commerce model can be analysed into a series of concurrent sequences, while these sequences are implemented by elementary transactions [7],[8],[9],[10]. In addition, four phases distinguish an e-commerce transaction. The knowledge phase, the intention phase, the contract phase and the settlement phase. Table 1 presents the four phases and the amount of the collected web pages, which were used as the training material. The total sample set consists of 3824 e-commerce pages, which were collected and validated by experts according to BMF. As a result, each web page depicted in Table 1 corresponds to one e-commerce type and one transaction phase. However, a respective training sample that consist of 2134 web pages and do not describe commercial transactions (web pages irrelative to web commerce transac-tions), was collected automatically using a meta-search engine tool. This tool collects randomly web pages from specified search engine directories and its functions are described in [11].

Table 1. Transaction phases and types of e-commerce pages according to the BMF

Transaction Phase - PT	e-commerce page type	web pages (per type)	web pages (per PT)
Knowledge	Query engines homepages	322	1305
	Directory pages	339	
	Product information pages	365	
	Registration pages	279	
Intention	Product catalogue pages	372	777
	Order – Payment pages	405	
Contracting	Terms and conditions pages	387	387
Settlement	Settlement monitoring pages	313	1355
	Digital delivery pages	364	
	Contact and complaint forms	358	
	After sales support pages	320	

3   Feature Selection

This section describes the feature extraction procedure for the training sample. The training sample consists of five classes from which, four of them correspond to the four BMF transaction phases and one class correspond to web pages that do not offer commercial services. Common information filtering techniques such as stop lists, character filters and suffix-stripping methods were initially used for reducing the large amount of the indexed terms. However, the Information Gain (IG) technique was adopted for feature selection. This technique measures the statistical dependence be-tween a term and the categorised class based on the entropy. Thus, terms with small information gain are discarded [12]. Rather than evaluating the entropy of a term distribution among a set of documents as is done for the signal-to-noise ratio technique, in the specific technique the entropy of the class distribution taken under consideration.

With the help of the IG technique 432 terms were finally selected in order to compose the vector that represents web pages (Web Page Vector WPV). The WPV characterise a web page by assigning a unique profile of weight values that depend on the im-portance of each term in the tested web page. In other words, weights are assigned to terms as statistical importance indicators. If m distinct terms are assigned for content identification, a web page is conceptually represented as an m-dimensional vector, named WPV. Equation 1, highlights the lnc formula used for the weighting mechanism, which is based on the SMART system as described in [13]. Web Page Vector is defined as $WPV_i = \{w_{i1}, w_{i1}, ..., w_{ik}\}$, while the weight of term k in the ith web page is normalized using the cosine length of the vector, where l equals to 432 and corresponds to the total amount of the used terms.

$$w_{ik}^{WPV} = (\log(tf_{ik}) + 1) \cdot (\sum_{k=1}^{282} [\log(tf_{ik}) + 1]^2)^{-1/2} \tag{1}$$

4   System Architecture

Generalised Regression Neural Networks (GRNNs) have the special ability to deal with sparse and non-stationary data whose statistical properties change over time. Due to their generality, they can be also used in various problems where non-linear relationships exist among inputs and outputs. The addressed problem can be considered to belong in this category since it is a document-mapping problem. A GRNN is designed to perform a non-linear regression analysis. Thus, if is the probability density function of the vector random variable x and its scalar random variable z, then the GRNN calculates the conditional mean of the output vector. The joint probability density function (pdf) is required to compute the above conditional mean. GRNN approximates the pdf from the training vectors using Parzen windows estimation, which are considered as Gaussian functions with a constant diagonal covariance matrix according to Equation 2.

$$E(z\backslash x) = \int_{-\infty}^{\infty} z \cdot f(x, z)dz \left/ \int_{-\infty}^{\infty} f(x, z)dz \right. , \tag{2}$$

where $f_p(x\backslash z) = ((2\pi\sigma^2)^{(N+1)/2})^{-1} \cdot P^{-1} \sum_{i=1}^{P} \left(e^{\frac{-D_i^2}{2\sigma^2}} \cdot e^{\frac{-(z-x_i)^2}{2\sigma^2}} \right)$

In the above equation P equals to the number of sample points x_1, N is the dimension of the vector of sample points, D_1 is the Euclidean distance between x and x_1 calculated by $D_i = \|x - x_i\| = (\sum_{i=1}^{N} (x - x_i)^2)^{\frac{1}{2}}$, where N is the amount of the input units to the network. Additionally, is a width parameter, which satisfies the asymptotic behaviour as the number of Parzen windows becomes large according to Equation 3 where S is the scale. When an estimated pdf is included in $E(z\backslash x)$, the substitution process defines Equation 4 in order to compute each component z_j.

$$\lim_{P \to \infty} (P \sigma^N(P)) = \infty \ and \ \lim_{P \to \infty} \sigma(P) = 0, \ when \ \sigma = \frac{S}{P^{E/N}}, 0 \le E < 1 \quad (3)$$

$$z_j(x) = (\sum_{i=1}^{P} c_i)^{-1} \sum_{i=1}^{P} z_j^i c_i, \ where \ c_i = e^{\frac{-D_i^2}{2\sigma^2}} \quad (4)$$

A clustering procedure is often incorporated in GRNN, where for any given sample x_1, instead of computing the new Gaussian kernel k_1 at centre x each time, the distance of that sample to the closest centre of a previously established kernel is found, and the old closest kernel $(k-1)_1$ is used again. Taking into account this approach, Equation 4 is transformed to Equation 5.

$$z_j(x) = (\sum_{i=1}^{P} B_i(k)c_i)^{-1} \sum_{i=1}^{P} A_i(k)c_i, \quad 1 \le j \le M, \quad (5)$$

where $A_i(k) = A_i(k-1) + z_j$, $B_i(k) = B_i(k-1) + 1$

The topology of the proposed neural network is 432-5958-5-5. The input layer consists of 432 nodes, which correspond to the number of the WPV terms. The second layer is the pattern layer consisting of 5958 that correspond to the training patterns. It follows the summation/division layer, which consists of 5 nodes that feed a same amount of processing elements in the output layer representing the 5 classes to be recognised. From the input to the pattern layer a training/test vector X is distributed, while the connection weights from the input layer to the kth unit in the pattern layer store the centre X_1 of the kth Gaussian kernel. In the pattern layer the summation function for the kth pattern unit computes the Euclidean distance D_k between the input vector and the stored centre X_1 and transforms it through the previously described exponential function c_1. Afterwards, the B coefficients are set as weights values to the remaining units in the next layer. Finally, the output layer receives inputs from the summation/division layer and outputs are estimated conditional means, computing the error on the basis of the desired output.

The generalised regression algorithm was implemented in C++ and trained in a Pentium IV, 2.4 GHz, 1024 MB RAM. The time needed for the completion of the training epoch, was approximately 3.1 minutes. During the training period, the beta coefficient for all the local approximators of the pattern layer, which was used to smooth the data being monitored, was set to 100 $(\beta = 1/2\sigma^2 = 100)$. In addition, the mean and the variance values of the randomised biases were equal to 0 and 0.5 respectively.

The values inside the parentheses in Table 2 correspond to the confusion matrix of the training epoch in percentage values. This matrix is defined by labelling the desired classification on the rows and the predicted classifications on the columns. Since the predicted classification has to be the same as the desired classification, the ideal situation was to have all the exemplars end up on the diagonal cells of the matrix. Therefore, the training confusion matrix displays

Table 2. Confusion Matrices: training (percentage values) / testing - absolute values

		Class assigned by the system					P (%)
		C_1	C_2	C_3	C_4	C_5	
Actual	C_1	(98,72)	(1,01)	(0)	(0,09)	(0,19)	**79,53**
class		1752	118	33	149	151	
	C_2	(1,31)	(98,63)	(0)	(0,05)	(0)	**78,42**
		123	1025	18	77	64	
	C_3	(0,04)	(0)	(99.83)	(0.13)	(0)	**81,07**
		43	17	501	34	23	
	C_4	(0,01)	(0)	(0)	(99,66)	(0,33)	**82,50**
		185	78	23	1966	131	
	C_5	(0,36)	(0)	(0,723)	(0,24)	(96,86)	**87,28**
		215	76	29	146	3197	

values, where each one corresponds to the percentage effect that a particular input has on a particular output. The proposed information system was tested with 10174 web pages Values not included in parentheses in Table 2 form the testing confusion matrix between the tested classes. The diagonal cells correspond to the correctly classified web pages for each class respectively (absolute values), while the other cells show the misclassified pages. In every row, the systems ability in terms of correct classification over an a priori known type of web pages is tested. The overall performance of the system outlines the ability to correctly classify the tested web pages in respect to the sample set for all the tested classes. Therefore, it is derived from the total amount of the correctly classified web pages residing in the diagonal cells, versus the total amount of the sample set (overall performance = 0.83). Generally, the implemented GRNN presents a high level of accuracy in testing most of the classes.

5   Conclusions

This paper proposes a generalised regression algorithm, which is implemented over a four layer Generalised Regression Neural Network and scopes to highlight and classify web commerce transactions. The classification is based on a well-known e-commerce framework according to which, an e-commerce model can be analysed into a series of concurrent sequences, while these sequences are implemented by elementary transactions. Except for classification purposes, the system can be exploited in many practical or research areas of e-commerce. This is due to the fact that using the proposed intelligent system commercial transactions can be quantified. Thus, the system can be either used locally in commercial servers for monitoring customer behaviour directly through local information or it can be launched independently to a portal, in order to survey and measure commercial activities, services and transactions on the web.

References

1. C.J. van Rijsbergen, Information Retrieval, Butterworths, London, Second Edition, 1979.
2. G. Salton, Automatic Text Processing, Addison-Wesley Publishing Company Inc, 1989.
3. Kohonen T., Kaski S., Lagus K., Salojarvi J., Honkela J., Paatero V. and Saarela A., Self organization of a massive document collection, IEEE Transactions on Neural Networks, 11(3):574-585, Special Issue on Neural Networks for Data Mining and Knowledge Discovery, May 2000.
4. Chung-Hsin Lin, Hsinchun Chen, An automatic indexing and neural network approach to concept retrieval and classification of multilingual (Chinese-English) documents, IEEE Transactions on Systems, Man and Cybernetics, Part B, pp. 75 - 88 Feb. 1996.
5. Rialle V., Meunier J., Oussedik S., Nault G., Semiotic and Modeling Computer Classifica-tion of Text with Genetic Algorithm: Analysis and first Results, Proceedings ISAS'97, pp. 325-30, 1997.
6. Anagnostopoulos I., Anagnostopoulos C., Papaleonidopoulos I., Loumos V. and Kayafas E., A proposed system for segmentation of information sources in portals and search engines repositories, 5th IEEE International Conference of Information Fusion 2000, IF2002, pp. 1450-1456, vol.2, 7-11 July 2002, Annapolis, Maryland, USA.
7. Klose M. and Lechner U., Design of Business Media - An integrated Model of Electronic Commerce, 5th Americas Conference on Information Systems (AMCIS'99), pp.115-117, 1999.
8. Schmid B.F., Lindemann, M.A, Elements of a reference model for electronic markets, Proceedings of the Thirty-First Hawaii International Conference on System Sciences, vol.4, pp. 193-201, 1998.
9. Schmid, B., What is new about the Digital Economy, Electronic Markets, vol.11, no.1, 04/2001.
10. Timmers, P, Gadient, Y., Schmid, B., Selz, D., Business Models for Electronic Markets, Electronic Commerce in Europe, EM - Electronic Markets, vol. 8, no.2, 07/1998.
11. Anagnostopoulos I., Psoroulas I., Loumos V. and Kayafas E., Implementing a customised meta-search interface for user query personalisation, IEEE 24th International Conference on Information Technology Interfaces, ITI 2002 pp. 79-84, June 24-27, 2002, Cav-tat/Dubrovnik, CROATIA.
12. Yang Y and Pedersen J (1997) A comparative study on feature selection in text categoriza-tion. In: Proceedings of the 14th International Conference in Machine Learning, ICML97, pp. 412 420, 1997, Nashville, TN, USA.
13. Buckley C, Salton G and Allan J (1993) Automatic retrieval with locality information using SMART. In: Proceedings of the 1st Text REtrieval Conference (TREC-1), pp. 59-72, 1993, Gaithersburg, MD, USA.

Tuples Extraction from HTML Using Logic Wrappers and Inductive Logic Programming

Costin Bădică[1], Amelia Bădică[2], and Elvira Popescu[1]

[1] University of Craiova, Software Engineering Department,
Bvd.Decebal 107, Craiova, RO-200440, Romania
{badica_costin, elvira_popescu}@software.ucv.ro
[2] University of Craiova, Business Information Systems Department,
A.I.Cuza 13, Craiova, RO-200585, Romania
ameliabd@yahoo.com

Abstract. This paper presents an approach for applying inductive logic programming to information extraction from HTML documents structured as unranked ordered trees. We consider information extraction from Web resources that are abstracted as providing sets of tuples. Our approach is based on defining a new class of wrappers as a special class of logic programs – *logic wrappers*. The approach is demonstrated with examples and experimental results in the area of collecting product information, highlighting the advantages and the limitations of the method.

1 Introduction

The Web was designed for human consumption rather than machine processing. This hinders the task of extracting useful information from it. Therefore the problem of automating information extraction (IE hereafter) from the Web has received a lot of attention in the last years ([1, 3, 6, 4, 11, 9]).

This paper deals with automating IE from HTML documents using inductive logic programming (ILP hereafter). IE is concerned with locating specific pieces of information in text documents including HTML and XML. A program that is actually used for performing the IE task is called a *wrapper* ([7]). ILP studies learning from examples within the framework provided by clausal logic.

IE from HTML uses two document models: a linear or string-based model and a tree-based model. It is appreciated that tree-based wrappers are more expressive than string-based wrappers ([11, 9]). In our work we consider HTML documents modeled as unranked ordered trees. IE approaches that adopted tree-based models were also reported in [6, 11, 3]. Recently, [9] proposed the combination of string and tree wrappers to yield more powerful wrappers.

The paper is a follow-up of our previous work reported in [1, 2]. In [1] we presented a methodology and experimental results on applying ILP to IE from HTML documents that represent printer information. The task was to extract single fields. In [2] we enhanced the original approach by enriching the target document representation and using an explicit set of negative examples, rather that treating all non-positive examples as negative examples.

P.S. Szczepaniak et al. (Eds.): AWIC 2005, LNAI 3528, pp. 44–50, 2005.

In this paper we adopt a relational data model of the information resources and we are focusing on the task of tuples extraction. Many Web resources can be abstracted in this way, including: search engines result pages, product catalogues, news sites, product information sheets, a.o. Their content is presented to the human user as HTML documents formatted using HTML tables or lists. We consider two problems: extracting tuples from a rectangular table and extracting tuples from a nested table with the imformation organized hierarchically.

Our paper is structured as follows. Section 2 contains some background on IE, tree-based document representations using logic programming and ILP. Section 3 contains a discussion of the problems addressed in our experiments and some experimental results. Section 4 concludes and points to future work.

2   Background

This section contains background on: IE, relational representation of XHTML documents, logic wrappers and the use of ILP for IE. More details are in [1].

2.1   The IE Process

We propose a generic IE process structured into the following sequence of stages: i) Collect HTML pages of interest using Web browsing and crawling and download them to a local repository; ii) Preprocess and convert the documents from HTML to XHTML; iii) Manually extract a few items and annotate accordingly the XHTML documents; iv) Parse the annotated XHTML documents and generate the input for the learner; v) Apply the learning algorithm and obtain the wrapper; vii) Compile the wrapper to an XML query language; viii) Apply the wrapper to extract new information from other documents.

Note that this IE process is parameterized according to the following dimensions: number of documents used for manual IE (stage iii), the learning technique (stages iv and v) and the IE engine (stages vii and viii).

2.2   L-Wrappers for IE from HTML

The idea of representing documents and wrappers using logic programming is not entirely new ([4, 5, 8, 12]). All of these approaches assume that the target document is represented as a list of tokens with features. We propose a relational representation of an XHTML document seen as an unranked ordered tree.

The *structure* of an XHTML document consists of a set of document nodes that are nested in a tree like structure. Each node has assigned a specific tag from a given finite set of tags Σ. There is a special tag $text \in \Sigma$ that designates a text node.

The *content* of an XHTML document consists of the actual text in the text elements and the attribute-value pairs attached to the other document elements.

We assign a unique identifier (an integer) to each node of the document tree. Let $\mathcal{N}$ be the set of all node identifiers.

The structure of an XHTML document is represented using three relations:

i) $child \subseteq \mathcal{N} \times \mathcal{N}$, $(child(P, C) = true) \Leftrightarrow (P$ is the parent of $C)$.
ii) $next \subseteq \mathcal{N} \times \mathcal{N}$, $(next(L, N) = true) \Leftrightarrow (L$ is the left sibling of $N)$.
iii) $tag \subseteq \mathcal{N} \times \Sigma$, $(tag(N, T) = true) \Leftrightarrow (T$ is the tag of node $N)$.

We introduce two sets to represent the content component of an XHTML document tree: the set $\mathcal{S}$ of content elements, which are the strings attached to text nodes and the values assigned to attributes, and the set $\mathcal{A}$ of attributes. The content of an XHTML document is then represented using two relations:

i) $content \subseteq \mathcal{N} \times \mathcal{S}$, $(content(N, S) = true) \Leftrightarrow (S$ is the string contained by the text node $N)$.
ii) $attribute\_value \subseteq \mathcal{N} \times \mathcal{A} \times \mathcal{S}$, $(attribute\_value(N, A, S) = true) \Leftrightarrow (S$ is the string value of the attribute A of the node $N)$.

Based on our experimental results reported in [2], we found useful to enhance the representation of the document structure with two new relations:

i) $first \subseteq \mathcal{N}$, $(first(X) = true) \Leftrightarrow (X$ is the first child of its parent node).
ii) $last \subseteq \mathcal{N}$, $(last(X) = true) \Leftrightarrow (X$ is the last child of its parent node).

This representation allows the definition of *L-wrappers* (i.e. *logic wrappers*).

Definition 1. *(L-wrapper) An* L-wrapper *is a logic program defining a relation* $extract(N_1, \ldots, N_k) \subseteq \mathcal{N} \times \ldots \times \mathcal{N}$. *For each clause, the head is* $extract(N_1, \ldots, N_k)$ *and the body is a conjunction of literals in a set* $\mathcal{R}$ *of relations.*

Every tuple of relation $extract$ is extracted by the wrapper. Note that relation $content$ is used to find the content of the extracted tuples. $attribute\_value$ could also be used in the clause bodies to check additional constraints on attributes of extracted nodes. Note also that in our case $\mathcal{R} = \{child, next, tag, first, last\}$.

The manual writing of L-wrappers is a tedious and error-prone process requiring a careful analysis of the target document. Fortunately, it is possible to learn L-wrappers with a general purpose learning program.

2.3   Learning L-Wrappers Using ILP

ILP is a combination of inductive machine learning with representation of theories as logic programs. In our experiments we have used FOIL – First Order Inductive Learner, an ILP program developed by J. R. Quinlan at the beginning of the '90s ([10]). In what follows we assume that the reader has some familiarity with FOIL. For a detailed description see [10].

We mapped our training data as input for FOIL. We assumed that in the training stage the user selects a single training document and performs a few extraction tasks on it. FOIL's input is split in three parts:

i) The definition of the relations arguments types. We used a single type that represents the set $\mathcal{N}$ of all the nodes found in the training document.

ii) The extensional definition of the target relation *extract*. The positive examples are the tuples manually extracted by the user. If negative examples are not provided explicitly then they are automatically generated by FOIL using the closed world assumption (i.e. all the other tuples that are not postive examples).

iii) The extensional definitions of the background relations *child*, *next*, *tag*, *first* and *last*. For convenience, we have replaced the relation *tag* with a set of relations r_σ, for all $\sigma \in \Sigma$, defined as $r_\sigma = \{N | tag(N, \sigma) = true\}$.

3   Experiments and Discussion

We performed experiments of learning L-wrappers for extracting printer information from Hewlett Packard's Web site. The information is represented in two column HTML tables (see figure 1). Each row contains a pair (feature name, feature value). Consecutive rows represent related features and are grouped in feature classes. For example there is a row with the feature name 'Print technology' and the feature value 'HP Thermal Inkjet'. This row has the feature class 'Print quality/technology'. So actually this table contains triples (feature class, feature name, feature value). Some triples may have identical feature classes.

In what follows we consider two experiments: i) tuples extraction from flat information resources, examplifying with pairs (feature name, feature value); ii) coping with hierarchical information by extracting pairs (feature class, feature name). We have used the same test data as in [1], only the learning tasks were changed. We used examples from a single training document with 28 tuples.

Speed/monthly volume	
Print speed, black (pages per minute)	Up to 15 ppm
Print speed, color (pages per minute)	Up to 11 ppm
Recommended monthly volume, maximum	12,000 pages
Print quality / technology	
Print technology	HP Thermal Inkjet
Print quality, black	up to 1200 x 600 dpi
Print quality, color	up to 1200 x 600 dpi on photo paper
Resolution technology	HP PhotoREt III
Paper handling / media	
Paper trays, std.	2
Paper trays, max.	2

Fig. 1. An XHTML document fragment and its graphic view

3.1   Tuples Extraction from Flat Information Resources

We performed an experiment of learning to extract the tuples containing the feature name and feature value from HP printer information sheets. The experimental results are reported in table 1, row 1.

Because the number of tuples excedes the size of FOIL's default tuple space, we explicitly set this size to a higher value (300000) and we used a random sample representing a fraction of the negative examples in the learning process.

Table 1. Experiments with tuples extraction

Ex.no.	No.pos.ex	Frac.neg.ex	Prec.	Rec.	No.lit.
1	24, 28	20 %	0.959	1	14
2	24, 28	20 %	1	1	15

The L-wrapper learnt consisted of a single clause:
$extract(A, B) \leftarrow tag(A, text) \wedge tag(B, text) \wedge child(C, A) \wedge child(D, B) \wedge$
$\quad child(E, C) \wedge child(F, E) \wedge child(G, D) \wedge child(H, G) \wedge child(I, F) \wedge$
$\quad child(J, I) \wedge next(J, K) \wedge first(J) \wedge child(K, L) \wedge child(L, H).$

This rule extracts all the pairs of text nodes such that the grand-grand-grand-grandparent of the first node (J) is the first child of its parent node and the left sibling of the grand-grand-grand-grandparent of the second node (K).

3.2   Tuples Extraction from Hierarchical Information Resources

The idea of modeling nested documents using a relational approach and building wrappers accordingly to this model is not entirely new; see [7].

In this section we present an experiment of learning to extract pairs (feature class, feature name) from printer information sheets. Note that because we may have many features in the same class, the information is hierarchically structured. The experimental results are reported in table 1, row 2.

The L-wrapper learnt consisted of a single clause:
$extract(A, B) \leftarrow child(C, A) \wedge child(D, B) \wedge tag(C, span) \wedge child(E, C) \wedge$
$\quad child(F, E) \wedge next(F, G) \wedge child(H, G) \wedge last(E) \wedge child(I, D) \wedge child(J, I) \wedge$
$\quad child(K, J) \wedge child(L, K) \wedge next(L, M) \wedge child(N, M) \wedge child(H, N).$

There is one difference from the flat case – how examples are collected. In this case, some examples will share the feature class. Moreover, in the general case, some fields will need to be selected repeatedly during the manual extraction process (like the feature class in the printer example). This can be avoided by designing the graphical user interface that guides the example selection such that the tuple previously selected is always saved and thus its fields may be reused in the next selection.

3.3   Discussion

In our experiments we used the closed world assumption to generate the negative examples. This means that each tuple not given as positive example, automatically counts as negative example. Let d be the size of the training document (i.e. the number of nodes) and let k be the tuple arity. The number of negative examples is proportional with d^k, i.e. it is exponential in the tuple arity. For example, our documents had about 1000 nodes. This means that for tuples of arity 3, the total number of negative examples is about 10^9.

For this reason we had problems with learning to extract tuples of arity greater than 2. Because the number of negative examples exceded the memory available, we were forced to use for learning a random sample representing a very small fraction (less than 0.1 %) of the total number of the negative examples. This had the effect of producing wrappers with a very low precision.

4   Conclusions

In this paper we have shown the advantages and limitations of applying ILP to learn L-wrappers for tuple extraction from HTML documents structured as trees. As future work we have in mind the investigation of the possibility to automatically translate our L-wrappers to an XML query language and to find clever methods to reduce the number of negative examples needed.

References

1. Bădică, C., Bădică, A.: Rule Learning for Feature Values Extraction from HTML Product Information Sheets. In: Boley, H., Antoniou, G. (eds): *Proc. RuleML'04*, Hiroshima, Japan. LNCS 3323, Springer-Verlag (2004) 37–48
2. Bădică, C., Popescu, E., Bădică, A.: Learning Logic Wrappers for Information Extraction from the Web. In: Papazoglou M., Yamazaki, K. (eds.) *Proc. SAINT'2005 Workshops. Computer Intelligence for Exabyte Scale Data Explosion*, Trento, Italy. IEEE Computer Society Press, (2005) 336–339
3. Chidlovskii, B.: Information Extraction from Tree Documents by Learning Subtree Delimiters. In: *Proc. IIWeb'03*, Acapulco, Mexico (2003), 3–8
4. Freitag, D.: Information extraction from HTML: application of a general machine learning approach. In: *Proc. AAAI'98*, (1998), 517–523
5. Junker, M., Sintek, M., Rinck, M.: Learning for Text Categorization and Information Extraction with ILP, In: *Proc. Workshop on Learning Language in Logic*, Bled, Slovenia, (1999)
6. Kosala, R., Bussche, J. van den, Bruynooghe, M., Blockeel, H.: Information Extraction in Structured Documents Using Tree Automata Induction. In: *Principles of Data Mining and Knowledge Discovery*, 6th *European Conf.*, Helsinki, Finland, LNAI 2431, Springer-Verlag (2002), 299–310
7. Kushmerick, N.: Wrapper induction: Efficiency and expressiveness. *Artificial Intelligence*, No.118, Elsevier Science (2000), 15–68
8. Kushmerick, N., Thomas, B.: Adaptive Information Extraction: Core Technologies for Information Agents, In: *Intelligent Information Agents R&D in Europe: An AgentLink perspective* (Klusch, Bergamaschi, Edwards & Petta, eds.). LNAI 2586, Springer-Verlag (2003), 79–103

9. Ikeda, D., Yamada, Y., Hirokawa, S.: Expressive Power of Tree and String Based Wrappers. In: *Proc. IIWeb'03*, Acapulco, Mexoco, (2003), 21-16
10. Quinlan, J. R., Cameron-Jones, R. M.: Induction of Logic Programs: FOIL and Related Systems, *New Generation Computing*, 13, (1995), 287–312
11. Sakamoto, H., Arimura, H., Arikawa, S.: Knowledge Discovery from Semistructured Texts. In: Arikawa, S., Shinohara, A. (eds.): *Progress in Discovery Science*. LNCS 2281, Springer-Verlag (2002) 586–599
12. Thomas, B.: Token-Templates and Logic Programs for Intelligent Web Search. *Intelligent Information Systems*. Special Issue: Methodologies for Intelligent Information Systems, 14(2/3) (2000), 241-261

Immune Systems in Multi-criterion Evolutionary Algorithm for Task Assignments in Distributed Computer System

Jerzy Balicki[1]

Naval University of Gdynia,
ul. Smidowicza 69, Gdynia 81-103, Poland
J.Balicki@amw.gdynia.pl,
http://www.amw.gdynia.pl

Abstract. In this paper, an improved model of the immune system to handle constraints in multi-criteria optimization problems has been proposed. The problem that is of interest to us is the new task assignment problem for a distributed computer system. Both a workload of a bottleneck computer and the cost of machines are minimized; in contrast, a reliability of the system is maximized. Moreover, constraints related to memory limits, task assignment and computer locations are imposed on the feasible task assignment. Finally, an evolutionary algorithm based on tabu search procedure and the immune system model is proposed to provide task assignments.

1 Introduction

Evolutionary algorithms (EAs) have to exploit a supplementary procedure to incorporate constraints into fitness function in order to conduct the search correctly. An approach based on the penalty function is the most commonly used to respect constraints. Similarly, the penalty technique is frequently used to handle constraints in multi-criteria evolutionary algorithms to find the Pareto-suboptimal outcomes. However, penalty functions have some familiar limitations, from which the most noteworthy is the complicatedness to identify appropriate penalty coefficients.

The homomorphous mappings have been proposed as the constraint-handling technique of EA to deal with parameter optimization problems in order to avoid some impenetrability related to the penalty function. Then, a constrained-handling scheme based on a model of the immune system have been designed to optimization problems with one criterion.

In this paper, we propose an improved model of the immune system to handle constraints in multi-criteria optimization problems. Both a workload of a bottleneck computer and the cost of machines are minimized; in contrast, a reliability of the system is maximized. Moreover, constraints related to memory limits, task assignment and computer locations are imposed on the feasible task assignment. Finally, an evolutionary algorithm based on tabu search procedure

P.S. Szczepaniak et al. (Eds.): AWIC 2005, LNAI 3528, pp. 51–56, 2005.

and the immune system model is proposed to provide task assignments to the distributed systems.

2   Immune System

The immune system can be seen as a distributed adaptive system that is capable for learning, using memory, and associative retrieval of information in recognition. Many local interactions provide, in consequence, fault tolerance, dynamism and adaptability [2]. A model of primary response in the attendance of a trespasser was discussed by Forrest et al. [7]. Besides, the model of secondary response related to memory was assembled by Smith [12]. Both detectors and antigens were represented as strings of symbols in the first computer model of the immune system by Farmer et al. [6].

The model of immune network and the negative selection algorithm are major models in which most of the current work is based [8]. Moreover, there are others used to simulate ability of the immune system to detect patterns in a noise environment, aptitude to discover and maintain diverse classes of patterns and skill to learn effectively, even when not all the potential types of invaders had been previously presented to the immune system [5].

Differential equations to simulate the dynamics of the lymphocytes by calculation the change of the concentration of lymphocytes' clones has been applied by Jerne [9]. Lymphocytes work as an interconnected network. On the other hand, the negative selection algorithm (NSA) for detection of changes has been developed by Forrest at el. [7]. This algorithm is based on the discrimination principle that is used to know what is a part of the immune system and what is not [8].

The NSA can be used to handle constraints by isolating the contemporary population in two groups [2]. Feasible solutions called "antigens" create the first cluster, and the second cluster of individuals consists of "antibodies" – infeasible solutions. For that reason, the NSA is applied to produce a set of detectors that determine the state of constraints.

We assume the fitness for antibodies is equal to zero. Then, a randomly chosen antigen G^- is compared against the σ antibodies that were selected without replacement. After that, the distance S between the antigen G^- and the antibody B^- is calculated due to the amount of similarity at the genotype level [2]:

$$S(G^-, B^-) \sum_{m=1}^{M} s_m(G^-, B^-), \tag{1}$$

where

- M - the length of the sequence representing the antigen G^- (the length of the antibody B^- is the same),
- $s_m = \begin{cases} 1 \ if \ G_m^- \ is \ a \ matching \ to \ B_m^- \ at \ position \ m, \\ 0 \ in \ the \ other \ case. \end{cases} m = \overline{1, M}$;

The fitness of the antibody with the highest matching magnitude S is increased by adding its amount of similarity. The antibodies are returned to the current population and the process of increasing the fitness of the winner is repeated typically tree times the number of antibodies. Each time, a randomly chosen antigen is compared against the same subset of antibodies.

Afterwards, a new population is constructed by reproduction, crossover and mutation without calculations of fitness. Above process is repeated until a convergence of population or until a maximal number of iterations is exceeded. Then, the final population of the NSA is returned to the external evolutionary algorithm.

The measure of genotype similarity between antigen and antibody depends on the representation. The measure of similarity for the binary representation can be re-defined for integer representation:

$$S'(G^-, B^-) = \sum_{m=1}^{M} |G_m^- - S_m^-|. \tag{2}$$

The negative selection algorithm is a modified genetic algorithm in which infeasible solutions that are similar to feasible ones are preferred in the current population. Although, almost all random selections are based on the uniform distribution, the pressure is directed to improve the fitness of appropriate infeasible solutions. Ranking procedure for the NSA has been described in [1]

3   Task Assignment

Let the negative selection algorithm with the ranking procedure be called NSA+. To test its ability to handle constraints, we consider a multicriteria optimization problem for task assignment in a distributed computer system [1].

Finding allocations of program modules may decrease the total time of a program execution by taking a benefit of the particular properties of some workstations or an advantage of the computer load. An adaptive evolutionary algorithm has been considered for solving multiobjective optimization problems related to task assignment that minimize Z_{max}– a workload of a bottleneck computer and F_2 – the cost of machines [1]. The total numerical performance of workstations is another criterion for assessment of task assignment and it has been involved to multicriteria task assignment problem in [1]. Moreover, a reliability R of the system is an additional criterion that is important to assess the quality of a task assignment.

In the considered problem, both a workload of a bottleneck computer and the cost of machines are minimized; in contrast, a reliability of the system is maximized. Moreover, constraints related to memory limits, task assignment and computer locations are imposed on the feasible task assignment.

A set of program modules $\{M_1, ..., M_m, ..., M_M\}$ communicated to each others is considered among the coherent computer network with computers located at the processing nodes from the set $W = \{w_1, ..., w_i, ..., w_I\}$. A set of program modules is mapped into the set of parallel performing tasks $\{T_1, ..., T_v, ..., T_V\}$ [13].

Let the task T_v be executed on computers taken from the set of available computer sorts. $\prod = \{\pi_1, ..., \pi_j, ..., \pi_J\}$. The overhead performing time of the task T_v by the computer π_j is represented by an item t_{vj}. Let π_j be failed independently due to an exponential distribution with rate λj. Computers can be allocated to nodes and tasks can be assigned to them in purpose to maximize the reliability function R defined, as below:

$$R(x) = \prod_{v=1}^{V} \prod_{i=1}^{I} \prod_{j=1}^{J} exp(-\lambda_j t_{vj} x_{vi}^m x_{ij}^\pi), \tag{3}$$

where

- $x_{ij}^\pi = \begin{cases} 1 \ if \ \ \pi_j^- \ is \ assigned \ to \ the \ \ w_i \\ 0 \ in \ \ the \ \ other \ \ case. \end{cases}$

- $x_{vi}^m = \begin{cases} 1 \ if \ \ task \ T_v \ is \ assigned \ to \ the \ \ w_i \\ 0 \ in \ \ the \ \ other \ \ case. \end{cases}$

- $x = [x_{11}^m, ..., x_{1I}^m, ..., x_{vi}^m, ..., x_{VI}^m, x_{11}^\pi, ...x_{1J}^\pi, ..., x_{ij}^\pi, ..., x_{I1}^\pi, ..., x_{Ij}^\pi, ..., x_{IJ}^\pi]^T.$

The workload $Z_{max(x)}$ of the bottleneck computer for the allocation x is provided by the subsequent formula:

$$z_{max}(x) = \begin{array}{c} max \\ i \in \overline{1,I} \end{array} \left\{ \sum_{j=1}^{J} \sum_{v=1}^{V} t_{vj} x_{vi}^m x_{ij}^\pi + \sum_{v=1}^{V} [\sum_{\substack{u=1 \\ u \notin v}}^{V}][\sum_{\substack{i=1 \\ k \notin i}}^{I}] \sum_{k=1}^{I} \tau_{vuik} x_{vi}^m x_{uk}^m \right\}, \tag{4}$$

- where τ_{vuik} –the total communication time between the task T_v assigned to the ith node and the T_u assigned to the kth node.

Let the following memories $z_1, ..., z_r, ..., z_R$ be available in an entire system and let d_{jr} be the capacity of memory z_r in the workstation π_j. We assume the task T_v reserves c_{vr} units of memory z_r and holds it during a program execution. Both values c_{vr} and d_{jr} are nonnegative and limited.

The memory limit in a machine cannot be exceeded in the ith node, what is written, as bellows:

$$\sum_{v=1}^{V} c_{vr} x_{vi}^m \leq \sum_{j=1}^{J} d_{jr} x_{ij}^\pi, \quad i = \overline{1,I}, \ \overline{1,R}. \tag{5}$$

The other measure of the task assignment is a cost of computers [1]:

$$F_2(x) = \sum_{i=1}^{I} \sum_{j=1}^{J} K_j X_{ij}^\pi, \tag{6}$$

where K_j corresponds to the cost of the computer π_j.

4   Tabu-Based Adaptive Evolutionary Algorithm Using NSA

Let (X, F, P) be the multi-criterion optimization question for finding the representation of Pareto-optimal solutions. It is established, as follows:

1. X - an admissible solution set

$$X = x \in B^{I(V+J)} | \sum_{v=1}^{V} c_{vr} x_{vi}^m < \sum_{j=1}^{J} d_{jr} x_{ij}^\pi, i = \overline{1, I}, r = \overline{1, R};$$

$$\sum_{i=1}^{I} x_{vi}^m = 1, v = \overline{1, V}; \sum_{j=1}^{J} x_{ij}^\pi = 1, i = \overline{1, I}$$

where $B = \{0, 1\}$
2. F - a quality vector criterion

$$F : X \to R^3, \tag{7}$$

where R–the set of real numbers,
$F_x = [- - R_x, Z_{max}(x), F_2(x)]^T$ for $x \in X$,
$R(x), Z_{max}(x), F_2$ (x) are calculated by (3), (4) and (6), respectively
3. P - the Pareto relation [9].

An overview of evolutionary algorithms for multiobjective optimization problems is submitted in [3, 4]. An analysis of the task assignments has been carried out for two evolutionary algorithms. The first one was an adaptive evolutionary algorithm with tabu mutation AMEA+ [1]. Tabu search algorithm [13] was applied as an additional mutation operator to decrease the workload of the bottleneck computer.

Better outcomes from the NSA are transformed into improving of solution quality obtained by the adaptive multicriteria evolutionary algorithm with tabu mutation AMEA*. This adaptive evolutionary algorithm with the NSA (AMEA*) gives better results than the AMEA+. After 200 generations, an average level of Pareto set obtaining is 1.4% for the AMEA*, 1.8% for the AMEA+. 30 test preliminary populations were prepared, and each algorithm starts 30 times from these populations.

5   Concluding Remarks

The tabu-based adaptive evolutionary algorithm with the negative selection algorithm can be applied for finding Pareto-optimal task allocations in a three-objective optimization problem with the maximization of the system reliability. In this problem, the workload of the bottleneck computer and the cost of computers are minimized.

The negative selection algorithm can be used to handle constraints and improve a quality of the outcomes obtained by an evolutionary algorithm. Our future works will concern on a development the NSA and evolutionary algorithms for finding Pareto-optimal solutions of the multiobjective optimization problems.

References

1. Balicki, J., Kitowski, Z.: Tabu-based evolutionary algorithm for effective program module assignment in parallel processing, WSEAS Transactions on Systems, Vol. 3 (2004) 119-124
2. Coello Coello, C. A., Cortes, N.C.: Use of Emulations of the Immune System to Handle Constraints in Evolutionary Algorithms, Knowledge and Information Systems. An International Journal, Vol. 1 (2001) 1-12
3. Coello Coello, C. A., Van Veldhuizen, D. A., Lamont, G.B.: Evolutionary Algorithms for Solving Multi-Objective Problems, Kluwer Academic Publishers, New York (2002)
4. Deb, K.: Multi-Objective Optimization using Evolutionary Algorithms, John Wiley & Sons, Chichester (2001)
5. D'haeseleer, P., et al.: An Immunological Approach to Change Detection. In Proc. of IEEE Symposium on Research in Security and Privacy, Oakland (1996)
6. Farmer, J.D., Packard, N.H., Perelson, A.S.: The Immune System, Adaptation, and Machine Learning. Physica D, Vol. 22 (1986) 187-204
7. Forrest, S., Perelson, A.S.: Genetic Algorithms and the Immune System. Lecture Notes in Computer Science (1991) 320-325
8. Helman, P. and Forrest, S.: An Efficient Algorithm for Generating Random Antibody Strings. Technical Report CS-94-07, The University of New Mexico, Albuquerque (1994)
9. Jerne, N.K.: The Immune System. Scientific American, Vol. 229, No. 1 (1973) 52-60
10. Kim, J. and Bentley, P. J.: Immune Memory in the Dynamic Clonal Selection Algorithm. Proc. of the First Int. Conf. on Artificial Immune Systems, Canterbury, (2002) 57-65
11. Koziel, S., Michalewicz, Z.: Evolutionary Algorithms, Homomorphous mapping, and Constrained Parameter Optimisation. Evolutionary Computation, Vol. 7 (1999) 19-44
12. Smith, D.: Towards a Model of Associative Recall in Immunological Memory. Technical Report 94-9, University of New Mexico, Albuquerque (1994)
13. Weglarz, J. (ed.): Recent Advances in Project Scheduling. Kluwer Academic Publishers, Dordrecht (1998)
14. Wierzchon, S. T.: Generating Optimal Repertoire of Antibody Strings in an Artificial Immune System. In M. Klopotek, M. Michalewicz and S. T. Wierzchon (eds.) Intelligent Information Systems. Springer Verlag, Heidelberg/New York (2000) 119-133
15. Zitzler, E., Deb, K., and Thiele, L.: Comparison of Multiobjective Evolutionary Algorithms: Empirical Results. Evolutionary Computation, Vol. 8, No. 2 (2000) 173-195

Ants in Web Searching Process

Urszula Boryczka

Institute of Computer Science, University of Silesia,
Będzińska 3, 41–200 Sosnowiec, Poland
phone/fax: (+48 32) 291 82 83
uboryczk@us.edu.pl

Abstract. In this paper, we propose a new ant–based searching algorithm called AntSearch. We describe a process of stigmergy and diffusion of pheromone, leading to a degree of self–organization brought
about through the independent actions and iterations of its individual
agents. We use it in the construction in our continually evolving system,
AntSearch. We discuss some of the issues raised and attempt to explain
some of its success as well as account for its failings. We analyze the
main characteristics of the algorithm and try to explain the influence of
parameters value on the behavior of this system.

1 Intoduction

This paper introduces AntSearch, a novel approach to the adaptive searching in
the Internet. AntSearch is a distributed, mobile agents system that was inspired
by recent work on the ant colony metaphor. This paper is organized as follows:
the section 2 gives a detailed description of stigmergy. The section 3 describes
the main principles and adaptations of ACS of different optimization problems.
The section 4 presents the AntSearch algorithm. In the section 5, we present
some of the results that have been obtained during the searching process. The
last section concludes and discusses future evolutions of AntSearch.

2 Ant Colony Optimization

The foraging behavior of ants [4, 5, 8] has inspired a novel approach to distributed
optimization, Ant Colony Optimization (ACO). Most of current ACO [2, 7] applications are either in combinatorial optimization or in communications networks
routing. Ant System (AS), the first ACO algorithm, was applied to the traveling
salesman problem (TSP). Although it had limited success from a performance
standpoint it opened up the road to improvements and new applications. Ant
colony System (ACS), a modified version of AS that extends AS and includes
local search routines, exhibits top performance on asymmetric TSPs. A whole
family of ACO algorithms is now applied to many different combinatorial optimization problems ranging from the quadratic assignment problem and the
sequential ordering problems to vehicle routing and graph coloring problems.

P.S. Szczepaniak et al. (Eds.): AWIC 2005, LNAI 3528, pp. 57–62, 2005.
© Springer-Verlag Berlin Heidelberg 2005

ACO algorithms for routing in communication networks, also called ant routing algorithms, have been particularly successful. This success is probably due to the dynamic nature of the routing problem which is well matched to the distributed and adaptive characteristics of ACO algorithms.

3   AntSearch System

AntSearch takes inspiration from previous work on artificial ant colonies techniques to solve combinatorial optimization problems [6]. The core ideas of these techniques are:

- the use of repeated and concurrent simulations carried out by a population of artificial agents called "ants" to generate new solutions to the problem
- the use by the agents of stochastic local search to build the solution in an incremented way
- the use of information collected during past simulations to direct future search for better solutions [3].

Overall, the effect of ants on the network is such that nodes (sites) which are visited frequently by predecessors will be favored nodes when building paths to route new links. This has the effect links close to the ant source node get higher reinforcement that are far away. There is a strong and complex interplay among routing nodes, routing of ants, updating the pheromone table. A schematic representation of these relationships is given in Fig.1.

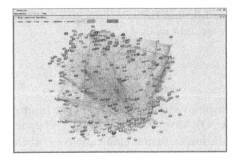

No of experim.	No of relevant nodes	% of all nodes	Completeness	Cost of retrieval
Type of net: 538 nodes, 9639 edges. High thematic cohesion				
1	40	7.435 %	52 %	11.7 %
2	14	2.6 %	57.1 %	9.85 %
3	17	3.159 %	82.3 %	25.4 %
Type of net: 542 nodes, 7655 edges. Low thematic cohesion.				
4	45	8.3 %	53,3 %	8.3 %
5	19	3.5 %	100 %	6.08 %
6	6	1.017%	83.3 %	12.5 %
Type of net: 563 nodes, 6382 edges. High thematic cohesion				
7	36	6.39 %	88 %	23.9 %
8	5	0.88 %	100 %	7.9 %
9	16	2.84 %	68.7 %	16.3 5
			average 76.08 %	13.55 %

Fig. 1. The schematic representation of ants' net

Fig. 2. Results

The idea presented in this article is similar to the Bilchev and Parmee approach [1]. Authors suggest considering a finite set of regions (initial links) at each iteration of the algorithm: agents are send to these regions, from which they explore random–proportionally selected directions within a coefficient of exploration and range of ant. Agents reinforce their paths according to their performance and coefficient of similarity/correlation. Trails evaporate and create a new region for exploration. This algorithm operates of three different levels:

- individual search strategy of individual agents
- the cooperation between ants using pheromone trails to focus on searching serendipitous and receptive neighborhood (cumulative coefficient RNRM)
- the exchange of information between different regions performed by some kind of "diffusion" similar to a crossover in a genetic algorithm. We define the ant range dedicated to the special part of the network (nodes). When some nodes will not be accepted as a "tastiest morsels" by the ant algorithm, so that the path leading to it will soon decay.

Search and optimal foraging decision–making of ants can be compare with bacterial swarm foraging behavior [9], where we observe the chemical attractant evaporation concerning the environment and another communication medium–a slime trail. We may observe the similar process of diffusion after chemotactic steps of presented simulations.

In order to design a more global approach and to avoid inefficient searching we introduce the following parameters:

- the initialization of the pheromone trail use the value depending on the Minimal Ant Trail — MAT
- we establish the value of pheromone for non–visited nodes on the value equal to Clear Node Trail — CNT. It makes an opportunity to create new regions
- the parameter NOA establishes the number of ants. Ants use the classical strategy of searching depending on the parameter EE (exploration/exploitation)
- agents use local pheromone updating rule exploiting the idea of evaporation — PD
- the ant range — AR parameter allows agents to route into unknown areas
- the evaluation function for document d (node) in our network is determine by the correlation between this document T_d and the query T_k. We add this value whenever it keeps within the value of parameter CWL.

Ant Search combines the quality, effectiveness of searching process as well as the synergetic effect obtains by pheromone changes. So the mechanism of diffusion the cumulative values of pheromone use the standard evaporation process:

1. when an agent visits a node, algorithm cumulates the value according to the validation of this document
2. this cumulative value will be diminished according to the discount factor (Storage Discount — SD)
3. the process of diffusion depends on the Storage Range factor (SR)
4. in case of relevant documents we have an opportunity to increase weights of the appropriate nodes (via the parameter RNRM $\in \langle 1, 10 \rangle$)

The following equation shows how the evaluation function is computed:

$$f_o(d, k) = (card(T_k \cap T_d) + f_{kc}(T_k, T_d)) \cdot R \tag{1}$$

where:

$$f_{kc}(T_k, T_d) = \sum_{i=0}^{card(T_k)} \sum_{j=0}^{card(T_d)} STC_{ij}$$

STC is a partially similarity function:

$$STC_{ij} = \begin{cases} f_{pt}(T_{k_i}, T_{d_j}) \text{ when } f_{pt}(T_{k_i}, T_{d_j}) > CWL \\ 0 \qquad\qquad \text{otherwise} \end{cases}$$

where $f_{pt}(T_{k_i}, T_{d_j})$ is equal to a number of the same characters within terms T_{k_i}, T_{d_j} and CWL is a correlation threshold.

$$R = \begin{cases} RNRM \text{ when } card \ (T_k \cap T_d) = card(T_k) \\ 1 \qquad\qquad \text{otherwise} \end{cases}$$

where T_k and T_d are the terms of a query and a document.

The local updating rule is performed as follows:

$$\tau_d(t + 1) = \tau_d(t) + \frac{MAT}{L_d} \tag{2}$$

where L_d indicates the number of visitors of node d.

The global pheromone updating rule is executed as follows:

$$\sum_{i=0}^{card(P)} \Delta\tau_{d_i} = PD \cdot \tau_{d_i} + \frac{MAT}{L_{d_i} + card(P) - i} \tag{3}$$

where:

- L_{d_i} indicates the number of visitors of node d_i
- MAT is a minimal ant trail
- $card(P)$ is the number of nodes belonging to path P

We consider a population of NOA ants. Ants are located in nodes of the highest rank values and they try to find the areas of their interest. The regions created during the search process correspond to the nodes (sites) which have the greater values of pheromone. The number of visitors and the correlation process corresponds to these values.

4   Experiments

To evaluate the performance of AntSearch, we have run experiments with following information networks: firstly we analyze Web site "Wirtualny Wszechswiat"

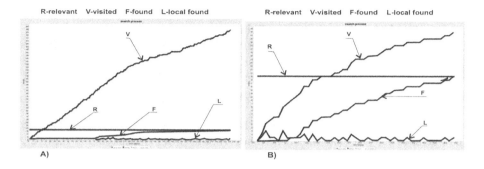

Fig. 3. Two examples of the search processes

(www.wiw.pl/astronomia) consists on 538 nodes and 9639 edges between these nodes. It is an example of a data set with a high thematic cohesion, so the results obtained during the search process should be optimistic. In AntSearch there are a number of parameters that need to be set. We set the following values: MAT = 0.2, CNT = 0.1, PD = 0.888, AR = 1.0, NOA = 6, CWL = 0.5, SR = 0.768, SD = 0.883, EE = 0.06, RNRM = 3. Secondly we explore the another type of data set: Polish BBC information service (www.BBC.pl) contains 542 nodes joining up with 655 edges. This network may be characterized by a high differentiation, without thematic cohesion. We establish the following values of the AntSearch parameters: MAT = 0.2, CNT = 0.172, PD = 0.798, AR = 1.0, NOA = 6, CWL = 0.5, SR = 0.768, SD = 0.833, EE = 0.06, RNRM = 3.

We have tested these networks with different sets of parameters. The final parameter settings have been determined by first optimizing the parameters on each of these examples of data networks separately and then averaging the parameters over the three different queries.

Fig.3 a) presents an example of a search process for a query: "A sphere in a planetary system". The number of a relevant nodes : 17–3.159% of a whole network. We analyze the first data set. As it shown in Fig.3 a), in the first steps of the performance of AntSearch agents could not find relevant documents, but after 200 iterations we obtain the completeness of searching process equal to 82.3% with the cost of the exploration this network — 25.4%. Fig.3 b) presents an example of search process for query: "50 years of Queen Elisabeth reign". Now we analyze a network with 19 relevant nodes that constitute only 3.5% of its total number of nodes. It occurs in the second data set, concerning BBC news. In this case algorithm shows really good performance. The completeness of the search process is higher than in the previous experiment. Now we obtain 100% of completeness with the cost of exploration — 6.08%. This good result obtained in this case we can explain by the fact, that this information is located in only one region and the query is formulated with a satisfying precision.

The conclusions below can be drawn from the tests we have performed, but the reader should keep in mind that these conclusions are limited to the tested networks. The number of ants in AntSearch does not seem to be a critical parameter in the case of a sequential implementation. The distribution of ants depends on the network size. Two properties of this approach seem to be crucial: the value of parameters: SR and SD are really important in the performing of the diffusion process. In addition, the values of parameters: CNT and PD guarantee fruitful communication between agents and they are quite important for the location of profitable regions. The lack of comparison in this phase of experimental study can be explained by the fact that we analyze a specific polish characteristics concerning search process. All in all, the experiments performed when testing the web sites suggest that the effectiveness (about 80%) is satisfying (see Fig.2). Preliminary tests of AntSearch on different queries seem to indicate that this algorithm can achieve robust performance for all the tested networks.

5   Conclusion

In this paper, we have proposed a new search algorithm inspired by the behavior of real ants. This algorithm has many features such as multiple local search processes concentrated around multiple regions, a strategy of pheromone diffusion sensitive to the success of evaluated nodes and the number of ants. Now we are using techniques of evolutionary biology to design information systems. These systems are designed to cooperate and interact with other memberships of the multi–agent system. AntSearch mimic natural systems use of stigmergy. We obtain the effectiveness of the searching process by the traveling through stigmergic medium–pheromone. Experimental studies suggest that AntSearch may achieve interesting results. We plan in the future to evaluate AntSearch with larger data sets and with several web sites to validate our approach.

References

1. G. Bilchev and I. C. Parmee. The ant colony metaphor for searching continuous design spaces. In *Proceedings of the AISB Workshop on Evolutionary Computing.* Springer–Verlag, Berlin, 1995.
2. E. Bonabeau, M. Dorigo, and G. Theraulaz. *Swarm Intelligence. From Natural to Artificial Systems.* Oxford University Press, 1999.
3. D. Corne, M. Dorigo, and F. Glover. *New Ideas in Optimization.* Mc–Graw–hill, 1999.
4. J.-L. Deneubourg. *Personal communication.* Université Libre de Bruxelles, Brussels, 2002.
5. J.-L. Deneubourg, S. Aron, S. Goss, and J.-M. Pasteels. The self–organizing exploratory pattern of the argentine ant. *Journal of Insect Behavior*, 3:159–168, 1990.
6. M. Dorigo and L. M. Gambardella. Ant colonies for the Traveling Salesman Problem. *Biosystems*, 43:73–81, 1997.
7. M. Dorigo and T. Stützle. *Ant Colony Optimization.* The MIT Press, 2004.
8. S. Goss, S. Aron, J.-L. Deneubourg, and J.-M. Pasteels. Self–organized shortcuts in the argentine ant. *Naturwissenschaften*, 76, 579–581.
9. K. M. Passino. *Biomimicry for Optimization, Control, and Automation.* Springer–Verlag, London, 2005.

Using Adaptive Fuzzy-Neural Control to Minimize Response Time in Cluster-Based Web Systems

Leszek Borzemski[1] and Krzysztof Zatwarnicki[2]

[1] Institute of Information Science and Engineering,
Wroclaw University of Technology, Wroclaw, Poland
`leszek.borzemski@pwr.wroc.pl`
[2] Department of Electrical Engineering and Automatic Control,
Technical University of Opole, Opole, Poland
`KZatwarnicki@po.opole.pl`

Abstract. We have developed content-aware request distribution algorithm called FARD which is a client-and-server-aware, dynamic and adaptive distribution policy in cluster-based Web systems. It assigns each incoming request to the server with the least expected response time. To estimate the expected response times it uses the fuzzy estimation mechanism. The system is adaptive as it uses a neural network learning ability for its adaptation. Simulations based on traces from the 1998 World Cup show that when we consider the response time, FARD can be more effective than the state-of-the-art content-aware policy LARD.

1 Introduction and Related Work

Cluster-based Web systems are commonly used in locally distributed architecture for Web sites. Web servers in a cluster work collectively as a single Web resource. Typical Web cluster architecture includes a Web switch that distributes user requests among Web servers. Our contribution is to propose and evaluate a fuzzy-neural based content-aware request distribution mechanism which minimizes request response time. Our algorithm is called FARD (Fuzzy Adaptive Request Distribution) [2]. To the best of our knowledge, no other works in the area of Web clusters use such approach to request distribution. Here we show new results concerning the performance evaluation of FARD using simulation. FARD assigns each incoming request to the server with the least expected response time, estimated at the moment for that individual request based on current knowledge on server state. It uses the fuzzy estimation mechanism with client and server awareness and employs a neural network for learning and adaptation. Due to learning model of collecting information needed for dispatching decisions, FARD-based Web switch learns itself the changes in cluster as well as in the workload.

The survey [4] presents the state-of-the-art of Web cluster technologies and research perspectives in the field. The authors conclude that the area of content-

P.S. Szczepaniak et al. (Eds.): AWIC 2005, LNAI 3528, pp. 63–68, 2005.

aware Web switch architectures needs further research, and new adaptive policies combining effectively client and server information have to be developed. There is also urgent need for quality-oriented request distribution strategies, more sophisticated but yet acceptable for implementation. The usage of AI methods is expected [1, 9], especially in context of *content-aware* switches that make use of request information, such as URL. We propose to use *fuzzy* and *neural networks* approaches to the problem solving [9]. Fuzzy approach may be especially profitable when a small amount of uncertain and imprecise information about system under consideration is provided whereas neural networks have learning and adaptive capabilities. These system modeling approaches have been widely used in studying several decision-making systems, also for computer networks and distributed systems, but not yet in Web switch design. For example, [5] proposes a quality-provisioning neural fuzzy connection admission controller for multimedia high-speed networks and [6] presents a fuzzy-decision based load balancing system for distributed object computing. The rest of this paper is organized as follows. Section 2 presents FARD mechanism. Section 3 shows the performance of FARD vs. RR and LARD algorithms. Section 4 includes final remarks.

2   FARD Distribution Policy

We consider two-way architecture of cluster-based Web system where all user requests arrive through the Web switch and the resulting resources are sent back also through the Web switch. We want to optimize the server response time as it is recognized and measured by the Web switch - it is the time between opening and closing of the TCP session that is established between the Web switch and a target Web server to get a resource. The requests are directed by FARD-based Web switch to the server that is expected to provide the fastest response time. We assume that the resources are fully replicated on all servers and each server can handle each request.

Fig. 1a shows the major components of FARD architecture: *Executor, MIN* and *Model of Server* modules. Each server has its own corresponding Model of Server (Fig. 1b). We propose to evaluate the server load by the combination of three independently observed load indexes: CPU load c, disk load d and LAN link load a (the number of active TCP connections). The server load is described by the triplet *(c, d, a)*. The values of first two elements of this index are expressed in percentage terms, the third one is discrete. They are represented in the *load table* as the triples *(Acl, Adm, Aan)*, where *Acl, Adm* and, *Aan* are fuzzy sets. Five fuzzy sets were defined for processor load, two for disc load and twelve for LAN link load. The crisp values for the first two inputs are given as percentage values. The membership functions for outputs are singletons (one element fuzzy sets), for which the membership degree is 1. Figures 1c, 1d and 1e show the membership functions. The requests x_i, $i=1,\ldots$, are serviced independently in the order of their arrival. When x_i request arrives, each Model of Server calculates its own estimator of the response time t_i^{*s}, $s = 1, .., S$ assuming that this request is to be serviced by the given server, and making use of current server load information $(c, d, a)^s, s = 1, .., S$ and the knowledge about the request x_i (type and size of the object). First, the request x_i is classified

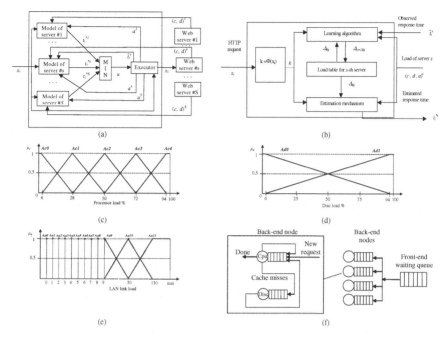

Fig. 1. FARD: (a) Architecture; (b) Model of Server module; (c), (d) Membership functions for inputs (c), processor load (d), LAN link load(e); (f) Model of cluster-based Web systems

to the k-th class using the classification function $\Phi(x_i)$. After then, the *estimation mechanism* determines the expected response time t_i^{*s} on the basis of the set Δ_{ikj} of elements in the k-th row of the load table for the s-th server, where $\Delta_{ikj}=\{t_{ikj}\}$, for given i, k and for *fired j's* , $j \in J^*$, $J^* \subset J$, where $J=\{1, \dots, 120\}$ is the set of indexes of rules defined in the rule base with 120 if-then rules. J^* is the set of indexes of rules in the rule base that are fired by a current crisp value of server load $(c, d, a)^s$ (i.e. such that $\mu_{Rj}(c, d, a)^s > 0$). Next, the MIN module determines the target server as the one for which the estimated response time is minimal. Our estimation mechanism is based on a fuzzy-neuro model and follows Mamdani's model [8]. The fuzzification block and the rule base are constructed like in typical fuzzy models, whereas in the deffuzification block we propose to use the artificial neuron. Each neuron works for a single rule. We have $K*S$ estimation mechanisms because we need to have an individual estimation mechanism for each class of objects in each Model of Server module. When the request is completed by the target server, then the Executor measures the response time, and uses as the observed value of response time $\tilde{t}_i^s$ for request x_i in the *learning algorithm* to recalculate the set $\Delta_{(i+1)kj}$ of new values of the response times, where $\Delta_{(i+1)kj}=\{t_{(i+1)kj}\}$, for given i, k and for *fired j's* , $j \in J^*$. Set $\Delta_{(i+1)kj}$ refines the old values stored in the k-th row of the load table of the s-th server. To teach the network we use traditional *error back propagation* algorithm. Distinct phases of learning and working that would be typical of neural networks are not present here. The system continuously adapts to the changes in the workload and Web cluster characteristics. Information about server loads is collected independently of request handling. Simultaneously, every τ seconds, the system refines server load information. Information about c and d is sent by each Web server to its Model of Server module whereas information about all $a's$ is collected and distributed centrally by the Executor.

3   Simulation

The model of a cluster-based Web system used in our simulation is shown in Fig. 1f. We assumed that both the Web switch and local area network were fast enough and did not introduce significant delay that might influence results. The main delay in request servicing was assumed to be introduced by Web servers. Our simulator runs using the same assumptions about CPU speed, amount of memory, number of disks and other parameters as described in [8]. The processing costs are calculated for Pentium II 300 MHz PC with FreeBSD 2.2.5. Connection establishment and teardown costs are set at 145 μs of CPU time each, while transmit processing incurs 40 μs per 512 bytes. Disc costs are the following: reading a file from disk has a latency of 28 ms, the disk transfer time is 410 μs per 4 KByte. Additionally, for files larger than 44 KBytes, an additional 14 ms (seek plus rotational latency) is charged for every 44 Kbytes of file length in excess of 44 KBytes. The Least Recently Used (LRU) cache replacement policy is used, however files with a size of more than 500 KB are never cached. The total memory size used for caching is 85 MB. For comparison reasons, we consider two well known dispatching policies: *Round Robin* (RR) [4] and *Locality Aware Request Distribution* (LARD) [8]. RR is content-blind baseline policy that allocates arriving requests based on a round robin discipline. LARD is known to be the best content-aware dynamic policy that is aimed to partite files among servers and increase RAM cache hit rate. We evaluate our algorithms via trace-driven simulation using real trace data from the 1998 World Cup Soccer web site. We use two data sets from June 26, 1998, both including about 4 800 000 requests. The first data set W1 (Fig. 2a) is taken from 15:34 to 16:18 and features the significant increase in the number of requests in a piece of time. The second data set W2 (Fig. 2b) is taken from 19:51 to 20:43 and is characterized by a balanced arrival of requests.

In the first simulation we used W1 workload and measured the average response times versus number of Web servers used in the cluster (Fig. 2c). It was shown that FARD outperforms LARD for small number of servers (up to 5 servers). Such configurations are representative for a two-layer Web switch global architecture where at the higher layer we have a content-blind switch distributing requests among several lower layer content-aware switches where each such switch supports a few servers only [4]. In case of RR policy our simulation showed that the response time for RR policy for 3, 4, 5 servers is more that 5, 4, 3 times worse than FARD, respectively. Fig. 2d shows the convergence characteristic of FARD for a cluster with four servers under W1 workload. The experiment showed the relative response time estimation error to vary from 20% to 70%, stabilizing at 20% after about 15 000

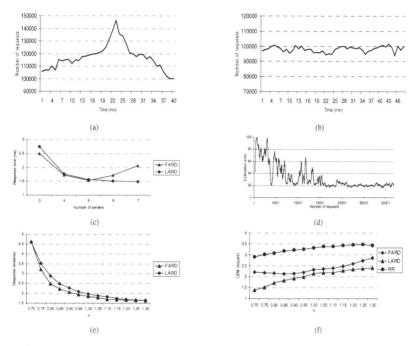

Fig. 2. (a),(b) Workload profiles; (c) Average response time v. # servers; (d) Estimation error v. # requests; (e) Average response time v. n; (f) LBM request index v. n

requests. The convergence time was not long even though this sudden increase in the number of requests.

The second simulation was performed for four-server cluster configuration using W2 workload. The inter-arrival time between two consecutive requests was calculated using the following formula: (the arrival time of current request minus the arrival time of the previous request)$*n$, where parameter n was taken from [0.7, 1.3]. Fig. 2e presents how FARD substantially outperforms LARD. The difference in performance in the context of average response time between FARD and LARD is up to 20% for heavy load. RR is comparatively very poor policy because it achieves the average response time almost 16 ms for n=0.7 and 6 ms for n=1.3. Fig. 2f illustrates that unfortunately FARD is not a good policy in the context of load balancing. As the load balancing measure we used the Load Balance Metric (LBM) [3] calculated for the load expressed by the number of requests serviced by the server. The LBM can range from 1 to at most the number of servers (i.e. 4). Small values of the LBM indicate better load balancing performance, i.e. smaller peak-to-mean load ratios, than large values - the optimal value is 1. However one should remember that the load balancing is not a primary aim of FARD as it optimizes the response time.

Content-aware distribution mechanisms introduce processing overhead at the Web switch that may cause severe throughput bottleneck. To evaluate this we developed the software Web switch (but still without proper optimization) equipped with all algorithms under consideration, and performed the stressing tests in a four-server Web cluster. The peak throughput achieved by RR and LARD was about 110 000 requests/sec, while FARD was able to process up to 90 000 requests/sec on the same hardware platform (Pentium 4 3GHz). The work in [4] shows that a throughput of 20 000 requests/sec is acceptable for good Web switches. Therefore, processing overhead introduced by FARD can be neglected.

4   Conclusions

We evaluated our Web request dispatching algorithm FARD. We showed that it is possible to creatively apply a neuro-fuzzy method when designing the content-aware Web switch. FARD optimizes request response time using the combination of individual load indexes as a single index to reflect the server load. Such approach is a new contribution in the context of Web clusters. FARD outperforms substantially RR policy. When considering the response time FARD can be more effective than LARD, the state-of-the-art content-aware Web switch policy.

References

1. Borzemski L.: Data Mining in Evaluation of Internet Path Performance. Innovations in Applied Artificial Intelligence. LNCS, Vol. 3029. Springer-Verlag Berlin (2004) 643-652
2. Borzemski L., Zatwarnicki K.: A fuzzy adaptive request distribution algorithm for cluster-based Web systems. Proc. of 11th Conf. on Parallel, Distributed and Network-based Processing, IEEE CS Press Los Alamitos (2003) 119-126
3. Bunt R., Eager D., Oster G., Wiliamson C.: Achieving load balance and effective caching in clustered web servers. Proc. 4th Int'l Web Caching Workshop (1999)
4. Cardellini V., Casalicchio E., Colajanni M., Yu P.S.: The state of the art in locally distributed Web-server systems. ACM Comp. Surv. Vol. 34, No. 2 (2002) 263-311
5. Cheng R.G., Chang C.J.: A QoS-provisioning neural fuzzy connection admission controller for multimedia networks. IEEE Trans. on Networking, vol. 7, no. 1, Feb. (1999) 111-121
6. Kwok Y.-K., Cheung L.-S: A new fuzzy-decision based load balancing system for distributed object computing. J. Parallel Distribut. Comput. 64 (2004) 238-253
7. Mamdani E.H.: Application of fuzzy logic to approximate reasoning using linguistic synthesis. IEEE Trans. on Computers, vol. C-26, No.12, Dec. (1977) 1182-1191
8. Pai V.S., Aront M., Banga G., Svendsen M., Druschel P., W. Zwaenpoel, E. Nahum, Locality-aware request distribution in cluster-based network servers. Proc. of 8th ACM Conf. on Arch. Support for Progr. Languages (1998)
9. Yager R.R., Filev D.: Essentials of fuzzy modeling and control, John Wiley and Sons, New York (1994)

Task Realization's Optimization with Earliness and Tardiness Penalties in Distributed Computation Systems

Wojciech Bożejko[1] and Mieczysław Wodecki[2]

[1] Institute of Engineering, Wrocław University of Technology,
Janiszewskiego 11-17, 50-372 Wrocław, Poland
`wbo@ict.pwr.wroc.pl`
[2] Institute of Computer Science, University of Wrocław,
Przemyckiego 20, 51-151 Wrocław, Poland
`mwd@ii.uni.wroc.pl`

Abstract. There are many service systems (especially in reservation systems, electronic commerce, in tasks synchronized directly with the Internet), where each task has to be executed in some fixed range of time. Exceeding the term is disadvantageous and causes additional penalties. Therefore, it is necessary to establish optimal sequence of tasks (which minimizes penalties) and its starting times. It amounts to some job scheduling problem with earliness and tardiness. Because usually tasks are received in the distributed system (in the web), so to solve the presented problem we propose a parallel coevolutionary algorithm based on the Lamarck evolution and the island model of migration.[*]

1 Introduction

There are some types of manufacturing systems, called Just In Time (*JIT*), where costs are connected not only with executing a job too late, but also too early. Such a situation takes place especially when tasks are connected directly with the Web, e.g. routing, agents, similarity classification, etc. This induces formulating many optimization problems with goal functions, where there is a penalty for both tardiness and earliness of a job. The problem of scheduling with earliness and tardiness (total weighted earliness/tardiness problem, *TWET*) is one of the most frequently considered in literature. In this problem each job from a set $J = \{1, 2, ..., n\}$ has to be processed, without interruption, on a machine, which can execute at most one job in every moment. By p_i we represent the execution time of a job $i \in J$, and by e_i and d_i we mean an adequately demanded earliest and latest moment of the finishing processing of a job. If a scheduling of jobs is established and C_i is the moment of finishing of a job i, then we call $E_i = \max\{0, e_i - C_i\}$ an *earliness* and $T_i = \max\{0, C_i - d_i\}$ a *tardiness*. The

---

[*] The work was supported by KBN Poland, within the grant No. T11A01624.

P.S. Szczepaniak et al. (Eds.): AWIC 2005, LNAI 3528, pp. 69–75, 2005.

expression $u_i E_i + w_i T$ is a *cost* of execution a job, where u_i and w_i $(i \in J)$ are nonnegative coefficients of a goal function. The problem consists in minimizing a sum of costs of jobs, that is the function $\sum_{i=1}^{n} (u_i E_i + w_i T_i)$. Such a problem is represented by $1|| \sum (u_i E_i + w_i T_i)$ in literature and it belongs to a strong NP-hard class (if we assume $u_i = 0$, $i = 1, 2, \ldots, n$, we will obtain a strong NP-hard problem $1|| \sum w_i T_i$ - Lawler [6] and Lenstra et al. [7]). Baker and Scudder [1] proved, that there can be an idle time in an optimal solution (jobs need not be processed directly one after another), that is $C_{i+1} - p_{i+1} \geq C_i$, $i = 1, 2, \ldots, n-1$. Solving the problem amounts to establishing a sequence of jobs and its starting times. Hoogeven and van de Velde [5] proposed an algorithm based on a branch and bound method. Because of exponentially growing computation's time, this algorithm can be used only to solve instances where the number of jobs is not greater than 20. Therefore in practice almost always approximate algorithms are used. The best of them are based on artificial intelligence methods. Calculations are performed in two stages:

1. Determining the scheduling of jobs (with no idle times).
2. Establishing jobs' optimal starting times.

There is an algorithm in the paper of Wan and Yen [9] based on this scheme. To determine scheduling a tabu search algorithm is used.

In this paper we consider a *TWET* problem additionally assuming that the machine begins execution of jobs in time zero and it works with no idle (*TWET-no-idle* problem). We present a parallel genetic algorithm (called coevolutionary), in which a part of a population is replaced with adequately local minima (so-called Lamarck evolution). The property of partitioning a permutation into subsequences (blocks) was used in an algorithm of determining local minima. This method decreases the size of a neighborhood to about 50% in a local optimization algorithm, it improves the solution's values and significantly speeds up computations.

Sections 2 contains a description of a genetic algorithm and local optimization algorithm. Subsequent sections describe computer simulations of sequential and parallel algorithms.

2 Evolutionary Algorithm Method

The evolutionary algorithm is a search procedure, based on the process of natural evolution following the principles of natural selection, crossover and survival. The method has been proposed and developed by Holland [4]. In the beginning, a population of individuals (solutions of the problem, for example permutations) is created. Each individual is evaluated according to the fitness function. Individuals with higher evaluations (more fitted, with a smaller goal function value) are selected to generate a new generation of this population. So, there are three essential steps of the genetic algorithm: (1) selection – choosing some subset of individuals, so-called parents, (2) crossover – combining parts from pairs of parents to generate new ones, (3) mutation – transformation that creates a new individual by small changes applied to an existing one taken from the population, (4) succession – determining of the next population. New individuals created by crossover or mutation replace all or a part of the old population. The process of evaluating fitness and creating a new population generation is repeated until a termination criterion is achieved.

Let P_0 be an initial population, k – number of iteration of the algorithm, P_k – population. Let P_k' be a set of parents – subset of the most fitted individuals of the population P_k. By the mechanism of crossover, the algorithm generates a set of offsprings P_k'' from the set P_k'. Next, some of the individuals from the set P_k'' are mutated. *Succession* operation consists in reducing P_k'' to the size $|P_0|$, forming the new population P_{k+1}. The algorithm stops after a fixed number of iterations. Of course the complexity of the algorithm depends on the number of iterations and the size of the population.

All operations in a coevolutionary algorithm (selection, crossover and succession) are executed locally, on some subsets of the current population called *islands*. It is a strongly decentralized model of an evolutionary algorithm. There are independent evolution processes on each of the islands, and communication takes place sporadically. Exchanging individuals between islands secures diversity of populations and it prevents fast imitating of an individual with a local minimum as its goal function. Additionally, the so-called Lamarck model of evolution is applied to intensify the optimization process. In each generation some part of the population is replaced by "their" local minima. From the current population some subset is drawn. Each individual of this subset is a starting solution for the local optimization algorithm. Therefore on each island a hybrid algorithm is applied, in which an evolutionary algorithm is used to determine the starting solutions for the local search algorithm.

Evolutionary algorithm
Number of iteration $k := 0$; $P_0 \leftarrow$ initial population;
repeat
    $P_k' \leftarrow$ Selection(P_k);　　　　　　　　　　*{Selection of parents}*
    $P_k'' \leftarrow$ Crossover(P_k');　　　　　　　　　*{Generating an offspring}*
    $P_k'' \leftarrow$ Mutation(P_k'');
    $A \leftarrow$ RandomSubSet(P_k'');　　　　　　　　*{Subpopulation}*
    $P_k'' \leftarrow P_k'' \cup$ LocalMinimumSet(A);
    $P_{k+1} \leftarrow$ Succession(P_k, P_k'')　　　　　　*{A new population}*
    $k := k + 1$;

until some termination condition is satisfied;

The *RandomSubSet* procedure determines a random subset A of elements of the current population P_k'', and the *LocalMinimumSet* procedure calculates a subset of local minima.

Because in the coevolutionary algorithm subpopulation develops on the islands independently, so calculations can be executed in the distributed web.

Parallel coevolutionary algorithm

The parallel algorithms based on the island model divide the population into a few subpopulations. Each of them is assigned to a different processor which performs a sequential genetic algorithm based on its own subpopulation. The crossover involves only individuals within the same population. Occasionally, the processor exchanges individuals through a migration operator. The main determinants of this model are: (1) size of the subpopulations, (2) topology of the connection network, (3) number of individuals to be exchanged, (4) frequency of exchanging.

The island model is characterized by a significant reduction of the communication time, compared to previous models. Shared memory is not required, so this model quite flexible.

Local Search Method

The local search (LS) method is a metaheuristic approach designed to find a near-optimal solution of combinatorial optimization problems. The basic version starts from an *initial solution* x^0. The elementary step of the method performs, for a given solution x^i, a search through the *neighborhood* $N(x^i)$ of x^i. The neighborhood $N(x^i)$ is defined by a move performed from x^i. The move transforms a solution into another solution. The aim of this elementary search is to find in $N(x^i)$ a solution x^{i+1} with the lowest cost functions. Then the search repeats from the best found solution, as a new starting one (see Glover and Laguna [3]).

Local search algorithm

Select a starting point: x; $x_{best} := x$;
repeat
    Select a point $y \in N(x)$ according to a given criterion
    based on the value of the goal function $F(y)$;
    $x := y$;
    if $F(y) < F(x_{best})$ **then** $x_{best} := y$;

until some termination condition is satisfied;

A fundamental element of the algorithm, which has a crucial influence on the quality and time of computation, is the neighborhood. The neighborhood is generated by the insert moves in the best local search algorithms with the permutation representation of the solution. Let k and l ($k \neq l$) be a pair of positions in a permutation. Insert move (*i-move*) i_l^k, consists in removing the element from the position k and next inserting it in the position l.

For the *TWET-no-idle* problem, each schedule of jobs can be represented by permutation $\pi = (\pi(1), \pi(2), \dots, \pi(n))$ of the set of jobs J. Let $S(n)$ denote the set of all such permutations. The total cost $\pi \in S(n)$ is $F(\pi) = \sum_{i=1}^{n} f_{\pi(i)}(C_{\pi(i)})$, where $C_{\pi(i)}$ is completed time of the job $\pi(i)$, $C_{\pi(i)} = \sum_{j=1}^{i} p_{\pi(j)}$. The job $\pi(i)$ is considered *early* if it is completed before its earliest moment of finishing $(C_{\pi(i)} < e_{\pi(i)})$, *on time* if $e_{\pi(i)} \leq C_{\pi(i)} \leq d_{\pi(i)}$, and *tardy* if the job is completed after its due date (i.e. $C_{\pi(i)} > d_{\pi(i)}$).

Each permutation $\pi \in S(n)$ is decomposed into subpermutations (subsequences of jobs) $\Omega = [B_1, B_2, \ldots, B_v]$ called *blocks* in π, each of them contains the jobs, where:

1. $B_i = (\pi(a_i), \pi(a_i + 1), \ldots, \pi(b_i - 1), \pi(b_i))$, and
   $b_i = a_{i-1} + 1, \; 1 \le i \le v, \; a_0 = 0, \; b_v = n$.

2. All the jobs $j \in B_i$ satisfy the following condition:

$$e_j > C_{\pi(b_i)}, \qquad\qquad \text{or} \qquad (C1)$$
$$e_j \le C_{\pi(b_{i-1})} + p_j \text{ and } d_j \ge C_{\pi(b_i)}, \qquad \text{or} \qquad (C2)$$
$$d_j < C_{\pi(b_{i-1})} + p_j. \qquad\qquad\qquad (C3)$$

3. B_i are maximal subsequences of π in which all the jobs satisfy either Condition $C1$ or Condition $C2$ or Condition $C3$.

By definition, there exist three types of blocks implied by either C1 or C2 or C3. To distinguish them, we will use the *E-block*, *O-block* and *T-block* notions respectively. For any block B in a partition Ω of permutation $\pi \in S(n)$, let

$$F_B(\pi) = \sum_{i \in B} (u_i E_i + w_i T_i).$$

Therefore, the value of a goal function

$$F(\pi) = \sum_{i=1}^{n} (u_i E_i + w_i T_i) = \sum_{B \in \Omega} F_B(\pi).$$

If B is a T-block, then every job inside is early. Therefore, an optimal sequence of the jobs within B of the permutation π (that is minimizing $F_B(\pi)$) can be obtained, using the well-known Weighted Shortest Processing Time (*WSPT*) rule, proposed by Smith [8]. The *WSPT* rule creates an optimal sequence of jobs in the non-increasing order of the ratios w_j/p_j. Similarly, if B is an E-block, than an optimal sequence of the jobs within can be obtained, using the Weighted Longest Processing Time (*WLPT*) rule which creates a sequence of jobs in the non-decreasing order of the ratios u_j/p_j.

Partition Ω of the permutation π is *ordered*, if there are jobs in the *WSPT* sequence in any T-block, and there are jobs in the *WLPT* sequence in any E-block.

Theorem 1. [2] Let Ω be an ordered partition of a permutation $\pi \in S(n)$ to blocks. If $\beta \in S(n)$ and $F(\beta) < F(\pi)$, so at least one job of some block of π was moved before the first or after the last job of this block in permutation β.

Note that Theorem 1 provides the necessary condition to obtain a permutation β from π such, that $F(\beta) < F(\pi)$.

Let $\Omega = [B_1, B_2, \ldots, B_v]$ be an ordered partition of the permutation $\pi \in S(n)$ to blocks. If a job $\pi(j) \in B_i$ ($B_i \in \Omega$), therefore moves which can improving goal function value consists in reordering a job $\pi(j)$ before the first or after the last job of this block. Let N_j^{bf} and N_j^{af} be sets of such moves ($N_j^{bf} = \emptyset$ for $j \in B_1$ and $N_j^{af} = \emptyset$ for $j \in B_v$). Therefore, the neighborhood of the permutation $\pi \in S(n)$,

$$N(\pi) = \bigcup_{j=1}^{n} N_j^{bf} \cup \bigcup_{j=1}^{n} N_j^{af}. \tag{1}$$

As computational experiments show, the neighborhood defined in (1) has a half smaller size than the neighborhood of all the insert moves.

3   Computational Experiments

We have tested the proposed algorithm on a set of randomly generated problems on a Sun Enterprise 4x400MHz using Ada95 language. For each job i, an integer processing time p_i was generated from the uniform distribution $[1, 100]$ and integer weights u_i and w_i were generated from the uniform distribution $[1, 10]$. Let $P = \sum_{i=1}^{n} p_i$. Distributions of earliness e_i and deadline d_i depend on P and two additional parameters L and R, which take on values from 0.2 to 1.0 in increments of 0.2. An integer deadline d_i was generated from the uniform distribution $[P(L - R/2), P(L + R/2)]$. Earliness e_i was generated as an integer from the uniform distribution $[0, d_i]$. Obtained solutions was compared to the well-known Earliest Due Date (EDD) constructive algorithm.

Table 1. Percentage relative deviation of parallel coevolutionary algorithm's solutions compared to the solutions of the EDD constructive algorithm

n	number of processors		
	1	2	4
40	-87.46%	-86.80%	-87.74%
50	-87.03%	-86.47%	-85.91%
100	-87.60%	-83.16%	-83.18%

The computational results can be found in Table 1. The number of iterations was counted as a sum of iterations on processors, and was permanently set to 500. For example, 4-processor implementations make 125 iterations on each of the 4 processors, so we can obtain comparable costs of computations. As we can see, parallel versions of the algorithm keep the quality of the obtained solutions, working in a shorter time. Because of small cost of the communication, the speedup parameter of the parallel algorithms is almost linear.

4   Conclusions

We have discussed a new approach to the single scheduling problem based on the parallel asynchronous coevolutionary algorithm. Compared to the sequential algorithm, parallelization shortes computation's time, keeping the quality of the obtained solutions.

References

1. Baker K.R., Scudder G.D.: Sequencing with earliness and tardiness penalties: a review, Operations Research 38 (1990), 22-36.
2. Bożejko W., Grabowski J., Wodecki M.: A block approach for single machine total weighted tardiness problem. Tabu search algorithm. (to appear)
3. Glover F., Laguna M.: Tabu Search, Kluwer, 1997.
4. Holland J.H., Adaptation in natural and artificial systems: Ann Arbor, University of Michigan Press, 1975.
5. Hoogeveen J.A., Van de Velde S.L.: A branch and bound algorithm for single-machine earliness-tardiness scheduling with idle time, INFORMS Journal on Computing 8 (1996), 402-412.
6. Lawler E.L.: A "pseudopolynomial" algorithm for sequencing jobs to minimize total tardiness, Annals of Discrete Mathematics 1 (1977), 331-342.
7. Lenstra J.J., Rinnoy KanA.H.G., Brucker P.: Complexity of machine scheduling problems, Annals of Discrete Mathematics 1 (1977), 343-362.
8. Smith W.E.:Various Optimizers for Single-Stage Production, Naval Research Logist Quartely 3(1956), 59-66.
9. Wan G., Yen B.P.C.: Tabu search for single machine scheduling with distinct due windows and weighted earliness/tardiness penalties, European Journal of Operational Research 142 (2002), 271-281.

Robust Fuzzy Clustering with Fuzzy Data

Bohdan S. Butkiewicz

Warsaw University of Technology,
Nowowiejska 15/19, 00-665 Warsaw, Poland,
`bb@ise.pw.edu.pl`,
WWW home page: `http://www.ise.pw.edu.pl/ bb/index.html`

Abstract. Proposed method of clustering is based on modified fuzzy c-means algorithm. In the paper features of input data are considered as linguistic variables. Any feature is described by set of fuzzy numbers. Thus, any input data representing a feature is a fuzzy number. The modified method allows finding the appropriate number of classes. Moreover, it uses improvements introducing in conventional fuzzy c-means algorithm increasing its robustness to the influence of outliers.

1 Introduction

The idea of fuzzy approach to clustering problems was proposed by Bellman, Kalaba and Zadeh. Now, clustering methods has been developed and used in different areas as electronics, astronomy, biology, medicine, information retrieval, and marketing. Good introduction and comparative study on the clustering topics can be fined in the works of Kaufmann and Rousseeuw [5], Everitt [8], Gordon [10], Jain *et al.* [4], Gao and Xie [9]. One of most popular methods used in clustering is fuzzy c-means method (FCM). The fuzzy c-means method was proposed by Dunn [3]. It was a modification of a technique introduced by Ball and Hall [1], the ISODATA process, called now hard c-means clustering (HCM). The method FCM allows crisp data elements to belong to several clusters in varying membership levels. In the conventional c-means clustering and also in fuzzy c-means clustering algorithms the number of clusters is constant. The number of clusters must be declared at the beginning. One problem with HCM is that it tends to stop in local minimum of the objective function and does not properly identify the cluster centers. FCM uses very similar technique to HCM, but is better than HCM because it is more robust to the local minima.

1.1 Conventional Fuzzy C-Means Algorithm

Consider a set of data x_i, $i = 1, ..., N$. Any data x_i represents a vector. Assume that data form c clusters. The membership of a data x_i in cluster c_j, $j = 1, .., c$ is denoted by $u_{ij} \in [0, 1]$. Thus, set of u_{ij} forms a membership matrix U. Each data x_i satisfies requirements

$$\sum_{j=1}^{c} u_{ij} = 1 \tag{1}$$

P.S. Szczepaniak et al. (Eds.): AWIC 2005, LNAI 3528, pp. 76–82, 2005.

$$0 < \sum_{i=1}^{N} u_{ij} < N \tag{2}$$

The FCM algorithm minimizes the objective function

$$J(U,V) = \sum_{i=1}^{N} \sum_{j=1}^{c} u_{ij}{}^{m} d_{ij}{}^{2} \tag{3}$$

where $d_{ij} = \| x_i - v_j \|$ is Euclidean distance between data x_i and center v_j of cluster c_j. Value m is the weighting exponent. For m=1 and discrete values of u_{ij} FCM is transformed into conventional HCM. Staring with arbitrary choused number c of clusters, called sometimes exemplars, and initial membership u_{ij} new cluster centers are calculated

$$v_j = \frac{\sum_{i=1}^{N} u_{ij}{}^{m} x_i}{\sum_{i=1}^{N} u_{ij}{}^{m}} \tag{4}$$

New membership matrix U is calculated using equation

$$u_{ij} = \left[\sum_{k=1}^{c} \left(\frac{d(x_i, v_j)}{d(x_i, v_k)} \right)^{\frac{2}{m-1}} \right]^{-1} \tag{5}$$

This procedure is repeated iteratively.

2   Robust FCM with Fuzzy Data

Consider input data set $X = (X_1, ..., X_N)$ where any data X_i is described by a vector $F_i = (f_{i1}, ..., f_{iL})$ of fuzzy features f_{il}. Any feature f_{il} represents a linguistic variable. Let any linguistic variable takes real numeric values. Thus, any feature is described by set of fuzzy numbers r_{ilk} with membership functions μ_{ilk}. Suppose that in considered situation the values of r_{ilk} and μ_{ilk} are known and they represent the fuzzy input data in actual situation. Therefore, for simplicity index k may be omitted. From other side consider set $C = (C_1, ..., C_c)$ of fuzzy clusters. Denote unknown centers of clusters as $v_1, ..., v_c$. Any data X_i can belong to any cluster C_j with unknown membership u_{ij}. The goal of robust fuzzy c-means (RFCM) algorithm is to find optimal number of clusters and centers of clusters to minimize objective function $J(U, V)$.

In the paper following procedure is proposed. Firstly, centers of fuzzy numbers are found. Any defuzzification procedure can be applied. Here, in simulation experiments trapezoidal fuzzy numbers with parameters $a_{1i}, a_{2i}, a_{3i}, a_{4i}$ are used. Thus, the centers are calculated as $x_i = (a_{1i} + a_{2i} + a_{3i} + a_{4i})/4$. Next, sufficient, surely to great number c_{max} of clusters is supposed and matrix of membership U. For example, without any previous knowledge u_{ij} can be equal to 1 or 0.5. To reduce impact of outliers (data placed vary far away from the cluster centers) the procedure proposed by Kersten [6] [7] who modified RFCM algorithm of Choi and Krishnapuram [2] is considered here to application. They proposed reduction of outliers using Huber function

$$\rho(x) = \begin{cases} x^2/2 & if \ | \ x \ | \leq 1 \\ | \ x \ | & if \ | \ x \ | > 1 \end{cases} \qquad (6)$$

Huber function is applied to distance measure $d(x_i, v_j)$ between data X_i and cluster C_j. In this paper is proposed another idea. Influence of outliers will be reduced after in other way using weighting factor. The function $\rho(x)$ has another goal. It fastens the searching for far big clusters. It has the form of

$$\rho(x) = \begin{cases} x^2/2 & if \ | \ x \ | \leq 1 \\ x^2 - 1/2 & if \ | \ x \ | > 1 \end{cases} \qquad (7)$$

New objective function is equal

$$J(U, V) = \sum_{i=1}^{N} \sum_{j=1}^{c} u_{ij}{}^{m} \rho(d(x_i, v_j)/\gamma) \qquad (8)$$

where γ is a scaling constant. The value of γ can be found experimentally or calculating standard deviation or median of distance. The choice of γ was not very critical.

The matrix of membership is updated in the following way

$$u_{ij} = \left[\sum_{k=1}^{c} \left(\frac{\rho(d(x_i, v_j)/\gamma)}{\rho(d(x_i, v_k)/\gamma)} \right)^{\frac{1}{m-1}} \right] \qquad (9)$$

Now, influence of outliers can be reduced using weighting function

$$w(x) = \begin{cases} 1 & if \ | \ x \ | \leq 1 \\ 1/x^2 & if \ | \ x \ | > 1 \end{cases} \qquad (10)$$

The weighting function proposed above is somewhat similar to Huber weighting function defined as $w = \rho'(x)/x$. For $| \ x \ | \leq 1$ the weight $w = 1$ and for $| \ x \ | > 1$ $w = 1/ \ | \ x \ |$. Applying inversely Huber definition $\rho'(x) = w(x)\,x$ to proposed weighting function it is possible to fined appropriate $\rho(x)$ as integral

$$\rho(x) = \begin{cases} x^2/2 & if \ | \ x \ | \leq 1 \\ ln(| \ x \ |) + 1/2 & if \ | \ x \ | > 1 \end{cases} \qquad (11)$$

However, using this definition of $\rho(x)$ the results obtained by simulation are not good. From this reason definitions (7) and (10) were accepted for proposed clustering algorithm. New centers of clusters are calculated as follows

$$v_j = \frac{\sum_{i=1}^{N} u_{ij}{}^{m} \, w(d(x_i, v_j)/\gamma) x_i}{\sum_{i=1}^{N} u_{ij}{}^{m} \, w(d(x_i, v_j)/\gamma)} \qquad (12)$$

Now, there are two possibilities - center of cluster can be crisp or fuzzy. More interesting is fuzzy center, because it may represent fuzziness of data belonging to the cluster. If membership function of the data have identical type it is reasonable to use the same type of membership for cluster center. In simulation experiments it was trapezoidal fuzzy number. Support of this number was calculated as weighted mean

$$a_{j1} = \frac{\sum_i^N a_{i1} u_{ij}}{\sum_i^N u_{ij}} \qquad a_{j4} = \frac{\sum_i^N a_{i4} u_{ij}}{\sum_i^N u_{ij}} \tag{13}$$

and similarly for the points a_{j2}, a_{j3} for α-cut equal to 1. It is not necessary to calculate these values during iteration. They can be found at the end of optimization procedure.

3 Merging Clusters Procedure

RFCM algorithm requires declaring maximal number of clusters. During any iteration merging procedure can diminish the number of clusters if the distance between their centers is small. Several method for merging procedure are proposed in literature. Here, merging criterion is based on conceptions of variation, cardinality, and compactness. Variation of the cluster C_j is defined in [11] as the weighted mean square of distance

$$\sigma_j = \sum_{i=1}^N u_{ij} \, d^2(x_i, v_j) \tag{14}$$

Fuzzy cardinality is a measure of the cluster size and is equal

$$n_j = \sum_{i=1}^N u_{ij} \tag{15}$$

Compactness of the cluster is a ratio

$$\pi_j = \frac{\sigma_j}{n_j} \tag{16}$$

Taking in consideration weighting constant m and modified distance definition (7) compactness must be change to the form of

$$\pi_j = \frac{\sum_{i=1}^N u_{ij}{}^m \, \rho(d(x_i, v_j)/\gamma)}{\sum_{i=1}^N u_{ij}{}^m} \tag{17}$$

Separation between two clusters C_j, C_k can be defined as Euclidean distance $d(v_j, v_k)$ between cluster centers v_j, v_k. Decision about merging two clusters is taking with help of validity index. Validity index proposed in [11] is defined as ratio

$$\omega_{jk} = \frac{d(v_j, v_k)}{\pi_j} \tag{18}$$

This definition is not symmetric on account of C_j, C_k. It seems that more reasonable definition is

$$\omega_{jk} = \frac{d(v_j, v_k)}{\sqrt{(\pi_j \pi_k)}} \tag{19}$$

This formula requires somewhat grater computing effort. Using modified distance definition the validity index take form of

$$\omega_{jk} = \frac{\rho[d(v_j, v_k)/\gamma]}{\sqrt{(\pi_j \pi_k)}} \tag{20}$$

During every iteration the validity index is calculated for any pair of clusters C_j, C_k and if $\omega_{jk} < \alpha$ then merging procedure is initiate. The value $\alpha = 1$ corresponds to situation when distance between clusters is equal to geometric mean of the cluster compactness. In practice the values in the range [0.1,0.35] work well. The center v_l of new cluster C_l is located in the weighted middle

$$v_l = \frac{v_j n_j + v_k n_k}{n_j + n_k} \tag{21}$$

Two old clusters are eliminated after merging. Membership values are recalculated and the RFCM procedure repeats. In the paper Euclidean distance is used, but generally the Minkowski distance can be applied.

4   Simulation Experiments

In the paper input data have probabilistic nature. Every data X_i is two dimensional vector of fuzzy trapezoidal numbers $x_i = (a_{i1}, a_{i2}, a_{i3}, a_{i4})$, and $y_i = (b_{i1}, b_{i2}, b_{i3}, b_{i4})$ on the plain $(x, y) = 640 \times 480$ pixels. Three kinds of probabilistic distributions were used: uniform, triangle, and circular. First, the values $a1$, $b1$ were generated with uniform [0,1] distribution. The values a_{i1}, b_{i1} with triangle density functions were generated using formulas of the type:
if $2 \leq c \leq 4$ then for $j := 1$ to c do begin $a1 := 10 + (j - 1) * 600/c + (300/c) * (1 + sign * sqr(a1))$; $b1 := 10 + 220 * (1 + sign1 * sqr(b1))$; end.
The values $sign$ and $sign1$ equal to 1 or -1 were changed during generation to obtain symmetrical probabilistic density. Other parameters of fuzzy numbers were obtained using formulas
a2:=a1+4+Random(5); a3:=a2+4+Random(5); a4:=a3+4+Random(5);
b2:=b1+3+Random(5); b3:=b2+3+Random(5); b4:=b3+3+Random(5);
 For circular distribution uniform density was used for radius and angle. Every time 5% or 15 % of data were generated as outliers with uniform distribution on hole plain. Following values were used $N = 250$, 500 or 1000, real number of

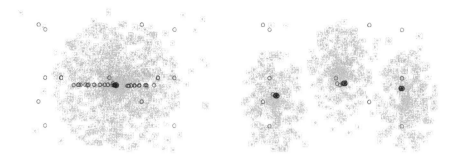

Fig. 1. Two examples of clustering results where starting value $c_{max} = 5$

clusters $c=1$, 2, 3, 4, maximal value $c_{max} = 5$ or 4. Some examples of results are presented in the Fig. 1. Gray and black circles show actual number of clusters and displacement of the cluster centers during iteration.

5   Conclusion

Generally, the algorithm works well. For number $N = 1000$ of fuzzy data, $c_{max} = 5$, and $c = 1..3$ it finds correct number of clusters and their centers very fast, after 10 to 20 iterations. Only for small $\epsilon \leq 0.001$ the number of iterations rises, but exact value (geometrical position on the plain) not differs practically. It can be seen that cluster centers are something moved to neighbor clusters from 'visual' centers, because of cluster fuzziness.

References

1. Ball G. H., Hall D. J.: ISODATA, a novel method of analysis and classification. Tech. Rep., Stanford University, Stanford CA (1965)
2. Choi Y., Kirishnapuram. Fuzzy and robust formulations of maximum-likelihood-based Gaussian mixture decomposition. Proc. Fifth IEEE Int. Conf. On Fuzzy Systems, New Orleans, LA (1996) 1899-19005
3. Dunn J.: A fuzzy relative of the ISIDATA process and it use in detecting compact well-separated clusters. Journal of Cybernetics **3** No. 3, (1973) 32-57
4. Jain A. K., Murty M. N., Flynn P. J.: Data Clustering: A Review. ACM Computer Surveys, **31** No. 3 (1999)
5. Kaufman L., Rousseeuw P. J.: Finding Groups in Data: An Introduction to Cluster Analysis. Wiley-Interscience, New York (1990)
6. Kersten P.: Fuzzy order statistics and their application to fuzzy clustering. IEEE Trans. Fuzzy Systenms, **7** No. 6 (1999) 708–712
7. Kersten P., Lee R., Verdi J., Carvalho R., Yankovich S.: Segmenting SAR images using fuzzy clustering. Proc. 19th Int. Conf. of the North American Fuzzy Information Processing Society, (2000) 105–108

8. Everitt B. S.: Cluster Analysis. Edward Arnold, London (1993)
9. Gao X., Xie W.: Advances in theory and application of fuzzy clustering. Chinese Science Bulletin, **45** No. 11 (2000) 961-970
10. Gordon A. D.: Classification. Chapman and Hall, London (1999)
11. Xie X. L., Beni G. A.: A validity measure for fuzzy clustering. IEEE Trans. on Pattern Analysis and Machine Intelligence, **13** No. 8 (1991) 841–847

Distributed Service Management
Based on Genetic Programming

Jing Chen[1], Zeng-zhi Li[1], and Yun-lan Wang[2]

[1] Institute of Computer Architecture and Network, Xi'an Jiaotong University,
Xi'an, 710049, P.R. China
`jingchen@263.net`
[2] Center for High Performance Computing, Northwestern Polytechnical University,
Xi'an, 710072, P.R. China

Abstract. An architecture for online discovery quantitative model of distributed service management based on genetic programming (GP) was proposed. The GP system was capable of constructing the quantitative models online without prior knowledge of the managed elements. The model can be updated continuously in response to the changes made in provider configurations and the evolution of business demands. The GP system chose a particular subset from the numerous metrics as the explanatory variables of the model. In order to evaluate the system, a prototype is implemented to estimate the online response times for Oracle Universal Database under a TPC-W workload. Of more than 500 Oracle performance metrics, the system model choose three most influential metrics that weight 76% of the variability of response time, illustrating the effectiveness of quantitative model constructing system and model constructing algorithms.

1   Introduction

Along with the growing acceptance of the web services, an evident trend [1] in service delivery is to move away from tightly coupled systems to structures of loosely coupled, dynamically bound distributed systems structure. In order to assure provided service quality, primary tasks to distributed service management are such as health monitoring to determine if the system in a safe operating region, early detection of service level agreement(SLA) violations, and on-going optimization of configurations to ensure good performance. All of these tasks require quantitative insights, preferably quantitative models that predict SLA metrics such as response time.Therefore, we first present a important concept in the research of quantitative model for distributed service management.

Definition of a quantitative model: In service management, for predicting important SLA parameter y, we select several (m) variables ($x_1, x_2, ..., x_m$ in general) from a set of candidate variables $\{x_1, x_2, ..., x_n\}$, and establish the quantitative relation model between y and $x_1, x_2, ..., x_m$. This model is called quantitative model. And the process is called the construction of the quantitative

P.S. Szczepaniak et al. (Eds.): AWIC 2005, LNAI 3528, pp. 83–88, 2005.

model. We refer y as the response variable and $x_i(1 \leq i \leq m)$ as the explanatory variables and $x_i(1 \leq i \leq n)$ as the candidate variables.

However, not only construction of these models requires a skilled analyst who understand the measurement data, configuration, and workloads, but also changes in any of these or the relationships between them mean that the model has to be reconstructed. Therefore, this paper presents the on-line discovery of quantitative models for service management based on genetic programming (GP)[2, 3]. The approach can construct the quantitative models on-line without prior knowledge of the managed elements, and it should be generic in that it discovers the explanatory variables to use.

2   Construction of Quantitative Models

Traditional solution for the construction of quantitative models is to find derivatives with formal equation group which is so called data imitation in Mathematics. But it is complicated in computing process, enormous in operation amount and not very accurate for higher-degree polynomial and multi-independent-variable (i.e., multidimensional space). The linear regression method also can be used here, but there is a premises that the linear correlation must exist between response variables and explanatory variables, so that it's not suitable when we don't know the correlation between two kinds of variables. In this paper, we construct the quantitative models with bintree coded genetic programming. Taking full advantage of wide searching space and only paying attention to the target function information of heredity algorithms, we can get the global optimizing solutions without deducing. At the same time, making use of the structure characteristics of bintree, the complexity and amount of operation are reduced greatly, so that it's suitable for on-line automatic quantitative models, and the models constructed have higher precision.

2.1   Coding Manner

Coding is the work first done by a heredity algorithm, that is transform the solution space of a problem with doable solutions to the searching space treated by the algorithm. This is the key to affect the other steps of the algorithm. Here we adopt bintree coding and make use of the characteristic of the bintree that it corresponds to the function expression one by one according as specific going through method. We take a random bintree met certain conditions as a solution to express a kind of function relation between response variables and explanatory variables. The bintree meets the requirement that each node is either an operand or an operator.

Operators: unitary operators : fabs, exp, log, atan, sin, cos;
              binary operators: +, -, *, /.
Operands: candidate variables,$x_1, x_2, ..., x_n$
Constants: random real number produced randomly.

2.2   Fitness Function

The heredity algorithm searches by each unit of the seed group only according to fitness function but not with any other exterior information, so that it's extremely important to select a suitable fitness function. For our topic, the smaller the difference between the values forecasted by the model and the measured values, the better the model is. Therefore, we take the sum of the squares of the differences between the forecasted values by models and the measured values as the fitness function, i.e. $\left\{ \sum_i \left(f(x_{i1}, x_{i2}, ..., x_{in}) - y_i \right)^2 \right\}^{-1}$, where f presents the function corresponding to the bintree; y_i presents measured value of ith sample response variable; $x_{ij}(j = 1, 2, ..., n)$ presents measured value of ith sample explanatory variable; and $f(x_{i1}, x_{i2}, ..., x_{in})$ presents value of the response variable forecasted by the model. Obviously, the more accurate is the quantitative model, the bigger the fitness value.

2.3   Design of the Selector

The selector adopt roulette selecting method. First, it finds the fitness value for every bintree, and sorts ascending the units of the bintree array according to their fitness values. Then, it finds the selected probability and cumulative probability of each bintree according to its fitness values. The selected probability of ith bintree is $P_i = \frac{f_i}{\sum_{i=1}^{M} f_i}$, where M represents the scale of the seed population and $f(i)$ is the fitness value of ith bintree. The cumulative probability of ith bintree is $acc[i] = \sum_{1 \le j \le i} acc[j]$. Finally, it determines all the selected bintrees according to cumulative probabilities. For selecting cross individual, multi-round choice is needed. Each round a symmetrical random number r in [0,1] is produce, which is used as the selecting pointer to determine the selected individual. If $acc[i-1] < $ r $ < acc[i]$ (acc is the array to store cumulative probabilities, and i is the position number of the current bintree in the array), then ith bintree is selected. After the selecting process, produced new group may include the same bintree, displaying that the eugenic individual has the stronger survival ability in the evolvement process.

2.4   Design of the Crossover

Crossing means genes recombined. It replaces and recombines part structures of two father individuals producing a new individual. (1)Selecting of crossing trees: First, assigning a random number in [0,1] to each bintree, if the number is smaller than the crossing rate, then corresponding bintree is selected. Then every pair of bintrees that border upon each other crosses in first-in-first-out sequence. If only one tree remains last, then it will be lost. (2)Crossing process of two bintrees: Crossing points are selected randomly for two bintrees (It can be any node of the bintree). Two new bintrees that the roots are the crossing points are exchanged each other; if crossed bintree exceed layer level, then it will be truncated, and the nodes on the layer level will be replaced by random operands. If the fitness value of above produced bintree is not existent or smaller than F_{min}, then this tree will be lost, and a suitable random bintree will be produced as the substitute.

2.5   Design of the Mutation

Selecting the mutation tree: Assigning a random number in [0,1] to each bintree, if the number is smaller than the mutation rate, then corresponding bintree is selected, and it will be mutated. Mutation process: The mutation point is selected randomly (it can be any node of the bintree). Disposing of mutation point: (1) If the mutation point selected randomly is a leaf, the we can randomly select one of the following two ways to process it: replacing it with any operand, or replacing it with a bintree produced randomly. (2) If the mutation point selected randomly is a ramification, then it is processed randomly according to its type. If the ramification is a monadic operator then it will be replaced with a randomly different monadic operator. If the ramification is a binary operator, then it will be replaced with a randomly different binary operator. The left and right subtrees that the roots are the mutation point will be mutated. If the fitness value of the mutation bintree is not existent or smaller than F_{min} , then this tree will be lost, and a suitable random bintree will be produced as the substitute.

3   Prototype and Performance

In this paper, the managed element is based on the WBEM[4] (Web-Based Enterprise Management) framework leaded by DMTF (Distributed Management Task Fore), its kernel part is CIM (Common Information Model) standard. The element in the prototype is the Oracle9i database management system running on a Linux platform, and the response variable is response time measured by an external probe[5]. The TPC-W[6] is used as the workload generator. The characteristics of the workload are modulated by varying the number of emulated browsers (EB) and also the workload mixes. For observing the prediction performance of GP experi-

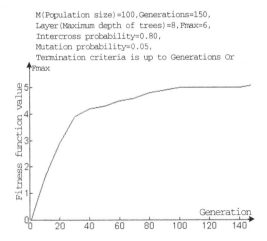

Fig. 1. The average value of fitness function in GP

ments results, we continued capturing the average value of fitness function ,it is shown in figure. For the final quantitative model, from more than 500 Oracle metrics, we choose 3 as the explanatory variables. The model produced is:

$$ResponseTime = 1.34 * ApplsExccutingInDBCurrently +$$
$$8.68 * 10^{-5} * TotalBufferpoolReadTime +$$
$$8.96 * 10^{-7} * TotalBufferpoolWriteTime$$

To evaluate data imitation veracity of the regression models, we employ the widely used r^2 metric . $r^2 = 1 - \sum_{1 \leq i \leq s} (y_i - \widetilde{y_i})^2 / \sum_{1 \leq i \leq s} (y_i - \overline{y})^2$, where s is the number of the samples, $\widetilde{y_i}(1 \leq i \leq s)$ is the observed value of the ith sample response variable, $y_i(1 \leq i \leq s)$ is the estimated value of the response variable, $\overline{y}$ is the average value of y. Metric r^2 quantifies the accuracy of the model through computing response viriable explained by the model. The domain of r^2 is [0,1]. $r^2 = 0$ expresses that there isn't any linear correlation between explanatory variables and response variables. $r^2 = 1$ means that the optimal model explaining capability.

We can find that for our model $r^2 = 0.76$, showing that the model established imitates 76% of the variability in the data, that is a fine imitation degree. Since the workload variation is mainly caused by varying the number of emulated browsers, the ApplsExecutingInDBCurrently metric is identified as most important. The other two are also relevant because reading/writing to bufferpools is often where most of the delay in the database occurs when processing queries. The relative importance of these metrics is consistent with the expectations of experienced database administrators.

4   Conclusion and Future Work

Quantitative models have considerable value in distributed service performance management. This paper propose an approach to on-line discovery of quantitative models without prior knowledge to managed elements. The metrics of the managed elements were built based on CIM. A subset of these metrics were selected as the explanatory variables through GP, then the quantitative model was built. The system taken Oracle database systems, which has the most quotient in market, as examples. Of the approximately 500 metrics available from the database system performance monitor, our system chooses 3 to construct a model that provides very good estimates of response times, and we demonstrated the approach through estimating the response times with TPC-W workload.

While our initial results are encouraging, much work remains. Currently, the response variable (e.g., response time, throughput) must be known when the Model Builder is invoked. We are extending our architecture to include extracting response variables from a service level agreement specification. Another direction is to adapt the model on-line, such as when there are changes in workloads and/or configuration (which may require change-point detection).Last, we want to scale our techniques to address multi-tiered eCommerce systems.

Acknowledgements

The authors gratefully acknowledge the suggestions of the reviewers and the hard work of the AWIC'2005 Program Committee.The authors also gratefully acknowledge the support of the National Natural Science Foundation of China(No.90304006), and the Specialized Research Fund for the Doctoral Program of Higher Education(SRFDP)(No. 20020698018).

References

1. Chen A G, Li X F. Thinking in services architecture for NGI[J]. Journal of Beijing University of Posts and Telecommunications, 2004, 27(Sup): 118-124.
2. John R. Koza, "Genetic programming: On the programming of computers by means of natural selection", MIT Press, Cambridge, MA, USA, 1992.
3. John R. Koza, "Genetic programming II: Automatic discovery of reusable programs", MIT Press, Cambridge, MA, USA, 1994.
4. Specification for CIM Operations over HTTP, Version 2.8. Distributed Management Task Force, May 2002.
   http://www.dmtf.org/standards/documents/WBEM/DSP200.html.
5. M. Basseville and I. Nikifirov. Detection of Abrupt Changes: Theory and Applications. Prentice Haa,1993.
6. Wayne D Smith. TPC-W: Benchmarking an ecommerce solution.
   http://www.tpc.org/tpcw.
7. Common Information Model(CIM) Version 2.8. Specification, Distributed Management Task Force, August 2002. http://www.dmtf.org/standard/cim_spec_v28/.
8. Standards Based Linux Instrumentation for Manageability Project.
   http://oss.software.ibm.com/developworks/projects/sblim/.
9. M. Debusmann and A. Keller. SLA-driven Management of Distributed Systems using the Common Information Model. In G.S.Goldszmidt and J. Schonwalder, editor, Proceedings of the 8th IFIP/IEEE International Symposium on Integraed Network Management. Kluwer Academic Publishers, March 2003.

Research on Path Clustering Based on the Access Interest of Users*

Chen Junjie and Wu Junjie

Taiyuan University of Technology, College of Computer and Software,
79 West Yingze Street, Taiyuan , 030024, Shanxi, China
chenjj@tyut.edu.cn

Abstract. Users with same interests can be classified by making use of clustering technology, based on the access path of users, the page access time of users, the resident time at page and URL of linking to the page in a web site. A new clustering algorithm is proposed by using access interests of users in the paper, in which the new interest degree, similitude degree, and clustering center will be defined. A true experiment has been completed making use of log files in the www.ty.sx.cn web site. Experiment results are successful.

1 Introduction

Internet is changing our life gradually and the future is a web world. How to attract more users and improve the users' browsing interest has been becoming the major work of web sites. At the same time, the higher demands have been put on the design and function of the web sites, in other words, web sites should have intelligence, ability to find out the required information quickly and exactly, ability to provide various service, to allow the users to customize the page according to their needs, to provide the information of product selling strategy for users, and so on. It is difficult to achieve all the function completely, and it needs to have great progress in some technology fields, for example, artificial intelligent and natural language understanding. An efficient way to solve the problem is to make use of the technology of web data mining to get the useful information.[2]

Data mining technology relates to structural data. However, web is an incompact distributed system, which has no central control, no uniform structure, no integrated restriction, no transaction management, no standard query language and data model, and can be extended unlimitedly.[3] In theory, it is difficult to mine useful information, and the information from web is also unascertainable. Whereas the log of web server have ideal structure, when users access the web sites, their browsed pages, access time and ID of users, etc, will be recorded into the log. Analyzing the web log, catching the delicate relations in the users' log,

---

* **Sponsored by** the grand science and technology research program of ministry of education (03020) and the Natural Science Foundation of Shanxi Province(20031038).

P.S. Szczepaniak et al. (Eds.): AWIC 2005, LNAI 3528, pp. 89–94, 2005.

finding out the common action of users' skimming through the web sites, mining the useful information, and then making use of these measures on web designs, will have great significance to improve the access count, to develop the market and carry out intelligent design of web.[4]

Log mining is to analyze and deal with server logs by making use of the idea of data mining. With the help of server log files, we can know the users' access pattern. It can help us analyze and investigate the rules of log records exteriorly, and improve web's structure and function, thereby construct adaptive web sites. It also can increase personality service and find out potential user colony by statistics and associated analysis.[6]

We need to analyze a data set, but we don't know the kind of partition. In this case, clustering is the better way. By clustering, we can identify district, and find out different users' characters from the path of users' access, thereby find unitary distributing model and interesting connection among the data attributes.

It's very important for the sequence of users' browse page to manage the web sites. From the view of the web sites managers, they always hope to have the consistency between users' browsing and page's hyperlink design.[7] The paper will introduce a new clustering algorithm based on access interest of users, and paying attention to access time, lasting time and source link. When the users browse every page, a superset of users' query transaction can be formed including all of the users' access path.

The minimal information we can collect from the users is users' access link stream, access time and staying time. Other information can be derived from known information.

2   Path Clustering Algorithm

Before clustering, you should preprocess the web site logs at first, and identify the users' transaction. First of all, data cleaning is completed, that is, logs should be turned into the credible and precise data, which are adapted to data mining, and the irrelevant items are deleted. Log records include users' IP address, users' ID, URL of users' request, request method, access time, transport protocols, transmission byte count, error code, etc. But users IP address, URL of users' request and access time are only relevant, other attributes can be taken out. There is always some assistant information, for example, image, sound, video, etc. in the URL except the straight matter of users' attention.

The aim of mining logs is to find out the users' common access pattern. If the records of assistant information are useless they can be deleted. It can be achieved by checking the suffixes of URL. All of gif, jpeg, cgi, etc. suffixes can be taken out if they are irrelevant. Of course, if pictures are main web contents, they have to be dealt with in other ways. Session identification is a kind of method at least.[1]

Session is a page stream of users' continue request. Different users' browse pages belong to different sessions.[8] If the same users' browse pages take longer time, it can be considered that users' access time is not only once, and timestamp timeout can be used. If the interval of users' browse page exceeds the timeout, it may be thought that a new user session begins. We can identify the users' transaction basing on it.

For data mining, users' session looks rough and is not accurate enough. It needs to turn session into the transaction having certain semantics. The paper adopts the most advanced URL to define transaction. As for every user's session, the beginning page is regarded as the starting point, and every most fronted path is as a kind of transaction. Finally all of the access transactions in the time sequence constitute transaction set, which can be used for mining.

Definition 1. *Users access transaction*

$$S = (l_1, \ldots, l_n) \tag{1}$$

Here:
n denotes the most length of this transaction.
l_i denotes the page i that some user browsed in this transaction $(1 \leq i \leq n)$

Definition 2. *Supposed that a user u, his access transaction is $S_u = (l_1, \ldots, l_n)$, corresponding staying time is $T_u = (t(l_1), \ldots, t(l_n))$, frequency of access page is $F_u = (f(l_1), \ldots, f(l_n))$, so the user's access transaction can be denoted as a triplet:$(S_u : T_u : F_u)$*

After data cleaning, session identification and transaction identification, clustering transaction set has been formed. Every user's access transaction is a path during the course of accessing web sites. The users' access transaction set is an access path set of all of the users to the web site during a period of time. After finding out users' access transaction set, we can go on clustering according to the path.

There is an interesting relation in users' access to web sites. The relation reflects the users' access interest. That is to say, these colony users' access interest and their access sequence have greater relativity. However, in the cause of the design of web sites, users' access transaction reflects their access interest naturally after considering the staying time and access frequency.[1]

Definition 3. *Interest degree (user interest to the page in the transaction), it can be expressed as follows:*

$$I_l = (n - l + 1) \times t(l) \times f(l) \tag{2}$$

Here:
n denotes transaction length
l denotes this page's position in the transaction
$t(l)$ denotes this page's staying time
$f(l) = \frac{see_l}{see_{all}}$ denotes this page's browsing frequency in detected time
see_l denotes access times of the page l in detect time
see_{all} denotes the total access times of all of the pages

In this transaction, if URL appears repeatedly, this page's interest degree needs to be accumulative, and only needs to keep down the address appeared in the first time.

Definition 4. *Supposed two transactions S_i and S_j, their similitude degree can be defined as follows:*

$$sim(S_i, S_j) = \cos(\theta_{(S_i,S_j)}) = \frac{< S_i, S_j >}{(< S_i, S_i >)^{\frac{1}{2}}(< S_j, S_j >)^{\frac{1}{2}}} \tag{3}$$

Here:

$$< S_i, S_j >=< (S_i : T_i), (S_j : T_j) >= \sum_{k=1}^{n} I_{i_k} I_{j_k}$$

$$= \sum_{k=1}^{n} (n_i - l_{i_k} + 1) \times t(l_{i_k}) \times f(l_{i_k}) \times (n_j - l_{j_k} + 1) \times t(l_{j_k}) \times f(l_{j_k})) \tag{4}$$

Definition 5. *Mapping the users' access transaction into vector*

$$V = (v_1, \cdots, v_n) \tag{5}$$

Here: $v_l = I_l = (n - l + 1) \times t(l) \times f(l)$

In order to calculate expediently, turn the uncertain length into certain length

$$V = (v_1, \cdots, v_n, 0, \cdots, 0) \tag{6}$$

Definition 6. *Mapping the users' access transaction into vector and forming matrix.*

$$A_{(m,n)} = \begin{pmatrix} V_1 \\ \cdot \\ \cdot \\ \cdot \\ V_m \end{pmatrix} \tag{7}$$

Here:
V_i denotes the vector defined by the formula (6) defined.$(1 \leq i \leq n)$
n denotes transaction length
m denotes the count of all the transaction

Definition 7. *Clustering count $k = r(A)$, it is order of the matrix $A(n,c)$*

Definition 8. *Clustering center $C = (c_1, \ldots, c_n)$*
Here: c_i denotes the page of the max interest degree of dimension in transaction of the clustering. Maybe the path represented by the transaction does not exist, but it stands for the natural center of this clustering.

The algorithm divides matrix $A_{(m,n)}$ into k clustering and makes the total similitude degree minimize between all of transactions of every clustering and this clustering center. The minimizing process can be expressed as follows:

1. Choosing the radix of $A_{(n,c)}$ as the first clustering center: $C_1, \ldots, C_n$
2. According to formula (3), counting the total similitude degree of clustering set, and distributing it. If there is no space vector to be chosen, the algorithm is end.
3. Adjusting clustering center, return to 2.

3   Experiment

The experiment makes use of www.ty.sx.cn logs as experimental object. The data include three day's data. The total data is 488M. We random access continuous 100000 data. Timeout is set as 15 minutes. At the same time, we have a contrastive experiment when staying time and access frequency is considered or not. We also consider that web sites need to attract users' access. So the experiment takes out the first page. The results are shown as Table 1.

Table 1. The results of the experiment

	Experiment times	1	2	3
	Users' access time	2004-05-12 06:29:33- 2004-05-12 07:22:16	2004-05-12 07:22:17- 2004-05-12 07:46:56	2004-05-12 08:11:45- 2004-05-12 08:36:00
	Records' count after log cleaning	5856	5939	6187
	Users' transaction count	213	200	157
	Average transaction length	3.0	6.0	10.0
Considering	Clustering count	27	26	35
	Average length of clustering center	7.0	6.0	15.0
	Average offset times of clustering center	28.0	25.0	30.0
Unconsidered	Clustering count	24	25	33
	Average length of clustering center	5.0	5.0	10.0
	Average offset times of clustering center	45.0	42.0	62.0

Experiment indicates: clustering count increased 7.5% averagely, it is useful to classify access users better; the average length of clustering center increased 37%, it is useful to classify web site's context better; the average offset times of clustering center reduced 59% averagely, it reduced clustering waste highly. Clustering effect is obvious. Web sites access time has great influence to the result of clustering, and has obvious clustering effect to access users of different time. With the increasing of clustering count, the average length of clustering center has increased obviously, so we can rather classify the access users, and satisfy the personality service. The average offset times of clustering center has reduced obviously. The algorithm efficiency is higher.

4   Conclusion and Future Work

The path clustering method the paper put forward is a kind of interested clustering means. It considers the interest of users' access path to web sites chiefly, which can help web sites improve their structure and content according to the analyzed results, at the same time, can lighten the users' burden by avoiding users' input and go on personality design exteriorly. The traditional viewpoint thinks that the page is a single information stream sending by server to client under the B/S structure, even if under the dynamic condition, it also can collect users' information by users' input, (for example, users' login information), we did not consider the client's buffering problem[5], and our imagination is to establish a proxy at client for dealing with this job, and to send this kind of information to server, which will be our next work.

References

1. Wang S., Gao W., Li J.T., Xie H. : Path Clustering: D is covering the knowledge in the Web site. Journal of Computer Research & Development. Vol.38 , No.4 (2001) 482–486
2. Song A.B., Hu K.F., Dong Y.S. : Research on Web log mining. Journal of Southeast University (Natural Science Edition). Vol.32, No.1 (2002) 15–18
3. Qian W.N., Zhou A.Y.: Analyzing Popular Clustering Algorithms from Different Viewpoints. Journal of Software. Vol.13, No.8 (2002) 1382–1394
4. Mobasher B., Dai H., Luo T., Nakagawa M. : Discovery and Evaluation of Aggregate Usage Profiles for Web Personalization. Data Mining and Knowledge Discovery,January. Vol.6, No.1 (2002) 61-82
5. Cadez I., Heckerman D., Meek C., Smyth P., White S. : Model-Based Clustering and Visualization of Navigation Patterns on a Web Site. Data Mining and Knowledge Discovery. Vol.7, No.4 (2003) 399-424
6. Grabmeier J., Rudolph A. : Techniques of Cluster Algorithms in Data Mining. Data Mining and Knowledge Discovery. Vol.6, No.4 (2002) 303-360
7. Cho Y.H., Kim J.K., Kim S.H. : A personalized recommender system based on web usage mining and decision tree induction. Expert Systems with Applications. Vol.23, No.3 (2002) 329-342
8. Tan P., Kumar V. : Discovery of Web Robot Sessions Based on Their Navigational Patterns. Data Mining and Knowledge Discovery. Vol.6, No.1 (2002) 9–35

A Request-Based Approach to Maintain Object Consistency in Content Distribution Network

Yan Chen, Zeng-zhi Li, Zhi-gang Liao, and Yun-lan Wang

Institute of Computer Architecture & Network,
Xi'an Jiaotong University, Xi'an 710049, China

Abstract. A novel request-based object consistency algorithm for Content Distribution Network (CDN) is proposed to ensure that locally cached data is consistent with that at the server. Interesting rate is proposed to indicate access rate of object, replica server polls Web server periodically and pull changes to object whose interesting rate equals to 1. Dynamic slip-window method is used to enable adjusting the size of refresh window according to request and modify rate in previous window. In order to make refresh interval more accuracy, object request clustering algorithm is proposed to optimize the basic algorithm. Simulated results show that this algorithm can take advantage of Content Distribution Network and significantly reduce the traffic generated as well as ensure object fidelity.

1   Introduction

An important problem in CDN (Content Distribution Network) is to maintain the freshness of cached objects that is to employ object consistency mechanisms that ensure replica servers are in-sync with Web server. Commonly used consistency mechanisms include: server-based "push" mechanisms and replica-based "pull" mechanisms.

A sever-based mechanism can offer high fidelity for rapidly changing data. However, it incurs a significant computational and state-space overhead resulting from a large number of open push connections. Thus, replica-based mechanism is widely used in CDNs. Most of such mechanisms adapt polling frequency to the rate at which objects change at Web server. However, a replica-based mechanism does not offer high fidelity when the data changes rapidly. Moreover, the replica-based mechanism generates significant levels of unnecessary traffic if objects are seldom accessed. In this paper, we propose a novel Request-based Object Consistency Algorithm (ROCA) that generates less polling traffic, in addition the introduction of clustering algorithm in our mechanism improve fidelity of objects.

2   Request-Based Object Consistency Algorithm (ROCA)

The purpose of object consistence algorithm is to ensure that users do not receive stale object from the replica server. To formally define consistency semantics,

P.S. Szczepaniak et al. (Eds.): AWIC 2005, LNAI 3528, pp. 95–100, 2005.

let s_t^a and p_t^a denote the version of object a at the Web server and replica server, respectively at time t. In such a scenario, a cached object is said to be strongly consistent with that at the server if $\forall t$, $P_t^a = S_t^a$. However, it is impossible to achieve strong consistency due to the existence of network delay. Nearly all consistency mechanism can only maintain Δ-consistency which means a cached object is never out-of-sync by more than Δ with the copy at the server. That is,

$$\forall t, \ \exists r, \ 0 \leq r \leq \Delta, \quad P_{t+r}^a = S_t^a \tag{1}$$

Interesting rate (IR) is defined to indicate access rate of object, Table 1 depicts two-level IR mechanism and its related consistency policy.

Table 1. Interesting rate of object

IR	Access rate	Refresh policy	Server to return object	Consistency degree
1	High	Refresh by TTR	Replica server	Δ−Consistency
0	Low	Do not refresh	Web server	Strong consistency

Fig. 1 depicts the flowchart of ROCA. The most important issue in ROCA is to adapt the TTR value (and thereby, the polling frequency) dynamically to the rate of update and request of the object.

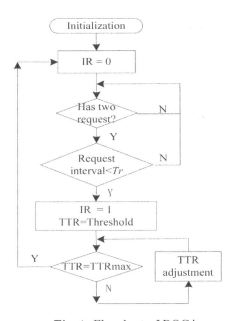

Fig. 1. Flowchart of ROCA

$TTRmin$ and $TTRmax$ represent lower and upper bounds on the TTR values. There are two main factors when determine the TTR value: update rate of Web server and request rate of client. Pc indicates the amount of request in last polling window, and Ps indicates whether the object be modified in last polling window.

After each poll, the algorithm updates TTR value based on the following cases:

Case 1 $Pc = 0$, then TTR $=$ TTR$\times 2^{w-1}$.

Where w is the amount of no-request polling window. Consequently, the TTR of an object that hasn't been accessed for a long period increases to $TTRmax$ rapidly.

Case 2 $Pc{\neq}0$ and $Ps{=}0$, then TTR $=$ TTR$+\varepsilon$.

Where $\varepsilon{\geq}0$, by choosing an appropriate value of ε, the algorithm can increase the TTR slightly or keep it unchanged.

Case 3 $Pc^{i-1}{\neq}0$ and $Ps^{i-1} =1$, then TTR $=$TTR $\times$ m, $0 < m < 1$.

3   Using Clustering Algorithm to Optimize ROCA

Although ROCA can ensure fidelity with lower cost, to adapt the value of TTR has a problem of delay. We introduce clustering algorithm to optimize ROCA, which can cluster weblog data of replica servers to discover groups of similar access patterns. We use concept hierarchy method to design dissimilarity of object that is depicted in Fig. 2.

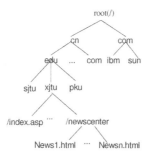

Fig. 2. Hierarchical Concept of object

Definition 1 (Property value) Suppose $O =\{O_1, O_2, \ldots, O_m\}$ is the set of object property, O_i is property of object i, $dom(O_i)$ is set of possible value of $O_i . o[O_i]$ is the projective of object o at O_i, that is the value of O_i.

Definition 2 (Concept hierarchy) The tree T_i that construct based on the elements of $dom(O_i)$ is defined as concept hierarchy. Suppose h is the depth of T_i, the layers are named as $1, 2, \ldots, h$. If the dissimilarity between layer i and layer $i+1$ is $W_{i,i+1}$, then $\forall x \in dom(O_i)$, the layer of x is denoted as $l(x)$.

Definition 3 (Dissimilarity of object) Suppose $\delta(Oname, Oname')$ is dissimilarity of object name and $\delta(Pc, Pc')$ is dissimilarity of access rate for object o and o', then the dissimilarity of these two object is define as:

$$\delta(o, o') = (|\delta(Oname, Oname')|)^\alpha + (|\delta(Pc, Pc')|)^\beta \quad 0 \leq \alpha, \beta \leq 1 \quad (2)$$

Definition 3.1 Dissimilarity of object name is defined as:

$$\delta(Oname, Oname') = 1 - \min(1, \frac{|Po \cap Po'|}{\max(1, \max(|Po|, |Po'|) - 1)})$$

Where Po indicates the path from root to o at the tree that shown in Fig. 2. Po indicates the length of the path or the number of links among the path.

Definition 3.2 Dissimilarity of access rate is defined as:

$$\delta(Pc, Pc') = \begin{cases} 1 - \frac{Pc}{Pc'}, & Pc' \geq Pc \\ 1 - \frac{Pc'}{Pc}, & Pc' < Pc \end{cases}$$

Where Pc, Pc' are the access rate of object o and o'.

Definition 4 (Class mode) Suppose X is the set of a classification group, the property value set denotes as $O = O_1, O_2, \ldots, O_m$. The mode of X is a vector $Q = [q_1, q_2, \ldots, q_m] \in \Omega$ that makes $D(Q, X) = \sum_{i=1}^{n} \delta(X_i, Q)$ be minimum.

Definition 5 (Object access clustering problem) Given a object access dataset D and an integer value k which is the number of clusters to be created. The clustering problem is to define a mapping: $D \rightarrow \{D_1, \ldots, D_k\}$ where $D = \cup_{i=1}^{k} D_i$ and $D_i \cap D_j = \phi, i \neq j$. If the mode of D_i is M_i, then the objective function of clustering is: $f = \sum_{i=1}^{k} D(D_i, M_i)$, the purpose of clustering is to minimize the value of f.

According to the characteristic of object consistency algorithm, we design an Object Access Clustering Algorithm OAKM, the algorithm is illustrate as:

1. Select an initial mode for each class;
2. Repeat
3. Put object o in the class to which the dissimilarity is minimum;
4. Update class modes depending on all objects belong to the class;
5. Re-caculate the dissimilarity of each object to all class modes, and put in the nearest class mode;
6. Until termination criteria is met.

The above OAKM algorithm is executed periodically. The clustering results are used to optimize ROCA in following steps.

1. Calculate the average TTR value of objects $TTRave$ in each class;
2. Using formula (3) to amend the TTR value of each object.

$$TTRnew = (a \times TTRave) + ((1 - a) \times TTRold) \quad (3)$$

Where $TTRnew$ and $TTRold$ are TTR value after and before amend. $0 \leq a \leq 1$, is adjustable value to determine the similarity of TTR among the same class.

4   Performance Evaluation

Our ROCA algorithm is evaluated using the following metrics: Request Fidelity (RF) and Bandwidth Consumption (BC) for useless polls.

$$RF = 1\text{- Number of violations/Number of requests} \quad (4)$$

$$BC = \text{Number of useless polls/Number of polls} \quad (5)$$

To generate the workload for our experiments, we use traces from NLANR[1]. Each request record in the trace provides information such as the time of request, the requested URL, the size of the object etc. Determining when objects are modified is crucial to consistency mechanisms. We employ an empirically derived model to generate synthetic write requests (use [2] for reference). Based on observations in [3], we divide objects into three types that *Image* almost never changed, while *application* objects changed quit often and for *text/html*, slightly over half the resources never changed, and most of the rest changed on each access after the first.

When select different value of a, we use clustering algorithm OAKM to optimize ROCA, the experimental results are show in Fig. 3. In our experiment we choose *text/html* object, the update interval of object is set to 900s. In Fig. 3, the *TTR* values which upper than *TTRmax* are filtered due to the clustering algorithm will not amend *TTR* value that upper than *TTRmax*. From Fig. 3 we can see that the values of *TTR* are more consistent with update rate after optimization.

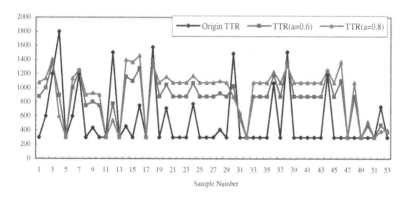

Fig. 3. The optimize results of clustering algorithm

Using evaluation factors that defined by formula (4) and (5), we compare ROCA with other approach, the results are depicted in Table 2. From Table 2 we see our ROCA has better performance in request fidelity and bandwidth consumption.

Table 2. comparison of different approach

Approach	ROCA	Using OAKM to optimize	Webserver "push" Ignore network delay	Periodic polling (Interval: 3600s)
RF	0.81	0.89	≈ 1	0.7
BC	0.2	0.17	0.78	0.85

(a)Image

Approach	ROCA	Using OAKM to optimize	Webserver "push" Ignore network delay	Periodic polling (Interval: 3600s)
RF	0.78	0.85	≈ 1	0.69
BC	0.36	0.31	0.61	0.75

(b)Text/html

Approach	ROCA	Using OAKM to optimize	Webserver "push" Ignore network delay	Periodic polling (Interval: 3600s)
RF	0.97	0.96	≈ 1	0.76
BC	0.81	0.78	0.97	0.96

(c)Application

5   Conclusion and Future Work

One of the key issues in CDN is how to manage the consistency of content at replicas with the origin server. In this paper, we proposed a novel approach in which the replica server determines consistency policy based on access rate of clients for each object. We explored clustering algorithm on TTR adjustment process by which we can determine the TTR value more accurately. Future work is expected to continue in optimize algorithm to adapt TTR according to bandwidth consumption and server workload.

References

1. NLANR, Weekly access logs at NLANR's proxy caches.
   ftp://ftp.ircache.net/Traces/.
2. A. Ninan. Maintaining Cache Consistency in Content Distribution Networks. Master's thesis, Department of Computer Science, Univ. of Massachusetts, June 2001.
3. F. Douglis, A. Feldmann, B. Krishnamurthy, and J.Mogul: Rate of change and other metrics: A live study of the World Wide Web. In Proc. Of USENIX Symp. on Internet Technologies and Systems, 147-158.

Testing the Effectiveness of Retrieval to Queries Using Polish Words with Diacritics

Kazimierz Choroś

Wrocław University of Technology, Faculty of Computer Science and Management,
Wyb. S. Wyspiańskiego 27, 50-370 Wrocław, Poland
choros@pwr.wroc.pl

Abstract. The development of network systems and the widespread access to the Internet generate the need for efficient tools of information retrieval. The globalisation of the Internet doesn't mean the unification of the languages used there even if we observe the dominance of English. Much information is accessible in other national languages which, however, for good understanding of the text, require the use of language specific characters, diacritical marks and/or accents. The results of testing the effectiveness of retrieval to queries expressed in Polish language using words with diacritics are presented. Then the influence of Polish local characters on the number of items retrieved by search engines is analysed and the reasons for using or not using diacritics is examined.

1 Introduction

The main value of an information retrieval system lies not in computer applications responsible for storing and retrieving relevant documents but in the amount and quality of information gathered in the system collections. These collections are changing in structures and formats. In the 70-ies the texts were stored using simple code tables, so that all text characters were capital letters. Language specific characters appeared much later. They are necessary not only for practical reasons but also for better understanding of the text. Furthermore, the use of local characters has a great influence on the system effectiveness. On the other hand, the search engines don't discriminate the texts accessible in the Internet according to the language used.

The analyses of Internet pages have shown that the great majority, more than 70% [8] of Internet information is in English. But the percentage of Internet users whose native language is English is much lower, only 35,2%. Only about 0,35% of Internet pages are in Polish, while Internet users who speak Polish account for 1,2% of the Internet population [13]. Even if the above numbers are only estimated, it is evident that non-English language pages and users cannot be ignored. The capabilities of search engines for non-English languages (Russian, French, Hungarian and Hebrew) were examined in [8]. The problem arises to what extent the national languages and specific local characters and words with diacritics influence the Internet search engine effectiveness.

P.S. Szczepaniak et al. (Eds.): AWIC 2005, LNAI 3528, pp. 101–106, 2005.

We can assume that a web or local system user is not interested in retrieval cost and other functional parameters of a computer application. The retrieval time can be neglected within reasonable limits, if the user needs relevant information so much that he is ready to wait even several minutes to get it. The only thing he strongly expects and demands is the information he needs. So, in this case the only measures of a system evaluation are measures reflecting the ability of the system to retrieve relevant information. The most important parameter of the retrieval process is its effectiveness expressed by standard measures, recall and precision [10]:

$$RECALL \quad R = \frac{RR}{ER} \quad and \quad PRECISION \quad P = \frac{RR}{SR} \tag{1}$$

where RR - the number of retrieved relevant items, ER - the number of all existing relevant documents and SR - the number of items in a system response.

Recall measures the proportion of relevant documents retrieved in response to a given query (i.e. the number of retrieved relevant documents divided by the total number of relevant documents contained in the collection, in the Web), whereas precision expresses which portion of retrieved documents is relevant for the user (i.e. the number of retrieved relevant documents divided by the total number of retrieved documents).

2   Recall Evaluation

The precision is easy to calculate, because we always know all the needed parameters and that is the reason why it is commonly used. But the other measure, recall, so fundamental for retrieval system evaluation creates some problems [3][4][5][7]. The cause is that we do not know how many relevant documents are stored in a system collection or how many relevant pages are accessible in the Internet. In experimental tests with small experimental collections this number is always known, but in a real situation it is impossible to re-examine the whole collection or all pages in the Web. This is the reason why even in present Web search engine evaluations, presented in computer magazines, this fundamental measure is not used. In a scientific approach, however, we cannot ignore it, even if some new measurements for search engine evaluation are proposed [12].

To establish the number of all relevant items in a huge collection (i.e. in the WWW net), the following strategies can be used:

- In local document collections sampling methods are very useful. In such a sampling process the main problem is to define a representative sample of a given collection. Such a technique is used for example in public opinion polls and market soundings. Such an approach is rather not possible to be applied in a Web environment.
- The other procedure consists in the application of test queries, prepared on the basis of selected documents introduced then to the collection. In a retrieval evaluation process only so "marked" documents are taken into account. This procedure is not possible to be applied in a Web environment either.

- The next possible method consists in a precise definition of the desired system response that should include known documents, identified or retrieved by another process, even without using computer retrieval system (paper catalogues, other private means of communication etc.).
- If in a given tested system there is more than one retrieval procedure, we can use them for comparing evaluations.
- The next method takes into account the inclusive nature of retrieval systems. Then the query should be generalised, so that it leads to retrieving a rather great number of items, but we hope that this numerous response contains almost all searched relevant documents which should be retrieved to the initial, precise query. This neighbourhood in a document space defined by a generalised query is assumed to be representative for the whole collection.
- The last procedure is very useful in a Web environment. The Internet can be browsed by several independent search engines. Their responses enable us to better evaluate the total number of relevant items in the Internet. To some extent, meta search engines can be applied. But in such a case we do not have an opportunity to choose a preferred search engine. Moreover, an additional analysis of response is necessary to avoid repetitions of items because of a generally low effectiveness of response aggregation.

3   Comparative Test Results

The last presented method was used to compare the effectiveness of 3 search engines very popular in Poland and oriented on Polish Web sides: ALTAVISTA, NETOSKOP (not functioning yet, the page serves the results obtained by Netsprint search engine) and ONET PL. The sum of relevant items retrieved in several other search engines was assumed as the number of all relevant items. Sometimes the queries were also generalized if a response was very small.

In the tests 8 queries in Polish language were used. The queries were totally different, but rather specific, so that the number of retrieved items was not limited by the system itself. That is, the queries were chosen in such a way that the system response contained less than 500 items and the users agreed to examine and evaluate the relevance of every item. The queries were formulated using all known techniques accessible in the information retrieval languages of the tested search engines, with the hope to get the optimum response. The results were averaged using macroprecision and they are presented in Fig.1 in the form of a Cranfield graph for 20 levels of recall (every 0.05), finally in the form of a continuous recall-precision graph.

The recall-precision graph shows that the effectiveness of Web search engines is relatively low and does not vary with different search engines. The main effort of search engine administrators is to ensure an adequate ranking of retrieved items, mainly in the first portions of retrieved items presented on the computer screen. For example the Onet search engine limits the system response only to the first 500 items.

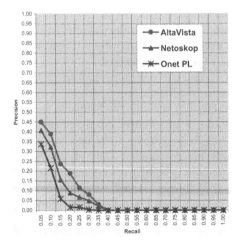

Fig. 1. Comparative results in the form of a Cranfield graph

4   Polish Diacritics

In Polish language there are several local characters with diacritic symbols, such as: ąćęłńóśźż. A diacritic is a symbol that does not occur independently, but always occurs with a character and is visually positioned in relation to another character, usually above or below. Diacritics are also sometimes referred to as accents. Polish diacritics come with such letters as: a, c, e, l, n, o, s, and z. There's the acute above c, n, o, s and z, the tail below a and e, the character l can be barred, and the dot could be put above z. Those diacritics represent concrete sounds of Polish.

In consequence, diacritics have the influence on the recall of the search. This problem has been already observed for Polish language [11], as well as for other languages using diacritics [1][2][6][8].

The number of items retrieved by the Web search engines varies (Tab. 1) depending on the use or non-use of diacritics. At the beginning, the moderators and strategists of search engines, which were not specially oriented on the Polish Internet made an assumption that the queries with and without local characters should lead to the same retrieval results. On one hand this assumption leads to the improvement of system recall, but on the other hand to the important increase in information noise. The meanings of words with and without diacritics are different. Moreover, if we omit a diacritic in a Polish word it can be mistakenly treated as a completely different word from another language. Therefore a change has been noticed [14] in the way the Google handles diacritics. In the past, words with no diacritics would match those with them and vice versa. Since 2001 we should use all diacritic variants of the word if we expect a high recall.

In the Google, which serves at present (as of Dec. 14, 2004) an enormous number 8,058,044,651 of indexed pages from all over the world, Polish words without diacritics are mistaken with other words in foreign languages. For example my name

Table 1. Numbers of the Internet pages retrieved for words with and without diacritics

	AltaVista	Google	Netsprint	Onet / Onet Pl
Choroś	601	1,560	850	341 / 269
Choros	96,300	103,000	230	21,059 / 87
dźwięk	540,000	1,110,000	140,000	117,643 / 67,037
dzwiek	60,000	57,200	31,000	12,892 / 12,190
gołoledź	1,620	4,210	750	825 / 241
gololedz	71	321	93	36 / 27
Łódź	1,240,000	2,240,000	440,000	269,600 / 132,690
Lodz	766,000	2,950,000	260,000	168,159 / 33,311
Wrocław	1,700,000	3,210,000	620,000	374,233 / 148,809
Wroclaw	795,000	1,860,000	270,000	175,532 / 38,049

without a diacritic becomes rather common Greek word 'choros', which means choir (chorus), although the etymology of my name has no connection with this Greek meaning.

Why do Polish words without diacritics appear also in the Polish Internet? There are several reasons for that. Many people using the Internet don't use local characters, because they are not used to using them. They have worked with computer systems for a long time and for a long time these systems have not offered them the local characters. Sometimes it is recommended to use a specific transcription if local characters are not available to avoid this kind of misunderstanding. For example in the Polish orthographic Internet dictionary prepared by the most respected editorial board Państwowe Wydawnictwo Naukowe [9], the Polish local characters could be transcribed by the use of the additional character ('), so we should then write: choros', dx'wie'k, gol'oledx', L'o'dx' and Wrocl'aw.

Many young people consciously don't use the local characters, having such a clumsy style, sometimes it is simply laziness or haste, because the use of local characters needs the simultaneous use of two keyboard keys or using additional keys. The analysis of the results shows that the important part of retrieved items without diacritics are the funny pages with jokes and private blogs. But not only laziness causes such a situation. Some very official Internet portals, for example of national journals, offer two kinds of their pages with and without diacritics. Some people, using old version of Internet browsers, or having troubles to configure their operating systems in an adequate way cannot display pages with diacritics correctly.

There is also another reason for not using the local characters, that is the names of computer files. The local characters were admitted in file names only recently. So, many computer users are used to not using such characters, mainly to avoid trouble on their computers or in file exchange in the network.

Finally, Polish words in foreign Internet services or journals are in general deprived of diacritics. Even it is recommended by the editors to avoid diacritics.

5   Conclusions

One of the reason for the low effectiveness of Internet search engines is the lack of consistency in using words with or without diacritics. There are many Internet services which offer us the information in national languages with or without local characters. The strategy to neglect these characters leads, however, to an increase in information noise, because the words in national languages are mistaken for other words in other languages.

There is also no consistency in using these local characters not only in official information services but mainly on rather free style private information pages, blogs, chats, forums, Internet discussions, commentaries etc.

The indexing procedures should take into account these facts. On the other hand, the Internet search engine users should be aware that the text containing the most relevant information could be without local characters. As a consequence, this information could be not retrieved or could be ranked low in a system response if we use the diacritics.

References

1. Bar-Ilan, J., Gutman, T.: How do search engines handle non-English queries? - A case study. WWW2003 Proc. of the Twelfth International World Wide Web Conference, available at:
http://www2003.org/cdrom/papers/alternate/P415/BARILAN.HTM
2. Brooks, T.A.: Orthography as a fundamental impediment to online information retrieval. J. ASIS **49** (8) (1998) 731-741
3. Can, F., Nuray, R., Sevdik, A.B.: Automatic performance evaluation of Web search engines. Inf. Proc. Man. **40** (3) (2004) 495-514
4. Choroś, K.: Effectiveness of Internet search engines (in Polish). Efektywność wyszukiwarek internetowych. In: Multimedialne i sieciowe systemy informacyjne. Ofic. Wyd. Polit. Wroc., Wrocław (2002) 115-123
5. Clarke, S.J., Willet, P.: Estimating the recall performance of Web search engines. ASLIB Proc. **49** (6) (1997) 184-189
6. Craven, T. C.: Variations in use of meta tag descriptions by Web pages in different languages. Inf. Proc. Man. **40** (3) (2004) 479-493
7. Fricke, M.: Measuring recall. J. of Inf. Science **24** (6) (1998) 409-417
8. Grefenstette, G, Nioche, J.: Estimation of English and non-English Language Use on the WWW. (Available at:http://arxiv.org/ftp/cs/papers/0006/0006032.pdf)
9. http://so.pwn.pl/
10. Salton, G., McGill, M.J.: Introduction to Modern information Retrieval. McGraw-Hill, Inc., New York 1983, p. 55, 164
11. Sroka, M.: Web search engines for Polish information retrieval: Questions of search capabilities and retrieval performance. Int. Inf. Lib. Res. **32** (2000), 87-98
12. Vaughan, L.: New measurements for search engine evaluation proposed and tested. Inf. Proc. Man. **40** (4) (2004) 677-691
13. www.global-reach.biz/globstats (Accessed on Nov. 12, 2004)
14. www.searchengineshowdown.com/newsarchive/000358.shtml (Accessed on Nov. 16, 2004)

Using a Neuro-Fuzzy Network
for Impulsive Noise Suppression
from Highly Distorted Images of WEB-TVs

Pınar Çivicioğlu

Erciyes University, Civil Aviation School,
Department of Aircraft Electrics and Electronics, Kayseri, Turkey
`civici@erciyes.edu.tr`

Abstract. This paper introduces a novel approach for denoising the images corrupted by Impulsive Noise (IN) by using a new nonlinear IN suppression filter, entitled **t**-nearest neighborhood pixels based **A**daptive-**F**uzzy **F**ilter (**t-AFF**). The proposed filter is based on *statistical impulse detection* and *nonlinear filtering* which uses Adaptive Neuro-Fuzzy Inference System as a missed data interpolant over the **t**-nearest neighbor pixels of the corrupted pixels. The impulse detection is realized by using the well-known *Edgington's goodness-of-fit test* which yields a decision about the impulsivity of each pixel. To demonstrate the capability of **t-AFF**, extensive simulations were realized revealing that the proposed filter achieves a better performance than the other filters mentioned in this paper in the cases of being effective in noise suppression and detail preservation, even when the images are highly corrupted by IN.

1   Introduction

Today WEB-TV broadcasting continues to grow exponentially causing the transmission quantity of images to increase. Images are often degraded by Impulsive Noise (IN) because of the errors caused by noisy sensors or transmission channels (i.e., WEB), thus suppression of IN is one of the most important issues in image and video restoration systems [1], [2]. In image denoising, a compromise has to be achieved between noise reduction and preserving significant image details. IN removal is an important task of image processing applications in many research and application areas such as *TV-Radio broadcasting*, *Radar Imaging*, *Astronomy*, *Avionics*, *Aerial Navigation* and *Remote Sensing*. In the last years, nonlinear approaches based on fuzzy systems [3] and artificial neural networks [4] have emerged as attractive alternatives to classical noise suppression techniques due to their advanced features and adaptive functionality. An important advantage of the fuzzy paradigm is knowledge representation and its ability of handling imprecise and inconsistent *real-world* data. A fuzzy system typically represents information in the form of rules that emulate human thinking and decision making whereas the key feature of artificial neural networks is knowledge acquisition.

P.S. Szczepaniak et al. (Eds.): AWIC 2005, LNAI 3528, pp. 107–113, 2005.

Therefore, a combination of the fuzzy and neural systems can play a very important role in information processing. In this paper, a novel approach is presented for the restoration of IN-corrupted images by the application of ANFIS [5] to nonlinear filtering. The task of impulse detection is a simple classification problem and in this paper, the Edgington's goodness-of-fit test (EGT) [6] has been used to check each pixel in order to detect whether it is distorted or not. Then, the proposed nonlinear filtering scheme is achieved for the distorted pixels, while the noise-free pixels are left unaltered. The **t-AFF**, proposed in this paper, differs from the other IN removal filters by performing the restoration of degraded images with no blurring even when the images are highly corrupted by IN [7], [8], [9], [10]. In order to test the success of the proposed filter, the performance of **t-AFF** is compared with the performances obtained by using *Progressive Switching Median Filter* (PSM) [7], *Yüksel's Fuzzy Filter* (YÜKSEL) [8], *Recursive Adaptive-Center Weighted Median Filter* (ACWMR) [9], and *Russo's if-then-else fuzzy reasoning filter* (RUSSO) [10].

2   Statistical Analysis of Impulsive Behavior of Pixels

Statistical tests are beneficial in the analysis of impulsive behavior of pixels, therefore, in this paper, impulsive behavior of the image pixels has been investigated with the use of statistical tests. Extensive simulations exposed that each intensity level within the real images possesses at least one best-fitted statistical distribution model. The statistical analysis has revealed that the well-known Normal Distribution (*ND*) [6], [11] appears to be the best statistical distribution model for the sample of intensity data, which are derived from [32x32] pixels sized unoverlapping blocks (bins) [12]. In this paper, The *EGT* has been used in order to statistically analyze the residuals of *ND* [6], [11]. The *ND* has been used to find out the pixels, which are suspected to be *corrupted* intensity levels in distorted image. In order to statistically analyze impulsive behavior [13] of the intensity levels, the image surface is divided into [32x32] pixels sized unoverlapping subimages. Extensive simulation results expose that [32x32] pixels sized bins are ideal for *EGT* test. For each intensity level, a *numerical set* denoting the number of the pixels, which possess this intensity level within the subimages, has been determined. This *numerical set* has been used for investigating the *EGT* value of an intensity level. It is observed empirically that the intensity levels, whose *EGT* is *greater* than the *threshold* **10.000 ± 2.000** belong to the *corrupted pixels*, respectively. The value of ±**2.000** denotes the deviation from the thresholds for *EGT* value, when a deviation from *ND* occurs. It is observed empirically that a deviation from the *ND* that is greater than the given threshold value indicates corruption. Therefore, the pixels whose *EGT* significance probability values are greater than the related thresholds are considered as *corrupted pixels*. The value of the *threshold* has been validated by the experimental results realized using almost 50 different real-world images under different impulsive noise densities. The noise detection procedure can be summarized as the decision rule of *if EGT* $(g) \geq 10.000 \pm 2.000$ *for an intensity level,* (g), *then the pixels possessing* (g) *are considered as corrupted.*

3   Adaptive Neuro-Fuzzy Inference System (ANFIS)

An ANFIS, is a fuzzy inference system implemented in the framework of adaptive networks [5]. An adaptive artificial-network is a superset of all kinds of feed-forward neural networks with supervised learning capability. ANFIS serves as a basis for constructing a set of fuzzy *if-then-else* rules with appropriate membership functions to generate the stipulated input-output pairs. In the proposed method, a combination of least-squares and backpropagation gradient descent methods have been used at the training phase of the fuzzy structures, in order to compute the parameters of the membership functions, which were used to model given set of inputs (x, y) and single-output g where (x, y) and g denote the spatial positions and intensity values of the pixels, respectively. The parameters of the ANFIS structures have been obtained for each of the t-nearest neighbor pixels of a corrupted pixel by training the ANFIS structures with 20 epochs. All the fuzzy structures have two triangular curve membership functions at their inputs and one linear membership function at their output. The computational structure of ANFIS is *not mentioned* in this paper in detail because many studies have been realized on ANFIS [5], [8].

4   Proposed Method

The computational algorithm of the **t-AFF** is given below step-by-step:

- Find the image coordinates, (x, y), of the corrupted pixels, which were determined by using *EGT* over the residuals of *ND* fitting.

   For each corrupted pixel perform the following steps,

- Find out the spatial positions of the *t-nearest neighbor uncorrupted pixels* for the related corrupted pixel.
- Use the spatial coordinates and gray values of the *t-nearest neighbor uncorrupted pixels* in order to train an ANFIS structure.
- Use the trained-ANFIS structure in order to make an estimation for the gray value of the corrupted pixel.
- Update the gray value of the corrupted pixel value with the value estimated in the previous step.

5   Experiments

A number of experiments were realized in order to evaluate the performance of the proposed **t-AFF** in comparison with the recently introduced and highly

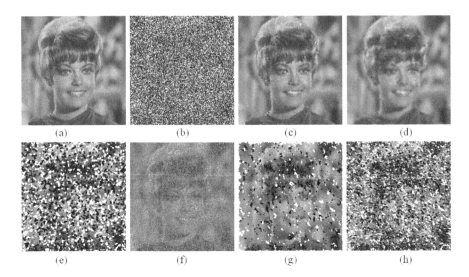

Fig. 1. The restored images of the Zelda Image for the Noise Density of 75%: (a) Original Image, (b) Corrupted Image at the noise density of 75%, (c) t-AFF (t=10), (d) t-AFF (t=15), (e) PSM, (f) YÜKSEL, (g) ACWMR, (h) RUSSO

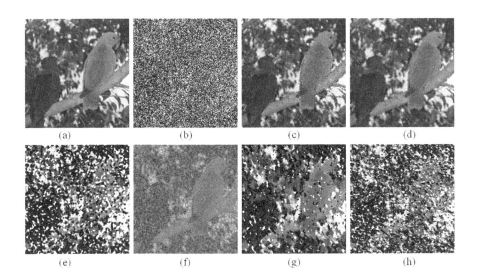

Fig. 2. The restored images of the Parrots Image for the Noise Density of 75%: (a) Original Image, (b) Corrupted Image at the noise density of 75%, (c) t-AFF (t=10), (d) t-AFF (t=15), (e) PSM, (f) YÜKSEL, (g) ACWMR, (h) RUSSO

approved IN suppression filters. The experiments were carried out on the well-known test images; *The Zelda* and *The Parrots*, which are 256x256 pixels sized and 8 bit per pixel. The test images were corrupted by IN at various noise densities ranging from 15% to 75%. The restoration results of test images for the noise density of 75% are illustrated in Fig.s 1-2, where it is clearly seen that, the noise suppression and detail preservation are satisfactorily compromised by using the proposed **t-AFF** even if the noise density is high (i.e. 75%). Restoration performances are quantitatively measured by the Mean-Squared-Error (MSE). The filters of PSM, YÜKSEL, ACWMR and RUSSO have been simulated as well for performance comparison with the proposed filter. The major improvement achieved by the proposed filter, **t-AFF**, has been demonstrated with extensive simulations of the mentioned test images corrupted at different noise densities. The experiments have been conducted for both $t=10$ nearest neighbor pixels and $t=15$ nearest neighbor pixels. As it is seen from the tables, the restoration performance of the proposed filter rises with t. Experimental studies show that $10 \leq t \leq 20$ supplies best restoration results. It is obviously seen from Tables 1-2 that **t-AFF** provides a substantial improvement compared with the simulated filters, especially at the high noise densities. The IN removal and detail preservation are best compromised by the **t-AFF**. Robustness is one of the most important requirements of modern image enhancement filters and the Tables 1-2 indicate that the proposed **t-AFF** provides robustness substantially across a wide variation of noise densities.

Table 1. Comparison of the restoration performances of the mentioned methods in MSE for **The Zelda** test image

Method	Noise Density				
	15%	30%	45%	60%	75%
Corrupted Image	2706.60	5343.10	8052.90	10741.00	13442.00
t-AFF (t=10)	5.11	17.66	97.546	163.71	233.91
t-AFF (t=15)	**4.97**	**11.29**	**23.02**	**42.11**	**58.06**
PSM	14.94	37.63	236.81	1713.40	6835.10
YÜKSEL	33.73	75.61	179.61	380.78	719.09
ACWMR	24.39	94.41	298.35	766.10	2476.90
RUSSO	28.70	151.87	665.67	2028.60	5084.00

Table 2. Comparison of the restoration performances of the mentioned methods in MSE for **The Parrots** test image

Method	Noise Density				
	15%	30%	45%	60%	75%
Corrupted Image	3048.60	6129.20	9343.40	12152.00	15491.00
t-AFF (t=10)	13.47	40.30	81.61	138.45	300.02
t-AFF (t=15)	**11.28**	**26.96**	**47.64**	**81.59**	**168.37**
PSM	84.25	175.08	497.65	1925.00	7482.30
YÜKSEL	156.31	273.58	535.32	966.35	1716.20
ACWMR	77.44	209.07	516.83	1255.70	3652.00
RUSSO	112.70	361.38	1035.30	2528.70	6171.00

6 Conclusions

In this paper, a simple-structured, high performance filter is proposed for the suppression of IN. It can be seen from the Tables 1-2 that the proposed **t-AFF** gives absolutely better restoration results and a higher resolution in the restored images when compared with the IN suppression filters mentioned in this paper. The effectiveness of the proposed filter in processing different images can easily be evaluated by appreciating the Tables 1-2 which demonstrate the restoration results of **t-AFF** and the comparison filters for images degraded by IN. The MSE values of the proposed **t-AFF** is smaller than the MSE values of comparison filters for all of the test images. In addition, the proposed **t-AFF** supplies more pleasing restoration results aspect of visual perception and also provides the best trade-off between IN suppression and image enhancement for detail preservation as can be seen from Fig.s 1-2. In order to reduce the computational cost, fuzzy structures in the proposed method use only four rules for each corrupted pixel.

References

1. Çivicioğlu, P., Alçı, M.: Impulsive Noise Suppression from Highly Distorted Images with Triangular Interpolants. AEU International Journal of Electronics and Communications, **58** (5) (2004) 311–318
2. Çivicioğlu, P., Alçı, M.: Edge Detection of Highly Distorted Images Suffering from Impulsive Noise. AEU International Journal of Electronics and Communications, **58** (6) (2004) 413–419
3. Russo, F.: Evolutionary Neural Fuzzy Systems for Data Filtering. IEEE Instrumentation and Measurement Technology Conference, **2** (1998) 826–830
4. Haykin, S.: Neural Networks: A Comprehensive Foundation. Macmillian College Publishing Company, New York, 1994
5. Jang, J.S.R.: Anfis: Adaptive-Network-Based Fuzzy Inference System. IEEE Transactions on Systems, Man and Cybernetics, **23** (3) (1993) 665–685
6. Edgington, E.S.: Randomization Tests. Third Edition, Revised and Expanded. Marcell-Deker Press, USA, 1995
7. Wang, Z., Zhang, D.: Progressive Switching Median Filter for the Removal of Impulse Noise from Highly Corrupted Images. IEEE Transactions on Circuits and Systems-II: Analog and Digital Signal Processing, **46** (1) (1999) 78–80
8. Yüksel, M.E., Baştürk, A.: Efficient Removal of Impulse Noise from Highly Corrupted Digital Images by a Simple Neuro-Fuzzy Operator. AEU International Journal of Electronics and Communications, **57** (3) (2003) 214–219
9. Chen, T., Wu, H.R.: Adaptive Impulse Detection Using Center Weighted Median Filters. IEEE Signal Processing Letters, **8** (1) (2001) 1–3
10. Russo, F., Ramponi, G.: A Fuzzy Filter for Images Corrupted by Impulse Noise, IEEE Signal Processing Letters. **6** (3) (1996) 168–170
11. Pok, G., Liu, J.C., Nair, A.S.: Selective Removal of Impulse Noise Based on Homogeneity Level Information. IEEE Trans. on Image Process., **12** (1) (2003) 85–92

12. Çivicioğlu, P., Alçı, M., Beşdok, E.: Using an Exact Radial Basis Function Artificial Neural Network for Impulsive Noise Suppression from Highly Distorted Image Databases. Lecture Notes in Artificial Intelligence, **LNCS 3261** (2004) 383–391
13. Brown, C.L., Zoubir, A.M.: Testing for Impulsive Behavior: A Bootstrap Approach. Digital Signal Processing, **11** (2) (2001) 120–132

Vector Retrieval Model for XML Document Based on Dynamic Partition of Information Units

Cui Li-zhen and Wang Hai-yang

School of Computer Science and Technology, Shandong University, Jinan, P.R. China
clz@dareway.com.cn

Abstract. XML document is applied in WEB application more and more. Because users can find what they need in numerous XML documents, technology of information retrieval based on XML document becomes a hot topic in information retrieval field now. Traditional technology of information retrieval based on XML document need define retrieval unit and retrieval result unit of the retrieval beforehand, and the dividing granularity is either too big or too small. In this paper we propose a retrieval method, which can dynamically partition information units in terms of the structure and semantic information of XML in vector space model. Therefore it reduces calculating workload efficiently and improves running efficiency of the entire retrieval system. The retrieval efficiency of this method is proved than the traditional one when they have the same accuracy. Finally, the results have been testified by experiment.

1   Introduction

As a standard document form, XML (eXtensible Markup Language) is more and more widely used in every field. Using unified method to present different structured data, XML makes the transform between different fields possible. We can see that, in the near future, there will be many kinds of document presented in XML. In order to provide user with the convenience of information retrieval in XML documents, XML documents information retrieval has became a hot research point. As a structured text document, XML has the same structure and delamination with its structure in physical organization, and the logic semantic present is contained in its text and structure too. Web information retrieval system can use the tag of the element to ensure its structure, and then ensure retrieval in the part needed, not like html, in which we treat it as a line in general and ignore its structure information. In order to use the information of semantic and structured XML documents, ensure the fit able retrieval and retrieval result unit, realize XML information retrieval based on key words, we need to know how to decide the size of the information unit using present technology and how to compute the similarity between the information unit and the query. In this paper, we present a retrieval method based on Vector Space Model for XML

P.S. Szczepaniak et al. (Eds.): AWIC 2005, LNAI 3528, pp. 114–119, 2005.

documents, with which the system can decide the information unit automatically. This method is based on Vector Space Model, it can use the structured and semantic information of XML documents well, and decide the granularity of information unit and compute the similarity between the information unit, to reduce the waste of system running resource and prompt the speed of information retrieval.

2   The VSM

Professor Salton had started the study on information retrieval, and proposed the classical computing model in field of information retrieval - Vector Space Modelshorted as VSM[1].

The expression of Vector Space Model is to extract character vectors from text terms, and give weight to them by a certain rule, e.g. we can present document d as $d(t_1, t_2, \ldots, t_n)$, in which t_k is term. We can use weight to qualify them, and present document d as $d(t_1, w_1, t_2, w_2, \ldots, t_n, w_n)$, shorted as $d(w_1, w_2, \ldots, w_n)$, the weight of term t_k is $w_k, 1 \leq k \leq n$.

For a given document $d(t_1, w_1, t_2, w_2, \ldots, t_n, w_n)$, $w_1, w_2, \ldots, w_n$ is an n dimensional space vector, $d(w_1, w_2, \ldots, w_n)$ is called as the Vector Space Model of document d. Then a text can be presented as a vector. We use a function $sim(d_i, d_j)$ to present the similarity between the document d_i and d_j as the relativity between them. We give the formula is:

$$Sim(D_i, D_j) = \cos\theta = \frac{\sum\limits_{k=1}^{n} w_{ik} \cdot w_{jk}}{\sqrt{\left(\sum\limits_{k=1}^{n} w_{ik}^2\right)\left(\sum\limits_{k=1}^{n} w_{jk}^2\right)}} \qquad (1)$$

In which, tf_{ik} is the frequency of t_k appeared in D_i, $\log(N/n_k + 0.01)$ is the presentation of the set of retrieval unit (N is the number of documents, n_k is the number of documents in which t_k appears); the denominator is to standard all of the ponderances to ensure the weight of term t_k is in $[0, 1]$.

3   XML Retrieval Based on Vector Space Model

In this section, we discuss our method in detail. First introduce the definition of information unit. Second, give the calculation method of the similarity between the information unit and the query.

3.1   The Definition of Information Unit

We need to define information unit, which is meaningful for users before we start information retrieval. Some traditional information retrieval methods deal with a whole document as a retrieval unit; the retrieval result unit is a set of documents that are suitable for query request [4]. It can provide users full-scale information; but for the large scale of the retrieval units, there would be too much information that users would not concern about, and then it leads to inaccurate retrieval results and information redundancy. The others deal with an element as a retrieval unit; the retrieval result unit is a set of elements that contain the information the query want most [6]. It can improve the retrieval precision, but for the large number and small scale of the retrieval units, it need consume too much system resource and cannot provide users enough information.

Here, we introduce a method which could automatically decide the information units suitable for the XML document retrieval based on the semantic and structure of the XML document. First, we convert a xml document to a logic structure. Then, we give the definition of information unit and result unit.

The Logic Structure Model of XML Document. A XML document can be converted to a tree structure with the relationship of hiberarchy and containing among elements. In this paper, we can convert the attribute to the parent/child relationship, and then describe as a vector tag graph, in which the parent nodes have several edges towards children nodes and the heading of the edge tells. Fig.1 showed an example of one XML document tree.

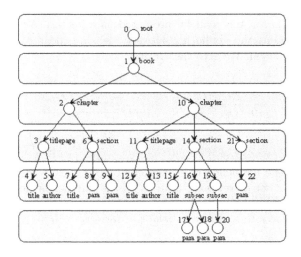

The Definition of Retrieval Unit. As shown above, a XML document is a structured semantic document, its structure character not only appears on its tags, also appears in the tag name. Afigure XML document to a XML document tree. Based on the analysis above, we define the re can be transferred trieval unit below:

Information retrieval system analyses the XML document with XML grammar parser, build XML document tree and pick-up the content in the element tags. When there is user inputting query to the system, it first matching the keywords to the content of the tag:

1. If matching succeeds, find out the highest node in them; treat all of its contained nodes as the retrieval unit of the document.
2. Else, if fail, define child nodes which have the most nodes in the XML structure tree as the retrieval result unit.

The Definition of Retrieval Result Unit. The retrieval result unit is the result provided to the user, it needs to be have the suitable size and serve enough information, not only a fragment of the XML document or XML document self. So, we define the retrieval result unit as follow:

1. For above case 1 of retrieval unit definition. The retrieval result unit is itself;
2. For above case 2 of retrieval unit definition. The retrieval result unit is the node which is on the way the retrieval node to the root node and have same element tag in its delamination (not include the retrieval node); if they are not exist, the retrieval result unit is the root node.

Using this method, we can get retrieval and retrieval result unit automatically from the XML document. The number of the retrieval unit does not larger than the number of the leaf node for every retrieval unit contains at least one leaf node; this resolved the problem of too many retrieval units in information retrieval. The number of the retrieval result unit does not larger than the number of the retrieval unit and have the suitable size for information retrieval, for every retrieval result unit contains at least one retrieval unit, they are the more meaningful result unit for the user to search. This resolved the problem of too large retrieval result unit scale and semantic redundancy or lack. At the same time it avoids to compute similarity between every leaf node and the query, save the running time, prompt the system running efficiency.

3.2   The Similarity Between the Information Unit and the Query

In order to computing the similarity between the document and the query, we need to compute the similarity between the retrieval unit and the query, map it to the tree structure and then compute the similarity between the retrieval result unit and the query, finally provide the users the retrieval result in descending order.

The Similarity Between Retrieval Unit and Query. For every retrieval unit, we abstract its entire containing context as text to get the vector of the document. When we input query to the system, a vector is generated.

Considering e_i, the information retrieval system computes the frequency all of the terms appear in the XML document, using the VSM method said in section 2 to get the vector of retrieval unit e_i is $D_i = (w_{i1}, w_{i2}, \ldots, w_{in})$.

When user input keywords to the information retrieval system as a query, the system generates a query vector $Q = (q_1, q_2, \ldots, q_n)$. If t_k is appears in query key words, then $q_k = 1$; else, $q_k = 0$. Using formula (1), we can get their similarity method:

$$Sim(D_i, D_j) = \cos\theta = \frac{\sum\limits_{k=1}^{n} w_{ik} \cdot q_k}{\sqrt{\left(\sum\limits_{k=1}^{n} w_{ik}^2\right)\left(\sum\limits_{k=1}^{n} q_k^2\right)}} \qquad (2)$$

The Similarity Between Retrieval Result Unit and Query. Every retrieval result unit contains at least a retrieval unit, so we need to use the structure reflecting relation between retrieval unit and retrieval result unit to get the similarity between retrieval result unit and query using the similarity between retrieval unit and query. We can get the similarity using the formula below:

$$Sim(D_n, Q) = f(Sim(D_{c_1}, Q), Sim(D_{c_1}, Q), \ldots, Sim(D_{c_m}, Q)) \qquad (3)$$

In which, $c_1, c_2, \ldots, c_m$ is the children of node n, $Sim(D_{c_k}, Q)$ is the similarity between subtree c_k and the query. In this paper we define function is:

$$f(s_1, s_2, \ldots, s_m) = 1 - \left(\frac{(1-s_1)^p + (1-s_2)^p + \ldots + (1-s_m)^p}{m}\right)^{\frac{1}{p}} \qquad (4)$$

For example, when a user input query keyword "information retrieval", we can use the above method, the document with the structure showed in Fig.1, the retrieval systems first pick-up the element tag content of the XML document, and compare with the query keywords. Since the four degree of the tree has the most number of element nodes, we tread every nodes of its parent as a retrieval unit. Then we can get document fragment including node3, node6, node11, node14, node21; get its retrieval result unit including node2, node10. Using formula (2), we can get the similarity between $d_3, d_6, d_{11}, d_{14}, d_{21}$ and query Q; using formula (3) and (4), get the similarity between d_2, d_10 and query Q. Finally, the results in descending order give the user the most related information.

Experiments and Method Analyses In the process above, for a certain XML document, all D_i is computed once, so during a retrieval process, the main computation is the similarity between D_i and Q. In our method, since there is a pretreatment before retrieval, we can get suitable retrieval unit and retrieval result unit for the query, the similarity computing is only between retrieval unit and retrieval result unit , we can compute similarity between every retrieval unit and query Q using formula (2), and then get similarity between every retrieval result unit and query Q using formula (3) , and the number of retrieval and retrieval result unit are much less than the number of leaf notes, so we can avoid much computing for similarity and improve the efficiency of the system. At the same time, we can confirm suitable retrieval result unit for the query, and compute dynamically suitable query result, which can improve the satisfaction of users. It is showed in the experiment that our method can define information unit automatically, reduce the consummations of system resource, and improve the efficiency of information retrieval.

4 Conclusions

XML retrieval has become one of the hot research points now. In this paper, we do research work on the technology of XML information retrieval based on VSM, and prompt a method that can define suitable retrieval unit in XML documents dynamically. This method uses XML document structure and realizes the XML information retrieval using VSM and keywords with unique retrieval technology. Based on the analysis of XML structure and semantic information, compared with the traditional XML retrieval technology, this method define information unit automatically, reduce the waste of system resource, and improve the efficiency of information retrieval.

In future, we will be dedicated to improve the precision of the whole system with good efficiency.

References

1. Salton, G., Wong, A.: A vector space model for automatic indexing. Communications of the ACM, 18(1975) 613-620
2. Lee, J.: Analyzig the Effectiveness of Extended Boolean Models in Information Retrieval. In Proc. of SIGIR-94, Dublin, Ireland (1994)182-190
3. Theobald, A., Weikem, G.: Adding relevance to XML. Proceedings of the 3rd International Workshop on Web and Database, Dallas, USA (2000) 105-124
4. Fuhr, N., Grobjohann, K.: XIRQL: A query language for information retrieval in XML documents. Proceedings of the 24th Annual International Conference on Research and development in Information Retrieval, New Orleans, USA (2001)172-180
5. Hayashi, Y., Tomita, J.: Searching text-rich XML documents with relevance ranking. ACM SIGIR 2000 Workshop on XML and Information Retrieval, Athens, Greece (2000)
6. Hatano, K., Kinutani, H., Yoshikawa, M., Uemura, S.: Information Retrieval System for XML Documents. Proceedings of the 13th International Conference on Database and Expert Systems Applications, Aix-En-Provence, France (2002)758-767

Flexible Querying with Fuzzy Projection

Krzysztof Dembczyński, Maciej Hapke, and Dominik Przybył

Institute of Computing Science, Poznań University of Technology,
60-965 Poznań, Poland
kdembczynski@cs.put.poznan.pl

Abstract. In the paper we present a new operation called fuzzy projection that extends flexible querying languages. It consists in fuzzification of tuples for all linguistic variables defined on domains of attributes specified in a query. In result, tuples with linguistic variables, instead of original values, are displayed. On the basis of fuzzy projection a specific fuzzy group-by operation is introduced. These two operations are implemented as a part of SQLf_j language based on SQLf introduced by Bosc and Pivert.

1 Introduction

Classical queries to database systems assume Boolean-logic based conditions. Such an approach requires from the user precise information about what she/he is looking for. Most common situation is that the query conditions are imprecise. A useful approach to handle imprecision is fuzzy set theory introduced by Zadeh [8]. The application of fuzzy sets in the area of databases systems has been widely addressed in the literature, see for example [1, 2, 4, 5, 6, 7].

There are some different proposals of fuzzy querying languages. For example, SQLf introduced by Bosc and Pivert [1] and SummarySQL [5] are straightforward extensions of the classical SQL, the most popular language of relational databases. The main feature of them is that they allow using fuzzy conditions in place of Boolean ones. Moreover, SummarySQL follows a popular concept of linguistic summaries in sense of Yager [6].

In the paper, we introduce a new operation called *fuzzy projection*. It consists in fuzzification of tuples, i.e. checking in what extent an attribute value belongs to all linguistic variables defined on domains of attributes specified in a query. As the result, tuples with linguistic variables, instead of original values, are displayed. On the basis of fuzzy projection we introduce a specific fuzzy group-by operation. It allows grouping tuples by linguistic variables. These two operations, fuzzy projection and fuzzy group-by, are implemented as a part of SQLf_j language (based on SQLf). Command-line application for processing SQLf_j queries is written in Java and built upon MySQL Server [3]. It can be applied in Internet services such as Amazon or eBay.

The paper is constructed as follows. In the section 2, the basic features of SQLf_j are presented. The section 3 contains description of fuzzy projection and fuzzy group-by. The paper is concluded in the last section.

P.S. Szczepaniak et al. (Eds.): AWIC 2005, LNAI 3528, pp. 120–125, 2005.

2   Features of SQLf_j

Let us explain main features of SQLf_j using an illustrative example. Assume that there is a job agency that maintains data about applicants (see Table 1). Fuzzy queries to this database will help to find the best workers. The example and the data are taken from [7].

Table 1. Workers

FName	LName	Age	Job_Type	Expertise	Salary
Bob	McLedon	23	Academic	AI	2200
Rob	Mucker	27	Industry	Expert Systems	3800
Nancy	McCay	40	Management	Statistics	3500
John	Hunt	55	Management	Robotics	6500

The imprecision in queries is represented using two approaches: a similarity-based and a possibility-based. The similarity-based approach uses linguistic terms (e.g. domain values of attributes Job_Type or Expertise). The imprecision of these terms is characterized by a similarity matrix, which records the degree of similarity between pairs of linguistic terms in a domain (see Table 2). Similarity-based approach was first introduced by Buckles and Petry [2]. The second possibility-based approach, requires changing the data representation to a representation of fuzzy attribute values. For example, if we have an attribute Age in a database, then originally this attribute will have numeric values. Following natural language we can introduce terms like *Young, Middle-aged, Old* that are characterized by corresponding linguistic variables such as those defined in Fig. 1. These two elements, similarity matrixes and linguistic variables, have to be defined by the user and stored in the system.

The attributes with linguistic variables defined on their domains and attributes associated with similarity matrixes (e.g. 'Age' and 'Expertise') are called *f-* and *s-attributes*, respectively. Such attributes are denoted with prefixes '~' or '#'. The set of linguistic variables defined on *f*-attribute is denoted as $D(\sim Name)$, and similarly, the set of linguistic terms defined on *s*-attribute is denoted as $D(\#Name)$, where *Name* is an attribute's name. The original domain of an attribute is denoted by $D(Name)$.

The result of a fuzzy query is a *fuzzy relation*. It means that each tuple t in the fuzzy relation, say R, is associated with its membership degree, denoted

Table 2. Similarity matrix for a domain of attribute Expertise

	Robotics	Expert Systems	AI	Statistics
Robotics	1.0	0.6	0.6	0.2
Expert Systems	0.6	1.0	0.9	0.2
AI	0.6	0.9	1.0	0.2
Statistics	0.2	0.2	0.2	1.0

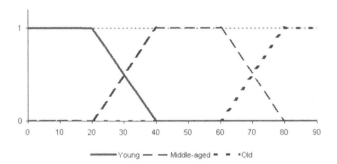

Fig. 1. Possibilistic distribution of linguistic variables on attribute `Age`

$\mu_R(t)$, that evaluates to what degree the tuple satisfies the query. Fuzzy relation is usually presented as a list of tuples ordered by decreasing membership degrees. Tuples with membership degree equal to 0 are not included to this list. The number of returned tuples may be limited by specifying a threshold for membership degree or a number of top t tuples with highest membership degree.

Let us present a typical query formulated in SQLf-j. Assume that the user is looking for *middle-aged* workers specialized in artificial intelligence. The query could be seen as follows:

```
SELECT THRESHOLD 0.2 LName, Age, Expertise FROM Workers
WHERE ~Age IS 'Middle-aged' AND #Expertise IS 'AI';
```

where '~' and '#' before attribute's name means that the condition concern f- and s-attribute, respectively. Such condition is referred to as *fuzzy condition*. The membership degree for each tuple t from the table `Workers` is computed as:

$$\mu_R(t) = \mu_{Middle-aged}(t_{[Age]}) \otimes \mu_{AI}(t_{[Expertise]}) =$$
$$= min(\mu_{Middle-aged}(t_{[Age]}), sim('\text{AI}', t_{[Expertise]})).$$

where $t_{[Name]}$ denotes the original value of t on corresponding attribute, $\mu_L(x)$ is a membership function, where $L \in D(\sim Name)$ and $x \in D(Name)$, sim is a function that returns the similarity degree between linguistic terms by taking it from the similarity matrix and $\otimes$ denotes t-norm (as default min operator is used) that is used for conjunction of fuzzy conditions.

In the example query, the threshold of membership degree is given by specifying it after keyword `THRESHOLD`. In result the user obtains applicants that are middle-aged and expertised in domains similar to '`AI`' with degree at least 0.2. Similarly, if the keyword `TOP` was used, then top t workers satisfying fuzzy conditions would be returned. Results are presented in Table 3 (left). Remark that `McLedon` is to young to be included in the results.

Table 3. Results of basic SQLf_j query (left) and fuzzy projection (right)

LName	Age	Expertise	degree
Hunt	55	Robotics	0.60
Mucker	27	Expert Systems	0.35
McCay	40	Statistics	0.20

LName	Age	~Age	degree
Hunt	55	Middle-aged	1.00
McCay	40	Middle-aged	1.00
McLedon	23	Young	0.85
McLedon	23	Middle-aged	0.15
Mucer	27	Young	0.65
Mucer	27	Middle-aged	0.35

3 Fuzzy Projection in SQLf_j

The projection of attributes is one of the main operation in relational databases. It returns all tuples, but only with attributes listed after keyword SELECT. The returned values are the same as those within original table. Taking into account fuzzy extensions of databases, it would make sense to obtain tuples with linguistic variables instead of original values and to retrieve an information about membership to *every* linguistic variable defined on the attribute's domain. In other words, we define an operation that proceed *fuzzyfication* for each tuple to every linguistic variable. It will be called *fuzzy projection*.

We distinguish two types of fuzzy projection. The first one concerns *f*-attributes. While the original domain of these attributes is *numeric* fuzzy projection exposes a tuple's membership degree to every linguistic variable defined on the attribute's domain. The second fuzzy projection is applied to *s*-attributes. Here the fuzzy projection exposes a tuple's similarity degree to every linguistic term defined on the attribute's domain. In other words, the fuzzy projection of both types is a transformation of a tuple with no-fuzzy values to several tuples, with the information of membership degree, that contain linguistic variables or terms instead of original values.

The attributes that are fuzzy projected are denoted using a prefix '~' (in the case of *f*-attributes), or a prefix '#' (in the case of *s*-attributes). Let us consider the following query, results of which are presented in Table 3 (right):

```
SELECT LName, Age, ~Age FROM Workers ORDER BY LName;
```

Consider the first tuple in the Table 1. The original values on attributes LName and Age are {McLedon,23}. In result of the fuzzy projection, this tuple is transformed to three fuzzy tuples containing linguistic variables defined on the domain of attribute Age. These new tuples are: {McLedon, 23, Young}, {McLedon, 23, Middle-aged}, {McLedon, 23, Old}. The membership degree is computed as $\mu_R(t) = \mu_L(t_{[Age]})$, where $L \in D(\sim Age)$. From the results one can easily read that McLedon belongs to young workers in degree 0.85, and to middle-aged workers in degree 0.15. Note that only tuples with membership function greater than 0 are presented. That is why the fuzzy tuple that defines McLedon's degree of membership to old workers is not shown.

Table 4. Results of multiple fuzzy projection (left) and fuzzy group-by (right)

LName	˜Age	#Expertise	degree
McLedon	Middle-aged	AI	0.15
McLedon	Middle-aged	Expert Systems	0.15
McLedon	Middle-aged	Robotics	0.15
McLedon	Middle-aged	Statistics	0.15
McLedon	Young	AI	0.85
McLedon	Young	Expert Systems	0.85
McLedon	Young	Robotics	0.60
McLedon	Young	Statistics	0.20

#Expertise	count(*)
AI	2
Expert Systems	2
Statistics	1
Robotics	1

Not only one attribute may be projected in this way. Consider the query below:

```
SELECT LName, ~Age, #Expertise FROM Workers
WHERE LName = 'McLedon' ORDER BY ~Age, #Expertise;
```

The original tuple is fuzzificated to all conjunctions of linguistic variables and terms defined on attributes Age and Expertise, respectively. The membership degree is computed then as $\mu_R(t) = \mu_L(t_{[Age]}) \otimes \mu_S(t_{[Expertise]})$, for each $L \in D(\sim Age)$ and $S \in D(\#Expertise)$. Results of the query are presented in Table 4 (left). Note that the tuples are sorted by linguistic variables and terms. The clause ORDER BY may involve the f- and s-attributes, but only in the case when the same attributes occur also in the fuzzy projection.

The fuzzy projection does not forbid fuzzy conditions. These two elements may occur together. The tuples satisfying the fuzzy conditions are then fuzzificated (or otherwise). The membership degree is computed as a t-norm (for example, using min operator) of membership degrees resulting from fuzzy projection and fuzzy conditions.

The fuzzy projection allows to define a simple *fuzzy group-by* operation. Consider the following query that returns all workers and for each of them her/his original and similar expertises with minimal degree 0.9:

```
SELECT THRESHOLD 0.9 LName, #Expertise FROM Workers;
```

Notice that the tuples being a result of the query could be grouped by the attribute '#Expertise'. The result of such grouping answers how many workers can be hired as experts in particular domain (e.g. AI) taking into account the fact of similarities between domains. The fuzzy group-by query is formulated as follows:

```
SELECT THRESHOLD 0.9 #Expertise, count(*) FROM Workers
GROUP BY #Expertise;
```

It is easy to check that with respect to threshold 0.9, two persons may work in the area of artificial intelligence or expert systems, and only one in robotics or in statistics. Results of this query contains exactly this information (see Table 4, right).

4   Conclusions

The fuzzy projection and fuzzy group-by are useful extension of flexible query-ing languages. These two features are implemented and work. The command-line application that proceeds SQLf_j queries is written in Java. It contains a parser module and a transformation module that translate SQLf_j queries into sophis-ticated SQL queries. In other words, the transformation algorithm allows to "simulate" the fuzzy queries in the relational database system. The application may be used as a middle-tier in Internet services such as *Amazon* or *eBay*. In this implementation MySQL Server is exploited in database system layer, but in general, any relational database system with JDBC support can be used. The presentation layer may be designed in such a way that it would support the user in many ways to construct fuzzy queries compatible with SQLf_j.

The prototype of Internet application for real estate office have been created. Next to classic queries like, e.g. "retrieve apartments which price $\leq$ 150000 Euros and size $\geq$ 100 m^2", the utilization of fuzzy queries is desirable. Then, the user may obtain not so restrictive results and the query can be formulated in more natural way, e.g. "retrieve big, low-priced apartments". Such possibility gives much bigger liberty to compose our preferences.

References

1. Bosc, P., Pivert, O.: SQLf: A Relational Database Language for Fuzzy Querying. IEEE Trans. on Fuzzy Systems **3** (1995) 1–17
2. Buckles, B. P., Petry, F. E.: A fuzzy representation of data for relational databases. Fuzzy Sets and Systems **5** (1982) 213–226
3. Dembczyński, K., Hapke, M., Przybył, D.: SQLf_j - a fuzzy querying language and application. Research Report RA-010/04, Poznań University of Technology (2004)
4. Kacprzyk, J., Zadrożny, S.: FQuery for Access: Fuzzy Querying for Windows-Based DBMS. In: Bosc, P., Kacprzyk, J. (eds.): Fuzziness in Database Management Systems, Physica-Verlag (1995)
5. Rasmussen, D. and Yager, R. R.: SummarySQL - A flexible fuzzy query language. Proceedings of the Second Workshop on Flexible Query-Answering Systems, Roskilde, Denmark (1996) 1–18
6. Yager, R. R.: A new approach to the summarization of data. Information Sciences **28** (1982) 69–86
7. Yen, Y., Langari, R.: Fuzzy Logic: Intelligence, Control and Information. Prentice Hall (1998)
8. Zadeh L.A.: Fuzzy Sets. Inform. and Control **8** (1965) 338–353.

Ontology Aided Query Expansion
for Retrieving Relevant Texts

Lipika Dey[1], Shailendra Singh[2], Romi Rai[1], and Saurabh Gupta[1]

[1] Department of Mathematics, IIT Delhi, Delhi - 110 016, India
`lipika@maths.iitd.ac.in`
[2] Samsung India Software Center, SIEL, Noida, India
`shailendra.s@samsung.com`

Abstract. Knowledge based approaches to text information retrieval are aimed at increasing the precision of retrieval. In this paper we show that query enhancement through the use of domain ontological structures can enhance the quality of retrieval to a large extent. We have presented a formal framework for extending user queries with domain ontological structures. The query-expansion mechanism has been implemented as a client-side query processor which can use any efficient search engine like Google or Alta Vista at the back end. The approach offers substantial performance gains. We have established the effectiveness of the approach experimentally through the use of single and multiple ontologies.

1 Introduction

The idea of semantic web [1] encourages the use of knowledge-rich structures to disambiguate world knowledge on-line. Presently, ontologies are providing the backbone for sharing domain knowledge among distributed users and applications and represent inter-relationship among domain concepts in a structured way and hence can be used for enhancing user queries to include more related concepts.

In this paper we have presented a formal mechanism to exploit ontological structures for extracting relevant information from unstructured web documents.The proposed system is based on a query expansion mechanism where ontological knowledge from one or more ontologies is used to expand original user queries with semantically related concepts. We have also presented a method to compute the relevance of the documents with respect to the original query. The proposed intelligent query-processing system accepts user queries through a graphical user interface, performs query expansion and extension using knowledge from one or more relevant ontology. The relevance of ontology is judged by semantic equivalence of query concepts and ontological concepts through the use of WordNet [3]. The transformed query is then passed on to google search engine and retrieved documents are ranked according to a new relevance computation function. It is observed that the retrieval precision is much more for the transformed query than the original query.

P.S. Szczepaniak et al. (Eds.): AWIC 2005, LNAI 3528, pp. 126–132, 2005.

The rest of the paper is organized as follows. In section 2 we have reviewed some related work in knowledge-based query processing. In sections 3 and 4 we have proposed a formal specification for ontology-based query enhancement and document grading. Section 5 presents results and performance analysis of our system.

2   Related Work

[9] proposed a general framework for retrieving relevant documents by using domain-specific semantic net of concepts and WordNet. [4] propose the use of part-of-speech patterns to reduce query ambiguity by considering the roles these words can assume and the role the user might be interested in. [6] proposed the integration of web-based and corpus-based techniques for question answering. [5] proposed annotation of the semantic web using natural language. [7] proposed ontology based information retrieval in which the meaning of a concept depends not only on its name but also on its properties and on its semantic relations with other concepts in an ontology. Since it is only natural that each ontology specifically describes a partial view of the world, integration of multiple knowledge is a key area of research. [8] proposes a system called OBSERVER which uses multiple pre-existing real-world domain ontologies and uses mechanisms to incrementally enrich answers by substituting original query terms with new terms mined through inter-ontological relationships like synonyms, hypernyms and hyponyms and it also estimates loss of information. Castano *et al.* proposed H-MATCH [2] an algorithm for dynamically matching ontologies in peer-based systems. [7] describes a linguistic based scheme for matching local ontologies and uses WordNet when a concept has multiple senses associated with it. In the next few sections, we describe our proposed system which aims at successfully integrating the use of ontologies for on-line information access.

3   Ontology Based Query Enhancement

To enhance a query with semantically related concepts, it is necessary to establish the semantic mappings by considering the overlap or equivalence of concepts present in the query and the ontological structures. Let the query-processing schema be represented by $\mathbf{Q}$.

Definition 3.1. The query processing schema $\mathbf{Q}$ is defined by a system ($\mathbf{L}$, $\mathbf{O}$, $\mathbf{M}$) where

$\mathbf{L}$ − is the global lexicon defining the vocabulary. This consists of all terms that can be present in the query. For our work, we have used Word Net as the general purpose Thesaurus. Any word recognized by Word Net is acceptable in query.

O - defines a set of ontologies whose locations are known to the system. Word Net is one of the ontologies which is set as a default. Besides, we have used other standard ontological structures like Wine ontology and Plant ontology, described in OWL, which can be linked to the system. Each ontology O_i in this set defines a set of concepts C_i and a set of relations R_i. C_i may consist of terms present in **L**, but may also contain new terms. R_i is a set of relations defined in the ontology O_i. These relations include all defined relations for the OWL language like class-subclass, class-property, union-of-property-values etc. **M** defines a set of mapping between entities (concepts) in query and ontological entities. We define a set of atomic mappings $M^a = \{\subseteq, \supseteq, \emptyset, \equiv, =, \approx\}$. These mappings correspond to the sub-class, super-class, not-related, synonymous, equal to and overlapping relations respectively.

There are two steps in our query-extension mechanism. The first step consists of *concept approximation* and the second step is that of *concept extension*. *Concept approximation* refers to the process of identifying similar concepts in the query and an underlying ontology. *Concept extension* refers to the process of enhancing the query with semantically close concepts to enlarge the target concept space. To accommodate different terminological relationships with varying degrees of affinity between concepts we define ρ *-approximation* to a target concept, where ρ is a specified terminological relationship.

Definition 3.2. The ρ - approximation to a target concept c^* within an identified ontology O is defined as the set of all concepts which are related by the relation ρ to c^*, where $\rho \in M$.

Thus ρ - approximation to c^* in $O = \{c \mid c \in O, \rho \in M \text{ and } c \, \rho \, c^* \text{ holds}\}$. The most commonly used ρ - approximations are those of equality and synonymy, in that order. Thus given a query and a specified domain, for each target concept in query, our system first identifies the concepts in the underlying ontologies. If these are found the corresponding nodes in the ontology structures act as starting points for the query-extension mechanism. If the target concepts are not found in the ontology, then concepts which are synonymous to the target concepts, are identified using the WordNet.

After identifying related concepts in the query and ontological structures, the next step is to extend the query with terminologically related concepts extracted from the ontology. Again, depending on the relationships between different concepts, different kinds of concept extensions can be obtained.

Definition 3.3. A β-extension of a concept c^* in ontology O_i is defined as the set of concepts $c \in O_i$, which are β-related to c^*, where $\beta \in R_i$.

According to the definition of relations defined over R as specified in the earlier section, β may be a simple or a composite relation. Since concept affinity cannot be uniform for different kinds of terminological relationships, it is required to define the degree of affinity for the different semantic extensions. In our application we have assumed the degree of affinity between two concepts to be inversely proportional to the distance between them. Finally, we associate the concept of a threshold for a concept to be in the target query. For a given user query, the final expanded query is produced as per the following definition.

Definition 3.4. For a given user query **q**, the final expanded query **q**/ is generated by including all ontological concepts **c**/ which are β-extensions of original query concepts **c** or their ρ-approximations, and are within semantic distance δ from them.

The query that is fed to the search engine is the final expanded query **q**/. Algorithm Enhance_query is used to build the enhanced query. The activation values of the concepts are used during document grading.

Algorithm Enhance_Query (Q, O)
Input: Query Q, Ontology tree O
Output: Activation levels of various concepts in enhanced query.
Let S $=\{s_1, s_2, \ldots, s_m\}$ be the set of synonyms of each concept q_i present in query **Q**, along with concepts present in **Q**.
Let d[i] be the minimum distance of each concept C_i from a fully activated node (having activation value 1.0) in ontology **O**.
    For each concept $C_i \in$ O
    C_j = parent(C_i) /* C_j is parent of C_i*/
    if $C_i \in$ S then d[i] =1.0, act_value[i]=1.0
    else if(R_{ij}=intersect_with || R_{ij}=disjoint_with || R_{ij}=equivalent_class)
    /*considering different relations in ontology */
    then act_value[i]=act_value[j];/* same activation value as parent */
    else if (R_{ij}=subClassOf) then
    if it has fully activated ancestor node
    act_value[i]=1.0/d[i]
    else act_value[i]=0.0
    elseif (R_{ij}==unionOf) then
    act_value[i]=act_value[i]/(total number of children of C_j with unionOf property)
    else act_value[i]=0.0; /*we don't bother with other properties like complementOf */
    Append Ci and act_value[i] to **A**
    End For
Append all synonyms which are not already present with activation value 1.0 to **A**.
Sort **A** alphabetically.
Return **A**.
End Algorithm

4   Grading the Retrieved Documents

Though the documents retrieved with the enhanced query are far more relevant, the arrangement of the documents is not perfect. Our system re-computes the relevance of a document as a weighted function of the distance between document concepts and concepts in the β-extension of the original query concepts. Thus similarity computation uses all concepts which are contextually related to the query concepts. Let $| E |$ denote the total number of concepts in the expanded query and E_i denote those concepts which are at distance i from the given query. Let D denote the set of all concepts(words) present in a document. $| E_i \cap D |$ denotes an intersection of concepts which are common between expanded query and the document. The final relevance of a document with respect to the original query is given by the following weighted sum.

$$\sum_{i=1}^{|E|} \frac{|E_i \cap D|}{|E|} * \frac{1}{i}\mu \qquad (1)$$

5   Experimental Results

In this section, we will present some results obtained with queries in the domains of wine ontology and plant ontology. We collected the top most two urls (www.hhmi.org/research/investigators/morrison.html,   www.sirinet.net/~jgjohnso/revchap31.html) retrieved by google with the original query "stem cell functions",and another two urls (www.ag.arizona.edu/pubs/garden/mg/botany/plantparts.html, www.plantphys.info/plants_human/stems.html) retrieved by "stem cell functions plant", without using any ontology, the document retrieved with our ontology-based expanded query and a document that was retrieved with the enhanced query but ranked 4th by Google and 1st by our mechanism. The last two are better than the earlier two, and could be obtained because of the semantically related scientific terms that could be appended to the original query using the ontology.

Figure 1 presents consolidated results on precision of retrieval obtained by evaluating the relevance of top 10 documents for 20 queries in the domain of "Wine" ontology (left) and 20 queries for plant ontology (right), in the form of area covered under each curve. The lightly shaded area corresponds to the precision of documents retrieved with enhanced query and the darker area is for the documents retrieved with original query without enhancement.

The average precision for wine domain increased from 45.5% for the original query to 67.5% for the enhanced query and from precision increase was 27.5% to 69% for plant domain. The accuracy of the relevance computation mechanism was found to be 87.5%.

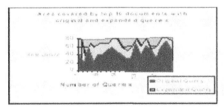 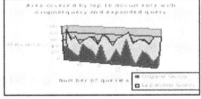

Fig. 1. Precision of retrieval with original and enhanced queries in (left) Wine (right) Plant domains

We have also used the query expansion technique to merge concepts from more than one ontology. This is done by merging the extended concept spaces identified from different ontologies along with all terminologically related concepts of the original query concepts i.e. merging the β-extension of query concepts over multiple ontologies. For example, given a query "Part of Alfalfa affected by Rust", the query is processed and enhanced using knowledge from two ontologies . "Rust is a kind of plant disease" is gathered from plant-disease ontology which stores information about parts of plants affected by various diseases. That Alfalfa is a kind of legume is gathered from plant taxonomy ontology.

 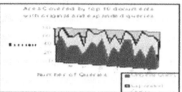

Fig. 2. Retrieval with merger of multiple ontologies (left) sample document (right) precision increase from 38 to 66.5%

Average precision was observed to increase from 38% to 66.5% for such queries and is shown in Figure 2 along with a snapshot of the relevant page retrieved by our system.

6   Conclusions

In this paper,we have proposed the design and implementation of an ontology-based text retrieval system. Ontology helps in the specification of context of a user query in a formal way. We have shown how query expansion within a controlled context approximation can lead to the retrieval of better documents even through the popular search engines. The retrieved documents are re-ranked by our system to compute the relevance of the documents with the original query concepts.

References

1. Berners-Lee, T., Hendler, J., and Lassila.,O., The Semantic Web. *Scientific American*, 284, (5): 34-43, 2001.
2. Castano,S. , Ferrara,A. and Montanelli.,S., H-MATCH: an Algorithm for Dynamically Matching Ontologies in Peer-based Systems. *http://www.cs.uic.edu/ ~ifc/SWDB/papers/Castano_etal.pdf,* 2003.
3. Fellbaum.,C., *WordNet: An Electronic Lexical Database.* Ed. Cristiane Fellbaum, The MIT Press, Cambridge, London, England, 1998.
4. Gonzalo,J., Verdejo,F., Chugur,I., and Cigarr'an,J., Indexing with WordNet synsets can improve text retrieval. In *Proceedings of the COLING/ACL '98 Workshop on Usage of WordNet for NLP*, 1998.
5. Katz,B. and Lin.,J., Annotating the Semantic Web Using Natural Language. In *Proceedings of 2nd Workshop on NLP and XML, COLING 2002*, Taipei, Taiwan, 2002.
6. Katz,B. , Lin,J., Loreto,D. and Hldebrandt.,W., Integrating Web-based and Corpus-based Techniques for Question Answering. In *Proceedings of Twelfth Text Retrieval Conference (TREC 2003)*, November 2003.
7. Magnini,B. , Serafini,L. and Speranza.,M. Linguistic Based Matching of Local Ontologies. *American Association for Artificial Intelligence*, 2002.

8. Mena,E., Kashyap,V., Illarramendi,A., and Sheth. ,A. Estimating Information Loss for Multi-Ontology based Query Processing. In *Proceedings of the Second and Interdisciplinary Workshop on Intelligent Information Integration* in conjunction with *European Conference on Artificial Intelligence*, Brighton, UK, August 1998.
9. Vorhees, E. Using WordNet to disambiguate Word Senses for Text retrieval. In *ACMSIGIR*, Pittsbourgh, PA, 1993.

WCVF: The Struggling Web Contents Visualization[*]

Santiago Eibe and Oscar Marbán

Facultad de Informática, UPM,
Campus de Montegancedo 28660, Boadilla del Monte, Spain
{seibe, omarban}@fi.upm.es

Abstract. Nowadays, humans and machines do not use the same format of knowledge representation. This gap is a serious problem in the human-machine interaction. More specifically, comprehension of text and images plays a key role in the process underlying Web navigation. This fact aim us to explode the aplication of intelligent methods that minimize the gap between the information that is showed to users and what they are able to understand and use, in a per-site and per-user basis.

1 Introduction

Providing information with explicit and formal descriptions of meaning about data structures, proceses, devices, and networks is not only needed for machine-use but also for human-consumption. However, current fundamental Semantic Web technology is computation-centered and uses mechanisms base on description logic, theorem proving, situation calculation, planning and so on. Since these technologies do not pay attention to humans who actually create and use Web contents, the high-quality and the widespread of this technology may not be guaranteed. In order to bring out real benefit for humans of the Semantic Web, we need to develop human-centered technologies that will bridge the gap between the human use and the computation-centered mechanisms. In this paper we are exploding methods to minimize this gap. We display knowledge used by machines in a specifically and personalized way to different users.

Information Visualization [6] is a new and rapidly growing research area which aims to provide visual depictions of very large information spaces. It covers interdisciplinary areas such as Information Retrieval [2, 4] or Human Computer Interaction [9]. One of the most active and promising application area for visualization is related to the visualization of semantics because the semantic contents of a web site can be used more advantageously for the visualisation of its information, since we already have the knowledge about the meaning and the existing relations between the concepts used in it. Therefore, the key is not to look for contents directly but to look for descriptions of contents.

---

[*] The work presented in this paper has been partially supported by UPM project ERDM - ref 14589.

P.S. Szczepaniak et al. (Eds.): AWIC 2005, LNAI 3528, pp. 133–139, 2005.

Traditionally, conceptual modeling provides the basis to formally identify the concepts that represents information needs of users. Database systems have been applying the concept of subschemas to provide multiple views of the same underlying information. However, the development of Web-based information systems differs from traditional software in several directions. Firstly, Web engineering has to take into account navigational and cognitive aspects that traditional software does not support. Thus, application of theories and models from basic cognitive research [11, 12] must play a key role in web development [12]. Secondly, Web development process requires visual models and a more standarized notation for this visualization.

Therefore, visualizing the Worl Wide Web requires new front-end tools to aid navigation and search interfaces that follows the structure of information. [1] presents tools to navigate through a set of documents that are clustered for different user needs and where each cluster is labelled with related words. The Atlas of Cyberspace [7] exposes an atlas showing the best maps and graphic representations of the Internet, WWW and Cyberspaces. In order to improve the organization of search results [8] proposes present *hierarchical faceted metadata* in an appealing and understandable way to general users. There have been several proposals where navigation have a peer role as, for instance, UWE [10]. More recently and joined to the advent of the Semantic Web some approaches as [5] and MoSeNa [3], are looking for semantic navigation structures modeling.

Research on personalization has led to development of systems that adapt themselves to the characteristics of their users. Case-Based Reasoning (CBR) [13] is an Artificial Intelligence method based on the idea of reusing past experience in a domain-specific library of problem-solution descriptions, known as cases. Usually, cases are represented as user stereotypes [14].

2   Web Contents Visualization Framework Objectives

Our proposal to improve Web usability is to provide a procedure to deploy web interfaces in an unified way, that caters both humans and machines, combining data and treatment exhibition in a per-site and per-user basis. The next list shows the main goals of the proposed architecture:

- Dynamic organization of web site structure based on metadata about users (per-user) and contents (per-site)
- Provide dynamically specialized interfaces combining both textual and non textual metaphors
- Support interactive browsing of contents by appropriate visualization of metadata about categories and relations related to organization of the site contents
- Possibility for users to interactively define new descriptions and annotations about contents
- Filter descriptions have to be provided by the system.. Users could choose a partial view and needs to know the available filters to select the most semantically significant contents

In order to be able to exchange the semantics of information distributed and shared among many users, the first requirement is to agree on how to explicitly model it. Therefore, we are going to define a two-layer framework named Web Contents Visualization Framework (WCVF) where symbols embedded in web contents are automatically deployed. The proposed architecture consists of two layers: Data Visualization Conceptual Model, DVCM, (only for human use) and Visualization Formal Model, VFM, (a machine directed layer).

2.1   DVCM: Modeling to Knowledge Visualization

Starting at the top level of the WVF architecture we propose an independent domain model to define visualization resources. Not to waste time searching for the right icon to represent specific information or activities. Given the frequency with which we encounter these interface design elements, we suppose that exist a common visual vocabulary that could aid in user comprehension. In fact, there are a few iconic symbols that have already achieved web convention status. This conceptual model defines these contents including the context where they are used. The basic assumption of the presented architecture is that the visualization of these semantics together with a personalized presentation is key to the success of users doing tasks at the site. Thus, each object on the navigator's screen that is a meaningful unit or a target for action must be included into the DVCM. Therefore, main features of DVCM are given following:

– DVCM describe objects as seen for site users but ignoring that features, such as colors or sizes
– structure and behaviour of the system are integrated
– simplicity: The symbol set of DVCM is reduced for readability
– human-oriented

   Therefore, the main components of a DVCM diagram are:

– Navigational Schemas (NS): NSs reflect what task users do at a site, according to an already known navigational pattern extracted by web mining or obtained by domain experts recomendation
– Visualization Objects (VO): The basic elements of any DVCM diagram. VOs are represented as a rectangle with a name (see fig 2) and, optionally, a URI
– Visualization Attributes (VA): Attributes represent any possible feature of VOs. VA are usually represented with a circle inside the rectangle (see figure 1)
– Visualization Events (VE): Events can be triggered by VO, state changes or external actions. VE are represented by a triangle
– Visualization Rules (VR): Rules in a DVCM diagram define the organization (structure) and the interactions (behavior) among the elements in the model
– Visualization Schemas (VS): VS are subsets of DVCM diagrams. Users scan pages constructing schematic representations to leverage the complexity of them. Thus, VS normally reflects that top-level schematic collections of VOs such as navigation bars, menus and window controls. Of course, several different VS can share VO, VA, VR, VE or all of them

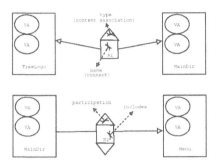

Fig. 1. Structural Rules

Visualization Objects (VO). At the Visualization Conceptual layer the information contained in a web site is like a geographic environment with a variety of representational objects and views: perspective, illustrative or diagrammatic, static or dynamic, etc. We are interested in how abstractions and representational conventions can be used to enhance sites usability. In this scenario VO would be classified in atomic VOs and compound VOs, content dependent (contextual) and independent, asociative, structural, specific or general and so on. Therefore, any VO will have a VA to indicate what kind VO is.

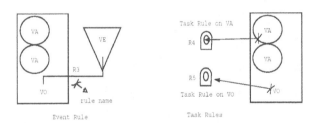

Fig. 2. Task and Event Rules

Visualization Rules (VR). VR can be of two main kinds:

– VO-VA Rules. These rules define the set of attributes that characterize a Visualization Object. They are represented both explicitly as a thin line or implicitly locating an inner circle into the VO
– VO-VO Rules. We distinguish between structural and procedimental:
   • structural VO-VO: rules that reflect structural relations among VO such as participation, specialization, metaphors, content association or metonimies. These rules are represented (see figure 1) as directed arcs from the source VO to the target VO and ended with a single edge
   • procedural VO-VO are intended to show behaviour representation and can be transformation rules (exploding/imploding VO, VO's state or

features change, etc.), enabling rules and connection rules. Both of them can be applied to tasks or events as in figure 2:

Visualization Schemas (VS). VS are important because users scan visually related regions rather than read site contents. There is not relation with web page concept so VS can exist at one page or one VS can extend to several pages.

2.2   VFM: Deconceptualization of Visualization Resources

The main goal of this layer is to build a formal model to represent and process the visualization resources defined in the DVCM. This step transforms the existing deconceptualization of objects to their perceptual sense. Therefore, VFM layer captures the perceptual structure of web site contents to simulate how visual attention is schedule among information stimuli. We choosed a stereotype-based user model because stereotype mimics intuitive human reasoning. In fact, one important advantage is that before knowing a new user in a detailed way, the system can make early assumptions about him.

User stereotypes require two types of information: captured properties and events or behavior that implies a particular stereotype. Both of them are elements of DVCM that we will translate in this layer. Therefore, VFM Stereotypes correspond to VS at DVCM and describe the 'information interests' of user which will be assigned to the prototypical stereotype.

VFM stereotypes are represented in the form of a frame containing slots and links between them:

– Slots correspond to VOs, VEs and hosts description values in facets. Facets represent VAs (simple or compound) defined at the DVCM level. Moreover, all facets have a weight which value indicates the relative degree of interest for the facet into the slot. The weight of the whole slot results of the sum of the weights of the facets
– Links represent rules, mostly VO-VO structural, defined at the DVCM level

VFM incorporate automatic learning using machine learning methods to help stereotypes to handle user.

Users are represented in the form of frames divided into header and body. Header contains some user's personal data and a list of matching stereotypes. The body is a collection of slots and links that allows for the creation and maintenance of facet's semantic networks.

User modelling process begins when an user description is available. This description is obtained by means of a form that is presented to the user when accesses the system for the first time. So, this description will be formed by a pattern of weights that results from each slot of the preliminary sterotype selected for the user from a case library and according to a specific metric. The number of weights in the pattern is the same as the number of slots in the stereotype. The case library contains the old stereotypes obtained primarily from Navigational Schemas (NS) and confirmed mining annotated web logs.

Basically, a classification of the user is performed in this preliminary phase. The classification algorithm assigns to the user a stereotype that most resembles their visualization preferences.

After the initial stereotype is assigned to the user begins the refine phase. One basic assumption of the proposal architecture is that users navigation is carried out selecting contents that they perceive as the most similar to the semantic representation of their current goal. We say that contents related in a some personal way belongs to the same context. Therefore, users can specify if the corresponding object supports the browsing process and the support degree.

3   Conclusions

In this paper we present WCVF, a visualization-centric architecture to improve web usability. Our framework unifies human and machine representations of knowledge modeling and the static and dinamyc aspects of web contents visualization. Moreover, this paper presents the principles of context-aware mechanisms to enable the application of intelligent methods to assist personalized navigation for different human users.

Future work will proceed in both theoretical and practical ways. The theory will focus on producing an initial specification that covers other important knowledge and system representation aspects. The practical work will confirm the advantages of our platform and guide future development.

References

1. P. Au, M. Carey, S. Sewraz, Y. Guo, and S. Rüger. New paradigms in information visualization. In *Research and Development in Information Retrieval*, 2000.
2. R. Baeza-Yates and B. Ribeiro. *Modern Information Retrieval*. ACM Press, 1999.
3. J. Becker, C. Brelage, K. Klose, and M. Thygs. Conceptual modeling of semantic navigation structures: the MoSeNa-approach. In *Proc of the 5th ACM Web information and data management*, pp 118–125. ACM Press, 2003.
4. P. Brusilovsky and C. Tasso. Preface to special issue on user modeling for web information retrieval. *User Model. User-Adapt. Interact.*, 14(2-3):147–157, 2004.
5. C. Cachero and N. Koch. Conceptual Navigation Analysis: a Device and Platform Independent Navigation Specification. In *In 2nd Int.Workshop (IWWOST02)*, 2002.
6. S. K. Card, J. D. Mackinlay, and B. Shneiderman. *Readings in Information Visualization: Using Vision To Think*. Morgan Kaufmann, 1999.
7. M. Dodge and R. Kitchin. *The Atlas of Cyberspace*. Addison-Wesley, 2002.
8. J. English, M. Hearst, R. Sinha, K. Swearingen, and P. Yee. Hierarchical faceted metadata in site search interfaces. In *Proc. Of ACM CHI 02*, 2002.
9. A. D. et al. *Human-Computer Interaction, 2nd Edition*. Prentice Hall, 1998.
10. R. Hennicker and N. Koch. Modeling the user interface of Web Applications with UML. In UML 2001, Kllen Druck+Verlag, 158-172, October 2001.
11. J. A. Jacko and A. Sears. *The human-computer interaction handbook: fundamentals, evolving technologies and emerging applications*. L. Erlbaum Ass, Inc., 2003.

12. E. Julie Ratner. *Human Factors and Web Development, Second Edition.* Lawrence Erlbaum Assoc, 2002.

13. D. B. Leake, editor. *Case-Based Reasoning: Experiences, Lessons, and Future Directions.* AAAI Press, Menlo Park, CA, 1996.

14. E. Rich. User modeling via stereotypes. In M. T. Maybury and W. Wahlster, editors, *Intelligent User Interface (Readings in).* Morgan Kaufman Publishers, Inc., San Francisco, California, 1998.

Ontology Based Web Crawling – A Novel Approach

S. Ganesh

Assistant System Engineer,
TCS Nortel- Product Test Tata Consultancy Services Ltd,
Mumbai 400 066, India
ganesh1.s@tcs.com

Abstract. The requirement of a web Crawler that downloads most relevant pages is still a major challenge in the field of Information Retrieval Systems. The use of link analysis algorithms as page rank and other Importance-metrics like back link count have shed a new approach in prioritizing the URL queue for downloading higher relevant pages. In this paper, the combination of these metrics along with a new metric called association-metric, which brings the use of Ontology for Crawling has been proposed and implemented. The use of domain dependent Ontology brings into effect the both semantic and link nature of the URL and its page .The association-metric estimates the semantic content of the URL based on the domain dependent ontology, which in turn strengthens the metric that is used for prioritizing the URL queue. In addition, after downloading the page, the association metric plays important role in estimating the relevancy of the links in that page. This new metric solves the major problem of finding the relevancy of the pages before the process of crawling, to an optimal level. The crawler developed based on the Association metric has shown encouraging results.

Keywords: Web Crawler, Ordering-metric, Importance-metrics, Association-metric, and Ontology.

1   Introduction

The worldwide web, having over millions of pages, continues to grow rapidly at a million pages per day and it also changes rapidly. This rapid growth of the worldwide web poses unprecedented scaling challenges for general-purpose crawlers and search engines. The increase in the number of accessible web pages by Internet users imposes the need for a technique to get only the relevant information. Crawler, which is a main component of a search engine, is a program that retrieves Web pages or a Web Cache [3]. Roughly, a crawler starts off with the URL for an initial page P_0. It retrieves P_0, extracts any URLs in it, and adds them to a queue of URLs to be scanned. Then the crawler gets URLs from the queue (in some order), and repeats the process. Every page that is scanned is given to a client that saves the pages, creates an index for the pages,

P.S. Szczepaniak et al. (Eds.): AWIC 2005, LNAI 3528, pp. 140–149, 2005.

or summarizes or analyzes the content of the pages. The design of a good crawler presents many challenges [4]. The most prominent challenge faced by the current web crawlers is to select important pages for downloading. The crawler cannot download all pages from the web. It is important for the crawler to select the pages and to visit "important" pages first by prioritizing the URLs in the queue properly. Other challenges are the proper refreshing strategy, minimizing the load on the websites crawled and parallelization of the crawling process. This paper deals with the challenge of prioritizing the URL queue for crawling more relevant pages based on the domain dependent ontology. This paper explores the possibility of merging the present prioritizing algorithms with the semantic nature of the URL, which has been obtained from the ontology through the association-metric. The following section 2 discusses the related work done so far on this challenge. Section 3 gives detailed description on the working of a web crawler and, various prioritizing algorithms. Section 4 deals with our work on this challenge and on the new prioritizing algorithm that is based on the ontology. System overview of developed crawler is described in section 5. Section 6 deals with the discussion of proposed Ordering metric.

2   Related Work

There has been considerable work done on prioritizing of the URL queue for efficient crawling. The performance of the existing prioritizing algorithms for crawling does not suit the requirements of the various kinds and levels of the users. The use of link analysis algorithms has solved the problem partially. The best-known example of such link analysis is the Page rank Algorithm successfully employed by the Google Search Engine [5]. The HITS algorithm proposed by Kleinberg [1] relies on query-time processing to deduce the hubs and authorities that exist in a sub graph of the web consisting of both the results to a query and the local neighborhood of these results. But page rank suffers from slow computation due to its recursive nature of its algorithm. The main draw back of Kleinberg's HITS algorithm is its query-time processing for crawling pages [1].

The recent work by *Junghoo Cho et al.*, claims that the evaluation of the importance of the page P as I(P) using some metrics solves to certain extent. These metrics are discussed in section 3 [3]. But these metrics' efficiency is affected by many factors like page rank, is less effective at start of the crawl process. Back link metric is proved to be less effective for Small domains. Similarity metric done by them evaluates only the textual similarity between the crawled pages with the driving query based on only few key words. The other approach for crawling higher relevant pages was by the use of neural networks [1]. Even this approach has not been established as the efficient crawling technique till now.

All these approaches solve the problem only partially .The combination of important metrics has not been explored explicitly [3].

3   Fundamentals

This section describes the basics of a web crawler and various importance metrics.

3.1   Web Crawler

WebCrawler receives a list of URLs to be downloaded and simply returns the full content of the HTML page or any errors, while trying to get the pages. The crawlers will process one URL from the queue at a time. The queue is prioritized based on the importance metrics discussed in the next section. The queue will be reordered according to the importance metric used after the downloading of each web page. All the pages may not be of equal interest to the client. So the pages should be associated with the importance of the page based on the metrics given below.

3.2   Importance Metrics

Given a Web page P, the importance of that page, $I(P)$, can be evaluated in one of the following ways:

1. ***Similarity to a Driving Query Q***. Based on a query Q which drives the crawling process *IS(P)* is defined to be the textual similarity between P and Q.
2. ***Backlink Count***. The value of *IB(P)* is the number of links to P that appear over the entire Web. Intuitively, a page P that is linked to by many pages is more important than one that is seldom referenced. A crawler may estimate the number of links to P that have been seen so far which is IB'(P) .
3. ***PageRank.*** The PageRank back link metric, *IR(P)*, recursively defines the importance of a page to be the weighted sum of the back links to it. PageRank is described in much greater detail in [3, 5].
   (a) ***Forward Link Count***. A metric *IF (P)* counts the number of links that emanate from P. Under this metric, a page with many outgoing links is very valuable, since it may be a Web directory. This metric can be computed directly from P.
   (b) ***Location Metric***. The *IL (P)* importance of page P is a function of its location, not of its contents. If URL u leads to P, then *IL (P)* is a function of u. URLs ending with ". com" or URL containing the string "home" may be deemed more useful.

4   Our Work

We have brought a new method of ordering the URL queue by combining both the link structure of the web and its semantic nature. Our work towards this challenge can be divided into following phases:

4.1   Combination Importance Metric:

The Importance metrics described in the previous section were combined to get a better composite metric. The simple combination of any two metrics obeys the results as published in [2]. The importance metric are evaluated for the Crawled pages, with this score the importance metric score for the URL u, O(u) is evaluated. The **combination Importance metric** is denoted by **CI(p)** where p is the page to be crawled.

This can be defined as follows:

$$CI(p) = a1\ IR(p) + a2\ IB(p) + a3\ IL(p) + a4\ IF(p)$$ Where a1, a2, a3, a4 are real constants that can be set properly to get an efficient CI (p). **CI' (p)** is defined as the metric evaluated for the downloaded or crawled page p. CI' $(p_1, p_2. \ldots .p_n)$ is evaluated for all the crawled pages $p_1, p_2. \ldots .p_n$. This Composite Importance metric is used with association metric for URL ordering.

4.2   Association metric

The use of the semantic nature of the web particularly the URL throws a new light in the URL ordering scheme. The Association metric is more like the similarity metric but it takes the semantic nature of the URL by the use of ontology.

4.2.1   Why Ontology? Ontology is one of the increasingly popular ways to structure information. Ontologies are also called graphs of concepts. Evaluation of association metric with the aid of the ontology that may be generic or domain dependent will surely give more relevant Results. The task can be achieved through the maintenance of a reference Ontology based on subject hierarchies may be collected from directories like yahoo and Open Directory Project. The Reference Ontology thus created will have the following associations like "is a", "part of", "has" relationships. The proposed metric evaluates the metric for the URL and the web pages crawled is discussed in section 6. The semantic metric for the URL u is evaluated based on its relevancy with the reference ontology. Once the page p of the URL u is downloaded the semantic metric for this page p is also calculated and maintained, as it will be a parent page for many links to be crawled. This calculation of the metric for the parent page helps in evaluating the relevancy of the link to be crawled or not even before the association metric for the link is calculated. AS (p) is same for all links from that page p but it differs for the links not extracted from this page. Hence we calculate two association metrics:

- **Association metric** for the URLs u_1 to u_n to be scanned
- **Association metric** for the downloaded parent page p_0.

The Association metric for URL u is denoted by **AS(u)** and the Association metric for page p crawled is denoted by **AS(p)**.

4.3   Ordering Metric O(u)

The **Ordering Metric O(u)** used for reordering the URL queue in our crawler is a composite metric defined as follows:

$$O(u) = b_1\ CI'(p) + b_2\ AS(u) + b_3\ [AS(p_1) + AS(p_2) + AS(p_3) + .. + AS(p_n)]$$, p_i is the ith Parent page of URL u to be crawled. Where b_1, b_2, b_3 are real constants to be evaluated from the results of our crawl. By varying these constants different results may be obtained. This O(u) metric is bound to give higher efficiency than all the priority algorithms as it combines both semantic and page-links nature of the web.

4.4   Pseudo code of Our Prioritizing Algorithm:

```
/*
    enqueue (url_queue, starting_url);
    While (not empty (url_queue))
    {url = dequeue(url_queue);
    page = crawl_page(url);
    enqueue (crawled_pages, (url, page));
    url_list = extract_urls (page);
```
For each page p in crawled_pages
If [page p has semantic associations with the keyword w in body or in title]
AS(p)= weighted association value
End loop
For each u in url_list
enqueue (links, (url, u));
If [u not in url_queue] and [(u,-) not in crawled_pages]
enqueue (url_queue, u);
If [url u has semantic associations with the keyword w]
AS(u)=weighted association value
CI(u)= pagerank[u]
O[u]= b₁ CI(u) + b₂ AS(u) + b₃ [AS(p₁) +AS(p₂) +.....+AS(pₙ)]
where p₁,p₂ ... pₙ are the parent pages to this url u
reorder_queue(url_queue); //based on O[u] }*/

5   System Overview

- **Importance Metric Evaluator:** Importance Metric Evaluator module is the important alteration that has been brought to the current crawling system. This module evaluates the importance of the pages to be crawled according to proposed Importance metric. In this module, the prioritizing algorithm based on the proposed Importance metric – **Association Metric** is implemented.

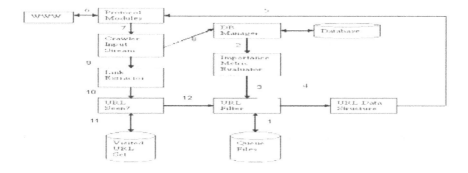

Fig. 5.1

- **URL Filter:** URL filter module is another new module not present in many crawling systems. Here the importance of the page for the current URL is calculated i.e. the ordering metric O(u) is calculated for the URL u based on the Importance metric value provided for u from the Importance metric evaluator

6   Implementation of the Ontology

In This Section the Implementation of our Ontology based Crawler is presented The Ontology used is similar to the hierarchical directory structure of google directory.
    The Ontology structure is as follows:

Fig. 6.1

The working of the algorithm devised has been discussed in this section with **Password Recovery** as a start title. Our crawler based on the association metric is to crawl web pages related to **Password Recovery**, a topic under network **security**. The ontology used here has a node for **security**, which comes under **computers** as shown fig 6.1. Before crawling, the ontology tree is traversed to the node pointing to **password recovery**. This forms the knowledge-path for our current crawl. The Ontology in our Crawler is currently based on the domain- **Computers**. It is a pure hierarchy based on the subject hierarchies for the Computers domain in ODP project http://www.dmoz.org//Computers The Open Directory Project (ODP) http://www.dmoz.org has been used because as it is an open source and has a less commercial bias. To implement this Ontology Structure, two text files are used. The first text file Ontology.txt establishes the parent-child Relationships i.e. "is a", "part of" relations of the Ontology in a simple way. To get the Associated Scores for each node in the Knowledge-Path, Score.txt is used. This text file gives integral scores for each node based on the depth it is present in the Ontology Structure. For Instance, Security is set 1 , which is at level 1 from the root http://www.dmoz.org//Computers and Hackers which is a child of Security gets the score 2 in the same way.

> Security Computers Security 1
> Hackers Security Hackers 2
> Cryptography Hackers Cryptography 3
> Password Recovery Cryptography Password Recovery 4
> Fig 6.2 Illustration of Ontology.txt Fig 6.3 Illustration of Score.txt The

initial parameters for the crawler namely number of pages to be crawled, the current topic of crawl - **Password Recovery** and the seed URL - http://www.dmoz.org//Computers are set before crawler starts. The Crawl and Stop model is followed .In this Crawler before it starts to crawl the **Knowledge-Path** for the current crawl is constructed based on the Ontology stored. The Ontology.txt is traversed to get the path for the current crawl - **Password Recovery.** The path is thus established: **Computers-Security-Hackers-Cryptography-Password Recovery.** This path decides and restricts the crawler's path for the current crawl. Also before the Crawling starts, the Scores for different keywords in the Knowledge-Path are calculated using Score.txt file. The scores thus established are as follows: **Security =1, Hackers=2, Cryptography=3, Password Recovery=4.** The Crawler is ready to crawl based on this **Knowledge-Path.**

The seed URL is downloaded first - http://www.dmoz.org//Computers and the new links are extracted and added to the queue. These new URLs are checked for the associations with the **Knowledge-Path**, if present the URL u is given the score based on the Keyword score that was evaluated before crawling. The crawler restricts to the **Knowledge –Path** by following this **URL Path:**
http://www.dmoz.org//Computers, http://www.dmoz.org/Computers/Security, http://www.dmoz.org//Computers/Security/Hacking,
http://www.dmoz.org//Computers/Security/Hacking/Cryptography,
http://www.dmoz.org/Cmputers/Security/Hacking/Cryptography/Password

7   Experiments and Results

The various algorithms were run on this crawler and the pages were downloaded. The crawler is written in Java. A Crawl and Stop model of crawler has been followed. The test bed is taken as the Open Directory Project. The comparison of various metrics is done based on the number of relevant and irrelevant pages and

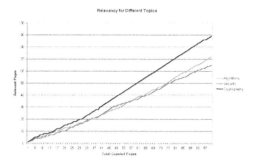

Fig. 7.1 Relevancy of Downloaded Pages Topic Wise

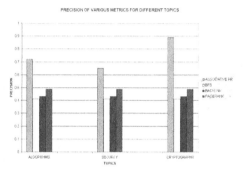

Fig. 7.2 Precision of Various Metrics

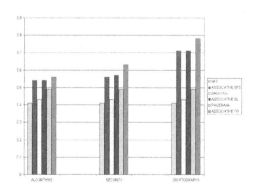

Fig. 7.3 Precisions of the Metrics with Association

the precision of the crawl. All these graphs establish the Associative metric has higher precision and relevancy than other metrics.

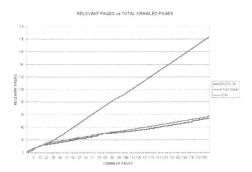

Fig. 7.4 Relevancies of Crawled Pages for same topic -security

8   Conclusion

The Web Crawler based on Importance-metrics developed has combined the semantic and link nature of the web for crawling. The new Ordering Metric proposed - **Association metric** which is based both on the semantic content of the URL u and all its parent pages along with the importance metric sheds a new method for prioritizing the URL queue for crawling by taking account both the semantic and link structure of the web. This new algorithm has the ability to solve the major problem of crawling relevant pages. This novel idea of bringing the ontology nature to the URL has never been explored so far. This proof-of-concept web crawler based on Importance-metrics has been developed successfully. This novel work is bound to bring a new dimension to the existing IR systems like search engine where crawling is purely based on the link structure of the web and keyword matching. The encouraging results shown by this crawler makes it more adept in the area of Focused Crawling. By making this crawler distributed, bringing in more relationships in the reference Ontology and updating the Ontology dynamically, it can be scaled to a powerful, generic web crawler. The scalability advantage for this crawler is bound to revolutionize the current crawling systems and the search engine architecture of having large storage structures. This crawler is a new leaf in the semantic web concept.

References

[1] Filippo Menczer, Gautam Pant and Padmini Srinivasan "Topical Web Crawlers: Evaluating Adaptive Algorithms" in ACM Transactions on Internet Technology The University of Iowa**36** (2003)

[2] S. Ganesh, M. Jayaraj, V. Kalyan, Srinivasa Murthy, G. Aghila, "Ontology based Web Crawler", In Proceedings of IEEE sponsored International Conference on Information Technology: coding and computing April 2004, Pondicherry Engineering College, India **287** (2004) 337–342

[3] Junghoo Cho, Hector Garcia-Molina, and Lawrence Page, "Efficient crawling through URL ordering", In Proceedings of the Seventh International World Wide Web Conference, pages 161–172, April 1998. **72** (1998) 161–172

[4] Monika R.Henzinger, "Algorithmic Challenges in Web Search Engines", Internet Mathematics Volume 1, pages 115-126, December 2002. **72** (2002) 115–126

[5] Sergey Brin and Lawrence Page, "The anatomy of a large-scale hyper textual Web search engine", In Proceedings of the Seventh International World Wide Web Conference, pages 107–117, April 1998. (bf 72) (1998) 107–117

Rough Set Based Data Mining Tasks Scheduling on Knowledge Grid

Kun Gao[1,2], Kexiong Chen[2], Meiqun Liu[3], and Jiaxun Chen[1]

[1] Information Science and Technology College, Donghua University,
1882 West Yan'an Road, Shanghai, P.R.C
gaokun@mail.dhu.edu.cn
[2] Aviation University of Air Force, P.R.C
[3] Administration of Radio Film and Television of Jilin Province, P.R.C

Abstract. An important aspect of scheduling data mining applications on Grid is the ability to accurately determine estimation of task completion time. In this paper, we present a holistic approach to estimation that uses rough sets theory to determine a similarity template and then compute a runtime estimate using identified similar task. The approach is based on frequencies of attributes appeared in discernibility matrix. Experimental result validates our hypothesis that rough sets provide an intuitively sound solution to the problem of scheduling tasks in Grid environment.

1 Introduction

A key aspect of scheduling data mining applications on Knowledge Grid [1] is the ability to accurately estimate their computation times. Such techniques can improve the performance of scheduling algorithms. For example, the Knowledge Grid provides a specialized broker of Grid resources for PDKD computations: given a user request for performing a Data Mining analysis, the broker takes allocation and scheduling decisions, and builds the execution plan, establishing the sequence of actions that have to be performed in order to prepare execution, actually execute the task, and return the results to the user. The execution plan has to satisfy given requirements and constraints. Once the execution plan is built, it is passed to the Grid Resource Management service for execution. Clearly, many different execution plans can be devised, and the RAEM service has to choose the one which maximizes or minimizes some metrics of interest. In its decision making process, this service has to accurately estimating applications computation times so as to improve the performance of scheduling algorithms.

Application runtime prediction algorithms operate on the principle that applications with similar characteristics have similar runtimes. Thus, we maintain a history of applications that have executed along with their respective runtimes. To estimate a given application's runtime, we identify similar applications in the history and then compute a statistical estimate of their runtimes. We use this as

P.S. Szczepaniak et al. (Eds.): AWIC 2005, LNAI 3528, pp. 150–155, 2005.

the predicted runtime. The fundamental problem with this approach is the definition of similarity; diverse views exist on the criteria that make two applications similar. For instance, we can say that two applications are similar because the same user on the same machine submitted them or because they have the same application name and are required to operate on the same size data. Thus, we must develop techniques that can effectively identify similar applications. Such techniques must be able to accurately choose applications' attributes that best determine similarity. Having identified a similarity template, the next step is to estimate the applications' runtime based on previous, similar applications. We can use statistical mean measures [2] to compute the prediction.

In order to accurately estimate the computation times of applications for improving the performance of scheduling algorithms, we propose to include in the Knowledge Grid service dynamic information about actual status of the Grid, the location of data sources, and the applications' attributes over specific data sources and so on. This information can be added as additional meta data associated with datasets, and collected by monitoring previous runs of the various software components on the specific datasets.

In this paper, we present a holistic approach to estimation that uses rough sets theory to determine a similarity template and then compute a runtime estimate using identified similar applications. We tested the technique on Grid-like. The rest of this paper is organised as follows: In section 2 we discuss the suitability of rough sets for identifying similarity templates to predict application run times. In section 3 we present our reduct algorithm and application runtime estimation algorithm. In section 4 we present some preliminary experimental results. Finally, in section 5 conclude this paper.

2   Rough Set Based Computation Times Estimation

Rough sets theory as a mathematical tool to deal with uncertainty in data provides us with a sound theoretical basis to determine the properties that define similarity. The history represents an information system in which the objects are the previous applications whose runtimes and other properties have been recorded. The attributes in the information system are these applications' properties. The decision attribute is the application runtime, and the other recorded properties constitute the condition attributes. This history model intuitively facilitates reasoning about the recorded properties so as to identify the dependency between the recorded attributes and the runtime. Thus, we can concretize similarity in terms of the condition attributes that are relevant and significant in determining the runtime. Thus, the set of attributes that have a strong dependency relation with the runtime can form a good similarity template. Rough sets operate entirely on the basis of the data that is available in the history and require no external additional information. Having cast the problem of application runtime as a rough information system, we can examine the fundamental concepts that are applicable in determining the similarity template.

The objective of similarity templates in application runtime estimation is to identify a set of characteristics on the basis of which we can compare applications. We could try identical matching, i.e. if n characteristics are recorded in the history, two applications are similar if they are identical with respect to all n properties. However, this considerably limits our ability to find similar applications because not all recorded properties are necessarily relevant in determining the runtime. Such an approach could also lead to errors, as applications that have important similarities might be considered dissimilar even if they differed in a characteristic that had little bearing on the runtime.

A reduct consists of the minimal set of condition attributes that have the same discerning power as the entire information system. A similarity template should consist of the most important set of attributes that determine the runtime without any superfluous attributes. In other words, the similarity template is equivalent to a reduct that includes the most significant attributes. Finding a reduct is similar to feature selection problem. All reducts of a dataset can be found by constructing a kind of discernibility function from the dataset and simplifying it. Unfortunately, it has been shown that finding minimal reduct or all reducts are both NP-hard problems. Some heuristics algorithms have been proposed. Hu gives an algorithm using significance of attribute as heuristics [3]. Some algorithms using genetic algorithm are also proposed. Starzyk use strong equivalence to simplify discernibility function [4]. However, there are no universal solutions. It's still an open problem in rough set theory.

Rough sets theory has highly suitable and appropriate constructs for identifying the properties that best define similarity for estimating application runtime. A similarity template must include attributes that significantly affect the runtime and eliminate those that don't. This ensures that the criteria with which we compare applications for similarity have a significant bearing on determining runtime. Consequently, applications that have the same characteristics with respect to these criteria will have similar runtimes. In this paper, we propose a simple but useful heuristic reduct algorithm using discernibility matrix. The algorithm is based on frequencies of attributes appeared in discernibility matrix.

3   Heuristic Reduct Algorithm and Application Runtime Estimation Algorithm

In this section, we present the reduct algorithm and application runtime estimation algorithm.Detail description of the rough set theory can be found in [5].

3.1   Heuristic Reduct Algorithm

The heuristic comes from the fact that intersection of a reduct and every items of discernibility matrix can not be empty. If there are any empty intersections between some item where c_{ij} with some reduct, object i and object j would be indiscernible to the reduct. And this contradicts the definition that reduct is the minimal attribute set discerning all objects.

In order to find reduct, a simple yet powerful method is to sort the discernibility matrix according to $|c_{ij}|$. As we know, if there is only one element in c_{ij}, it must be a member of the reduct. We can image that attributes in shorter and frequent $|c_{ij}|$ contribute more classification power to the reduct. After sorting, we can first pick up more powerful attributes and more likely get optimal reduct.

The sort procedure is like this. First, all the same entries in the discernibility matrix are merged and their frequency is recorded. Then the matrix is sorted according to the length of every entry. If two entries have the same length, more frequent entry takes precedence.

When generating the discernibility matrix, the frequency of every individual attribute is also counted for later use. The frequencies are used in helping picking up attribute when it is needed to pick up one attribute from some entry to insert into the reduct. The idea is that a more frequent attribute is more likely to be a member of the reduct. The counting process is weighted. Similarly, attributes appeared in shorter entry get higher weight. When a new entry c is computed, the frequency of the corresponding attribute $f(a)$ is updated as $f(a) = f(a)+|A|/|c|$, for every $a \in c$; where $|A|$ is total attribute of information system.

Fig. 1 is a heuristic reduct algorithm written in pseudo-code. In line 2, when a new entry c of M is computed, $count(a_i)$ is updated. $count(a_i) := count(a_i) + n/|c|$ for every $a_i \in |c|$. In line 3, the same entries are merged and M is sorted according to the length and frequency of every entry. Line 4-9 traverses M and generates the reduct.

Input: an information system $(U, A \cup \{d\})$, where $A = \cup a_i, i = 1, \cdots, n$.
Output: a reduct Red.
01. $Red = \Phi, count(a_i) = 0$, for $i = 1, \cdots, n$;
02. Generate discernibility matrix M and count frequency of every attribute $count(a_i)$;
03. Merge and sort discernibility matrix M;
04. For every entry m in M do
05. If $(m \cap Red == \Phi)$
06. select attribute a with maximal $count(a)$ in m
07. $Red = Red \cup \{a\}$
08. Endif
09. EndFor
10. Return Red

Fig. 1. Heuristic Reduct Algorithm

3.2 Application Runtime Estimation Algorithm

Let's now look at the estimation algorithm as a whole. Its input is a history record of application characteristics collected over time, specifically including actual recorded runtimes, and a task T with known parameters whose runtime we wish to estimate. Fig. 2 offers a formal view of the estimation algorithm. As we explained previously, the entire process of identifying similarity templates and matching tasks to similar tasks is based on rough sets theory, thereby providing an appropriate solution with a strong mathematical underpinning.

Input: History of tasks=H, Current task for which the runtime has to be estimated=T.
Output: Estimated runtime EST.
1. Partition H such that the runtime is the decision attribute and all the other recorded characteristics are the condition attributes.
2. Apply the rough set algorithm to the history and generate a similarity template ST.
3. Let $HT = H + T$, where H and T are union compatible.
4. Compute equivalence classes of HT with respect to ST.
5. Identify the equivalence class EQT to which T belongs.
6. Compute the mean of the recorded runtimes EST in H for all objects in EQT.

Fig. 2. Application Runtime Estimation Algorithm

4   Rough Set Based Tasks Scheduling and Some Preliminary Results

We adopted the MCT(Minimum Completion Time)[6]+rough set approach to validate that our hypothesis is feasible and efficient. The mapper does not consider node multitasking, and is responsible for choosing the schedule for computations involved in the execution of a given task, but also of starting tasks and checking their completion. The MCT mapping heuristics is very simple. Each time a task is submitted, the mapper evaluates the expected ready time of each machine. The expected ready time is an estimate of the ready time, the earliest time a given resource is ready after the execution of jobs previously assigned to it. Such estimate is based on both estimated and actual execution times of all the tasks that have been assigned to the resource in the past. To update resource ready times, when computations involved in the execution of a task complete, a report is sent to the mapper. The mapper then evaluate all possible execution plans for other task and chooses the one that reduce the completion time of the task. To evaluate our MCT scheduler that exploits rough set as a technique for performance prediction, we designed a simulation framework that allowed us to compare our approach with a Blind mapping strategy, which does not base its decisions on performance predictions at all. Since the blind strategy is unaware of predicted runtime, so it scheduled tasks according the principle of FCFS (first come first serve).

The simulated environment is composed of fifteen machines installed with GT3. Those machines have different physical configurations, operating systems and bandwidth of network. We used histories with 500 records as the condition attributes for estimation applications runtime. Data Ming tasks to be scheduled arrive in a burst, according to an exponential distribution, and have random execution costs. Datasets are all of medium size, and are randomly located on those machines. Fig. 3 shows the improvements in makespans obtained by our technique over the blind one when the percentage of heavy tasks is varied.

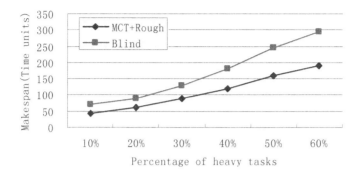

Fig. 3. Preliminary Experimental Results

5   Conclusion

Accurately estimating the computation times of applications is a key component of successful scheduling. The rough set theory provides a formal framework for data mining. It has several favorite features such as representing knowledge in a clear mathematical manner, deriving rules only from facts present in data and reducing information systems to its simplest form, etc. Our experiments showed that a rough sets based approach has good results for scheduling tasks in a grid environment. Such technique can improve the performance of scheduling algorithms and help estimate queue times.

References

1. D. Talia and M. Cannataro.: Knowledge grid: An architecture for distributed knowledge discovery. Comm. of the ACM, 2002
2. W. Smith ,V. Taylor, and I. Foster.:Using Runtime Predictions to Estimate Queue Wait Times and Improve Scheduler Performance,Job Scheduling Strategies for Parallel Processing , LNCS 1659,Springer-Verlag, 1999
3. X.Hu.:Knowledge discovery in databases: An attribute-oriented rough set approach, Ph.D thesis, Regina university, 1995
4. J.Starzyk, D.E.Nelson, K.Sturtz.:Reduct generation in information systems, Bulletin of international rough set society, volume 3, 1998
5. S.K.Pal, A.Skowron.:Rough Fuzzy Hybridization-A new trend in decision-making, Springer, 1999
6. Tracy D. Braun, Howard Jay Siegel, Noah Beck.:A Comparison of Eleven Static Heuristics for Mapping a Class of Independent Tasks onto Heterogeneous Distributed Computing Systems, Journal of Parallel and Distributed Computing, 2001

Global Stability Affected by Migration Behavior of Web Entities in the Bio-network Architecture

Lei Gao[1] and Yongsheng Ding[1,2,*]

[1] College of Information Sciences and Technology,
[2] Engineering Research Center of Digitized Textile and Fashion Technology,
Ministry of Education,
Donghua University, Shanghai 200051, P. R. China
*ysding@dhu.edu.cn

Abstract. We envision that an application or service of the evolving web is emerged from a collection of distributed and autonomous web entities. These entities follows a single set of behavior rules (e.g. migration, reproduction, and death) and implements a functional component related to its web service. To better understand the effect of migration behaviors on service emergence, we establish a mathematical model for the global migration behavior of web entities. By analyzing the model, we bring to light that some interesting properties of stable distribution of web entities. We also find out the relation between the migration rates and the number of web entities in the stable distribution. These conclusions provide us with an effective measure to improve the global quality of emergent services. The study in this paper also benefits the future deployment of an Internet-scale agent system that holds thousands of agents, hosts, and migratory movements of agents.

1 Introduction

The web, once solely a repository for text and images, is evolving into a worldwide integrated platform for computing, data storage, communication, entertainment, e-business, and so on [1]. The applications of the evolving web are expected to be autonomous, self-evolutionary, and adaptable to dynamic web environments. Such a web application can be looked upon as a dynamic service integrator, which knits a number of initially distinct web entities into a complex service bundle for offering a new service.

In our previous work [2, 3], we have applied some principles and mechanisms of biological systems (such as ecosystems and immune systems) to build the bio-network architecture and a novel middleware platform. The platform achieves built-in mechanisms to support desired requirements such as self-organization, adaptability, and self-evolution of complex web applications and services. We believe that the solution can provide the evolving web with the abilities to cope with its complexity including scalability, robustness and inherently adaptability.

P.S. Szczepaniak et al. (Eds.): AWIC 2005, LNAI 3528, pp. 156–162, 2005.

In the bio-network architecture, a web application or service can emerge from a collection of distributed and autonomous web entities (mobile agent) that like the creatures living in a large biological system. We call these web entities as bio-entities. Each bio-entity follows a simple set of behavior rules (e.g. migration, reproduction, mutation, and death) and implements a functional component related to its web service. These bio-entities can interact with each other to provide a useful service. We have introduced credit mechanism (which plays a role as that currency does in economy or energy does in ecology) to control and manage the behaviors of a bio-entity [2, 3].

To better design behavior rules of the bio-entities to emerge a desired application or service, it is necessary to study the effect of bio-entity behaviors from a global and macro aspect. Moreover, in the near future, Internet-scale agent systems will appear with vast numbers of agents that communicate, manipulate objects, and move across machines [4]. To aim at tackling these aspects, some exploring researches have been done, such as to solve agent migration between non-identical platforms [5]. However, to deal with an agent system that is geographically dispersed across a wide-area network, it is also a beneficial work to study the macro dynamic distribution of mobile entities between locations.

In this paper, we establish a mathematical model to discuss the global stability mainly affected by migration behavior of the bio-entities, and analyze the relation between bio-entity migration rates and global distribution of the bio-entities. The rest of this paper is organized as follows. Section 2 gives out a brief overview of the bio-network architecture. In Section 3, after proposing the global migration model, we also give out the model analysis from two aspects: (1) the global stable distribution of the bio-entities and (2) the effect of bio-entity migration rates on global stability. Finally, this paper concludes our efforts.

2   The Bio-network Architecture

From the top down, the layered bio-network architecture includes Bio-entity Survivable Environment, Bio-network Core Services, Bio-network Low-level Functional Modules, Java Virtual Machine, and a heterogeneous distributed system established in a network node for deploying wide-area web applications.

(1) Bio-network Survivable Environment layer is runtime environment for deploying and executing the bio-entities. Technically, such a bio-entity is a combination of a Java object, an execution thread, a remote interface for a network communication, and a self-description. (2) The Bio-network Core Service layer provides a set of general-purpose runtime services that are frequently used by bio-entities. They include naming service, community niche sensing service, bio-entity migration service, evolution state management service, credit-driven control service, and so on. These services alleviate the bio-entities from low-level operations and also allow the bio-entities to be lightweight by separating them from routine work. (3) In Bio-network Low-level Functional Modules layer, local resource management modules manage resources of networks and systems. The ideal situation would place a bio-network platform on every device as a

network node. Bio-network Low-level Functional Modules are just a bridge to maintain access to local resources. However, the bio-network platforms require a fair amount of common resources such as CPU power and memory, so they currently run on desktop-sized computers or more advanced computers.

Some nodes can form a community niche that refers to a logically defined area where the bio-entities can learn from their surrounding environment. A bio-entity may sense which bio-entities are in the community niche, what services they perform, and which resources it can access. This helps a bio-entity create a new application or join an existing community. Physical proximity among network nodes is used to define a community niche in this paper.

The bio-network platform provides the Bio-entity Migration Service, which implements the functionalities necessary to support the migration behavior of the bio-entities. The migration behavior involves determining where and when to migrate by considering the cost/benefit tradeoff of migrating towards an adjacent community niche. The migration will be used to find useful partner bio-entities, near the source of service requests, and acquire new relationships.

3   The Global Migration Model of Bio-entities and Its Stability Analysis

3.1   The Global Migration Model

In this paper, we study the bio-entities that provide the same or similar type of service. These bio-entities are distributed in different community niches. Assume that the total number of community niches is n, the initial time is t_0, and the time interval is Δt. At t_k time, the number of bio-entities in Niche i is $x_i(t_k)$, where $t_k = t_0 + k \cdot \Delta t$, $i = 1, 2, \ldots, n$ and $k = 0, 1, 2 \ldots$. Thus, $X(t_k) = [x_1(t_k), x_2(t_k), \ldots, x_n(t_k)]$ is called as community niche distribution vector for the number of bio-entities at t_k time.

In the bio-network architecture, to deal with the users' requests effectively, an excellent bio-entity can be copied through the replication behavior or a child bio-entity can be produced by two parent bio-entities through the reproduction behavior. In addition, bio-entities may die because of old age or lack of credit value. If they have enough credit units, they will exist longer and even produce a new bio-entity to provide satisfying services. On the contrary, the bio-entities who own few credit units will die quickly. The users' requests in each community niche are relatively unvarying. So, the bio-entities in the same community niche have the same birth rate and death rate. Assume that the birth rate and the death rate of bio-entities in Niche i are respectively b_i and d_i. So, in Niche i, the natural increase rate $c_i = b_i - d_i (i = 1, 2, \ldots, n)$. When the service requests are sufficient, the bio-entities will keep active and c_i will not be less than 0. Due to the difference of community niches, such as the number of service requests, the bio-entities in different community niches have different natural increase rate.

We assume the migration rate from Niche i to Niche j is $m_{ij}(0 \le m_{ij} \le 1)$.

When $i = j$, m_{ij} stands for the stay rate. Obvious, we have $\sum_{j=1}^{n} m_{ij} = 1$. Thus, at t_{k+1} time, the number of bio-entities in Niche i can be expressed as follows:

$$x_i(t_{k+1}) = (1+c_1)m_{1i}x_1(t_k) + (1+c_2)m_{2i}x_2(t_k) + \ldots (1+c_n)m_{ni}x_n(t_k) \quad (1)$$

where $i = 1, 2, \ldots, n$ and $k = 0, 1, 2 \ldots$. The community niche distribution vector for the number of bio-entities at t_{k+1} time is

$$X(t_{k+1}) = [x_1(t_{k+1}), x_2(t_{k+1}), \ldots, x_n(t_{k+1})] \quad (2)$$

From Equation (1) and (2), we can obtain

$$X(t_{k+1}) = L \cdot X(t_k) \quad (3)$$

where $L = [(1+c_j)m_{ji}]_{n \times n}$ $(j = 1, 2, \ldots, n, c_j \geq 0$ and $m_{ji} > 0)$.

We can iterate Equation (3) and obtain $X(t_{k+1}) = L \cdot X(t_k) = L^2 \cdot X(t_{k-1}) = \ldots = L^{k+1} \cdot X(t_0))$, namely,

$$X(t_k) = L^k \cdot X(t_0) \quad (4)$$

where $X(t_0)$ is the initial community niche distribution vector.

In real deployment, the migration modes of the bio-entities, the network topologies, and the distribution of service requests are diversified, so we attempt to propose a general model from a global and macro aspect to study the distribution of the bio-entities. In the next section, we will discuss the Equation (4) for obtaining interesting results.

3.2   Global Stable Distribution of the Bio-entities

In Equation (4), $L \in \Re^{n \times n}$ is a *nonnegative matrix* whenever each $(1+c_j)m_{ji} \geq 0$(each $c_j \geq 0$ and $m_{ji} \geq 0$). According to Ferron-Frobenius Theory of Nonnegative Matrices [6], there exists a unique positive eigenvalue λ_1 with the corresponding eigenvector $\xi_1 = (\alpha_1, \alpha_2, \ldots, \alpha_n)^T$ in Equation (4). In addition, λ_1 has the greatest absolute value of any other eigenvalue (real or complex).

Suppose that n distinct eigenvalues of L are $\lambda_1, \lambda_2, \ldots, \lambda_n$ and their corresponding eigenvectors are $\xi_1, \xi_2, \ldots, \xi_n$. Let $P = (\xi_1, \xi_2, \ldots, \xi_n)$, because the columns of P are independent, P is invertible and we can diagonalize L as $L = Pdiag(\lambda_1, \lambda_2, \ldots, \lambda_n)P^{-1}$. Thus, $\frac{1}{\lambda_1^k}X(t_k) = \frac{1}{\lambda_1^k}L^k \cdot X(t_0)$
$= \frac{1}{\lambda_1^k}Pdiag(\lambda_1^k, \lambda_2^k, \ldots, \lambda_n^k)P^{-1}X(t_0)$ and then we obtain the following equation:

$$\frac{1}{\lambda_1^k}X(t_k) = Pdiag(1, \frac{\lambda_2^k}{\lambda_1^k}, \ldots, \frac{\lambda_n^k}{\lambda_1^k})P^{-1}X(t_0) \quad (5)$$

Due to $\lambda_1 > |\lambda_2| \geq |\lambda_3| \geq \ldots |\lambda_n|$, $\lim_{k \to \infty}(\frac{\lambda_i}{\lambda_1}) = 0$ $(i = 2, 3, \ldots, n)$. So, from Equation (5), we can obtain $\lim_{k \to \infty}\frac{1}{\lambda_1}X(t_k) = Pdiag(1, 0, \ldots, 0)P^{-1}X(t_0)$
$= (\xi_1, \xi_2, \ldots, \xi_n)diag(1, 0, \ldots, 0)P^{-1}X(t_0)$. We define the vector $P^{-1}X(t_0)$ to be $P^{-1}X(t_0) = (e, *, \ldots, *)$. Inserting this result in the above equation,

$$\lim_{k \to \infty} \frac{1}{\lambda_1} X(t_k) = (\xi_1, \xi_2, \ldots, \xi_n) diag(1, 0, \ldots, 0)(e, *, \ldots, *) \tag{6}$$

where e is a constant. When t_k is great enough, Equation (6) is expressed as:

$$X(t_k) \approx \lambda_1^k e \xi_1 \tag{7}$$

or

$$X(t_k) \approx \lambda_1 X(t_{k-1}) \tag{8}$$

From Equation (7) and (8), we can come to some interesting conclusions:

(i) With the increase of time, the community niche distribution for the number of bio-entities $X(t_k)$ tends to a stable status. Its stable distribution vector is $\xi_1 = (\alpha_1, \alpha_2, \ldots, \alpha_n)^T$.

(ii) With the increase of time, the total increase rate for the number of bio-entities at the time is also tends to a stable status. The limitation of total increase rate is $(\lambda_1 - 1)$. When the eigenvalue $\lambda_1 > 1$, the total number of bio-entities increase. When $\lambda_1 = 1$, the total number of bio-entities does not vary. When $\lambda_1 < 1$, the total number of bio-entities decrease.

(iii) Being standardized, each sub-vector of ξ_1 can act as a measurement, standing for the attraction of each community niche to an individual bio-entity.

(iv) If $c_1 = c_2 = \ldots = c_n = c$, i.e., the variation of the number of bio-entities is the same in each community niche, thus, $L = [(1 + c_j)m_{ji}]_{n \times n} = (1 + c)M$ (where $M = (m_{ji})_{n \times n}$). Due to $0 \leq m_{ij} \leq 1$ and $\sum_{j=1}^{n} m_{ij} = 1$, it is easy to prove that the greatest eigenvalue of M is 1. So, greatest eigenvalue of L is $1 + c$, that is, $\lambda_1 = 1 + c$. At this time, with the increase of time, the variation of the number of the bio-entities is a constant c. It is also the meaning of natural increase rate.

3.3   Effect of Bio-entity Migration Rates on Global Stability

If the migration rate $m_{fi} \geq m_{fj} (f = 1, 2, \ldots, n)$, there exists $x_i(t_{k+1}) = \sum_{f=1}^{n} (1 + c_f)m_{fi}x_f(t_k) \geq \sum_{f=1}^{n} (1 + c_f)m_{fj}x_f(t_k) = x_j(t_{k+1})$.

According to Conclusion (i), when $t_k \to \infty$, $X(t_k)$ tends to a stable distribution $\xi_1 = (\alpha_1, \alpha_2, \ldots, \alpha_n)$. So, there exists $\alpha_i > \alpha_j$.

Thus, we arrive to the following conclusion:

(v) If the bio-entity migration rate to a community niche is greater, the number of bio-entities in this community niche is greater in the stable distribution.

Besides, from Equation (1) and (2), the sum of bio-entities in all community niches at t_{k+1} time $S(t_{k+1}) = \sum_{i=1}^{n} x_i(t_{k+1})$

$$= \sum_{i=1}^{n} (\sum_{f=1}^{n} (1 + c_f)m_{fi}x_f(t_k)) = \sum_{f=1}^{n} [(1 + c_f)(\sum_{i=1}^{n} m_{fi})x_f(t_k)] \tag{9}$$

Because $\sum_{i=1}^{n} m_{fi} = 1$, Equation (9) can be expressed as

$$S(t_{k+1}) = \sum_{f=1}^{n}(1 + c_f)x_f(t_k) \tag{10}$$

Equation (10) demonstrates that,

(vi) during Δt, the variation of the number of global bio-entities is composed of each variation of the number of bio-entities in each community niche.

According Conclusion (v) and (vi), increasing the bio-entity migration rate to a beneficial community niche (with greater natural increase rate c_i) can make the sum of bio-entities in all community niches $S(t_k)$ greater.

4   Conclusions

We build a mathematical model for the global migration behavior of web entities. By analyzing the model, we bring to light that the total increase rate and the distribution for the number of bio-entities will finally reach a stable status. Some interesting properties of global stable distribution for the bio-entities are also revealed. We also find out the relation between the migration rates and the number of bio-entities in the stable distribution. The conclusion that increasing the migration rate to a beneficial community niche helps increase the total number of bio-entities, can provide us with an effective measure to improve the global quality of services. The study presented in this paper not only favors the design of composite application in the bio-network architecture, but also benefits the future deployment of an Internet-scale agent system that holds thousands of agents, hosts, and migratory movements of agents.

Acknowledgments. This work is supported by the National Nature Science Foundation of China (No. 60474037 and 60004006), Program for New Century Excellent Talents in University, and Specialized Research Fund for the Doctoral Program of Higher Education from Educational Committee of China (No. 20030255009).

References

1. McIlraith, S. A., Son, T. C., and Zeng, H.: Semantic web services. IEEE Intelligent Systems.**16** (2001) 46–53
2. Gao, L., Ding, Y.-S., and Ren, L.-H.: A novel ecological network-based computation platform as grid middleware system. Int. J. Intelligent Systems. **19** (2004) 859–884
3. Zhang, X.-F., Ding, Y.-S., Ren, L.-H., and Gao, L.: Immune emergent computation-based bio-Network architecture and its simulation platform. Info. Sci. submitted
4. Wijngaards, N. J. E., Overeinder, B. J., van Steen, M., and Brazier, F. M. T.: Supporting Internet-scale multi-agent systems, Data and Knowledge Engineering. **41** (2002) 229–245

5. Groot, D. R. A., Brazier, F. M. T., and Overeinder, B. J.: Cross-platform generative agent migration. In EUNITE 2004, Aachen, Germany. (2004) 356–363
6. Meyer, C.D.: Matrix Analysis and Applied Linear Algebra. SIAM Press. (2000)

The Cartographer Algorithm for Processing and Querying Description Logics Ontologies

Krzysztof Goczyla, Teresa Grabowska,
Wojciech Waloszek, and Michal Zawadzki

Gdansk University of Technology, Department of Software Engineering,
ul. Gabriela Narutowicza 11/12, 80-952 Gdansk, Poland
{kris, tegra, wowal, michawa}@eti.pg.gda.pl

Abstract. One of the most popular formalisms of describing knowledge is Description Logics. It has become even more popular when OWL standard has emerged. The paper presents a new reasoning algorithm - the Cartographer Algorithm - that allows for inferring implicit knowledge from a terminology (TBox) and assertions (ABox) of an ontology. The paper describes the way of processing ontologies in terms of binary signatures and an efficient way of querying ontologies containing numerous individuals. In addition, results of experiments comparing the Cartographer Algorithm with other reasoners are presented.

1 Introduction

While the Internet grows larger and more popular, the problem of structuring data and delivering new knowledge is becoming more and more important. The information society we live in demands immediate access to all possible information about any subject. The Semantic Web [1] idea has become an important step towards fulfilling these requirements. Within the Semantic Web a new language for describing data semantics - OWL Web Ontology Language [2] - has been developed. Although OWL is based on Description Logics (DL) [3], it has some new features adjusting DL to practical Web environment. OWL provides a syntactically uniform way of building ontologies, both in its terminological (TBox) and assertional (ABox) part. XML syntax of OWL data is advantageous for interoperability and readability. Unfortunately, to describe ontological knowledge in the Web is not enough. Much research effort concentrates on developing algorithms that can infer new knowledge from large ontologies containing numerous instances. This paper presents a new reasoning algorithm - the Cartographer Algorithm (called simply: Cartographer) - that is based on an idea of "knowledge cartography". The idea, primarily invented by Wojciech Waloszek, has been further worked out by the authors of this paper within a European Union 6th Framework Program project PIPS (*Personal Information Platform for Life and Health Services*, Contract No 507019). The main goal of PIPS is to create a Web infrastructure to support health and promote healthy life style among European communities. An essential part of PIPS is a Knowledge Management Subsystem

P.S. Szczepaniak et al. (Eds.): AWIC 2005, LNAI 3528, pp. 163–169, 2005.

with an inference engine based on Cartographer. So, Cartographer was primarily devised for processing food and health ontologies, but it turns out to be general enough to be used in any application domain.

2   The Cartographer Algorithm

Motivation behind the knowledge cartography is based on the three assumptions:

1. Terminological part of the knowledge base (TBox) is updated so rarely that it might be considered constant in time.
2. A knowledge base is queried much more often than updated (by updating we understand addition of new ABox assertions). Therefore performance of information retrieval is crucial, while performance of updating is less critical.
3. A knowledge base should be able to hold and efficiently process information about large numbers of individuals.

On the basis of these assumptions a cartographic approach has been developed. It aims at storing in the knowledge base as many conclusions about concepts and individuals as possible. The conclusions can be quickly retrieved in the process of query answering and remain valid due to the fact that terminology cannot be updated. By proper organisation of the knowledge base the same conclusions can be applied to any number of individuals, facilitating information retrieval and reducing size of the base.

The knowledge cartography takes its name after a map of concepts. A map of concepts is basically a description of interrelationships between concepts in a terminology. The map is created in the course of knowledge base creation. A map of concepts can be graphically represented in a form similar to a Venn diagram (Fig. 1). Each atomic region (i.e. a region that does not contain any other region) represents a unique valid intersection of base concepts. By valid we mean an intersection that is satisfiable with respect to a given terminology. Intersections of concepts that are not allowed by terminological axioms are excluded from the map (as in Fig. 1b, where two additional axioms eliminated four regions from the map). Cartographer calculates a number of valid atomic regions n and assigns each atomic region a subsequent integer number from the range $[1, n]$. Because any region in the map consists of some number of atomic regions it can be represented by an array of binary digits of length n with "1"s in positions mapped to contained atomic regions and "0"s elsewhere.

Using this technique we can assign any concept in the terminology a signature - an array of binary digits representing a region covered by the concept in the map. In this way we can describe any combination of complement, union and intersection of described concepts by simply mapping these operations to Boolean negation, disjunction and conjunction.

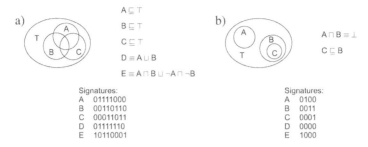

$A \sqsubseteq \top$

$B \sqsubseteq \top$

$C \sqsubseteq \top$

$D \equiv A \sqcup B$

$E \equiv A \sqcap B \sqcup \neg A \sqcap \neg B$

$A \sqcap B \equiv \bot$

$C \sqsubseteq B$

Signatures:
A   01111000
B   00110110
C   00011011
D   01111110
E   10110001

Signatures:
A   0100
B   0011
C   0001
D   0000
E   1000

Fig. 1. A map of concepts (a) with two terminological axioms added (b)

Formally, we define a function s from concepts to elements of a Boolean algebra $\mathbb{B}^n = \{0,1\}^n$. Atomic regions are counterparts of atoms of the algebra, i.e. arrays of "0"s with a sole "1". For any concepts C and D the following equalities hold:

$$s(\neg C) = \neg s(C), \; s(C \sqcap D) = s(C) \wedge s(D), \; s(C \sqcup D) = s(C) \vee s(D) \quad (1)$$

We can also prove the following equivalent statements:

$$C \sqsubseteq D \Leftrightarrow s(C) \vee s(D) = s(D), \; C \sqsubseteq D \Leftrightarrow s(C) \wedge s(D) = s(C) \quad (2)$$

The result (2) is very important because it means that having calculated signatures for concepts in a terminology one can solve any TBox reasoning problem (after reducing it to subsumption [3]) by signature calculations.

As for now we have not taken roles into consideration. In our approach we treat every construct of the form $\exists R.C$ as an atomic concept. This may however lead to some incorrect results, as shown in Fig. 2a. According to the terminology an individual cannot belong to $\exists R.B$ not belonging to $\exists R.A$ (because each member of B is a member of A). The described approach, applied directly, leads to generation of spurious atomic regions. In order to avoid this effect we perform postprocessing (details are omitted here). We also support $\forall R.C$ construct in the same way, by converting $\forall R.C$ into $\neg \exists R.\neg C$.

Using the presented approach, we can describe any $\mathcal{ALC}$ terminology in terms of signatures. It is worth stressing that a terminology need not to be definitorial. The method works well with terminologies that contain cycles (i.e. with concepts whose definitions cannot be expressed in terms of base concepts).

The same techniques can be applied to ABox. We can assign each individual a in ABox a signature of the most specific concept (we denote this concept C_a; this concept need not to be defined explicitly). Processing a new concept assertion $C(a)$ requires recalculation of the signature $s(C_a)$ by assigning it a new value $s(C_a) \wedge s(C)$. Processing a role assertion is slightly more complex and its details are omitted here for brevity.

After determination of signatures for individuals we can reduce ABox reasoning problems to TBox reasoning problems which in turn can be solved by signature calculations. For example, an instance checking problem (check if an

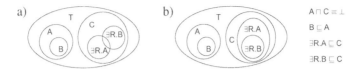

Fig. 2. Incorrect (a) and correct (b) assignment of roles to regions

individual a is a member of a concept C) can be reduced to a question whether the concept C_a is subsumed by the concept C.

3   Time/Space Complexity of Cartographer

The space and time complexity of processing a terminology by Cartographer is in the worst case exponential. Indeed, the maximum number of regions that the space can be divided into by n concepts is 2^n, which results in signatures of such a length. The corresponding terminology would consist of n concepts that are not related to each other at all. However, such a case is very rare in practical terminologies (if found at all). Specifically, this would mean that any subset of concepts may have common instances, because no pair of concepts is declared disjoint. For instance, consider the terminology $\mathcal{T}$ containing one root concept and three direct subconcepts (axioms 1, 2, and 3 below):

1. $Bird \sqsubseteq Animal$
2. $Fish \sqsubseteq Animal$
3. $Mammal \sqsubseteq Animal$

4. $Bird \sqcap Fish \equiv \bot$
5. $Bird \sqcap Mammal \equiv \bot$
6. $Fish \sqcap Mammal \equiv \bot$

In this terminology, $Bird$, $Fish$ and $Mammal$ are unrelated, which means that we could declare one individual to be simultaneously a bird and a fish. Such a terminology would create a domain space with 9 regions (Fig. 3a). Let us add three disjoints to $\mathcal{T}$ (axioms 4, 5, and 6 above). The number of regions in the domain space decreased to 5 (Fig. 3b). Actually, $\mathcal{T}$ is now a pure tree taxonomy, which reflects reality among animals. If the number of subconcepts is m and the order of terminological axioms is similar to the above (i.e. disjoints after inclusions), then the number of regions first reaches the peak of $1+2^m$, and then drops to the final $m + 2$. From this example it is clear that the order of axioms in the terminology definition is crucial for time/space complexity of processing a terminology. It is easy to check that if the axioms of $\mathcal{T}$ are processed in the following order: $(4, 5, 6, 1, 2, 3)$, the number of regions never exceeds 7. In general, for a terminology with 1 superconcept and m disjoint subconcepts, the maximal number of regions during "disjoints-first" processing of axioms is $2(m - 1) + 3$.

Our exemplary terminology $\mathcal{T}$ is very simple - it is just a two-level tree. For such a structure it is easy to find an optimal order of axioms processing. Practical terminologies may be much more complicated. They do not have to be trees, as subconcepts of several superconcepts are common in practice. Moreover, existence of general equalities in a terminology may cause a terminology to become

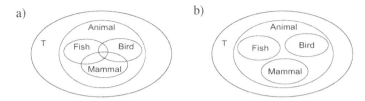

Fig. 3. The division of a domain space for $\mathcal{T}$: a) without disjoints, and b) with disjoints

cyclic. As a result, determining the optimal ordering of axioms for Cartographer is not easy and is currently under investigation.

4   Related Work

There are many tools for reasoning over DL ontologies available as open source software. Eminent representatives are: RACER [4], FaCT [5], and Jena2 Toolkit [6]. In their inference engines RACER and FaCT use structural subsumption and tableaux algorithms for TBox reasoning [3] with different optimisations, while Jena performs reasoning over RDF triples. We performed extensive tests of these tools, particularly checking their capabilities of reasoning over DL Knowledge Bases with large ABoxes. FaCT does not support ABoxes at all, so reasoning can be performed only on a DL terminology. RACER and Jena do support ABox, but they are not scalable. There is also a commercial product called Cerebra [7] that reportedly is based on FaCT optimised and enhanced with capabilities of reasoning over ABox. However, producers of Cerebra do not provide an evaluation version of their system, so we were not able to check it against our benchmark ontologies.

Table 1 presents results of experiments on different sets of individuals. Experiments compared times of loading ontologies and processing queries by Jena, RACER and Cartographer. The examined ontologies consisted of a simple TBox and ABoxes of different sizes. RACER was unable to load an OWL TBox, so the data was provided in KRSS format. The tests were performed on a PC with Celeron 2.4 GHz and 256 MB RAM. The back-end of Cartographer for storing ABox was a PostgreSQL database.

The main difference between analysed reasoning algorithms is related to time of loading ontology. The time of loading ontology is longer for Cartographer. In return we obtain a very short time of response. While RACER was unable to answer a query when 1000 individuals have been loaded, Cartographercould process the same query for 11000 individuals in 1.4 second.

Besides experiments carried out on benchmark ontologies, Cartographer has been successfully used for reasoning over a real-life ontology developed within the PIPS project. The number of concepts defined in the PIPS ontology is approx. 650 and the number of individuals is about two times higher.

Table 1. Results of efficiency experiments. Hyphens denote that the activity could not be completed within 2 hours

	Loading time [s]			Query-processing time [s]		
Size of ABox	400	1000	3800	400	1000	3800
Jena	1	22	-	6	250	-
RACER	3	4	5	58	-	-
Cartographer	43	122	465	<1	<1	1

5   Summary

According to the test results, Cartographer has fulfilled efficiency requirements. However, Cartographer has also some limitations, related to 1) The problem of choosing a proper order of axioms to be processed; 2) Expressiveness of supported ontologies; 3) Time of loading ABox assertions. The first issue has been discussed in Sect. 3. The second issue concerns the problem of which constructs can be used to define a terminology. With respect to DL description languages the set of supported constructs is similar to that defined for $\mathcal{ALC}$ language except that Cartographer lacks of possibility of use of $\exists R.C$ and $\forall R.C$ constructs in queries and assertions as long as such concepts have not appeared in the terminology. With respect to OWL DL language, Cartographer does not support such constructs as: cardinality constraints; symmetric, transitive and functional roles; role hierarchy; and datatype properties. The third issue mentioned above is connected with assumption that performance of information retrieval is crucial, while performance of updating is less critical.

Our present work concentrates on overcoming the above limitations. We are gradually extending expressivness of supported constructs. In particular, we are working on coupling the PIPS Inference Engine based on Cartographer with a relational database where attribute values for individuals are to be stored. This will further extend scalability of the PIPS Knowledge Base.

The other aspects we are currently working on are application of knowledge cartography to ontology alignment and query reformulation in a distributed knowledge base. Another research focuses on embedding trust issues into the knowledge base.

References

1. Semantic Web Initiatives, http://www.semantic-web.org/.
2. OWL - Web Ontology Language Guide. W3C, 2004, http://www.w3.org/TR/2004/REC-owl-guide-20040210/.
3. Baader F. A., McGuness D. L., Nardi D., Patel-Schneider P. F.: *The Description Logic Handbook: Theory, implementation, and applications*, Cambridge University Press, 2003.
4. Racer Semantic Middleware for Industrial Projects Based on RDF/OWL, a W3C Standard, http://www.cs.concordia.ca/~haarslev/racer/.

5. I. Horrocks: FaCT Reference Manual v1.6, August 1998, Included in FaCT archive from http://www.cs.man.ac.uk/~horrocks/FaCT/.
6. A Semantic Web Framework for Java, http://jena.sourceforge.net/.
7. Cerebra Server, http://www.networkinference.com/products/cerebra_business/.

On Association Rules Mining Algorithms with Data Privacy Preserving

Marcin Gorawski and Karol Stachurski

Silesian University of Technology, Institute of Computer Science,
Akademicka 16, 44-100 Gliwice, Poland
MGorawski@polsl.pl, KStachurski@ikp.info

Abstract. Data privacy becomes more and more important in data mining models designing. The concept of privacy preserving when performing data mining in distributed environment assumes that none of the databases shares its private data with the others. In our paper we analyze efficiency of two algorithms of privacy association rule mining in distributed data base. The algorithms are: HPSU (Horizontal Partitioning Secure Union) using horizontally partitioned database and VPSI (Vertical Partitioning Secure Intersection) using vertically partitioned database. To protect private data, HPSU uses secure union, and VPSI uses secure intersection. We implemented a system automatically performing analyses of these two algorithms using the same data. We point out possibilities of modifying the algorithms and discus the impact of these modifi-cations on the data privacy level.

1 Introdution

Nowadays every corporation uses knowledge hidden in its huge databases [6]. The quality of analyzed data has a big impact on the results. The better quality of analyzed data the better benefit gained. However, the data collected in a single database describes only part of the entire business process. In most cases the company collaborates with other companies. The databases of these firms contain data related to the company. The best known example is the Ford and Firestone case [3]. The issue was that in some cars the tires cracked at high speed. Neither company pleaded guilty; the solution assuming sharing private data was not accepted.

The solution in such cases is to conduct the privacy preserving data mining process. The implemented algorithms, partially designed by us and basing on the FDM algorithm [4], discover association rules in a distributed database of transactions and preserve private data leakage.

These algorithms are applicable for web mining, where a customer can be much better identified by many internet companies than in real world. With these algorithms, internet sellers and web searching companies are able to make much better forecast of the customer's behavior, without disclosing private data.

P.S. Szczepaniak et al. (Eds.): AWIC 2005, LNAI 3528, pp. 170–175, 2005.

2   Association Rule Mining

An association rule is an expression $A \Rightarrow B$, where A and B are itemsets. The support of the itemset is the percent of transactions in DB that contain the itemset. The support of the association rule is the support of the $(A \cup B)$ itemset. The confidence of the association rule is equal to a conditional probability $\sigma(A \cup B)/\sigma A$. The association rule is strong when its support exceeds the minimal support threshold, and is confident, when its confidence exceeds the minimal confidence threshold.

3   Hiding Data Methods

Commutative encryption [1] - Both algorithms use encryption and decryption of item-sets. Additionally, VPSI uses encryption of tid-lists. These operations are handled by Pohlig-Hellman's encryption algorithm. The crucial feature of the algorithm is the commutation which assures that the result does not depend on the order of encryption or decryption: $D1D2E1E2(x) = x$, where En is the encryption by the site n, a Dn is the decryption by the site n.

3.1   Secure Sum

The goal of this method [2] is to securely calculate the following expression:

$$S = \sum_{i=1}^{l} x_i$$

where l is a number of the sites, x_i is the value of a site i. If none of x_i is revealed to the other sites, the data privacy is preserved.

3.2   Secure Union

The goal of this method is to securely calculate an union of sets:

$$U = \bigcup_{i=1}^{l} z_i$$

where l is a number of the sites, z_i is the set of the a site i. If none of z_i is revealed to the other sites, the data privacy is preserved. Furthermore, the number of sites containing particular unencrypted item is hidden.

3.3   Secure Intersection

This method, like previous ones, bases on circuit computation. It securely computes the size of the intersection of sets, but unlike secure union, it uses only encryption. The goal is to calculate the following expression:

$$C = \left| \bigcap_{i=1}^{l} z_i \right|$$

where l is a number of the sites, z_i is the set of the a site i. If none of z_i is revealed to the other sites, the data privacy is sustained.

4   HPSU Algorithm

The HPSU (Horizontal Partitioning Secure Union) [1] discovers association rules in horizontally partitioned database of transactions, with secure union of itemsets. All globally large itemsets are discovered and all strong and confident association rules are evaluated. The algorithm uses the $bottom - up$ method to form sets of candidates in each iteration, starting from 1-itemsets. In the next iterations, Apriori property [5] is used to prune not large itemsets in early phase. Instead of exact support and exact confidence, the algorithm determines if the value exceeds the threshold or not.

5   VPSI Algorithm

The VPSI (Vertical Partitioning Secure Intersection) uses vertically partitioned database and secure set intersection. Like HPSU, the VPSI discovers all frequent itemsets and all strong and confident association rules. It also uses Apriori property and the $bottom - up$ method to form candidates. In opposite to the HPSU, algorithm, the VPSI computes the exact support of the itemsets and the exact confidence of the association rules. It uses secure intersection of lists of transactions in order to compute the count of the itemset.

6   Tests

In our tests we used four PC servers. Each server ran an Oracle database. The machines were connected by the 100MB/s Ethernet network. The configuration of each server was as follows: Windows XP, Oracle 10i, 512Mb RAM, Athlon XP 2000+.

Our goal was to measure the execution time and the amount of transferred data dur-ing the execution. Four databases of transactions were used; each containing the following number of transactions: 300k, 600k, 900k, 1200k. Each transaction contained at most 30 items.

Figures 1 and 2 present the execution times of both algorithms in function of a minimal support. The times are roughly proportional to the number of transitions, hence the algorithms are scalable with respect to the number of transactions. As shown in the graphs, the execution time of the HPSU algorithm is much greater than the execution time of the VPSI algorithm. The reason is the necessity of transferring tid-lists in the VPSI. The big amount of transferred data is not an issue though. The most time consuming operations are tid-lists generation from the databases, tid-lists encryption and tid-lists intersection.

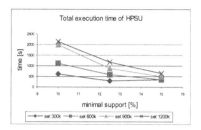

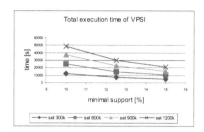

Fig. 1. Total execution time of HPSU algorithm

Fig. 2. Total execution time of VPSI algorithm

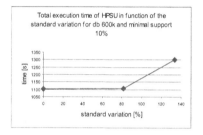

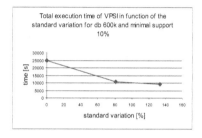

Fig. 3. Total execution time of HPSU in function of the standard variation

Fig. 4. Total execution time of VPSI in function of the standard variation

Figure 3 presents the impact of the data balancing on the HPSU algorithm execution time. The time increases with the standard variation. The estimation of the standard variation is based on the number of transactions in the particular nodes. The time increase is a result of the synchronization in the algorithm. Some operations can not be started until the previous operation was finished in all nodes. If the execution time of the previous operation strongly depends on the number of transactions, the slowest node delays the next operation.

Figure 4 presents the impact of the data balancing on the VPSI algorithm execution time. In this case the estimation of the standard variation is based on the number of items in particular nodes. The total execution time decreases as the stan-dard variation increases. The number of itemsets, created from the items located in one site, increases with the standard variation. For these itemsets, it is not need to compute the support with secure set intersection. The support is estimated locally in one node only. Hence the execution time decreases.

Figure 5 presents the amount of transferred data of HPSU. The value does not depend on the number of transactions. It depends only on the number of analyzed sets, because only objects of itemsets are transferred. In VPSI, figure 6, the total amount of transferred data strongly depends on the number of transactions. He reason is the need of sending transaction object, for each transaction, in process of global support evaluation. This is the main drawback of VPSI. As in case of execution time, HPSU outperforms VPSI with respect to amount of transferred

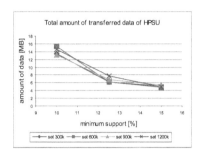

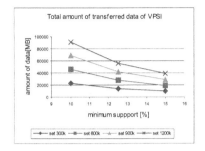

Fig. 5. Total amount of transferred data of HPSU algorithm

Fig. 6. Total amount of transferred data of VPSI algorithm

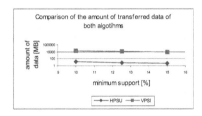

Fig. 7. Comparison of the amount of transferred data of both algotihms

data. The amount of data transferred in the VPSI algorithm is much greater than in the HPSU algorithm. Although, such a big amount of data doesn't have a significant impact on the algorithm efficiency.

7   Conclusions, Modifications and Open Problems

The user may not use some data privacy preserving methods in order to improve the efficiency.

The method using non-itemsets is rather time-consuming when there is a lot of items. This tradeoff improves the execution of the encryption and decryption. But it is important to notice that execution time of performing encryption and decryption is shorter than the time of local pruning. The bigger profit can be gained in the VPSI case. The algorithm extends the generated tid-lists to randomly chosen size from the range of the actual size to the number of transactions. When the itemsets have gener-ally low support, the execution time can strongly increase.

Another optimization of the VPSI algorithm is an early detection of not large item-sets. The operation of secure set intersection is partitioned. The entire transaction list is divided into hunks. Each partition of tids is processed as described in the paper. It's possible to detect early that the itemset will not be a globally large itemset. The profit depends on the minimum support parameter. For instance, the execution time would be decreased approximately by half for the minimum support of 50.

The HPSU algorithm was proved to be more efficient than the VPSI algorithm with respect to the execution time and the amount of transferred data. Unfortunately, the algorithms depend on data partitioning. The main advantages are the scalability with respect to the number of transactions and the number of globally large itemsets. The algorithms work with any number of sites. The VPSI algorithm outperforms the HPSU algorithm in terms of estimation of the exact support of an itemset and exact confi-dence of a given association rule.

Although the algorithms are scalable and they are applicable for analyses on very large databases, there is a lot of unsolved problems. The most important concerns adapting the algorithms to the other secure computation models. The current considered model assumes there is no collusion and every site provides correct input data and follows the protocol consequently. The other algorithms consider input data replacement, collusion or protocol interruption.

References

1. Murat Kantarcioglu Chris Clifton: Privacy-preserving Distributed Mining of Asso-ciatio Rules on Horizontally Partitioned Data, Purdue University Department of Computer Sci-ences 250 N University St West Lafayette, IN 47907-2066 January 30, 2003
2. Chris Clifton, Murat Kantarcioglu, Jaideep Vaidya, Xiaodong Lin, Michael Y. Zhu Tools for Privacy Preserving Distributed Data Mining
3. Jaideep Vaidya Chris Clifton: Privacy Preserving Association Rule Mining in Ver-tically Partitioned Data
4. 11. D. Cheung et al.: A Fast Distributed Algorithm for Mining Association Rules, Proc.4th Int'l Conf. Parallel and Distributed Information Systems, IEEE Computer Soc. Press, Los Alamitos, Calif., 1996, pp. 31-42.
5. Hua Zhu: On-Line Analitycal Mining of Association Rules, B.S., University of Sceince and Technology China 1995
6. Data Mining - Report by Sudeshna Basu, Georgia State University Fall 1997

Using Artificial Neural Networks for Processing Data Gained via OpenDAP and Consolidated from Different Databases on Distributed Servers

Aleksander Górny[1,3] and Magdalena Tkacz[1,2,3]

[1] Medical University of Silesia, IT Center,
Poniatowskiego 15, 40-055 Katowice, Poland
gorny@slam.katowice.pl,
[2] University of Silesia, Institute of Computer Science,
Będzińska 39, 41-200 Sosnowiec, Poland
tkacz@us.edu.pl
[3] Medical University of Silesia, Chair and Division of Bionics,
41-200 Sosnowiec, Ostrogórska 30, Poland

Abstract. This paper presents an idea of collecting and then processing a differential data obtained from heterogeneous systems via OpenDAP. Special attention was concentrated on case when obtained data, if collected into consoled, one big set becomes an incomplete dataset (e.g. because of absention of some data in particular asked database) - in such case application of neural networks for processing was proposed. In this paper a basic information about Data Access Protocol are presented too.

1 Introduction

Nowadays there is no problem with access to information - the main problem is even not to find them - a problem is to filter it, because in response to our query to the search engine we get links to many websites of specialized institutions, but to web pages of ordinary users, too. Solving problems with excessive information can be distinguished into two main trends. One is working out new algorithms and methods of classification, grouping, searching and filtering information. The second one refers to different kinds of utilization existing network infrastructure through developing new methods, exchanging and sharing distributed in the network information with taking advantage of existing mechanisms - protocols and known and friendly to users frontends. Almost all of today used databases are well specified and developed. There are clear methods and rules of using them, special languages to define a query (e.g. SQL). All those tools are effective when data are stored in one physical place, e.g. on one machine, or on several machines but connected together, e.g. arrays or cluster of servers. In many sciences, information about objects of studies are stored in many small, local institute's databases. It is clear that to carry out deep examination, as many as possible information about an object or structure will be desired. It can be done in a situation when institutes and universities will be able to gain access to the other institutes database.

P.S. Szczepaniak et al. (Eds.): AWIC 2005, LNAI 3528, pp. 176–182, 2005.

In the past years, when network was not so wide-spread, all institutions have been making databases for its own use, with his own solution. Assortment of offerable and available solution as a database engines, as well as operating systems was the reason for such heterogeneous environment, too. All of that make problems of interoperating among all already made databases "a little" complex.

2   Background and Motivation

As a computer scientist, we had been asked for advice for accessing many databases in one turn, and then, when the suitable data were retrieved, how to make them in a form of one, useful set of data - with minimal human effort. The considered problems were: to gain data form different meterogical stations, and basing on them forecasting of heavy rains which can cause a landslides which can be dangerous to people. The second one was similar to the previous one, but system should gain data from geophysical stations and helps to forecast earthquakes. The third and fourth differ from previous ones: at present there are many researches carried out in problem on decode the human genome. The forth is about collection of different kinds of images, especially images that are from tomography, RTG, NMR [7]. In such case there is a need to freely search and access classified with specified diseases images. All those problems can be reduced to one situation shown in Fig. 1. Usually every client computer can use

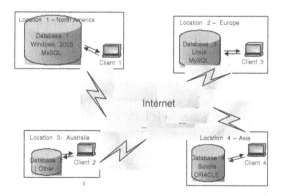

Fig. 1. Generalization of all problems - schema

only database of its own, but does not have access to other resources on other locations. The key is that we have heterogeneous environment physically connected via WAN (Internet). The submitted problems make us to start thinking how to solve them. The first two systems should automatically and continuously gain data from measuring points in different locations, process them and - when special conditions appear - to generate something alike alarm - to the appropriate man on duty, which then should examine the situation in more details. The advantage of that solution is that computer can continuously analyze data in that same way, with the same precision 24 hours a day, for the whole years. It should work as a kind of decision support system, but it should be a self-learning system and should have the ability to generalize data, moreover - it should work in the realtime. These two problems required us to think about both transferring and exchanging data, and a problem of processing them later. The third and fourth problem requires different approach - here, the only problem was to solve interoperation among databases.

3   Data Access Protocol

First of all we start to investigate what have been done in distributed data or database systems fields. We found an OpenDAP project [1]. OpenDAP is a framework for scientific data networking and provides free software, which makes possible retrieving data from remote databases regardless of local storage format. It allows to make your data accessible to other scientists too. A tool for transforming existing applications into OpenDAP clients is also provided. In this project a DAP (Data Access Protocol), which specification [3] was published as RFC (with category of proposed community standard) was used. DAP is a data transmission protocol which was specifically designed for transferring a science data (both C++ and Java implementation of DAP are available). This protocol has been used by DODS (Distributed Oceanographic Data System a part of National Virtual Ocean Data System [2]) since 1995 and from this time was suited to the other fields in Earth Sciences. DAP was developed in such a way to hide the implementation details in database systems in different organizations - this should allow clients to be free from taking into consideration of what data are stored and where they are stored, regardless of the format and type of database - and of the size of the database. The only (may be difficult to someone) thing to do to provide exchanging data using DAP is the necessity of installing and configuring special programs, a kind of service - DAP server and DAP client, because this protocol corresponds to HTTP and MIME standard and works with "client-server" method: client makes request of the server, server responds with some information. Both requests and responses are send via HTTP, so DAP is a stateless protocol, as a HTTP is. Requests and responses used by DAP are outlined in Table 1. However, the server may support additional request-response pairs, and may provide additional functions considered useful for clients. Data representation may be one of the following type [3]:

- Atomic variable:
  - Integer : Byte, Int16, UInt16, Int32, UInt32;
  - Floating Point : Float32, Float64;
  - String : String, URL;
- Constructor Variable:
  - Array;
  - Structure;
  - Grid;
  - Sequence.

Table 1. Requests and responses used by DAP [3]

Request	Response
DDS	DDS or Error - Dataset Description Structure
DAS	DAS or Error - Dataset Attribute Structure
DataDDS	DataDDS or Error - Data Dataset Descriptor Structure
Server version	Version information as text
Help	Help text discribing all request-response pairs

Additionally, any data attributes can be either atomic or constructor type, but may not be a multidimensional array. A variable name must contain only US-ASCII characters (a-z, A-Z, 0-9,_ ,! ,~ ,* ,' ,- ,''). Selection of the data is making DAP selectional operators. Operators are: $<$ 'less than', $<=$ 'less than or equal', $>$ 'greater than', $>=$ 'greater than or equal', $=$ 'equal', $!=$ 'not equal', $=\tilde{}$ 'regular expressions match'. Possibility of using a certain operator depends on data type. As shown above, DAP provides very flexible structure for data type definition, so we can freely decide what datatype definition will be appropriate for our needs. These definitions can be completely independed from datatype and structure used in local database systems. This flexible method for datatype definitions makes DAP useful either in exchanging a numerical data [statistics, measurements with wide range of precisions, alike a string or symbolic - in for example defined grammar in a special language [7]. In that way a problem of retrieving data from different and distributed databases looks to be solved.

4   Processing an Incomplete Data

Next problem to solve, was how to process dataset obtained as a result of compiled answers from querying the databases into one comprehensive database. assuming that we want to query each database about 3 objects, each characterized by 5 attributes, respectively. In reality we often work with hundreds or thousands of objects and with hundreds attributes. When we are lucky - we obtain a complete and coherent dataset which can be processed in a known way and standard database methods. Even when we do not have 'a priori' dependences between parameters, we can use e.g. artificial neural networks [4], [5], [6]. If we are less lucky - we have a dataset with duplicated data. After application of some filters and deletion excessive data, we can work with that database as with the previous one - using known tools and methods. In more complex or wide areas of investigations, as a final dataset we can obtain dataset in a form shown in Fig. 2. In case of making query to the database, an answer may be incomplete or falsified - and then thought out as useless. In that case we cannot directly apply any of standard methods of automatically processing the data. We should

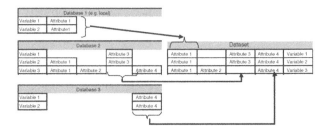

Fig. 2. Dataset obtained as a result of querying different database

remember that processing was required in the first and the second examples - and the system should work all the time without human interaction or action. It requires choosing such method which will allow on it. We know [8], [9], [10] that suitable, properly trained artificial neural network (e.g. multilayer perceptron with backpropagation algorithm) is able to predict some parameters basing on such kind of data. In [10] it was presented in details how to prepare such kind of dataset and how different neural networks, trained with different algorithms work with datasets of forms showed in figure. Exemplary effect - which shows the difference between real and predicted values, is shown in Figure 3. As seen

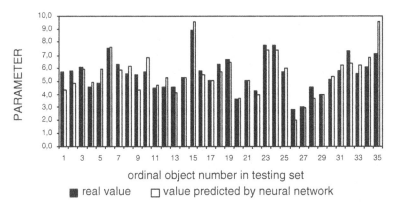

Fig. 3. Exemplary comparisons between real values and values predicted by neural network trained on incomplete dataset [10]

as in figure 3 differences are acceptable, and this is why we recommend such solution for usage in that situation (incomplete data).

5   Conclusions

After that considerations we know how to gain data form different platforms (heterogeneous environment) through the network, and we know what method can be used to process data - even in a least comfortable situation when dataset is incomplete. After compiling them into a one, big dataset, the two things remain to be done: the first - to apply the proposed by us (and described above) solution in testing environment and check out how it works in practice, e.g. what about network load, about reliability, what is the required bandwidth for comfortable use. It is interesting to test to use this solution via GPRS connection (mobile phone or smartphone with PDA together). It should be useful if you want to have access to data if you are in the field. Another questions are about possibility of utilization and cooperation of proposed method with existing databases - GIS (getting data from GIS databases based on GPRS position, and next connecting with the closest database in measuring point to gain the most recent and appropriate data). So we now can state that exchanging and accessing data among universities and research centers using existing internetwork infrastructure and protocols is possible form technical point of view. It does not depend on environment used for building databases and network environment. Additionally, processing an incomplete data (obtained as a compiled from different sources set of data) is possible with usage of neural networks.

References

1. http://www.opendap.org/ - OpenDAP project webpage
2. http://www.po.gso.uri.edu/tracking/vodhub/vodhubhome.html - The National Ocean Data System webpage
3. Gallagher J., Potter N., Sgouros T., Hankin S, Flierl G.: The Data Access Protocol-DAP 2.0. ESE-RFC 004.0.03 Category: Proposed Community Standard, 2004/09/14 (NASA Standard Process Group webpage: http://spg.gsfc.nasa.gov)
4. Horzyk A., Tadeusiewicz R.: Self-Optimizing Neural Network, in F. Yin, J. Wang, Ch. Guo (eds.): Advances in Neural Networks - ISNN 2004, Lecture Notes in Computer Science, Vol. 3173, Springer-Verlag, Berlin - Heidelberg - New York, 2004, Part I, pp. 150 - 155
5. Tadeusiewicz R., Lula P.: Neural Network Analysis of Time Series Data, Informatica - An International Journal of Computing and Informatics, vol. 25, nr. 1, 2001, pp. 3-10
6. Tadeusiewicz R.: Applications of Neural Networks in the Diagnosis of Pathological Speech, Chapter (No 11) in book: Lisboa P.J.G., Ifeachor E.C, Szczepaniak P.S. (Eds.): Artificial Neural Networks in Biomedicine, Springer-Verlag, Heidelberg 2000, pp. 141 - 150
7. Tadeusiewicz R, Ogiela M.: Medical Image Understanding. Studies in Fuzziness and Soft Computing, vol.156, Springer-Verlag, Berlin - Heidelberg - New York, 2004
8. Tkacz Magdalena (1999): Processing an incomplete data using artificial neural networks. International Workshop Control and Information Technology, IWCIT 1999. Ostrava, Technical University 1999

9. Tkacz Magdalena (2001): Processing an incomplete and random data using artificial neural networks. International Workshop Control and Information Technology, IWCIT 2001. Ostrava, Technical University 2001

10. Tkacz Magdalena (2004): Geoenvironmental modelling with artificial intelligence methods in case of hybrid geothermal system. Doctorate dissertation, Sosnowiec, Uniwersytet Śląski 2004.

A Technique for Learning Similarities on Complex Structures with Applications to Extracting Ontologies

Michał Grabowski and Andrzej Szałas

The College of Economics and Computer Science,
Olsztyn, Poland
mich@mimuw.edu.pl, sz@ida.liu.se

Abstract. A general similarity-based algorithm for extracting ontologies from data has been provided in [1]. The algorithm works over arbitrary approximation spaces, modeling notions of similarity and mereological part-of relations (see, e.g., [2, 3, 4, 5]). In the current paper we propose a novel technique of machine learning similarity on tuples on the basis of similarities on attribute domains. The technique reflects intuitions behind tolerance spaces of [6] and similarity spaces of [7]. We illustrate the use of the technique in extracting ontologies from data.

1 Introduction

Ontologies are considered essential to the semantic web, where meaningful information retrieval requires ontology-based search engines. Many ontologies are being prepared by domain experts, who apply the existing tools (for an overview see, e.g., [8]). On the other hand, the construction of ontologies is a difficult and time-consuming task and there is a need for automated extraction of ontologies from available data sources (see, e.g., [9, 10, 11, 12]). The existing approaches mainly focus on extracting ontologies from sources like texts, folder/database structures, XML schemas or URLs saved in a bookmark list, with the main emphasis on text analysis. However, ontologies can also be extracted on the basis of the existing database contents. For example, one might expect to obtain useful ontologies for e-commerce analyzing huge databases of clients' behavior patterns.

One of the important techniques for extracting ontologies is based on incorporating known or machine learned similarities between complex objects and sets of objects. A basis for the approach of this paper is an abstract algorithm for generating ontologies, working over arbitrary domains, which has been proposed in [1]. More precisely, in [1] it is assumed that the underlying approximation spaces are given. Approximation spaces have frequently been considered in the literature (see, e.g., [2, 3, 4, 5]) as a tool for modelling similarities, approximations and mereological part-of relationships between sets and relations. In most approaches based on approximation spaces one benefits due to abstracting from particular similarity measures. On the other hand, one faces here a more general problem of obtaining well-behaved similarity measures on complex structures, based on similarities defined on more elementary domains, like domains of simple attributes or sensor measurements (see, e.g., [13, 14, 15, 16, 17]). Of course, it is relatively easier to provide or machine learn similarities on elementary domains.

P.S. Szczepaniak et al. (Eds.): AWIC 2005, LNAI 3528, pp. 183–189, 2005.

In [1] the general approach is exemplified by tolerance spaces, as defined in [6], where the similarity relation is reflexive and symmetric. Tolerance spaces are also useful in the context of heterogenous perceptual capabilities of agents, as shown in [18, 19].

In the current paper we propose a technique for machine learning similarities on complex structures. The starting point is the notion of similarity spaces of [7], which are a direct generalization of tolerance spaces. On the basis of similarity spaces on elementary domains, one can machine learn similarity spaces on tuples as well as approximation spaces, which make the algorithm of [1] applicable. Here we assume that similarity spaces for base domains are given. The base domains can be simple, like numbers, or complex, like tuples or sets. What we require is that a notion of similarity on elements of those domains is provided, e.g., obtained by recursively using the technique we propose. Then we construct a model for machine learning similarity spaces for tuples over elementary domains, based on solving corresponding optimization problems. For simplicity we focus on the case, where attributes are weighted (for related approaches see, e.g., [14, 15, 16]) and lead to linear models.[1] On the basis of the machine learned similarities one can construct a lattice of concepts, using the algorithm of [1].

The paper is organized as follows. In Section 2 we first recall notions related to similarity spaces and approximation spaces. Next we provide a construction of approximation spaces based on similarity spaces. In Section 3 we introduce a novel technique for machine learning similarities on tuples and sets. In Section 4 we briefly recall the basic algorithm of [1]. Section 5 provides an example of extracting ontologies from data using the introduced machine learning techniques in conjunction with the algorithm of [1]. Finally, Section 6 concludes the paper.

2   Similarity Spaces and Approximation Spaces

Similarity spaces, considered in [7] generalize the concept of tolerance spaces, as defined in [6].

Definition 1. *By a similarity function on a set U we mean any function $\sigma : U \times U \longrightarrow [0, 1]$. A similarity space is defined as the tuple $S = \langle U, \sigma, p \rangle$, consisting of a nonempty set U, called the* domain *of S, a similarity function σ, and a similarity threshold $p \in [0, 1]$. By a similarity neighborhood of $u \in U$ wrt S, denoted by $n_S(u)$, we understand the set $\{v \in U \mid \sigma(u, v) \geq p\}$.*   ◁

Approximation spaces are substantial in the approach to ontology generation of [1].

Definition 2. *By an* approximation space *we understand any tuple $\langle U, I, \nu \rangle$, where:*

- *U is a nonempty set of objects, called a* domain
- *$I : U \longrightarrow 2^U$ is an* uncertainty function
- *$\nu : 2^U \times 2^U \longrightarrow [0, 1]$ is an* inclusion function.   ◁

---

[1] It should, however, be emphasized that linear models might be too restricted for large data sets, where non-linear similarity functions might be required. Our technique for machine learning weights and similarity thresholds can easily be adopted to non-linear cases, however, with a risk of a substantial increase of the complexity of the approach.

The intuitive meaning of $I(u)$ is the set of objects "similar", in some sense, to $u,$. The inclusion function $\nu(U_1, U_2)$ provides a degree of inclusion of U_1 in U_2.

Approximation spaces can be constructed using similarity spaces. Such a construction allows us to formulate a model for machine learning similarities on complex structures, based on similarities on simpler structures.

Definition 3. *Let* $S = \langle U, \sigma, p \rangle$ *be a similarity space. By a canonical approximation space induced by* S *we understand the approximation space* $\langle U, I, \nu \rangle$*, where, for any* $u \in U$, $I(u) \stackrel{def}{=} n_S(u)$ *and for any* $U_1, U_2 \subseteq U$,

$$
\nu(U_1, U_2) \stackrel{def}{=} \begin{cases} \dfrac{|\{u_1 \in U_1 : \exists u_2 \in U_2[u_1 \in n_S(u_2)]\}|}{|U_1|} & \text{if } U_1 \neq \emptyset \\ 1 & \text{otherwise,} \end{cases}
$$

where $|.|$ *denotes the cardinality of a set.*   ◁

3   Machine Learning Similarities on Tuples

Consider k-tuples over $U_1 \times U_2 \times \ldots \times U_k$, where $U_1, U_2, \ldots, U_k$ are arbitrary sets (domains of given attributes, which can also consist of arbitrary complex structures). Using notation $\bar{t}$, where $\bar{t} \in U_1 \times U_2 \times \ldots \times U_k$, we assume that $\bar{t} = \langle t_1, t_2, \ldots, t_k \rangle$.

Let us assume that similarity spaces $S_1 = \langle U_1, \sigma_1, p_1 \rangle$, $S_2 = \langle U_2, \sigma_2, p_2 \rangle$, …, $S_k = \langle U_k, \sigma_k, p_k \rangle$ on domains $U_1, U_2, \ldots, U_k$ are given.

Suppose that an expert has classified chosen tuples to belong to similarity neighborhoods $N_1, \ldots N_r$, assuming that $N_1, \ldots N_r$ are pairwise disjoint. The goal is to find a similarity space $S = \langle U_1 \times U_2 \times \ldots \times U_k, \sigma, p \rangle$, satisfying conditions:

(a) for any $1 \leq i \leq r$ and tuples $\bar{t}, \bar{t}' \in N_i$, we have that $\sigma(\bar{t}, \bar{t}') \geq p$ (i.e., S identifies $\bar{t}$ with $\bar{t}'$)

(b) for any $1 \leq i \neq j \leq r$ and tuples $\bar{t} \in N_i, \bar{t}' \in N_j$, we have that $\sigma(\bar{t}, \bar{t}') < p$ (i.e., S distinguishes $\bar{t}$ from $\bar{t}'$).

In general, one would like to build $\sigma \stackrel{def}{=} \Gamma(S_1, S_2, \ldots, S_k)$, for some operator Γ, suitably parameterized. Then requirements (a) and (b) lead to the following optimization problem, where parameters of Γ together with p are to be found and p is required to be minimal, maximal, or user-chosen number from interval $[0, 1]$:

(a') for all $1 \leq j \leq r$ and $\bar{t}, \bar{t}' \in N_j$, $\Gamma(S_1, S_2, \ldots, S_k)(t_l, t_l') \geq p$
(b') for all $1 \leq i \neq j \leq r$ and $\bar{t} \in N_i, \bar{t}' \in N_j$, $0 \leq \Gamma(S_1, S_2, \ldots, S_k)(t_l, t_l') < p$.

Observe that the similarity threshold p, proposed as a substantial part of tolerance spaces in [6] and similarity spaces in [7], plays a crucial role in the proposed models. The maximal value of p provides us with the smallest similarity neighborhoods while the minimal value of p provides us with the largest similarity neighborhoods. Of course, one can accept any threshold between the minimal and maximal value of p. However, parameters have to be recomputed for each such threshold.

In what follows, for simplicity, we concentrate on looking for a suitable σ which is a weighted (linear) combination of similarities on attributes, $\sigma(\bar{t}, \bar{t}') = \sum_{1 \leq l \leq k} w_l \sigma_l(t_l, t_l')$.

We then search for $w_1, w_2, \ldots, w_k$ as well as maximal and minimal $0 \leq p \leq 1$ satisfying:

(a") for all $1 \leq j \leq r$ and $\bar{t}, \bar{t}' \in N_j$, $\sum_{1 \leq l \leq k} w_l \sigma_l(t_l, t_l') \geq p$

(b") for all $1 \leq i \neq j \leq r$ and $\bar{t} \in N_i, \bar{t}' \in N_j, 0 \leq \sum_{1 \leq l \leq k} w_l \sigma_l(t_l, t_l') < p.$

Such optimization problems are linear, which makes them solvable in deterministic polynomial time wrt the size of the model. The resulting similarity spaces are then given by (with p_m being maximal, minimal or user-chosen p, respectively),

$$\left\langle U_1 \times U_2 \times \ldots \times U_k, \frac{\sum_{1 \leq l \leq k} w_l \sigma_l(t_l, t_l')}{\sum_{1 \leq l \leq k} |w_l|}, \frac{p_m}{\sum_{1 \leq l \leq k} |w_l|} \right\rangle.$$

4   The Algorithm for Extracting Ontologies

The following algorithm of [1] generates an ontology from an approximation space, where the domain of individuals in the approximation space is viewed as the initial data set. Observe that the standard inclusion serves to generate partial ordering on concepts (interpreted as "to be more specific/general than").

– Input: an approximation space $AS = \langle U, I, \nu \rangle$
– Output: an ontology $\mathcal{O} = \langle U, \mathcal{C}, \subseteq \rangle$
– Algorithm:
  1. $\mathcal{C} := \{I(u) \mid u \in U\}$;
     $i := 0; AS_i := AS; \mathcal{C}_i := \mathcal{C}$;
  2. while new concepts are added to $\mathcal{C}$ do
     begin
        $AS_{i+1} := 2^{AS_i}; \mathcal{C}_{i+1} := \emptyset$;
        for all $u \in \mathcal{C}_i$ do
        begin
           $\mathcal{C} := \mathcal{C} \cup flat(I_{i+1}(u))$;
           $\mathcal{C}_{i+1} := \mathcal{C}_{i+1} \cup I_{i+1}(u)$
        end;
        $i := i + 1$;
     end;
  3. $\mathcal{C} := \mathcal{C} \cup \{\emptyset, U\}$.

Notation:

For $AS = \langle U, I, \nu \rangle$, let $2^{AS} \stackrel{\text{def}}{=} \langle 2^U, I', \nu' \rangle$, where

– $I'(S) \stackrel{\text{def}}{=} \{T \in 2^U \mid \nu(S, T) > 0\}$
– ν' is defined by analogy with Definition 3.

$$P_i(U) \stackrel{\text{def}}{=} \begin{cases} U & \text{when } i = 0 \\ 2^{P_{i-1}(U)} & \text{when } i > 0 \end{cases}$$

A *flat representation* of a finite set $X \in P_n(U)$, denoted by $flat(X)$, is defined inductively:

$$flat(X) \stackrel{\text{def}}{=} \begin{cases} \{u\} & \text{for } X = u \in U \\ \bigcup_{Y \in X} flat(Y) & \text{for } X \in P_n \text{ with } n > 1. \end{cases}$$

For example,

$flat(\{\{\{4\}\}, \{\{3\}, \{4, 5\}\}\}) = \{3, 4, 5\}.$

5   An Example

Consider the data set of [20].[2] The conditional attributes:

- age of the patient ('age'): young (y), pre-presbyopic (pp) presbyopic (p)
- spectacle prescription ('presc'): myope (m), hypermetrope (h)
- astigmatic ('ast'): false (f), true (t)
- tear production rate ('tear'): reduced (r), normal (n).

Table 1. Training data and similarities on attribute values

nr	age	presc	ast	tear	dec	nr	age	presc	ast	tear	dec	similarities
1	p	m	t	n	1	5	pp	m	f	n	2	$\sigma_{age}(y, pp) = 0.7, \sigma_{age}(y, p) = 0.3$
2	pp	m	t	n	1	6	y	m	f	n	2	$\sigma_{age}(p, pp) = 0.8$
3	y	h	t	n	1	7	p	h	f	r	3	$\sigma_{presc}(m, h) = 0.4$
4	p	h	f	n	2	8	y	m	f	r	3	$\sigma_{ast}(f, t) = 0.0, \sigma_{tear}(r, n) = 0.5$

The decision attribute (dec) values, representing expert's decisions, are [20]: hard contact lenses (1), soft contact lenses (2) and no contact lenses (3). For simplicity we consider only training data and similarities on attribute values[3] gathered in Table 1. We then consider the following set of inequalities, where $p \geq 0$:

$(1, 2)\ \sigma_{age}(p, pp)w_1 + \sigma_{presc}(m, m)w_2 + \sigma_{ast}(t, t)w_3 + \sigma_{tear}(n, n)w_4 \geq p$

$(1, 3)\ \sigma_{age}(p, y)w_1\ \ + \sigma_{presc}(m, h)w_2\ \ + \sigma_{ast}(t, t)w_3 + \sigma_{tear}(n, n)w_4 \geq p$

$(2, 3)\ \sigma_{age}(pp, y)w_1 + \sigma_{presc}(m, h)w_2\ \ + \sigma_{ast}(t, t)w_3 + \sigma_{tear}(n, n)w_4 \geq p$

$\cdots$

$(6, 7)\ 0 \leq \sigma_{age}(y, p)w_1 + \sigma_{presc}(m, h)w_2\ \ + \sigma_{ast}(f, f)w_3 + \sigma_{tear}(n, r)w_4 < p$

$(6, 8)\ 0 \leq \sigma_{age}(y, y)w_1 + \sigma_{presc}(m, m)w_2 + \sigma_{ast}(f, f)w_3 + \sigma_{tear}(n, r)w_4 < p$

Assuming accuracy 0.01, we obtain:

$$-\text{the maximal } p \text{ is } 1.0 \text{ for } w_1 = 0.0, w_2 = 0.0, w_3 = 0.04, w_4 = 0.96 \qquad (1)$$

$$-\text{the minimal } p \text{ is } 0.12 \text{ for } w_1 = 0.0, w_2 = 0.0, w_3 = 0.04, w_4 = 0.08. \qquad (2)$$

Table 2. Further data for ontology extraction

nr	age	presc	ast	tear	nr	age	presc	ast	tear	nr	age	presc	ast	tear	nr	age	presc	ast	tear
9	y	m	t	n	13	p	h	t	n	17	pp	h	f	r	21	pp	m	t	r
10	pp	h	f	n	14	p	m	f	r	18	pp	h	t	r	22	y	h	f	r
11	y	h	f	n	15	p	m	f	n	19	pp	h	t	n	23	y	h	t	r
12	p	h	t	r	16	p	m	t	r	20	pp	m	f	r	24	y	m	t	r

The resulting ontology generated on the data set presented in Tables 1 and 2 is (with tolerance threshold for the similarities on sets equal to 0.96):

---

[2] For the full description see also ftp://ftp.ics.uci.edu/pub/machine-learning-databases/lenses/.

[3] We assume reflexivity ($\sigma(x, x) = 1$) and symmetry ($\sigma(x, y) = \sigma(y, x)$), too.

- for the maximal p (case (1)), we have concepts $C_0 = \emptyset$, $C_1 = \{1, 2, 3, 9, 13, 19\}$, $C_2 = \{4, 5, 6, 10, 11, 15\}$, $C_3 = \{7, 8, 14, 17, 20, 22\}$, $C_4 = \{12, 16, 18, 21, 2, 24\}$, $C_5 = C_1 \cup C_2$, $C_6 = C_3 \cup C_4$, $C_7 = \{1, 2, \ldots, 24\}$, ordered by inclusion (here the ontology reflects the domination of attribute 'tear' over other attributes)
- for the minimal p (case (2)), we have $C_0, C_1, C_2, C_3, C_4, C_5, C_7$ and $C_8 = C_2 \cup C_3$, $C_9 = C_1 \cup C_4$, also ordered by inclusion (here 'ast' is more substantial than above).

6   Conclusions

In the current paper we have shown a novel technique for machine learning similarities on tuples on the basis of similarities on base domains. We have shown an application of the method to extracting ontologies from data, using the algorithm of [1]. However, due to the page limit, we have restricted our considerations to crisp concepts, linear models based on weighting attributes and to a simple but illustrative example. Also the problem of machine learning similarities on sets deserves further attention. We plan to address these problems in a full version of this paper.

References

1. Doherty, P., Grabowski, M., Łukaszewicz, W., Szałas, A.: Towards a framework for approximate ontologies. Fundamenta Informaticae **57** (2003) 147–165
2. Catteano, G.: Abstract approximation spaces for rough theories. In Polkowski, L., Skowron, A., eds.: Rough Sets in Knowledge Discovery 1: Meth. and Appl. (1998) 59–98
3. Duentsch, I., Gediga, G.: Uncertainty measures of rough set prediction. Artificial Intelligence **106** (1998) 77–107
4. Skowron, A., Stepaniuk, J.: Generalized approximation spaces. In Lin, T., Wildberger, A., eds.: Soft Computing: Rough Sets, Fuzzy Logic, Neural Networks, Uncertainty Management, Knowledge Discovery. (1995) 18–21
5. Skowron, A., Stepaniuk, J.: Tolerance approximation spaces. Fundamenta Informaticae **27** (1996) 245–253
6. Doherty, P., Łukaszewicz, W., Szałas, A.: Tolerance spaces and approximative representational structures. In Günter, A., Kruse, R., Neumann, B., eds.: Proc. of the 26th German Conf. on Artificial Intelligence KI'2003. Volume 2821 of LNAI. (2003) 475–489
7. Doherty, P., Szałas, A.: On the correspondence between approximations and similarity. In Tsumoto, S., Slowinski, R., Komorowski, J., Grzymala-Busse, J., eds.: Proc. 4th Conf. RSCTC'2004. Volume 3066 of LNAI. (2004) 143–152
8. Gómez-Pérez, A., Fernández-López, M., Corcho, O.: Ontological Engineering with Examples from the Areas of Knowlegge Management, e-Commerce and the Semantic Web. Springer (2004)
9. Cimiano, P., Hotho, A., Staab, S.: Comparing conceptual, divisive and agglomerative clustering for learning taxonomies from text. In Mantaras, R., Saitta, L., eds.: Proc. ECAI'2004. (2004) 435–439
10. Lamparter, S., Ehrig, M., Tempich, C.: Knowledge extraction from classification schemas. In Meersman, R., Tari, Z., eds.: Proc. of CoopIS/DOA/ODBASE'2004. Volume 3290 of LNCS. (2004) 618–636

11. Maedche, A., Staab, S.: Measuring similarity between ontologies. In: Proc. of the EKAW-2002. Volume 2473 of LNCS/LNAI. (2002) 251–263
12. Maedche, A., Staab, S.: Comparing ontologies - similarity measures and a comparison study. Institute AIFB, University of Karlsruhe, Internal Report (2001)
13. Wang, X., De Baets, B., Kerre, E.: A comparative study of similarity measures. Fuzzy Sets and Systems **73** (1995) 259–268
14. Wettschereck, D., Aha, D.W., Mohri, T.: A review and empirical evaluation of feature weighting methods for a class of lazy learning algorithms. Artificial Intelligence Review **11** (1997) 273–314
15. Kononenko, I.: Estimating attributes: Analysis and extensions of RELIEF. In: European Conference on Machine Learning. (1994) 171–182
16. Stahl, A.: Approximation of utility functions by learning similarity measures. In Lenski, W., ed.: Logic versus Approximation. Volume 3075 of LNCS. (2004) 150–172
17. Nguyen, S.H.: Regularity Analysis and its Applications in Data Mining. Ph.D. Thesis. University of Warsaw (1999)
18. Doherty, P., Łukaszewicz, W., Szałas, A.: Approximative query techniques for agents with heterogeneous ontologies and perceptive capabilities. In Dubois, D., Welty, C., Williams, M.A., eds.: Proc. of 9th Int. Conf. KR'2004. (2004) 459–468
19. Doherty, P., Łukaszewicz, W., Szałas, A.: Approximate databases and query techniques for agents with heterogenous perceptual capabilities. In: Proc. of the 7th Int. Conf. on Information Fusion, FUSION'2004. (2004) 175–182
20. Cendrowska, J.: PRISM: An algorithm for inducing modular rules. Int. J. Man-Mach. Stud. **27** (1987) 349–370

Conceptual Query Expansion

Orland Hoeber, Xue-Dong Yang, and Yiyu Yao

University of Regina, Regina, SK S4S 0A2, Canada
Orland.Hoeber@uregina.ca

Abstract. Query expansion has been extensively studied as a technique for increasing information retrieval performance. However, due to the volume of documents available on the web, many of the techniques that have been successful in traditional information retrieval systems do not scale well to web information retrieval. We propose a new technique based on conceptual semantic theories, in contrast to the structuralist semantic theories upon which other techniques are based. The source of the query expansion information is the concept network knowledge base. Query terms are matched to those contained in the concept network, from which concepts are deduced and additional query terms are selected. In this paper, we describe the theoretical basis for this in-progress research, along with some preliminary results.

1 Introduction

Query expansion is a technique for dealing with the word mismatch problem in information retrieval systems. In general, the word mismatch problem is a result of different terms being used in reference to a single concept, both in the documents and in the user queries[1]. Query expansion is the process of adding additional terms to the original query in order to improve retrieval performance [2]. Through query expansion, the effects of the word mismatch problem are reduced, resulting in a higher ratio of relevant documents in the retrieval results (precision) and a higher ratio of the relevant documents from the collection that are retrieved (recall).

Recent studies have shown that users have difficulties choosing good terms to add to their query, even when presented with a list of potentially good terms [3]. Therefore, we focus on automatic query expansion techniques. The general process for automatic query expansion begins with matching the terms from the user query to a knowledge base. From this knowledge base, the best new terms are added to the query automatically, and the expanded query is then used.

A number of different techniques for automatic query expansion have been proposed in recent years. In work by Qiu & Frei [4], a similarity thesaurus was constructed based on the similarity of term pairs across the complete document collection. New terms to be added were based on similarity to all rather than individual query terms. In Voorhees' system [5], the queries were expanded using the term relationships encoded in the WordNet thesaurus [6], a lexical-semantic knowledge base. The relationships used were the synonym, hypernym/hyponym and meronym/

P.S. Szczepaniak et al. (Eds.): AWIC 2005, LNAI 3528, pp. 190–196, 2005.

holonym relationships among nouns. Xu & Croft [7] used the top ranked documents returned by the original query as the knowledge base for the query expansion. In this technique, the co-occurrence of terms was calculated using only the passages that contained the query terms, rather than the whole document.

Information retrieval of web documents poses a number of problems for these query expansion techniques. Due to the extremely large volume of documents on the web, analysis of the entire collection (e.g. [4]) is not feasible. In addition, web queries are very short, often consisting of only two or three words [8]. Techniques that have reported success with longer queries (e.g. [7]) may not prove to be very effective with short queries. A third difficulty is that the collection of web documents is very general, necessitating a very general knowledge base. However, a knowledge base which is too general (e.g. [5]) can result in terms being added to the query that are not actually related to the user's query terms in the document collection.

Our approach is to use a concept network to generate a conceptual query expansion for web information retrieval. This is ongoing research being conducted as part of a larger research project consisting of meta-searching, clustering, and visual representations of the search results based on the concepts intended by the user's queries, rather than just the specific terms in the query.

Briefly, a concept network is a bipartite graph consisting of two classes of nodes: concepts and phrases. Such a concept network can be constructed through the statistical analysis of concept-phrase co-occurrence in a concept hierarchy such as the Open Directory Project [9]. Within the concept network, weighted edges between the concepts and the phrases represent the degree to which the phrase has shown to be a good indicator of the concept. Query expansion is performed by selecting additional phrases from those that are connected to the same concepts as the user's query phrases. Weight thresholds ensure that only concepts that are strongly connected to the user's query phrases are selected, and only phrases that are strongly connected to these concepts are included in the expanded query.

By basing the construction of our concept network knowledge base on a human-reviewed subset of the entire collection of web documents (i.e, the Open Directory Project), we avoid the complications introduced by the size of the web, and the generality of the collection. The short queries that are common in web information retrieval remain a problem; there may not be enough evidence in a short query to clearly indicate a single concept. Our larger research project addresses this problem by allowing users to interactively refine their query in a visual manner.

2   Theoretical Basis for the Concept Network

Semantics, the study of the meanings of words in a language, provides many theories that attempt to explain the meaning of a word or phrase. Of interest for query expansion are the structuralist theories of meaning and the conceptual theories of meaning [10].

The structuralist theories hold that in order to understand the meaning of a word, one has to understand how it functions together with, and in contrast to, other related words. The meaning of a word consists of the relationships it has with other words in the language (i.e., synonyms, homonyms, polysems, antonyms, etc.). In order for two people to communicate, they must have a similar understanding of how the words they use are related to other words in the language [10].

In the conceptual theories, the meaning of a word is the concept in the mind of the person using that word; communication is possible via a shared connection between words and concepts. That is, there is a mapping between the set of words in the vocabulary and the set of concepts in the minds of the users. While there will not be a single unique mapping that all users of a language share, the individual mappings must be similar to one another with respect to the vocabulary used in order for communication to occur [10].

Both of these theories infer the meanings of words used by an individual with respect to other objects. That is, the semantics of words are not provided by definitions, reference to instances, or their use, as we are normally accustomed; rather the meaning of words are provided by their relationship to other objects. These theories differ in the type of objects to which words are related (i.e., other words in the structuralist theories, higher-level concepts in the conceptual theories). We note that with the conceptual theories, one can infer a relationship between a pair of words if there is a concept which they have in common. The level of detail of this common concept provides a clue to the degree to which the terms are related: terms linked through a high-level (general) concept may have a weak relationship, whereas terms linked through a low-level (specific) concept may have a strong relationship.

Previous work on query expansion, both those that rely on a general thesaurus as the basis for the query expansion [5], and those that rely on the construction of a specialized thesaurus from the text of the corpus being searched [4, 7], follow the structuralist theories. Queries are expanded to include additional terms that are related to the original terms in the thesaurus. The success of these techniques varies depending on whether the query expansion is manually chosen or automatic, as well as the specificity of the thesaurus used.

Other theoretical approaches for formally specifying concepts in terms of intensions and extensions, such as formal concept analysis [11], have a basis in the conceptual theories. For example, applying formal concept analysis to information retrieval, the intension of a concept is the set of terms that are present in all the documents that represent the extension of the concept. Terms do not have a direct relationship to one another; they have an implied relationship through a common concept. However, such approaches are vulnerable to the word mismatch problem, and the size of the collection of documents in web information retrieval.

In this research, we hypothesize that the mappings between words and concepts proposed by the conceptual theories provides a more effective connection between words (via a common concept) than the thesaurus-based approach of the structuralist theories. Basing the query expansion on such a mapping results in a conceptual query expansion where the basis for the expansion are the concepts intended by the original query.

3   The Concept Network

We define a concept network as a weighted bipartite graph that links concept nodes to phrase nodes. More formally, a concept network $CN = \{C, P, E\}$ consists of a set of concept nodes C, a set of phrase nodes P and a set of edges $E = \{c_i, p_j, w_{ij}\}$, where $c_i \in C$, $p_j \in P$, and c_i and p_j are related with a weight w_{ij}. The weight w_{ij} of an edge in the concept network represents the degree to which the phrase represents the intension of the concept.

While hand-crafting a concept network is possible, it is only feasible for a small set of concepts and phrases. However, given a well defined set of concepts, and a set of documents assigned to these concepts, a concept network can be automatically constructed as shown below. During this process, a bag-of-words approach is used to count the occurrences of noun phrases within each document. The noun phrase frequency is used to calculate the weight values w_{ij}.

For example, consider the set of documents $D_i = \{d_{i1}, \ldots, d_{in}\}$ which are a subset of the extension of the concept $c_i \in C$. For each document d_{ik}, the set of phrases used in this document is $P_{ik} = \{p_{1,ik}, \ldots, p_{m,ik}\}$. We define a function $f(d_{ik}, p_j)$ as the occurrence count of phrase p_j in document d_{ik}. The value for the edge weight between concept c_i and phrase p_j is given by:

$$w_{ij} = \frac{\sum_{k=1}^{n} \frac{f(d_{ik}, p_j)}{\sum_{l=1}^{m} f(d_{ik}, p_{l,ik})}}{n}$$

After all the concepts for which we are given document sets have been analysed, we normalize the edge weights from each phrase in the concept network. For a phrase p_i that is connected to r concepts whose index is given by the relation $f(x)$, $x = 1 \ldots r$, the normalization is performed via the simple calculation:

$$w_{ij} = \frac{w_{ij}}{\sum_{k=1}^{r} w_{if(k)}}$$

Using the normalized average noun phrase frequency rather than a simple total of the noun phrase occurrences reduces the impact of the different document sizes and different numbers of documents that represent a concept in the calculation of the weight values. In particular, without this calculation, a single large document could provide phrase weights that overshadow the weights provided by a number of smaller documents; a similar situation is avoided for concepts that have a large number of documents. Further, without the normalization, common phrases that are included in many documents for many concepts would have a very high weight value, even though these phrases are of little value in describing the concept. With normalization, the weights for these common terms will be significantly reduced.

We note that the automatic construction of a concept network represents the training phase of this system. In our preliminary research, we used subsets of the Open Directory Project as the training data to construct preliminary concept networks automatically.

4 Conceptual Query Expansion Using the Concept Network

Given a concept network $CN = \{C, P, E\}$, and a query $Q = \{q_1, \ldots, q_n\}$ consisting of query phrases q_i, the process of constructing a query expansion is as follows:

1. Match the query phrases q_i to the phrase set P to obtain a $P' \subseteq P$.
2. Obtain the set of concepts $C' \subseteq C$ which are connected to the phrases in P'. We use two parameters to control this operation: a weight threshold w_e, and an phrase ratio PR. First, all the concepts that are connected to the phrases in P' with a weight greater than w_e are chosen as candidate concepts in C'. Each of these concepts are then evaluated to determine the ratio of the phrases in P' to which they are connected with a weight greater then w_e. If this ratio is less than PR, the candidate concept is dropped from C'.
3. Obtain the set of phrases $P'' \subseteq P$ which are connected to the concepts C'. We use a weight threshold parameter w_d to control this operation. All phrases that are connected to the concepts in C' with a weight greater than w_d are chosen as the phrases in P''.
4. Perform a union of the original query phrases and the new set of phrases to obtain the query expansion: $QE = Q \cup P''$.

For example, consider the concept network in Figure 1, which was constructed automatically from a subset of the Open Directory Project, as described in the previous section. In this figure, the concepts are represented by the shaded boxes, and the phrases are represented by the ovals. In the interest of clarity, distance is used to represent the edge weights, rather than displaying the weight values; phrases with very low weights (i.e., very common phrases that are used in the documents of many concepts) are excluded from this figure. Suppose we are given a user query $Q = \{$ "information", "visualization", "problems", "software", weight thresholds $w_e = 0.05$ and $w_d = 0.1$, and phrase ratio of $PR = 75\%$.

In the first step, this user query is matched to the phrases in the concept network to arrive at $P' = \{$ "information", "visualization", "software"$\}$. In the second step, we follow only the edges that have a weight greater w_e to obtain our set of candidate concepts $C' = \{$ "computer graphics", "distributed computing", "artificial intelligence"$\}$. The candidate concept "computer graphics" is connected to 100% of the phrases with a weight greater than w_e; "distributed computing" is connected to 33%; and "artificial intelligence" is connected to 66%. Since these last two concepts have phrase ratios less than our phrase ratio parameter PR, they are dropped from the set, resulting in $C' = \{$ "computer graphics"$\}$.

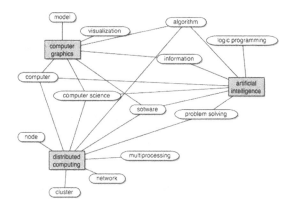

Fig. 1. A sample concept network constructed automatically from a subset of the Open Directory Project

In the third step, we follow the edges that have a weight greater than w_d to obtain our phrases that are related to the concepts in C', resulting in $P'' =\{$"computer", "model", "visualization"$\}$. In the final step, we merge the original query and these concept phrases, giving us $QE =\{$"information", "visualization", "problems", "software", "computer", "model"$\}$.

The end result is a query expansion that has included phrases only from the concepts that the system decided were related to the original query. Such a query will be much more specific to the deduced concepts than the original query. We anticipate that this query will result in a set of documents that are more relevant to the actual information need of the user. Research regarding the effectiveness of this system, along with determining appropriate settings for the parameters w_e, w_d, and PR under various conditions, is ongoing.

5   Conclusion

In this paper, we presented an overview of our ongoing research on the use of a concept network as the knowledge base for inducing a query expansion based on the concepts deduced from the original query terms. We acknowledge that the quality of this conceptual query expansion depends on the quality of the concept network; we are working towards the automatic construction of a large, high quality concept network using the Open Directory Project as the source of concept extensions.

Future work includes determining appropriate initial values for the parameters that control the conceptual query expansion process, measuring the performance of conceptual query expansion using test collections such as the TREC Web Track collections [12], using conceptual query expansion in a meta-search and clustering system, and using the concept network as a basis for the visualization of search results.

References

1. Furnas, G.W., Landauer, T.K., Gomez, L.M., Dumais, S.T.: The vocabulary problem in human-system communication. Communications of the ACM **30** (1987)
2. Efthimiadis, E.N.: Query expansion. Annual Review of Information Systems and Technology (ARIST) **31** (1996)
3. Ruthven, I.: Re-examining the potential effectiveness of interactive query expansion. In: Proceedings of the ACM SIGIR Conference on Research and Development in Information Retrieval. (2003)
4. Qiu, Y., Frei, H.P.: Concept based query expansion. In: Proceedings of the ACM SIGIR Conference on Research and Development in Information Retrieval. (1993)
5. Voorhees, E.M.: Query expansion using lexical-semantic relations. In: Proceedings of the ACM SIGIR Conference on Research and Development in Information Retrieval. (1994)
6. Miller, G.A.: Wordnet: a lexical database for english. Communications of the ACM **38** (1995)
7. Xu, J., Croft, W.B.: Improving the effectiveness of information retrieval with local context analysis. ACM Transactions on Information Systems **18** (2000)
8. Spink, A., Wolfram, D., Jansen, B.J., Saracevic, T.: Searching the web: the public and their queries. Journal of the American Society for Information Science and Technology **52** (2001)
9. Project, O.D.: A human-edited directory of web pages, http://www.dmoz.org/ (2004)
10. Goddard, C.: Semantic Analysis: A Practical Introduction. Oxford University Press (1998)
11. Ganter, B., Wille, R.: Formal Concept Analysis: mathematical foundations. Springer-Verlag (1999)
12. Voorhees, E.M.: Overview of trec 2003. In: The Twelfth Text REtrieval Conference (TREC 2003), National Institute of Standards and Technology Special Publication (2003)

A General Framework of Targeted Marketing

Jiajin Huang[1], Ning Zhong[2], Y.Y. Yao[3], and Chunnian Liu[1]

[1] Multimedia and Intelligent Software Technology Beijing Municipal Key Laboratory,
College of Computer Science and Technology, Beijing University of Technology,
100022, Beijing, P.R. China
`hjj@emails.bjut.edu.cn`
[2] Department of Information Engineering, Maebashi Institute of Technology,
Maebashi-City 371-0816, Japan
`zhong@maebashi-it.ac.jp`
[3] Department of Computer Science, University of Regina,
Regina, Saskatchewan, Canada S4S 0A2
`yyao@cs.uregina.ca`

Abstract. In this paper, inspired by a unified probabilistic model of information retrieval, we propose a general framework of targeted marketing by considering three types of information, namely, the customer profiles, the product profiles, and the transaction databases. The notion of market value functions is introduced, which measure the potential value or profit of marketing a product to a customer. Four sub-models are examined for the estimation of a market value function. Based on market value functions, two targeted marketing strategies, namely, customer-oriented targeted marketing and product-oriented targeted marketing, are suggested. This paper focuses on the conceptual development of the framework. The detailed computation of a market value function and the evaluation of the proposed framework will be reported in another paper.

1 Introduction

Targeted marketing typically involves the identification of a relative small group of potential buyers from a huge pool of customers, or the identification of a relative small set of items from a huge pool of products [7]. It is an important area of application for data mining [10] and a crucial area of Web Intelligence for e-business portals [9, 11]. Data mining techniques are often used to achieve the goal of targeted marketing [10]. For example, using transaction database, we can find the associations between items purchased together. According to the discovered association, when a customer has purchased one set of items, we can recommend the associated items as the targeted products [4]. This application of items association is simple and effective. However, its effectiveness is limited due to a lack of consideration of the customer features and product characteristics.

For a more complete and realistic model of targeted marketing, one needs to consider at least three types of information and knowledge. They are the customer features represented by customer profiles, the product characteristics

P.S. Szczepaniak et al. (Eds.): AWIC 2005, LNAI 3528, pp. 197–203, 2005.

represented by product profiles, and the transaction data that link customers and products. Together, they provide useful and necessary information for Customer Relation Management (CRM). Typically, customer profiles are used for the purpose of personalization; the product profiles are used for stock management; and transaction table is used for recommendation [1]. There does not exist a common framework that combines the three types of information in a unified manner.

The main objective of this paper is to propose a general framework of targeted marketing by using all three types of information. The model is inspired by a probabilistic model of information retrieval developed by Robertson *et al.* [6]. However, instead of using the concept of the probability of relevance, we introduce the notion of market values. A market value function measures the degree of connection of a product and a customer with respect to their potential value or profit. Based on the general model of Robertson *et al.*, we can also identify four sub-models for targeted marketing. The four models describe relationships between a class of products and a class of customers, between a class of customers and a single product, between a single customer and a class of products, and between a single product and a single customer, respectively.

We introduce two targeted marketing strategies: the customer-oriented targeted marketing and the product-oriented targeted marketing. Given a product or a group of products, the customer-oriented strategy ranks a set of customers based on the market value function. On the other hand, given a customer or a group of customers, the product-oriented strategy ranks a set of products. The two strategies are complementary to each other, and serve the common goal of achieving more profits through targeted marketing.

In this paper, due to space limitation, we only deal with the conceptual development of the model. The detailed computation of market value function and the evaluation are under way and will be reported in future publications.

2   The Formulation of the Model

There are many issues and steps to be considered in targeted marketing [1]. For the formulation of our framework, we consider three related issues, the collection of data and information sources stored as information tables, the analysis of multiple information tables (i.e., constructing models for estimating market value functions), and the application of the results from analysis for targeted marketing (i.e., designing targeted marketing strategies according to a market value function).

2.1   Information Sources

There are at least three types of information and knowledge for targeted marketing. They are the customer features represented by customer profiles, the product characteristics represented by product profiles, and the transaction data. For customer profile, there are two kinds of information. One is demographic information which is given explicitly by customers. The other is implicit information derived from transaction data, for example customers' preference. For product profile, generally, it is related to inherent properties of a product. For transaction data, it represents customers' options about products. On the one hand, options can be given explicitly. For example, we know whether a customer has bought a product from purchase records. On the other hand, options can also be derived from implicit information such as Web log, cookies by using Web usage mining approach.

Formally, the three types of information can be represented as information tables. The rows of the tables correspond to objects of the universe, the columns correspond to their attributes, and each cell is the value of an object with respect to an attribute. Take a movie database as an example [12]. An alternative solution of processing the database as follows. Customer profile table shows information about age, gender, education. *etc.* of customers. Product profile table shows properties of movies, such as title, genre, and so on. Transaction table shows customers' options about movies which are made on a 5-star scale. In this example, options are represented as "0" or "1", where "0" denotes that the customer has not bought the movie while "1" denotes that the customer has bought the movie. Let $c_1, c_2...$ denote customers and $m_1, m_2...$ denote movies. The relationship among the three tables is shown in Figure 1. From Figure 1, we can see that customer profile table and product profile table represent information about customers and movies in transaction table, respectively, and on the other hand, transaction table links customer profile table and product profile table. Together, they provide useful information for targeted marketing.

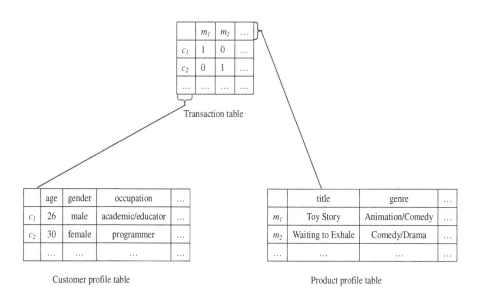

Fig. 1. An Example of Information Source for Targeted Marketing

2.2   Models for Estimating Market Value Functions

For the purpose of targeted marketing, we can analyze the available multiple information tables from various aspects. Although different types and forms of knowledge can be obtained, we suggest the use of market value functions (mvf) as a representation of the results of such an analysis. A market value function can be in different forms, depending on the assumption of a particular model. In general, it is a two place function taking customer and product as its arguments. The market values can be interpreted by more familiar concepts, such as risk, cost, value, profit, understandability, actionability, *etc.*, and they compute the potential market gains from marketing a particular product (or a group of products) to a particular customer (or a group of customers).

In order to study market value functions, we adopt an information retrieval model proposed by Robertson *et al.* [6], which consists of four sub-models as shown in Figure 2. In this figure, let c be a single customer, C a class of customers, p a single product and P a class of products. On the one hand, given a product, we may group together customers according to the customers profile or their transaction, then estimate market value $mvf(C, p)$ by using model1. The underlying assumption is that similar type of customers tend to have similar preferences. On the other hand, given a customer, we may group product together according to their properties, then estimate market value $mvf(c, P)$ by using model2. Alternatively, we can cluster customers and products respectively, and then estimate market value $mvf(C, P)$ by using model0. Based on the above three models, we can estimate market value $mvf(c, p)$ by using model3 which describes the relationship between a given customer c and a given product p.

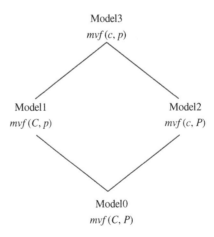

Fig. 2. The targeted marketing model

The applicability of each sub-model depends on the available information. If transaction data and customer profile are available, we can estimate $mvf(C, p)$

by using model1. If transaction data and product profile are available, we can estimate $mvf(c, P)$ by using model2. If all of the above three types of information are available, we can obtain the information of each class of customers and each class of products and estimate $mvf(C, P)$ by using model0. We can combines all of the information for estimating $mvf(c, p)$ by using model3.

2.3   Two Targeted Marketing Strategies

Based on the proposed model, we can estimate market value which measures the degree of the connection of a particular customer (or a group of customers) and a particular product (or a group of products) with respect to their potential value or profit. According to a market value function, we can rank customers based on their market values for a given product (or a group of products). On the other hand, we can also rank products for a given customer (or a group of customers). The former marketed targeting strategy is called customer-oriented targeted marketing and the latter is called products-oriented targeted marketing.

Customer-oriented targeted marketing We can rank customers one by one by using $mvf(c, p)$ for a given product, or rank customers group by group by using $mvf(C, p)$ and $mvf(C, P)$ for a given product and a given group of products, respectively, or rank customers one by one by using $mvf(c, P)$ for a given group of products. A cut-off point of the ranked list may be chosen based on various criteria such as financial constraints. We can select top customers before the cut-off point as targeted customers for promotion.

Product-oriented targeted marketing The ranked list of products for a given customer and a given group of customers can be obtained by using $mvf(c, p)$ and $mvf(C, p)$, respectively. The ranked list of groups of products can also be obtained by using $mvf(c, P)$ and $mvf(C, P)$ for a given customer and a given group of customers, respectively.

3   Relationship to Existing Work

There is a close relationship between our model and three basic approaches, namely, collaborative filtering, content-based filtering and demographic-based filtering. Collaborative filtering is to recommend new products to a given customer based on what both the customer and like-minded customers have bought [2]. Content-based filtering is to recommend products which are similar to what a given customer has bought [3]. Demographic-based filtering is to use demographic customer information to identify potential customers [5]. Obviously, collaborative and content-based recommendation are products-oriented targeted marketing and demographic-based recommendation is customers-oriented targeted marketing. Hybrid recommender systems which combine these three approaches have been used to deal with more information and knowledge available [3, 5]. Our model describes a general framework for targeted marketing, covering these existing approaches. In addition, explanation-oriented data mining uses customer features and product characteristics to search for an explanation for the association discovered from transaction table [8]. It provides an alternative solution for explaining the existence of the patterns.

4   Conclusions

Targeted or direct marketing is an important profit-driven marketing strategy involving the identification of a group of most profitable customers or products. It is an interdisciplinary study that combines marketing methods and database, data analysis, and data mining technologies. This paper presents a general framework for targeted marketing. In the framework, customer features, product characteristics and transaction data are used to build four sub-models for the estimation of market value functions. Based on market value functions, two targeted marketing strategies are suggested. According to a market value function, the customer-oriented strategy ranks customers with respect to a product, and the product-oriented strategy ranks products with respect to a customer. This paper only deals with the conceptual development of the model. Future work includes detailed computation of a market value function and the evaluation.

Acknowledgement

The above works are partially supported by Open Foundation of Multimedia and Intelligent Software Technology Beijing Municipal Key Laboratory , the NSFC major research program: "Basic Theory and Core Techniques of Non-Canonical Knowledge" (60496322), the Natural Science Foundation of China (69883001) and Beijing Municipal Natural Science Foundation (4022003).

References

1. Associates, D.S.: *The New Direct Marketing*, McGraw-Hill (1999)
2. Breese, J, Hecherman, D, Kadie, C.: "Empirical analysis of predictive algorithms for collaborative filtering", *Proc. the 14th Conference on Uncertainty in Artificial Intelligence (UAI'98)* (1998), 43–52
3. Balabanovic, M., Shoham, Y.: "Fab: Content-based, Collaborative Recommendation", *Communications of the ACM*, 40 (1997), 66–72
4. Han, J.W., Kamber, M.: *Data Mining Concepts and Techniques*, Higher Education Press and Morgan Kaufmann Publishers (2002)
5. Pazzani, M.J.: "A Framework for Collaborative, Content-based and Demograhic Filtering", *Artificial Intelligence Review*, 13(5-6) (1999), 393–408
6. Robertson, S.E., Maron, M.E. and Cooper, W.S.: "Probability of Relevance: A Unification of Two Competing Models for Document Retrieval", *Information Technology: Research and Development*, 1 (1982), 1–21
7. Yao, Y.Y., Zhong, N., Huang, J., Ou, C, Liu, C.: "Using Market Value Functions for Targeted Marketing Data Mining", *International Journal of Pattern Recognition and Artificial Intelligence*, 16(8) (2002), 1117–1131

8. Yao, Y.Y., Zhao, Y, Maguire, R.B.: "Explanation Oriented Association Mining Using Rough Set Theory", *Proc. RSFDGrC 2003*, LNAI 2639, Springer (2003), 165–172
9. Zhong, N.: "Towards Web Intelligence", Menassalvas, R.E. , Segovia, J., Szczepaniak, P.S. (eds.): *Advances in Web Intelligence*, LNAI 2663, Springer (2003), 1–14
10. Zhong, N., Yao, Y.Y., Liu, C, Huang, J., Ou, C.: "Data Mining for Targeted Marketing", Zhong, N., Liu, J.(eds.): *Intelligent Technologies for Information Analysis*, Springer (2004), 109–134
11. Zhong, N., Liu, J., Yao, Y.Y. (eds.): *Web Intelligence*, Springer (2003)
12. http://www.movielens.org/

Rough Sets Approach to Medical Diagnosis System

Grzegorz Ilczuk[1] and Alicja Wakulicz-Deja[2]

[1] HEITEC AG Systemhaus fuer Automatisierung und Informationstechnologie,
Werner-von-Siemens-Strasse 61, 91052 Erlangen, Germany
Grzegorz.Ilczuk@ilczuk.com,
[2] Institut of Informatics University of Silesia,
Bedzinska 39, 41-200 Sosnowiec, Poland
wakulicz@us.edu.pl

Abstract. Pawlak's Rough Sets Theory is one of many mathematical approaches to handle imprecision and uncertainty. The main advantage of the theory over other techniques is that it does not need any preliminary or additional information about analyzed data. This feature of rough set theory favors its usage in decision systems where new relations among data must be uncovered. In this paper we use data from a medical data set containing information about heart diseases and applied drugs to construct a decision system, test its classification accuracy and propose a methodology to improve an accurateness and a testability of generated "if-then" decision rules.

1 Introduction

Nowadays capabilities of generating and collecting data within computer systems are growing rapidly. Gathered data are stored in huge and powerful database systems. Common for database systems is that they do not offer enough possibilities to analyze data they manage. An analysis of such information is a scope of research for Data Mining [3]. This process groups identical properties of datasets in classes. Such classes are distinguishable through values of their attributes. At the end of this process *classification rules*, which classify each class according to values of its attributes, are calculated. If preconditions of a rule are satisfied by an object from dataset, then it belongs to a certain class.

Currently a lot of research effort is directed toward the invention of new algorithms and much less into gaining experience in applying them to important practical applications. Therefore in our research we focus on a complete system which provides an insight into understanding the relations between complex medical data. Key elements of this system are: importing and converting narrative text information into a data understandable by standard machine learning algorithms, selection of strong attributes based on user's criteria and generation of easily verifiable und understandable by humans decision rules. In this paper we focus on following elements of the described system: generation of decision rules with Grzymala-Busse LEM2 algorithm [4] and post-processing of

P.S. Szczepaniak et al. (Eds.): AWIC 2005, LNAI 3528, pp. 204–210, 2005.

achieved rules to improve their accuracy. Additionally readability of the generated decision rules and their appliance in a medical domain is experts from an electrocardiology clinic.

2   Basic Notions

Information system [5, 6] is a pair $\mathbf{A} = (U, A)$ where U is a non-empty, finite set called the universe and A is a non-empty, finite set of *attributes*, i.e. $a : U \rightarrow V_a$ for $a \in A$, where V_a is called the *value set* of attribute a. Elements of U are called *objects*.

It is convenient to treat an information system as a two-dimensional array (matrix) in which rows relate to the corresponding objects and columns include the values of attributes on objects. This representation of information system allows to describe each object in a single row of the information table [1].

The special case of information systems called *decision system* is defined as $\mathbf{A} = (U, A \cup \{d\})$, where $d \notin A$ is a distinguished attribute called *decision* and elements of A are called *conditions*.

A *decision rule* is defined as $r = (a_{i1} = v_1) \wedge \ldots \wedge (a_{im} = v_m) \Rightarrow (d = k)$ where $1 \leq i_1 < \ldots < i_m \leq |A|, v_i \in V_{ai}$. We say an object matches a rule if its attributes satisfy all *atomic formulas* $(a_{ij} = v_j)$ of the rule. A rule is called minimal consistent with $\mathbf{A}$ when any decision rule r' created from r by removing one of atomic formula of r is not consistent with $\mathbf{A}$.

3   Data Material

Data used in this case study are collected from Electrocardiology Clinic of Silesian Medical Academy in Katowice-the leading electrocardiology clinic in Poland specializing in hospitalization of severe heart diseases. Data of 2039 patients in average age over 70 hospitalized between 2003 and 2004 is used in this publication. Most of these patients have combination of several diseases mostly as a consequence of high blood pressure, diagnosed in more then 70% cases. High blood pressure workloads the heart and arteries and if continues for a long time damages the heart, arteries, blood vessels of the brain and kidneys, resulting in stroke, heart failure, kidney failure or heart attack. Other common group of heart diseases are abnormal heart rhythms (arrhythmias) caused by problems with the electrical system, which instead of steady, rhythmic beat generate long-lasting or transient impulses, which are too fast or too slow, which can lead to sudden cardiac death. Another heart disease is cardiomyopathy (damage of heart muscle) cause by an infection or a heart attack. All patients in the used dataset were, because of their severe heart disease, under drug treatment. Often a combination of two or more following groups of drugs were used:

1. Angiotensin Converting Enzyme (ACE) Inhibitors, which open wider blood vessels so blood can flow through more easily. These drugs act by blocking formation of angiotensin, a hormone that causes tightening of arteries and sodium retention
2. Beta-blockers, change force and frequency of the heartbeat thus reducing workload and pressure on the heart and blood vessels
3. Statins (HMG-CoA reductase inhibitors), block an enzyme (HMG-CoA reductase) responsible for making cholesterol thus reducing level of LDL cholesterol
4. Nitrates, they relax smooth muscle and widen blood vessels what makes the blood flow better, reduces blood pressure, reduces the workload on the heart and allows more oxygen-rich blood to reach the heart muscle
5. Diuretics, which reduce the amount of water and sodium in the body are not only used in high blood pressure disease but also as a heart stroke prevention

Medical expert's knowledge about heart diseases and correlation between them allowed us to build a decision table from medical reports written in narrative text. The described system has following attributes:

1. **tds_ATT** - Atrial fibrillation and flutter
2. **tds_CIHD** - Chronic ischaemic heart disease
   1-Atherosclerotic heart disease or Aneurysm of heart
   2-Ischaemic cardiomyopathy
   4-Myocardial infarction in past
3. **tds_SSS** - Sick Sinus Syndrome
4. **tds_AVB** - Atrioventricular block and left, right bundle-branch
   1-Atrioventricular block first degree or Left, Right bundle-branch block
   2-Atrioventricular block second and third degree
5. **tds_HYPERENSION** - Hypertension and Hypertensive heart diseases
   1-Hypertension
   2-Hypertrophic cardiomyopathy
6. **tds_ANGINAP** - Angina pectoris
   1-Unstable
   2-Chronic (CSS I,II)
   4-Severe chronic (CSS III,IV)
7. **tds_PTACH** - Paroxysmal tachycardia
   1-Supraventricular tachycardia
   2-Ventricular tachycardia
8. **tds_MAS** - Stokes-Adams Syndrome
9. **tds_VALVEDIS** - Valve disorders
   1-Mitral valve disorders
   2-Aortic valve disorders
   4-Tricuspid valve disorders
10. **tds_CEREBD** - Cerebrovascular diseases
11. **tds_DIABETES** - Diabetes
12. **tds_HYPERCHOL** - Hypercholesterolaemia

A value of each attribute is set to 1 if a disease coded by an attribute, was diagnosed and to 0 otherwise. If an attribute codes more then one disease then a value of the attribute is a logical OR operation on each diagnosed disease. This coding allows to group within an attribute heart diseases originated from similar causes.

Three decision tables were build from presented decision system, each containing twelve described input attributes and one of three following decision attributes:

1. **tds_ACE** - Prescription of ACE Inhibitor (1-if prescribed, 0-otherwise)
2. **tds_BBloker** - Prescription of Beta-bloker (1-if prescribed, 0-otherwise)
3. **tds_Statin** - Prescription of Statin (1-if prescribed, 0-otherwise)

The choice of decision attributes reflects a usage frequency of drugs and their importance in medical treatment in the electro cardiology clinic.

4   Test Environment

During experiments described in this paper an RSES (Rough Set Exploration System) [2] environment in version 2.1.1 was used. All decision rules were generated using LEM2 [4] algorithm, which shows a better total accuracy in medical datasets over a pure covering algorithm and an exhaustive algorithm based on boolean reasoning approach [7]. For a rule generation each of three decision tables (one for each decision attribute) was divided into two tables, one containing 60% and the other 40% of data from the original table. Rules generated based on attribute values of the *train table* (containing 60% of records) were then tested on the *test table* according to the *train-and-test* procedure.

Following two-phased methodology was used to find the strongest decision rules:

1. For each of three train tables five covering ratios (1.0, 0.95, 0.9, 0.8, 0.7) and five rule shortening ratios (1.0 0.9, 0.8, 0.7, 0.6) were used for rule generation, thus resulting in 25 rule sets for each of three train tables. Covering ratio (cover parameter) defines expected degree of coverage of the training set by derived rules. Shortening ratio is a coefficient between 0 and 1, which determines how "aggressive" the shortening procedure should be, where 1.0 means no shortening occurs and values toward zero mean that the algorithm attempts to maximally shorten reducts. This definition of shortening ratio means in fact a threshold imposed on the relative size of positive region after shortening [2]. At the end of the phase five combination of covering and shortening ratio , which gave the best total accuracy and total coverage were chosen for the phase two.
2. During this phase from all three original decision tables an decision attribute was removed. Then missing values of each decision attribute were calculated based on rule sets selected in the phase one. As a result five tables with reproduced values of decision attribute were created for each of three decision

attributes. A table with the lowest rate of missing values was considered as the best solution and the rule set used to create the table was proved by medical experts from the electrocardiology clinic.

5   Results

Results after calculating the 25 rule sets for each decision attribute show, that the best total accuracy was achieved for rule shortening ratio between 0.8 and 0.7. The best results for a generation of missing decision attributes in phase two were achieved for covering ratio 0.95. Both results indicate that a certain level of roughness must be used in order to improve accuracy of calculated rules for uncertain datasets. Summary results are shown in the table 1. A few of the strongest rules for the tds_ACE=1 class are shown in the table 2.

Table 1. Results for all three decision attributes

Covering ratio	Shortening ratio	Total accuracy/ Total coverage	Accuracy 0/ Coverage 0	Accuracy 1/ Coverage 1
Decision attribute:tds_ACE				
0.95	0.80	0.767/0.988	0.473/0.977	0.907/0.993
Decision attribute:tds_BBloker				
0.95	0.70	0.667/0.956	0.413/0.942	0.850/0.966
Decision attribute:tds_Statin				
0.95	0.70	0.665/0.958	0.831/0.965	0.455/0.950

Table 2. The strongest decision rules for the tds_ACE=1 class

Rule	Support
(tds_HYPERENSION=1)	693
(tds_MAS=1) & (tds_DIABETES=1)	121
(tds_CIHD=1) & (tds_DIABETES=1)	131
(tds_MAS=1) & (tds_ANGINAP=2) & (tds_HYPERCHOL=0)	83
(tds_DIABETES=1) & (tds_AVB=0)	77
(tds_MAS=1) & (tds_AVB=1)	62
(tds_HYPERCHOL=1) & (tds_DIABETES=1)	73
(tds_MAS=0) & (tds_HYPERENSION=1) & (tds_AVB=2)	76

Results presented in the table 1 show that the decision system classifies objects from the test table with the best accuracy (over 76%) for decision attribute tds_ACE. Correct classification of attributes tds_BBloker and tds_Statin reached about 67% total accuracy. Satisfactory results of 90% accuracy for tds_ACE=1 class and 85% for tds_BBloker=1 class shows that the choice of attributes in the decision table was correct.

On the other hand, results for the class tds_Statin=1 with 45% accuracy indicate that for this drug the decision table must be extended with some additional information to allow more accurate classification. Medical experts when confronted with achieved results also pointed out, that Statins are widely used as a prevention drug against heart diseases and thus their usage is not always based on current, diagnosed state of a patient. As a result there is not enough information in the decision table for accurate classification of the tds_Statin decision attribute. Decision rules for classes tds_ACE=1, tds_BBloker=1 and tds_Statin=1 were shown to medical experts from the electrocardiology clinic, who based on rule conditions predicted the decisions. The observed difference between human and computer classification was in a range from 15-20%.

The achieved results show that the applied rule shortening and generalization process results in short and strong decision rules, which provide not only a good accuracy but are also easily verifiable by medical experts.

6   Conclusions

In this paper we shown a decision system built based on information form narrative medical reports. Attributes of this system were selected based on the knowledge of domain experts. We used LEM2 algorithm to generate several sets of decision rules with different values of shortening and covering parameters and achieved the best accuracy of the generated rules for covering ratio equal 0.95 and shortening ratio between 0.7 and 0.8. Generated using these parameters decision rules were short and easily understandable and therefore could be quickly tested by domain experts. This verification shown that the knowledge stored in the data set used as a source for the presented decision table was correctly retrieved and the described methodology results in strong, short and easily verifiable decision rules.

Our further research will be focused on removing noisy and irrelevant information by selecting subsets of strong attributes from an extended version of the presented decision table.

References

1. Bargiela Andrzej, P.W.: Granular Computing: An Introduction. Kluwer Academic Publishers (2003)
2. Bazan, J.G., Szczuka, M.S.: Rses and rseslib - a collection of tools for rough set computations. Lecture Notes in Computer Science **2005** (2000) 106–113
3. Chen, M.S., Han, J., Yu, P.S.: Data mining: An overview from a database perspective. IEEE Trans. Knowl. Data Eng. **8** (1996) 866–883

4. Grzymala-Busse, J.W.: A new version of the rule induction system lers. Fundam. Inform. **31** (1997) 27–39
5. Pawlak, Z.: Rough sets. International Journal of Computer and Information Sciences **11** (1982) 341–356
6. Pawlak, Z.: Knowledge and uncertainty: A rough set approach. Workshops in Computing (1993) 34–42
7. Wakulicz-Deja, Paszek: Applying rough set theory to multi stage medical diagnosing. FUNDINF: Fundamenta Informatica **54** (2003) 387–408

Towards a Synergistic Combination of Web-Based and Data-Driven Decision Support Systems via Linguistic Data Summaries

Janusz Kacprzyk[1,2] and Sławomir Zadrożny[1,2]

[1] Systems Research Institute, Polish Academy of Sciences,
ul. Newelska 6, 01–447 Warsaw, Poland
[2] Warsaw School of Information Technology (WSISiZ),
ul. Newelska 6, 01–447 Warsaw, Poland
{kacprzyk, zadrozny}@ibspan.waw.pl

Abstract. We show how to combine the concepts of a Web based and a dta-driven decision support system as an effective and efficient hybrid solution. We advocate the use of linguistic database summaries, within the proposed DSS framework, for grasping the essence of large sets of data. We present an implementation for a computer retailer.

1   Introduction

One can basically distinguish the following types of DSSs: (1) dta-driven, (2) communication driven and group DSSs, (3) document driven, (4) model driven, (5) knowledge driven, (6) Web based and interorganizational. *dta-driven DSSs-communication Driven DSSs* use network and communications technologies to facilitate collaboration and communication, *Group DSSs* are interactive systems that facilitate solution of unstructured problems by a set of decision-makers working together, *document driven DSSs* integrate a variety of storage and processing technologies for a complete document retrieval and analysis, *model driven DSSs* emphasize access to and manipulation of a model, e.g., statistical, financial, optimization; use data and parameters, *knowledge driven DSSs* are interactive systems with specialized problem-solving expertise about a particular domain, *Web based DSSs* deliver decision support related information and/or tools to a manager/analyst using a "thin-client" Web browser (e.g., MS Internet Explorer), the TCP/IP protocol, etc.

We can summarize the benefits from the use of the Web technology as: it provides a distributed infrastructure for information processing, it can deliver timely, secure information and tools with a popular user-friendly interface (e.g., MS Internet Explorer), it has no time or geographic restrictions as the users can access Web based systems at any time, any place, the users can control and retrieve results remotely and instantly, etc. (cf. Yao et al. [21]).

The architecture of a Web based DSS may be depicted as in Fig. 1. This is a (thin) clint/server structure. The users are clients on the top layer. The lower

P.S. Szczepaniak et al. (Eds.): AWIC 2005, LNAI 3528, pp. 211–217, 2005.

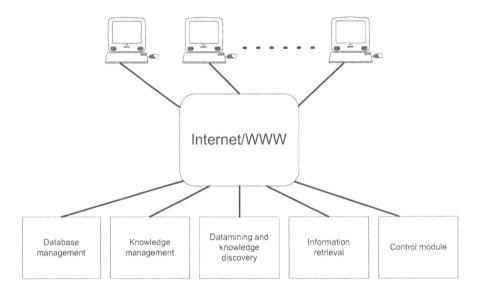

Fig. 1. Architecture of a Web based DSS

layers are similar to conventional DSSs since a a Web based DSS is a DSS with the Web and Internet as the interface. Notice that data and user results are divided which leads to a secure and standardized system. From another perspective, Web based DSSs can be divided into three levels that concern: (1) a support for personal activities, (2) an organizational support, and (3) a collaboration between organizations or decision making by a group like in group DSSs.

Here we will concentrate on a combination of Web based and dta-driven DSSs. We will advocate such a hybrid solution as the one that may provide an added values and synergy, and that fuzzy linguistic database summaries, and indirectly fuzzy querying, can open new vistas in Web based and dta-driven DSSs. We show an implementation for a sales database of a computer retailer, and that the linguistic summaries may be very useful.

2   Linguistic Data Summaries Using Fuzzy Logic with Linguistic Quantifiers

In Yagers approach (cf. Yager [19], Kacprzyk and Yager [3], and Kacprzyk, Yager and Zadrożny [4]) to linguistic data(base) summaries we have: (1) $Y = \{y_1, \ldots, y_n\}$ is a set of objects (records) in a database, e.g., the set of workers, (2) $A = \{A_1, \ldots, A_m\}$ is a set of attributes characterizing objects from Y, e.g., salary, age, etc. in a database of workers, and $A_j(y_i)$ denotes a value of attribute A_j for object y_i, and a linguistic summary of data set D contains: (1) a summarizer S, i.e. an attribute together with a linguistic value (fuzzy predicate) as, e.g., low salary for attribute salary, (2) a quantity in agreement Q, i.e. a linguistic quantifier (e.g. most), (3) truth (validity) $T \in [0,1]$ of the summary (e.g. 0.7), and – optionally – (4) a qualifier R as, e.g., young for age.

Thus, the linguistic summary, of a simpler and richer (with a qualifier), form may be exemplified by

$$T(\text{most of employees earn low salary}) = 0.7 \qquad (1)$$
$$T(\text{most of young employees earn low salary}) = 0.7$$

The core of a linguistic summary is a *linguistically quantified proposition* in the sense of Zadeh [23] which, corresponding to (2), may be written as

$$Qy\text{'s are } S \quad \text{and} \quad QRy\text{'s are } S \qquad (2)$$

and T may be calculated by using Zadehs calculus of linguistically quantified statements (cf. [23]), Yagers OWA operators [20], etc.

Using Zadeh's calculus, a (proportional, nondecreasing) linguistic quantifier Q is assumed to be a fuzzy set in the interval $[0,1]$ and the truth values (from $[0,1]$) of (2) are calculated, respectively, as

$$\text{truth}(Qy\text{'s are } S) = \mu_Q\left[\frac{1}{n}\sum_{i=1}^{n}\mu_S(y_i)\right] \qquad (3)$$

$$\text{truth}(QRy\text{'s are } S) = \mu_Q\left[\frac{\sum_{i=1}^{n}(\mu_R(y_i) \wedge \mu_S(y_i))}{\sum_{i=1}^{n}\mu_R(y_i)}\right]$$

Both S and R are simplified, atomic, referring to one attribute but can be extended to involve a confluence of attribute values as, e.g, "young and well paid", and also in addition to T, a degree of imprecision (fuzziness), a degree of covering, a degree of appropriateness, a length of a summary, etc. may be added (cf. Kacprzyk and Yager [3]).

Recently, Zadeh [22] introduced the concept of a *protoform* that is highly relevant in this context. Basically, a protoform is defined as a more or less abstract prototype (template) of a linguistically quantified proposition type. The most abstract protoforms correspond to (2), while (2) are examples of fully instantiated protoforms. Thus, evidently, protoforms form a hierarchy. As proposed by Kacprzyk and Zadrożny [16], the concept of a protoform may be taken as a guiding paradigm for the design of a user interface supporting the mining of linguistic summaries. The user specifies a protoform of linguistic summaries sought. Basically, the more abstract protoform the less should be assumed about the summaries sought. In Table 1 basic types of protoforms/linguistic summaries are shown, corresponding to protoforms of a more and more abstract form.

3   Generation of Linguistic Database Summaries – A Fuzzy Querying Approach

The generation of linguistic summaries may be more or less automatic. At the one extreme, the system may both construct and verify the summaries (this cor-

Table 1. Classification of protoforms/linguistic summaries

Type	Protoform	Given	Sought
0	QRy's are S	All	validity T
1	Qy's are S	S	Q
2	QRy's are S	S and R	Q
3	Qy's are S	Q and structure of S	linguistic values in S
4	QRy's are S	Q, R and structure of S	linguistic values in S
5	QRy's are S	Nothing	S, R and Q

responds to Type 5 protoforms/summaries in Table 1). At the other extreme, the user proposes a summary and the system only verifies its validity (which corresponds to Type 0 protoforms/summaries in Table 1). In Kacprzyk and Zadrożnys [6, 7] approach, the interactivity, i.e. user assistance, is in the definition of summarizers (indication of attributes and their combinations). This proceeds via a user interface of a fuzzy querying add-on. In Kacprzyk and Zadrożny [8, 9, 10], a conventional database management system is used and a fuzzy querying tool, FQUERY (for Access), is developed to allow for queries with fuzzy (linguistic) elements. Thus, the derivation of a linguistic summary of the type considered may proceed in an interactive (user-assisted) as: (1) the user formulates a set of linguistic summaries of interest (relevance) using the fuzzy querying add-on, (2) the system retrieves records from the database and calculates the validity of each summary adopted, and (3) a most appropriate linguistic summary is chosen. Type 0 and Type 1 linguistic summaries may be easily produced by a simple extension of FQUERY for Access as the user has to construct a query, a candidate summary, and it is to be determined which fraction of rows matches that query (and which linguistic quantifier best denotes this fraction, in case of Type 1). Type 3 summaries require much more effort as their primary goal is to determine typical (exceptional) values of an attribute (combination of attributes), and query/summarizer S consists of only one simple condition built of the attribute whose typical (exceptional) value is sought. Type 5 summaries represent the most general form considered, i.e. fuzzy rules. The summaries of Type 1 and 3 have been implemented as an extension to Kacprzyk and Zadrożnys [11, 12, 13] FQUERY for Access.

4 An Implementation for a Computer Retailer

This application concerns a sales database of a computer retailer, and the DSS proposed is both dta-driven because it operates on a set of data, and Web based as it uses a Web browser interface to formulate queries (summaries proposed) and to use of external data available from free and commercial Internet sources.

We will only briefly present some results of running the system. First, suppose that we are interested in a relation between the commission and the type of goods sold. The best linguistic summaries obtained are as shown in Table 2. As we can

Table 2. Linguistic summaries expressing relations between the group of products and commission

Summary
About 1/3 of sales of network elements is with a high commission
About 1/2 of sales of computers is with a medium commission
Much sales of accessories is with a high commission
Much sales of components is with a low commission
About 1/2 of sales of software is with a low commission
About 1/3 of sales of computers is with a low commission
A few sales of components is without commission
A few sales of computers is with a high commission
Very few sales of printers is with a high commission

see, the results can be very helpful, for instance while negotiating commissions for various products sold.

If we are interested in relations between the groups of products and times of sale, then we obtain the summaries as in Table 3. Notice that in this case the summaries are much less obvious than in the former case expressing relations between the group of product and commission. But, again, they provide very useful information.

Table 3. Linguistic summaries expressing relations between the groups of products and times of sale

Summary
About 1/3 of sales of computers is by the end of year
About 1/2 of sales in autumn is of accessories
About 1/3 of sales of network elements is in the beginning of year
Very few sales of network elements is by the end of year
Very few sales of software is in the beginning of year
About 1/2 of sales in the beginning of year is of accessories
About 1/3 of sales in the summer is of accessories
About 1/3 of sales of peripherals is in the spring period
About 1/3 of sales of software is by the end of year
About 1/3 of sales of network elements is in the spring period
About 1/3 of sales in the summer period is of components
Very few sales of network elements is in the autumn period
A few sales of software is in the summer period

Then, the user has suggested that since his company does not operate in a vacuum, some external data (e.g. on climate, economy) can be relevant and should be taken into account. We have extended the system to include data on wheather, available freely on the Web, and a Web based DSS has turned

Table 4. Linguistic summaries expressing relations between the attributes: group of products, time of sale, temperature, precipitacion, and type of customers

Summary
Very few sales of software in hot days to individual customers
About 1/2 of sales of accessories in rainy days on weekends by the end of the year
About 1/3 of sales of computers in rainy days to individual customers

out to be a convenient setting. For instance, if we are interested in relations between group of products, time of sale, temperature, precipitacion, and type of customers, the best linguistic summaries are as shown in Table 4. Notice that the use of external data gives a new quality to linguistic summaries, and provides much insight into relevant relations.

5   Concluding Remarks

We have proposed how to combine two types of DSSs: a web-based and a dta-driven, and the idea of a linguistic summary to obtain a more effective and efficient decision making support. The use of (quasi)natural language and a high level summarization may considerably help the decision maker. Moreover, the concept of Zadeh's protoforms may provide a further level of gnerality and abstraction. We have also presented an application for a computer retailer.

References

1. P. Bosc, D. Dubois, O. Pivert, H. Prade and M. de Calmes. Fuzzy summarization of data using fuzzy cardinalities. Proceedings of IPMU 2002, pp. 1553 - 1559, Annecy, France, 2002.
2. R. George and R. Srikanth. A soft computing approach to intensional answering in databases. Information Sciences, 92, 313 - 328, 1996.
3. J. Kacprzyk and R.R. Yager: Linguistic summaries of data using fuzzy logic. International Journal of General Systems, 30, 33 - 154, 2001.
4. J. Kacprzyk, R.R. Yager and S. Zadrożny. A fuzzy logic based approach to linguistic summaries of databases. International Journal of Applied Mathematics and Computer Science, 10, 813 - 834, 2000.
5. J. Kacprzyk and S. Zadrożny. Protoforms of linguistic data summaries: towards more general natural-language-based data mining tools. In A. Abraham, J. Ruiz-del-Solar, M. Koeppen (Eds.): Soft Computing Systems, pp. 417 - 425, IOS Press, Amsterdam, 2002.
6. J. Kacprzyk and S. Zadrożny. Data Mining via Linguistic Summaries of Data: An Interactive Approach. In T. Yamakawa and G. Matsumoto (Eds.): Methodologies for the Conception, Design and Application of Soft Computing. Proc. of IIZUKA98, pp. 668 - 671, Iizuka, Japan, 1998.
7. J. Kacprzyk and S. Zadrożny. Data mining via linguistic summaries of databases: an interactive approach. In L. Ding (Ed.): A New Paradigm of Knowledge Engineering by Soft Computing, pp. 325-345, World Scientific, Singapore, 2001.

8. J. Kacprzyk and S. Zadrożny. FQUERY for Access: fuzzy querying for a Windows-based DBMS. In P. Bosc and J. Kacprzyk (Eds.): Fuzziness in Database Management Systems, pp. 415-433, Springer-Verlag, Heidelberg, 1995.

9. J. Kacprzyk and S. Zadrożny. The paradigm of computing with words in intelligent database querying. In L.A. Zadeh and J. Kacprzyk (Eds.): Computing with Words in Information/Intelligent Systems. Part 2. Foundations, pp. 382 - 398, Springer-Verlag, Heidelberg and New York, 1999.

10. J. Kacprzyk and S. Zadrożny. Computing with words in intelligent database querying: standalone and Internet-based applications. Information Sciences, 134, 71 - 109, 2001.

11. J. Kacprzyk and S. Zadrożny. Computing with words: towards a new generation of linguistic querying and summarization of databases. In P. Sinčak and J. Vaščak (Eds.): Quo Vadis Computational Intelligence?, pp. 144 - 175, Springer-Verlag, Heidelberg and New York, 2000.

12. J. Kacprzyk and S. Zadrożny. On a fuzzy querying and data mining interface, Kybernetika, 36, 657 - 670, 2000.

13. J. Kacprzyk J. and S. Zadrożny. On combining intelligent querying and data mining using fuzzy logic concepts. In G. Bordogna and G. Pasi (Eds.): Recent Research Issues on the Management of Fuzziness in Databases, pp. 67 - 81, Springer–Verlag, Heidelberg and New York, 2000.

14. J. Kacprzyk and S. Zadrożny. On linguistic approaches in flexible querying and mining of association rules. In H.L. Larsen, J. Kacprzyk, S. Zadrożny, T. Andreasen and H. Christiansen (Eds.): Flexible Query Answering Systems. Recent Advances, pp. 475 - 484, Springer-Verlag, Heidelberg and New York, 2001.

15. J. Kacprzyk and S. Zadrożny. Linguistic summarization of data sets using association rules. Proceedings of The IEEE International Conference on Fuzzy Systems, pp. 702 - 707, St. Louis, USA, 2003.

16. J. Kacprzyk and S. Zadrożny. Fuzzy linguistic data summaries as a human consistent, user adaptable solution to data mining. In B. Gabryś, K. Leiviskä and J. Strackeljan (Eds.): Do Smart Adaptive Systems Exist? Best Practice for Selection and Combination of Intelligent Methods. Springer-verlag, Heidelberg and New York, 2005 (in press).

17. D. Rasmussen and R.R. Yager. Finding fuzzy and gradual functional dependencies with SummarySQL. Fuzzy Sets and Systems, 106, 131 - 142, 1999.

18. G. Raschia and N. Mouaddib. SAINTETIQ: a fuzzy set-based approach to database summarization. Fuzzy Sets and Systems, 129, 137 - 162, 2002.

19. R.R. Yager: A new approach to the summarization of data. Information Sciences, 28, pp. 69 - 86, 1982.

20. R.R. Yager and J. Kacprzyk (Eds.): The Ordered Weighted Averaging Operators: Theory and Applications. Kluwer, Boston, 1997.

21. Y.Y. Yao, N. Zhong, J. Liu and S. Ohsuga. Web Intelligence (WI): research challenges and trends in the new information age. In Web Intelligence: Research and Development, LNAI 2198, Springer, Berlin, pp. 1 - 17, 2001.

22. L.A. Zadeh. A prototype-centered approach to adding deduction capabilities to search engines - the concept of a protoform. BISC Seminar, 2002, University of California, Berkeley, 2002.

23. L.A. Zadeh. A computational approach to fuzzy quantifiers in natural languages. Computers and Mathematics with Applications. 9, 149 - 184, 1983.

24. L.A. Zadeh and J. Kacprzyk (Eds.): Computing with Words in Information/Intelligent Systems. Part 1. Foundations. Part 2. Applications, Springer – Verlag, Heidelberg and New York, 1999.

WindOwls – Adaptive System for the Integration of Recommendation Methods in E-Commerce

Przemysław Kazienko and Paweł Kołodziejski

Wrocław University of Technology, Institute of Applied Informatics,
Wybrzeże S. Wyspiańskiego 27, 50-370 Wrocław, Poland
kazienko@pwr.wroc.pl, super@hot.pl

Abstract. WindOwls, the new hybrid system of personalized product recommendation in e-commerce, by integrating various methods, is presented in the paper. Each e-commerce user has assigned their own weights corresponding to particular methods. Due to the permanent and personalized adaptation of these weights, WindOwls can adjust the influence of individual methods. Testing implementation and evaluation of recommendation efficiency are also described.

1 Introduction

Recommendation systems are an important part of recent e-commerce. They enable the increase of sales by suggesting to users selected products from the offer. The problem how to choose the most suitable items, possibly with respect to the user's inclinations, is a challenging research problem. Four fundamental approaches to recommendation can be mentioned: demographic filtering, collaborative and content-based recommendation, and simplified statistical approaches [7]. In demographic recommendation, users are classified based on their personal data, which they themselves provided during the registration process [10]. Alternatively, this data can be extracted from the purchasing history, survey responses, etc. Each product is assigned to one or more classes with a certain weight and the user is suggested with items from the class closest to their profile. Collaborative recommendation is typically based on item ratings explicitly delivered by users. The system recommends products, which have been evaluated positively by another similar user or by a set of such users, whose ratings are in the strongest correlation with the current user [3]. Content-based recommendation focuses on the similarity between products, usually taking into account their features like textual descriptions [6], hyperlinks, related ratings [12], or co-occurrence in the same purchased transactions or web user sessions [5]. Items that are the closest to the most recently processed, are ones suggested regardless of user preferences. In the statistical approach, the user is shown products based on some statistical factors; usually popularity measures like average or summary ratings, and numbers of sold units [13]. Most recommendation methods have significant limitations. Collaborative and some content-based filtering methods

P.S. Szczepaniak et al. (Eds.): AWIC 2005, LNAI 3528, pp. 218–224, 2005.

hardly cope with new users and new products, for which there is no appropriate data (ratings or purchases). Yet another analogue weakness is the problem of sparseness. It could be difficult to estimate reliable correlations between a product and a user in the environment with large amounts of empty data. This may also result in a recommendation list that is too short [5]. As the remedy for these and other shortcomings, many hybrid systems were proposed [2, 3, 4, 7]. The integration of recommendation methods was usually performed in the not adaptive way, i.e. the contribution of each method was either unchangeable over the course of time either independent from the user. The opposite approach was proposed in [11] by the introduction of a coordinator agent. It gathers ordered suggestion lists from three recommendation agents and it integrates them combining with weights. A weight corresponding to the particular agent is periodically updated according to the popularity of suggestions delivered by that agent. This approach was extended, concretized and first of all personalized in the described below WindOwls system, in which an individual set of weights is separately assigned to, and constantly updated for each user. The overall idea of the use of weights for items and their adaptation according to the user behavior was used by Bollacker *et al.* in the CiteSeer system for scientific literature [1].

2   Personalized Integration of Recommendation Methods

A single recommendation method can offer either ephemeral or persistent personalization. The former is based only on a current session and can deliver a different list on every web page but be the same for all users. Persistent personalization uses the history of user's behaviour and generates different product list for each user, but it works only with logged in users [13]. The main goal of WindOwls system is to overcome shortcomings of a single method and to deliver full personalization, which could offer every user different product lists which change during navigation. It simultaneously depends on watched products (content-based, ephemeral personalization), history of user's behaviour (e.g. ratings) and user's likes and dislikes (persistent personalization) as well as on effectiveness of previous recommendations for the given user (adapted personalization). To achieve full personalization, WindOwls system combines association rules for ephemeral content-based personalization and collaborative and demographic filtering for persistent one. Thus, WindOwls is a complete hybrid recommendation system integrating many independent recommendation methods in personalized and adaptive way. It exploits weights that are dynamically recalculated according to the effectiveness of recommendation. It means that the more effective the particular method is, the bigger the weight it will have. This results in a bigger influence on the final recommendation list. Another unique feature of WindOwls system is its personalization capability. Every user has its own personal set of weights corresponding to the method's usefulness for this individual. The system also uses its knowledge gained from previous users to better suit its new ones. When WindOwls is running for the first time weights of all methods are set to system base values determined by constant initial parameters. After some users join the system, these system base weights are recalculated. First, the average value for each method is estimated from weight sets of all users. Next, these values are normalized so that their sum is the same as at the beginning. Every new user starts from system base weights as initial values. Once a user gets his own weights set, only his personal behavior has an influence on it. The work of WindOwls starts with the user's interaction (Fig. 1). The context of interaction (the requested page URL and the user identifier UID) determines which conditions have been fulfilled and, in consequence, which methods are allowed to present their recommendation lists. The context is also utilized by some methods e.g. collaborative filtering uses UID while association rules require URL. The WindOwls system is capable of integrating any number of methods, although in the implementation, only five have been used. If a user is logged in, the system exploits collaborative and demographic recommendations — only in this case WindOwls has the appropriate source data. Otherwise, two simple statistical methods are used: "the best rated" and "the best buy". Collaborative filtering makes use of ratings inserted previously by registered users while demographic recommendation is based on matching personal data: likes and dislikes, pre-owned products, annual expenses on certain category, etc. To improve recommendation quality, also association rules were introduced. They reflect cases in which a given product was purchased together with the set of another ones frequently enough that this set might be recommended on the web page describing the given product. This recommendation technique is a kind of content-based method, which generates a different but static list on every product page. Its biggest disadvantage is that it can be used only on product pages and not on the other ones, e.g. news pages or so-called white pages [6]. The system assumption is that one product page corresponds to exactly one product from the e-commerce offer. Other kinds of relationships were studied in [6]. Note that all other considered recommendation methods are insensitive to the type of the requested page. Each method is independent from all others and it is provided by WindOwls only with the context data (URL, UID).

All methods relay, for further processing, their own list of recommended products with assigned appropriate scores for each. This method prerequisite is a positive value of every score. Having received these lists, WindOwls integrates, normalizes and orders them using both the obtained scores and weight set belonging to the given user:

$$f_{jkl} = \frac{1}{\max_{kl}} \sum_{i=1}^{M} w_{ik} \cdot s_{ijkl}, \quad s_{ijkl} \geq 0, \tag{1}$$

where: f_{jkl} — the final score of product j for user k in context (page) l; w_{ik} — the current weight of the method i for user k; s_{ijkl} — the score of product j assigned by the recommendation method i for user k with respect to context l; M — the number methods, in the implementation $M = 5$; $\max_{kl}$ — maximum value of score s_{ijkl} among scores returned by method i — the top one in ranking i. Factor $1/\max_{kl}$ is used to flatten different domains of methods to the range $[0, 1]$, i.e. the first item in the ranking of each method receives the value 1.

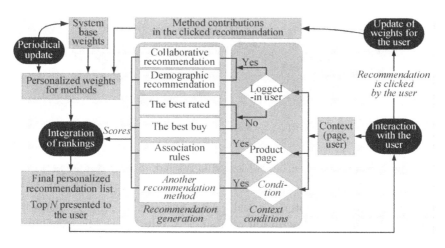

Fig. 1. Personalized integration of various methods of recommendation

Note that the context determines also the product, in the case when the user requests a product page. Each method delivers only K items (products) to reduce processing and it appears that K equal to about $N \cdot M$ would be enough; where N is the number of recommendations suggested to user. $N = 3$ and $K = 10$ were assumed in the implementation. Due to method preconditions, only three recommendation methods are able to supply suggestions at the same time. The greater K is, the less efficient is the system but the more accurate are obtained scores.

The top N candidates from the final recommendation list are presented to the user. Additionally, the system stores component scores for each of N items displayed to the user until the next user's request. If a user chooses one of recommendations linking to product j, WindOwls checks what score s_{ijk} had each i-th method in recommending this product and it adequately updates weights of all methods in the set of user k:

$$w_{ik}^{(1)} = w_i^{(0)} + s_{ijk}, \text{ after the first click on recommendation by user } k,$$
$$w_{ik}^{(n+1)} = w_{ik}^{(n)} + s_{ijk}, \text{ after the } (n+1)\text{-th click.} \tag{2}$$

where: $w_{ik}^{(1)}$, $w_{ik}^{(n)}$, $w_{ik}^{(n+1)}$ — the weight of method i for user k after the first, n-th and $n+1$ user click on recommendation, respectively; $w_i^{(0)}$ — the system base weight for method i; s_{ijk} — the score of the clicked, j-th product assigned by method i for user k.

After user's interaction, the described cycle repeats.

3   Implementation and Evaluation

The WindOwls system was implemented as an e-commerce windsurfing website (www.windowls.smellme.netlook.pl). It contains sections with news, articles, shop and settings. On the settings page users can change their personal

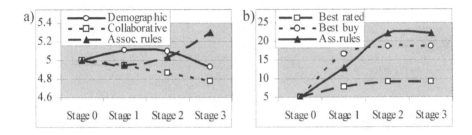

Fig. 2. System base weights for logged in (a) and not logged in users (b)

information about their interests used for demographic filtering. A typical page in the shop contains a description of a single product with the possibility of buying or rating it. The average rating of the product provided by other users and three or less (if not available) recommendations are always visible. Every user is presented with an individual recommendation list that changes on each page during navigation. Furthermore, even the same user on the same page can be proposed with different products due to the possible changes in their personal weights (2) or updates in methods source data.

The WindOwls system was evaluated by 40 registered, logged in users in a real life simulation. They were invited on the specialized news group to use the website, and to rank and purchase products. In total, 42 products were bought and 63 ranks were delivered. Besides, 25 not registered users, who only browsed through the e-commerce offer, used the system. Test data, which consisted of the set of 273 users clicks on recommendation within 102 user sessions, was divided into two groups: related to logged in users (Fig. 2a) and not logged in ones (Fig. 2b). System base weights on four stages were considered: at the beginning $w_i^{(0)} = 5$ were assigned to every method (stage 0), after 1/3 of all clicks (stage 1), after 2/3 of clicks (stage 2) and for all registered users clicks on recommendations (stage 3). System base weights were recalculated before each stage based on all users' personal weights (w_{ik}), but normalization was performed only in the logged in mode. After stage 1, with a very limited number of users and their interactions, demographic filtering provided best recommendations for logged in users (Fig. 2a). After more users created accounts and delivered much information to the system, association rules started to gain an advantage. The best buy at first and association rules after stage 1 appeared to be the most effective recommendation method for not logged in users (Fig. 2b). Other tests and results can be found in [9].

4   Conclusions and Future Work

The WindOwls hybrid system appeared to be effective in adapting to the user's needs and its main advantage over single recommendation method is full personalization that provides users with a dynamic list of products most likely to be interesting. Due to the update of weights of recommendation methods, WindOwls includes new adaptive capabilities that allow it to reward most efficient methods and discard others. It is open for introduction of new recommendation methods based for example either on user navigation patterns [5, 7] or on textual content of web pages [6].

Future work will focus on negative feedback available in some methods (e.g. badly ranked products in collaborative filtering). It would benefit the system to utilize such opinions and to lower the score of bad products even if other methods show them as recommendable. At this approach, the system would have to resign from using only K best items from each method, because it cuts off most of negative rated products. All recommendation methods need their base knowledge to be periodically updated offline because new ratings, users and products would appear. Some of them share the same source data, so the update process should be synchronized among all methods [8]. Differences in normalized weights of methods are very small; at the test end, they did not exceed 10% (Fig. 2a). It is the effect of respecting weights of users that did not click any recommendations. It will be improved in the next version of the system.

References

1. Bollacker K.D., Lawrence S., Lee Giles C.: Discovering Relevant Scientific Literature on The Web. IEEE Intelligent Systems, **15** (2) (2000) 42–47.
2. Cho Y.H., Kim J.K., Kim S.H.: A personalized recommender system based on web usage mining and decision tree induction. Expert Systems with Applications **23** (2002) 329–342.
3. Ha, S.H.: Helping Online Customers Decide through Web Personalization. IEEE Intelligent Systems **17** (6) (2002) 34–43.
4. Jung K.-Y, Jung J.J., Lee J.H.: Discovery of User Preference in Personalized Design Recommender System through Combining Collaborative Filtering and Content Based Filtering. DS'03, LNCS **2843**, Springer Verlag (2003) 320–327.
5. Kazienko P.: Product Recommendation in E-Commerce Using Direct and Indirect Confidence for Historical User Sessions. DS'04, LNAI **3245** (2004) 255–269.
6. Kazienko P., Kiewra M.: Integration of Relational Databases and Web Site Content for Product and Page Recommendation. IDEAS '04, IEEE Computer Society (2004) 111–116.
7. Kazienko P., Kiewra M.: Personalized Recommendation of Web Pages. Chapter 10 in: Nguyen T. (ed.) Intelligent Technologies for Inconsistent Knowledge Processing. Advanced Knowledge International, Adelaide, South Australia (2004) 163–183.
8. Kazienko P., Kiewra M.: ROSA — Multi-agent System for Web Services Personalization. AWIC'03, LNAI **2663**, Springer (2003) 297–306.
9. Kołodziejski P.: Methods of Product Recommendation in E-commerce. Master Thesis. Wrocław Univeristy of Technology (2004), in Polish.
10. Krulwich, B.: Lifestyle Finder: Intelligent User Profiling Using Large-Scale Demographic Data. AI Magazine **18** (2) (1997) 37–45.

11. Lim M., Kim J.: An Adaptive Recommendation System with a Coordinator Agent. WI 2001, LNAI **2198**, Springer Verlag (2001) 438–442.
12. Mooney R. J., Roy L.: Content-based book recommending using learning for text categorization. Fifth ACM Conference on Digital Libraries (2000) 195–204.
13. Schafer, J.B., Konstan, J.A., Riedl J.: E-Commerce Recommendation Applications. Data Mining and Knowledge Discovery **5** (1/2) (2001) 115–153.

Automated Keyphrase Extraction: Assisting Students in the Search for Online Materials

John Kilbride and Eleni Mangina

Department of Computer Science,
University College Dublin,
Belfield, Dublin 4, Ireland

Abstract. A high percentage of today's students use the World Wide Web (WWW) on a regular basis as a source for information, learning materials and references. In order to find reliable and trustworthy material students must sift through the millions of pages available on the web. Search engines can greatly reduce the number of documents a student must navigate through. In order to use search engines and find reliable resources efficiently, students must learn a number of search techniques. As students gain experience, they will gradually build up a model of certain sites and the quality and types of content they contain. Classmates often collaborate with one another in the search for materials recommending books, web-sites and other resources to one another. This paper describes a system designed to assist students of a web-based learning environment, while searching for online materials. This is achieved by either acting autonomously or assisting users to create queries, perform searches and filter the search results.

1 Introduction

A high percentage of students are now using the WWW on a daily basis as a source for information, learning materials, references and examples. Students must sift through the millions of pages available on the web in search of relevant materials. The problem of navigating the web in search of relevant documents is referred to as the information overload problem [10]. Search engines like Google [1] and Yahoo! [5] can reduce the amount of documents a student must go through. Utilizing these search engines efficiently requires an experienced user capable of creating the appropriate queries. Students must learn how to formulate queries in order to reduce the search space to a realistic size. For example querying Google with the string 'The Irish War of Independence' returns over half a million documents. If we search for the specific event in which we are interested in such as 'The Irish War of Independence, the 1916 Rising' reduces the search space to under twenty thousand documents.

Learning how to construct effective queries and narrow the search space to a manageable number of documents is only one of a number of methods students

P.S. Szczepaniak et al. (Eds.): AWIC 2005, LNAI 3528, pp. 225–230, 2005.

master in order to find appropriate resources. Over time as students gain experience, they will gradually establish a collection of preferred or trusted sites. When searching for materials and resources online students will often search through one of these preferred sites first before resorting to searching the WWW. Students often collaborate with one another in the search for materials recommending books, web-sites and other resources to one another. Collaborative filtering has been applied to several problems domains such as filtering news stories [12] and [7], online-shopping [8] and recommender systems for items such as music [2] and television programs [13]. With collaborative filtering these systems can recommended new stories etc., by making informed recommendations given minimal amounts of information about the current user.

This paper describes a system designed to reduce the amount of time students in an online learning environment such as Moodle [3] spend searching for additional learning materials. The system can be divided into three phases, the keyphrase extraction phase, the search phase and the filtering phase. By automating or assisting the users to compose queries based on the materials they are viewing, the system retrieves a list of documents related to the subject area. These resulting documents are then filtered using feedback supplied by the students. Finally the top ranked remaining links will be presented as a list of hyper-links beside the resource the user is currently viewing (see Section 3).

The remainder of this paper describes a system designed to reduce the effort and time students must spend searching for reliable resources on the WWW. This is achieved by assisting students to compose queries and filtering the search results using student feedback. Section two describes briefly some work on keyphrase extraction and document summarization and the reasoning behind the select of KEA (Keyphrase Extraction Algorithm) for keyphrase extraction. Section three gives an overview of the system and details how the KEA learning algorithm has been applied to the problem of finding supplementary materials. Section four describes how KEA works, section five the conclusions drawn from initial results on the extraction of keyphrases. Finally section five discusses several possible areas for future work including individualized keyphrase extraction models based on feedback from individual users, and improvements to the filtering phase of the system.

2   Related Work

This paper concentrates of the automated extraction of keyphrases from educational documents with the overall system aiming to reduce the amount of time students spend looking for reliable supplementary material on the web. Several algorithms are available for retrieving keyphrases including GenEx [14] and KEA [15]. Both GenEx and KEA use similar approaches in the search of keyphrases, based on various machine learning techniques. Turney experiments with C4.5 and GenEx (A Hybrid Genetic Algorithm for Keyphrase Extraction), while Witten et al. examined both Naive Bayes (KEA) and C4.5 (KEA-C4.5). The Naive Bayes based KEA and GenEx performed best. [6] contains a more complete evaluation of the prominent keyphrase, keyword and summarization algorithms. KEA was chosen ahead of GenEx because of its simplicity, efficiency and effectiveness. KEA requires minimal training data, approaching its optimal performance level when given only 20-50 training documents. KEA also generalizes well when the training data is from a different domain to the test data, although performance does suffer slightly as a result. KEA uses only two simple attributes, is less computationally expensive than GenEx and performs equally well. The next section describes the overall system and where KEA fits into the system in order to extract key-phrases.

3   Retrieving Related Documents from the Web

The overall system uses KEA to extract candidate keyphrases from the documents being viewed by students. These keyphrases are then passed as queries to google to retrieve related documents which may be of interest to the student. The system shown in Figure 1 can be divided into three stages: the keyphrase extraction stage, the search stage and the results filtering stage.

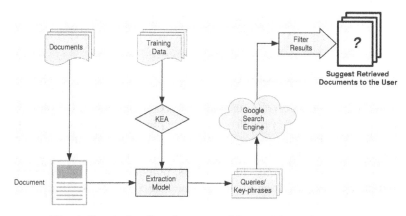

Fig. 1. Retrieving Supplementary Material from the WWW

A keyphrase can consist of any number of words extracted from the selected piece of text. In this case keyphrases consisting of three or more words are sought as the basis for queries. Initially training is performed offline, training data in the form of documents and their associated keyphrases are supplied to KEA so that a keyphrase extraction model can be built. Once an extraction model has been established then keyphrases can be extracted from any given document. The keyphrase extraction stage begins when a student selects one of course documents available to them. The system then uses KEA and one of the extraction models available to compose a short list of keyphrases. The highest ranked keyphrase is then passed as a query into the Google search engine. The returned links are then filtered using any relevant feedback returned by the students who have previously viewed the page (or its hosting site) being recommended. The top ranked results are then presented as a list of recommended links on the page the student is currently viewing. The list of keyphrases are also presented here so the student can select a number of different search term. If necessary, the student can edit the keyphrases before submitting the query to Google in order to find more specific information, this process is illustrated in Figure 2.

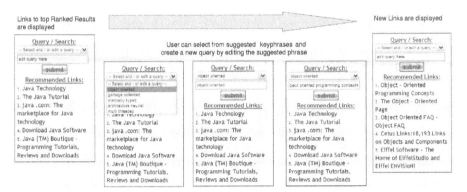

Fig. 2. Query Refinement and Document Retrieval

4   Keyphrase Extraction

KEA runs in two stages, training and extraction. During the training stage a number of examples are provided and a keyphrase extraction model is constructed. In the extraction phase a number of keyphrases are automatically assigned to a chosen document using an appropriate extraction model. KEA first cleans the input text removing brackets, numbers, punctuation marks etc. Candidate keyphrases are then identified using three rules (see [15]). Each word in a candidate phrase is then case folded using Lovins stemming algorithm [9]. Two attributes are then calculated for each phrase TFxIDF and first occurrence (newer versions also use a third attribute keyphrase frequency). A Naive Bayes model [11] is then used to classify candidate keyphrases into two classes; keyphrase and not-keyphrase. A number of experiments have been conducted to examine the effects of varying the parameters used by KEA when creating a keyphrase extraction model. For these experiments each new keyphrase extraction model was run against a collection of documents and their pre-assigned keyphrases. Three main document sets where constructed: CSTR, CSGen and Arts/History. The CSTR set contains a collection of Computer Science Technical Reports dealing mainly with network related topics. The CSGen model is a collection of short documents from several loosely related disciplines in Computer Science. Finally the Arts/History set contains extracts from texts on a wide variety of unrelated subjects.

Table 1. Key Experimental Results

Training Set	Test Set	5-Keyphrase Extraction	15-Keyphrase Extraction
CSTR	CSTR	0.6 +/- 0.7	0.88 +/- 0.87
CSTR	CSGen	0.37 +/- 0.62	0.5 +/- 0.74
CSGen	CSGen	0.43 +/- 0.65	0.49 +/- 0.73
CSGen	CSTR	0.6 +/- 0.7	0.89 +/- 0.91
CSGen	Arts/History	0.3 +/- 0.46	0.33 +/- 0.48

5 Conclusions

The results shown in Table 1 contain the average number of correctly identified keyphrases. The results show how the performance of the KEA algorithm varies given the correlation of the domains from which the training and test documents have been drawn. These experiments highlight a number of interesting results. The first experiment was performed using data drawn from the CSTR documents. It highlights the performance of KEA given domain specific training data. The second set of results highlights that domain specific extraction models perform poorly when extracting keyphrases from more general document sets. The forth experiment demonstrates that general domain models can perform as well as domain specific models, although further investigation is required to examine how generalized extraction models can become. The final experiment illustrates that any given extraction model will obtain a minimal level of performance even in completely unrelated domains. Upon closer examination of the extracted keyphrases another interesting result came to light. As the number of keyphrases being extracted increases so does the average number of correctly extracted keyphrases. While this may seem an obvious result it highlights an area where post processing results could lead to ranking the correct keyphrases higher in the results list. Examining the output closer identifies that KEA extracts a number of similar keyphrases for which it has calculated similar scores. For one document the following phrases were extracted, "summary of installing", "summary of installing network", "summary of installing network cards", "installing network cards in server", all with an equal score of 0.1371. Clearly these could all be resolved to a single keyphrase "Installing Network Cards" with a score equal to the sum of the all keyphrases resolved to the new keyphrase. Current development is examining the possible combination of similar keyphrases using n-gram tiling [4] to combat this problem.

6 Future Work

Future work will look at the generation of subject specific keyphrase extraction models as well as personalized and updated extraction models by utilizing user adjusted queries as part of the training data for newer extraction models. The final stage which filters the documents returned by Google based on student feedback needs to be extended. The current system uses student feedback as its only source of filtering information. Information about a students level of knowledge of the current or a related topic and his/her similarity to other students who have provided feedback could be employed to improve the suitability of the final suggested documents.

References

1. Sergey Brin and Lawrence Page. The anatomy of a large-scale hypertextual Web search engine. *Computer Networks and ISDN Systems*, 30(1–7):107–117, 1998.
2. William W. Cohen and Wei Fan. Web-collaborative filtering: recommending music by crawling the Web. *Computer Networks (Amsterdam, Netherlands: 1999)*, 33(1–6):685–698, 2000.
3. Martin Dougmais and Peter C. Taylor. Moodle: Using learning communities to create an open source course management system. In *Proc. of ED-MEDIA 2003: World Conference on Educational Multimedia, Hypermedia and Telecommunications*, 2003.
4. Susan Dumais, Michele Banko, Eric Brill, Jimmy Lin, and Andrew Ng. Web question answering: Is more always better? In *Proceedings of the 25th Annual International ACM SIGIR Conference on Research and Development in Information Retrieval*. ACM, 2002.
5. David Filo and Jerry Yang. Yahoo! search engine. http://www.yahoo.com.
6. Eibe Frank, Gordon W. Paynter, Ian H. Witten, Carl Gutwin, and Craig G. Nevill-Manning. Domain-specific keyphrase extraction. In *Proc. Sixteenth International Joint Conference on Artificial Intelligence*, pages 668–673, San Francisco, CA, 1999. Morgan Kaufmann Publishers.
7. Ken Lang. NewsWeeder: learning to filter netnews. In *Proceedings of the 12th International Conference on Machine Learning*, pages 331–339. Morgan Kaufmann publishers Inc.: San Mateo, CA, USA, 1995.
8. Greg Linden, Brent Smith, and Jeremy York. Amazon.com recommendations: Item-to-item collaborative filtering. http://dsonline.computer.org/0301/d/wp1lind.htm.
9. Julie B. Lovins. Development of a stemming algorithm. *Mechanical Translation and Computational Linguistics*, 11:22–31, 1968.
10. Pattie Maes. Agents that reduce work and information overload. *Communications of the ACM*, 37(7):30–40, 1994.
11. Tom Mitchell. *Machine Learning*. McGraw Hill, 1997.
12. P. Resnick, N. Iacovou, M. Suchak, P. Bergstorm, and J. Riedl. GroupLens: An Open Architecture for Collaborative Filtering of Netnews. In *Proceedings of ACM 1994 Conference on Computer Supported Cooperative Work*, pages 175–186, Chapel Hill, North Carolina, 1994. ACM.
13. Barry Smyth and Paul Cotter. A personalised television listings service. *Communications of the ACM*, 43(8):107–111, 2000.
14. Peter Turney. Learning to extract keyphrases from text. Technical Report Technical Report ERB-1057, Institute for Information Technology, National Research Council of Canada, 1999.
15. Ian H. Witten, Gordon W. Paynter, Eibe Frank, Carl Gutwin, and Craig G. Nevill-Manning. KEA: Practical automatic keyphrase extraction. In *ACM DL*, pages 254–255, 1999.

Adaptive Tuning of PID Controller for Multivariable System Using Bacterial Foraging Based Optimization

Dong Hwa Kim[1] and Jae Hoon Cho[2]

[1] Dept. of Instrumentation and Control Eng.,
Hanbat National University,
16-1 San Duckmyong-Dong Yuseong-Gu,
Daejeon City, Korea 305-719,
kimdh@hanbat.ac.kr
[2] Hanbat National University

Abstract. In this paper, design approach of PID controller with multivariable system is proposed using bacterial foraging based optimal algorithm. To tune PID controller for multivariable system, disturbance rejection conditions based on H_∞ are illustrated and the performance of response based on the bacterial foraging is computed for the designed PID controller as ITSE (Integral of time weighted squared error). Hence, parameters of PID controller are selected by bacterial foraging based optimal algorithm to obtain the required response.

1 Introduction

A Proportional – Integral – Derivative (PID) controller has been widely used in the most industrial processes despite continual advances in control theory. This is not only due to the simple structure which is theoretically easy to understand but also to the fact that the tuning technique provides adequate performance in the vast majority of applications. However, it cannot effectively control such a complicated or fast running system such as multivariable system, since the response of a plant depends on only the three parameters (P, I, and D) and its gain has to be manually tuned by trial and error in the industrial world. Most of the PID tuning rules developed in the past years use the conventional method such as frequency-response methods [1]. This method needs a highly technical experience to apply since they provide simple tuning formulae to determine the PID controller parameters. Despite the fact that many PID tuning methods are available for achieving the specified GPM, they can be divided into two categories. On the other hand, since natural selection of bacterial foraging tends to eliminate animals with poor foraging strategies for locating, handling, and ingesting food, optimization models can be provided for social foraging where groups of parameters communicate to cooperatively forage in engineering. That is, biological information processing systems such as human beings have many

P.S. Szczepaniak et al. (Eds.): AWIC 2005, LNAI 3528, pp. 231–235, 2005.

interesting functions and are expected to provide various feasible ideas to engineering fields. In this paper, an intelligent tuning method of PID controller
for multivariable system by bacterial foraging based optimal algorithm is suggested for robust control with disturbance rejection function on control system
of multivariable control loop.

2   PID Controller Tuning with Disturbance Rejection Function

2.1   Condition for Disturbance Rejection

In Fig. ??, the disturbance rejection constraint can be given by [?, ?]

$$\max_{d(t)\in D} \frac{\|Y\|}{\|d\|} = \left\| \frac{w(s)}{1+K(s,c)G(s)} \right\|_\infty < \delta. \tag{1}$$

Here, $\delta < 1$ is constant defining by the desired rejection level and $\|\cdot\|_\infty$
denotes the H_∞-norm, which is defined as $\|G(s)\|_\infty = \max_{w\in[0,\infty)} |G(jw)|$.
The disturbance rejection constraint becomes

$$\left\| \frac{w(s)}{1+K(s,c)G(s)} \right\|_\infty =$$
$$= \max_{w\in[0,\infty)} \left(\frac{w(jw)w(-jw)}{1+K(jw,c)G(jw,c)K(-jw,c)G(-jw,c)} \right)^{0.5} = \tag{2}$$
$$= \max_{w\in[0,\infty)} (\sigma(w,c))^{0.5}$$

The controller $K(s,c)$ is written as $K(s,c) = c_1 + \frac{c_2}{s} + c_3 s$ and the vector c
of the controller parameter is given by $c = [c_1, c_2, c_3]^T$. Hence, the condition for
disturbance rejection is given as $\max_{w\in[0,\infty)} (\sigma(w,c))^{0.5} < \delta$.

2.2   Performance Index for Disturbance Rejection Controller Design

The performance index defined as ITSE (Integral of the Time-Weighted Square
of the Error) is written by

$$PI = \int_0^\infty t\,(E(t))^2\,dt, \quad E(s) = \frac{B(s)}{A(s)} = \frac{\sum_{j=0}^m b_j s^{m-1}}{\sum_{i=0}^n a_i s^{n-1}} \tag{3}$$

Because $E(s)$ contains the parameters of the controller (c) and plant, the
value of performance index, PI for a system of nth order can be minimized by
adjusting the vector c as $\min_c PI(c)$. The optimal tuning proposed in this paper
is to find the vector c, such that the ITSE performance index, $PI(c)$ is a minimum
using bacterial algorithm and the constraint $\max_{w\in[0,\infty)} (\sigma(w,c))^{0.5} < \delta$ is
satisfied through real coded bacterial algorithms.

3 Behavior Characteristics and Modeling of Bacteria Foraging

3.1 Overview of Chemotactic Behavior of E. coli

This paper considers the foraging behavior of E. coli, which is a common type of bacteria as in reference 4-5. Its behavior to move comes from a set of up to six rigid 100-200 rps spinning flagella, each driven as a biological motor. An E. coli bacterium alternates between running and tumbling. Running speed is 10-20 μm/sec, but they cannot swim straight. Mutations in E. coli affect the reproductive efficiency at different temperatures, and occur at a rate of about 10^{-7} per gene and per generation. E. coli occasionally engages in a conjugation that affects the characteristics of a population of bacteria. Since there are many types of taxes that are used by bacteria such as, aerotaxis (it are attracted to oxygen), light (phototaxis), temperature (thermotaxis), magnetotaxis (it it can be affected by magnetic lines of flux. Some bacteria can change their shape and number of flagella which is based on the medium to reconfigure in order to ensure efficient foraging in a variety of media.

3.2 Optimization Function of Bacterial Swarm Foraging

The main goal based on bacterial foraging is to apply in order to find the minimum of $P(\phi), \phi \in R^n$, not in the gradient $\nabla P(\phi)$. Here, when ϕ is the position of a bacterium, and $J(\phi)$ is an attractant-repellant profile. A neutral medium, and the presence of noxious substances, respectively can showed by

$$H(j, k, l) = \{\phi^i(j, k, l) | i = 1, 2, \ldots, N\}. \tag{4}$$

Equation represents the positions of each member in the population of the N bacteria at the jth chemotactic step, kth reproduction step, and lth elimination-dispersal event. Let $P(i, j, k, l)$ denote the cost at the location of the ith bacterium $\phi^i(j, k, l) \in R^n$. Reference [?, ?] let

$$\phi^i = (j + 1, k, l) = \phi^i(j, k, l) + C((i)\phi(j)), \tag{5}$$

so that $C(i) > 0$ is the size of the step taken in the random direction specified by the tumble. If at $\phi^i(j + 1, k, l)$ the cost $J(i, j + 1, k, l)$ is better (lower) than at $\phi^i(j, k, l)$, then another chemotactic step of size $C(i)$ in this same direction will be taken and repeated up to a maximum number of steps N_s. N_s is the length of the lifetime of the bacteria measured by the number of chemotactic steps. Functions $P_c^i(\phi), i = 1, 2, \ldots, s$, to model the cell-to-cell signaling via an attractant and a repellant is represented by

$$
\begin{aligned}
P_c(\phi) = \sum_{i=1}^{N} P_{cc}^i = \sum_{i=1}^{N} & \left[-L_{attract} \exp\left(-\delta_{attract} \sum_{j=1}^{n} (\phi_j - \phi_j^i)^2 \right) \right] \\
& + \sum_{i=1}^{N} \left[-K_{repellant} \exp\left(-\delta_{attract} \sum_{j=1}^{n} (\phi_j - \phi_j^i)^2 \right) \right],
\end{aligned} \tag{6}
$$

When we where $\phi = [\phi_1, \ldots, \phi_p]^T$ s a point on the optimization domain, $L_{attract}$ is the depth of the attractant released by the cell and $\delta_{attract}$ is a measure of the width of the attractant signal. $K_{repellant} = L_{attract}$ is the height of the repellant effect magnitude), and $\delta_{attract}$ is a measure of the width of the repellant. The expression of $P_c(\phi)$ means that its value does not depend on the nutrient concentration at position ϕ. In tuning the parameter M, it is normally found that, when M is very large, $P_{ar}(\phi)$ is much larger than $J(\phi)$, and thus the profile of the search space is dominated by the chemical attractant secreted by E. coli. This paper describes the method in the form of an algorithm to search optimal value of PID parameter.

[step 1] Initialize parameters n, N, N_C, N_S, N_{re}, N_{ed}, P_{ed}, $C(i)(i = 1, 2, \ldots, N)$, ϕ^i, and random values of PID parameter. Where, n: Dimension of the search space (Each Parameter of PID controller), N: The number of bacteria in the population, N_C: chemotactic steps, N_{re}: The number of reproduction steps, N_{ed}: the number of elimination-dispersal events, P_{ed}: elimination-dispersal with probability, $C(i)$: the size of the step taken in the random direction specified by the tumble. The controller parameter is searched in the range of Kp=[0 30], Ti=[0 30], and Td=[0 30].
[step 2] Elimination-dispersal loop: $l = l + 1$
[step 3] Reproduction loop: $k = k + 1$
[step 4] Chemotaxis loop: $j = j + 1$
[step 5] If $j < N_C$, go to step 3. In this case, continue chemotaxis, since the life of the bacteria is not over.
[step 6] Reproduction:
[step 7] If $k < N_{re}$, go to [step 3]. In this case, we have not reached the number of specified reproduction steps, so we start the next generation in the chemotactic loop.
[step 8] Elimination-dispersal: For $i = 1, 2, \ldots, N$ with probability P_{ed}, eliminate and disperse each bacterium. To do this, if you eliminate a bacterium, simply disperse one to a random location on the optimization domain. If $l < N_{ed}$, then go to [step 2]; otherwise end.

4   Simulation and Discussions

Fig. ?? shows the step response to variation of chemotactic step size. When step size is 0.15 response is best response. Fig. ?? illustrates search process of optimal parameters of PID controller by bacteria foraging (by Ns). Fig. ?? is representing search process of performance index (ITSE) by bacteria foraging and Fig. ?? is comparison of result by IA (Immune Algorithm), curve by FNN (Fuzzy Neural Network), and result by bacteria foraging suggested in this paper.

5   Conclusions

Up to now, the PID controller has been used to operate the process loops including multivariable system. However, achieving an optimal PID gain is very difficult for

Table 1. Comparison of PID parameter and ITSE of each optimal algorithm

	Kp	Ti	ITSE
FNN	0.29	1.11	0.026
IA	0.56	1.9	0.022
Ba	0.66	0.14	0.0046

the control loop with disturbances. Since the gain of the PID controller has to be tuned manually by trial and error. Since natural selection of animal tends to eliminate animals with poor foraging strategies for locating, handling, and ingesting food, they obtain enough food to enable them to reproduce after many generations, poor foraging strategies are either eliminated or shaped into good ones redesigned. Therefore, optimization approach can be provided for social foraging where groups of parameters communicate to cooperatively forage in engineering. In this paper, an intelligent tuning method of PID controller by bacterial foraging based optimal algorithm is suggested for robust control with disturbance rejection function on multivariable control system. Simulation results are showing satisfactory responses. The object function can be minimized by gain selection for control, and the variety gain is obtained as shown in Table 1. The suggested controller can also be used effectively in the control system as seen from Figs. ??-??.

References

1. Ya-Gang Wang: PI tuning for processes with large dead time. Proceeding of the ACC, Chicago Illinois, June (2000) 4274-4278
2. K. J. Astrom, T. Hagglund, C. C. Hang, and W. K. Ho: Automatic Tuning and Adaptation for PID Controllers-A Survey. IFAC J. Control Eng. Practice 1(4) (1993) 699-714.
3. J. X. Xu, C. Liu, and C. C. Hang: Tuning of Fuzzy PI Controllers Based on Gain/Phase Margin Specifications and ITAE Index. ISA Transactions 35 (1996) 79-91.
4. Dong Hwa Kim: Intelligent tuning of a PID controller with robust disturbance rejection function using an immune algorithm. Proc. Int. Conf. Knowledge-based intelligent information and engineering systems. Springer-Verlag (2004) 57-63.
5. K. M. Passino: Biomimicry of Bacterial Foraging for Distributed Optimization University . Press, Princeton, New Jersey (2001).
6. K. M. Passino: Biomimicry of Bacterial Foraging for Distributed Optimization and Control. IEEE Control Systems Magazine (2002).

Context-Aware Access Control Mechanism for Ubiquitous Applications

Young-Gab Kim[1], Chang-Joo Mon[2], Dongwon Jeong[3], Jeong-Oog Lee[2], Chee-Yang Song[4], and Doo-Kwon Baik[1],[**]

[1] Department of Computer Science and Engineering , Korea University,
Anam-dong 5-ga, Seongbuk-gu, 136-701, Seoul, Korea
{ygkim, baik}@software.korea.ac.kr
[2] Department of Computer Science, Konkuk University,
322 Danwol-dong, Chungju-si, Chungcheongbuk-do, 380-701, Korea
{mcj, ljo}@kku.ac.kr
[3] Department of Informatics & Statistics, Kunsan National University,
San 68, Miryong-dong, Gunsan, Jeolabuk-do, 573-701, Korea
djeong@kunsan.ac.kr
[4] IP Media Service Division, Marketing and Technology Laboratory, Korea Telecom,
17, Woomyeon-dong, Seocho-gu, Seoul, 137-792, Korea
songyang@kt.co.kr

Abstract. With a rapid development of ubiquitous computing technology in the home and community, users can access information anytime and anywhere via personal devices such as PDA and internet mobile phone. Similarly, more flexible access control is required in the ubiquitous applications. In this paper, we propose a context-aware access control mechanism, which dynamically grants and adapts permissions to users according to the current context. We extend the role-based access control(RBAC) model to deal with the context information in ubiquitous environment. Unlike the traditional RBAC, the proposed access control mechanism can consider context information such as location, time and system resources by the context-aware agent and state checking matrix(SCM).

1 Introduction

With rapid development of ubiquitous computing technology in the home and community, users can access information anytime and anywhere via personal devices such as PDA. Sometimes it may be necessary to provide a multiresolution access mechanism so that users with different levels of clearances have different access privilege in the ubiquitous environment. That is, more flexible access control is required in the ubiquitous applications.

Access control[1] can take many forms. The basic model of access control is the Access Control Matrix(ACM)[2]. The ACM specifies individual relation-

---

[**] The Corresponding Author.

P.S. Szczepaniak et al. (Eds.): AWIC 2005, LNAI 3528, pp. 236–242, 2005.

ships between entities wishing access subjects and the system resources they with to access object. Current access control mechanisms do not implement the ACM directly. Most access control mechanisms in current use are based on models, such as access control lists or capabilities[2], which have direct relationship with the access control matrix. However, this model is inadequate for ubiquitous applications because it doesn't consider context information such as location, time, system resources and so on. In a ubiquitous environment, users are mobile and access resources using small mobile devices and intelligent appliances. This means that the context information of the user is highly dynamic, and it is possible to grant a user access privilege without considering the user's current condition. Therefore, a fine-grained access control mechanism that dynamically adjusts changes of context information of users is required.

This paper proposes a context-aware access control mechanism, which dynamically grants and adapts permissions to users according to current context. We extend the role-based access control(RBAC)[3] model to deal with the context information in an ubiquitous environment. The proposed mechanism dynamically adjusts role assignments(UA) and permission assignments(PA) based on current context information.

2   Background and Related Work

The concept of RBAC begins with multi-user and multi-application on-line system pioneered in the 1970s[3]. The RBAC model has four elements: users, roles permission and sessions. A users represents a human activity or an autonomous agent, while a role is a job function or job title within the organization with some associated semantics regarding the authority and responsibility conferred on a member of the role. A permission is an approval of a particular mode of access to one or more objects in the system. Each session is a mapping of one user to possibly many roles. In other words, a user establishes a session during which the user activates some subset of roles. The basic concept of RBAC is that users are assigned to roles, permissions are assigned to roles and users acquire permissions by being members of roles. In RBAC model, user-role and permission-role assignment can be many-to-many. However, RBAC can be configured to support a wide variety of access control policies, including traditional discretionary access control(DAC) and mandatory access control(MAC), as well as organization-specific policies[4]. Therefore, in this paper, we extend RBAC to provide context-aware access control mechanisms for ubiquitous applications.

There are several research efforts to take additional factors into consideration when make access control decision. [5] proposed a distributed authorization service using their Generalized Access Control Language(GACL). In GACL, they use the notion of system load as the determining factor in certain access control decisions, so that, for example, certain programs can only be executed when there is enough system capacity available. However, GACL does not consider context information as a key factor in their access control mechanism.

[6, 7] proposed the Generalized Role Based Access Control(GRBAC) model. GRBAC extends the power of traditional RBAC by applying to all the entities, which are subject, object and environment, although a traditional RBAC only applies the role to the subject. GRBAC uses context information as a factor in making access decisions. Especially, [7] extend the model beyond time by introducing location and system status as constraints. In GRBAC, the definition of environment roles allows the model to partially address problem we described, but it may not be feasible in practice because the potential large amount of environment roles make the system hard to maintain.

[8] proposed the Dynamic Access Control Model(DRBAC) for dealing with context information. In DRBAC model, they only presented the concept and requirement of the DRBAC without showing the practical usage in the applications.

3   Requirements and Basic Concept of Context-Aware Access Control Model

As mentioned above, the traditional RBAC models do not directly adapt the requirements of the ubiquitous application. In the RBAC model, the user is assigned a subset of roles when the user begins a session. During a session, although roles can be activated or deactivated based on constraints such as role conflict or prerequisite roles, the user's access privilege is not changed based on context information. To maintain system security for a ubiquitous application, it is necessary to dynamically adapt access permissions granted to users when context information changes. That is, access control in ubiquitous environment should meet two requirements. First, user's access privileges must change when the user's context, such as location and time, changes. Second, a resource must adjust its access permission when its system information, such as network bandwidth and memory usage, changes[8]. Context-aware access control model proposed in this paper meets these two requirements. It extends the traditional RBAC model to use dynamic context information while making access control decision. Fig. 1 show the basic concept of context-aware access control mechanism.

Basically user is assigned roles and roles are assigned permissions as in the RBAC model. Thus, user acquires permissions through the roles. Default UA is a mapping that assigns a role to a user. Each user is assigned a set of roles. Default PA is a mapping that assigns a permission to a role. Every role is assigned a set of permissions. That is, default role is assigned to users by the traditional RBAC, and then the role is activated or deactivated according to the change of context information of users. The context information is used to decide which role is active and which permission is active for that role. As shown in Fig 1, these default UA and PA are changed to context-aware UA and PA by applying the state checking matrix(SCM) to deal with context information. As a result, we can get the changed relations, which are user and permission assignments like context-aware UA and context-aware PA. That is, we can dynamically grant and

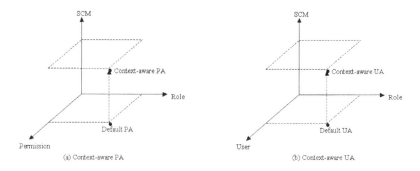

Fig. 1. Context-aware PA and Context-aware UA

adapt permissions to users according to the context information of users. More detail description will be presented in the following section.

4   Context-Aware Access Control Model

The proposed access control model for ubiquitous applications extends the traditional RBAC via some functional components. Fig. 2 shows global structure of context-aware access control mechanism in ubiquitous environment.

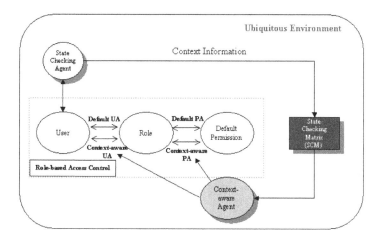

Fig. 2. Context-aware Access Control Model in Ubiquitous Environment

There are traditional RBAC and three important components: State checking agent, state checking matrix(SCM) and context-aware agent. State checking agent maintains the role subset for each user. It plays a role in monitoring the environment status of the user and dynamically changing the active role of the user.

State checking matrix deals with the context information such location, time, and resources such as network bandwidth and memory usage. Therefore, it activates or deactivates the specific role of the user. Context-aware agent maintains the permission subset for each role. It monitors the change of the state checking matrix and dynamically changes defaults the PA and UA to context-aware PA and UA as soon as SCM decides the activeness of the role for the user.

SCM is the key component to decide of user's access privileges in the context-aware access control model. It decides the activeness of roles for the user by mapping the status of context information such as location and time when user's context information changes. SCM for making access control decision forms as shown in Fig. 3 and 4. Fig. 3 depicts an example of SCM for context of user's location and Fig. 4 depicts an example of SCM for context of user's time.

	$Location_1$	$Location_2$	$Location_3$	$Location_4$
$User(R_1)$	Active	inactive	Inactive	Inactive
$Admin(R_2)$	Active	Active	Inactive	Active
$Pub(R_3)$	Inactive	Active	Active	Inactive

Fig. 3. SCM for location context

	$Time_1$	$Time_2$	$Time_3$	$Time_4$
$User(R_1)$	Active	Active	Inactive	Inactive
$Admin(R_2)$	Active	Active	Active	Active
$Pub(R_3)$	Inactive	Active	Active	Inactive

Fig. 4. SCM for time context

The row of SMC means elements of context information and the column of SCM means roles of the users. Making access control decision depends on a pair of context information. User's role is only active when all elements of context information are active. In the above example for SCM, user's role is only active when location and time are active. The concept of activeness of role can be described as follows:

$$\text{Activeness of role} = Context(Context_1, Context_2, \ldots, Context_n)$$
$$= \text{Context(Active, Active, \ldots, Active)} = \text{Active} \cdots\cdots(1)$$

In the case of context information is location and time, we can describe the activeness of role as follows by (1):

$$\text{Activeness of role} = \text{Context(Location, Time)}$$
$$= \text{Context(Active, Active)} = \text{Active} \cdots\cdots (2)$$

We propose an application scenario and describe how SCM would perform in the ubiquitous applications. Let us suppose that a smart building of university has many rooms including faculty office, administration office, conference rooms, classrooms and laboratories. Sensors in the building can capture, process and store a variety of information about the building, the users and their activities. Ubiquitous applications in such an environment allow the users, who can be faculty, staff, students and administrators, to access resources or information from any locations at anytime while inside this building using mobile devices and wireless networks. To make access control decision, user credentials are the basis for all the access control decisions. Furthermore, user's context information and application state should also be considered. To apply to context-aware access control model, let us suppose that $Location_1$ is faculty offices, $Location_2$ is administration office and $Location_3$ is conference room and $Location_4$ is classroom. For example, if a professor currently has a role set R_1, R_2, R_3 assigned by RBAC and then moves to administration office($Location_2$) at $Time_4$, the professor's role will be R_2 because the roles R_1 and R_3 by will be deactivated per (2). The activeness of roles are mapped into as follows:

Activeness of R_1 = $(Location_2, Time_4)$ = (Inactive, Inactive) = Inactive
Activeness of R_2 = $(Location_2, Time_4)$ = (Active, Active) = Active
Activeness of R_3 = $(Location_2, Time_4)$ = (Active, Inactive) = Inactive

Although we just apply to two elements(location and time) of context information in this example, we can extend scale of the context information easily by adding the SCM for required context information such as special event, system resource, network state, network security configuration and so on.

5   Conclusion and Future Work

In this paper, we presented the context-aware access control model for ubiquitous applications. The proposed access control model extends the RBAC model and dynamically adjusts role assignments and permission assignments based on the context information of the user. Much of this paper is focused on providing dynamically access control decision according to current context information. State checking matrix(SCM) in context-aware access control model is used to deal with context information and decides the activeness of roles for the user by mapping the status of context information such as location and time when user's context information changes. A desirable extension to this work is to make context-aware agents that are controlled by intelligent algorithms such as fuzzy or NN-based algorithm.

References

1. R.S. Sandhu and P. Samarati, Access control: Principles and practice, IEEE Communications Magazine, 32(9), pages 40-48, 1994

2. M.A. Harrson, W.L. Ruzzo, and J.D. Ullman. Protection in operation systems. Communications of the ACM, 19(8), pages 461-471, August 1976
3. R. S. Sandhu, E. J. Coynek, H. L. Feinsteink, C. E. Youmank, Role-Based Access Control Models, IEEE Computer, Volume 29, Number 2, February 1996, pages 38-47
4. David F. Feraiolo, D.Richard Kuhn, Ramaswamy Chandramouli, Role-Based Access Control, Artech House, INC, 2003
5. T. Y. C. Woo and Simon S. Lam. Designing a distributed authorization service. In Proceedings of IEEE INFOCOM, 1998.
6. M. J. Moyer M. J. Covington and M. Ahamad. Generalized role-based access control for securing future applications. In proceedings of NISSC 2000, October 2000.
7. M. J. Covington, W. Long, S. Srinivasan, A. K. Dey, M. Ahamad, G.D. Abowd, Securing Context-aware Applications Using Environment Roles, In proceedings of SACMAT'01, May 2001
8. G. Zhang, M. Parashar, Context-aware Dynamic Access Control for Pervasive Applications, In proceedings of the CNDS2004

On Application of Neural Networks
for S-Boxes Design

Piotr Kotlarz[1,2]

[1] Kazimierz Wielki University, Bydgoszcz,
[2] Zbigniew Kotulski,
Institute of Fundamental Technological Research
of the Polish Academy of Sciences,
Institute of Telecommunications of WUT, Warsaw

Abstract. In the paper a new schedule of S-boxes design is considered. We start from motivation from block cipher practice. Then, the most popular S-box design criteria are presented, especially a possibility of application of Boolean bent-functions. Finally, we propose integrating neural networks (playing a role of Boolean functions with appropriate properties) in the design process.

1   Foundations

Almost all modern block ciphers have iterative structure. This means that the complicated encryption of a block of text is due to multiple iterations of a simple round function. In the case of Feistel permutation, which was introduced in Lucifer and then widespread in 1977 through American standard DES [1], the input 64-bit block is divided into two 32-bits sub-blocks L_i and R_i. The round transformation, represented as:

$$L_i = R_{i-1},$$
$$R_i = L_{i-1} \oplus f\left(R_{i-1}, K_i\right), \tag{1}$$

substitutes the right subblock R_{i-1} the from previous round as the left subblock L_i at present and calculates bit-wise XOR of the left subblock L_{i-1} from the previous round with the output of the round function f taken on the right subblock R_{i-1} from the previous round and the round key K_i, substituting the result as the new right subblock R_i. Such a structure makes the cipher invertible (if decrypting we put the round keys in inverse order) and secure, provided the round function f has specific properties. These properties (e.g., diffusion and confusion, see [2]) make that during multiple iterations the plaintext bits mix strongly with themselves and bits of the secret key, so they cannot be reconstructed from the ciphertext without knowledge of the key. Usually, the two properties are realized in the round function by two layers of transformations: the diffusion by permutations and the confusion by key-dependent non-linear transformations. Description of permutations is quite simple (it is a table of substitutions), while

P.S. Szczepaniak et al. (Eds.): AWIC 2005, LNAI 3528, pp. 243–248, 2005.

writing down an arbitrary non-linear transformation mapping n bits block (e.g., $n = 32$ for DES) on n bits block is very complicated.

The problem of non-linear maps was practically solved by the concept of substitution boxes (S-boxes). For example, in DES (and earlier in Lucifer) the confusion layer contains a number of parallel S-boxes. Each S-box transforms 6 bit inputs to 4 bit output. It is a table of 4 rows and 16 columns. The elements of the table are the outputs (elements of the set $\{0, 1, 2, ..., 15\}$), equivalent to 4 bit blocks $\{0000, 0001, ..., 1111\}$. The element of the table is chosen according to the value of the input block: two bits (the first and the last) point the row number while the outstanding four bits give the number of the column. In the whole layer DES uses 8 different S-boxes.

The idea of application of S-boxes of proved to be very fruitful in constructing cryptographic algorithms. For example, in new American encryption standard AES [3] 16×16 S-boxes were applied. The Russian encryption standard GOST [4] also uses a layer of S-boxes, but with content left to the users' invention. S-boxes are used not only in block ciphers but also in certain stream ciphers [5] and hash algorithms.

In the cryptographic practice there is no mathematically precise theory of the S-boxes design. However, there are some intuitive rules and conditions imposed on the S-boxes. Returning to the classical example of DES we can give some properties of all its eight S-boxes:

- No S-box is a linear of affine function of its input (they are non-linear functions)
- Every row in any S-box is a permutation (it contains equal number of zeros and ones)
- Changing one bit of input we change at least two bits of the output of S-box (the avalanche property)
- If one input bit is fixed, an S-box minimizes the difference of zeros and ones on the output.

The particular properties of the S-boxes presented above resulted in more general properties of the whole DES cipher: its (maximally possible) resistance to the linear [6] and differential [7] cryptanalysis. This result became a foundation of a practical method of constructing S-boxes: first one should generate the S-box putting its contents at random and then test its statistical properties (as a binary map) to obtain the maximal resistance against the two attacks. The assumed dimension of the S-box and some prior constraints on the S-boxes must be carefully discussed in the context of a cryptographic algorithm the S-box is to be installed. The higher dimension of the S-box, its statistical analysis more complicated both for the algorithm designer and a hostile cryptanalyst.

At present the methods of S-boxes design are based on two parallel methodologies. The first one uses mainly mathematical theories and statistical investigations, while the other is additionally supported by practitioners experience To find a link between the both methodologies we propose the application of the neural networks learning methodology in the S-box design procedure.

2   Neural Networks

Neural networks are a form of multiprocessor matrices with simple processing elements, simple scalar messages and adaptive interaction between elements. The working element of the network is neuron. Its mathematical model is presented at Fig. 1.

$$net = \sum_{i=1}^{n} x_i w_i,$$
$$x = [x_1, x_2, ..., x_n]^T,$$
$$w = [w_1, w_2, ..., w_n]^T$$

Fig. 1. The mathematical model of neuron

The weighted sum of the inputs x is calculated to compose the activation of the neuron net, (also called the post-synaptic potential). The activation signal is passed through an activation (or transfer) function f to generate the output of the neuron. Eq. (2) shows two examples of activation function: the step function (discrete unipolar) f_p and sigmoid (continuous unipolar) f_s ones.

$$f_p(x) = \begin{cases} 1, \sum\limits_{i=1}^{n} x_i w_i \geq p \\ 0, \sum\limits_{i=1}^{n} x_i w_i < p \end{cases}, \quad f_s(x) = \frac{1}{1 + \exp\left\{-\alpha \left(\sum\limits_{i=1}^{n} x_i w_i\right)\right\}}. \quad (2)$$

The training of a neuron or a neural network can be performed with a number of methods. One of them is learning according to the back-propagated delta rule with supervision. The aim of the training is minimizing the sum squared error between the desired output and the actual output.

$$x(i) = [x_1(i), x_2(i), ..., x_m(i)]^T$$
$$y(i) = [y_1(i), y_2(i), ..., y_m(i)]^T$$
$$\bar{y}(i) = [\bar{y}_1(i), \bar{y}_2(i), ..., \bar{y}_m(i)]^T$$
$$d_j(i) = y_j(i) - \bar{y}_j(i)$$
$$w'_j = w_j + \eta d_j(i) x_j, \quad j = 1...m$$
$$E = \frac{1}{2} \sum_{i=1}^{n} \sum_{j=1}^{m} d_j^2(i)$$

Fig. 2. The neural network training process

Fig. 2 drafts a schedule of training a neural network with $m-$bit inputs and $m-$bit outputs. At the figure, $\bar{x}, \bar{y}$ is the training set (a set of n vector inputs and desired outputs) and i is the number of its element, y is the actual output, $d_j(i)$ is a ith cycle error of the jth coordinate, wj is the weight of jth input, x is the input vector, η is the learning rate and E is the sum squared error. More details about neural networks can be found in the literature (see, e.g. [9]).

3   S-Boxes Design

S-boxes are critical security elements of the Feistel-type ciphers (see [10]) and other cascade algorithms. Well-designed S-box is a strongly non-linear Boolean (vector) map with the avalanche property. In the literature one can find some practical methods of the S-box design [11], [12], but they are rather specific than universal. Among others, one of the most promising seems to be application of Boolean bent-functions (see, e.g., [13], [14]).

The Boolean functions is defined as:

$$f : (Z_2)^n \rightarrow Z_2, \ Z_2 = GF(2). \tag{3}$$

To be the bent-function, the Boolean function must additionally be non-linear and balanced (it should output the equal number of zeros and ones when its argument goes over the whole range). More precisely, a Boolean function is the bent-function (or perfectly nonlinear) if the function $f(x) \oplus f(x \oplus a)$ is balanced for every $a \in (Z_2)^n$ such that $1 \leq hwt(a) \leq n$.

The balance of a Boolean function is a fundamental property from the cryptography point of view (see [15]). In the language of Hamming measures the function f is balanced if $hwt(f) = 2^{n-1}$. The Hamming measure of a binary string is the number of ones in this string. For the Boolean function f, its Hamming measure is the number of ones in its truth table. The Hamming distance of two Boolean functions f and g is defined as $d(f, g) = hwt(f \oplus g) = \sum_x f(x) \oplus g(x)$

where the summation is over the whole argument's range.

4   Neural Networks and the Bent-Functions

As we remarked, cryptographically secure S-boxes must satisfy certain conditions. Thy critical property is the balance of outputs. This means in fact, that the S-box can be considered as a black box which transforms any input vector into a balanced vector in a non-predictable way (what translates in practice as non-linear). Now we will show that such an security element can be realized by specific neural networks.

To solve the construction problem we start from the 2×2 S-box (two bits input and two bits output of a Boolean function) We expect, that the S-box produces a balanced output for an arbitrary input. The sample truth table in such a case can be represented as:

x_1	x_2	y_1	y_2
0	0	0	1
0	1	1	0
1	0	1	0
1	1	0	1

The Hamming measure of this table is 2, by definition of the measure. As it is seen from the table, the output of the vector-valued Boolean function is with such a truth table would be balanced.

To realize the balanced Boolean function we apply certain two-layers neural network. First we start from one block of the network. The first layer of the block is a pair of neurons with the sigmoid activation functions f_s and the other is a single neuron with step activation function f_p (see Fig. 3).

$$y = \begin{cases} 0 \text{ for } f_s(x_i w_i) < 0 \\ 1 \text{ for } f_s(x_i w_i) \geq 0 \end{cases}$$

Fig. 3. Neural network for the one-output bent-function

Combining two such blocks (Fig.4) and training each of them with different training set we obtain the network which outputs the balanced binary vector irrespective of the values of the input binary data.

Fig. 4. Neural network for two-outputs bent-function

Now we can take the neural blocks presented at Figs. 3, 4 and combine them into larger structures realizing certain functions. As a simple example we built a network of 189 neurons (Fig.3) to obtain a selector choosing elements from S-box of DES. Compiled with a standard neural network it gave neural representation of the S-box. Certainly, such a network should be optimized to reduce number of "neural cells". This will be the subject of future research.

The balance and avalanche property are fundamental for S-boxes, but they do not suffice their security. The other important property of Boolean functions and S-boxes is the correlation resistance. This property generalizes the balance property. We say that the function f of n arguments has the correlation resistance of order m $(1 \leq m \leq n)$ if the output $f(x)$ is statistically independent of any m chosen elements of x. In the language of information (see [15]) we can write this as

$$H(f(x)) - H(f(x)|x_1, x_2, ..., x_i) = 0. \tag{4}$$

Testing the property (4) can be additional, except of the balance property, easy to implement training condition of the neural network modelling an S-box. Let us remark the training procedure could be performed without exact knowledge of the modelled function, only on the basis of very general requirements lied on it.

5 Summary

In the paper we presented an idea of application of neural networks for constructing S-boxes, the critical security elements of block ciphers and other private key cryptographic algorithms. This element is most difficult to realize by a neural network. The others elements of block ciphers like permutations and linear substitutions are much easier. Thus, realization of the whole algorithm is only a technical problem. The other potentially fruitful possibility of application of neural networks in cryptology is testing cryptographic algorithms. This problem along with improvement of the approach presented in this paper would be the subject of our future research.

References

[1] FIPS 46-3, Data Encryption Standard (DES), NIST 1999.
[2] Z. Kotulski, Construction of block ciphers: new possibilities. (Polish) *Mat. Stosow.* No. 4(45) (2003), pp. 1-24.
[3] FIPS 197, Advanced Encryption Standard (AES), NIST 2001.
[4] GOST 28147-89, Cryptographic Protection for Data Processing Systems. Cryptographic Transformation Algorithm, Government Standard of the U.S.S.R. 1990.
[5] L. Gan, S. Simmons, S. Tavares, A new family of stream ciphers based on cascades small S-boxes, IEEE (1997).
[6] M. Matsui, Linear Cryptanalysis Method for DES Cipher, LNCS Advances in Cryptology, EUROCRYPT'93, pp. 386-397, Springer-Verlag, Berlin 1993.
[7] E. Biham, A. Shamir, Differential Cryptanalysis of Data Encryption Standard, Springer Verlag, Berlin 1993.
[8] C. M. Adams, S. E. Tavares, Designing S-boxes for Ciphers Resistant to Differential Cryptanalysis.
[9] A. Horzyk, R. Tadeusiewicz, Self-Optimizing Neural Networks, in: F. Yin, J. Wang, Ch. Guo [Eds.]: Advances in Neural Networks - ISNN 2004, pp.150-155, LNCS 3173, Springer, Berlin 2004.
[10] L.R. Knudsen, Practically Secure Feistel Ciphers, in: R.Anderson [Ed.], Fast Software Encryption, LNCS 809, pp. 211-222, Springer-Verlag, Berlin 1994.
[11] A F Webster, S E Tavares, On the design of S-boxes, LNCS 218 Advances in Cryptology—CRYPTO'85, pp.523-534, Springer-Verlag, Berlin 1985.
[12] S. Mister, C. Adams, Practical S-Box Design, Workshop on Selected Areas in Cryptography (SAC '96) Workshop Record, Queens University, 1996, pp. 61–76.
[13] C.M. Adams and S.E. Tavares, The Use of Bent Sequences do Achieve Higher Order Strict Criterion in S-Box Design TRTR 90-013 Jan. 1990.
[14] A. Grocholewska-Czurylo, Avalanche and propagation properties of random bent Boolean functions, Proc. RMCIS 2003, p.9.3, Zegrze 2003.
[15] J. Szmidt, Cryptographic properties of the Boolean functions, Proceedings of the 5th National Conference on Cryptography ENIGMA 2001, Warsaw 2001.

Migration Integrity Rules in Open Systems

Dariusz Król[1] and Bogusław Szlachetko[2]

[1]Faculty of Computer Science and Management, Wrocław University of Technology,
Wyb. Wyspiańskiego 27, 50-370 Wrocław, Poland
[2] Faculty of Electronics, Wrocław University of Technology, Wyb. Wyspiańskiego 27,
50-370 Wrocław, Poland
{Dariusz.Krol, Boguslaw.Szlachetko}@pwr.wroc.pl

Abstract. Multi-class Object Methodology allows objects to change their structure and behavior with respect to semantic integrity. This paper examines the problem of object constraint satisfaction. Two aspects of object constraints are analyzed in detail. The first aspect refers to multi-class feature of objects, and the second is related to the migration of multi-class objects. The expanding approach compared to existing solutions is relied on standardizing the elementary notions: object and constraint. The major contribution is: objects are allowed to change during their lifetime and migrate between systems, also constraints are allowed to change and migrate. The sequence of migration is depending on operation order.

1 Introduction

Multi-class Object Methodology is a concept for simplifying object migration between different systems (see [9, 10]). We need keep in mind that all existing concepts in integrity modeling, both more natural and pure artificial, must evolve or die. To bypass the gap between objects and constraints, a unify object notation should be used to define, change and migrate. In order to achieve it we need to add new features to object and constraint definition. In this regard, we are encouraged by the modeling language for dynamic systems and dynamic constraints [13].

The goal of this paper is to provide a formal approach to migration objects in a Web environment that relies on a multi-class dependencies to reflect the behavior and state, and to show how different results could be achieved in this framework during migration transaction.

The evolution on the object level consists of such operation as object moving or object adding [12]. Between classes and objects different relationships, such as inheritance or preference etc., may occur. Because of these relationships an object schema mentions a complicated and nested net in which the nodes represent classes and objects, and the edges - different relationships between them. One should note that in this kind of nets each operation which moves or adds elements requires a very expensive reconstruction.

P.S. Szczepaniak et al. (Eds.): AWIC 2005, LNAI 3528, pp. 249–253, 2005.

In MOM we have to take into consideration constraints not appearing in others environments. At first satisfaction for object-sub-object association, i.e. Student could be simultaneous Graduate, but Pupil not. At second satisfaction for migration path, i.e. Student could migrate to Graduate, and next to Lecturer, but it is impossible that Graduate could stay Student again.

In this paper we propose a new constraint model which enables to specify the notions of semantic integrity between objects. There are three possibilities to describe constraints: constraints could be defined in instances, classes and special constraints-objects. On this basement it is possible to define effective mechanisms for dynamic evolution also in distributed environments.

The rest of the paper is organized as follows. In Section 2 we describe the formal notation of Multi-class Constraint. In Section 3 different examples of migration paths are presented and discussed. Finally, Section 4 presents our conclusions and future works.

2   Formal Approach to Object Integrity

Suppose we have a database of a factory assembling vehicles in a certain country. We can see the following examples of value propagation:

Definition 1. *By a multi-class object x we call an expression*

$$(id(x), Sub(x), Sup(x), A_{Sub}(x), v(x), M(x)) \tag{1}$$

where $id(x)$ - object identifier of x, $Sub(x)$ - set of sub-objects identifiers of x, $Sup(x)$ - set of sup-objects identifiers of x, $A_{Sub}(x)$ - set of attributes described sub-objects of x, $v(x)$ - value of x, $M(x)$ - set of methods of x, where:

$$(\forall x, y \in OBJ)(id(x) = id(y) \Leftrightarrow v(x) = v(y) \wedge Sub(x) = Sub(y) \wedge Sup(x) \tag{2}$$
$$= Sup(y) \wedge M(x) = M(y) \wedge A_{Sub}(x) = A_{Sub}(y))$$
$$(\forall x, y \in OBJ)(id(y) \in Sub(x) \Rightarrow id(x) \notin Sub(y)) \tag{3}$$
$$(\forall x, y \in OBJ)(id(y) \in Sup(x) \Rightarrow id(x) \notin Sup(y)) \tag{4}$$
$$(\forall x, y \in OBJ)(id(y) \in Sub(x) \Rightarrow id(x) \in Sup(y)) \tag{5}$$
$$(\forall x, y \in OBJ)(id(y) \in Sub(x) \Rightarrow A(y) \supseteq A_{Sub}(x) \vee A_{Sub}(y) \supseteq A_{Sub}(x)) \tag{6}$$
$$v(x) : A(x) \rightarrow V(x) \quad \text{where} \quad a \in A(x), v \in V_a(x) \tag{7}$$

Between object there are relation called object-sub-object relation.

Definition 2. *We call that objects x and y are in object-sub-object relation, if $y \in Sub(x)$. We denote object-sub-object relation as $x \angle y$.*

If object-sub-object relation is restricted to object-class relation we will obtain classical inheritance relation.

Definition 3. *Object-sub-object relation we call inheritance relation, iff $(x \angle y)$ and $A_{Sub}(y) \supseteq A_{Sub}(x)$. We denote inheritance relation as $x \leq y$.*

Definition 4. *By a multi-class constraint x we call an expression*

$$(id(x), Sub(x), Sup(x), A_{Sub}(x), v(x), M(x)) \tag{8}$$

where $Sub(x) = Sup(x) = A_{Sub}(x) = \emptyset$,
where $id(x)$ - *object identifier of* x, $Sub(x)$ - *set of sub-objects identifiers of* x, $Sup(x)$ - *set of sup-objects identifiers of* x, $A_{Sub}(x)$ - *set of attributes described sub-objects of* x, $v(x)$ - *value of* x,
where $a \in \{Apply, Not\ apply, Covers, Covered\ with\} \wedge V_{Apply} \subseteq OBJ \wedge V_{Not\ apply} \subseteq OBJ \wedge V_{Covers} \subseteq OGR \wedge V_{Covered\ with} \in CONSTR$,
$M(x)$ - *set of methods of* x,
where

$$\forall\, x, y \in V_{Apply} \Rightarrow \neg(x \leq y \vee x \geq y \vee x \angle y \vee y \angle x) \tag{9}$$

$$\forall\, x, y \in V_{Not\ apply} \Rightarrow \neg(x \leq y \vee x \geq y \vee x \angle y \vee y \angle x) \tag{10}$$

$$\forall\, x \in V_{Apply} \Rightarrow x \notin V_{Not\ apply} \tag{11}$$

$$\forall\, x \in V_{Not\ apply} \Rightarrow x \notin V_{Apply} \tag{12}$$

$$\forall\, x \in V_{Not\ apply} \Rightarrow \exists y \in V_{Apply} \wedge (y \leq x \vee y \angle x) \tag{13}$$

$$\forall\, x \,\exists y : \; x \in V_{Covers}(y) \Rightarrow V_{Covered\ with}(x) = y \tag{14}$$

Example 1. If we study inter-object associations there is a need for mutually exclusive objects (15), (16) or mutually inclusive objects (17).

$$\forall x \in Sub(Pupil) : (\; x \in Sub(Class_{2a}) \Rightarrow x \notin Sub(Class_{2b})) \tag{15}$$

$$\forall x \in Sub(Pupil) : (\; x \in Sub(Class_{2b}) \Rightarrow x \notin Sub(Class_{2a})) \tag{16}$$

$$\forall x \in Sub(Pupil) : (\; x \in Sub(Math_{circle}) \Rightarrow x \in Sub(Class_{2a}) \vee \tag{17}$$
$$x \in Sub(Class_{2b}))$$

3   Migration Problem

Migration process could be in special case nonsense. In particular each path start (a) from any class to superclass (b) from any class to subclass (c) from any class to another class, but not superclass or subclass.

Lets see the following objects: Person, Male, Female. The migration path of type (a) or (b) for Person and Female is without sense. Also the migration type (c) is impossible since Male and Female are semantic exclusive. The next problem is the direction of the change, ie. object Children migrates to Adult but not back.

The fundamental question is for data integrity after migration process is completed. In open systems [8] we use the following operators:

$$Object_1 \; \frac{Object_2}{Add} \; Object_3 \tag{18}$$

$$Object_1 \frac{Object_2}{Delete} Object_3 \tag{19}$$

$$Object_1 \frac{Object_2}{Move} Object_3 \tag{20}$$

In some situations the migration process especially move operator could cause some integrity problems. Lets see the following example.

Example 2. We have the following objects:

$$(K, \ Sub(K), \ \{Z\}, \ \{Surname, \ Date \ of \ birth\}, \ \emptyset, \ M(K)), \tag{21}$$
$$(S, \ Sub(S), \ Sup(S), \ \{Surname, \ Address\}, \ \emptyset, \ M(S)), \tag{22}$$
$$(M, \ Sub(M), \ \{Z\}, \ \{Surname, \ Date \ of \ birth\}, \ \emptyset, \ M(M)), \tag{23}$$
$$(Z, \ \{K, \ M\}, \ Sup(Z), \ \{Surname, \ Date \ of \ birth\}, \ \emptyset, \ M(Z)), \tag{24}$$

and the object

$$(Pupil_1, \ \emptyset, \ \{K\}, \ \emptyset, \ < Name : Rob, \ Surname : Clark, \tag{25}$$
$$Date \ of \ birth : 1991, \ Gender : M, \ Note : 5.0, 4.0, 3.5 >, \ \emptyset).$$

Moreover

$$(Surname, K) = (Surname, S) = (Surname, M) \tag{26}$$

and

$$(Date \ of \ birth, K) = (Date \ of \ birth, M) = (Date \ of \ birth, Z). \tag{27}$$

Lets compare the operation

$$(K \ \frac{Pupil_1}{Move} \ M) \tag{28}$$

with a sequence

$$(K \ \frac{Pupil_1}{Move} \ S) \tag{29}$$

$$(S \ \frac{Pupil_1}{Move} \ M) \tag{30}$$

After *Move* sequence object $Pupil_1$ is the following:

$$(Pupil_1, \ \emptyset, \ \{K\}, \ \emptyset, \ < Name : Rob, \ Surname : Clark, \tag{31}$$
$$Date \ of \ birth : 1991, \ Gender : M, \ Note : 5.0, 4.0, 3.5 >, \ \emptyset).$$

4   Discussion

This paper outlines simple migration integrity rules for objects in open systems. We believe that this approach to follow migration paths is very promising for future work. From a practical point of view we are studying the behavior of objects in Web systems.

Future work will tackle the problem of mining associations rules using multi-class methodology. It is necessary to get to know what can be done not only with object structures but also with object behavior.

Our approach seems specific only for multi-object environment, but could be simple modified and adopted to similar multi-agent environment and distributed systems [9].

References

1. Arregui, D., Pacull, F., Willamowski J.: Rule-Based Transactional Object Migration over a Reflective Middleware. Lecture Notes in Computer Science **2218** (2001) 179–196
2. Behm, A., Geppert, A., Dittrich K.R.: Algebraic Database Migration to Object Technology. Lecture Notes in Computer Science **1920** (2000) 440–453
3. Bertino E., Guerrini G., Merlo I.: Extending the ODMG Object Model with Triggers. IEEE Transactions on Knowledge and Data Engineering **16** (2004) 170–188
4. Castellani X., Jiang H., Billionnet A.: Method for the analysis and design of class characteristic migrations during object system evolution. Information Systems **26** (2001) 237–257
5. Corradi A.: Parallel Objects Migration: A Fine Grained Approach to Lad Distribution. Journal of Parallel and Distributed Computing **60** (2000) 48–71
6. Dori D.: ViSWeb - the Visual Semantic Web: unifying human and machine knowledge representations with Object-Process Methodology. The VLDB Journal **13** (2004) 120–147
7. Jurisica I., Mylopoulos J., Yu E.: Ontologies for Knowledge Management: An Information System perspective. Knowledge and Information Systems **6** (2004) 380–401
8. Krivokapic N., Islinger M., Kemper A.: Migrating Autonomous Objects in a WAN Environment. Journal of Intelligent Information Systems **15** (2000) 221–251
9. Król D.: Migration mechanism for multi-class object in multi-agent systems. Lecture Notes in Artificial Intelligence **3214** (2004) 1165–1171
10. Król, D., Nguyen N. T., Danilowicz Cz.,: Migration of multi-class objects in information systems. Advanced in soft computing (2002) 403–412
11. Noy N.F., Klein M.: Ontology Evolution: Not the Same as Schema Evolution. Knowledge and Information Systems **6** (2004) 428–440
12. Sapir A., Gudes E. Dynamic Relationships and Their Propagation and Concurrency Semantics in object-Oriented Databases. Lecture Notes in Computer Science **1649** (1999) 94–111
13. Su J.: Dynamic Constraints and Object Migration. In Proceedings of the 17th International VLDB Conference (1991) 233–242
14. Zadeh L. A. : Web Intelligence, World Knowledge and Fuzzy Logic. Lecture Notes in Artificial Intelligence **3214** (2004) 1–5

Fulltext-Image Watermarking Using Improved DWT and HVS Based on JPEG Compression

Wongoo Lee, Byungsun Choi, Seounghyeon Lee, and Jaekwang Lee

Dept. of Computer Engineering, University of Hannam,
133 Ojong-Dong, Daeduk-Gu, Taejeon, 306-791, Korea
{wglee, bschoi, shlee, jklee}@netwk.hannam.ac.kr

Abstract. As multimedia data and their applications are rapidly distributed on the Web, the research on watermark insertion and integrity vigorously increases. In this paper, discrete wavelet transformation dissolves an original image into the 3-levels of low, middle, and high bandwidths. Human visual system with the significant coefficients extracted from the middle obtains enhanced image quality and robustness using watermark insertion. In the end, experimental results show that various attacks cannot destroy pre-inserted watermark and recovered image is of good quality by measuring PSNR.

1 Introduction

As demand for digital fulltext-image with fast development of super high-speed communication network is increasing in digital contents industry, its scale is increasing exponentially every year. However, this fulltext-image is illegally reprinting and distributing widely, and this brings about the problems of its copyrights and proprietary rights[1][2]. Consequently, we design robust watermarking algorithm, which can resist a various attacks, construct digital fulltext-image framework for copyright service, and apply them in our digital fulltext-image protection system. To do this, first, we reconstructs the value-chain structure of digital contents industry about Framework from manufacturing of digital contents to its consumption and suggest integrated model and reference model about digital original text service by rearranging the subjects. Also, we construct digital fulltext-image service system based on reference model and reconstruct interface that is occurred between subjects. Second, we implement digital fulltext-image protection system that apply watermark/fingerprint algorithm that can be protect the copyright of digital fulltext.

2 Digital Watermarking Algorithms

At inserting watermark, HVS, designed by Lewis and Knowles, is system to insert imperceptible watermark with considering a various characteristics of our eye including retinal and neural network.

P.S. Szczepaniak et al. (Eds.): AWIC 2005, LNAI 3528, pp. 254–259, 2005.

We can insert watermark of big size at less insensitive part of our eye based on this characteristics, design watermarking algorithm with this. Existing algorithms proposed[8] applied JND(Just Noticeable Difference) which present minimal difference for someone to detect between two signals. However, this method has weak points that it enables to apply to only black and white picture and robustness become worse by inserting watermark without having regard to the effects of sight of a DWT coefficient. In this paper, we decreased computational load and had a little effect on image by selecting specific coefficient in middle frequency band. Also, we improve robustness by using Gaussian random vector that has the advantage of no pattern guessing, no dependency, and no relationship. In the end, we show that PSNR value of suggested technique is superior to it of existing techniques by way of experiment.

2.1 Watermark Inserting Algorithm Using HVS

We select specific coefficient. Of middle frequency band by using DWT, then look around the series of process to insert watermark by applying HVS. Fig.1 shows the process to insert watermark.

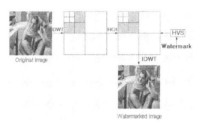

Fig. 1. The process of watermark insertion

[Step 1] To insert watermark in image, first we disjoint it into three levels through the process of DWT. We use our wavelet filter with the 9/7 tab which is suggested by Antonini as above Fig.1. I_1^0, I_1^1, I_1^2, middle frequency filled with gray color, is frequency band where watermark is inserted. We inserted watermark into middle frequency band because watermark inserted in that place is extracted in the high ratio after any image processing and the image inserted in the watermark is distorted in the low ratio than other band relatively.

[Step 2] To insert robust watermark, visually significant coefficient is selected. At this time, ROI found by using the principles of MTWC is inserted. Here, the visually significant coefficient has generally large value and remain a little change after image processing such as compression. If this coefficient is changed, the image through reverse DWT processing differs largely from original image.

The processing to find visually significant coefficient is the followings;

(a) At initial step, initial critical valule (T_s) of the band in which watermark is inserted. At this time, the critical value is the half of the largest coefficient ($C_{\max}$) which has the largest absolute value of coefficients in the band; $T_s = C_{\max}/2$.

(b) To find the significant coefficient, If $C_s(i,j) > T_s$ through comparing all coefficient $C_s(i,j)$ with critical values, it select as the significant coefficient.

(c) If all watermarks are not inserted, above processing repeat itself from step (a) until all of them is inserted.

[Step 3] Inserting watermarking using HVS: The property of HVS applies to visually significant coefficient which is selected from middle frequency where watermark is inserted(i.e. I_1^0, I_1^1 and I_1^2 band). The merit of this method is to enable to decrease computational load than other algorithms because watermark is not inserted to all coefficients and to have a little effect on image. Inserting of watermark is the processing to insert the information of watermark. This processing is the followings;

$$C_s(i,j) = C_s(i,j) + \alpha \cdot q(i,j) \cdot W_k$$

C_s is the original coefficient selected, C_s's is the coefficient with watermark, and α is parameter to present the strength of watermark and $\alpha \in (0.0, 3.0)$. q(i,j) is weighting function using HVS, W_k is watermark and used Gaussian random vector that its mean is 0 and its dispersion is 1. The merit of Gaussian random vector is to become independent to each other, to have no relation with each other, and not to guess pattern. The watermark can use string, image, logo and random string according to a property of algorithms.

2.2   Watermark Detection Algorithm

We describe the method to decide whether watermark is inserted or not and to judge its validity by extracting it in image.

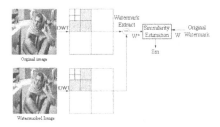

Fig. 2. The extraction process of watermark

Fig. 2 shows the process diagram to extract watermark, the process can be describes as followings;

(1) Call original image and image including watermark
(2) Decompose each frequency into three levels through DWT process for above two images
(3) Extract watermark through comparing two image decomposed by (2)
(4) Measure the similarity through measuring formula of similarity
(5) Decide whether watermark is inserted or not through comparing the estimated similarity value with critical value estimated by experimentation

$$C\left(W, W^*\right) = \frac{W \cdot W^*}{\sqrt{W \cdot W}}$$

C is similarity, W is watermark before it is inserted, W^* is watermark after it is extracted. If $C \geq$ critical value, we decide that watermark is inserted. Otherwise, we decide that it is not. Here, the critical value is obtained by experimentation but computation.

3   The Experimentation and the Results

We divide original image into 4-levels of sub-band image by using the biorthogonal wavelet filter[7][8], then insert and detect watermark in ROI(Region of Interest) through HVS(Human Visual System). At this time, we use 512*512, 256 gray color of "Barbara" image as experimented image. First,we experiment the invisibility of watermark. Fig. 3(a) shows original "Barbara" image, and Fig. 3(b) shows "Barbara" image with watermark. The difference of two images is scarcely as shown by Fig. 3. Also, [Fig. 3](c) shows "Barbara" image which apply JPEG compression(30:1) and decompression method to image in Fig. 3(b).

Fig. 3. Invisibility experimentation of image

(a) is original "Barbara" image, (b) is "Barbara" image with watermark(PSNR 45.68), and (c) is "Barbara" image applying JPEG compression(30:1) and decompression method(PSNR 26.38Db).

Fig. 4 shows various attack techniques for image. And we can see that the 299 units of a forged watermark have no response as shown by Fig. 5.

Our method considerably improves PSNR value than the method using HVS technique. The PSNR value of our method is similar to the PSNR value of the method using ROI technique, but it improves robustness than the method using ROI technique. The experimental result of the robustness for each method is shown by below the experimental result. We set up middle frequency band as the

(a)Blurring   (b)Sharpening   (c)Gaussian noise   (d)Cropping

Fig. 4. The results of various attacks

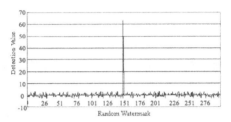

Fig. 5. The experimented result of the unique of watermark

Table 1. Comparative tables for experimental results of our method

Image	Our method	ROI method	HVS method
Lena	51.62 dB	53.08 dB	42.12 dB
Barbara	45.68 dB	47.19 dB	39.60 dB
Bridge	41.90 dB	43.03 dB	38.18 dB
Gold hill	42.89 dB	43.37 dB	39.37 dB
Air plane	39.50 dB	39.79 dB	36.82 dB

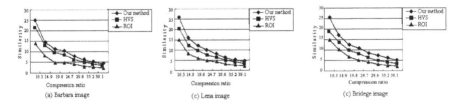

Fig. 6. The experimental result of JPEG compression and the similarity for image

region to insert the same strength of watermark and the watermark to compare the performance when the condition is on the same level at this experimentation.

We can see that our method improves the robustness than the method using HVS technique as shown by Fig. 6(a)(b)(c). Also, we can see that the PSNR value of the restored image has the highest value, but its robustness has the lowest value.

4   Conclusion

To protect copyright, digital watermarking techniques are suggested. In step, we designed robust watermarking algorithm, which could resist a various attack, construct digital fulltext-image framework for copyright service, and apply them in our digital fulltext-image protection system.

Thus, discrete wavelet transformation dissolves an original image into the 3-levels of low, middle, and high bandwidths. Human visual system with the significant coefficients extracted from the middle obtains enhanced image quality and robustness using watermark insertion. In the end, experimental results show that various attacks cannot destroy pre-inserted watermark and recovered image is of good quality by measuring PSNR values.

Acknowledgement

This work was supported by a grand No.R12-2003-004-02004-0 from Ministry of Commerce, Industry and Energy of the Korean Government.

References

1. Tae-Jung Kim, Sang-Kuk Kim and You-Jin Song: Standards Trends of Contents Right Protection and Its Related technology. KISSC review, Vol.14, No.1, (2004) 91–106
2. Korea Institute of Science and Technology Information: Research and Implementation for the Protection of Fulltext DataBase. (2003) 15–71
3. D. Kirovski, H. Malvar, Y. Yacobi: A dual watermark-fingerprint system. IEEE multimedia, Vol.11, No.3, (2004) 59–73
4. Martin Kutter, Sviatoslav Voloshynovskiy and Alexander herrigel: The watermark copy attack. proceedings of SPIE : Security and watermarking of multimedia content II, Vol.3971, (2000)
5. Syscop: http://www.crcg.edu/syscop/
6. DOI(Digital Object Identifier): http://www.doi.org
7. yiwei Wang, john F. Doherty, Robert E: "A Wavelet-based Watermarking Algorithm for Ownership Verification of Digital Images. IEEE Transactions on image procession 2002, (2002)
8. M. Antonini, M. Barlaud. P. Mathieu and I. Daubechies: Image Coding using Wavelet Transform. IEEE Transactions on Image Processing, Vol.1, No.3, (1992) 205–220

Active Network Approach for Web Caching[*]

Zhigang Liao[1], Zengzhi Li[1], Tao Zhan[2], and Yan Chen[1]

[1] Institute of Computer Architecture & Network,
Xi'an Jiaotong University, Xi'an 710049, China
[2] Computer Science and Technology Department,
Northwest Polytechnical University, Xi'an 710072, China

Abstract. Web caching is an effective way to save network bandwidth and promote network performance. In traditional network, strong consistency and collaboration mechanism establishment are two major problems. AWC (Active Networking Caching) is a distributed service based on active network. Each cache traces of server and makes a virtual link between cache and server. Different servers can share their branch nodes, so AWC will cause fewer burdens than conventional solution. AWC provides a lightweight way to coordinate distributed caches. Cache nodes needn't communicate with other caches to share storage for the sibling cache nodes share their storage. It can reduce the cost of collaboration establishing. The simulation results shows AWC cost less network bandwidth for state tracking between server and caches.

1 Introduction

Although web is one of the most important approaches to publish information, users suffer from net congestion and server overload. Web caching is a good approach to save bandwidth and improve performance. However it still has many problems. Content consistency and content sharing are two of them. Unfortunately, by traditional network, it is difficult to solve them from the base.

As novel programmable network architecture, active network [1] provides dynamic generalization of network services by injecting code and/or policy into shared nodes of the network. Compare to conventional network, active network can develop new network protocol and service easily. In this paper, we introduce an active service called AWC (Active Web Caching) based on ANTS[2] to provide a flexible architecture for proxies and the original server.

2 Related Works and Web Caching Challenges

Content Consistency. Many research works have been done to solve content consistency problem. PER (Poll Each Read) [3] has strong consistency but it cannot bring much benefit on performance. TTL (Time to Live) [3], also called

---

[*] This paper is supported by the Nation Science Foundation of China (No.60173059).

Expire, can improve performance greatly but it can only provide weak consistency. These two methods are client driven and can be easily deployed in the Internet. Invalidation [4][5] and Lease[6] is another kind of approach driven by server. Server keeps track of the proxies caching its content. When content is modified, server will notify all related proxy to expire or fresh the content. Invalidation can get strong consistency with only a little more cost than client driven methods[5]. Leases [6] make a mixture of Invalidation and TTL. When looking deep into the these methods, we found it still has a vital fault. In the WWW, a proxy server may be severed from origin server temporarily or for a long vocation. During this vocation, if objects are modified in origin server, there is no mean to notify the proxy. In conclusion, since the proxy cannot trace the state of origin server especially connectivity to origin server at any time, so it cannot make reaction to fault in time.

Collaboration. Individual cache may work well but it meets challenge of huge storage volume since the information from different server will accumulate day by day. Cooperative caching mechanisms have been proposed to solve this problem. The architecture of these mechanisms can be divided into three categories [3]: hierarchical caching architecture, distributed caching architecture and hybrid caching architecture.For hierarchical caching architecture, the caching system forms a tree structure. For distributed caching system the storage is shared among caches. And the hybrid caching architecture is a combination of two architectures mentioned above. ICP (Internet Cache Protocol, RFC 2186) is a typical example that offers a mechanism for establishing complex cache hierarchies. Though these methods can improve the performance of web cache effectively, to configure a hierarchical web cache is a time consuming work and sometimes it is difficult to coordinate. In [7]the author indicates that approximately only 10% of requests will be cache hits in neighbor caches while there are approximately 30-50% local hit rates typically seen by most caches.

3   Active Web Cache Mechanisms

3.1   Status Tracking

AWC provides an active mean for status tracking between server and cache nodes. Assume a cache node wants to keep track with server's state. Firstly, it sends request capsule to the server. As well as server receiving the request, it sends back a reply capsule; each node on the route from server to the cache node will activate the AWC Service. The service will monitor the next and the previous node to see whether the neighbor is available. As shown in figure 1, it becomes a dual link from the server to the cache node. This makes a group of node pairs. In figure 1, it has generated three node pairs: (CacheNode, AN1), (AN1, AN2) and (AN2, Server). The normal state is that all nodes in the link connected together and the service is working. If the service on the server were down, the adjacent node, in this case AN2, will aware of the failure and notify the client along the link. All nodes that receive the message will release the resource.

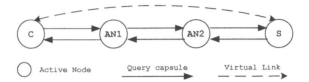

Fig. 1. Each node keeps track with adjacent nodes, and makes a virtual link between server and cache node

Multiple cache nodes can share link in the same route end to end. As shown in figure 2, the route from C1 to S is [C1, R1, R5, S] and the route from C2 to S is [C2, R1, R5, S]; they can share pair (R1, R5) and (R5, S). R1 and R5, as they are active routers, can easily record share information and save network bandwidth especially in large scale networks.

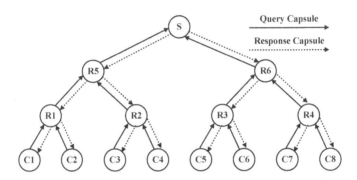

Fig. 2. By AWC, the query and response are distributed to each active router; so the server has a fixed burden no matter the number of cache nodes

Information sharing. The share level is determined by (1) network topology and (2) deployment of the related server. Tree is a usual topology applied in Internet. For convenience, full binary tree is considered as network topology in following discussion. The server is the root node; all cache nodes make up the leaves and middle nodes (usually router) make the branch. Let T be a full binary tree. Let $m + 1$ be the levels of T and let n_j be the total node number in the level $j (0 \le j \le m)$. Then n_j should be:2^j. Let P be amount of query packet that a cache node sent per second and let S be the size of a query packet. We assume the response packet has the same size with the query packet. In traditional way, the server will receive query packets from all cache nodes and then send response packet to respective node. So the throughput in the server$B_s = 2PSn_m = 2^{m+1}PS$. To compare, for AWC, the throughput in the server $B_{s'} = 2PSn_1 = 4PS$.

It is obvious that Bs' is a constant whereas Bs will increase greatly if the levels of tree increase. Moreover, information can be shared among different servers. Figure 3 shows an example for sharing information between two services which deployed in different nodes.

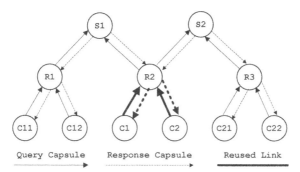

Fig. 3. Virtual link information can be shared for different service. The links colored blue are shared by two different servers

3.2   Collaboration

In AWC, collaboration is setup dynamically. Caches, servers and routers form a tree structure when the status tracking working. The server act as root while the caches act as leaves of tree Conforming to current network architecture, the sibling caches are usually near in geography and bandwidth of link connecting them are relatively wide. So a simple and effective way is to share the content of sibling caches.

Sibling Establishing and Cancel. As shown in figure 2, for example, C1 and C2 will share content with each other. C1 and C2 do not know each other at first, their relationship is established dynamically when they track the same server. When C1 sends tracking information to the server, R1 register C1 in its memory. Following the same step, C2 will also be registered in R1. All sibling relationships will be registered in branch nodes. If a sibling cache cancels caching for the servers, it won't track the server any more and it sends a capsule to its parent node with cancel information. The branch node receives the request and then removes the item of the request cache.

Sharing Mechanism. Taking figure 2 as an example, C1 and C2 share their content. If C1 receives some content from S, it will send a message to R1, and then R1 sends the information to every sibling nodes of C1. In this case, C2 will receive the message and know that the content has been cached by C1. The C2 will index the content to C1 saving to the memory pool. When C2 receives a request for the content index to C1, it forwards the request to C1 instead of S.

When a new comer, denoted as Cn, inserted into network and act as a sibling of C1 and C2, it has no idea about what content have been cached by its siblings. In AWC, Cn doesn't synchronize to the sibling nodes. It just does nothing but the cache work just like C1 and C2. When a client requests for some content of S reaching to it, it fetches them from S and cache it in the memory pool. And then, just as C1 and C2 will do, Cn sends the cache information to R1, and R1 sends the information to all child nodes. If C1 and C2 have indexed the content they will do nothing, otherwise they will index the content pointing to Cn.

4   Simulation Results

We evaluate the performance for status tracking using J-Sim [8]. The network topology of simulation is similar to figure 2, a full binary tree. The level of tree is set to 5 so there are total 63 nodes in the simulation. The bandwidth of whole network is configured as 64kbps and all link propagation delay are set to 0.0050. There are two goals for the simulation. One is to test for the realtime capability and the other one is the cost of keeping the track, i.e. how much bandwidth in server side will be consumed.

A set of simulations were made and the simulations were set by following steps:

1. At the start point, each leaf node, 32 nodes in total, works as cache node for the server. All cache nodes keep tracks with the server's status.
2. During the simulation, every non-leaf node may break from the network by random. When a node breaks from network, it sends a signal to a recording component that is assistant component just for recording information.
3. When caching nodes get aware of the connectivity to server being down they will send a message to the recording component. The message contains the information of which nodes being down.
4. Step (2) and (3) continue until the simulation time is over.

The variant of simulations is interval of PingCapsule. The total simulation was set to 600 seconds. Table 1 shows the simulation results.

Table 1. Simulation results for realtime capability of AWC

Item	1(s)	2(s)	3(s)	4(s)	5(s)	6(s)	7(s)	8(s)	9(s)	10(s)
Aver. Time(s)	2.438	5.060	7.240	9.717	12.25	15.02	17.59	19.88	22.87	26.42
Max time(s)	2.990	5.939	8.854	11.90	14.90	17.89	20.73	23.99	26.84	29.92
Min time(s)	2.200	4.215	6.217	8.233	10.39	12.78	14.54	16.42	18.36	20.39

From table 1 we can see that clients can keep track with server in comply with query interval. Figure 4 indicates the whole throughput in the server side by different intervals during the simulations. The shorter the interval is, the more bandwidth consumes.

5   Conclusions

AWC makes effort on strong content consistency and caching node collaboration. By utilizing the advantage of active networking technology, AWC can be constructed dynamically and consume relatively low bandwidth. So it is suitable for large scale network circumstances.

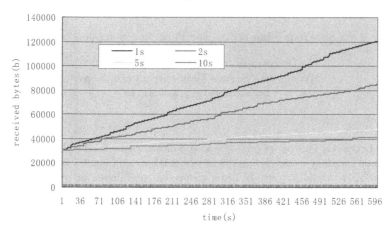

Fig. 4. Throughput of server by query interval 1s, 2s, 5s and 10s

References

1. David L Tennenhouse, Jonathan M Smith, W David Sincoskie et al.: A Survey of Active Network Research. IEEE Communication Magazine, Jan 1997, 35(1): 80-86.
2. David Wetheral.: Service Introduction in Active Networks. PhD Thesis, Massachusetts Institute of Technology, April 1999.
3. Mingkuan Liu, FeiYue Wang, Zeng D., Lizhi Yang.: An overview of World Wide Web caching. Systems, Man, and Cybernetics, 2001 Volume: 5, Page(s): 3045-3050
4. Balachander Krishnamurthy Craig E. Wills.: Study of Piggyback Cache Validation for Proxy Caches in the World Wide Web. USENIX Symposium on Internet Technologies and Systems (1997)
5. C. Liu and P. Cao: Maintaining strong cache consistency in the World Wide Web. Proc. of the 17th IEEE International Conference on Distributed Computing Systems, May 1997.
6. C. Gray and D. Cheriton.: Leases: An Efficient Fault Tolerant Mechanism for Distributed File Cache Consistency. Proceedings of the Twelfth ACM Symposium on Operating Systems Principles, pages 202-210, 1989.
7. Duane Wessels and K. Claffy.: ICP and the Squid Web Cache. IEEE JOURNAL ON SELECTED AREAS IN COMMUNICATIONS, VOL. 16, NO. 3, APRIL 1998
8. Hung-ying Tyan.: Design, Realization and Evaluation of a Component-based Compositional Software Architecture for Network Simulation. USA: The Ohio State University, 2002.

Document Retrieval Using Semantic Relation in Domain Ontology

Soo-Yeon Lim, Seong-Bae Park, and Sang-Jo Lee

Department of Computer Engineering,
Kyungpook National University, Daegu, Korea
nadalsy@sejong.knu.ac.kr

Abstract. This paper proposes a semiautomatic method to build a domain ontology using the results of text analysis and applies it to a document retrieval system. In order to present usefulness for retrieving a document using the hierarchical relations in an ontology, this study compares a typical keyword based retrieval method with an ontology based retrieval method, which uses related information in an ontology for a related feedback. As a result, the latter shows the improvement of precision and recall by 4.97% and 0.78% respectively.

1 Introduction

An ontology can be defined by a set of knowledge terms that include a simple rule, semantic relation, and words for a specific subject. That is, an ontology can be expressed by the concepts, which are related to a domain, features, which express the concept, relation between the concepts, and constraints of the features.

This paper builds a domain ontology with the semantic relation that exists in an ontology by extracting a semantic group and hierarchical structure after classifying and analyzing the patterns of terminology that appeared in a Korean document as a type of compound noun [6]. A built ontology can be used in various fields. This paper proposes an ontology that classifies words related to a specific subject by using a hierarchical structure for a method to improve the performance of retrieving a document. A retrieval engine can be used as a base of inference to use the retrieval function using the concept and rule defined in the ontology. In order to experiment this retrieval engine, the texts that exists in a set of documents related to the pharmacy field are used as an object of the experiment.

2 Building a Domain Ontology

A development of an ontology indicates a configuration area of an ontology by considering the characteristics of domain and usage of ontology, and then defines the detailed items that will be included in an ontology for the queries that an ontology will answer. In order to perform this process, it is a definition of the

P.S. Szczepaniak et al. (Eds.): AWIC 2005, LNAI 3528, pp. 266–271, 2005.

concepts and structure through a conference with the specialists of domain is required and builds by using these results. In an actual application system, it is necessary to an ontology that includes a specific knowledge for each domain. This paper selected the pharmacy field as an experiment domain and limited a document that existed in the pharmacy domain for learning.

2.1   Process for Building an Ontology

The relation that will append the concepts of the pharmacy ontology, which will be built using the results of the documents that exist in the pharmacy database (http://www.druginfo.co.kr) and the results will be configured. The collected documents will form concepts according to the tag that is attached after the transformation process to fit the configured structure using a semi-structurized(tagging) document.The building process of the proposed ontology consists of three steps as follows.

Base Ontology.   For building an ontology, a designer decides a minor node, which is located in the upper level, and builds an ontology based on it and extends it. It is called by a base ontology. This paper configures a base ontology using 48 words as shown in Fig. 1.

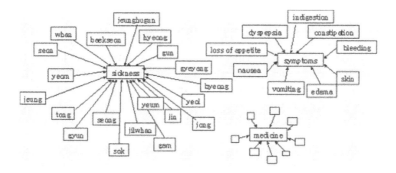

Fig. 1. Configuration of a base ontology

Extraction of Concepts.   In order to remove the stop words, the stop words list was made by using 181 words by considering the morphological characteristics of Korean language. The extracted nouns from an ontology that is a kind of network with a lot of words mean the concept of ontology. The tags and verbs present the relation between the concepts and act as a network, which plays a role in the connection of the concepts to each other.

Addition of Relations.   This paper introduces two methods in order to give a relation for the extracted concepts. The one is using the value of tag attached at the front of text, and the other is using the verb by extracting it from the text. Table 1 and Table 2 show 15 types of semantic relations according to the value of the attached tag and 18 semantic relations by the high frequency of verbs.

The relationship between the extracted verbs and nouns can be verified by the co-occurrence information.

Table 1. Types of the semantic relations for the values of the tag

Semantic Relations			
producedBy	hasKind	hasSideEffect	hasColor
hasInsCode	hasForm	byMean	hasContra
hasComCode	hasEffect	byAmount	byAge
hasClsCode	hasMethod	byUnit	

Table 2. Types of the semantic relations for the high frequency of verbs

Semantic Relations				
appear	rise	control	beWorse	prevent
take	infect	inject	use	relax
cure	noTake	cause	improve	return
reduce	accompany	maintain		

2.2   Extend of Ontology

A built ontology can be extended by other resources, such as other ontologies, thesaurus, and dictionaries. It is possible to reduce the time and cost to extend an ontology by applying the predefined concepts and rules by using the existing resources. This paper uses an abbreviated dictionary for medicine terminology (http: //www.nurscape.net/nurscape/dic/frames.html) and Doosan World Encyclopedia Encyber (http://www.encyber.com/) to extend the pharmacy ontology. The process consists of 3 steps, such as the import, extract, and append.

3   Application for Retrieving a Document

A built ontology can be used in various fields. We propose a method that will improve the effect of retrieving a document using this ontology. This paper uses a hierarchical relation for the process of user relevance feedback in the ontology. The query will be extended by using the terminologies, which appeared as a hyponym information in the ontology that related to the inputted queries, and calculates the weights for the rewritten question. In this process, the hyponym retrieval level to retrieve the nodes in the ontology was set by 2. Our document retrieval system consists of two modules. They are a preprocessing module and a retrieval module.

In order to compare the retrieval performance, a set of the upper 30 correct answered documents for the 10 questions by introducing the 5 specialists' advices about 430 documents was configured. Then, the rates of recall and precision for each query were produced based on this configuration.

4 Experiments and Evaluation

The experiment was applied by the extraction method proposed in this paper for the text in the pharmacy domain.

4.1 Recognition of Terminology

The documents used in this experiment are 21,113. From the results of the document analysis, the numbers of extracted terminology are 55,870. It covers about 70.8% for the total extracted nouns. This means that the rate of terminology is very high in a specific domain. There is good recognition for the terminologies that appeared and addition of 2,864 hyponym concepts after applying the extraction algorithm proposed in this paper in which the average level of the nodes, which existed in the ontology is 1.8.

The extracted terminologies can be investigated by three specialists by hand and evaluated by the precision. The precision of the singleton term is 92.57% that shows a relatively good performance compared with the proposed algorithm. And the average precision of the multi-word term terminologies was 79.96%. From the results of the experiment, 574 concepts were added.

4.2 Evaluation of the Retrieval Performance

In order to present the effectiveness for retrieving a document using the proposed method, this study compares the two methods. The one is a keyword based retrieval method by using the traditional method of , and the other is an ontology based retrieval method by using the hierarchical information that exists in the ontology to a relevance feedback.

An experiment reference collection and evaluation scale is used to evaluate an information retrieval system. This paper collects 430 health/disease information documents from the home page of Korean Medical Association (http://www.kma.org) in order to configure a reference collection and configures an information query using 10 questions. The experiment was carried for the 430

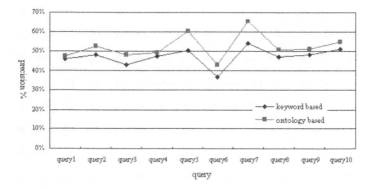

Fig. 2. comparison of the precision

documents extraction. The objective of the experiment was to produce the recall and precision for the 10 questions in which a set of correct answers for each inputted question was defined in order of the documents set by the specialists. Fig. 2 presents the comparison of the distributions of the precision for the inputted queries using the two methods mentioned above.

5   Conclusions

This paper proposes a semiautomatic method to build a domain ontology using the results of text analysis and applies it to a document retrieval system. This paper especially proposes a method to process the ontologies that were combined with a specific nouns or suffices in order to extract the concepts and relations for building the pharmacy ontology after analyzing the types of ontologies appeared in the relevant documents. Keyword based document retrieval system that gives weights by using the frequency information compared with an ontology based document retrieval system that uses relevant information existed in the ontology to a relevant feedback in order to verify the effectiveness of the hierarchical relation in the ontology. From the evaluation of the retrieval performance, it can be seen that the precision increased by 4.97% while the recall was maintained as similar to other one. This means that if the hierarchical relation in the ontology is used as relevant feedback information, the precision will be improved.

It is necessary to modify and extend the ontology in order to process a more precise processing of an query. 33 semantic relations defined in the present pharmacy ontology may be short. In this case, it is necessary to redefine other semantic relations required in a specific domain and extend the pharmacy ontology.

Acknowledgement

This work was supported by Korea Research Foundation Grant (KRF-2004-003-D00365).

References

1. Baeza-Yates, R. and Robeiro-Neto, B.: Modern Information Retrieval. ACM Press, New York, NY, USA, 1999.
2. Bettina, B., Andreas, H., Gerd, S.: Towards Semantic Web Mining. International Semantic Web Conference, 2002.
3. Kang, S. J. and Lee, J. H.: Semi-Automatic Practical Ontology Construction by Using a Thesaurus, Computational Dictionaries, and Large Corpora. ACL 2001 Workshop on Human Language Technology and Knowledge Management, Toulouse, France, 2001.
4. Klavans, J. and Muresan, S., "DEFINDER:Rule-Based Methods for the Extraction of Medical Terminology and their Associated Definitions from On-line Text," Proceedings of AMIA Symposium, pp. 201-202, 2000.

5. Missikoff, M., Velardi, P. and Fabriani, P., "Text Mining Techniques to Automatically Enrich a Domain Ontology," Applied Intelligence, Vol. 18, pp. 322-340, 2003.
6. Soo-Yeon Lim, Mu-Hee Song, Sang-Jo Lee, "Domain-specific Ontology Construction by Terminology Processing," Journal of the Korea Information Science Society(B), Journal of the Korea Information Science Society Vol. 31, No. 3, pp. 353-360, 2004.

An Anti-noise Text Categorization Method Based on Support Vector Machines*

Lin Chen, Jie Huang, and Zheng-Hu Gong

School of Computer Science, National University of Defense Technology,
410073 Changsha, China
chenlin@nudt.edu.cn, agnes_nudt@hotmail.com

Abstract. Text categorization has become one of the key techniques for handling and organizing web data. Though the native features of SVM (Support Vector Machines) are better than Naive Bayes' for text categorization in theory, the classification precision of SVM is lower than Bayesian method in real world. This paper tries to find out the mysteries by analyzing the shortages of SVM, and presents an anti-noise SVM method. The improved method has two characteristics: 1) It chooses the optimal n-dimension classifying hyperspace. 2) It separates noise samples by preprocessing, and trains the classifier using noise free samples. Compared with naive Bayes method, the classification precision of anti-noise SVM is increased about 3 to 9 percent.

1 Introduction

With the rapid growth of Internet, text categorization has become one of the key techniques for handling and organizing text data. A lot of statistical classification and machine learning techniques have been applied in text categorization. These include Naive Bayes models [1, 2], nearest neighbor classifiers [3], decision trees [4], neural networks [5], symbolic rule learning [6] and SVM Learning [7, 8].

In the paper, we are intent to find out how to improve precision of SVM by comparing it with Naive Bayes method in text categorization. The naive virtues of SVM make it more appropriate for text categorization than Bayesian method in theory. However, under the condition that training samples have noises, the hyperplane constructed will badly deviate from real optimal hyperplane. The paper presents an anti-noise classifying method based on SVM. The improved method optimizes high dimension space first, and then builds classifier by removing noises from training samples. Experiments prove that the classifying precision of anti-noise SVM increased about 3 to 9 percent than Bayesian method.

---

* This work is supported by the National Grand Fundamental Research 973 Program of China under Grant No. 2003CB314802.

P.S. Szczepaniak et al. (Eds.): AWIC 2005, LNAI 3528, pp. 272–278, 2005.

2   Measurements and Analyze

2.1   Comparison with Bayesian Methods

Thorsten Joachims [7] provides several advantages of SVM for text categorization.

1. SVM has potential to handle High dimensional input space.
2. SVM can process relevant features effectively.
3. SVM is born to classify two kinds of samples.
4. SVM is well suitable for problems with dense concepts and sparse instances.

We choose 1000 texts about news and science as test samples, and select 200 texts from candidates as training samples. When comparing two methods, the result in reality can not support the standpoint in [7]. In the following tables, n represents number of features we selected.

Table 1. Comparision of SVM and Bayesian method

	Precision of SVM				Precision of Bayesian method			
	n=300	n=800	n=1000	n=1500	n=300	n=800	n=1000	n=1500
true positives	85.3%	88.5%	90.9%	93.1%	87.1%	89.4%	93.9%	96.6%
false positives	86.2%	87.6%	92.6%	92.2%	88.7%	90.3%	94.1%	95.9%

2.2   Shortages of SVM

SVM has better nature features than Naive Bayes, but in real world, it gets opposite results. We try to find out mysteries by analyzing the shortages of SVM. At last, we draw following conclusions.

1. **SVM has no criteria in feature choice.**
   SVM can classify text perfectly. However, if it uses every words emerged in text simply as a dimension of hyperspace, the computation of hyperplane will be very difficult and classification precision will be low. Thus, one of our research emphases is how to choose important and useful features to optimize multi-dimension space.
2. **The anti-noise ability of SVM is weak.**
   Although SVM is treated as a good text categorization method, its anti-noise ability is very weak. Support Vector is a training sample with shortest distance to the hyperplane. The number of support vector is small, but it contains all information needed for classification. Classifying effect is decided by minority support vectors in the samples, so removing or reducing the samples that are not support vectors has no influence on the classifier. If a noise sample is treated as support vector, it will largely reduce classification precision of SVM. If we get rid of noise-samples first, then train SVM by optimized samples, we can achieve higher classifying precision.

3   SVM Based Anti-noise Text Categorization Methods

In order to obtain higher precision, we need to get over shortages of SVM. In this section, we enhance the methods from two aspects.

3.1   Constructing an Optimal Classifying Hyperspace

Efficiency and effect of SVM is largely influenced by the number of dimension and every dimension of hyperspace. Although SVM has advantages in text categorization, it has no criteria in dimension choice. This section uses statistical method to choose the most important features as dimensions of classification space.

Texts consist of words. Frequency of a word can be treated as a dimension of hyperspace. Nevertheless, the number of words in texts is very large in general. Which words are chosen as dimensions of hyperspace is very difficult to decide.

As figure 1 shows, upper circles denote samples in class C, and lower squares denote samples in class $\bar{C}$. We know that hyperspace in figure 1(b) is better than figure 1(a)'s for difference between C and $\bar{C}$ is more apparent.

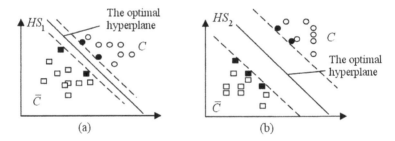

Fig. 1. (a) n-dimension hyperspace HS_1 (b) n-dimension hyperspace HS_2

Therefore, we need a criterion to choose certain words according to initial learning samples and construct optimal hyperspace for classification.

Assuming HS as n-dimension hyperspace, each dimension is frequency of a word.

Definition 1. *Barycentre of samples that belong to class C in HS is*

$$B_C = \sum_{d \in Sample \cap C} t \bigg/ |Sample \cap C|, t = (Fr_d(w_1), Fr_d(w_2), ..., Fr_d(w_n))\ denotes$$

a sample point in n-dimension hyperspace HS, $Fr_d(w_i)$ denotes frequency of word w_i in text d.

Definition 2. *We call HS_C as the optimal classifying n-dimension hyperspace about C, iff $|B_C - B_{\bar{C}}|$ for all samples is maximum under some w_i, and set cardinality of $|w_i|$ is n.*

Definition 3. *The prior odds on class C as $O(C) = P(C)/P(\neg C)$, $O(C)$ measures the predictive or prospective support according to C by background knowledge alone. In practice, we can calculate the prior odds on C by the following formula [9].*

$$O(C) = |\{t|t \in C \cap t \in Sample\}|/|\{t|t \notin C \cap t \in Sample\} \tag{1}$$

Definition 4. *Defining the likelihood ratio of word w on C as:*

$$L(w|C) = P(w|C) \,/\, P(w|\neg C) \tag{2}$$

$L(w|C)$ denotes the retrospective support given to by evidence actually observed. $P(w|C)$ denotes the average frequency of word in sample texts.

Theorem 1. *The posterior odds are given by the product as follow:*

$$O(C|w) = L(w|C) \,/\, O(C) \tag{3}$$

In practice, we can calculate $P(w|C)$ by frequency of w in samples of C and $P(w|\neg C)$ by frequency of w in $\bar{C}$. At last, we can work out $O(C|w)$ from equation (1)(2)(3). $O(C|w)$ represents the effect of classifying according to w's frequency.

Theorem 2. *When choosing first n maximum $O(C|w)$, we can construct optimal hyperspace HS_C by corresponding $Fr(w_i)$ as a dimension. HS_C represents a hyperspace in which the different between C and $\bar{C}$ is the most apparent.*

Text d in HS_C can be calculated by $t_{HS_C} = (Fr(w_1), Fr(w_2), \ldots, Fr(w_n))$, and w_i is one of n maximum $O(C|w_i)$ words.

3.2 Improving Anti-noise Ability of SVM

SVM has high classification precision under conditions with no noises. In noisy conditions, the precision reduces largely. As Figure 2(a) shows, point x is a noise sample in an n-dimension hyperspace. Although x belong to positive samples, it is largely different from other positive samples. If we consider x as a support vector when computing optimal hyperplane, it will make the hyperplane deviate from real optimal hyperplane largely. Classification precision is affected seriously.

Although x is positive one in samples, its characteristic is much more different from other positive samples and may be close to negative samples under some conditions. That is, the corresponding point x in high dimension space is an outlier. Noises in negative samples have the same characteristic. If we eliminate these noises in samples before training SVM, the classification precision will increase largely. As Figure 2(b) shows, we can get more reasonable optimal hyperplane after ignoring the influence of x when training.

In order to construct an anti-noise text classifier, we present a method that filter noise samples by outlier detection in high dimensional space before training SVM.

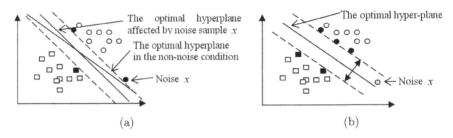

Fig. 2. (a)Noise x effect the optimal hyperplane (b)The optimal hyperplane when ignoring noise x

Supposing D is a classified sample set, o, p, q are samples in D, $d(p, q)$ represents the distance between samples p and q [10].

Definition 5. k *distance of sample* p, k-$dist(p)$. $d(p, o)$ *represents the distance between sample* p *and sample* o *in set* D. *If there are at least* k *samples* $o' \in D$ *subject to* $d(p, o') \leq d(p, o)$ *and at most* $k - 1$ *samples* $o' \in D$ *subject to* $d(p, o') < d(p, o)$, *which called* k *distance of sample* p, k-$dist(p)$.

Definition 6. k *nearest neighbors of sample* p, $N_k(p)$. *The sample set in set* D *whose distance to* p *do not exceed* k-$dist(p)$: $N_k(p) = \{q \in D \setminus \{p\}, d(p, q) \leq k$-$dist(p))\}$.

Definition 7. *Local density of sample* p, $den_k(p)$. *Local density of sample* p *represents reciprocal of* $N_k(p)$ *average* k-$dist$, *that is* $den_k(p) = 1/avg\{k$-$dist(q)|q \in N_k(p)\}$.

Definition 8. *Local outlier coefficient of sample* p, $LOF_k(p)$. *Local outlier coefficient of sample* p *represents the ratio between average density of* $N_k(p)$ *and* $den_k(p)$, *that is* $LOF_k(p) = avg\{den_k(q)|q \in N_k(p)\}/den_k(p)$. *Local outlier coefficient reflects discrete case of sample* p *relative to* k *nearest neighbors around.*

In order to separate noise samples, we need to calculate $LOF_k(t)$ for each text t in class C and $\bar{C}$, if $LOF_k(x_t)$ is greater than threshold θ, we conclude that t is an outlier, that is, text t is noise in samples.

At last, we get a reasonable classification function $H(x) = sgn(\omega^* x + b^*)$ by filtering noise samples.

4   Validity Test

Considering the problem of classifying texts C, we partition the training samples into set C and $\bar{C}$ manually first. Then, we select n words according to section 3.1, and then remove noise samples according to threshold θ by calculating $LOF_k(t)$

for each text in C or $\bar{C}$. At last, classification function $H(x) = sgn(\omega^*x + b^*)$ is obtained. We select 1000 test samples and 200 training samples as section 2.1. We test the method by using parameter n (n is the number of dimension) and $\theta = 20\%$.

Table 2. Precision of anti-noise method by different parameter n and $\theta = 20\%$

	n=300	n=800	n=1000	n=1500
true positives	96.7%	97.8%	99.5%	99.8%
false positives	97.2%	98.1%	99.7%	99.9%

From table 1, we can conclude SVM fit text categorization better in theory, but its precision is worse than Bayesian method in practice. And we also can find that precision of classifier increased about 6 to 11 percent after we apply anti-noise method. And anti-noise SVM method shows its advantage in text categorization, the precision of classifier increased about 3 to 9 percent compared with Naive Bayes method.

5 Conclusions

The paper enhances classification precision of support vector machines by pre-processing samples. It makes SVM can be used in conditions that samples contain noises. It proved that classification precision of anti-noise SVM increased about 3 to 9 percent.

References

1. Ion Androutsopoulos, John Koutsias, Konstantinos V.: Chandrinos, George Paliouras and Constantine D. Spyropoulos. An Evaluation of Naive Bayesian Anti-Spam Filtering. (2000)
2. Cross Validation for the naive Bayes Classifier of SPAM. http://stat-www.berkeley.edu/users/nolan/stat133/Spr04/Projects/SpamPart2.pdf (2004)
3. Lewim D., Ringuuette, M.: A comparison of two learning algorithms for text categorization. In Thirds Annual Symposium on Document Analysis and Information Retrieval. (1994) 81–93
4. Sholom M. Weiss, etc.: Maximizing Text-Mining Performance, IEEE Intelligent Systems. (1999) 2–8
5. Zhou Z., Chen S., Chen Z.: FANNC: A fast adaptive neural network classifier. International Journal of Knowledge and Information Systems. **2** (2000) 115–129
6. J.Kiven, M.Warmuth, and P.Auer.: The perception algorithm vs. window: Linear vs. logarithmic mistake bounds when few input variables are relevant. In Conference on Computational Learning Theory. (1995)
7. Thorsten Joachims.: Text Categorization with Support Vector Machines: Learning with Many Relevant Features. Proceedings of ECML-98, 10th European Conference on Machine Learning. (1997).

8. A. Basu, C. Watters, and M. Shepherd.: Support Vector Machines for Text Categorization. Proceedings of the 36th Hawaii International Conference on System Sciences. (2003)

9. Judea Pearl.: Probabilistic Reasoning in Intelligent Systems: Networks of Plausible Inference. ISBD 0-934613-73-7. (1988)

10. XU LongFei, XIONG JunLi etc.: Study on Algorithm for Rough Set based Outlier Detection in high Dimension Space, Computer Science. **30** (2003) (in Chinese).

Increasing Profitability: Voice-Based Browsing to Recommendation System Web Services

Hendrik T. Macedo and Jacques Robin

Universidade Federal de Pernambuco, Recife, Brazil
{htm, jr}@cin.ufpe.br

Abstract. We present a mediator Web service to provide voice-based access to recommendation systems through voice portals. The mediator allows requests for recommendation to be forwarded from the voice portal to the recommendation system Web service and uses natural language generation to summarizes the recommendation results and potential follow-ups as a VoiceXML dialog that is sent back to the portal. Since the mediator must be independent of the recommendation application, the semantics of the concepts used in the two services is reconciled by ontology-mediation: the mediator publishes its general recommendation system's ontology of entities and queries and the recommendation system Web service, in turn, attaches specific entities and services it provides, as specialization of concepts of the published general ontology that the mediator is able to convey as a natural language dialog.

1 Introduction

Computational *Recommendation Systems* [1] have emerged in response to the technological possibilities and human needs created by the web. A recommendation system (RS) makes use of information filtering techniques to progressively acquire the user preferences and profile concerning a set of products or services to generate personalized recommendations.

Most current implemented RSs, however, are desktop-driven application and do not allow for an pervasive access manner, which prunes the profitability of the system. The trend towards ever more compact devices coupled with the emergence of voice portals and VoiceXML [2] makes voice-browsing the most promising approach to deliver content at any time, any place. It is the only convenient option for mobile and landline phones and it can be integrated with traditional visual browsing to deliver more information more efficiently to higher-end devices such as PDA, laptops and desktops.

Undoubtedly, recommendations is a typical example of content for which ubiquitous access has clear practical added value. Imagine, for instance, that you went to a multiplex theater with friends but the movie you had selected to see gets sold-out while you are waiting on line. Would not it be handy to access your favorite movie recommendation system through your mobile phone to get alternative suggestions among the other movies playing at that multiplex?

P.S. Szczepaniak et al. (Eds.): AWIC 2005, LNAI 3528, pp. 279–285, 2005.

In this paper we describe the VERBS (Voice-Enabled Recommendation Browsing Service) interface we are currently developing to enable vocal access to whatever RSs published as Web services. We show how computational linguistics technologies, such as domain and linguistic knowledge based Natural Language Generation (NLG) [6] and Web engineering technologies, such as Web Services, VoiceXML, and Web Ontologies [9] can be harmoniously combined into a mediator Web service for ubiquitous access to RSs through voice portals. VERBS is implemented upon the MAVERICK architecture [3], a general software architecture to provide ubiquitous access to personalized Web content.

2   Voice-Enabling Recommendation System Web Services

Our work proposes an innovative mechanism to provide voice-based access to computational RSs that is published as Web services. In essence, Web services is a versatile framework for building distributed information systems through the assembly of components that are independently deployed on the web. It uses a lightweight XML-based protocol called SOAP (Simple Object Access Protocol) for exchange of information in such decentralized, distributed environment.

VERBS works as a mediator service between the RS Web service and the voice portal. The operations described in the RS Web service interface (iRS) (Fig. 1 (a)) are accessible by VERBS (Fig. 1 (b)).

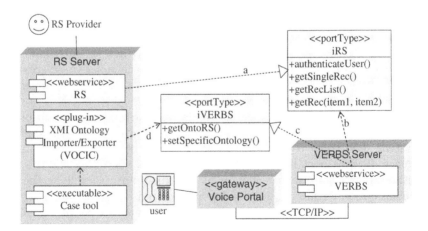

Fig. 1. VERBS works as a mediator service between the recommendation system (RS) and the voice portal

A VERBS session scenario takes place as follows: (1) a pre-registered user calls the recommendation service number from any ordinary phone; (2) the Voice

Portal send the user information identification to VERBS, which in turn, will (3) authenticate the user within the respective recommendation system (RS) and(4) call one of the operations described in the RS service interface (iRS); finally, (5) VERBS will carry on the generation of the navigable VoiceXML document from the XML-encoded content in the SOAP message sent as result to the call of referred operation.

2.1   NLG to Support Scalable Automated Generation of Voice-Browsing Dialogs

VoiceXML allows voice Web application developers to reuse as black-box components encapsulating complex, low-level computational linguistic technologies such as ASR, TTS and domain-specific grammar parsing [4]. However, to dynamically generate a VoiceXML dialog from an underlying content providing application to present customized content to the user in ubiquitously browsable form involves issues dealt with by a higher-level computational linguistic technology: Natural Language Generators (NLG). The input of an NLG is generally twofold. It includes (1) some information represented in a computational language and (2) a communicative goal (e.g., greeting the user, answering a request, issuing a warning). From such an input, an NLG automatically generates a natural language utterance. Such an utterance can be a turn in a dialog or a multiple page monologue. It can also be a written text or a spoken utterance. An example spoken dialog that can be generated by VERBS while interfacing a RS Web service is given in Fig. 2.

System-led menu-based dialog:

System turn: Welcome to LokFacil movie recommendation system Mr. Anderson. If at anytime during our dialog you want to switch interaction mode say "switch". If you are confused about anything say "help". First, would you like me to recommend (1) *a single movie* or (2) *a list of movies*?

User turn: A single movie.

System turn: OK, I recommend you Matrix Reloaded. Now would you like (1) *more information about this movie* or (2) *the reason for this recommendation.*

User turn: More information about this movie.

System turn: Matrix Reloaded is the first sequel of the 1999 cyberpunk science-fiction blockbuster The Matrix. It stars Keanu Reeves, Lawrence Fishburne, Carrie-Ann Moss, Monica Belluci and Lambert Wilson. It is directed by the Wachowski Brothers and features groundbreaking computerized special effects. It shows the second chapter of humanity's epic struggle for freedom and survival against autonomous machines that have enslaved humans as biological batteries spending their life anesthetized in forcefully induced virtual reality dreams.

System turn: Do you want to know why I picked this movie for you?

User hangs up.

Fig. 2. Voice-based browsing dialog example

The first sentence of this dialog does not convey any information but only satisfies the communicative goal of greeting the user. The communicative goal of the third system turn, in the meantime, is to respond to the request for more information about the movie just recommended in the second system turn.

VoiceXML allows fine tuning the level of user initiative in a dialog to the size of computational grammars and lexicons of non-prohibitive development cost. It also allows packaging all the related content for a variety of information needs into a single document, leaving the user selecting and ordering its exposure to the relevant units through voice navigation choices. Automating dialog generation using VoiceXML is thus far closer to the task of hypertext generation [7], than to that of classical natural language question-answering interfaces focused on sentence interpretation [4]. Due to its emphasis on generating a coherent, multi-paragraph discourse, hypertext generation, and thus VoiceXML dialog generation must rely on the more complex but more scalable and reuse fostering phrase-based text generation (PBTG) approach of NLG, rather than on canned text or template matching [5].

This PBTG approach to mediate between a Web content providing service, such as recommendation ones, and a voice portal is entirely new. Previous work [8], proposed instead on a machine translation approach that reused a classical dynamic HTML generation infrastructure, together a generic HTML to VoiceXML translation system. We believe that for even mildly sophisticated information needs, voice-browsing differs too radically from visual browsing as a sensory and cognitive experience for such an approach to robustly produce voice-browsing dialogs that are effective enough for practical applications.

2.2   Ontologies to Integrate Independently Developed Web Services

An ontology specifies the entity classes of a given conceptual domain, together with their properties, relationships and constraints. It must use a representation language that allows both a human community to share a precise, unambiguous under common understanding of the domain and software agents to perform automated reasoning about it. Conceptual knowledge bases, for instance, presented in most NLG systems are full-fledged ontologies.

We adopt a three-tier ontology mediation to reconcile the semantics of the concepts used in such a RS Web service and the VERBS itself, since it must be independent of the RS Web service. In the first tier, we have the application domain itself (ex: the movies domain); in the second tier, we have the RS service domain; in the third tier we have the RS-specific concepts. The VERBS publishes an ontology and the RS Web service attaches the specific entities and services it provides, as specialization of concepts of this published ontology.

The general ontology VERBS publishes is the General Recommendation System Ontology (OntoRS)[1] that has been formally modelled as UML/OCL artifacts following the initiative of using UML for knowledge representation in artificial intelligence applications and semantic web ontologies [10].

OntoRS models general recommendation domain concepts such as users, items, common machine learning-based recommendation algorithms, user rat-

---

[1] Due to the lack of space, OntoRS will be detailed in a further paper.

ings for items and the recommended items themselves, as well as, typical recommendation services.

As an illustrative example, we show how the ontology mediation works in the VERBS/LokFácil[2] case study. Fig. 3 shows an illustrative simplified example of a chunk of the OntoRS, made available by VERBS, and the coupling of the LokFacil system's ontology.

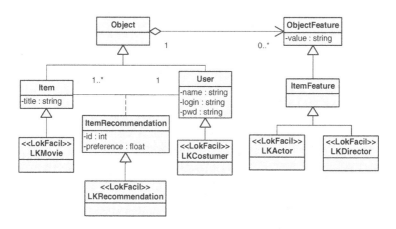

Fig. 3. OntoRS and LokFacil ontology coupling. In the diagram, one or more items are recommended to the user. Each recommendation has an id and a preference value that the system predicts the user will give to the referred item

Since recommendation in VERBS is based on OntoRS, a movie recommendation and some features, such as director and actor, for instance, would be represented in VERBS as an instance of the ItemRecommendation class associated with two instances of ItemFeature class. In order to enable the recommendation of a movie and its features, the developer of LokFacil system should specify that the class LKMovie is a kind of Item in VERBS ontology and, similarly, LKDirector and LKActor are kinds of ItemFeatures.

3   Human-Assisted Ontology Composition

The scenario described so far clearly points out the need for a component where developers can manually extend the ontology that the VERBS publishes with the specific one of their recommendation applications. We have called such component as Visual Ontology Coupling Interface Component (VOCIC).

---

[2] LokFacil is a movie recommendation system developed in our laboratory at Universidade Federal de Pernambuco.

The VOCIC works as an application plug-in for any industry available UML case tool that imports such ontology and exports the merged ontology back;the import/export process is totally based on the XML Metadata Interchange (XMI).

In the VERBS/LokFacil case study, the content provider uses the VOCIC plug-in to access OntoRS that VERBS publishes (see Fig. 1 (c) and (d)), and which resides in the VERBS server. The content provider visually specifies the specific RS ontology in terms of the OntoRS by means of a case tool with the VOCIC plug-in. Thus, the VOCIC accesses the setSpecificOntology() operation defined in the VERBS port to set the resulting merged ontology. As a result, the respective RS web service is potentially able to bear a vocal interface.

4   Conclusion

We presented VERBS, a mediator web service to provide voice interface for recommendation systems published as Web services. VERBS combines a vast array of technologies from software engineering and web engineering to computational linguistics and shows how these can be integrated into an innovative synergy to connect independently developed RS Web services and voice portals. We describe, in particular, how the ontology-mediation based on UML, OCL an XMI takes place within VERBS and the need for a component where RSs' developers can manually extend the ontology that the VERBS publishes with the specific one of their recommendation applications.

References

1. Resnick, P. and Varian, H. R. (Eds.): Recommender System. In Communications of the ACM, vol. 40, no. 3, (entire issue). (1997).
2. McGlashan, S. et al.: Voice Extensible Markup Language (VoiceXML) Version 2.0, W3C Working Draft. World Wide Web Consortium. (2001).
3. Macedo, H. and Robin, J.: A Mediator Architecture Providing Ubiquitous Access to Web Content via Voice Portals, Web Services, Ontologies and Natural Language Generation. In Proceedings of 3rd International Information and Telecommunication Technologies Symposium (I2TS'04). São Carlos -SP, Brazil (2004).
4. Dale, R., Moisi, H. and Somers, H. (Eds.): Handbook of Natural Language Processing, Marcel Dekker (2000).
5. Cole, R. A., Mariani, J., Uszkoreit, H., Zaenen, A. and Zue, V. (eds.): Survey of the State of the Art in Human Language Technology. Kluwer, Dordrecht (1996).
6. Reiter, E. and Dale, R.: Building Applied Natural Language Generation Systems, Cambridge University Press (2000).
7. Favero, E. and Robin, J.: HYSSOP: Natural Language Generation Meets Knowledge Discovery in Databases. (IIWAS'2001), Linz, Austria (2001)
8. Annamalai, N., Gupta, G. and Prabhakaran, B.: Accessing Documents via Audio: An Extensible Transcoder for HTML to VoiceXML Conversion. ICCHP (2004).

9. Fensel, D. and Brodie, M. Ontologies: the Silver Bullet for Knowledge Management and Electronic Commerce, Springer-Verlag (2003).

10. Cranefield, S. and Purvis, M.: UML as an ontology modelling language. In Proceedings of the Workshop on Intelligent Information Integration, 16th International Joint Conference on Artificial Intelligence (IJCAI-99) (1999).

Effectiveness and Relevancy Measures Under Modal Cardinality for Intuitionistic Fuzzy Sets

Jacek Manko

XXXI LO, Kruczkowskiego 4, 93-236 Lodz, Poland
matmamaster@o2.pl

Abstract. The paper focuses on the application of the modal logic operators of "necessity" and "possibility" to determining the concept of a cardinality of an intuitionistic fuzzy set. As a consequence, the operators are used for constructing the ratio-based effectiveness and relevancy indices in Web-searching process.

Keywords: Fuzzy set and its cardinality, intuitionistic fuzzy set, modal logic operators "necessity" and "possibility", effectiveness and relevancy indices.

1 Introduction

The fuzzy sets theory was introduced to enable the description of the notions and objects which are unsharply-defined in the everyday language. When L. A. Zadeh published his first paper on fuzzy sets [18] in 1965, hardly anyone could realise how spontaneously it was going to develop. The opponents of this theory suspected the hidden form of probability in the theory of fuzzy sets. At the same time they misunderstood idea of its being random and its imprecise (fuzzy) description. The classical meaning of the notion of a set and sets theory, introduced in 1878 by G. Cantor, is based on a two-valued logic. In this sense, each element can belong to a set or not, and there is no other possibility. In many real life situations such formulation is not flexible enough and does not really describe them. It forced the invention of a new logic and new notion of a set. Among the great number of logicians and philosophers, who contributed to the evolution of this new kind of logic, so called the many-valued logic, there were Polish scientists: J. Lukasiewicz [12,13] and T. Kotarbinski [14] and also A. Tarski [17] and Z. Zawirski [19].

One of the consequences of logic evolution was the idea of a fuzzy set. It was to describe the situations and notions which were unclear, imprecise or unprecisely described or defined. By a fuzzy set L in a universum $U \neq \emptyset$ we mean the structure [18] $L = \{(x, \mu_L(x)) : x \in U\}$, where $\mu_L : U \to [0,1]$ is the membership function of the set L and the number $\mu_L(x) \in [0,1]$ denotes the degree of belonging an object x to the fuzzy set L.

Undoubtedly, one of the not strictly defined notion in the fuzzy sets theory is the notion of a cardinality of such a set, i.e. the exact number of its elements. It

P.S. Szczepaniak et al. (Eds.): AWIC 2005, LNAI 3528, pp. 286–292, 2005.

is closely connected with the membership degree of such an element to a fuzzy set. The first attempt to define the problem of cardinality of a fuzzy set was the conception by A. de Luca and S. Termini published in 1972 [11]. According to their idea, when $U = \{x_1, x_2, \ldots, x_N\}$ is the finite universum (in the usual sense) and L is a fuzzy set in U, then the number

$$|L| = \sum_{i=1}^{N} \mu_L(x_i) \tag{1}$$

is meant as a cardinality of L. It is obvious that when L is a set in a classical sense, i.e. $\mu_L(x) \in \{0, 1\}$, the formula (1) denotes the cardinality (the power) of the usual (crisp) finite set.

For the thirty years of development of the fuzzy set theory there have appeared various conceptions and modifications of the fuzziness. One of more successful was the conception by K. Atanassov of an intuitionistic fuzzy set in 1983 [1, 2, 3, 4]. Fuzzy sets and their methods in relation to Web applications were earlier considered in [21, 22, 23].

In this paper, we refer to the concept of interval cardinality and interval probability of an intuitionistic fuzzy set proposed in [15, 16]. We attain the similar results, but ours are motivated by logical operators, which are very specific for modal logic. The paper is strictly connected to the results proposed in [8] and [9]. As a consequence of the defined cardinality the effectiveness and relevancy [10] indices are proposed in terms of intuitionistic fuzzy calculus.

2   Intuitionistic Fuzzy Sets

Let $U \neq \emptyset$ be a set in common sense and let U be the universum for our considerations.

By an intuitionistic fuzzy set A in U we mean the object [1, 2, 3, 4]:

$$A = \{(x, \mu_A(x), \nu_A(x)) : x \in U\} \tag{2}$$

where $\mu_A, \nu_A : U \rightarrow [0, 1]$ are the membership and the non-membership function of an element x to the set A respectively, while the condition

$$0 \leq \mu_A(x) + \nu_A(x) \leq 1 \text{ for all } x \in U \tag{3}$$

is fullfiled.

The difference $\pi_A(x) = 1 - \mu_A(x) + \nu_A(x)$ is called an intuitionistic fuzzy index and the number $\pi_A(x) \in [0, 1]$ should be treated as a hesitancy margin connected with the evaluation degree while qualify or not each element x to a set A. It is one of the most important and original idea distinguishing the intuitionistic fuzzy sets theory form the fuzzy sets theory. The family of all intuitionistic fuzzy sets in U is denoted by $IFS(U)$.

For $A, B \in IFS(U)$ we have [1, 2, 3, 4]:

$$A \cup B = \{(x, \mu_A(x) \vee \mu_B(x), \nu_A(x) \wedge \nu_B(x)) : x \in U\} \tag{4}$$

$$A \cap B = \{(x, \mu_A(x) \wedge \mu_B(x), \nu_A(x) \vee \nu_B(x)) : x \in U\} \qquad (5)$$

$$A^C = \{(x, \nu_A(x), \mu_A(x)) : x \in U\} \qquad (6)$$

where the symbols $\vee$ and $\wedge$ stand for maximum and minimum respectively and A^C denotes the complement of the intuitionistic fuzzy set (2).

There are some specific arguments that distinguish the intuitionistic fuzzy sets theory and the fuzzy sets theory. One of them are the operators transforming an intuitionistic fuzzy set into a fuzzy set. The most typical examples are Atanassovs operators described in [5] called "necessity" and "possibility" and defined as:

$$\square A = \{(x, \mu_A(x), 1 - \mu_A(x)) : x \in U\} \qquad (7)$$

$$\lozenge A = \{(x, 1 - \nu_A(x), \nu_A(x)) : x \in U\} \qquad (8)$$

Notice that sets obtained via (7) and (8) from an intuitionistic fuzzy set are typical Zadehs fuzzy sets. The operators "$\square$" and "$\lozenge$" indicate that these operators are meaningless in the case of fuzzy sets and they demonstrate the fact that intuitionistic fuzzy sets are the proper extension of the ordinary fuzzy sets.

3   Cardinality of an Intuitionistic Fuzzy Set

Let $U = \{x_1, x_2, \ldots, x_N\}$ be a finite crisp set treated as our consideration set and let $A \in IFS(U)$ be an intuitionistic fuzzy set described by the defining functions μ_A, ν_A, π_A.

We define the cardinalities of the set A:

$$card_{nec}(A) = card(\square A) = \sum_{i=1}^{N} \mu_A(x_i) \qquad (9)$$

$$card_{pos}(A) = card(\lozenge A) = \sum_{i=1}^{N} (1 - \nu_A(x_i)) \qquad (10)$$

The formula (9) is treated as the least (certain) cardinality of A and the formula (10) as the biggest (possible) cardinality of A. The formulae (9) and (10) are mathematicaly equivalent with (1).

Let us notice, that the formula (10) can be written as

$$card_{pos}(A) = card(\lozenge A) = \sum_{i=1}^{N} (\mu_A(x_i) + \pi_A(x_i)) \qquad (11)$$

while $\mu_A(x_i) + \nu_A(x_i) + \pi_A(x_i) = 1$ according to (3).

Then, by the cardinality of an intuitionistic fuzzy set A we mean a number $card(A)$ such that

$$card(A) \in [card_{nec}(A), card_{pos}(A)] \qquad (12)$$

The cardinality of the intuitionistic fuzzy set (12) treated here as a closed interval is, in some sense, similar to the conception described in [15, 16], but it arises from the intuitionistic fuzzy logic and is based on specific modal operators. The number (9) we interpret as a guarantee (doubtless, certain) cardinality of A meanwhile the number (10) we should treat as a possible (permitting) cardinality of A where the hesitancy margin $\pi(x_i)$ is the element which emphasises our conviction of membership x_i to A.

It is not difficult to notice that

$$card_{nec}(A^C) = \sum_{i=1}^{N} \nu_A(x_i) \tag{13}$$

$$card_{pos}(A^C) = \sum_{i=1}^{N} (\nu_A(x_i) + \pi_A(x_i)) \tag{14}$$

and therefore

$$card(A^C) \in \left[card_{nec}(A^C), card_{pos}(A^C)\right] \tag{15}$$

Moreover, we have

$$0 \leq card_{nec}(A) \leq N \tag{16}$$

$$0 \leq card_{pos}(A) \leq N \tag{17}$$

and

$$card_{nec}(A) + card_{pos}(A^C) = N \tag{18}$$

$$card_{pos}(A) + card_{nec}(A^C) = N \tag{19}$$

Let us notice that the problem of the cardinality of an intuitionistic fuzzy set was discussed earlier in [6, 7, 15, 16].

4   A Concept of Ratio-Based Effectiveness and Relevancy Measures

Textual data in the Web and other sets of documents are mostly partly standarised, i.e. they are characterised by some kind of form and contents cohesion recognised by a computer only concerning the syntax or sometimes semantics of keywords. Very frequently, the lack of elasticity happens, which is connected with natural language requirements, for example the Slavonic inflection. Computer tools required to search some needed notions retrieve the sets of documents which are not always compatible with the criterium of their importance or "adequacy". There is always some risk of "noising" the displayed information by unneeded auxiliary terms as prepositions and conjunctions etc. (the elements of the so-called stop-list), and also accidental analogy of the words resulting from their similar structure.

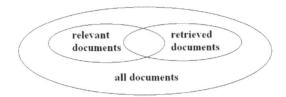

Fig. 1. The dependance between the documents retrieved and documents that are relevant

The propositional measures of precision of displayed results in the process of searching the set of text documents are [10]:

$$precision = \frac{|\{relevant\_doc\} \cap \{retrieved\_doc\}|}{|\{retrieved\_doc\}|} \tag{20}$$

$$effectiveness = \frac{|\{relevant\_doc\} \cap \{retrieved\_doc\}|}{|\{relevant\_doc\}|} \tag{21}$$

The precision index (20) describes the ratio of the amount of documents retrieved and relevant that are connected to the querry, to the actual amount of all retrieved documents.

The effectiveness index (21) informs about the number of relevant and retrieved documents to the total number of relevant documents.

However, the above construction is based on the strict assignment of a document to a chosen class (relevant or not). Hence, the diversification of levels of relevancy is not possible in that approach. Thus, we intend to provide a little bit more flexible mechanism allowing to determine the membership of a document to the class with respect to the criteria it fulfils, as well as to the criteria it does not.

Let us denote by A the set of all relevant documents and by B the set of all retrieved documents found by some mechanism. The set B is a finite set in a common sense (a crisp set), i.e. its membership function takes values in $\{0, 1\}$, while A can be treated as an intuitionistic fuzzy set, where the number $\mu_A(d_i)$ denotes the membership degree of a document d_i to the set of all relevant documents, $\nu_A(d_i)$ denotes the non-membership degree and $\pi_A(d_i)$ is the hesitancy margin of classification of d_i as the relevant document. Criteria of constructing membership and non-membership functions may depend on various documents' properties; the most known methods are based on lists terms called keywords, e.g. term frequency matrix [10], or string matching methods (Hamming or Edit distance, trigrams methods, etc.) [20].

We define then the so-called precision index as a number from the interval

$$precision \in [precision_{nec}, precision_{pos}] \tag{22}$$

where

$$precision_{nec} = card((\Box A) \cap B)/card(B) \tag{23}$$

and
$$precision_{pos} = card((\Diamond A) \cap B)/card(B) \tag{24}$$

The symbol "$\cap$" is defined in (5); the symbol $card$ denotes the cardinality of a fuzzy set given by (1).

Formula (23) characterises the guaranteed precision and formula (24) gives the highest possible matching connected to the precision of searching documents.

Similarly we define the effectiveness index as a number from the interval

$$effectiveness \in [effectiveness_{nec}, effectiveness_{pos}] \tag{25}$$

where
$$effectiveness_{nec} = card((\Box A) \cap B)/card(\Box A) \tag{26}$$

and
$$effectiveness_{pos} = card((\Diamond A) \cap B)/card(\Box A) \tag{27}$$

The concept of the precision and effectiveness indices as a number from the closed intervals is intuitively rooted in all the situations where it is very difficult to match the proper precision degree as a single number and the range is more convenient.

5   Concluding Remarks

The defined in (20)-(27) interval indices have been proposed. Their usefulness in Web-searching process and intuitiveness have been remarked. They allow to match the hesitancy when it is necessery to answer whether found documents are relevant to the given query. In the future, it is worth to decrease the range of introduced intervals.

References

1. Atanassov K.: *Intuitionistic fuzzy sets*, ITKRs Scientific Session, Sophia, June 1983, Deposed in Central Sci. Techn. Library of Bulg. Acad. of Science, 1697/84 (in Bulg.).
2. Atanassov K., Stoeva S.: *Intuitionistic fuzzy sets*, Proc. of Polish Symp. on Interval and Fuzzy Mathematics, Wydawn. Politechniki Poznanskiej, August 26-29.1983, Eds: J. Albrycht and W. Wisniewski, Pozna1985, 23-26.
3. Atanassov K.: *Intuitionistic fuzzy sets*, Fuzzy Sets and Systems 20, 1986, 87-96.
4. Atanassov K.: *Intuitionistic Fuzzy Sets: Theory and Applications*, Springer Verlag, 1999.
5. Atanassov K.: New operations defined over the intuitionistic fuzzy sets, Fuzzy Sets and Systems 61, 1994, 50-52.
6. Gerstenkorn T., Manko J.: *Remarks on the classical probability of bifuzzy events*, CASYS Intern. J. of Computing Anticipatory Systems, Ed. by Daniel D. Dubois Univ. of Liege, Belgium, 4th Intern. Conf. on Computing Anticipatory Systems, HEC Liege (Belgium), August 7-12, 2000, Partial Proc., Vol. 8, 190-196.

7. Gerstenkorn T., Manko J.: *A problem of bifuzzy probability of bifuzzy events*, BUSE-FAL 76, 1998, 41-47.

8. Gerstenkorn T., Manko J.: *Probability of intuitionistic fuzzy events with help of modal operators* (to be printed)

9. Gerstenkorn T., Manko J.: *Probabilities of intuitionistic fuzzy events*, 1st Warsaw Intern. Seminar on Intelligent Systems (WISIS 2004), May 21, 2004, Systems Research Inst., Inst. of Computer Science Polish Acad. Sciences, Warsaw 2004.

10. Han J., Kamber M.: *Data Mining: Concepts and Techniques*, Morgan Kaufman Publishers, 2001.

11. de Luca A., Termini S.: *A defnition of the non-probabilistic entropy in the setting of fuzzy sets theory*, Inform. and Control 20, 1972, 301-312.

12. Lukasiewicz J.: *O logice trojwartosciowej*, Ruch Filozoficzny V, 1920, 170-171 (in Polish).

13. Lukasiewicz J.: *Selected Works*, North Holland and PWN, Warsaw 1970.

14. Kotarbinski T.: *Elementy teorii poznania, logiki formalnej i metodologii nauk*, Zaklad im. Ossolinskich, Lwow 1929 (in Polish).

15. Szmidt E., Kacprzyk J., *Intuitionistic fuzzy linguistic quantifiers*, Notes on IFS 3, 1998, 111-122.

16. Szmidt E., Kacprzyk J., *Intuitionistic fuzzy events and their probabilities*, Notes on IFS 4, 1998, 68-72.

17. Tarski A.: *Der Aussapenkalkeul und die Topologie*, Fund. Math., XXXI, 1938.

18. Zadeh L. A.: *Fuzzy sets*, Inform. and Control 8, 1965, 338-353.

19. Zawirski Z.: *Geneza i rozwoj logiki intuicjonistycznej*, Kwart. Filozof. XVI, 1946 (in Polish).

20. Mitra S., Acharya T. *Data Mining. Multimedia, Soft Computing, and Bioinformatics*, 2003, John Wiley and Sons, Inc. Publication.

21. Menasalvas E., Segovia J., Szczepaniak P.S. (Eds), *Advances in Web Intelligence*, Proceedings of the First International Atlantic Web Intelligence - AWIC'2003, Series: Lecture Notes in Artificial Intelligence, Springer-Verlag, Berlin, Heidelberg, New York, 2003, ISBN 3-54040124-5

22. Favela J., Menasalvas E., Chavez E. (Eds), *Advances in Web Intelligence*, Proceedings of the Second International Atlantic Web Intelligence - AWIC'2004, Series: Lecture Notes in Artificial Intelligence - LNAI 3034, Springer-Verlag, Berlin, Heidelberg, New York, 2004, ISBN 3-540-22009-7

23. Loia V., Nikravesh M., Zadeh L.A. (Eds), *Fuzzy Logic and the Internet*, Series: Studies in Fuzziness and Soft Computing, Springer-Verlag, Berlin, Heidelberg, New York, 2004, ISBN 3-540-20180-7

A Simple, Structure-Sensitive Approach for Web Document Classification

Alex Markov and Mark Last

Ben-Gurion University of Negev,
Department of Information Systems Engineering,
Beer-Sheva 84105, Israel

Abstract. In this paper we describe a new approach to classification of web documents. Most web classification methods are based on the vector space document representation of information retrieval. Recently the graph based web document representation model was shown to outperform the traditional vector representation using k-Nearest Neighbor (k-NN) classification algorithm. Here we suggest a new hybrid approach to web document classification built upon both, graph and vector representations. K-NN algorithm and three benchmark document collections were used to compare this method to graph and vector based methods separately. Results demonstrate that we succeed in most cases to outperform graph and vector approaches in terms of classification accuracy along with a significant reduction in classification time.

1   Introduction

Automated classification of previously unseen data items has been an active research area for many years. Many efficient and scalable classification techniques were developed in the scope of Artificial intelligence [6] and Data mining [1] Those techniques are used in wide range of research domains including web document categorization.

Most web categorization methods come from information retrieval where the "vector space model" for document representation [10] is typically used. According to this model, vocabulary is constructed from words located in the training document set. Each document D_i presented by vector $(d_{i1}, d_{i2} \ldots d_{i|d|})$ where number of vector dimensions $|d|$ is equal to number of terms in vocabulary. Advantage of such representation model is that it can be used by most of algorithms for classification. For instance many methods for distance or similarity calculation between two vectors were developed [1], [2], [6] so *lazy* k-NN algorithm can easily be used with one of those methods.

Such vector collection can also be transformed into one of conventional classification models. Examples of available classification models include decision trees [8], [9] IFN - info-fuzzy networks [4], artificial neural networks, NBC - Naïve Bayes Classifier [6] and many others. Those models associate vector collection with attribute table where every term in dictionary is an attribute and each $d_{i,j}$ is the value

P.S. Szczepaniak et al. (Eds.): AWIC 2005, LNAI 3528, pp. 293–298, 2005.

of attribute j in document i. Examples of applications of such approach to text documents can be found in [5], [13]. Ability to create a model is extremely important for systems where classification needs to be done online.

However, this popular method of document representation does not capture important structural information, such as the order and proximity of term occurrence or the location of a term within the document. Vector space, as most other existing information retrieval methods, also ignores the fact that web documents contains markup elements (HTML tags), which are an additional source of information. Thus, HTML tags can be used for identification of hyperlinks, title, underlined or bold text etc. This kind of structural information may be critical for accurate internet page classification.

In order to overcome the limitations of the vector-space model, several methods of representing web document content using graphs instead of vectors were introduced [11], [12]. The main benefit of the proposed graph-based techniques is that they allow us to keep the inherent structural information of the original document. Ability to calculate similarity between two graphs allows to classify graphs with some distance based *lazy* algorithms like k-NN, but available eager algorithms (like ID3 and C4.5) work only with vectors and cannot induce even a simple classification model from a graph structure. On the other hand, *lazy* algorithms are very problematic in terms of classification time and cannot be used for online massive classification of web documents represented by graphs.

In this paper we present a new method of web document representation, based on frequent sub-graph extraction, that can help us to overcome problems of both, vector space and graph techniques. Our method has two main benefits: (1) we keep important structural web page information by extracting relevant sub-graphs from a graph that represents this page; (2) we can use most eager classification algorithms for inducing a classification model because, eventually, a web document is represented by a simple vector with Boolean values.

The methodology we propose in this work is based on frequent sub-graph recognition. As a general data structure, a graph can be used to model many complex relationships in data. Frequent sub-graph extraction or graph frequent pattern mining has been active research area in recent years. [7] is an example of using graphs for chemical compounds representation where labeled nodes represent different atoms and edges - different types of bounds among them. Most popular sub-structure detection algorithms based on BFS and DFS approaches are presented in [3] and [14] respectively.

This paper is organized as follows. In Section 2 we explain, step by step, text representation approach and classification method for obtained vector set. Benchmark document collections and comparative results describes in Section 3. Some conclusions are presented in Section 4.

2   Web Based Document Representation and Classification

In [11] five different ways for graph document representation were introduced. All those are based on the adjacency of terms in a web document. In our work the *standard* graph representation was used because of the best results shown by this method compared to other techniques. Under the *standard* method each unique term (keyword) appearing in the document becomes a node in the graph representing that document. Each node is labeled with the term it represents. The node labels in a document graph are unique, since a single node is created for each keyword even if a term appears more than once in the text. If word a immediately precedes word b somewhere in a "section" s of the document, then there is a directed edge from the node corresponding to term a to the node corresponding to term b with an edge label s. An edge is not created between two words if they are separated by certain punctuation marks (such as periods). Sections defined for the standard representation are: *title*, which contains the text related to the document's title and any provided keywords (meta-data); *link*, which is text that appears in hyper-links on the document; and *text*, which comprises any of the visible text in the document.

The first, document representation stage, begins with a training collection of labeled documents $D = (D_1 \ldots D_{|D|})$ and a set of categories as $C = (c_1 \ldots c_{|c|})$, where each document $D_i \in D; 1 \leq i \leq |D|$ belongs to one and only one category $c_v \in C; 1 \leq v \leq |c|$. Three main actions need to be done at this stage execution. First - graph generation where graph representation of document is generated and a set of labeled graphs $G = (g_1 \ldots g_{|D|})$ is obtained. It is possible to use a limited graph size by defining parameter N, which is the maximum number of nodes in the graph, and using only N most frequent terms for graph construction, or use all document terms except stop words. Second - extraction of relevant attributes (sub-graphs). Main goal of this stage is to find the attributes that are relevant for classification. We used simple Naïve approach for this particular work. The Naïve method is based on a simple postulate that an attribute explains the category best if it is frequent in that category. A set of relevant attributes was created from frequent sub-graphs of each category as follows. All graphs in G, representing the web documents, were divided into $|c|$ groups by the class attribute value. FSG algorithm [3] for frequent sub-graphs extraction was applied to each group with a predefined threshold value t_{min} of minimal frequency. Every sub-graph more frequent than t_{min} was chosen by the algorithm as a predictive attribute. A group of attribute sub-graphs was denoted as $G' = (g'_1 \ldots g'_{|g'|})$. Third - text representation, that is representation of all document graphs as vectors of Boolean features corresponding to every sub-graph in G' ("1" - a sub-graph from the set appears in a graph). A set of binary vectors $V = (v_1 \ldots v_{|D|})$ is the output of this stage. Since we deal with vectors, a lot of distance or similarity measures as Cosine [10], Manhattan Distance [1] etc are available.

3   Comparative Evaluation of Results

In order to evaluate the performance of proposed method we performed several experiments on three different benchmark collections of web documents, called the F-series, the J-series, and the K-series. We obtained the same collections that were used in [11] and [12] for comparative evaluation. Documents in those collections

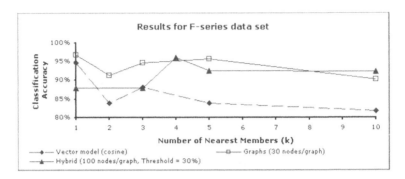

Fig. 1. Comparative results for the F-series

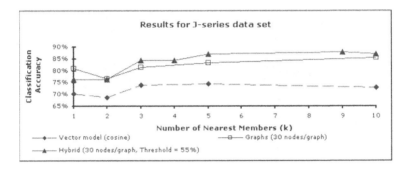

Fig. 2. Comparative results for the J-series

were originally news pages hosted at Yahoo (www.yahoo.com) and thay were down-loaded from ftp://ftp.cs.umn.edu/dept/user/boley/PDDPdata/.

To evaluate our classification approach we used k-NN as classification algorithm and Manhattan Distance [1] as distance measure. Manhattan Distance was cho-sen because of its ability to work with Boolean vectors and calculated as follows: $Distance(i,j) = |d_{i1} - d_{j1}| + |d_{i2} - d_{j2}| + \ldots + |d_{i|d|} - d_{j|d|}|$. Accuracy results of vector space and graph-based models were taken from [12]. Here we present only the most accurate results obtained in [12] for each model and collection. In all cases *leave-one-out* method was used for accuracy evaluation. In our approach different combinations of Graph Size N and Minimum Sub-graph Frequency Threshold t_{min} were used in search for maximum accuracy. As shown in Fig. 2 and Fig. 3, our hybrid method tends to outperform graph and vector methods in terms of classification ac-curacy. Especially, in J series (see Fig. 2), the hybrid approach has reached better accuracy for almost all values of k. We also measured and compared the execution time needed to classify one document for the K-series data set, which was the most time-consuming for each method. Results are presented in Table. 1. Average time to classify one document for vector and graph models was taken from [11]. That time for our *hybrid* method was calculated under the same system conditions for more than 50 experiments.

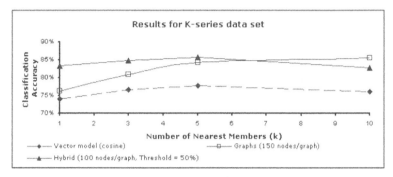

Fig. 3. Comparative results for the K-series

Timing results were taken for higher accuracy cases with each method. Such improvement in execution time can be explained by the fact that we used shorter vectors (156 dimensions) in contrast with 1458 in the vector space model to reach nearly the same accuracy. In addition, our vectors take binary values, giving us the ability to use *xor* function for calculating the Manhattan Distance between each two vectors as follows: $Distance(i,j) = |d_{i1} \otimes d_{j1}| + |d_{i2} \otimes d_{j2}| + \ldots + |d_{i|d|} \otimes d_{j|d|}|$, which is computationally faster than calculating the cosine distance between non-binary vectors.

Table 1. Average time to classify one K-series document for each method

Method	Average time to classify one document
Vector (cosine)	7.8 seconds
Graphs, 100 nodes/graph	24.62 seconds
Hybrid, 100 nodes/graph, $t_{min} = 50\%$	0.012 seconds

4   Conclusions

This paper has empirically compared three different representations of web documents in terms of classification accuracy and execution time. The proposed *hybrid* approach was found to be more accurate in most cases and generally much faster than its vector-space and graph-based counterparts. Finding the optimal Graph Size N and Minimum Sub-graph Frequency Threshold t_{min} is a subject for our future research. In addition, we are going to classify web documents using our *hybrid* representation with model-based algorithms such as ID3 or Naïve Bayes. We expect an additional reduction of classification time as a result of using the hybrid representation with these algorithms.

Acknowledgments

This work was partially supported by the National Institute for Systems Test and Productivity at University of South Florida under the USA Space and Naval

Warfare Systems Command Grant No. N00039-01-1-2248. We thank Dr. Adam Schenker for his technical assistance.

References

[1] J. Han, M. Kamber, "Data Mining Concepts and Techniques", Morgan Kaufmann 2001.

[2] A.K. Jain, M.N. Murty, and P.J. Flynn, "Data Clustering: A Review", ACM Computing Surveys, Vol. 31, No. 3, 1999

[3] M. Kuramochi and G. Karypis, "'An Efficient Algorithm for Discovering Frequent Subgraphs", Technical Report TR♯ 02-26, Dept. of Computer Science and Engineering, University of Minnesota, 2002.

[4] O.Maimon, and M.Last, Knowledge Discovery and Data Mining - The Info-Fuzzy Network (IFN) Methodology, Kluwer Academic Publishers, 2000.

[5] A. McCallum, K. Nigam, "A Comparison of Event Models for Naive Bayes Text Classification", AAAI-98 Workshop on Learning for Text Categorization, 1998.

[6] T. M. Mitchell, "Machine Learning", McGraw-Hill, 1997.

[7] D. Mukund, M. Kuramochi and G. Karypis, "Frequent sub-structure-based approaches for classifying chemical compounds", ICDM 2003, Third IEEE International Conference, 2003.

[8] J.R. Quinlan, "Induction of Decision Trees", Machine Learning, 1:81–106, 1986.

[9] J.R. Quinlan, "C4.5: Programs for Machine Learning", 1993.

[10] G. Salton, A. Wong, and C. Yang, "A vector space model for automatic indexing", Communications of the ACM, 18(11):613–620, 1971.

[11] A. Schenker, "Graph-Theoretic Techniques for Web Content Mining", Ph.D. Thesis, University of South Florida, 2003.

[12] A. Schenker, M. Last, H. Bunke, A. Kandel, "Classification of Web Documents Using Graph Matching", International Journal of Pattern Recognition and Artificial Intelligence, Special Issue on Graph Matching in Computer Vision and Pattern Recognition, Vol. 18, No. 3, pp. 475-496, 2004.

[13] S. M. Weiss, C. Apte, F. J. Damerau, D. E. Johnson, F. J. Oles, T. Goetz and T. Hampp, "Maximizing Text-Mining Performance", IEEE Intelligent Systems, Vol.14, No.4. Jul. /Aug. 1999. Pp.63-69.

[14] X. Yan and J. H. Gspan," Graph-based substructure pattern mining", Technical Report UIUCDCS-R-2002-2296, Department of Computer Science, University of Illinois at UrbanaChampaign, 2002.

A Reinforcement Learning Approach for QoS Based Routing Packets in Integrated Service Web Based Systems

Abdelhamid Mellouk and Saïd Hoceini

Computer Science and Robotics Lab – LIIA,
Université Paris XII, IUT de Créteil-Vitry,
120-122, Rue Paul Armangot - 94400 Vitry / Seine - France
Tel.: 01 41 80 73 75 - fax. : 01 41 80 73 76
mellouk@univ-paris12.fr

Abstract. Routing packets is a relevant issue for maintaining good performance and successsfully operating in a web based systems. This problem is naturally formulated as a dynamig programming problem, which, however, is too complex to be solved exactly. We proposed here two adaptive routing algorithms based on reinforcement learning. In the first algorithm, we have used a neural network to approximate a reinforcement signal, allowing the learner to incorporate various parameters into its distance estimation such as local queue size. Moreover, each router uses an on line learning module to optimize the path in terms of average packet delivery time, by taking into account the waiting queue states of neighboring routers. In the second step, the exploration of paths is limited to N-Best non loop paths in term of hops number (number of routers in a path) leading to a substantial reduction of convergence time. The performances of the proposed algorithms are evaluated experimentally for different levels of traffic's load and compared to standard shortest path and Q-routing algorithms. Our Approaches proves superior to a classical algorithms and are able to route efficiently even when critical aspects of the simulation, such as the network load, are allowed to vary dynamically.

1   Introduction

Web's solutions used the media Internet which has become the most important communication infrastructure of today's human society. It enables the world-wide users (individual, group and organizational) to access and exchange remote information scattered over the world. A routing algorithm consists of determining the next node to which a packet should be forwarded toward its destination by choosing the best optimal path according to given criteria. Traditionnal routing protocols calculate the shortest path based on a single metric (e.g. hop count) to detremine path between source and destination. However, the emergence of many kinds of flows in web solutions and realtime services, requiring Quality of Service (QoS, such as bounded delay, bounded delay jitter, and/or bounded loss ratio) better than Best Effort, raises the question wether path

P.S. Szczepaniak et al. (Eds.): AWIC 2005, LNAI 3528, pp. 299–305, 2005.

selection can be improved when QoS requirements are taken into account. A mechanism of routing packets must determinating the path of flow based on knowledge of both the network ressource availability and the QoS requirements of the flow. The deployment of QoS-based routing will increase the dynamics of path selection which make the network traffic less predictable. The Integrated Services architecture[1], with its flow-based reservations, is not scalable to the core of the transporting many kinds of flow integrated in web solution. Therefore, QoS-based routing solutions, which establish QoS paths for flows, such as QOSPF[2], are also not applicable for the core of web solution. The Differentiated Services concept, with its scalabilty and simplicity, can provide QoS in the core of the Internet's web solution. Furthermore, the traffic engineering features of MPLS [3] can also provide QoS-based routing for trunk traffic. In case of Integrated Services are deployed in the access part of the network, flow-based QoS routing can further enhance the service offering. However, when QoS-based routing is deployed without a ressource reservation mecfhanism, it becomes more complicated to obtain the QoS requirements, after the QoS path has been established.

For a network node to be able to make an optimal routing decision, according to relevant performance criteria, it requires an accurate prediction of the network dynamics during propagation of the message through the network. This, however, is impossible unless the routing algorithm is capable of adapting to network state changes in almost real time. So, it is necessary to develop a new intelligent and adaptive routing algorithm. This problem is naturally formulated as a dynamic programming problem, which is too complex to be solved exactly[4, 5]. In our approach, we use the methodology of reinforcement learning (RL) introduced by Sutton [6] to approximate the value function of dynamic programming. One of pioneering works related to this kind of approaches concerns Q-Routing algorithm [7] based on Q-learning technique [6]. Only a few Q values are current while most of the Q values in the network are unreliable. For this purpose, other algorithms have been proposed like Confidence based Q-Routing (CQ-Routing) or Dual Reinforcement Q-Routing (DRQ-Routing)[8]. All these routing algorithms use a table to estimate Q values. However, the size of the table depends on the number of destination nodes existing in the network. Thus, this approach is not well suited when we are concerned with a state-space of high dimensionality.

In this paper, we propose a Q-routing algorithm optimizing the average packet delivery time, based on Neural Network (NN) ensuring the prediction of parameters depending on traffic variations. Compared to the approaches based on a Q-table, the Q-value is approximated by a reinforcement learning based neural network, allowing the learner to incorporate various parameters such as local queue size and time of day, into its distance estimation. The Q-Neural Routing algorithm is presented in detail in section 2. All these routing algorithms explore all the network environment and do not take into account loop problem in a way leading to large time of convergence algorithm. To address this drawback and reducing computational time, we present in section 3 the N-Best Q-Routing algorithm. The performances of Q-Routing, Q-Neural Routing and N-Best Q-Routing algorithms are evaluated experimentally in section 4 and compared to the standard shortest paths routing algorithm.

2   Q-Neural Routing Approach

In our routing algorithm, the objective is to minimize the average packet delivery time. Consequently, the reinforcement signal which is chosen corresponds to the estimated time to transfer a packet to its destination. Typically, the packet delivery time includes three variables: The packet transmission time, the packet treatment time in the router and the latency in the waiting queue.

2.1   Evaluation of the Reinforcement Signal

Let's denote by $Q(s, y, d)$ the estimated time by the router s so that the packet p reaches its destination d through the router y. This parameter does not include the latency in the waiting queue of the router s. The packet is sent to the router y which determines the optimal path to send this packet.

The reinforcement signal T employed in the Q-learning algorithm can be defined as the minimum of the sum of the estimated $Q(y, x, d)$ sent by the router x neighbor of router y and the latency in waiting queue q_y corresponding to router y.

$$T = \min_{x \in neighbor of y} \{ q_y + Q(y, x, d) \} \tag{1}$$

Once the choice of the next router made, the router y puts the packet in the waiting queue, and sends back the value T as a reinforcement signal to the router s. It can therefore update its reinforcement function as:

$$\Delta Q(s, y, d) = \eta(\alpha + T - Q(s, y, d)) \tag{2}$$

So, the new estimation $Q'(s, y, d$ can be written as follows:

$$Q'(s, y, d) = Q(s, y, d)(1 - \eta) + \eta(T + \alpha) \tag{3}$$

α and η are respectively, the packet transmission time between s and y, and the learning rate. In our neural network, the input cells correspond to the destination addresses d and the waiting queue states. The outputs are the estimated packet transfer times passing through the neighbors of the considered router. The algorithm derived from this architecture is called Q-Neural Routing and can be described according to the following steps:

When receiving a packet of information:

1. *Extract a destination IP address,*
2. *Calculate Neural Network outputs,*
3. *Select the smallest output value and get an IP address of the associated router,*
4. *Send the packet to this router,*
5. *Get an IP address of the precedent router,*
6. *Create and send the packet as a reinforcement signal.*

On reception of a reinforcement signal packet:

1. *Extract a Q estimated value computed by the neighbor,*
2. *Extract a destination IP address,*
3. *Neural Network updating using a retropropagation algorithm based on gradient method,*
4. *Destroy the reinforcement packet.*

3   N-Best Optimal Paths Q-Routing Approach

A Q-Neural Routing needs a rather large computational time and space memory. In the goal of reducing the complexity of our algorithm, we proposed an hybrid approach combining neural networks and reducing the search space to N-Best no loop paths in terms of hops number reducing. This approach requires each router to maintain a link state database, which is essentially a map of the network topology. When a network link changes its state (i.e., goes up or down, or its utilization is increased or decreased), the network is flooded with a link state advertisement (LSA) message [9]. This message can be issued periodically or when the actual link state change exceeds a certain relative or absolute threshold. Obviously, there is tradeoff between the frequency of state updates (the accuracy of the link state database) and the cost of performing those updates. In our model, the link state information is updated when the actual link state change. Once the link state database at each router updated, the router computes the N-Best optimal paths and determines the best one from Q-Routing algorithm.

3.1   Constructing N-Best Paths

Several papers discuss the algorithms for finding N-Best paths [5, 10]. Our solution is based on a label setting algorithm (based on the optimality principle and being a generalization of Dijkstra's algorithm) [11]. The space complexity is O(Nm), where N

```
/* S the source node
* K –set of nodes in network
* X – the label set
* Count_i – Number of paths from S to I
* elm – Affected number to assigned label
* P – Paths list from S to destination (D)
* N – paths number to compute
* h – corresponding between node and affected
label number */
/* Initialisation */
count_i = 0   /* for all i ∈ N */
elem = 1
h(elem) = s
h^{-1}(s) = {elem}
distance_{elem} = 0
X = {elem}
P^N = 0
While (count_t < N and X != { })
begin
      /* find a label lb from X, such that
      distance_{lb}<= distance_{lb1} ,∀ lb1 ∈ X*/
      X = X – {lb}
      i = h(lb)
      count_i = count_i + 1
      if (i == D) then
      /* if the node I is the destination node D */
      begin
            p = path for 1 to lb
```

```
            P^N = P^N U {h(p)}
      end
      if (count_i <= N )then
      begin
            for each arc(i,j) ∈ A
            begin
            /* Verify if new label does not
               result in loop */
               v=lb
               While (h(v) != s)
               begin
                     if (h(v) == j) then
                           goto do_not_add
                     v = previous_v
               end
               /* Save information from
                  new label */
               elem = elem + 1
               distance_{elem}= distance_n + c_{ij}
               previous_{elem}= lb
               h(elem) = j
               h^{-1}(j) = h^{-1}(j) U {elem}
               X = X U {elem}
               do_not_add:
            end
      end
end
```

is the number of paths and m is the number of edges. By using a pertinent data structure, the time complexity can be kept at the same level $O(Nm)$ [11]. We modify the algorithm to find the N-Best non-loop paths as follows: Let a DAG $(K; A)$ denote a network with k nodes and m edges, where $K = \{1, \ldots, k\}$, and $A = \{a_{ij}/j, i \in K\}$. The problem is to find the top N paths from source s to all the other nodes. Let's define a label set X and a one-to-many projection $h: K \rightarrow X$, meaning that each node $i \in K$ corresponds to a set of labels $h(i)$, each element of which represents a path from s to i.

4   Implementation and Simulation Results

To show the efficiency and evaluate the performances of our approach, an implementation has been performed on OPNET software of MIL3 Company where the protocol specification language is based on a formal description of a finite state automaton. The proposed approaches have been compared to that based on standard Q-routing and shortest paths routing policies (such as RIP).

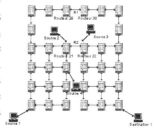

The topology of the network employed here for simulations, which used in many papers (such as [7]), includes 33 interconnected nodes. Two kinds of traffic have been studied: low load and high load of the network. In the first case, a low rate flow is sent to node destination-1, from nodes source-1 and source-4. From the previous case, we have created conditions of congestion of the network. Thus, a high rate flow is generated by nodes source-2 and source-3.

This topology shows the two possible ways R-1 (routers-29 and routers-30) and R-2 (routers-21 and routers-22) to route the packets between the left part and the right part of the network. Performances of algorithms are evaluated in terms of average packet delivery time. Fig. 1 illustrates the obtained results when source-2 and source-3 send information packets during 10 minutes.

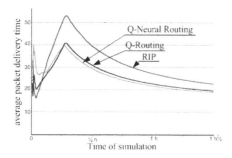

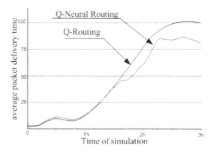

Fig. 1. Congestion after 10 minutes   **Fig. 2.** Congestion after 60 minutes

From fig.1, one can see, clearly, that after an initialization period, the Q-routing and Q-Neural routing algorithms, exhibit better performances than RIP. Thus, packet average packet delivery time obtained by Q-routing algorithm and Q-Neural routing algorithm is reduced of respectively 23,6% and 27,3% compared to RIP routing policy. These results confirm that RIP algorithm lead to weak performances due to packets delayed in the waiting queues of the routers. Moreover, this policy does not take into account the load of the network. On the other hand, when a way of destination is saturated, Q-routing and Q-Neural routing algorithms allow the selection of a new one to avoid this congestion.

Fig. 2 illustrates the average packet delivery time obtained when a congestion of the network is generated during 60 minutes. Thus, in the case where the number of packets is more important, the Q-Neural routing algorithm gives better results compared to Q-routing algorithm. For example, after 2 hours of simulation, Q-Neural routing exhibits a performance of 20% higher than that of Q-routing. Indeed, the utilization of waiting queue state of the neighbouring routers in the decision of routing, allows anticipation of routers congestion.

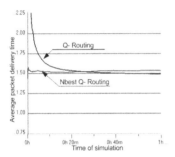
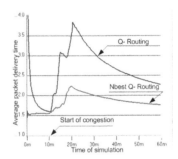

Fig. 3. Network with a low load   **Fig. 4.** Network with a high load

On the other hand, results about the combined Neural Networks Best Optimal Paths called N-Best paths Q-routing algorithm are given in fig. 3 & 4. From fig. 4, one can see, clearly, that after an initialization period, the N-Best Q- Routing exhibit better performances than standard Q-Routing algorithms. Thus, packet average packet delivery time obtained by N-Best paths Q-routing algorithm is reduced by 30, 2% compared to Q-routing algorithm. These results confirm that Q-Routing algorithm has weak performances due to speed of adaptation of the routers.

Moreover, this policy does not take into account the loop problem in way of destination. On the other hand, N-Best paths Q-routing algorithms explore only the N-Best paths. In the case of a low load (fig 3), one can note that after a period of initialization, performances of these algorithms are approximately the same.

5   Conclusion

In this paper, a flow based routing approach on neural networks is proposed. This approach offers advantages compared to standard routing policy and Q-routing algorithm, like the reduction of the memory space for the storage of secondary paths, and a reasonable computing time for alternative paths research. The Q-value is approximated by a reinforcement learning based neural network of a fixed size. The learning algorithm is based on the minimization of the average packet delivery time, by taking into account the waiting queue state. For reducing the computational time, a flow based routing approach conbining neural networks and short optimal path called N-Best optimal paths Q-Routing algorithm is proposed. This approach offer advantage compared to standard Q-Routing algorithm, like the reduction of the exploration paths for update Q-value, and a reasonable computing time for alternative paths research. The learning algorithm is based on find N-Best paths and the minimization of the average packet delivery time on these paths. Simulation results show better performances of the our algorithm comparatively to standard shortest paths routing and Q-routing algorithms.

References

1. P. P. White, "RSVP and Integrated Services in the Internet: A Tutorial", IEEE Com. Mag.,May 1997.
2. E. Crawley, R. Nair, B. Rajagopalan, H. Sandick, "A Framework for QoS-based Routing in the Internet", RFC2386, IETF, August 1998.
3. W. Stallings, "MPLS" , Internet Protocol Journal, Vol. 4, nr. 3, September 2001.
4. R.G. Gallager "A minimum delay routing algorithm using distributed computations", IEEE Transactions on Communications, Vol. COM-25, 1977.
5. A.E. Ozdaglar, D. P. Bertsekas "Optimal Solution of Integer Multicommodity Flow Problem with Application in Optical Networks", Proc. Of Symposium on Global Optimisation, June 2003.
6. R.S. Sutton and A. G. Barto, "Reinforcement Learning" MIT Press, 1997.
7. J. A. Boyan and M. L. Littman, "Packet Routing in Dynamically Changing Networks: A Reinforcement Learning Approach." InAdvances in Neural Information Processing Systems 6, 1994.
8. S. Kumar and R. Miikkualainen, " Confidence-based Q-routing: an on-queue adaptive routing algorithm" In Proceedings of Neural Networks in Engineering, 1998.
9. J. Yanxia, N. Ioanis, and G. Pawel, " Multiple path QoS Routing" Proc. Int. Conf. Communications (ICC2001), IEEE, June 2001.
10. A. Mellouk and P. Gallinari, "Discriminative training for improved neural prediction system" In IEEE Int. Acoustic, Speech and Signal Processing, 1995.
11. V. Lemaire and F. Clérot, "Estimation of the Blocking probabilities in an ATM Network Node Using Artificial Neural Networks for Connection Admission Control." In International Tel. traffic Congress, volume 16, Edinburgh 1999.

Goal Directed Web Services

Alfredo Milani, Marco Baioletti, and Valentina Poggioni

Department of Mathematics and Computer Science,
University of Perugia, Via Vanvitelli 1, Perugia, Italy
milani@dipmat.unipg.it

Abstract. In this paper a system for goal directed integration of web services based on automated planning is presented. The increasing number of web services available on the net poses the problem of having efficient tools in order to integrate existing services for obtaining complex services which reflect user goals and needs. In this scenario, automated planning techniques represent promising components of such dynamical and evolutionary systems. In the proposed architectural model, web services and user goals are modeled as planning operators and goals, while the generated solution plans are used for directly generating web service scripts. An extended planning model based on the notion of output variable has been introduced in order to take into account of results produced by services invocations. A technique called semantic wrapper has been developed for modeling services as operators. The implementation of P4WS, a planner with output variables which demonstrated the model is described and experimental results are presented.

1 Introduction

Web services [2] consist of software services designed for being remotely invoked over the web by other software components and/or services. Currently web services are increasingly available on the net and they cover a variety of purposes which range from information retrieval services to services which produce relevant effects in the real world. They are based on XML technologies [10] and they represent a software layer which allows access to distributed resources in a platform independent, reusable way. The problem of having flexible tools for integrating web services in order to realize complex tasks has been only partial addressed with the definition, currently under development, of appropriate script languages [14]. The expected explosion of web services which will characterizes the next internet scenario poses the problem of developing tools for the automatic integration of collection of an increasing number of web services in order to realize user goals which change dynamically over time. In this evolutionary and dynamical scenario, state of the art techniques for automatic synthesis of plans of actions [3, 1, 4] can be used to realize a double purpose: a personalized integration based on user/application desired goals and preferences, and an effective mechanism for integrating new web services as they appear on the net.

In Section 2 the planning model and the overall architecture of the system are described; a special techniques for modeling input/output interfaces of web

P.S. Szczepaniak et al. (Eds.): AWIC 2005, LNAI 3528, pp. 306–312, 2005.

services, based on the concept of semantics wrapper and on the notion of output planning variables, is introduced in Section 3; the P4WS planner, an implementation of the planner for Web services is presented in Section 4; finally, experiments, relationships with previous works and future developments are discussed in Section 5 and in Section 6.

2   A Planning Based Architecture for Web services

A web service can be characterized as the remote invocation of a method which resides in an object over the web. The SOAP protocol [11, 13] provides a uniform XML based interface for remote methods invocation, for passing input parameters and for returning output data to the caller. The possibility of invoking remote methods in a transparent uniform way allows a new approach to distributed programming, in fact new personalized services can be obtained by exploiting and integrating existing web services producing new relevant behaviour. Our purpose is to realize an automation integration of web services which is dynamically generated on the base of user goals and needs.

Classical planning problem [3] is posed as a tuple (I, G, O), where I is the logical description of the initial state, G the goal state description and O the set of domain operators (operators define state-to-state transitions and are described in terms of preconditions and effects). A planning problem consists of generating a solution plan P, i.e. a partially ordered set of actions (operators instances) that, if executed, transform the initial state I into a state which reaches G.

Our approach to automatic web service integration relies on the basic idea of modeling each web service as a planning operator and describing the user goals and the input knowledge respectively as goals and initial state of a planning problem. The generated solution plan will represent the calls to the web services needed for satisfying user goals. In Fig.1 it is shown the architecture of the system for automatic web service generation and integration. The *Goal Acquisition Interface* module transforms user goals into planning goals and initial states; *Semantics Wrappers* are used to model services as planning domain operators; the

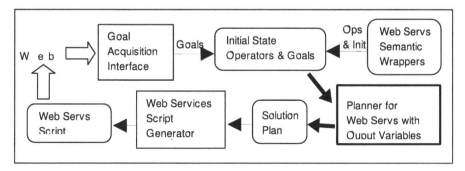

Fig. 1. The Web Services Planning Architecture

Planner with Output Variables module is responsible of generating the solution plan which is then mapped, by *Script Generator* module, into an actual script which realizes the web services calls.

3   A Planning Model with Output Variables

The basic element which characterizes this planning model from the classical ones is the introduction of the concept of output variables, which are needed in order to model web service outputs.

3.1   Describing Operators by Semantics Wrappers

A planning operator which describes a web service must characterize the behaviour of the service in term of preconditions and effects. Informations about web service methods invocations are described in WSDL (web service description language) [2, 12, 14] documents associated with the service, but unfortunately they often provide purely syntactic information which cannot be directly used to build operator descriptions. We call semantics wrapper an operator description derived from a WSDL by adding the semantics information allowing to use the web service as a planning operator.

We can assume, for instance, that `Satellite_Picture` is a web service which provides satellite information given the geographical coordinates of the area of interest. A pure syntactical description of the method `getSatPicture` is the following Java-like declaration: `GifPicture getSatPicture(float lat, float long, float width, float length)`. A semantics wrapper of the method should specify that, `lat` and `long` are latitudes and longitudes and that if the pair (`lat`,`long`) represents the coordinates of an object, then the returned picture refers to the same object. A suitable semantics wrapper for the `getAPicture` method could be:

```
(operator: getSatpicture
    (parameters: ?lat ?long ?object)
    (output parameters: !picture)
    (precond (coordinates_of ?object ?lat ?long))
    (effects (and (gif_picture !picture)(ImageOf ?object !picture)) ) )
```

It must be noted that in the above description we introduce a special descriptor and notation for the output parameter: `!picture`. In state of the art planners existing in the literature [1, 4, 14] actions which generate output variables are not modeled, i.e. it is not allowed to specify in an effect a parameter which is not named in the preconditions. The reason is that usually effects estabilish properties over ground terms, the semantics of action execution is given forward, from preconditions to effects, then the preconditions binding mechanism is not able to specify which value should hold the output parameter.

3.2   Output Variables

The problem of representing output variables can be solved by observing that is not strictly necessary to know their values in order to built a plan. Output variables [15] can be seen as placeholders for objects which will be known at execution time. The solution we propose is based on the assumption that web services have a deterministic behaviour, i.e. they produce the same output for a given input. The solution consists in associating for each ground tuple of operator parameters in the plangraph [4, 1], one unique ground symbol to each output variable. Neverthless the assumption of deterministic web service behaviour has certain limitations, for most real applications this limitation is not relevant because of the following property.

Property: *If a plan includes at most one instance of an operator for a given combination of its input parameters, deterministic operators are equivalent to non deterministic ones.*

3.3 Planning Problems with Output Variables

A goal is denoted by a conjunction of conditions which must hold in the final state. In the web service framework it is significant to be able to specify output variables in the problem final goals. The problem of binding output variables in the goal is solved by the technique of modifying the planning problem by introducing a dummy operator `final_op` which has the dummy effect `final_goal` (which is the new final goal) and it has the original goals as preconditions. Given this characterization for output variable the standard definitions of the planning models [3] hold in this extension. In our framework a planning problem with output variables is then characterized by a tuple (I,G,O) where the goal corresponds to the single `final_goal`, the set O include the special operator `final_op` and output variables are allowed in domain operators.

4   Implementing a Planner for Web Services

Currently, we have experimented two implementations of P4WS, our planner for web services, one based on Blackbox [4] and one based on DPPLAN [1]. The semantics for output variables is realized by a technique developed by the authors as an extension of domain compilation technique [8]. For each output variable `!var` appearing in an operator `op`, the artificial precondition (`output ?var`) and the effect `not(output ?var)` are added; then each occurrence of `!var` in `op` is then substituted with an occurrence of normal input variable `?var`. For example, the former operator `getSatpicture` is compiled in standard PDDL as:

```
(operator: getSatpicture
    (parameters: ?lat ?long ?object ?picture)
    (precond (and (coordinates_of ?object ?lat ?long) (output ?picture)) )
    (effects (and (gif_picture ?picture) (ImageOf ?object ?picture)
                  (not (output ?picture)) ) )
```

5   Experiments and Related Works

We have experimented the P4WS planner in a domain in which a set of Web Services is encoded by the semantic wrappers technique; in this domain[1] three classes of web service integration problems have been designed:

p1 Built a web page with picture of a given town and weather conditions for a given date

p2 Choose an hotel in a given town based on user preferences and reserve it

p3 Conjunctions of the goals for p1 and p2 for an increasing number of cities, we have tried from 2 to 30 cities at the same time.

In order to point out the feature of the generated solution plans we show in Fig.2 a simple plan for the goal (and (ImageOf !pict1 rome) (ImageOf !pict2 florence) (Weather rome 12/4/2003 !WeatherCond1) (hotel_in Rome !hotel1) (reserved !hotel1 12/2/2003 !reservation_number)). The problem consists of finding two picture, respectively of Florence and Rome, reserving an hotel in Rome for 12/4/2003 and getting weather info for the same date. The plan consists

```
1.  city_info(florence, lat1, lat2, mayor1, points_of_interest1)
1.  city_info(rome, lat3, lat4, mayor2, points_of_interest2)
2.  WeatherInfo(rome, lat3, lat4, 12/2/2003, weather_cond1)
2.  getSatellitePicture(florence, lat1, lat2, picture1)
2.  getSatellitePicture(rome, lat3, lat4, picture2)
2.  getHotels(rome, hotel_list1)
3.  BestBargain(rome, user_pref, hotel_list1, hotel1)
4.  ReserveHotel(rome, hotel1, 12/2/2003, reservation_number1)
5.  Final_op(picture1, picture2, weather_cond1, hotel1,
    reservation_number1)
```

Fig. 2. A Web Service Plan Generated by P4WS

of eight operators instances executed in four steps. The resulting solution points out the parallel structure of the web service calls (e.g. a parallel or asyncronous set of calls can be generated for the four calls at step 2) and optimises the number of web service calls. The execution time of both implemented planners for the given problems is very efficient and satisfactory and does not show to be sensible to the used planner (see Fig.3).

The use of planning for integrating software resources in order to realize automatic script generation has been experimented in the Multivicar planner developed at JPL [6] for image processing, in the case of Multivicar, the planner was used to generated scripts which were furtherly modified by human operators. In [5] a planner is used, with similar techniques, for organizing personalized training materials for spacecraft crews.

---

[1] Available at www.dipmat.unipg/ milani/p4ws

Problem	P4WS based on Blackbox	P4WS based on DPPLAN
P1	0.05	0.03
P2	0.04	0.03
P3 #cities=2	0.06	0.07
P3 #cities=5	0.15	0.09
P3 #cities=10	0.27	0.14
P3 #cities=20	0.34	0.18
P3 #cities=30	0.52	0.24

Fig. 3. Experimental Results

6 Conclusions

This paper shows that automated planning techniques can be successfully applied to goal directed automatic integration of web services. In this framework semantics wrapper are used to model web service as planning operators in term of logical preconditions/effects. A special technique for planning with output variables has been developed, in order to denote and manage output resulting from web service calls. A realized implementation P4WS has been presented and experimented.

In order to have more efficient implementation and avoiding the explosion of the dimensions of the plangraph, we have under development a modified version of DPPLAN [1] and Blackbox [4] which modifies the operators instantiation mechanism of the plangraph. Moreover future developments will proceed following three main directions: development of planning techniques which allow plan of web services with iterations and conditionals; automatic acquisition of knowledge about online services and integration with the semantics web ontologies; integration with languages for Web services flow control.

References

1. Baioletti M., Marcugini S. and Milani A. *DPPlan: An Alghoritm for Fast Solution Extraction from a Planning Graph.* In Proceedings of AIPS-2000, AAAI Press, 2000, Menlo Park, California, USA, ISBN 1-57735-111-8.
2. Cauldwell, Chawla, Chopra, Damschen, Dix, Hong, Norton, Ogbuji, Olander, Richman, Saunders, Zaev. *Professional XML Web Services*, Wrox, 2001
3. Fikes R.E., Nilsson N.J. *STRIPS: A new approach to the application of theorem proving to problem solving.* In Artificial Intelligence, 2(3/4), 1971.
4. H.Kautz, B.Selman, *BLACKBOX: A New Approach to the Application of Theorem Proving to Problem Solving.* In Proceeding of Planning as Combinatorial Search, AIPS-98, Pittsburgh, PA, 1998, AAAI Press.
5. T.J.Grant, M.Verhoef, L.P.Gale, *AI Planning for Just-In-Time Training in Space: ESA's Integrated Learning System.* In Proceedings of 1st NASA Workshop on Planning and Scheduling for Space, Oxnard, CA, Oct 1997.
6. S.Chien et al. *The Multimission VICAR Planner: A Knowledge-based System for Automated Image Processing*, NASA Science Information Systems, Issue 38.

7. A.Milani, et al. *NetWatcher: A Software Agent for Monitoring Events on the Web*, In Int. J. of Information Theories and Applications, Vol 6, n.3 1999 ISSN 1310.

8. A.Milani, S.Marcugini, M.Baioletti. *Encoding Planning Constraints into Partial Order Planning Domain*, In Proceeding of KR98, pp.608-616, Morgan Kauffmann 1998, ISBN 1-55860-554-1.

9. A.Milani, S.Marcugini. *Stockbot: a Monitoring and Acting Software Agent for Stock Markets*, Int.J.of Intell.System in Accounting, Finance and Management, Vol 8,Isuue 1, 1999, Wiley&Son 1999.

10. Didier Martin et al. *Professional XML*, Wrox Press Ltd, 2000

11. W3C, *SOAP 1.1 Note*, www.w3.org/TR/SOAP, May 8 2001

12. W3C, *WSDL 1.1 Note*, www.w3.org/TR/WSDL, March 15 2001

13. James Snell, Doug Tidwell, Pavel Kulchenko. *Programming Web Services With Soap*, O'Reilly Internet Series, 2001.

14. Microsoft Corporation. *Global XML Web Services Architecture White Paper*, Ottobre 2001.

15. Golden, O. Etzioni, and D. Weld. *Xii: Planning with universal quantification and incomplete information*, In Proceedings of the 4th International Conference on Principles of Knowledge Representation and Reasoning, KR'94, 1994.

16. A. Milani, S. Marcugini. *Planning Technologies for the Web Environment: Perspectives and Research Issues*, International Journal on Information Theories and Apllications, vol.10, n.1. 36-43, ISBN 1310-0513.

Optimizing Collaborative Filtering Recommender Systems

Sung-Hwan Min and Ingoo Han

Graduate School of Management,
Korea Advanced Institute of Science and Technology,
207-43 Cheongrangri-dong, Dongdaemun-gu, Seoul 130-722, Korea
shmin@kgsm.kaist.ac.kr

Abstract. Collaborative filtering (CF) is the most successful recommendation technique, which has been used in a number of different applications. In traditional CF, the ratings of all items are equally weighted when similarity measure is calculated. But, if the importance of features (or items) is different respectively, feature weighting structure needs to be changed according to the importance of features. This paper presents a GA based feature weighting method. Through this weighting method, we can focus on the good items while removing bad ones or reducing their impacts.

1 Introduction

Collaborative filtering (CF) is the most successful recommendation technique, which has been used in a number of different applications such as recommending movies, articles, products, Web pages [1, 5]. CF is built on the assumption that a good way to predict the preference of the active consumer for a target product is to find other consumers who have similar preferences, and then use those similar consumer's preferences for that product to make a prediction [3].

In traditional CF, the ratings of all items are equally weighted when similarity measure is calculated as shown in Eq.(1).

$$S_{a,u} = \frac{\sum_i (r_{a,i} - \overline{r}_a)(r_{u,i} - \overline{r}_u)}{\sqrt{(\sum_i (r_{a,i} - \overline{r}_a)^2)}\sqrt{\sum_i (r_{u,i} - \overline{r}_u)^2}} \,, (where -1 \leq S_{a,u} \leq 1) \tag{1}$$

In the above equation $S_{a,u}$ is the similarity between the active user and each of the other users who have the co-rated items with the active user A, i is the index of each item that both user A and user U have rated, $r_{a,i}$ is the rating of user A for item i and $r_{u,i}$ is the rating of user U for item i. And, $\overline{r}_a$ denotes the average rating of active user A, $\overline{r}_u$ is the average of the other user's ratings. This similarity is generally used to select the nearest neighbors who have the most similar tastes in order of the values of $S_{a,u}$. But, if importance of features is different respectively, feature weighting structure needs to be changed according to the importance of features. This paper presents a GA based feature weighting

P.S. Szczepaniak et al. (Eds.): AWIC 2005, LNAI 3528, pp. 313–319, 2005.

method. Through this weighting method, we can focus on the good items while removing bad ones or reducing their impacts. Ratings on a 'good product' are highly relevant to the preference for the target product, while a 'bad product' is irrelevant or noisy in prediction for the target product. Introduction of the proposed feature weighting method may be useful to improve the accuracy of prediction.

2   Genetic Algorithm (GA)

GA is an artificial intelligence procedure based on the theory of natural selection and evolution. GA uses the idea of survival of the fittest by progressively accepting better solutions to the problems [2]. GA simultaneously possesses a large amount of candidate solutions to a problem, called population. The key feature of a GA is the manipulation of a population whose individuals are characterized by possessing a chromosome. Two important issues in GA are the genetic coding used to define the problem and the evaluation function, called the fitness function. Each individual solution in GA is represented by a string called the chromosome. Initial solution population could be generated randomly, which evolve to the next generation by genetic operators such as selection, crossover and mutation. The solutions coded by strings are evaluated by the fitness function. Selection operator allows strings with higher fitness to appear with higher probability in the next generation [4]. Crossover is performed between two selected individuals, called parents, by exchanging parts of their strings, starting from a randomly chosen crossover point. This operator tends to enable to the evolutionary process to move toward promising regions of the search space. Mutation is used to search further space of problem and to avoid local convergence of the GA [6].

GA has been extensively researched and applied to many combinatorial optimization problems. Furthermore GA has been increasingly applied in conjunction with other AI techniques such as neural network and CBR. Various problems of neural network design have been optimized using GA. GA has been also used in conjunction with CBR to select relevant input variables and tune the parameters of CBR. But few studies have dealt with integration of GA and CF, though there is a great potential for useful applications in this area. In this study, we present a GA based feature weighting method. Through this weighting method, we can focus on the good items while removing bad ones or reducing their impacts.

3   Hybrid GA-CF Model

Finding an appropriate feature weight for CF plays an important role on the performance of CF. But, it is not known beforehand which values are the best for CF. Optimizing feature weight of CF is crucial for the best prediction performance. This paper proposes the GA as the method of optimizing feature weight

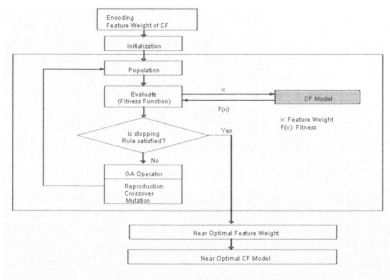

Fig. 1. Overall Procedure of GA-CF

of CF. Fig. 1 shows the overall procedure of the proposed model which optimizes feature weight for CF. The procedure starts with the randomly selected
chromosomes which represent feature weight for CF. Each new chromosome is
evaluated by sending it to the CF model. These feature weight is used in similarity calculation step as shown in Eq. (2).

$$S_{a,u} = \frac{\sum_i fw_i \cdot (r_{a,i} - \overline{r}_a)(r_{u,i} - \overline{r}_u)}{\sqrt{(\sum_i (r_{a,i} - \overline{r}_a)^2)}\sqrt{\sum_i (r_{u,i} - \overline{r}_u)^2}} \tag{2}$$

The CF model uses these feature weights for all items in order to obtain the
predictive accuracy. The predictive accuracy is used as the fitness function and
is evolved by GA. The chromosomes for feature weight are encoded as strings
standing for some weight of the original feature set list. Each value of the chromosome represents the importance of the corresponding feature. 1 means the
corresponding feature is the most important, whereas 0 means it is not important and not used in similarity calculation step. The value of feature weight
indicates how important the feature (or item) is.

Fig. 2 shows examples of encoding for GA. Each of the selected feature weight
is evaluated using an CF model. This process is iterated until the best feature
weight is found. The data set is divided into a training set and a validation
portion. Training set (T) consists of both T_1 and T_2. GA evolves a number
of populations. Each population consists of sets of feature weights. The fitness

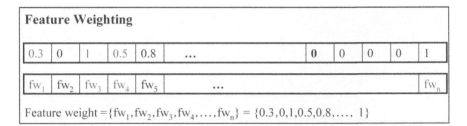

Fig. 2. Examples of Encoding for GA

of an individual of the population is based on the performance of a CF model. CF model is trained on T_1 using only the feature weight of the individual. The fitness is the prediction accuracy of CF model over T_2. At each generation new individuals are created and inserted into the population by selecting fit parents which are mutated and recombined. During the evolution, the simple crossover operator (traditional 1-point crossover) is used. Mutation operator just flips a specific bit. With elite survival strategy, we reserve elite not only between generations but also in the operation of crossover and mutation so that we can obtain all the benefit of GA operation. The details of the proposed model in an algorithmic form are explained in Table 1.

4   Experimental Evaluation

We conducted experiments to evaluate the proposed model. For experiments we used the EachMovie database, provided by Compaq Systems Research Center (http://www.research.compaq.com/SRC/eachmovie). We used Mean Absolute Error (MAE) as our choice of evaluation metric to report prediction experiments because it is commonly used and easy to interpret. First we selected 1200 users with more than 100 rated items. We divided the data set into a training set and a test portion.

Before starting full experimental evaluation of different algorithms we investigated the sensitivity to different parameters. We fixed the optimum values of these parameters from the sensitivity plots and used them for the rest of the experiments. The size of the neighborhood has a significant impact on the prediction quality [3]. To determine the sensitivity to this parameter, we performed an experiment where we varied the number of neighbors to be used and computed MAE. Our results are shown in Fig. 3. We can observe that the size of neighborhood does affect the quality of prediction. The CF algorithm improves as we increase the neighborhood size from 10 to 40. After that, the rate of increase diminishes and the curve tends to be flat. We used 70 as our choice of neighborhood size. To compare the performance of the proposed GA based CF algorithm we used the traditional CF algorithm as the benchmark model. The traditional CF recommendation employs the Pearson nearest neighbor algorithm.

Table 1. Step of GA-CF

Step 1.Define the string (or chromosome)
Vi = (s,t,,r)(Feature weights of CF model are encoded into chromosomes)
Step 2. Define population size (N_{pop}), probability of crossover (P_c) and
probability of mutation (P_m).
Step 3. Generate the initial population of N_{pop} chromosomes randomly.
Step 4. While stopping condition is false, do Step 4- 8.
Step 5. Decode j_{th} chromosome (j = 1,2, , N_{pop}) to obtain the corresponding
feature weights
Step 6. Apply V_j to the CF model to compute the output, Ok.
Step 7. Evaluate fitness, F_j of the j_{th} chromosome using Ok
(Fitness function: Average predictive accuracy)
Step 8. Calculate total fitness function of population
TF = $\sum_{i=1}^{N_{pop}} F_i(V_i)$
Step 9. Reproduction
9.1 Compute $q_i = F_i (V_i)$/TF
9.2 Calculate cumulative probability
9.3 Generate random number r between [0, 1]. If r < q1 , then select first string
(V1), otherwise, select j_{th} string such that $q_{j-1} < r < q_j$
Step 10. Generate offspring population by performing crossover and mutation on
parent pairs
10.1 Crossover: Generate random number r_1 between [0, 1] for a new string.
If $r_1 < P_c$, then operate crossover
10.2 Mutation: Generate random number r2 between [0, 1] and select the bit
for mutation randomly. If $r_2 < P_m$, then operate mutation for the bit.
Step 11. Stop the iterative step when the terminal condition is reached.

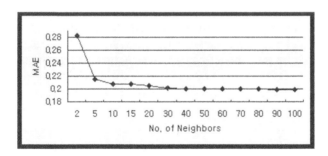

Fig. 3. Sensitivity to the Neighborhood Size

Table 2. Performance results

Model		MAE
Proposed Model	GACF	0.19837
Traditional Model	TCF	0.19917

Table 3. Paired t-test

Model	p-value
TCF	
GACF	0.036**

** Significant at the .05 level

Table 2 shows the results of experiment. In Table 2, GACF describes the proposed GA based CF model and TCF means the traditional CF model. Table 2 presents the performance of the competing models according to the metric of mean square error of recommendation. It can be observed that the proposed GA based CF algorithm outperforms the traditional CF algorithm. In addition, a set of pairwise t-tests in Table 3 indicates that the differences were statistically significant. GA based CF reflects better user preference than traditional CF at the 5% significance level. These results show that the proposed GA based CF algorithm is more accurate than the traditional CF algorithm.

5   Conclusion

Due to the explosion of e-commerce, recommender systems are rapidly becoming a core tool to accelerate cross-selling and strengthen customer loyalty. This study focused on improving the performance of recommender system by optimizing feature weight of CF. This paper presents a GA based feature weighting method. Through this weighting method, we can focus on the good items while removing bad ones or reducing their impacts.

We conducted an experiment to evaluate the proposed model on the Each-Movie data set and compared them with the traditional CF algorithm. The results show the proposed model's improvement in making recommendations.

In our future work, we intend to optimize feature weight and parameters of CF simultaneously. We would also like to expand this model to apply to the instance selection problems.

References

1. Breese, J.S., Heckerman, D., Kadie, C. (1998). Empirical Analysis of Predictive Algorithms for Collaborative Filtering. Proceedings of the 14th Conference on Uncertainty in Artificial Intelligence (UAI-98), pp. 43-52.
2. Goldberg, D. E., Genetic Algorithms in Search, Optimization and Machine Learning (Addison-Wesley, New York 1989)
3. Herlocker, J.L., Konstan, J.A. and Riedl, J., (2000). Explaining collaborative filtering recommendations. Proceedings on the ACM 2000 Conference on Computer Supported Cooperative Work, (pp. 241-250). Philadelphia.
4. Holland, J. H., Adaptation in natural and artificial systems (The University of Michigan Press, Ann Arbor, 1975)

5. Sarwar,B.M., Konstan,J.A., Borchers,A., Herlocker,J.L., Miller,B.N., Ried1,J. (1998). Using filtering agents to improve prediction quality in the grouplens research collaborative filtering system. Proceedings of CSCW'98. Seattle, WA.
6. Tang, K. S., Man, K. F., Kwong, S., He, Q., Genetic Algorithms and Their Applications, IEEE Signal Processing Magazine 13 (1996) 22-37.
7. http://www.research.compaq.com/SRC/eachmovie

Intelligent Reputation Assessment for Participants of Web-Based Customer-to-Customer Auctions

Mikołaj Morzy, Marek Wojciechowski, and Maciej Zakrzewicz

Institute of Computing Science,
Poznań University of Technology, Piotrowo 3A, 60-965 Poznań, Poland
{Mikolaj.Morzy, Marek.Wojciechowski, Maciej.Zakrzewicz}@cs.put.poznan.pl

Abstract. The Internet witnesses the unprecedent boom of customer-to-customer e-commerce. Most online auction providers use simple participation counts for reputation rating, thus enabling dishonest participants to cheat. In this paper we propose a novel definition of reputation and credibility of C2C e-commerce participants and we present an algorithm for reputation rating estimation. We conduct several experiments on real-world data which prove the feasibility of our algorithm.

1 Introduction

The Internet is quickly becoming an important arena of a novel type of merchandise called electronic commerce, or e-commerce for short. One of the most important models of e-commerce is customer-to-customer commerce representing auctions. We investigate the fundamental property of the C2C model, namely, the credibility of participants. Indeed, trust, fairness, and credibility are perceived by the users as crucial issues in online trading through C2C channels. The anonymity provided by the Internet tempts the participants into dishonest behavior. Unfortunately, currently used reputation reporting mechanisms are not satisfactory and can be easily deceived by malicious participants. Most popular auction sites use a simple participation counter for reputation reporting. Other users are allowed to see this counter along with textual comments and ratings (usually labeled with "negative", "neutral", and "positive"). In order to avoid unfairly high or low ratings only users who truly finalized an auction can mutually post comments and ratings.

In this paper we introduce a novel approach to reputation estimation. We propose to use a data mining technique to analyze the graph of connections between participants to derive knowledge about the credibility of each participant. Our method efficiently discovers most common types of frauds that occur in online auctions. Our accomplishments are twofold. First, we propose a novel definition of the reputation based on credibility of contractors and we present an efficient algorithm to compute it. Second, we empirically prove the practical usability of our algorithm by mining a large volume of real-world data obtained from a

P.S. Szczepaniak et al. (Eds.): AWIC 2005, LNAI 3528, pp. 320–326, 2005.

leading Polish online auction provider. In addition, we perform a controlled fraud and we show how our method quickly discovers malevolent behavior.

This paper is organized as follows. In Section 2 we present the related work on the subject. Section 3 contains definitions of basic notions used throughout the paper. We describe our algorithm in details in Section 4 and we present the results of the empirical evaluation of the algorithm in Section 5. The paper concludes with future work agenda in Section 6.

2   Related Work

Reputation systems [1] are a practical way of building trust in environments with high anonymity and low trustworthiness of participants. Contemporary Web-based auction systems rely on simple trust models with credibility of participants assessed by counting comments received after each transaction. In [3] Malaga presented a critical analysis of such simple models, identifying several problems that should be solved, including the subjective nature of feedbacks, the credibility of feedbacks, the lack of feedback's context, the lack of differentiation of recent and older feedbacks, and the lack of incentives for a participant to rate the trading partner. Several solutions have been proposed to address at least some of the limitations of current feedback-based models. In [2], the authors introduced a complaint-only trust management method, based on the fact that users are more eager to provide negative comments if they are not satisfied, than to give positive feedback. Another method presented in [4] differentiates comments by taking into account the credibility of the rater, assuming that the rating is of good quality if it is consistent with the majority of ratings. In [5] a novel trust model called PeerTrust was proposed. The presented model includes several trust parameters, such as feedback in terms of satisfaction, number of transactions, credibility of feedback, transaction context, and community context. Credibility of feedback in PeerTrust is assessed differently than in [4]. The idea is to give more weight to feedbacks from more credible participants.

Somewhat related to the problem of reputation assessment in e-commerce systems is the problem of evaluating importance of Web pages. Examples of algorithms for judging the importance of pages are PageRank [7] and HITS [6]. Our method for credibility assessment is somehow similar to the later algorithm. HITS divides the pages into authorities (covering a certain topic) and hubs (directory-like pages linking to authorities). In our method, we apply a similar distinction, dividing auction participants into sellers and buyers, and we use adjacency matrices to recursively compute the credibility of participants.

3   Basic Constructs

Given a set of buyers $B = \{b_1, b_2, \ldots, b_n\}$ and a set of sellers $S = \{s_1, s_2, \ldots, s_m\}$. Let c denote a comment, $c \in \{-1, 0, 1\}$, where each value represents the "negative", "neutral", and "positive" comment, respectively. Given a set of auctions $A = \{a_1, a_2, \ldots, a_p\}$. An auction is a tuple $a_i = \langle b_j, s_k, c \rangle$ where $b_j \in B \wedge s_k \in S$.

Let $S(b_j)$ represent the set of sellers who sold an item to the buyer b_j. We denote the *support* of the buyer b_j as $support(b_j) = |S(b_j)|$. Let $B(s_k)$ represent the set of buyers who bought an item from the seller s_k. We denote the *support* of the seller s_k as $support(s_k) = |B(s_k)|$. According to this formulation, the support of the participant (either buyer or seller) is identical to the reputation measure currently employed by leading online auction providers.

Given a $m \times n$ matrix M_S. Each entry in the matrix represents the flow of support from the seller to the buyer in a finalized auction. Entries in the matrix M_S are initialized as follows.

$$\forall\, i \in \langle 1, m \rangle\ \ M_S[i, j] = \frac{1}{support(b_j)}\ \ \textit{if } \langle b_j, s_i, c \rangle \in A,\ 0\ \textit{otherwise}$$

Given a $m \times n$ matrix M_B. Each entry in the matrix represents the flow of support from the buyer to the seller in a finalized auction. Entries in the matrix M_B are initialized as follows.

$$\forall\, j \in \langle 1, n \rangle\ \ M_B[i, j] = \frac{1}{support(s_i)}\ \ \textit{if } \langle b_j, s_i, c \rangle \in A,\ 0\ \textit{otherwise}$$

Given a vector $S_C = [s_1, s_2, \ldots, s_m]$ of seller credibility ratings. Initially, all sellers receive the same credibility of 1. Analogously, given a vector of buyer credibility ratings $B_C = [b_1, b_2, \ldots, b_n]$. Initially, all buyers receive the same credibility of 1. Upon the termination of the algorithm vectors S_C and B_C contain diversified credibility ratings for sellers and buyers, respectively. A reputation rating for a buyer b_j is a tuple $R(b_j) = \langle C_-, C_0, C_+ \rangle$. Each component represents the sum of credibilities of sellers participating in transactions with a given buyer and posting a negative, neutral, or positive comment, respectively. Formally, $C_- = \sum_k S_C[k]$ where $\langle b_j, s_k, -1 \rangle \in A$, $C_0 = \sum_k S_C[k]$ where $\langle b_j, s_k, 0 \rangle \in A$, and $C_+ = \sum_k S_C[k]$ where $\langle b_j, s_k, +1 \rangle \in A$. Reputation rating for a seller can be defined analogously.

4   Iterative Reputation Assessment Algorithm

Our method of reputation rating is based on the following recursive definition of credibility. A given buyer is highly credible if the buyer participates in many auctions involving credible sellers. Analogously, a given seller is credible if the seller participates in many auctions involving credible buyers. Since there is no *a priori* estimation of credibility of participants, we assume that initially all participants receive equal credibility. Then, we iteratively recompute the credibility of sellers and buyers in the following way. In each iteration we distribute the current credibility of each buyer among participating sellers. Next, we update the credibility of all sellers by aggregating the credibility collected from participating buyers. After this update we propagate the current credibility of sellers to buyers and we refresh the appropriate ratings. We repeat this procedure several times until the credibility of sellers and buyers converge. Alternatively, the procedure can be repeated a given number of times. After assessing the credibility of all participants the credibility ratings are used together with past comments to derive proper reputation ratings by aggregating the credibility of contractors grouped by the type of the comment issued after the transaction. The intuition behind the algorithm is that the credibility of "good" buyers quickly aggregates in "good" sellers and *vice versa*. Initial ratings consisting of simple participation counts are quickly replaced by the true credibility which reflects the importance of every participant. The outline of the algorithm is presented in Fig. 1.

Require: $A = \{a_1, a_2, \ldots, a_p\}$, the set of finalized auctions
Require: $B = \{b_1, b_2, \ldots, b_n\}$, the set of buyers
Require: $S = \{s_1, s_2, \ldots, s_m\}$, the set of sellers
Require: M_S, M_B, matrices representing the structure of the inter-participant network
Require: S_C, B_C, vectors representing the credibility of participants
1: Initialize matrices M_S, M_B and vectors S_C, B_C appropriately
2: **repeat**
3:      **for all** $s_k \in S$ **do**
4:          $S_C[s_k] = \sum_{j=1}^n M_S[j,k] * B_C[b_j]$
5:      **end for**
6:      **for all** $b_j \in B$ **do**
7:          $B_C[b_j] = \sum_{k=1}^m M_B[j,k] * S_C[s_k]$
8:      **end for**
9: **until** vectors S_C and B_C converge
10: Output S_C and B_C as credibility ratings
11: Compute reputation ratings $R(b_j)$, $R(s_k)$ $\forall b_j \in B$, $\forall s_k \in S$ using S_C, B_C, and A

Fig. 1. Iterative Reputation Assessment Algorithm

5   Empirical Results

Here we present the results achieved on real datasets. The datasets have been acquired from www.allegro.pl, the leading Polish provider of online auctions. The datasets contain information on 400 000 participants and over 2 000 000 terminated auctions. All experiments are conducted on Pentium IV 2.4 GHz with 480 MB RAM. Data are stored and preprocessed using Oracle 9i database.

Figures 2 and 3 present the scaling of the algorithm. We differentiate the number of users from 1 000 to 100 000. The performance of the algorithm is satisfactory even for large user communities. We attribute the performance of the algorithm to the delegation of the most computationally expensive parts of the algorithm to the database engine and replacing the procedural processing with recursive SQL processing. The second test verifies the scalability of the algorithm with respect to the number of auctions. As can be seen, the execution time of the algorithm is almost linear.

Figures 4 and 5 present the convergence of credibility computed by our algorithm. Figure 4 depicts the changes of credibility in subsequent iterations for a

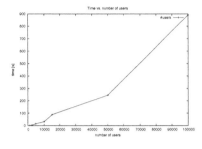

Fig. 2. Time vs. #users

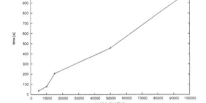

Fig. 3. Time vs. #auctions

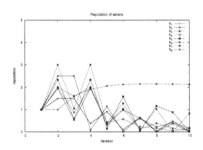

Fig. 4. Credibility of sellers

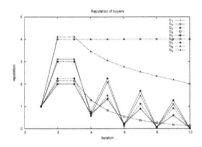

Fig. 5. Credibility of buyers

selected subset of sellers. We choose the sellers with the highest standard deviation to include in the figure, so the figure presents only the most atypical sellers. For the vast majority of sellers the changes in credibility are much smoother and the final credibility estimation stabilizes after a few iterations. The results of a similar selection for buyers are depicted in Fig. 5. Again, the estimation of credibility quickly converges and the rating stabilizes after only a few iterations.

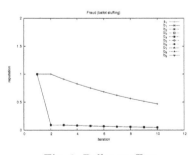

Fig. 6. Ballot stuffing

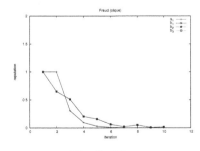

Fig. 7. Clique

In the next experiment we are simulating ballot stuffing. A dishonest seller s_1 decides to create dummy buyers $b_1, \ldots, b_{10}$ to inflate his/her reputation rating.

Additionally, the seller s_1 participates in auctions with buyers from outside the group. Figure 6 presents the credibility estimation for the group of participants involved in cheating. Estimates for all involved buyers are exactly the same, because those buyers are indistinguishable from the point of view of the topology of relationships. Already in the second iteration the algorithm discovers that buyers $b_1, \ldots, b_{10}$ are not credible, since they do not receive any feedback from sellers other than s_1. The seller s_1 initially aggregates all credibility from the buyers $b_1, \ldots, b_{10}$, but the credibility of the seller diminishes over time, causing the credibility of the buyers $b_1, \ldots, b_{10}$ to drop even further. The credibility of the seller s_1 slowly evaporates through the relationship with buyers from outside the group and no new credibility flows in from other sellers or buyers.

The next experiment represents a plot to form a clique. A dishonest seller tries to outwit the system by creating a set of virtual buyers and interconnects them to form a clique (one can easily imagine registering few users and finalizing low cost auctions between them to make them pretend as credible and active participants of auctions). Figure 7 presents the credibility ratings for seller s_1 and a group of buyers b_1, b_2, and b_3 involved in a clique plot. The algorithm discovers the fraud and determines that the real credibility of participants is low. Therefore, after a few iterations the deceiving group receives a low credibility rating. This result is probably even more desirable than the previous one, because the clique cheating is more dangerous to honest auction participants and harder to discover using manual analysis methods.

6   Conclusions

In this paper we have presented a novel algorithm for reputation rating of online auction participants, which evaluates the reputation based on the network of inter-participant relationships using a recursive definition of credibility. The experiments prove the practical usability of the solution. Our future work agenda includes extension of the algorithm to safeguard against artificial lifting of bids by dummy buyers created by dishonest sellers. We also plan to scale the algorithm to allow for real-time analysis of huge amounts of data.

References

1. P. Resnick, R. Zeckhauser, E. Friedman, K. Kuwabara. *Reputation systems*. Communications, of the ACM, 43(12), 2000.
2. K. Aberer and Z. Despotovic. *Managing trust in a peer-to-peer information system*. In Proc. of the ACM CIKM, pp. 310-317, 2001.
3. R. A. Malaga. *Web-based reputation management systems: Problems and suggested solutions*. Electronic Commerce Research, 1(4), 2001.
4. M. Chen and J. P. Singh. *Computing and using reputations for Internet ratings*. In 3rd ACM Conference on Electronic Commerce, 2001.
5. L. Xiong, L. Liu. *A Reputation-Based Trust Model for Peer-to-Peer eCommerce Communities*. In IEEE Conf. on Electronic Commerce (CEC'03), Newport Beach, USA, June, 2003.

6. J.Kleinberg, *Authoritative Sources in a Hyperlinked Environment*. Proc. 9th Ann. ACM-SIAM Symp. Discrete Algorithms, ACM Press, New York, 1998.
7. L. Page, S. Brin, R. Motwani, T. Winograd, *The PageRank Citation Ranking: Bringing Order to The Web*. Stanford Digital Library Technologies Project, 1998.

Awareness and Coordination for Web Cooperative Authoring

Aslam Muhammad[1], Ana María Martínez Enríquez[1], and
Dominique Decouchant[2]

[1] Depto de Ingeniería Eléctrica, CINVESTAV-IPN, D. F., México
[2] Laboratoire "Logiciels, Systèmes, Réseaux", Grenoble, France
muhammad@computacion.cs.cinvestav.mx, ammartin@cinvestav.mx,
Dominique.Decouchant@timag.fr

Abstract. This paper presents our approach to design and provide elaborated awareness coordination functions for cooperative production of complex Web shared documents. We designed a Group Awareness Inference Engine (GAIE) that catches working focus of collaborators and then deduces some of their potential interests for communication to enhance coordination and cooperative production.

Keywords: Web Co-Authoring, Events, Work Focus, Inference Engine, Context-Based Communication.

1 Introduction

In Web-based cooperative work three domains are related: production, communication and coordination [4]. Having better functionalities in one of them entail an enhancement in the others e.g., a better quality production is possible if users have advanced facilities for communication and coordination.

The Web-based Cooperative Writing Applications (WCWAs) like BSCW [1], AllianceWeb [2], EquiText [7], REDUCE [8] allow authors to asynchronously produce (download, modify, and upload) shared documents from different locations. Concerning communication support, BSCW offers Instant Messaging, whereas EquiText and REDUCE provides (e-mail) asynchronous communications.

In the synchronous communication the people have the possibility to waste time until they convey on a specific point of discussion. In case of an asynchronous communication (e.g. e-mail), they spend time sending messages with linked information until they obtain a final agreement. Coordination is a main feature that must be provided by an adapted communication service to enhance the shared and cooperative production.

In this paper, we describe AllianceWeb, a cooperative writing application for which a group awareness support is developed. The co-authors can use a synchronous communication service guided by a dynamic and precise work focus system related to author productions. The goal of this service is to enhance the coordination.

P.S. Szczepaniak et al. (Eds.): AWIC 2005, LNAI 3528, pp. 327–333, 2005.

The architecture of the AllianceWeb includes a dedicated Group Awareness Inference Engine (GAIE), designed following Artificial Intelligence principles, and whose goal is to deduce important facts from the cooperative environments of collaborators (section 2). The awareness coordination facilities, depending upon the interest of collaborators, determine a dynamic and specific context under which co-authors can establish quasi synchronous communications (section 3). Finally, conclusions and important open issues are highlighted in section 4.

2   The AllianceWeb / GAIE Architecture

AllianceWeb allows co-authors to produce complex HTML/XML documents. Based on the structure, a document is partitioned in sharing units called "fragments" such as title, introduction, paragraphs, lists, sections, and figures for a chapter document.

A fragment has associated co-authors and their roles [M-Manager, W-Writer, R-Reader, N-Null] to act on it. At a time, only one author can act with the "writer" or "manager" role on a fragment in contrast to "readers". The document partitioning ensures the consistency of cooperative contributions. For example, two users can produce two different paragraphs of the same document section.

Producing with AllianceWeb, co-authors perform different actions according to assigned roles like starting a cooperative session, opening a shared document, modifying it. All actions of a co-author are represented as "events".

The events are captured, managed and delivered by a Distributed Event Management Service (DEMS) [3] that serves as a intermediate agent among event generating and event requiring applications (Fig. 1).

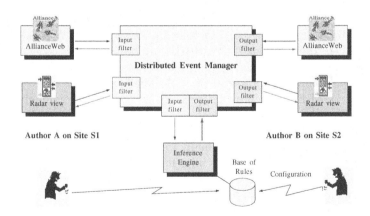

Fig. 1. The Distributed Event Management Service (DEMS)

In order to coordinate cooperative and non-cooperative applications, the DEMS distinguishes two types of applications: "*producers*" that follow a "Connect-Put-Disconnect" mechanism to deliver events; and "*consumers*" that follow a

"Connect-Get-Disconnect" protocol to retrieve and consume events from the DEMS. All events are memorized by a dedicated storage space in a chronological order to supply them to interested consumer applications.

From the DEMS point of view, AllianceWeb is a groupware "producer". The generated events represent actions like: *document handling, authoring, decoration, fragmentation*, and *assignment of editing roles*.

The GAIE engine is a "consumer" that deduces the state of each user's environment and his preferences, proposes him actions to adapt his environment, and provides new facts about the shared production to enhance it.

For instance, when a user is busy, he can turn off the synchronous communication service but if another user wants to communicate with the former, the GAIE engine recommends the later to modify his preferences. The action is supported by the following rule written in the first order predicate logic [5]:

StartRule "Requesting a user to modify his communication preferences"
If author (fragment_1) = x /* x is author of fragment_1 */
   session_on (x) = "true" /* x is producing */
   sync_comm (x) = "true" /* communication is enabled */
   comm_interest (x) = y /* x wants to communicate with y */
   session_on (y) = "true"
   sync_comm (y) = "false"
Then
   announce (y) ← "a co-author is interested to communicate"
EndRule

The principles of the GAIE operation is as follow:

- Retrieving session or editing events for deduction of new facts,
- Deducting facts to present synthetic perception of shared entities,
- Proposing actions to co-authors to modify their environments like establishing contextual communication.

The GAIE engine notifies starting and terminating session, production in a session, and so on. Additionally, the engine optimizes communication between two users when they manifest specific interest to establish a communication centered on a particular context as we see in the following scenario.

Jorge reviews a document part while Carmin, with the writing role, writes a formula in this partition. Jorge wants to suggest a modification in this formula. He desires to highlight his point of interest on the Carmin's display and to establish a synchronous communication with her.

This scenario shows the requirements needed by co-authors to establish a synchronous communication centered under a particular context of their shared production. Now we describe how the GAIE engine determines the work focus under which users have the possibility to communicate.

3   Context-Based Communication

A collaborator is able to read and to annotate a document part produced by other users as shown in the above scenario. The reader suggests some modifications and to better understanding, wants to establish a synchronous communication with the producer to discuss their point of view. The shared document is present on the display of the two collaborators, and the GAIE engine takes advantage of that to transmit the focus of interest on both displays.

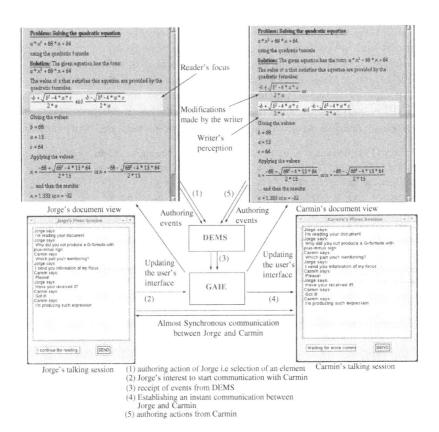

Fig. 2. Co-Author Work Focus and Perception

Suppose the reader takes the initiative to establish communication, and selects a part as a point of discussion (Fig. 2). The GAIE engine receives authoring events from the DEMS, and sends the determined selection to the other author display with whom he wants to establish a communication. Thus, the two co-authors can continue the discussion focused on the selected point, since both have a consistent perception of the shared information. The GAIE applies the following rule:

```
StartRule "The work focused communication"
If author (fragment_1) = x
   author (fragment_1) = y
   sync_comm (x) = "true"
```

```
   session_on (y) = "true"
   action (y) = "select_element" /* y's action is a selection */
Then
   display_environment (x) ← send (selected_element)
   announce (y) ← get_selected_part
         /* Selected element is displayed in y's environment */
EndRule
```

The user can highlight one or more textual, mathematical or graphical elements. The unique identifier of the selected elements within the framework of shared document are determined and transmitted. A selection is dynamic and may be a part of a textual paragraph, several elements of a graphical object, some terms of a formula, a row or a column from a complex table. In the case of partial textual selection, the positions of the first and the last characters within the element will be highlighted on all concerned environments.

In general, the GAIE engine dynamically determines the work focus of a co-author depending upon his production and executed actions. When a user modifies a fragment and this modification affects current contextual focus, the GAIE updates it in all concerned environment. For instance, changes in a figure entail modifications in its descriptions and hence, the concerned collaborators are informed. In case a co-author does not agree on modifications, he can start a synchronous communication with producers. The following rule is applied:

```
StartRule "Perception of a co-author"
If author (fragment_1) = x
   session_on (x) = "true"
   sync_comm (x) = "true"
Then
   announce (x) ← "Information received for contextual focus"
         /* x perceives the contextual focus */
EndRule
```

The individuals presence notification is resolved by Internet Messaging and Presence (IM&P) services [6]. Users of this service must have the list of his colleagues with whom he wants to talk. When a user starts his session, a notification is sent to all on-line users. A user can see the presence of all his partners and in quasi real time mode he knows if they are on-line or off-line. Out of the present users, some may be active, away or busy. A user can also change his status ("not in office" or "in-meeting").

In our architecture, we integrate this messaging service, such that when a user opens his collaborative session, the IM&P service is launched. Thus, when the GAIE engine recovers the selection event and it determines that users open a synchronous communication, the particular rule is triggered.

4   Conclusions and Perspectives

In cooperative work, the awareness coordination plays an important role and addresses a hard problem. Up to now, several WCWAs provide asynchronous communication services like EquiText [7] and REDUCE [8]. But, writing e-mail seems to be laborious when co-authors have to concentrate on a point within the complex production. Other application like BSCW system [1] launches a (synchronous) chat session among collaborators. Nevertheless, out of the kind of communication, it is also important to deduce the point of discussion, in order as quickly as possible to center it. This was our main aim pursued in this research.

In our approach based on artificial intelligence principles, the GAIE engine takes events as a piece of knowledge to deduce other important knowledge to adapt the environment of the user and to have awareness about the evolution of the shared production. In case of any change of the goal pursued by our application, and to extend its functionalities, it is only necessary to modify the base of rules, that are the input data of the GAIE.

Coordination is essential to any groupware system, thus we will extend our platform including complex information as contextual-based communication, like multimedia. We have to address issues such as filter the people who communicate with, transforming from 1:N to 1:1, blocking unconcerned people. The research is focusing on future needs for the Web-based cooperative production e.g. using mobile communication technologies and protocols.

References

1. Bentley, R., Applet, W., Bushbach, U. Hinrichs, E., Kerr, D., Sikkel, K., Trevor, J., and Woetzel, G., "Basic Support for Cooperative Work on the World Wide Web", *Int. Journal of Human Computer Studies: Special Issue on Novel Applications of the WWW,* Academic Press, Cambridge, vol. 46, num. 6, pp. 827-846, June 1997.
2. Decouchant D., Favela J. and Martínez Enríquez A. M., "PIÑAS: A Middleware for Web Distributed Cooperative Authoring", *In Proc. of SAINT'2001, the 2001 Symposium on Applications and the Internet,* IEEE Computer Society and IPJ Information Processing Society of Japan, San Diego, CA, USA, pp. 187-194, 8-12 January 2001.
3. Decouchant, D., Martínez Enríquez, A. M., Favela, J., Morán A L., Mendoza, S., Jafar, S., "A Distributed Event Service for Adaptive Group Awareness", *In Proc. of MICAI'2002, the 2nd Mexican International Conference on Artificial Intelligence,* LNAI 2313, pp. 506-515, April 2002.
4. Ellis, C. A., Gibbs, S. J., Rein, G. L., "Groupware: Some Issues and Experiences", *Communication of the ACM,* vol. 34, num. 1, pp. 38-58, January 1991.
5. Feigenbaum, E. A., McCorduck, P., *"The Fifth Generation: Artificial Intelligence and Japan's Computer Challenge to the World",* Addison-Wesley, 1983.
6. Godefroid, O., Herbsleb, J. D., Jagadeesan, L. J., Li. D., "Ensuring Privacy in Presence Awareness Systems: An Automated Verification Approach", *In Proc. of CSCW'2000, the Conference on Computer Supported Cooperative Work,* ACM Press, Philadelphia, PE, USA, pp. 59-68, December 2000.

7. Rizzi, C. B., Alonso, C. M. C., Hassan, E. B., Tarouco, L M. R., and DE Seixas, L. M. J., "EquiText: A helping tool in the elaboration of collaborative texts", *In Proc. of SITE'2000, the 11th International Conference,* San Diego, CA, USA, 2000.
8. Yang, Y., Sun, C., Zhang, Y., Jia, X., "Real-time cooperative editing on the internet", *IEEE Internet Computing,* vol. 4, num. 3, May-June 2000.

Security Systems Design and Analysis Using an Integrated Rule-Based Systems Approach[*]

Grzegorz J. Nalepa[1] and Antoni Ligęza[1]

Institute of Automatics,
AGH University of Science and Technology,
Al. Mickiewicza 30, 30-059 Kraków, Poland
{gjn, ligeza}@agh.edu.pl

Abstract. The paper discusses the applications of rule-based systems (RBS) theory in the field of web security systems. It discusses rule-based foundations of these systems and presents an original solution for the RBS design and analysis. Furthermore, the present and possible future applications of this approach to security systems are discussed. Proper design and analysis methods of the security systems can significantly improve their important features such as reliability and correctness.

1 Introduction

Security and privacy are some of the most important concerns in todays web systems. The use of advanced security systems includes (but is not restricted to) access control, intrusion detection, and traffic monitoring and limiting.

In the field of security systems features such as reliability, safety, correctness, and stability are of key importance. They may be assured in different ways, depending on a given class of security system. The most common approach is to provide appropriate administration tools, sometimes accompanied with design and analysis facilities. These tools are usually dedicated to particular system class. They are based more on an engineering practise rather than on a deeper theoretical knowledge about the system structure and its properties.

Note that multiple implementations of security systems share common scientific foundations: rule-based systems (RBSs for short) theory. This theory has been studied for many years in the field of Artificial Intelligence [1, 2]. A comprehensive discussion of RBS theory and practice has recently been given in [3]. Number of approaches to the design as well as *formal* analysis and verification of RBSs have been developed. It may be asserted, that advanced design and formal analysis of RBS underlying the security systems can significantly improve their important features such as reliability, safety, correctness, and stability. The main original contribution of this paper is an outline of a computer-aided methodology for design and verification of security systems.

---

[*] Research supported from a KBN Research Project No.: 4 T11C 035 24.

P.S. Szczepaniak et al. (Eds.): AWIC 2005, LNAI 3528, pp. 334–340, 2005.

An original application of RBS design methods in the field of computer security (firewall systems) was proposed in [4]. It was based on the original research of new visual design and formal analysis methods of RBS, presented in [5]. This paper presents the continuation of the research introduced in [4]. However, it significantly extends the ideas presented there, by presenting a complete RBS design approach, accompanied with a CASE tool, discussed in detail in [6]. An original idea presented in this paper consists in applying formal RBS design and analysis methods to the design of real-life computer security systems.

The paper briefly discusses RBS in Sect. 2. Then in Sect. 3 rule-based foundations of security systems are analyzed. A complete solution for RBS design and analysis is presented in Sect. 4. The present and possible future applications of this approach to computer security systems (including web security) are discussed in Sect. 5. The concluding remarks are given in Sect. 6.

2   Rule-Based Systems

Multiple computer security systems have rule-based foundations. Rule-Based Systems (RBS) constitute a powerful tool for specification of knowledge in design and implementation of systems in the domains such as system monitoring, intelligent control, decision support, situation classification, and operational knowledge encoding. For the state-of-the-art in RBSs see [1, 2, 3].

Although the rule-based programming paradigm seems relatively conceptually simple, in case of real-life systems it is a hard and tedious task to design and implement a rule-based system that works in a correct way. A practical implementation of rule-based systems encounters two main problems. The first one consists in the well-known difficulties with obtaining a precise knowledge specification. Specific knowledge representation structures and abstract knowledge representations may be used to help to overcome this problem. The second problem concerns the analysis, verification and validation of knowledge. By making the analysis of the knowledge base a part of ongoing knowledge acquisition and review process, system developers can minimize the time and resources devoted to development of such systems. In order to assure safe, reliable and efficient performance, analysis and verification of selected qualitative properties (e.g. completeness, consistency, determinism) should be carried out [7, 8, 5].

Practical design of non-trivial rule-based systems requires a systematic, structured and consistent approach. The paper discusses a complete, integrated RBS design methodology, including a new original knowledge representation method called XTT [6]. This methodology is supported by a visual CASE tool called Mirella [6]. The approach can significantly improve RBS design and analysis process. It has been practically applied in selected security systems.

3   Selected Security Systems

A modern secure web and network infrastructure includes a number of security systems [9], including: access control, traffic monitoring and limiting, and intrusion detection systems. As it was asserted in Sect. 1, a number of these systems have rule-based foundations.

A concept common in modern access control systems is the Mandatory Access Control (MAC) [9]. Several practical implementations for the open source systems have been studied. They include FreeBSD MAC (`www.freebsd.org`) and Linux RSBAC (Rule Set Based Access Control) (`www.rsbac.org`). Other projects such as GrSecurity ACL (Access Control Lists) (`www.grsecurity.net`) for Linux and NSA SELinux (Security Enhanced) (`www.nsa.gov/selinux`) have even broader scope functionality. MAC systems use rule sets called polices in order to control access to every facility provided by the system.

Network firewalls are the main component of every network infrastructure. They allow for real-time traffic monitoring and limiting on the low level. They are in fact optimized real-time rule-based control systems [4]. Firewalls use internally precompiled structured rule-base, a security policy. There are several important firewall implementations to be considered: Linux NetFilter (`www.netfilter.org`), FreeBSD IP Filter (IPF), and OpenBSD (`www.openbsd.org`) PF (Packet Filter). They all provide similar functionality including statefull packet filtering and network address translation.

Automatic intrusion detection systems (IDS) [9] play a critical role in web monitoring and surveillance systems. An example of such system is Snort (`www.snort.org`), a network intrusion detection system. It uses rule-based knowledge describing security incidents in order to detect security breaches in real-time.

From theoretical perspective, which takes into account RBS theory, all of the security systems mentioned in this section are rule-based systems. They use *decision rules* as knowledge representation method. Most of them, namely firewalls, are *forward-chaining systems*, whereas some, such as IDS also employ *backward-chaining* reasoning. Since even now the design of such system is often close to hand craft activity, it seems reasonable to apply novel visual design and analysis tools to assure satisfactory quality of the resulting knowledge base.

4   Integrated RBS Design and Analysis Process

The existing RBS design methods and tools have limitations mostly in the following three areas: knowledge representation methods, framework for analysis and verification of system properties, integrated computer tools supporting the design process. To overcome these limitations a new approach has been proposed and developed in [6]. The approach includes three main components: a new knowledge representation method (XTT), an integrated RBS design and implementation process, as well as a computer tool supporting it (Mirella).

The main idea behind new visual knowledge representation language called Extended Tabular-Trees (XTT) aims at combining some of the existing approaches such as decision-tables and decision-trees by building a special hierarchy of Object-Attribute-Tables. An early proposal of this approach was presented in [5]. The XTT was invented with the goals to integrate the system design and verification stages; further, it supports the implementation stage through introducing the possibility of automatic code generation.

The language has some unique features such as: simplicity and transparency, due to an intuitive visual knowledge specification, hierarchical, tree-like representation, highly efficient way of visualization with high data density, power of the decision table representation, flexibility with respect to knowledge manipulation, and direct knowledge representation mapping into Prolog and rule-based systems. The language plays a key role in the new approach to RBS design.

The proposed approach follows the structural methodology for RBS design. It is simultaneously a top-down approach, which allows for incorporating hierarchical design. In the approach the following 3 design phases are identified:

1. Conceptual design, in which the basic structure of the system is identified, along with data and control flow, as well as main operating contexts, objects and attributes; this allows for further defining the headers of XTT tables.
2. Logical design, which involves building table rows (corresponding to rules), connecting tables; the XTT structure can be incrementally built, *analyzed*, and possibly *verified* and *optimized* on-line.
3. Physical design, in which a preliminary implementation is done by building a Prolog code (or any other target language since the approach is of generic character), which can be executed, compiled, debugged and possibly translated to system-specific representation.

One of the most important features of this approach is the separation of logical and physical aspects of the design, which also allows for a transparent, hierarchical design process. On the other hand, the process integrates RBS development phases from the design to the implementation.

Mirella [6] is an intelligent visual design tool supporting on-line verification of RBSs, based of the XTT knowledge representation. It is oriented towards designing reliable and safe RBSs in general. It supports all of the stages of the process discussed above. The main goal of the tool is to move the design procedure to a more abstract, logical and graphical level, where knowledge specification is based on use of abstract rule representation. The designed graphical specification is automatically translated into a predefined XML (XTTML) knowledge format, so the designer can focus on logical specification of safety and reliability; simultaneously, practical code can be generated for a wide class of systems. On the other hand, formal aspects such as completeness, determinism, etc. may be automatically verified on-line during the design using Prolog-based engine, so that its verifiable characteristics are preserved.

Mirella manages knowledge about the designed system on three different levels: XTT is used for visual design and knowledge representation, Prolog is used for corresponding formal system description, while XML-based language supports machine readable knowledge encoding and possible transformations.

5   Applications in Reliable Security Systems

The approach discussed in Sect. 4 was developed in order to provide a unified process for a large class of RBSs with security systems in mind. In fact, in [6] a complete study of a benchmark firewall system has been provided.

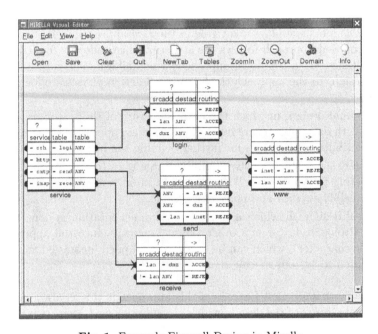

Fig. 1. Example Firewall Design in Mirella

The example system is a common in SOHO setups 3 subnetwork case with Internet, Intranet and DMZ (DeMilitarized Zone) blocks [9]. A complete security policy has been designed in Mirella using the XTT representation. An example of a design session is given in Fig. 1. A logical Prolog-based representation has been automatically generated; an excerpt of the specification is shown below.

```
rule(1,1,[f(aService,atomic,ssh)],[f(aTable,atomic,login)],[],[],2,5).
rule(1,2,[f(aService,atomic,http)],[f(aTable,atomic,www)],[],[],3,8).
rule(1,3,[f(aService,atomic,smtp)],[f(aTable,atomic,send)],[],[],4,11).
rule(1,4,[f(aService,atomic,imap)],[f(aTable,atomic,receive)],[],[],5,14).
```

Formal verification and analysis facilities provided with Mirella allowed for formal firewall analysis, which showed that the system is complete and deterministic. On the other hand a possible optimization (rule reduction) was detected. Mirella also allowed for interactive system simulation. A firewall design in Mirella is structured and hierarchical.

Mirella would eventually allow to formulate a unified description of certain subclass of systems, e.g. firewalls. Such a description would include a set of predefined system attributes (in this case firewall-specific, such as network addresses). It would be also possible to translate XTTML firewall representation to a number of different target implementations, e.g. NetFilter, or IPF.

Firewalls are just one of the security system classes described in Sect. 3. An ongoing effort aims at designing and analyzing MAC and IDS systems in Mirella (mirella.ia.agh.edu.pl). However, these cases are more complicated. The differences between different MAC models are far greater that in the case of firewalls. While preliminary models addressing particular implementation can be built, it is more difficult to provide a unified model.

Basing on the results presented in [6] it may be concluded that visual design facilities provided by Mirella can improve RBS design process thanks to XTT knowledge representation and transformation features. Possibility of formal verification and analysis leads to improved system reliability.

6   Concluding Remarks

In this paper practical applications of rule-based systems theory to security systems have been discussed. The paper discusses a selection of rule-based security systems including access control, intrusion detection, and traffic monitoring systems. It introduces a complete, integrated RBS design methodology, including the new knowledge representation method called XTT, and visual CASE tool called Mirella. This methodology has been applied to number of RBS classes including rule-based security systems. The paper discusses how an advanced design and formal analysis of RBS underlying the security systems can significantly improve their mission-critical features such as reliability and correctness.

References

1. Liebowitz, J., ed.: The Handbook of Applied Expert Systems. CRC Press, Boca Raton (1998)
2. Hopgood, A.A.: Intelligent Systems for Engineers and Scientists. 2nd edn. CRC Press, Boca Raton London New York Washington, D.C. (2001)
3. Ligęza, A.: Logical Foundations for Rule-Based Systems. Uczelniane Wydawnictwa Naukowo-Dydaktyczne AGH w Krakowie, Kraków (2005)
4. Nalepa, G.J., Ligęza, A.: Designing reliable web security systems using rule-based systems approach. In Menasalvas, E., Segovia, J., Szczepaniak, P.S., eds.: Advances in Web Intelligence. AWIC 2003, Madrid, Spain, May 5-6, 2003. Volume LNAI 2663., Berlin, Heidelberg, New York, Springer-Verlag (2003) 124–133
5. Ligęza, A., Wojnicki, I., Nalepa, G.: Tab-trees: a case tool for design of extended tabular systems. In et al., H.M., ed.: Database and Expert Systems Applications. Volume LNCS 2113 of Lecture Notes in Computer Sciences. Springer-Verlag, Berlin (2001) 422–431
6. Nalepa, G.J.: Meta-Level Approach to Integrated Process of Design and Implementation of Rule-Based Systems. PhD thesis, AGH University of Science and Technology, AGH Institute of Automatics, Cracow, Poland (2004)

7. van Harmelen, F.: Applying rule-based anomalies to kads inference structures. ECAI'96 Workshop on Validation, Verification and Refinement of Knowledge-Based Systems (1996) 41–46

8. Ligęza, A.: Logical support for design of rule-based systems. reliability and quality issues. In Rousset, M., ed.: ECAI-96 Workshop on Validation, Verification and Refinment of Knowledge-based Systems. Volume W2. ECAI'96, Budapest (1996) 28–34

9. Garfinkel, S., Spafford, G., Schwartz, A.: Practical Unix and Internet Security. 3rd edn. O'Reilly and Associates (2003)

On Two Possible Roles of Type-2 Fuzzy Sets in Linguistic Summaries

Adam Niewiadomski

Institute of Computer Science, Technical University of Lodz
aniewiadomski@ics.p.lodz.pl

Abstract. The paper contains the propositions of employing type-2 fuzzy sets in linguistic summaries of databases. This new approach is the promising extension for ordinary linguistic summaries [1][4][14] and for recently introduced interval-valued linguistic summaries [11]. The two original concepts of *a type-2 summarizer* and *a type-2 linguistic quantifier* are proposed as the extensions for ordinary and interval-valued corresponding constructs. This innovation is supposed to provide better handling of natural language uncertainties that are impossible to be modelled with ordinary fuzzy sets. An application on sample data is presented.

1 Linguistic Summaries of Data

Effective analysing and grasping huge amount of data, contemporarily present in different — mostly Web — sources, definitely exceeds human skills. Frequently applied methods are based on expressing raw and unprocessed numerical information in human consistent and linguistic terms. The solution to the problem of distilling the most crucial information from vast numbers of records was proposed by Yager, who formulated the concept of *a linguistic summary of a database* [14] [15]. It is based on the idea of a linguistic variable [16] and on its exemplification — a fuzzy quantifier [17].

To summarize a database linguistically means *to build a natural language sentence which describes the amount of records manifesting chosen attributes*. The general form of a linguistic summary is

$$Q \ P \ \text{are/have} \ S \ [T] \tag{1}$$

where the symbols are interpreted: Q is a determination of amount (a quantity in agreement), the so-called *linguistic quantifier*, which is a linguistic variable itself, e.g. ABOUT HALF, FEW, MORE THAN 50. P is the subject of the summary — it refers to objects described by records, e.g. workers, cars. S is a feature of interest, the so-called *summarizer* expressed with a fuzzy set, e.g. HIGH SALARY, AVERAGE SPEED. T is a quality measure for the summary, *degree of truth* or *the truth of a summary*, which describes reliability of the quantity pronouncement Q for the feature S. It is a real number from $[0,1]$ and it is interpreted as the

P.S. Szczepaniak et al. (Eds.): AWIC 2005, LNAI 3528, pp. 341–347, 2005.

level of confidence for the given summary. Summarizers and fuzzy quantifiers are linguistic expressions handled by fuzzy logic [16] [17].

Improvements and enhancements of Yager ideas are widely presented in the literature. George and Srikanth proposed building summarizers of more than one properties under *t*-norms [1] (e.g. *Many cars are cheap* AND *poorly equipped*). Further significant extensions are given in [2] [3] [5]. Numerous implementations and applications are also presented, e.g. FQUERY — the add-on to Microsoft Access [2]. New methods for computing the goodness of a summary are given in [3] [5]. Interval-valued forms for fuzzy quantifiers and summarizers are given in [11]. The attempt of summarizing textual databases with the textual form of a summarizer is presented in [12].

2   Type-2 Fuzzy Sets

The concept of a *Type-2 Fuzzy Set* (FST2) was given at first by Zadeh in 1975 [16]. The idea has stayed forgotten for long years, until in 1998 Karnik and Mendel [6] [7] introduced the foundations of type-2 fuzzy logic systems. Since there various practical applications have been introduced [10] [13] and useful remarks on operations on FST2 and on subsystems of FST2 (as Interval Type-2 Fuzzy Sets [8] [9]) have been given.

Ordinary fuzzy sets, whose membership functions (MFs) are crisp sets themselves, do not provide sufficient support for many kinds of uncertainty that appears in linguistic descriptions of numerical quantities or in subjectively expressed amounts, dimensions, etc. Karnik and Mendel in [7], assuming that *words (numbers, descriptions, linguistic quantities) can mean different things to different people*, proposed to increase the number of degrees of freedom for fuzzy logic systems arguing that adding at least one may provide a measure of dispersion for totally certain (till now) membership functions of type-1.

The main idea of a type-2 fuzzy set is based on extending an ordinary and crisp itself type-1 MF to a type-2 MF. A MF of type-2 is a family of fuzzy sets of type-1, where each FST1 is assigned to one element of a universe of discourse. Formally, let $\mathcal{X}$ be a universe of discourse. A fuzzy set of type-2 $\tilde{A}$ in $\mathcal{X}$ is of the form

$$\tilde{A} = \int\limits_{x \in \mathcal{X}} \int\limits_{u \in J_x} \frac{\mu_{\tilde{A}}(x, u)}{(x, u)}, \quad u \in J_x \tag{2}$$

where $\mu_{\tilde{A}} : \mathcal{X} \times J_x \to [0, 1]$ is the type-2 MF of $\tilde{A}$, and $J_x \subseteq [0, 1]$ is the set of primary membership degrees of $x \in \mathcal{X}$.

The MF of type-2 $\mu_{\tilde{A}}$ depends on two arguments, x and u, where $x \in \mathcal{X}$, and u is its primary membership degree. Unlike in Zadeh's fuzzy sets where u is a certain number, in a FST2 an element u has its own membership degree, which is treated as *a grade of possibility* that u well describes a membership degree of x. This additional degree is expressed as a value of secondary membership function $\mu_x(u)$, where $\mu_x : J_x \to [0, 1]$, which may be the same or specific for each $x \in \mathcal{X}$.

Hence, in fuzzy sets of type-2 we diversify *primary membership functions* (PMF) and *secondary membership functions* (SMF). The former always depends on the variable $x \in \mathcal{X}$, while the latter depends in fact on two variables, x and u, so we denote it as $\mu_x(u)$. Now, it is possible to rewrite (2) with u and μ_x symbols:

$$\tilde{A} = \{< x, u, \mu_x(u) >: x \in \mathcal{X}, u \in J_x \subseteq [0,1]\} \tag{3}$$

Let us show these concepts on a very basic example:

Example 1. Let $\mathcal{X} = \{2, 3, 4, 5\}$ be the discreet universe of discourse, set of scores obtained in a test $(2$ — the lowest, 5 — the highest). The FST2 $\tilde{B}$ modelling the predicate *an adequate score for a test* is proposed as

$$\tilde{B} = \Big\{ \frac{1}{2, 0.5} + \frac{0.7}{2, 0.1} + \frac{0.1}{2, 0.0} + \frac{0.9}{3, 1.0} + \frac{0.3}{3, 0.1} + \frac{0.5}{3, 0.3} +$$
$$+ \frac{0.5}{4, 0.3} + \frac{0.6}{4, 0.7} + \frac{0.8}{4, 1.0} + \frac{0.9}{5, 0.0} + \frac{0.9}{5, 1.0} + \frac{0.5}{5, 0.8} \Big\} \tag{4}$$

where the nominator in each fraction is secondary membership of $< x, u >$, $x \in \{2, 3, 4, 5\}$, the first number in the denominator — a primary membership u, and the second in the denominator is its primary memberhip u.

The example shows also that each element of $\mathcal{X}$ is described by a set of pairs of values, comming, for instance, from different experts. The primary membership degree for "2" is the fuzzy set itself of the form $\{\frac{0.1}{0.0} + \frac{0.7}{0.1} + \frac{1.0}{0.5}\}$, and determined in $J_2 = \{0.0, 0.1, 0.5\} \subset [0, 1]$, where 0.1, 0.7, and 1.0 are secondary membership levels specific for each pair $< 2, u >$, $u \in J_2$. Further, the primary membership for "3" is the fuzzy set $\{\frac{0.3}{0.1} + \frac{0.5}{0.3} + \frac{0.9}{1.0}\}$ established in $J_3 = \{0.1, 0.3, 1.0\}$. J_4, J_5 — analogously.

PMFs as well as SMFs are usually designed with respect to given problems in order to represent uncertain data as well as it is possible. However, there exist a few typical shapes for SMFs, used as the most typical and standard solutions in type-2 FLSs [6] [7]. Especially, standard SMFs are of the shapes which determine some of the most known types of FST2. Hence, one may discuss *Gaussian fuzzy sets of type-2, triangular or interval FST2, trapezoidal, sigmoidal,* etc.

3   Generating Summaries with Fuzzy Sets of Type-2

Summarizers and quantifiers expressing linguistic statements in (1) are ordinary fuzzy sets. However, this manner of modelling imprecise data may be insufficient to express some more complicated structures, which is argued in Section 2. Therefore, the introduction to summaries employing interval-valued summarizers and quantifiers is given in [11].

This section is the next step to generalize the mechanisms for constructing linguistic summaries: it contains the description of the manner in which fuzzy sets of type-2 can express summarizers and quantifiers.

3.1   Type-2 Summarizer

Each property or feature which is too imprecise to be modelled with a membership function of type-1, may be expressed as a fuzzy set of type-2 in the same universe of discourse. Zadeh [16] points at two types of statements, which should be estimated as ordinary fuzzy sets and type-2 fuzzy sets, respectively. The latter are characterized by a high grade of subjectivity and impreciseness. It especially concerns the cases in which the ambiguity of different opinions makes it impossible to determine a set of membership grades without any additional characteristics assigned to them.

Such a situation may be exemplified as follows: suppose that a paper is submitted to a conference (a journal) by a scientist. The paper is checked, evaluated, and commented by a few reviewers. Naturally, they frequently differ in their opinions, points of view, etc., so the paper is finally evaluated with different scores. However, each of these scores is obtained from a few partial results (e.g. within the scale lowest=0.0, 0.2, 0.4, 0.6, 0.8, highest=1.0), e.g. ratings for motivation, originality, validity of the paper, etc.; see Tab. 1.

Table 1. Sample evaluation of paper by reviewers

	Reviewer 1	Reviewer 2	Reviewer 3
Motivation	0.8	0.6	0.4
Originality	0.8	0.8	0.2
Significance	0.6	0.6	0.2
Validity	0.8	0.6	0
Presentation	0.6	0.8	0.4
OVERALL RATING	**0.8**	**0.6**	**0.2**

The table shows that the position *Validity* is of the most influence on a final result. Let us assume that a score for *Validity* is of 0.6 weight, and another scores — of 0.1 weights. We may express the overall rating for the considered paper as the fuzzy set of type-2 $\tilde{M}$ in $\mathcal{X} = \{Rev.1, Rev.2, Rev.3\}$

$$\tilde{M} = \left\{ \frac{0.8}{Rev.1, 0.8} + \frac{0.2}{Rev.1, 0.6} + \frac{0.8}{Rev.2, 0.6} + \frac{0.2}{Rev.2, 0.8} + \right.$$
$$\left. + \frac{0.6}{Rev.3, 0.0} + \frac{0.2}{Rev.3, 0.2} + \frac{0.2}{Rev.3, 0.4} \right\} \tag{5}$$

where $J_{Rev.1} = \{0.8, 0.6\}$ is the set of primary memberships for the element $Rev.1$.

The values $\mu_{Rev.1}(0.8) = 0.8$ and $\mu_{Rev.1}(0.6) = 0.2$ are the secondary memberships, where 0.8 for $Rev.1, 0.8$ comes from $0.6+0.1+0.1$ (the sum of weights for the 0.8 score), and 0.2 for $Rev.2, 0.6$ is the result of $0.1+0.1$. The sets $J_{Rev.2} = \{0.6, 0.8\}$ and $J_{Rev.3} = \{0.0, 0.2, 0.4\}$ contain primary memberships for $Rev.2, Rev.3$, respectively, and their corresponding secondary memberships are shown as the second stands in the denominators in (5). $\tilde{M}$ is a model for the statement *acceptable* which describes whether the paper is valid enough to be published.

The secondary membership levels of type-2 fuzzy sets may be interpreted in many manners. One of them is *a weight* of an opinion, as shown above. Another interpretation is to look at secondary memberships as at *levels of possibility* that primary memberships well characterize given phenomena; this variant is presented in [6]. Let us reconstruct the given example with secondary memberships viewed as *possibilities*; in this case the additional index named *a level of confidence* is assigned to each reviewer due to the scale: lowest=0.0, 0.2, 0.4, 0.6, 0.8, highest=1.0. A confidence level should be interpreted as a *possibility* that a given rating well describes the *acceptability* of the paper. See Table 2.

Table 2. Sample scores given by reviewers with different levels of confidence

	Reviewer 1	Reviewer 2	Reviewer 3
OVERALL RATING	**0.8**	**0.6**	**0.2**
Level of confidence	0.6	0.8	1.0

Summarizers of type-2 can also be based on more than one attribute. The meet operation [6] should be performed to intersect FST2 modelling single attributes. Such a realization promises that an obtained summarizer of type-2 is a generalization of the approach given in [1]. Combining type-1 attributes with type-2 attributes is also possible; many systems work on data of mixed types: crisp, type-1, type-2, etc. When input data are of both types, it is necessary to "upgrade" all attributes of type-1 to type-2 by adding secondary membership levels (unities) to each primary membership. The conversion of FST1 into FST2 in $\mathcal{X}$ is symbolically written as

$$A = \int_{x \in \mathcal{X}} \frac{\mu_A(x)}{x} \Rightarrow \tilde{A} = \int_{x \in \mathcal{X}} \int_{u \in J_x} \frac{1}{x, \mu_A(x)} \quad J_x \subseteq [0, 1] \tag{6}$$

where $u = \mu_A(x)$ is the primary membership level of x to the ordinary fuzzy set A, and unities in the numerators in (6) are the secondary memberships.

3.2   Type-2 Fuzzy Quantifier

The idea of a fuzzy quantifier of type-2 — which actually is a generalization of a type-1 (Zadeh's) fuzzy quantifier [17] — is constructed similarly to the idea of a type-2 fuzzy summarizer. If the description of modelling multi-sourced data with fuzzy sets of type-2 given in the previous section may be seen as the exemplification of *a linguistic variable of type-2*, one may view at linguistic quantifiers as at special cases of these variables.

Type-2 quantifiers may be, analogously to ordinary fuzzy quantifiers, *absolute*, e.g. LESS THAN 1000, ABOUT 50 or *relative*, e.g. ABOUT 3/4, MORE-LESS A HALF. The former kind is determined in any positive universe of discourse $\mathcal{X} \subseteq \mathcal{R}^+ \cup \{0\}$, and the latter — in the $[0, 1]$ interval. It is worth underlining that the qualification of a quantifier as relative or as absolute depends only on the form of its domain, and does not depend on its secondary membership function(s).

The following example of a type-2 fuzzy quantifier may be given: the statement *slightly less than 10* is being modelled. Let us assume that the four membership functions are proposed by four experts as given in Fig. 1.

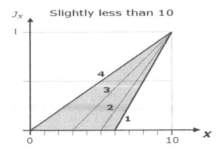

Fig. 1. The fuzzy quantifier of type-2 *slightly less than 10*

If assumed that experts are of different levels of confidence (compare the corresponding example in Section 3.1), one may assign additional indices to their opinions — secondary membership levels for the four primary membership functions (from the lower to the upper) are, for instance: 1, 0.7, 0.4, and 0.8, respectively. Hence, one may interpret these numbers as *possibility levels* that the functions $\mu_1,...,\mu_4$ properly characterize the modelled quantity in agreement. The compatibility level for the sample statement "5 is slightly less than 10" is the fuzzy set of the form

$$\mu(5) = \left\{ \frac{1}{0} + \frac{0.7}{0} + \frac{0.4}{0.28} + \frac{0.8}{0.5} \right\} \tag{7}$$

where $\mu : \mathcal{X} \rightarrow [0,1] \times [0,1]$ is the type-2 MF due to (2).

4   Conclusions

The original type-2-fuzzy-based extension for linguistic summaries of databases has been proposed. The elements of type-2 fuzzy sets have been employed in handling uncertainty appearing in sample data of the natural provenience. The new approach is supposed to provide human consistent tools for grasping and analysing large sets of data.

References

1. George, R., Srikanth, R.: Data Summarization Using Genetic Algorithms and Fuzzy Logic. In: Herrera F., Verdegay J. L. (Eds.), Genetic Algorithms and Soft Computing, Physica–Verlag, Heidelberg (1996) 599–611

2. Kacprzyk, J., Zadrożny, S.: FQUERY for Access: Fuzzy Querying for Windows-based DBMS. In: Bosc P., Kacprzyk J. (Eds.): Fuzziness in Database Management Systems, Physica-Verlag, Heidelberg (1995) 415–433

3. Kacprzyk, J., Strykowski, P.: Linguistic Data Summaries for Intelligent Decision Support, Proceeding of EFDAN'99. 4-th European Workshop on Fuzzy Decision Analysis and Recognition Technology for Management, Planning and Optimization, Dortmund, (1999) 3–12

4. Kacprzyk, J., Yager, R.R.: Linguistic summaries of data using fuzzy logic. International Journal of General Systems **30** (2001) 133–154

5. Kacprzyk J., Yager R.R., Zadrożny S.: Fuzzy linguistic summaries of databases for an efficient business data analysis and decision support. In: Abramowicz W., Żurada J. (Eds.) Knowledge Discovery for Business Information Systems. Kluwer, Boston, (2001) 129–152

6. Karnik, N.N., Mendel, J.M.: An Introduction to Type-2 Fuzzy Logic Systems. University of Southern California, Los Angeles (1998)

7. Karnik, N.N., Mendel, J.M.: Type-2 Fuzzy Logic Systems. IEEE Transactions on Fuzzy Systems, vol. **7**, no. **6** (1999) 643–658

8. Karnik, N.N., Mendel, J.M.: Operations on type-2 fuzzy sets. Fuzzy Sets and Systems **122** (2001) 327–348

9. Liang, Q., Mendel, J.M.: Interval Type-2 Fuzzy Logic Systems. Theory and Design. IEEE Transactions on Fuzzy Systems, vol. **8**, No. **5** (2000) 535–550

10. Liang, Q., Mendel, J.M.: Equalization of Non-linear Time-Varying Chanels Using Type-2 Fuzzy Adaptive Filters. IEEE Transactions on Fuzzy Systems, vol. **8**, No. **5** (2000) 551–563

11. Niewiadomski, A.: Interval-valued linguistic variables. An application to linguistic summaries (to appear).

12. Ochelska, J., Niewiadomski, A., Szczepaniak, P. S.: Linguistic Summaries Applied To Medical Textual Databases, Dept. of Electronics & Computer Systems, University of Silesia (2001) 125–130

13. de Tre, G., de Caluwe, R.: Level-2 fuzzy sets and their usefulness in object-oriented database modelling. Fuzzy Sets and Systems **140** (2003) 29–49

14. Yager, R. R.: A new approach to the summarization of data. Information Sciences **28** (1982) 69–86

15. Yager, R. R., Ford, M., Canas, A. J.: On linguistic summaries of data. In: Piatetsky-Shapiro G., Frawley W.J. (Eds.) Knowledge discovery in databases. AAAI Press, the MIT Press (1991) 347–363

16. Zadeh, L.A.: The concept of linguistic variable and its application for approximate reasoning (I). Information Science **8** (1975) 199–249

17. Zadeh, L.A.: A computational approach to fuzzy quantifiers in natural languages. Computers and Maths with Applications **9** (1983) 149–184

Fuzzy Sets-Based Retranslation of Numerical Data in E-Learning

Adam Niewiadomski[1,2] and Bartosz Rybusiński[1]

[1] Institute of Computer Science, Technical University of Lodz, Poland
aniewiadomski@ics.p.lodz.pl,
ichtio@stud.ics.p.lodz.pl
[2] Academy of Humanities and Economics, Lodz, Poland
aniewiadomski@wshe.lodz.pl

Abstract. Since e-learning is becoming more and more popular, there is a need to improve and widen information techniques that support e-teachers. Presently, the automated and intelligent examining procedures are essential for this support. We present the new soft-computing procedures of rating e-tests in German. The *clou* of this paper is *the retranslation algorithm* transforming raw numerical data into human consistent terms. The retranslation associated with fuzzy template matching is supposed to be a reliable solution giving satisfactory outputs. The results of the retranslation process are expressed in natural language, which makes them understandable and useful also for technologically non-advanced personnel.

1 Introduction

1.1 Fuzzy Sets and Interval-Valued Fuzzy Sets

Well known Zadeh fuzzy sets are present in computer sciences since 1965 [14]. Various extensions for fuzzy sets have been proposed, e.g. *L*-fuzzy sets [3], intuitionistic fuzzy sets [1], type-2 fuzzy sets [5], nevertheless, in this approach, we deal with two types: ordinary, i.e. Zadeh fuzzy sets, and interval-valued fuzzy sets (IVFS for short) [4] [13]. While the definition of the former is classic, the brief formalization of the latter is given: let $\mathcal{X}$ be a universe of discourse. An interval-valued fuzzy set A in $\mathcal{X}$ is a set of ordered triples of the form

$$A =_{df} \{< x, \underline{\mu}_A(x), \overline{\mu}_A(x) >: x \in \mathcal{X}; \underline{\mu}, \overline{\mu} : \mathcal{X} \to [0,1]\} \tag{1}$$

The gist of an IVFS is to assign two, instead of one, membership degrees to each element of $\mathcal{X}$: *the lower membership* and *the upper membership*. Due to the name of this type of fuzzy sets, $\underline{\mu}(x)$ and $\overline{\mu}(x)$ have the interpretation of lower and upper bounds (respectively) of an interval in which a membership value for an x is contained. IVFSs are used when the precise determination of a membership degree is impossible with respect to the nature of modelled phenomena.

P.S. Szczepaniak et al. (Eds.): AWIC 2005, LNAI 3528, pp. 348–354, 2005.

1.2   Operations on Interval Data

The structure of interval-valued vector (IVV) is proposed to store intervals as membership levels. Let $k \in \mathcal{N}$. Vector $V = [v_i], i \leq k$ built of k elements is called *interval-valued vector* in $(Int(R))^k$, iff each v_i is an interval in $Int(R)$, i.e. $v_i = [\underline{v}_i, \overline{v}_i] \in Int(\mathcal{R}), \underline{v}_i \leq \overline{v}_i$, for each $i = 1, 2, ..., k$. Thus, vector V is of the form:

$$V = \{[\underline{v}_1, \overline{v}_1], [\underline{v}_2, \overline{v}_2], ..., [\underline{v}_k, \overline{v}_k]\} \tag{2}$$

It may be needed to type-reduce interval-valued data, which means that one particular crisp number is to be extracted from the interval. Such a conversion is especially useful in the experiments described in Section 3 where comparisons of signals consisting of crisp numbers are needed. Especially, for IVV $V = \{[\underline{v}_1, \overline{v}_1], [\underline{v}_2, \overline{v}_2], ..., [\underline{v}_n, \overline{v}_n]\}, n \in \mathcal{N}, V \in Int(\mathcal{R})^n$ the following operations on V are called type-reductions

$$TR_{OPT}(V) = \{\overline{v}_1, \overline{v}_2, ..., \overline{v}_n\} \tag{3}$$

$$TR_{PES}(V) = \{\underline{v}_1, \underline{v}_2, ..., \underline{v}_n\} \tag{4}$$

As seen, type-reductions convert an IVV to a classic vector by taking the most optimistic option — the upper bound of an interval, or the most pessimistic — the lower bound. Another type-reductions, e.g. based on a weighted average of $\overline{\mu}$ and $\underline{\mu}$ are also possible [5].

The set of a few intervals describing the same phenomenon (e.g. degree of membership) may be converted to one interval value via computing the median of them. Let IVV $V = \{v_1, v_2, ..., v_k\}, V \in Int(\mathcal{R})^k$. The median of V denoted as $med(V)$ is computed as

$$med(V) = v_i \in V \text{ such that}$$

$$card(\{v_j \in V : v_j \prec v_i\}) = card(\{v_h \in V : v_i \prec v_h\}) = \left\lfloor \frac{k}{2} \right\rfloor \tag{5}$$

where function $\lfloor \frac{k}{2} \rfloor = n$ ("floor of $\frac{k}{2}$") is the biggest natural number n such that $n \leq \frac{k}{2}$, and the relation "$\prec$" between intervals a and b is defined as

$$a \prec b \leftrightarrow \underline{a} \leq \underline{b} \wedge \overline{a} \leq \overline{b} \tag{6}$$

Another methods of comparing intervals are given in [12]. Also the arithmetic or the weighted average may be used here, nevertheless, the median seems to be most robust estimator.

2   Retranslation as Data Interpretation

The process of *retranslation* may be briefly characterized as follows: it is the conversion of raw numerical data into terms from natural language. Assuming that some facts, perceptions, or measurements were transcribed to figures and

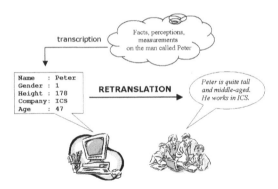

Fig. 1. Retranslation of numerical data

symbols to simplify their storage, the retranslation is the opposite process and may be qualified as a kind of knowledge acquisition; see Fig. 1.

Methods of retranslation are not described generally by global formulae and/or algorithms. They are usually designed according to the problem which is to be solved. From this point of view retranslation methods are very close to membership functions designed for fuzzy sets. In fact, retranslation via fuzzy sets is based mostly on finding proper membership functions mapping spectra of numerical values into discreet sets of linguistic and/or human consistent terms. The most known examples of retranslation are linguistic variables and fuzzy linguistic quantifiers introduced by Zadeh [15] [16].

3   Implementation

The study of the current literature shows that contemporary e-testing methods lacks of intelligent testing and scoring procedures. In fact, even if the teacher is widely supported by various multimedia technology, checking and rating exams must still be done manually. Some attempts of automation may be observed in rating single and multiple choice tests, but they can hardly be named *intelligent*, since they rely on Hamming distance only. Therefore, we describe the experiment employing intelligent template matching and retranslating obtained results into human consistent terms.

3.1   Experiment Construction

The presented experiment is based on German language vocabulary tests. The set of 33 questions is proposed. The tasks for a student is to complete a full correct and sensible from a set of mixed words (for details see [9]). Experts propose also the set of 240 correct, partially correct, and incorrect answers to these questions. All answers are scored by four matching algorithms (scores are from $[0,1]$) and by three experts (scores are from the scale 0=lowest, 0.5, 1, 1.5, 2.0=highest). The obtained results are denoted as $A_1 = \{a_{1,1}, a_{1,2},..., a_{1,240}\}$, $A_2, ..., A_4$, and $E_1 = \{e_{1,1}, e_{1,2},..., e_{1,240}\}$, E_2, E_3. The most characteristic point of the experiment, is that while the algorithms provide single numbers as the outputs (so $A_1, ..., A_4$ are the classic vectors), the experts frequently give intervals, e.g. 1–1.5 (so E_1, E_2, E_3 are IVVs), which is equivalent to some natural hesitation in rating. The imprecise predicate *correct answer* is modelled with the obtained vectors, since $A_1, ..., A_4$ are treated as ordinary fuzzy sets and E_1, E_2, E_3 as IVFSs.

3.2 Scoring Algorithms

The scoring algorithms are based on so-called n-gram method [2] and on its generalization [6] [10]. The method allows to compare strings with respect to their common subsequences of different lengths — n-grams — and to interpret results in terms of fuzzy similarity relations. The attempts of using this class of algorithms in distance testing are presented in [8] and [9].

Finally, four algorithms are chosen to the experiment: 1-n-grams, 2-grams, 2-3-grams, and 3-grams.

3.3 Retranslating Algorithm Results

The crucial part of the experiment is to *interpret*, or more thoroughly: to *retranslate* numbers obtained via Algorithms 1–4 into scores. These numbers are understood as *similarity level between an answer and a template of correctness*. However, a non-retranslated result, e.g. 0.63, is hardly understandable for the technologically non-advanced users. Also an e-teacher expects rather ready-to-use diagnosis as *answer correct*, or at least a number and/or a symbol, which expresses the level of correctness basing on his/her perception, than a number being a similarity level. Moreover, scores are so deeply rooted in human mind that — even if expressed with numbers or letters — they are viewed rather as human consistent statements than as numbers. For this reason, a selection of ranges 0.0–0.5; 0.5–1.0; 1.0–1.5; 1.5–2.0 to be used in retranslation methods is made as those which are the most commonly used by examiners in manual tests rating.

Thus, some methods of retranslation algorithm results into scores, which are ready to be accepted or rejected by a tutor, are presented.

"FloorCeil" Retranslation Retranslation "FloorCeil" is based on fitting the result obtained from algorithm to the closest of crisp scores $\{0, 0.5, 1, 1.5, 2\}$. This manner strictly corresponds with natural human behaviour while scoring: if one is not sure about his opinion, but can express it as interval, just a choice between the lower and the upper bound of this interval should be made.

Retranslating via Intervals with Type-Reduction Another way of retranslation — retranslation via intervals — is even less complicated than "FloorCeil". While "FloorCeil" algorithm requires determining crisp scores as final results, this manner of retranslation simply maintains intervals as scores (in this particular case interval bounds are multiplied by 2 to satisfy the assumption about scale of scoring). The formula of retranslation via intervals is

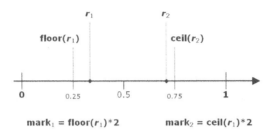

Fig. 2. FloorCeil retranslation

$$
score = \begin{cases} [0,0.5], \text{ if } r \in [0, 0.25] \\ [0.5,1], \text{ if } r \in [0.25, 0.5] \\ [1,1.5], \text{ if } r \in [0.5, 0.75] \\ [1.5,2], \text{ if } r \in [0.75, 1] \end{cases} \tag{7}
$$

Because obtaining scores from the scale $\{0, 0.5, 1, 1.5, 2\}$ is intended, only two variants of type-reduction, optimistic (3) and pessimistic (4) are used.

Scores Without Retranslation (Direct Results) This "non-existing" re-translation is made for comparison of algorithm scores in their pure (non-retranslated) form to interval-valued type-reduced expert scores. The obtained results help to establish some arguments for and/or against the necessity of retranslation.

3.4   Comparison

The present state of the art unfortunately lacks of methods for automated scoring e-tests. The comparison of results may be performed via statistical methods (as given) or via the linguistic summaries, as presented in [7].
Here, we present the statisitical methods of comparison. The scores obtained via algorithms and the scores collected from experts (expert opinions are computed as $E = med\{E_1, E_2, E_3\}$) are compared according to three similarity measures: the correlation coefficient r_{cc}, the minimum-maximum r_{mm}, and the arithmetic average-minimum method r_{am} [11]. The weighted average for r_{cc}, r_{mm}, and r_{am} with the weights $w_1 = 0.5$, $w_2 = 0.25$, and $w_3 = 0.25$ is temporarily used to determine the overall performance (OP) of the algorithm A_n, $n = 1, 2, 3, 4$:

$$
OP(A_n) = 0.5 \cdot r_{cc}(E, A_n) + 0.25 \cdot r_{mm}(E, A_n) + 0.25 \cdot r_{am}(E, A_n) \tag{8}
$$

The purpose of this computation is to find the strength of similarity connections between expert and algorithm opinions.

3.5   Results

The results of comparison for non-retranslated and for retranslated scores given by algorithms 1–4 are presented in Tab. 3.5

Table 1. OP similarity coefficients for the algorithms

Algorithm	Direct	FloorCeil	IV optimistic	IV pessimistic
1	**0,82**	**0,90**	**0,88**	**0,85**
2	0,83	0,85	0,83	0,84
3	0,83	0,83	0,84	0,83
4	0,80	0,80	0,81	0,80

As it can be observed, the strongest similarity to experts opinion is presented by non-retranslated results of algorithm 2. However, the FloorCeil and the interval-valued optimistic retranslations significantly improves the results of algorithm 1, which can be finally selected as the closest to expert opinions. This is also important with respect to the fact that if the retranslation were not performed, the wrong (weaker) algorithm would be chosen as the rating tool.

Also the results from algorithm 2 retranslated through the FloorCeil method and from algorithm 1 retranslated through interval-valued pessimistic method can provide quite reliable methods of automated rating.

4   Conclusions and Further Work Directions

The results of the experiment presented in this article show that the retranslation is able to improve significantly the procedures based on artificial intelligence. In particular, the retranslation shall be used in the final presentation of outputs to make them understandable and user-friendly. Advanced retranslation and interpretation procedures, based on fuzzy sets of type-2, are currently being developed by the authors.

References

1. Atanassov K.T.: Intuitionistic fuzzy sets. Fuzzy Sets and Systems **20** (1986) 87–96
2. Bandemer H., Gottwald S.: Fuzzy Sets, Fuzzy Logic, Fuzzy Methods with Applications. (1995) John Wiley & Sons
3. Goguen J.: L-fuzzy sets. Journal Math. Anal. Appl. **18** (1967) 145–174
4. Gorzalczany M.B.: A method of inference in approximate reasoning based on interval-valued fuzzy sets. Fuzzy Sets and Systems **21** (1987) 1–17
5. Karnik N.N., Mendel J.M.: Type-2 Fuzzy Logic Systems. IEEE Transactions on Fuzzy Systems, Vol. **7**, No. **6** (1999) 643–658
6. Niewiadomski A.: Intuitionistic fuzzy sets in text document comparison. PhD Dissertation, Institute of Systems Research, Polish Academy of Sciences, (2001) Warsaw, Poland (in Polish)
7. Niewiadomski A., Bartyzel M., Szczepaniak P.S.: Linguistic Summaries of Databases in Evaluating Algorithms for Automated Distance Testing (in Polish, in print).
8. Niewiadomski A., Grzybowski R.: Fuzzy measures of text similarity in automated evaluation of exams tests. Theoretical and Applied Computer Science, **5** (2003) 193–200 (in Polish)

9. Niewiadomski A., Rybusiński B., Sakowski K., Grzybowski R.: The application of multivalued similarity relations to automated evaluation of grammar tests. In: Academy On-line — e-learning, methodics, technologies, management (to appear; in Polish)

10. Niewiadomski A., Szczepaniak P.S.: Fuzzy Similarity in E-Commerce Domains. In: Segovia J., Szczepaniak P.S., Niedźwiedziński M.: E-Commerce and Intelligent Methods. Springer-Verlag (2002) 96–102

11. Ross T.J.: Fuzzy Logic with Engineering Applications. McGraw Hill Inc. (1995)

12. Sengupta A., Pal T.K., Chakraborty D.: Interpretation of inequality constraints involving interval cooeficients and a solution to interval linear programming. Fuzzy Sets and Systems **119** (2001) 129–138

13. Turksen I.B.: Interval-valued fuzzy sets based on normal forms. Fuzzy Sets and Systems **20** (1986) 191–210

14. Zadeh L.A.: Fuzzy Sets. Information and Control **8** (1965) 338–353

15. Zadeh L.A.: The concept of linguistic variable and its application for approximate reasoning (I). Information Science **8** (1975) 199–249

16. Zadeh L.A.: A computational approach to fuzzy quantifiers in natural languages. Computers and Maths with Applications **9** (1983) 149–184

Optimizing a Data Warehouse
Using Evolutionary Computation

Maciej Osiński

Faculty of Mathematics, Informatics and Mechanics,
Warsaw University,
Banacha 2, 02-097 Warsaw, Poland
m.osinski@zodiac.mimuw.edu.pl

Abstract. A data warehouse stores huge amounts of data collected from multiple sources and enables users to query that data for analytical and reporting purposes. Data in a data warehouse can be represented as a multidimensional cube.

Data warehouse queries tend to be very complex, thus their evaluation requires long hours. Precomputing a proper set of the queries (building subcubes) may significantly reduce the query execution time, though it requires additional storage space as well as maintenance time for updating the subcubes. Creating suitable indexes on the subcubes may have additional impact on the query evaluation time.

Proposed approach involves using evolutionary computation to select the set of subcubes and indexes that would minimize the query execution time, given a set of queries and available storage space limit.

1 Introduction

A data warehouse stores data collected from multiple sources and allows users to submit complex queries for analytical purposes. To answer these queries, the data warehouse engine needs to select a subset of data and aggregate it. But for various techniques of speeding up query evaluation, this process would take long hours. As each query may be associated with a view built on the base cube, a common technique involves precomputing a set of such views and storing them as materialized views (often called subcubes). Furthermore, the materialized views may have indexes, which additionally reduce the query execution time. Storing precomputed results requires extra storage space and maintenance time.

Gupta [1] states the problem (selecting a set of subcubes for materializing to minimize the evaluation time of a given set of queries under storage space limitation) as NP-complete. Thus, to solve the problem for a large number of possible subcubes within a reasonable amount of time, heuristic methods are usually used. I used evolutionary computation to solve this problem [2]. Evolutionary computation is based on a widely applied heuristic method called genetic algorithms (see [3] or [4]).

P.S. Szczepaniak et al. (Eds.): AWIC 2005, LNAI 3528, pp. 355–360, 2005.

2   Related Work

Most of the related work focus either on modifications of the greedy algorithm [1], [5] or on heuristically pruning the search space and using exhaustive search methods [6]. The greedy algorithm has certain limitations, including long time of execution for a large amount of subcubes and the possibility of omitting good solutions because of its "greedy" nature.

Lee and Hammer [7] used genetic algorithms to solve the problem of selecting subcubes to precompute and indicated choosing a set of indexes to create as a possible extension to their work. First tests of my framework for selecting both the subcubes and indexes exposed the need to use more sophisticated techniques of evolutionary computation (described in section 4) instead of classic genetic algorithms.

3   OLAP Model

I assume the knowledge of number of distinct values of each attribute. If not, it could be estimated [8]. Attributes are grouped into dimensions (e.g. dimension time contains attributes: year, month, week, etc.). The partial order of attributes (indicating whether one attribute can be computed by aggregating another) within a dimension is called a hierarchy. Each dimension contains the most aggregated "ALL" attribute with exactly 1 value. For more detailed OLAP model see e.g. [1], [9].

Cost model described in [5] has been used to calculate the storage space for subcubes and indexes as well as the query evaluation time.

A subcube is described by a set of attributes (one for each dimension) it is aggregated by. The size of a subcube is calculated as a product of distinct values of its attributes.

Each subcube may have indexes created on a subset of the set of attributes it is aggregated by. The order of attributes in the index matters. The size occupied by an index is assumed to be equal to the size of its subcube (details in [5]).

3.1   Queries

A query is described by a set of attributes it is aggregated by and its subset – set of attributes used for selecting rows in the "where" condition. Each query is assigned its weight, which indicates its importance.

The set of queries to analyze and their weights may be obtained from the data warehouse logs [11] or by modeling and predicting user behavior [10].

Cost of answering a query is estimated as the number of rows that need to be processed in order to answer the query (the linear model [5]). If a subcube chosen for answering a query has an index which prefix is the same as a subset of attributes in the where condition of the query, then the cost of answering the query is equal to the subcube size divided by the number of distinct values in this prefix. Otherwise, the cost of answering a query using a given subcube is equal to the size of this subcube. If a query cannot be answered using a given subcube, cost of answering is set to $+\infty$. A query cannot be answered using a given subcube if at least one of the attributes the query is grouped by is less aggregated than an appropriate attribute of the subcube.

For example, a subcube aggregated by T_year, C_customer, S_ALL, P_type (100 000 rows) with and index (C_customer, P_type) occupies 200 000 units of storage space. To answer a query aggregated by C_region and S_region with a where condition on C_region , 100 000 rows need to be processed as index cannot be used. However, answering a query aggregated by T_year and C_customer with a where condition on C_customer and T_year requires processing of only $\frac{100000}{500} = 200$ rows as a prefix of the index can be used.

3.2   Motivating Example

The motivating example is a simplified version of the TPC-R [12] benchmark. The dimensions, attributes and distinct values are:

- TIME: T_ALL(1) – T_year(4) – T_quarter(16) – T_month(48) – T_week(200)
- CUSTOMER: C_ALL(1) – C_region(8) – C_nation(40) – C_customer(500)
- SUPPLIER: S_ALL(1) – S_region(5) – S_nation(30) – S_supplier(50)
- PART: P_ALL(1) – P_type(50) – P_part(100).

There are 240 possible subcubes and 2^{240} possible combinations of subcubes to materialize. The base cube has $200*500*50*100 = 5*10^8$ rows. 20 queries were submitted for evaluation. Each query had a weight between 0 and 1. The cost of answering all queries using the base cube was $1.65*10^9$.

4   Genetic Algorithms and Evolutionary Computation

4.1   Genetic Algorithms

The idea behind genetic algorithms is to represent possible solutions of a problem as chromosomes, encoding features of the solution as genes. A new population is generated from the old one based on the fitness function until a given condition is met (e.g. a feasible solution is found or a given amount of time passed). Chromosomes are allowed to exchange genes (cross-over) and change values of genes (mutation) with a given probability. The population size may be fixed (e.g. 200 chromosomes) or not. In the latter case, each chromosome is assigned a maximum age based on the fitness function.

One of the major problems with genetic algorithms is the premature convergence, which takes place when a suboptimal solution dominates in the population and prevents other solutions (possibly better) from evaluating.

The approach suggested by Lee & Hammer in [7] involved encoding chromosomes as strings of boolean values, indicating whether a subcube should be materialized or not. This solution was not feasible for selecting indexes. Furthermore, first tests exposed the necessity to apply techniques of reducing premature convergence as well as using data structures and operations dedicated for this problem rather then basic genetic algorithms techniques.

4.2   Genes and Chromosomes

A chromosome consists of genes. Each gene represents a subcube to be materialized (Fig. 1). Two types of mutation have been used: external (add or remove subcubes) and internal (add or remove an index within an existing subcube). After adding an index, the indexes that are no longer neccessary (as they are prefixes of the new index) are removed. The probability of the internal mutation increases with the pass of time (number of generation).

The cross-over operation is performed between similar chromosomes (implementation of species [4]). The similarity is defined as the number of common genes. The role of species increases with the pass of time. Tests proved species to be helpful in maintaining population variety.

The fitness of a chromosome is calculated as the difference between the cost of answering queries using the base cube and using subcubes and indexes represented by the genes of this chromosome. Chromosomes are allowed to exceed storage space limit by 10%. The penalty for exceeding storage limit increases with the pass of time. Chromosomes that that exceeded the limit by more than 10% have randomly chosen genes removed.

4.3   Communities

Chromosomes are split into subpopulations (called communities), evaluated within these communities and exchanged between chromosomes. There are fixed size communities and variable size communities. Experiments revealed that the fixed size communities would more often find near-optimal solutions while the variable size ones would keep variety and have better average results. Fixed size communities use the remainder stochastic sampling model [4] to select the new population. Communities exchange chromosomes through a swap area (Fig. 1).

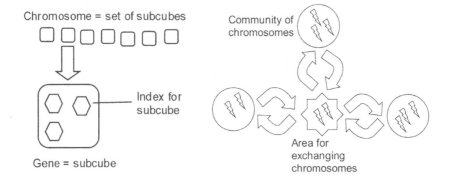

Fig. 1. Chromosomes, genes and communities

5 Experiment

The experiment phase involved developing a protype implementation and running a set of tests for the cube described in section 3.2. Tests were supposed to show how well did various configurations of the community based algorithm perform for 3 values of the storage space limitation (small, medium and large one). Each test was repeated at least 5 times. The results show the best and the average result for each test configuration. Time for each test execution was limited to 6 minutes, though usually it required 1 to 3 minutes. All test configurations where given a similar time for execution, therefore the amount of chromosomes within a community differed for different configurations. Hardly any progress has been observed after 40 generations, so the number of generations was limited to 50. The cross-over probability was set to 0.4 and the mutation probability was set to 0.01 and 0.05.

The prototype was implemented in Java, using the Eclipse IDE. It included: the greedy algorithm (selecting subcubes and indexes [5]), Lee & Hammer genetic algorithm (selecting subcubes [7]) and my community based algorithm. Experiments were carried out using a Celeron 2GHz PC running Windows XP.

Table 1. Sample results – minimal and average cost (in thousands of processed rows) of answering a set of queries for 3 values of storage space limit

Mode: Greedy – Gupta's greedy algorithm, Genetic – Lee & Hammer genetic algorithm, Fn Vm – community based algorithm with n fixed size communities and m variable size communities.

Exchange – ratio of chromosomes exchanged with other communities.

Mutation – mutation ratio

Mode	Exchange	Mutation	Small		Medium		Large	
			Min	Avg	Min	Avg	Min	Avg
Greedy	—	—	458465	458465	9440	9440	144	144
Genetic	—	—	514265	619305	514019	710668	514756	658119
F1 V1	0	0.01	469530	492720	4830	21392	324	1139
F1 V1	0.01	0.01	460248	501930	5482	14241	434	1065
F1 V1	0.1	0.01	493969	528036	2461	24933	434	1065
F1 V1	0.1	0.05	455326	501183	13284	22100	466	1409
F1 V1	0.2	0.05	467957	510122	12247	32272	535	1823
F2 V2	0.1	0.05	468121	510652	6183	18923	487	832
F4 V4	0.01	0.01	469121	503850	5233	23063	542	657
F4 V4	0.1	0.01	468448	503732	9253	26608	659	969
F4 V4	0.2	0.05	502186	522631	6651	20180	201	646
F8 V4	0.1	0.05	468003	497019	9193	23243	254	795
F8 V4	0.2	0.05	464341	520345	5590	24769	480	849
F8 V8	0.01	0.01	468038	513427	5383	19743	377	1500
F8 V8	0.1	0.01	468615	530597	5327	27570	243	644
F8 V8	0.1	0.05	458219	497786	5304	16415	241	707
F8 V8	0.2	0.05	468107	507997	8528	22828	573	908

6 Results

I was looking for configurations of the community based algorithm that often generate good results (better than the greedy algorithm), despite using randomized methods. Sample results are presented in Tab. 1. Tests shown that configurations with small number of big communities (e.g. 2048 chromosomes) produce worse results than configurations with a few smaller communities (suboptimal solutions dominate easier in the first case). Configurations with 6 to 16 communities, 64 to 256 chromosomes and exchange ration between 1% and 10% produce generally good results.

The basic genetic algorithm performs well only for a small limit of storage space, as other algorithms cannot make much use of indexes in this case.

7 Conclusion

An extended version of the Lee & Hammer genetic algorithm is proposed. The experiment shown that the new algorithm produces feasible solutions within a reasonable amount of time (in this case 1 to 5 minutes for 240 possible subcubes) and therefore is an interesting alternative for both the exhaustive search methods and the greedy algorithm. Furthermore, thanks to the use of techniques for maintaining population variety, it very often produces acceptable results.

References

1. Gupta, H.: Selection of Views to Materialize in a Data Warehouse, Proceedings of the International Conference on Database Theory, Delphi, (1997), 98–112.
2. Osiński, M.: Optymalizacja wykorzystania przekrojów hiperkostek w hurtowni danych, Master Thesis, Warsaw University, (2005).
3. Goldberg, D.: Genetic Algorithms in Search, Optimization, and Machine Learning, Addison-Wesley, 1989.
4. Michalewicz, Z.: Genetic Algorithms + Data Structures = Evolution Programs, Springer-Verlag, 1996.
5. Gupta, H., Harinarayan, V., Rajaraman, A., Ullman, J.D.: Index Selection for OLAP, Proceedings of the XIII Conference on Data Engineering, (1997), 208–219.
6. Theodoratos, D., Sellis, T.K.: Data Warehouse Configuration, Proceedings of the 23rd International Conference on Very Large Data Bases, (1997), 126–135.
7. Lee, M., Hammer, J.: Speeding Up Warehouse Physical Design Using a Randomized Algorithm, University of Florida, Technical Report, 1999.
8. Shukla, A., Deshpande, P.M., Naughton, J.F., Ramasamy, K.: Storage Estimation for Multidimensional Aggregates in the Presence of Hierarchies, VLDB, Bombay, (1996), 522–531.
9. Vassiliadis, P., Sellis, T.: A Survey on Logical Models for OLAP Databases, ACM SIGMOD Record, 28:4, (1999), 64–69.
10. Sapia, C.: On Modeling and Predicting User Behavior in OLAP Systems, Proc. CaiSE99 Workshop on Design and Management of Data Warehouses, (1999).
11. Application Response Measurement, http://www.opengroup.org, 1998.
12. Transaction Processing Performance Council, http://www.tpc.org/tpcr.

Specifying Schema Mappings for Query Reformulation in Data Integration Systems

Tadeusz Pankowski[1,2]

[1] Institute of Control and Information Engineering,
Poznań University of Technology, Poland
[2] Faculty of Mathematics and Computer Science,
Adam Mickiewicz University, Poznań, Poland
tadeusz.pankowski@put.poznan.pl

Abstract. In data integration systems there is a problem of answering queries through a target schema, given a set of mappings between source schemas and the target schema, and given that the data is at the sources. This is of special importance when integrated sources, e.g. from Web data repositories, have overlapping data and its merging is necessary. We propose a language for specifying a class of mappings between source and target schemas, and design rewriting rules which reformulate a target query to a query over data sources based on the mappings.

1 Introduction

The main problem of data integration systems is to combine data from different sources, and to provide the user with a unified view of these data [2, 3, 9]. We assume that there is a set of *source schemas* describing real data, and a *target schema* (or *mediated schema*) that is a virtual and reconciled view of the underlying sources. This allows the user for uniformly querying many different sources through one common interface (target schema). There are two approaches to answer queries in such environment: *view materialization* and *query reformulation*. The former assumes that a materialized instance of the target schema is available. In the latter, a query is reformulated in such a way that it can be processed against underlying sources, and partial answers are merged to obtain the final result. To realize query reformulation, relationships or *schema mappings* must first be established between the source schemas and the target schema.

In this paper we propose a method for specifying schema mappings and show how this specification can be used for query reformulation in data integration systems. We follow the GAV (*global-as-view*) approach and assume that both source and target are XML data. A schema mapping is specified by a high-level language XDMap which is an extension of XDTrans [5]. We propose four rewriting rules which reformulate a target query to a query over data sources. This reformulation is based on the mappings and some target constraints.

The rest of the paper is organized as follows: In Section 2 we define XDMap as a language for specifying mappings between schemas. In Section 3 we show

P.S. Szczepaniak et al. (Eds.): AWIC 2005, LNAI 3528, pp. 361–366, 2005.

how mapping between schemas can be defined and used for query reformulation. Section 4 concludes the paper.

2   XDMap - A Language for Schema Mapping Specification

To define schema mapping we will use a language called XDMap, which is an extended version of our XML data transformation language XDTrans [5]. We will consider mappings over XML data, so the syntax and semantics of the language is oriented towards the tree nature of XML. According to W3C standard, any XML document can be represented as a data tree [?], where a node conforms to one of the seven node types: *root, element, attribute, text, namespace, processing instruction*, and *comment*. In this paper, we restrict our attention to four first of them. Every node has a unique *node identifier (nid)* - to obtain an unique node identifier we will use Skolem functions.

Definition 1. *A data tree is an expression defined by the syntax:*

$$
\begin{aligned}
&data\ tree ::= nid(tree),\\
&tree \qquad ::= e\text{-}tree \mid a\text{-}tree \mid t\text{-}tree,\\
&e\text{-}tree \quad ::= \langle e, nid\rangle(tree, ..., tree), \qquad (element\ tree),\\
&a\text{-}tree \quad ::= \langle a, nid\rangle(s), \qquad\qquad\qquad (attribute\ tree),\\
&t\text{-}tree \quad ::= nid(s), \qquad\qquad\qquad\quad (text\ tree),
\end{aligned}
$$

where nid, e, a, and s are from, respectively, a set $\mathcal{N}$ of node identifiers, a set Σ_E of element labels, a set Σ_A of attribute labels, and a set $\mathcal{S}$ of string values. By $\mathcal{D}_{\Sigma,\mathcal{S}}(\mathcal{N})$, where $\Sigma = \Sigma_E \cup \Sigma_A$, will be denoted a set of all data trees over Σ and $\mathcal{S}$ with node identifiers from $\mathcal{N}$. □

Further on we assume that $\mathcal{C}$ is a set of *non-terminal symbols* called *concepts*, $\mathcal{P}$ is a set of *XPath expressions* in which *variables* can appear, and $\mathcal{F}$ is a set of Skolem functions. Any invocation $SF(x_1, ..., x_n)$ of a Skolem function SF returns the same node identifier for the same values of arguments $x_1, ..., x_n$. For different Skolem functions and for different values of arguments returned identifiers are distinct.

The goal of *schema mapping* is to define a conversion of a set of source schemas (data tree types) into an expected set of target schemas. A mapping can be specified by a set of *mapping rules*. Every rule determines a type of expected *final* or *intermediate* result tree in a form of a *tree expression*.

Definition 2. *A tree expression over alphabets Σ, $\mathcal{C}$, $\mathcal{S}$, $\mathcal{P}$ and $\mathcal{F}$ conforms to the following syntax:*

$$\tau ::= s \mid E \mid SF(...)(s) \mid \langle a, SF(...)\rangle(s) \mid \langle e, SF(...)\rangle(\tau, ..., \tau) \mid C(E, ..., E),$$

where: $s \in \mathcal{S}$, $E \in \mathcal{P}$, $SF \in \mathcal{F}$, $a \in \Sigma_A$, $e \in \Sigma_E$, $C \in \mathcal{C}$. The set of all tree expressions will be denoted by $T_{\Sigma,\mathcal{S}}(\mathcal{C}, \mathcal{P}, \mathcal{F})$. □

Definition 3. *A mapping specification language is a system*

$$XDMap = (\Sigma, \mathcal{C}, \mathcal{S}, \mathcal{F}, \text{START}, \mathcal{P}, \mathcal{R}),$$

where $\text{START} \in \mathcal{C}$ *is the initial concept, and* $\mathcal{R}$ *is a finite set of rules of the form:*
$$(C, (\$v_1 : E_1, ..., \$v_p : E_p)) \rightarrow \tau, ..., \tau,$$
where $C \in \mathcal{C}$, *any* E *(possibly with subscripts) is from* $\mathcal{P}$, $\$v$ *(possibly with subscripts) is a variable,* $\tau \in \mathcal{T}_{\Sigma, \mathcal{S}}(C, \mathcal{P}, \mathcal{F})$, *and every variable occurring in the body occurs also in the head of the rule.*   □

The head of a rule includes a concept C which will be rewritten by the body of the rule. A rule with concept C in the head *defines* this concept. We assume that any concept in a given set of rules must be defined, and that every concept has exactly one definition. Thus, our system is deterministic. Recursive definitions for concepts are also allowed. There must be exactly one rule, the *initialization rule*, defining the initial concept START. In order to refer to the root of a document we use "@doc/".

3   Schema Mapping and Rewriting Rules

In Figure 1 we have a source schema, two target schemas and mappings between them. Constraints in Figure 1 can easily be deduced from the mapping specification. Target schemas are defined as views over the source, so the GAV approach is applied. The mapping explicitly tells the system how to retrieve the data when one wants to evaluate the various elements of the target schema. This idea is effective whenever the data integration system is based on a set of sources that is stable.

The first rule tells that the start non-terminal concept START denoting the expected target, is to be replaced by two target trees. The first target tree starts with the outermost element "<students>...</students> and the students node is uniquely determined by the Skolem function $STS()$. The subtree pointed to by the node is denoted by non-terminal tree expression STUDENT($\$x$), where the current context node is bound to variable $\$x$ and is passed to the rule defining the concept STUDENT (i.e. to the second rule). The precise semantics for transformation rules where Skolem functions are not given explicitly is defined in [5].

In Figure 2 we define rewriting rules for reformulating the target query into a source query (or a set of source queries) based on the mapping rules and constraints. The reformulation is achieved by iteratively applying rewriting rules to a target query. We use the following notations: $tgtE$ and $srcE$ denote XPath expressions on target and source schema, respectively; $SF_{tgtE}(L_{\$x})$ denotes the Skolem function associated to path expression $tgtE$ in mapping specification, and $L_{\$x}$ denotes a list of arguments of the function. For example, $CES(\$x/\text{Id}, \$x/\text{Course})$ is associated to @tgt/students/student/CourEvals; $[\$z \mapsto \$x]$ is a *replacement operation* replacing occurrences of target variable $\$z$ with source variable $\$x$; $L_{\$x}[\$x \rightarrow \$x']$ denotes the result of substitution all occurrences of $\$x$ in $L_{\$x}$

Source and target schemas:

```
src:                    tgt:                    tgt:
    Students                Students                Evals
        Student*                Student*                Eval*
            Id                      StId                    EvalId
            Name                    StName                  Course
            Course                  CourEvals               Grade
            Grade                   EvalId*
```

Mappings:

$(\text{START}, \$x : @\text{src/Students}) \rightarrow \langle @\text{tgt/Students}, STS()\rangle(\text{STUDENT}(\$x)),$
$\qquad\qquad\qquad\qquad\qquad \langle @\text{tgt/Evals}, EVS()\rangle(\text{EVAL}(\$x))$
$(\text{STUDENT}, \$x : \text{Student}) \rightarrow \langle\text{Student}, STU(\$x/\text{Id})\rangle($
$\qquad\qquad\qquad\qquad \langle\text{StId}, STI(\$x/\text{Id})\rangle(\$x/\text{Id}),$
$\qquad\qquad\qquad\qquad \langle\text{StName}, STN(\$x/\text{Id}, \$x/\text{Name})\rangle(\$x/\text{Name}),$
$\qquad\qquad\qquad\qquad \langle\text{CourEvals}, CES(\$x/\text{Id}, \$x/\text{Course})\rangle(\text{EVALID}(\$x)))$
$(\text{EVALID}, \$x : .) \rightarrow \langle\text{EvalId}, EVI(\$x/\text{Id}, \$x/\text{Course})\rangle(value(\$x/\text{Id}, \$x/\text{Course}))$
$(\text{EVAL}, \$x : \text{Student}) \rightarrow \langle\text{Eval}, EVA(\$x/\text{Id}, \$x/\text{Course})\rangle(\text{EVALID}(\$x),$
$\qquad\qquad\qquad\qquad \langle\text{Course}, COU(\$x/\text{Id}, \$x/\text{Course})\rangle(\$x/\text{Course}),$
$\qquad\qquad\qquad\qquad \langle\text{Grade}, GRA(\$x/\text{Id}, \$x/\text{Course}, \$x/\text{Grade})\rangle(\$x/\text{Grade}))$

Constraints:

STS = @tgt/Students	EVI = CES/EvalId	EVS = @tgt/Evals
STU = STS/Student		EVA = EVS/Eval
STI = STU/StId		EID = EVA/EvalId
STN = STU/StName		COU = EVA/Course
CES = STU/CourEvals		GRA = EVA/Grade

Fig. 1. Source and target schemas, mappings and constraints

with $\$x'$. An expression of the form $SF_{tgtE}(L_{\$x})$, $value(tgtE) = L_{\$x}.k$ means, that the text value associated to a path $tgtE$ is equal to the *k-th* component of the argument list $L_{\$x}$ of the Skolem function $SF_{tgtE}(L_{\$x})$ associated to $tgtE$.

$(\text{R1}) \quad \dfrac{\$z : tgtE, SF_{tgtE}(L_{\$x}), \$x : srcE}{\$x : srcE, [\$z \mapsto \$x]}$

$(\text{R2}) \quad \dfrac{\$z : \$y/tgtE, SF_{\$y/tgtE}(L_{\$x}, L'_{\$x}) = SF_{\$y}(L_{\$x})/tgtE, \$x : srcE, [\$y \mapsto \$y']}{\$x : srcE \wedge L_{\$x} = (L_{\$x}[\$x \rightarrow \$y']), [\$z \mapsto \$x]}$

$(\text{R3}) \quad \dfrac{\$x/tgtE_1 = \$y/tgtE_2}{R5(\$x/tgtE_1) = R5(\$y/tgtE_2)}$

$(\text{R4}) \quad \dfrac{\$x/tgtE, SF_{\$x/tgtE}(L_{\$x}), value(\$x/tgtE) = L_{\$x}.k}{R5(\$x/tgtE).k}$

$(\text{R5}) \quad \dfrac{\$y/tgtE, SF_{\$y/tgtE}(L_{\$x}) = SF_{\$y}(L'_{\$x})/tgtE, [\$y \mapsto \$y']}{L_{\$x}[\$x \rightarrow \$y']}$

Fig. 2. Rewriting rules

Target query Q:

```
(1) for     $s in @tgt/Students/Student
(2)         $c in $s/CourEvals
(3)         $e in @tgt/Evals/Eval
(4) where   $c/EvalId=$e/EvalId
(5) return  {$s/StName}
(6)         {$e/Course}
(7)         {$e/Grade}
```

Application of rewriting rules to query Q:

$$(1) \quad \frac{\$s : @tgt/Students/Student, \; STU(\$s'/Id), \; \$s' : @src/Students/Student}{\$s' : @src/Students/Student, \; [\$s \mapsto \$s']}$$

$$(2) \quad \frac{\$c : \$s/CourEvals, \; CES(\$c'/Id, \$c'/Course) = STU(\$c'/Id)/CourEvals,}{\$c' : @src/Students/Student, \; [\$s \mapsto \$s']} \atop {\$c' : @src/Students/Student \wedge c'/Id = s'/Id, [\$c \mapsto \$c']}$$

$$(3) \quad \frac{\$e : @tgt/Evals/Eval, \; EVA(\$e'/Id, \$e'/Course), \$e' : @src/Students/Student}{\$e' : @src/Students/Student, \; [\$e \mapsto \$e']}$$

$$(4) \quad \frac{\$c/EvalId = \$e/EvalId}{(\$c'/Id, \$c'/Course) = (\$e'/Id, \$e'/Course)}$$

$$(5) \quad \frac{\$s/StName}{s'/Name} \qquad\qquad (6) \quad \frac{\$e/Course}{e'/Course} \qquad\qquad (7) \quad \frac{\$e/Grade}{e'/Grade}$$

For (5), we have the following inference performed by invocation of (R5):

$$(R5) \quad \frac{\$s/StName, \; STN(\$x/Id, \$x/Name) = STU(\$x/Id)/StName, [s \mapsto s']}{(\$s'/Id, \$s'/Name)}$$

Reformulated query Q:

```
for     $s' in @src/Students/Student
        $c' in @src/Students/Student
        $e' in @src/Students/Student
where   $c'/Id=$e'/Id
        ∧ $c'/Course=$e'/Course
        ∧ $c'/Id=$s'/Id
return  {$s'/Name}
        {$e'/Course}
        {$e'/Grade}
```

Fig. 3. Reformulation of a target query to a source query

The two first rules are used to reformulate variable definitions from the **for** clause of the query. (R3) is used to rewrite an atomic equality from the **where** clause, and (R4) is applied to rewrite terms from the **return** part of the query. Rule (R5) is an auxiliary rule invoked by (R3) and (R4).

In Figure 3 we show application of rewriting rules to reformulate a query.

4   Conclusion

The problem of schema mapping and query reformulation has received considerable attention in recent years especially in the context of data integration, where data from various heterogeneous sources has to be transformed into data structured under a target (or mediated) schema. In relational data integration systems mappings have been defined in the form of GAV (*global-as-view*) or LAV (*local-as-view*) [3, 8]. Schema mappings have been also investigated in more general data integration scenarios [1, 4, 7]. Mappings are often specified in a high-level declarative way that state how groups of related elements in a source schema correspond to groups of related elements in the target schema [9].

Novelty of this paper is as follows: (1) we propose a language XDMap for specifying schema mappings, the language involves Skolem functions and allows for expressing a rich set of data restructuring operations (among other grouping and merging); (2) we propose rewriting rules for reformulating target queries into queries over source data, rewriting algorithm is illustrated by an example.

The proposed approach can be used when the source schemas are known. When these are not available some other methods based on schema discovery and domain ontologies should be applied. Such a case we discuss in [6].

References

1. Fagin, R., Popa, L., Kolaitis, P., Tan, W.-C.: Composing Schema Mappings: Second-Order Dependencies to the Rescue, *Proc. of the 23th ACM SIGMOD Symposium on Principles of Database Systems (PODS 2004)*, 2004, 83–94.
2. Halevy, A. Y.: Answering queries using views: A survey, *The VLDB Journal*, **10**(4), 2001, 270–294.
3. Lenzerini, M.: Data integration: a theoretical perspective, *ACM SIGMOD Symposium on Principles of Database Systems (PODS 2002)*, 2002, 233–246.
4. Madhavan, J., Halevy, A. Y.: Composing mappings among data sources, *Proc. of the 29th International Conference on Very Large Data Bases, VLDB 2003, Berlin, Germany*, 2003, 572–583.
5. Pankowski, T.: A High-Level Language for Specifying XML Data Transformations, In: Advances in Databases and Information Systems, ADBIS 2004, *Lecture Notes in Computer Science*, **3255**, 2004, 159–172.
6. Pankowski, T., Hunt, E.: Data Merging in Life Science Data Integration Systems, *Intelligent Information Systems, New Trends in Intelligent Information Processing and Web Mining*, Advances in Soft Computing, Springer Verlag, 2005.
7. Tatarinov, I., Halevy, A.: Efficient query reformulation in peer data management systems, *Proc. of the 2004 ACM SIGMOD International Conference on Management of Data*, 2004, 539–550.
8. Ullman, J. D.: Information Integration Using Logical Views. In: Database Theory - ICDT 1997, *Lecture Notes in Computer Science*, **1186**, 1997, 19–40.
9. Yu, C., Popa, L.: Constraint-based XML query rewriting for data integration, *Proc. of the 2004 ACM SIGMOD International Conference on Management of Data*, 2004, 371–382.

XKMS-Based Key Management for Open LBS in Web Services Environment

Namje Park[1], Howon Kim[1], Kyoil Chung[1],
Seungjoo Kim[2], and Dongho Won[2]

[1] Information Security Research Division, ETRI,
161 Gajeong-dong, Yuseong-gu, Daejeon, 305-350, Korea
{namjepark, khw, kyoil}@etri.re.kr
[2] School of Information and Communication Engineering, Sungkyunkwan University,
300 Chunchun-dong, Jangan-gu, Suwon-si, Gyeonggi-do, 440-746, Korea
skim@ece.skku.ac.kr, dhwon@dosan.skku.ac.kr

Abstract. As the killer application of the wireless internet, the LBS (Location-based Services) has reconsidered technology about location determination technology, LBS middleware server for various application, and diverse contents processing technology. For this kind of LBS, the role of security service is very important in the LBS that store and manage the location information of mobile devices and support various application services using those location information. And in all phases of these functions that include acquisition of location information, storage and management of location information, user management including authentication and information security, and management of the large-capacity location information database, safe security service must be provided. This paper describes a key management architecture based on XML standards for securing access to location based information and services. The main characteristic of the approach is that it build on a number of XML-based standards.

1 Introduction

Recently, with the rapid development of mobile communication technology and wide spread of mobile devices such as cellular phones equipped with a GPS (Global Positioning System) receiver, PDA, notebook PCs, LBS technology which uses location information of mobile devices is being more important.

LBS requests can span multiple security domains. Trust relationships among these domains play an important role in the outcome of such end-to-end traversals. A service needs to make its access requirements available to interested client entities, so that they understand how to securely request access to it. Trust between end points can be presumed, based on topological assumptions or explicit, specified as policies and enforced through exchange of some trust-forming credentials. In a LBS environment, presumed trust is rarely feasible due to the dynamic and distributed nature of virtual organizations relationships. Trust establishment may be a one-time activity per session or it may be evaluated dynamically on every request. The dynamic nature of the LBS in some cases can make it impossible to establish trust relationships among sites prior to application

P.S. Szczepaniak et al. (Eds.): AWIC 2005, LNAI 3528, pp. 367–373, 2005.

execution. Given that the participating domains may have different security infrastructures it is necessary to realize the required trust relationships through some form of federation among the security mechanisms.

Furthermore, an open LBS service infrastructure will extend the use of the LBS technology or services to business areas using web services technology. Therefore, differential resource access is a necessary operation for users to enable them to share their resources securely and willingly.

This paper describes a security approach to open LBS to validate certificates based on the current LBS environment using the web services security mechanism, presents a location-based platform that can block information leak and provide safe LBS, and analyzes authentication and security service between service systems and presents relevant application methods.

2 Service Architecture for Secure Open LBS

Web services can be used to provide mobile security solutions by standardizing and integrating leading security solutions using XML messaging. XML messaging is considered the leading choice for a wireless communication protocol. In fact, there are security protocols for mobile applications that are based on XML messaging. Some of these include SAML (Security Assertion Markup Language), which is a protocol for transporting

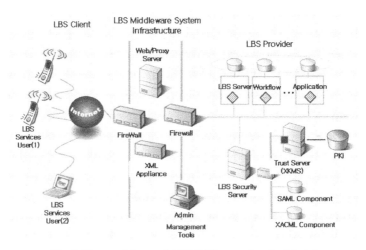

Fig. 1. Proposed Secure LBS Middleware Service Model

authentication and authorization information in an XML message. It can be used to provide single sign-on web services. On the other hand, XML signatures define how to sign part or all of an XML document digitally to guarantee data integrity. The public key distributed with XML signatures can be wrapped in XKMS (XML Key Management Specification) formats. In addition, XML encryption enables applications to encrypt part or all of an XML document using references to pre-agreed symmetric keys. Endorsed by IBM and microsoft, ws-security is a complete solution to providing security to web services. It is based on XML signatures, XML encryption, and same authentication and authorization scheme as SAML[1,11,12].

Security technology for LBS is currently based on KLP (Korea Location Protocol). Communication between the LBS platform and application service providers should be examined from the safety viewpoint vis-à-vis web services security technology[11]. As shown in the security service model of the LBS platform in figure 1, the platform should have an internal interface module that carries out authentication and security functions to provide the LBS application service safely to the users.

3   Secure LBS Services Transaction Models

3.1   Invocation Process of Security Protocol

Three types of principals are involved in the proposed protocol: LBS application (server/client), SAML processor, and XKMS server (including PKI). The proposed invocation process for the secure LBS security service consists of two parts: initialization protocol and invocation protocol[6,8,9].

The initialization protocol is a prerequisite for invoking LBS web services securely. Through the initialization protocol, all principals in the proposed protocol set the security environments for their web services (Fig. 2).

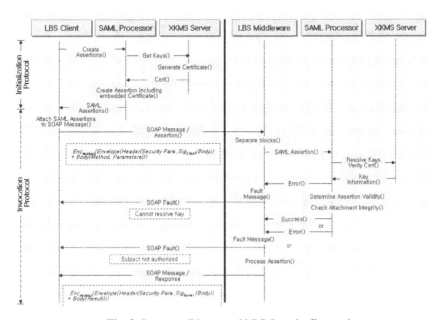

Fig. 2. Sequence Diagram of LBS Security Protocol

The following is the flow of setting the security environments: The client first registers information for using web services. It then gets its id/password, which will be used for verifying its identity when it calls web services via a secure channel. The client gets SAML assertions and installs a security module to configure its security environments and to make a secure SOAP message. It then generates a key pair for digital signature and registers its public key to a CA.

The client creates a SOAP message containing authentication information, method information, and XML signature. XML then encrypts and sends to a server such message. The message is in the following form: $Enc_{session}(Envelope\ (Header\ (SecurityParameters,\ Sig_{client}(Body))+Body(Method,\ Parameters))))$, where $Sig_x(y)$ denotes the result of applying x' s private key function (i.e., the signature generation function) to y. The protocol shown in figure 2 shows the use of end-to-end bulk encryption [4,5].

SAML also has such policy mechanism, whereas XACML (eXtensible Access Control Markup Language) provides a very flexible policy mechanism that is applicable to any resource type. For the proposed implementing model, SAML provides a standardized method of exchanging authentication and authorization information securely by creating assertions from the output of XKMS (e.g., assertion validation service in XKMS). XACML replaces the policy part of SAML (Fig. 3). Once the three assertions are created and sent to the protected resource, verification of authentication and authorization at the visiting site is no longer necessary. SSO (Single Sign-On) is a main contribution of SAML in distributed security systems[2,10].

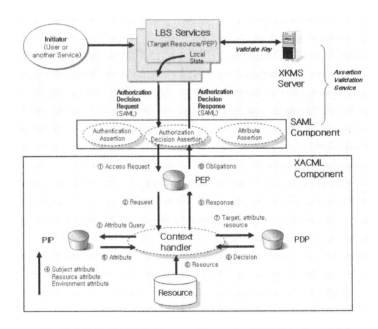

Fig. 3. SAML/XACML Message Flow using XKMS in Open LBS

3.2 Flow Certificate Validation Service in XKMS

Three validation processing methods consist of two steps: determination, which means accessing a repository and retrieving the certificate and construction of the path, and; validation, which means ensuring that each certificate in the path has integrity, each certificate is within its validity period, and each certificate has not been revoked [3,4,13]. In CVM (Certificate Validation Server Module), the client delegates subtasks (e.g., only path discovery) or entire task (e.g., path discovery and path validation) of certificate path processing to a server as shown in figure 4.

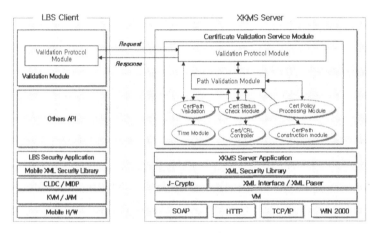

Fig. 4. CVM Components in XKMS

4 Simulations

We designed and implemented a test software, which focuses on security for open LBS services and messaging, and then targets system performance for the business scenarios mentioned in the previous section under a secure and reliable environment

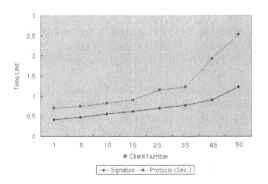

Fig. 5. Simulation Result of XKMS Protocol

Figure 5 showed difference for 0.2 seconds that compare average transfer time between client and server of XML encryption & decryption by XML signature base on LBS security library. According as increase client number on the whole, showed phenomenon that increase until 0.3 seconds

Figure 5 is change of average transmission time according as increase client number in whole protocol environment. If client number increases, we can see that average transfer time increases on the whole. And average transfer time increases rapidly in case of client number is more than 45. Therefore, client number that can process stably in computer on testbed environment grasped about 40(at the same time). When compare difference of signature time and protocol time, time of XML signature module is occupying and shows the importance of signature module about 60% of whole protocol time.

5 Conclusion

This paper sought to present a location-based platform that can block information leak and provide safe LBS as well as to establish methods for authentication and security application between service systems for presentation. Toward this end, LBS security requirements were examined and analyzed. In particular, the trend of technology and standard was analyzed to provide safe LBS. To formulate an authentication method as well as a security technology application method for LBS on MLP (Mobile Location Protocol), MLP security elements were identified based on LBS security requirements by defining the MLP security structure, which serves as the basis for KLP.

A novel security approach to open LBS was proposed to validate certificates based on the current LBS security environment using XKMS and SAML and XACML in XML security. This service model allows a client to offload certificate handling to the server and to enable the central administration of XKMS polices. To obtain timely certificate status information, the server uses several methods such as CRL (Certificate Revocation List), OCSP, etc. The proposed approach is expected to be a model for the future security system that offers open LBS security.

References

1. W3C Working Draft: XML Key Management Specification Version 2.0. (2003)
2. E. Faldella and M.Prandini: A Novel Approach to On-Line Status Authentication of Public Key Certificates. in Proc. the 16th Annual Computer Security Applications Conference (2000)
3. Y. Elley, et. Al, Building Certification Paths: Forward vs. Reverse. Proc. the Network and Distributed System Security Symposium Conference (2001)
4. M. Naor and K. Nissim: Certificate Revocation and Certificate Update. IEEE Journal on Selected Areas in Communications, 18 (4) (2000)
5. Euinam Huh, Jihye Kim, Hyeju Kim, Kiyoung Moon: Policy based on grid security infrastructure implementation for dirrerential resource access. ISOC Conference. (2003)
6. Yuichi Nakamur, et. Al.: Toward the Integration of web services security on enterprise environments. IEEE SAINT Conference (2002)

7. Boudewijn R. Haverkort John: Performance of Computer Communication Systems: A Model-Based Approach. Wiley & Sons (1999)
8. Sung-Min Lee et.al.: TY*SecureWS:An Integrated Web Service Security Solution Based on Java. Lecture Notes in Computer Science, Vol. 2738. (2003) 186-195
9. Minsoo Lee, et. Al: A Secure Web Services for Location based Services in Wireless Networks. Networking2004 (2004)
10. Junseok Lee, et. Al.: A DRM Framework for Distributing Digital Contents through the Internet. ETRI Journal, Vol.25, No.6 (2003) 423-436
11. Namje Park, et. Al.: The Security Consideration and Guideline for Open LBS using XML Security Mechanism. ASTAP 04/FR08/EG.IS/06. (2004)
12. Wooyong Han, et. Al.: A Gateway and Framework for Telematics Systems Idependent on Mobile Networks. ETRI Journal, Vol.27, No.1 (2005) 106-109
13. Jose L. Munoz et. Al.: Using OCSP to Secure Certificate-Using transactions in M-Commerce. Lecture Notes in Computer Science, Vol. 2846. (2003) 280-292

A Trust Model Based on Bayesian Approach

Jian-Jun Qi[1], Zeng-Zhi Li[1], and Ling Wei[2]

[1] Institute of Computer Architecture and Network,
Xi'an Jiaotong University, Xi'an, 710049, PR China
qjjwv@nwu.edu.cn
[2] Department of Mathematics, Northwest University,
Xi'an, 710069, PR China

Abstract. Trust plays a vital role in web-based systems in which entities act in an autonomous and flexible manner. This paper proposes a novel trust model based on Bayesian approach for web-based systems. The relationships between entities are classified into 4 kinds according to what if there are recommendations and/or direct interactions. For these 4 situations, the estimator of the successful cooperation probability (SCP) between entities is analyzed by using Bayesian approach. Finally, we take the estimator as the basis of an entity trusting in another and obtain the entity's relatively fixed cooperation system which consists of all of its potential partners in the future.

1 Introduction

The topic of trust in cyber-societies attracts increasing attention in the academic community and the industrial community in recent years[1, 2, 3, 4, 5]. Trust is undoubtedly a very important feature of human life. Luhmann has ever said, "A complete absence of trust would prevent even getting up in the morning" [6]. Similarly, trust is also important to effective interactions in web-based systems, such as e-commerce, peer-to-peer computing, the semantic web, recommender systems [1, 2], which have much in common with human society. In a web-based system, there are many entities which need to interact with one another. They act in an autonomous and flexible manner. They are likely to be unreliable, and maybe know nothing about each other. In order to facilitate interactions in such systems, trust must be addressed. Trust is a crucial part of decision making for web-based systems.

Up to now, several trust models have been published. For example, Beth's model using direct and recommendation trust [7], Manchala's model using fuzzy logic [8], Jøsang's model using subjective logic [9], and so on. In this paper, we present a Bayesian trust model for web-based systems. Our idea is to find an important feature of trust within such systems, that is the successful cooperation probability (SCP) between two entities, and to try to estimate it. Where, the Bayesian method supports a statistical evidence for trust analysis. In [10], Mui, L. et al. constructed a rating system for distributed systems using Bayesian method. In [11], Jøsang, A. et al. formed a reputation system also using Bayesian

P.S. Szczepaniak et al. (Eds.): AWIC 2005, LNAI 3528, pp. 374–379, 2005.

method. Although they both use Bayesian method, the selection of the parameters in Beta prior distribution are not analyzed. We discuss it in this paper.

Section 2 gives our trust model, estimates SCP in 4 different situations through analyzing the parameters in Beta prior distribution, and analyzes how to obtain an entity's cooperation system based on the estimator. The study is rounded off with a thought on future works in section 3.

2   The Trust Model Using Bayesian Approach

In this section, the trust model is given in detail. For an entity, it maybe have experiences with another one, or it can request recommendations about that one from its partners. According to this, we classify the relationships between two entities into 4 kinds. Then, we analyze the estimator of SCP in these different situations using Bayesian approach. Finally, We take the estimator as the basis of an entity (we call it "master entity") trusting in another and obtain its relative fixed cooperation system which consists of all of the master entity's potential partners in the future.

2.1   Basic Trust

In [13], Boon, S.D. and Holmes, J.G. proposed that an entity has a "basic" trust, which is derived from past experiences in all situations, and has a value in the range $[-1, +1)$. Good experiences lead to a greater disposition to trust, and vice versa. Marsh S.P. [12] developed this idea in his PhD thesis. In fact, the basic trust of an entity, which embodies its trusting disposition, is the basis of the entity affiliating with others.

In this paper, we define the value of basic trust in the range $[0, 1]$. The basic trust of an entity x is denoted by BT_x. We assume that an entity's basic trust is a fixed value during a period of time. In general, we call the entity is an optimist if BT_x is larger than 0.5, pessimist if BT_x is smaller than 0.5, realist if BT_x is equal to 0.5. Of course, the classification may not be so strict. For example, if BT_x is in $[0.4, 0.6]$ in real world, we can say x is a realist. For these three kinds of different entities, we will give different estimator of SCP in the following.

2.2   The Bayesian Model for Estimating SCP

Trust is always connected with some specified context. For example, a student may trust his mathematics teacher to solve an equation, while he would not trust him to operate on his heart. Here, for the sake of simplicity, we only consider a system within the same context during a period Δt.

For two entities x and y, the successful cooperation probability between them is denoted by θ. There may have direct interactions between them, there may also have other intermediate entities and each of them has direct experiences with x and y. On the one hand, if there are direct interactions between x and y, we can obtain direct probability of successful cooperation, which is called interaction probability, and denoted by θ_{int}. On the other hand, if there is an intermediate entity z between x and y, and there are interactions between x and z, z and y, then, we can also obtain an indirect probability of successful cooperation between x and y, which is called recommendation probability, and denoted by θ_{rec}. So, there are two kinds of probabilities of successful cooperation. They are entity x's direct and indirect experiences with entity y respectively. We will combine these two kinds of probabilities to be the estimator of successful cooperation probability. That is,

$$\widehat{\theta} = a\widehat{\theta}_{rec} + b\widehat{\theta}_{int} \tag{1}$$

where, a and b satisfy $a, b \in [0, 1], a + b = 1$. They are weights to represent the importance of these two probabilities respectively and are decided by the personal characteristics of the entity x.

With respect to recommendation probability, we use the following formula to be its estimator:

$$\widehat{\theta_{rec}} = \frac{r_1}{n_1} \times \frac{r_2}{n_2} \tag{2}$$

in which, n_1 (n_2) is the number of interaction between x and z (z and y), and r_1 (r_2) is the number of successful cooperation.

For the interaction probability, here we use Bayesian approach to compute its estimator.

Suppose that the probability of successful cooperation between them is modelled with a Beta prior distribution, which is used to represent probability distribution of binary events [14]. The Beta density function is,

$$p(\theta/\alpha, \beta) = Beta(\alpha, \beta) = \frac{\Gamma(\alpha + \beta)}{\Gamma(\alpha)\Gamma(\beta)} \theta^{\alpha-1}(1 - \theta)^{\beta-1} \tag{3}$$

where $0 < \theta < 1$ and $\alpha, \beta > 0$.

If we get a sample X, here we mean that there are $n = r+s$ times cooperation, in which, r times are successful and s times are unsuccessful. Then, we obtain the following likelihood function from the sample.

$$L(\theta/X) = \theta^r (1 - \theta)^s \tag{4}$$

So, we get the posterior density function $g(\theta/X)$ of successful cooperation probability .

$$g(\theta/X) \propto L(\theta/X)p(\theta/\alpha, \beta) = Beta(\alpha + r, \beta + s) \tag{5}$$

Under square loss function, we get the Bayesian estimator of the probability, which is,

$$\widehat{\theta}_{int} = E(\theta/X) = \frac{\alpha + r}{\alpha + \beta + n} \tag{6}$$

Now, we can use (1) to obtain the final estimator of successful cooperation probability under the same context during a period Δt, which have the following meanings. On the one hand, it is like a summary about past experience during the period Δt. On the other hand, it can be taken as an instructor of x's trusting in y to decide if x will select y to be its partner in the future, and further, it will form a relatively steady cooperation system with respect to x. It will be discussed in the following section.

2.3   Analyzing 4 Kinds of Relationships Between Two Entities

In the web-based system, the relationships between two entities, x and y, can be classified into 4 kinds according to what if there are recommendations and/or direct interactions between them. In this subsection, we will study these different relationships through analyzing the parameters of Beta distribution to obtain the final estimator of SCP.

Let $Rec = 1$ (or 0) represent there is (not) an intermediate entity z between x and y, $Int = 1$ (or 0) represent there are (not) interactions between x and y. Then, the 4 kinds of relationships can be described as: 1. $Rec = 0$, $Int = 0$; 2. $Rec = 1$, $Int = 0$; 3. $Rec = 1$, $Int = 1$; 4. $Rec = 0$, $Int = 1$. We analyze them one by one.

1. $Rec = \mathbf{0}$, $Int = \mathbf{0}$. It means there is neither recommendation nor interaction between x and y. So, we should select Uniform distribution (i.e. $Beta(1,1)$), the no-information prior distribution, to be prior distribution of SCP. So, the estimator of SCP is $\widehat{\theta} = 1/2$.

2. $Rec = \mathbf{1}$, $Int = \mathbf{0}$. In this situation, there is an intermediate z between x and y, but no direct interaction between them. If n_1 (n_2) is the number of direct interaction between x and z (z and y), and r_1 (r_2) is the number of successful cooperation, then the estimator of $\widehat{\theta}_{rec}$ is still as (2). Because here are no interaction between x and y, we let $\alpha = \beta = 1$ to estimate $\widehat{\theta}_{int}$. So, the final estimator of SCP is $\widehat{\theta} = a\widehat{\theta}_{rec} + b \times 1/2$.

3. $Rec = \mathbf{1}$, $Int = \mathbf{1}$. Here, there not only has an intermediate entity z but also has direct interactions between x and y. Then, the estimator of SCP is still as (1). But it should be noted that the existence of the intermediate entity z makes x know y well, which will increase the successful cooperation probability between them. So, we should select the parameters α and β to make the Beta prior distribution to be an increasing function with respect to the probability variable θ. Except $\alpha = 1$ or $\beta = 1$, the value of these parameters can be divided into 4 kinds: $\alpha < 1$ and $\beta < 1$; $\alpha > 1$ and $\beta > 1$; $\alpha < 1$ and $\beta > 1$; $\alpha > 1$ and $\beta < 1$. In which, only $\alpha > 1$, $\beta < 1$ satisfy the request. So, the final estimator of SCP is (1) but should be with $\alpha > 1$, $\beta < 1$.

4. $Rec = \mathbf{0}$, $Int = \mathbf{1}$. In this situation, there only has interactions between x and y, so the final estimator of probability is $\widehat{\theta} = \frac{\alpha+r}{\alpha+\beta+n}$. Based on the basic trust BT_x of the entity x, we can select proper parameters in the estimator. For example, if $BT_x > 0.5$, which means that the entity x is an optimist and would like to trust others, then we should choose such two parameters $\alpha > 1, \beta < 1$ that the Beta prior distribution is an increasing function. Similarly, if $BT_x < 0.5$ (or $BT_x = 0.5$), we choose such $\alpha < 1, \beta > 1$ (or $\alpha = \beta = 1$) that the Beta prior distribution is a decreasing function (or uniform).

2.4   Forming a Cooperation System

The obtained estimator of SCP can give instruction for x's future cooperation. For example, the higher the estimator is, the more possible x select y to be its partner in the future.

If we find an increasing function about the estimator to be trust function, the cooperation system of entity x can be formed. For example, suppose $T_x(y) = f(\theta)$, an increasing function about θ, is x's trusting in y. For an entity y, if $T_x(y) > T_0$, y will be added into x's cooperation system. Where, T_0 is trust threshold. After a period of time, there will be a relatively steady system.

3   Conclusion and Future Work

In this paper, we present a Bayesian trust model for web-based systems. This model is easy to master and has statistical basis. In this model, we consider not only objective elements but also subjective elements. At the same time, we classified the situations between x and y into 4 kinds and analyze them respectively. Finally, we try to give a method to find an entity's cooperation system.

In the future, we will perform a detailed simulation evaluation to evaluate the performance of our trust model and to compare it with other models. We will also work at applying our model into the semantic web to address its security issues.

Acknowledgements

The authors gratefully acknowledge the suggestions of the reviewers and the hard work of the AWIC'2005 Program Committee. The authors also gratefully acknowledge the support of the National Natural Science Foundation of China (No.60173059), and the Natural Scientific Research Project of the Education Department of Shaanxi Province in China (No.04JK131).

References

1. T. Grandison and M. Sloman. A survey of trust in internet applications. IEEE Communications Surveys and Tutorials, 4(4):2-16, 2000.
2. A. Jøsang, R. Ismail, and C. Boyd. A Survey of Trust and Reputation Systems for Online Service Provision (to appear). Decision Support Systems, 2005.
3. Jurca, R., Faltings, B., An Incentive Compatible Reputation Mechanism. In Proceedings of the 6th Int. Workshop on Deception Fraud and Trust in Agent Societies (at AAMAS'03). ACM, 2003.
4. Kamvar, S.D., Schlosser, M.T., and Garcia-Molina, H., The EigenTrust Algorithm for Reputation Management in P2P Networks. In proceedings of the 12th International World Wide Web Conference, Budapest, May 2003.

5. Buchegger, S., Le Boudec, J.Y., The Effect of Rumor Spreading in Reputation Systems for Mobile Ad-hoc Networks. In Proceedings of the Workshop on Modeling and Optimization in Mobile, Ad Hoc and Wireless Networks, March 2003.
6. Luhmann, N., Trust and Power. Chichester: John Wiley & Sons. 1982.
7. Beth, T., Borcherding, M. and Klein, B., Valuation of trust in open networks. IN proceedings of the Europesn Symposium on Research in Computer Security, Brighton, UK, 1994. Springer-Verlag.
8. Manchala, D.W., Trust metrics, models and protocols for electronic commerce transactions. In The 18th International Conference on Distributed Computing Systems, page 312, 1998.
9. Jøsang, A., A logic for uncertain probabilities. International Journal of Uncertainty, Fuzziness and Knowledge-Based Systems, 9(3):279-311, 2001.
10. Mui, L., Mohtashemi, M., Ang, C., Szolovits, P. and Halberstadt, A., Ratings in Distributed Systems: A Bayesian Approach. In Proceedings of the Workshop on Information Technologies and Systems (WITS), 2001.
11. Jøsang, A. and Ismail, R., The Beta Reputation System. In Proceedings of the 15th Bled Electronic Commerce Conference, Bled, Slovenia, June 2002.
12. Marsh, S.P.,Formalising Trust as a Computational Concept. PhD thesis, University of Stirling, UK, 1994.
13. Boon, S.D., & Holmes, J.G., The dynamics of interpersonal trust: resolving uncertainty in the face of risk. In: Hinde R.A., & Groebel J.(eds), Cooperation and Prosocial Behaviour. Cambridge University Press. 1991.
14. Stone, C.J., A Course in Probability and Statistics. Wadsworth Publishing Company, 1996.

Automatic Assignment of Wikipedia Encyclopedic Entries to WordNet Synsets*

Maria Ruiz-Casado, Enrique Alfonseca, and Pablo Castells

Computer Science Dep., Universidad Autonoma de Madrid,
28049 Madrid, Spain
{Maria.Ruiz, Enrique.Alfonseca, Pablo.Castells}@uam.es

Abstract. We describe an approach taken for automatically associating entries from an on-line encyclopedia with concepts in an ontology or a lexical semantic network. It has been tested with the Simple English Wikipedia and WordNet, although it can be used with other resources. The accuracy in disambiguating the sense of the encyclopedia entries reaches 91.11% (83.89% for polysemous words). It will be applied to enriching ontologies with encyclopedic knowledge.

1 Introduction

The huge availability of data in the World Wide Web (WWW), and its exponential growth from the past few years, has made the search, retrieval and maintenance of the information a hard and time consuming task, specially when these tasks (or part of them) have to be carried out manually. One of the difficulties that prevents the complete automatising of those processes [1] is the fact that the contents in the WWW are presented mainly in natural language, whose meaning ambiguities are hard to be processed by a machine.

The Semantic Web (SW) appears as an effort to extend the web with machine readable contents and automated services far beyond current capabilities [2]. In order to make explicit the meaning underlaying the data, and therefore processable by a machine, a common practise is the annotation of certain words, pages or other web resources using an ontology. Sometimes, the ontologies have to include a high amount of information, or they undergo a rapid evolution. This would be the case of the automatic annotation of news, where the domain is very vast and changing. Therefore, it would be highly desirable to automatise or semi-automatise the acquisition of the ontologies themselves. This problem has been object of recent increasing interest, and new approaches [3] for automatic ontology enrichment and population are being developed, which combine resources and techniques from Natural Language Processing, Information Extraction, Machine Learning and Text Mining.

Text Data Mining, defined as the problem of finding novel pieces of information inside textual data [4], is a research area motivated in part by the large amounts of text available. When the source for mining is the World Wide Web, Text Mining is

---

* This work has been sponsored by CICYT, project number TIC2002-01948.

P.S. Szczepaniak et al. (Eds.): AWIC 2005, LNAI 3528, pp. 380–386, 2005.

usually called *web mining*. Text and web mining techniques have been used previously for automatically populating ontologies and lexical semantic networks with concepts [5, 6, 7, 8, 3]. In order to construct ontologies semi-automatically, it is necessary to define a similarity metric between concepts that can be used to organise them. A popular procedure is based on the distributional semantics hypothesis, which states that the meaning of two words is highly related to the contexts in which they can appear [9]. In this way, we can assume that the meaning of a word is somehow encoded in the contexts in which we have observed it. A useful formalism for representing contexts is the Vector Space Model [10] (VSM), where a word is described as the bag of the terms which co-occur with it in texts [11, 12] or inside dictionary definitions [13]. There are some possible variations, such as collecting only terms which hold some head-modifier syntactic relationship [14, 15].

Apart from enriching existing ontologies with new concepts, it is also possible to try to discover semi-automatically new relationships between the concepts that already belong to the ontology. To this aim, concept definitions and glosses have been found very useful, as they are usually concise descriptions of the concepts and include the most salient information about them [16]. This has already been applied to the WordNet lexical semantic network [17], which is structured as a directed graph, where nodes represent concepts (called *synsets*, or synonym sets), arcs represent relationships, and each synset is annotated with a gloss. In fact, concept glosses have also been found useful in many other problems, such as Automatic Text Summarisation or Question Answering [18] On the other hand, WordNet glosses have been sometimes criticised, as they do not follow any common pattern and some of them are not very informative. This problem appears, with a higher extent, in the multilingual EuroWordNet [19], where many of the glosses are nonexistent. Therefore, a procedure for automatically extending them would be desirable.

In this paper, we present a procedure for automatically enriching an existing lexical semantic network with on-line encyclopedic information that defines the concepts. The network chosen is WordNet, given that it is currently used in many applications, although the procedure is general enough to be used with other ontologies. The encyclopedia chosen is the Wikipedia, in its Simple English version[1]. The syntactic structures found in Simple English are easier to handle by a parser than those in fully unrestricted text, so the definitions will be easier to process in the future.

2   Procedure

The system built crawls the Simple English Wikipedia collecting definition entries, and associates each entry to a WordNet synset. The processing performed is the following:

1. Retrieve a web page from the encyclopedia.
2. Clean the page from everything except the entry (remove all the menus and navigation links).

---

[1] http://simple.wikipedia.org/wiki/Main_Page

3. Analyse the entry with a part-of-speech tagger and a stemmer [20]. Remove all the closed-class words (everything except nouns, verbs, adjectives and adverbs).
4. Attach the definition to the synset in WordNet that it is defining. We may encounter several cases:

   - There is only one synset in WordNet containing the word described in the entry. This is the case, for instance, of the entry *Abraham Lincoln*. This case is trivial, as the encyclopedia entry can be simply associated with that synset.
   - It may also be the case that the term described in the encyclopedia does not appear in WordNet. In this case, the entry is ignored.
   - Finally, it may happen that there are several synsets in WordNet containing the word described in the entry. In this case, it is necessary to discover which is the correct sense with which the word is used in the entry.

The last case is a classical problem in Natural Language Processing called *Word Sense Disambiguation* [21] (WSD). It generally uses some metric of similarity between the word to disambiguate (in our case, the Wikipedia entry) and each one of the possibilities (the possible WordNet synsets). Different approaches use co-occurrence information [22], all WordNet relationships [23], or just is-a relations (the *hyperonymy* relationship, which relates a concept with others that are more general) [24], with various success rates. Also, some results indicate that WordNet glosses are useful in calculating the semantic similarity [25].

In our problem, we want to find a similarity metric between encyclopedia entries and WordNet synsets. If they refer to the same concept, we can expect that there will be much in common between the two definitions. This is the reason why the approach followed is mainly a comparison between the two glosses:

1. Represent the Wikipedia entry as a vector e using the Vector Space Model, where each dimension corresponds to a word, and the coordinate for that dimension is the frequency of the word in the entry.
2. Let $S = \{s_1, s_2, ..., s_n\}$ be the set of WordNet synsets containing the term defined in the Wikipedia entry.
3. Represent each synset s_i as the set of words in its gloss: $G_i = \{t_1, t_2, ..., t_{k_i}\}$.
4. Let $N = 1$
5. Extend the sets G_i with the synonym words in each synset s_i and its hyperonyms to a depth of N levels.
6. Weight each term t in every set G_i by comparing it with the glosses for the other senses. In this way, a numerical vector v_i, containing the term weights, is calculated for each G_i. In the experiments, two weight functions have been tried: tf·idf and χ^2 [22].
7. Choose the sense such that the similarity between e and v_i is the largest. Two similarity metrics between the two vectors have been tested: the dot product [26, pg. 18] and the cosine. If there is a tie between two or more senses, increment N and go back to step 5.

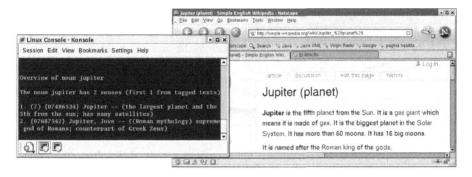

Fig. 1. Entry for *Jupiter (planet)* in the Wikipedia, and WordNet glosses for the synsets that contain the term *Jupiter*

3 Evaluation

The algorithm has been evaluated with a sample of the Simple English Wikipedia entries, as available on November 15, 2004. The version of WordNet used is 1.7. From 1841 Wikipedia terms, 612 did not appear in WordNet, 631 were found in WordNet with only one possible sense (they are monosemous) and 598 Wikipedia terms were found in WordNet with more than one sense (they are polysemous). Figure 1 shows an example of a polysemous term. The following evaluations have been performed:

3.1 Evaluation Procedure

Monosemous terms For these terms, the algorithm just associates each Wikipedia entry with the only WordNet synset containing it. A sample, containing the first 180 monosemous terms from Wikipedia, has been manually evaluated, to check whether this assignment is correct.

Polysemous terms In this case, for each Wikipedia entry there were several candidate senses in WordNet, one of which will be chosen by the algorithm. A sample with the first 180 polysemous terms from Wikipedia was manually annotated with the correct sense[2]. In a few cases, the Wikipedia entry included several senses at the same time, because either (a) the wikipedia contained two different definitions in the same entry, or (b) the WordNet senses were so fine-grained that they could be considered the same sense. Regarding this last point, some authors have proposed a previous clustering of the WordNet senses before attempting WSD, to reduce the fine granularity [27]. In these cases, all the right senses are annotated, so the algorithm will be considered correct if it chooses one of them.

The following baseline experiments and configurations have been tested:

---

[2] The tagged dataset is available under request at maria.ruiz@uam.es

Table 1. Results obtained for the disambiguation. The first row shows the results only for the polysemous words, and the second one shows the results for all entries in the Wikipedia for which there is at least one synset in WordNet containing the term. The first two columns are the baselines, the third column shows Lesk's algorithm results, and the other eight columns contain the results of the eight configurations tested in our approach

	Baselines			Our approach							
				Dot product				Cosine			
				Stemming		No stemming		Stemming		No stemming	
	Random	SEMCOR	Lesk	tf·idf	χ^2	tf·idf	χ^2	tf·idf	χ^2	tf·idf	χ^2
Polysem.	40.10	65.56	72.78	**83.89**	80.56	77.78	77.78	80.56	81.11	78.33	76.67
All	69.22	81.95	85.56	**91.11**	89.45	88.06	88.06	89.45	89.72	88.33	87.50

- The first baseline consists of a random assignment.
- The second baseline chooses the most common sense of the word in the sense-tagged SEMCOR corpus. This is a set of texts in which every word has been manually annotated with the sense with which it is used, and it can be used to find which is the most common sense of a word in a general text.
- Thirdly, we have implemented Lesk's WSD algorithm [28]. Before applying it, words have been stemmed. Ties between several senses are resolved by choosing SEMCOR's most common sense.
- Our procedure has been tested with three possible variations: two choices for the weight function (tf·idf and χ^2), two possible similarity metrics (cosine and dot product), and either stemming or using the lexical form of the words.

3.2   Results

With respect to the monosemous terms, 177 out of the 180 assignments were correct, which means an accuracy of 98.33%. Only in three cases the concept defined by the Wikipedia entry was different to the WordNet sense that contained the same term.

Table 1 summarises the accuracy of the different tests for the polysemous terms and for all terms (monosemous and polysemous). These are consistently better than other results reported in WSD, something which may be attributed to the fact that we are comparing two definitions which are supposed to be similar, rather than comparing a definition with an appearance of a term in a generic text. As can be seen, stemming always improves the results; the best score (83.89%) is statistically significantly higher than any of the scores obtained without stemming at 95% confidence. In many cases, also, tf·idf is better than the χ^2 weight function. Regarding the distance metric, the dot product provides the best result overall, although it does not outperform the cosine in all the configurations.

4   Conclusions and Future Work

In this work we propose a procedure for automatically extending an existing ontology or lexical semantic network with encyclopedic definitions obtained from the web. The approach has been tested with WordNet 1.7 and the Simple English Wikipedia, an Internet encyclopedia built in a collaborative way. We have shown that, for this task, it is possible to reach accuracy rates as high as 91% (83.89% for polysemous words). Interestingly, this result is much higher than the current state-of-the-art for general Word Sense Disambiguation of words inside a text (a more difficult problem), and it shows that current techniques can be applied successfully for automatic disambiguation of encyclopedia entries. We consider this task as a stage previous to knowledge acquisition from a combination of ontologies and encyclopedic knowledge, and opens the following research lines:

1. Analyse the entries that we have associated to WordNet synsets, in order to extract automatically relationships from them, such as *location, instrument, telic* (purpose) or *author*.
2. Generalise the experiment to other ontologies and encyclopedias, and see whether this technique can also be applied to other kinds of texts.
3. Concerning the Wikipedia entries which were not found in WordNet, it would be interesting to explore ways to semi-automatically extend the lexical network with these new terms [5, 6, 8].
4. In the few cases where an entry refers to several synsets in WordNet, divide it distinguishing which fragments of the entry refer to each possible sense.

References

[1] Ding, Y., Fensel, D., Klein, M.C.A., Omelayenko, B.: The semantic web: yet another hip? Data Knowledge Engineering **41** (2002) 205–227
[2] Berners-Lee, T., Hendler, J., Lassila, O.: The semantic web - a new form of web content that is meaningful to computers will unleash a revolution of new possibilities. Scientific American **284** (2001) 34–43
[3] Gómez-Pérez, A., Macho, D.M., Alfonseca, E., nez, R.N., Blascoe, I., Staab, S., Corcho, O., Ding, Y., Paralic, J., Troncy, R.: Ontoweb deliverable 1.5: A survey of ontology learning methods and techniques (2003)
[4] Hearst, M.A. The Oxford Handbook of Computational Linguistics. In: Text Data Mining. Oxford University Press (2003) 616–628
[5] Rigau, G.: Automatic Acquisition of Lexical Knowledge from MRDs. PhD Thesis, Departament de Llenguatges i Sistemes Informàtics, Universitat Politècnica de Catalunya (1998)
[6] Hearst, M.A. In: Automated Discovery of WordNet Relations. In Christiane Fellbaum (Ed.) WordNet: An Electronic Lexical Database. MIT Press (1998) 132–152
[7] Agirre, E., Ansa, O., Martínez, D., Hovy, E.: Enriching wordnet concepts with topic signatures. In: Proceedings of the NAACL workshop on WordNet and Other lexical Resources: Applications, Extensions and Customizations, Pittsburg (2001)
[8] Alfonseca, E., Manandhar, S.: Extending a lexical ontology by a combination of distributional semantics signatures. In: Knowledge Engineering and Knowledge Management. Volume 2473 of Lecture Notes in Artificial Intelligence. Springer Verlag (2002) 1–7

[9] Firth, J.: A synopsys of linguistic theory 1930-1955. In F. Palmer (ed.), Selected Papers of J. R. Firth. Longman, London (1957)

[10] Salton, G.: Automatic text processing. Addison-Wesley (1989)

[11] Church, K., Gale, W., Hanks, P., Hindle, D.: 6. In: Using Statistics in Lexical Analysis. In U. Zernik (ed.), Lexical Acquisition: Exploiting On-line Resources to Build a Lexicon. Lawrence Erlbaum Associates, Hillsdale, New Jersey (1991) 115–164

[12] Lin, C.Y.: Robust Automated Topic Identification. Ph.D. Thesis. University of Southern California (1997)

[13] Wilks, Y., Fass, D.C., Guo, C.M., McDonald, J.E., Plate, T., Slator, B.M.: Providing machine tractable dictionary tools. Journal of Computers and Translation (1990)

[14] Lee, L.: Similarity-Based Approaches to Natural Language Processing. Ph.D. thesis. Harvard University Technical Report TR-11-97 (1997)

[15] Faure, D., Nédellec, C.: A corpus-based conceptual clustering method for verb frames and ontology acquisition. In: LREC workshop on Adapting lexical and corpus resources to sublanguages and applications, Granada, Spain (1998)

[16] Harabagiu, S., Moldovan, D.I.: Knowledge processing. In: WordNet: An Electronic Lexical Database. MIT Press (1998) 379–405

[17] Miller, G.A.: WordNet: A lexical database for English. Communications of the ACM **38** (1995) 39–41

[18] Rus, V.: Logic Form For WordNet Glosses and Application to Question Answering. Ph.D. thesis. Computer Science Department, Southern Methodist University (2002)

[19] Vossen, P.: EuroWordNet - A Multilingual Database with Lexical Semantic Networks. Kluwer Academic Publishers (1998)

[20] Alfonseca, E.: Wraetlic user guide version 1.0 (2003)

[21] Ide, N., Véronis, J.: Introduction to the special issue on word sense disambiguation: the state of the art. Computational Linguistics **24** (1998) 1–40

[22] Manning, C.D., Schütze, H.: Foundations of statistical Natural Language Processing. MIT Press (2001)

[23] Hirst, G., St-Onge, D.: Lexical chains as representations of context for the detection and correction of malapropisms. In: WordNet: an electronic lexical database. MIT Press (1998)

[24] Resnik, P.K.: Disambiguating noun groupings with respect to wordnet senses. In: Proceedings of the Third Workshop on Very Large Corpora, Somerset, ACL (1995) 54–68

[25] Mihalcea, R., Moldovan, D.: A method for word sense disambiguation of unrestricted text. In: Proceedings of ACL'99, Maryland, NY (1999)

[26] Kilgarriff, A., Rosenzweig, J.: Framework and results for english SENSEVAL. Computer and the Humanities (2000) 15–48

[27] Agirre, E., de Lacalle, O.L.: Clustering wordnet word senses. In: Recent Advances in Natural Language Processing III. (2004)

[28] Lesk, M.: Automatic sense disambiguation using machine readable dictionaries. In: Proceedings of the 5th International Conference on Systems Documentation. (1986) 24–26

Using Existing Website Ontologies to Assist Navigation and Exploration

Guy Saward, Mahmood Shah, and Tracy Hall

School of Computer Science,
University of Hertfordshire College Lane,
Hatfield, AL10 9AB, UK
{g.r.saward, m.1.shah, t.hall}@herts.ac.uk

Abstract. Success in navigating websites is highly related to the structure of sites, which may be described by an ontology or classification. We present the *naviguidance* method, which exploits this structure in browsing and searching to improve usability, and three case studies where *naviguidance* has been applied to real Internet information systems.

1 Introduction

The problem of information overload is widely recognized and reported, as are its extreme manifestation as "web" or "search rage" [1].Many approaches exist to understand and solve this problem including novel visualizations, improved relevance algorithms, web log mining, and personalization. More recently the semantic web project addresses it by enriching the structure of information.

Rather than creating additional structure, in this paper we describe a method for using the structure already present in web sites to aid user navigation, exploration and learning. Called *naviguidance*, it uses an initial search to guide users to the most relevant information, similar to work by Olston and Chi [2]. In contrast to Olston and Chi, we focus on the explicit browsable navigation structure (rather than individual page links) as a way of identifying and highlighting the most relevant navigation choices.

Our work focuses on new information retrieval methods and interface designs through the synthesis of existing models, and their application in a number of Internet Information Systems (IIS) domains including websites, digital libraries and intranets. Section 2 presents related work while section 3 describes the generic *naviguidance* method and architecture. Section 4 contains case studies of specific *naviguidance* implementations before we conclude in section 5.

2 Related Work

Our work builds on widely used models of information retrieval and system acceptance. The first provides tools for investigating how users navigate complex

P.S. Szczepaniak et al. (Eds.): AWIC 2005, LNAI 3528, pp. 387–393, 2005.

information sources like websites, while the second provides insight into what makes users adopt or revisit particular sites. This is particularly important in the Internet's open market where many alternative providers may supply particular information, products or services.

The Role of Navigation in System Acceptance. The Technology Acceptance Model (TAM) [3, 4] highlights the importance of effective navigation. TAM predicts that users only use systems they both perceive to be easy to use (PEU) and perceive to be useful (PU). Therefore, effective navigation systems not only need to make a system easy to use, they need to demonstrate the usefulness of the system.

Navigation Issues. The problems of current information retrieval methods are well known [2] and usually center on two key issues: difficulties in interpreting browsable options correctly, and difficulties in specifying searches effectively.

Difficulty in browsing arises when there is no clear perceived match between a site and a task [5] and users get lost. Exploration can improve task/site match but may require too much effort. Search difficulties come from limited user input and a focus on a small subset of results. Over-precise queries return too few results [7] and limited PU, while imprecise queries generate too many options to review and low PEU.

Ontologies and Navigation. Ontologies are a key component of the semantic web. Although rich ontologies support data exchange or reasoning [8], query expansion and complex visualization, we are interested in a pragmatic interpretation of website structure or classification schemes as ontologies [9] to support simple visualization.

3   Naviguidance

The objectives of *naviguidance* are to assist and encourage exploration of IIS. The former should impact the Perceived Ease of Use (PEU), as defined by TAM, while the latter should promote understanding of the breadth of site content, thereby increasing Perceived Usefulness (PU). This should improve users' attitudes to using the system and increase overall site usage. Our approach is based on the following principles derived from our IIS design experience, e.g. [10].

Naviguidance uses the site ontology in: filtering search results to increase search effectiveness; and directing users in browsing. This aids the interpretation

Table 1. Principles for the design of navigation methods

Browse Principles	Search Principles
Give user full control of browsing	Exploit "good enough" search results
Show whole taxonomy when browsing	Specify search context via categories
Re-use existing static structure	Specify context after search
Explore structure from the top	Support more general queries

of browse labels as well as reducing the need to specify searches so exactly. This is done by using an existing site search engine to highlight the parts of the site ontology that contain items relevant to a particular query. The method is described with reference to an abstract architecture (Fig.1).

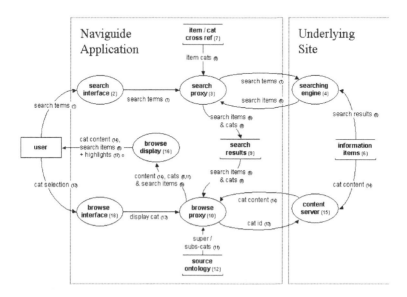

Fig. 1. A logical view of the *naviguidance* architecture

Naviguidance has the following steps [(n) refers to items in Fig. 1]:

1. The user executes a search (1) using the naviguide search interface (2).
2. A proxy search service (3) passes the query to the site search engine (4).
3. Search results (5) are selected from available items (6) and returned to the proxy.
4. The proxy cross-references the results with the site ontology (7) and the results with their associated categories (8) are stored (9).
5. A browse proxy (10) extracts sub/super-categories (11) from the taxonomy (12) .
6. In parallel, the browse proxy uses the current location in the site (13) to retrieve the basic content (14) to display from the site's content server (15).
7. A display process (16) determines which search results to show and categories to highlight (17) in the browsable content displayed to the user.
8. Browsing a new category in display (18) updates it content via steps 5 to 7.

As the user browses through the site ontology, the browse proxy in conjunction with the display process fetches the content to display and uses the site ontology to keep relevant categories highlighted. In addition, the search results will be continually filtered to show the search results related to the current category. In this way, the naviguide process continually highlights the parts of the site where search results are located, thereby guiding users in their browsing to the most relevant parts of the site. Crucially, highlighting is done within the current site design, rather than as a separate element [11], using an existing structure rather than a dynamic clustering.

4   Case Studies

Naviguidance has been implemented for a variety of systems including the Open Directory Project, a grocery e-commerce site and telephone directory. Three applications are described here to show *naviguidance* can be implemented using a variety of technologies and architectures for both the *naviguidance* application and underlying system. In addition, it shows *naviguidance* applied to a variety of different ontologies that are displayed in a number of different ways. The first two studies use an Apache / Tomcat / Java proxy server architecture. The third uses client-side Javascript.

Fig. 2. (a). Navigation bar for GA system showing highlights for "maternity pay" query. (b). Navigation bar for MR system showing highlights for "pushchair" query

Case Study 1: A Global Airline (GA). This study used GA's Lotus Notes intranet. GA wished to assess the effectiveness of previous design changes to the site structure, and to assess the feasibility enhancing the existing search engine. This gave us the opportunity to build an add-on *naviguidance* system and to evaluate it alongside the current GA system [12]. The system included basic category highlighting and filtering of search results as described above. In addition item counts were shown for each category and users could also choose to exclude certain categories of results.

The site ontology is displayed as a collection of links in a navigation bar (see Fig.2a) with a single level shown at a time. The current location in the ontology is shown as a breadcrumb trail. Recommendations for browsing the ontology are generated using a Lotus Notes search and highlighted in a contrasting text style and arrowhead images, although the user (as with any *naviguidance* system) is free to browse whichever category they choose given all the available options are shown at all times.

Case Study 2: A Multiple Retailer (MR). This study used the e-commerce site of a Multiple Retailer (MR) developed using Java, JSP and Oracle to sell over 30,000 health, beauty and related products. A review of recent changes to the site gave us the opportunity to evaluate the need for, and effectiveness of *naviguidance* [13].

The architecture for MR followed the GA study but the presentation of the site ontology was different. The MR site used up to three nested navigation bars on the left of the screen to provide backtracking to previously seen category, a pop-up look ahead menu to select lower levels in the ontology, and a bread crumb trail showing the current location. Fig. 2b shows a two level display for the "Baby" category.

The *naviguidance* for MR was a simplified version of the GA system and did not include category item counts or category exclusion filters. Highlighting of recommended browse categories in both the navigation bars and pop-up menus was done with a contrasting text style and a prefixed ">" character in the category name.

Case Study 3: A Naviguidable OPAC (NaviCat). This study uses the online public access catalogue (OPAC) of a library system. The OPAC provides access to items including books, journals and electronic journals. The study is part of an investigation of the factors driving the use of competing information sources such as subject specific portals and Internet search engines. In particular we wish to evaluate if improved subject based searching and browsing can promote the use of high quality academic sources. NaviCat has just been developed and is about to be evaluated.

NaviCat uses a frameset (see Fig. 3) to display the standard OPAC content alongside the site ontology, which uses Dewey classification. The ontology is shown as an expandable directory tree that can be expanded or collapsed as needed. This allows users to explicitly browse the implicit ontology. Search results and classes are taken from the OPAC page and used to select the categories to highlight. The highlighting uses the same style as the GA system. Clicking on a specific category removes unrelated search results from the OPAC display. For example, clicking on "Management & PR" in Fig. 3 removes the third search result (related to law) and 24 other results not related to e-commerce (the query used) and management (the category selected).

5   Findings

Our findings relate to the ability to implement a *naviguidance* system for existing IIS, and to the effectiveness of *naviguidance* in improving the use of IIS. The case studies show the *naviguidance* can be built on top of a variety of existing systems that have a search engine, a browsable structure, and a means of cross referencing the two.

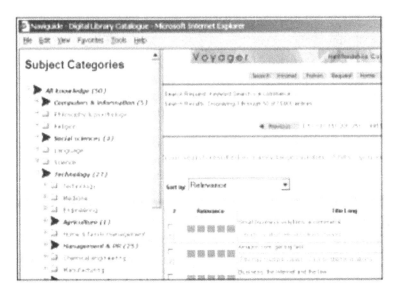

Fig. 3. The NaviCat interface showing site ontology (on left) and standard OPAC search results (on right). Highlighted ontology categories show the classification or location of search results

Naviguidance's impact on system use was assessed through individual user analysis (with 54 subjects) of the GA and MR systems. These show a positive user attitude towards *naviguidance*. After improving search relevance, this was rated the most useful development ahead of: limiting search by topic; increasing results detail; and increasing the number of search results shown. This implies that users want fewer, more relevant search results and that *naviguidance* is useful way of achieving this.

Although 60% of users thought *naviguidance* would help find information more quickly, this is not proved. No *significant* difference was found using task measures such as speed, completion rate or ease. However, ease of use was significantly correlated with knowledge or expectation of where items were located in the ontology.

Furthermore users who were more successful in browsing the site were more successful in acquiring this knowledge. The result is a virtuous circle where more browsing leads to more *successful* browsing. By encouraging users to engage with a site's ontology, *naviguidance* does appear to have a role in successfully promoting the use of particular sites. A long-term trial of NaviCat provides the opportunity to test this.

References

[1]   D. Sullivan, "WebTop Search Rage Study," The Search Engine Report, February 5, 2001.
[2]   C. Olston and E. H. Chi, "ScentTrails: Integrating Browsing and Searching on the Web," ACM Transactions on Computer-Human Interaction, vol. 10, pp. 177-197, 2003.

[3]   F. D. Davis, "Perceived Usefulness, Perceived Ease of Use, and User Acceptance of Information Technology," MIS Quarterly, vol. 13, pp. 318-341, 1989.

[4]   H. v. d. Heijden, "e-Tam: A revision of the Technology Acceptance Model to explain revisits," Vrije Universiteit, Amsterdam Research Memorandum 2000-29, 2000.

[5]   M. A. Katz and M. D. Byrne, "Effects of Scent and Breadth on Use of Site-Specific Search on E-Commerce Web Sites," ACM Trans. on CHI, vol. 10, pp. 198-220, 2003.

[6]   B. J. Rhodes and P. Maes, "Just-in-time information retrieval agents," IBM Systems Journal, vol. 39, 2000.

[7]   H. Stelmaszewska and A. Blandford, "Patterns of interactions: user behaviour in response to search results," presented at JCDL Workshop on Usability, 2002.

[8]   C. Brewster and K. O'Hara, "Knowledge representation with ontologies: the present and future," IEEE Intelligent Systems, vol. 19, pp. 72-81, 2004.

[9]   D. Fensel, D. L. McGuiness, E. Schulten, W. K. Ng;, G. P. Lim;, and G. Yan;, "Ontologies and electronic commerce," IEEE Intelligent Systems, vol. 16, pp. 8-14, 2001.

[10]   G. Saward, "Navigating Heterogeneous Knowledge Sources in a Customer Service Environment," in Internet-Based Organizational Memory and KM, Idea Group, 2000.

[11]   B. Richard, P. Tchounikine, and P. Jacoboni, "An architecture to support navigation and propose tips within a dedicated Web site," 1st Int'l Atlantic Web Intelligence Conf, 2003.

[12]   G. Saward, T. Barker, and T. Hall, "Changing Designs for Internet Information System Navigation, Usability and Acceptance," Uni. of Hertfordshire Tech Report, 2004.

[13]   G. Saward, T. Hall, and T. Barker, "Information Scent as a Measure of Usability," presented at 10th International Software Metrics Symposium, Chicago, 2004.

Fuzzy Constraint Based Answer Validation

Steven Schockaert, Martine De Cock, and Etienne E. Kerre

Ghent University, Department of Applied Mathematics and Computer Science,
Fuzziness and Uncertainty Research Unit,
Krijgslaan 281 - S9, B-9000 Gent, Belgium
{Steven.Schockaert, Martine.DeCock, Etienne.Kerre}@ugent.be

Abstract. Answer validation is an important component of any question answering system. In this paper we show how the formalism of prioritized fuzzy constraint satisfaction allows to unify and generalize some common validation strategies. Moreover, answer candidates are represented by fuzzy sets, which allows to handle imprecise answers.

1 Introduction

Question answering systems try to improve the functionality of search engines by providing an exact answer to a user's question, rather than a list of documents. A typical question answering system consists of a question analysis module, a search engine, an answer extraction module and an answer validation module. At least two fundamentally different ways to handle answer validation are used by current systems. Corpus–based methods (e.g. [5]) rely on a deep linguistic analysis of the question and the answer candidates, while redundancy–based methods (e.g. [2],[3],[6]) rely on the massive amount of information available on the web. This paper will focus on the latter kind of methods.

Since it is reasonable to assume that on the web, the answer to most questions is stated in a lot of documents, we can assume that there will be documents in which the answer is formulated in a simple way. As a consequence, simple answer extraction algorithms often suffice. However, simplicity comes with a price; a lot of web pages contain incorrect information, so the answer validation process used in corpus–based methods is not appropriate. Most redundancy–based methods apply some kind of voting: the answer which occurs most often is considered the most likely answer to be correct. This approach has the disadvantage of favouring short, unspecific, answers (e.g. "1928" over "July 26, 1928"). Some systems (e.g. [2],[6]) therefore apply heuristics to boost the scores of specific answers. These heuristics would treat an occurrence of "1928" as evidence for "July 26, 1928" which, in our opinion, is not a fully satisfactory approach.

In this paper we propose an alternative voting scheme, which separates positive and negative information about the feasibility of the answer candidates. To this end, we represent answer candidates as fuzzy sets and define a degree of inconsistency and a degree of inclusion between answer candidates. We show how this scheme can be further refined by asking additional questions and enforcing fuzzy constraints on the results.

P.S. Szczepaniak et al. (Eds.): AWIC 2005, LNAI 3528, pp. 394–400, 2005.

2   Answer Comparison

Let's consider the question "When was the Mona Lisa painted?". When examining the first few snippets returned by Google[1] for this question, we find answers like "the 1500s", "1506", "1503–1506", ... It is clear that simple string equality won't yield very good results in this case. Instead we will represent each answer as a fuzzy set in a suitable universe which enables us to handle differences in granularity (e.g. "July 26, 1928" vs. "1928"), intervals (e.g. "1503–1506", "the 1920s") and vague descriptions (e.g. "the late 1920s", "around 1930").

Recall that a fuzzy set A on a universe U is a mapping from U to the unit interval $[0, 1]$. If $A(u) = 1$ for some u in U, A is called normalised. To generalize the logical conjunction to the unit interval $[0, 1]$, we have a large class of $[0, 1]^2 - [0, 1]$ mappings, called t-norms at our disposal. Likewise, logical implication can be generalized by a class of $[0, 1]^2 - [0, 1]$ mappings called implicators. For further details on t-norms and implicators we refer to [8].

Let a_1 and a_2 be two fuzzy sets in the universe $\mathcal{D}$ of dates, the degree of inclusion $incl(a_1, a_2)$ and the degree of contradiction $contr(a_1, a_2)$ between a_1 and a_2 can be given by

$$incl(a_1, a_2) = \inf_{u \in \mathcal{D}} I(a_1(u), a_2(u)) \qquad contr(a_1, a_2) = 1 - \sup_{u \in \mathcal{D}} T(a_1(u), a_2(u))$$

where I is an implicator and T is a t-norm. In our implementation we used the Lukasiewicz implicator I_W defined by $I_W(x, y) = \min(1, 1 - x + y)$ and the t-norm T_M defined by $T_M(x, y) = \min(x, y)$ for x and y in $[0, 1]$. For each answer candidate a we can define the degree $pos(a)$ to which this answer is confirmed by the other candidates and the degree $neg(a)$ to which this answer is inconsistent with the other candidates:

$$pos(a) = \frac{1}{n} \sum_{i=1}^{n} incl(a_i, a) \qquad neg(a) = \frac{1}{n} \sum_{i=1}^{n} contr(a_i, a)$$

where $(a_1, a_2, \ldots, a_n)$ is the list of all answer candidates ($a_i = a_j$ may hold for some $i \neq j$, i.e. an answer candidate can occur several times). We interpret $pos(a)$ as the degree of feasibility of an answer candidate and $neg(a)$ as the degree of inconsistency, where $pos(a) = 1 - neg(a)$ doesn't hold in general. If I is a border implicator and all answer candidates are normalised then $pos(a) + neg(a) \leq 1$ holds. As a consequence, the set of answer candidates can be represented by an intuitionistic fuzzy set [1].

3   Refining the Answer Scores

Asking additional questions Prager et al. [9] introduced the idea to (automatically) ask additional questions in order to estimate the feasibility of an answer

---
[1] http://www.google.com

candidate. To answer the question "When did Leonardo da Vinci paint the Mona Lisa?", Prager et al. suggest to ask the additional questions "When was Leonardo da Vinci born?" and "When did Leonardo da Vinci die", which gives us the variables X_{work}, X_{born} and X_{died}. The possible instantiations of these variables are the answer candidates of the corresponding questions. All answer triplets that do not satisfy the following constraints[2] are rejected in [9]:

$$X_{born} + 7 \leq X_{died} \leq X_{born} + 100 \tag{1}$$
$$X_{work} \leq X_{died} \leq X_{work} + 100 \tag{2}$$
$$X_{born} + 7 \leq X_{work} \leq X_{born} + 100 \tag{3}$$

The use of crisp constraints has the disadvantage that a lot of world knowledge can not be expressed. For example, by using this kind of rather arbitrary threshold values, we can not express that it is more likely that someone became 70 years old than that someone became 8 years old. Another problem with this approach is how to combine the frequency counts of the answer candidates of the three variables X_{work}, X_{born} and X_{died}. In this section we show how both problems can be solved by using prioritized fuzzy constraints.

Prioritized fuzzy constraint satisfaction Let X_1, X_2, ..., X_n be variables taking values in the finite domains D_1, D_2, ..., D_n respectively. A fuzzy constraint c is a mapping from $D_1 \times D_2 \times ... \times D_n$ to the unit interval $[0, 1]$. For a constraint c and an instantiation $(x_1, x_2, ..., x_n) \in D_1 \times D_2 \times ... \times D_n$ of the variables, $c(x_1, x_2, ..., x_n)$ is interpreted as the degree to which the constraint c is satisfied by this instantiation. In [4] the notion of prioritized fuzzy constraint is introduced by assigning a priority to each constraint, which can be interpreted as the degree of importance of the constraint. Let α_i in $[0, 1]$ be the priority of constraint c_i ($i \in \{1, 2, ..., m\}$), the degree of joint satisfaction of the constraints $c_1, c_2, ..., c_m$ by an instantiation $(x_1, x_2, ..., x_n)$ can then be defined by [7]:

$$C(x_1, x_2, ..., x_n) = \prod_{i=1}^{m} P(\alpha_i, c_i(x_1, x_2, ..., x_n)) \tag{4}$$

where P is $[0, 1]^2 - [0, 1]$ mapping called a priority operator. It is easy to see that the notion of a priority operator as defined in [7] corresponds to that of a border implicator.

Constructing the fuzzy constraints As a fuzzification of inequality (1) for example, we used the fuzzy constraint c_1 defined by

$$c_1(x_b, x_d) = incl(x_d \ominus_T x_b, f) \tag{5}$$

where (x_b, x_d) is an instantiation of (X_{born}, X_{died}); x_b and x_d are fuzzy sets in the universe of dates $\mathcal{D}$. According to the extension principle of Zadeh [10], $x_d \ominus x_b$ is the fuzzy set in the universe of real numbers $\mathbb{R}$ defined for d in $\mathbb{R}$ by

---

[2] Prager et al. [9] consider only crisp answer candidates, corresponding to a year.

$$(x_d \ominus_T x_b)(d) = \sup_{d_1 - d_2 = d} T(x_d(d_1), x_b(d_2)) \tag{6}$$

where T is a t-norm. The result of the date subtraction $d_1 - d_2$ is treated as a real number respresenting the number of years between the date d_1 and the date d_2. The fuzzy set f in the universe $\mathbb{R}$ reflects life expectation expressed in years and is defined for d in $\mathbb{R}$ by

$$f(d) = \begin{cases} \frac{d}{30} & \text{if } 0 \leq d \leq 30 \\ 1 & \text{if } 30 \leq d \leq 90 \\ \frac{120-d}{30} & \text{if } 90 \leq d \leq 120 \\ 0 & \text{otherwise} \end{cases} \tag{7}$$

Fuzzification of (2) and (3) can be treated analogously. The priority of each of these fuzzy constraints is 1.

For a variable X, corresponding to a question with answer candidates x_1, $x_2, \ldots, x_n$, we can impose the unary constraint c_X, defined for each answer candidate x by[3]

$$c_X(x) = \frac{1 - neg(x)}{1 - neg(a^*)} \tag{8}$$

where $neg(a^*) = \inf_{a \in \mathcal{A}} neg(a)$ and $\mathcal{A}$ is the set of all answer candidates. The priority of this constraint can be interpreted as the reliability of the frequency count. In other words, if the number of answer candidates is high (resp. low) the priority should be high (resp. low) too. A possible definition of the priority α_X of the constraint c_X is given by $\alpha_X = \frac{n}{n+K}$ where n is the number of (not necessarily distinct) answer candidates as before, and $K > 0$ is a constant.

Yet another type of fuzzy constraints that can be imposed is based on co-occurrence. Consider the question "When was the Mona Lisa painted". In this case there is a fourth variable X_{pers} representing the painter of the Mona Lisa. If x_w is an answer candidate for the date that some person x_p painted the Mona Lisa, then we can assume that a lot of the sentences containing a date that is entailed by x_w in a set of documents about the "Mona Lisa" should contain a reference to x_p. We can express this by enforcing the constraint c_{assoc}, defined by

$$c_{assoc}(x_w, x_p) = \frac{assoc(x_w, x_p)}{\sup_{(x^W, x^P)} assoc(x^W, x^P)} \tag{9}$$

where the supremum in (9) is taken over all possible instantiations (x^W, x^P) of (X_W, X_P) and $assoc(x_w, x_p)$ measures the extent to which sentences containing a date that is entailed by x_w tend to contain a reference to x_p.

---

[3] We will consider only constraints that are normalised (i.e. constraints for which there exists at least one possible instantiation that fully satisfies the constraint).

Putting the pieces together Let $\{c_1, c_2, \ldots, c_m\}$ be the set of all considered constraints and let $X_1, X_2, \ldots, X_n$ be the variables that are considered relevant to the user's question. The degree $neg_C(x_1, x_2, \ldots, x_n)$ of infeasibility of an answer tuple $(x_1, x_2, \ldots, x_n)$ is then given by

$$neg_C(x_1, x_2, \ldots, x_n) = 1 - C(x_1, x_2, \ldots, x_n) \qquad (10)$$

where C is defined as in (4). For notational simplicity we use $c(x_1, x_2, \ldots, x_n)$ even when the constraint c doesn't refer to all x_i $(1 \le i \le n)$. The degree of feasibility $pos_C(x_1, x_2, \ldots, x_n)$ of an answer tuple $(x_1, x_2, \ldots, x_n)$ is defined by

$$pos_C(x_1, x_2, \ldots, x_n) = \prod_{i=1}^{n} pos(x_i) \qquad (11)$$

4   Experimental Results

To implement the ideas presented in this paper we extracted answer candidates using a simple pattern matching algorithm. Given the title of some work of art, possible creation dates and possible creators along with their birthdate and death date, are extracted from the snippets returned by Google for some (automatically generated) queries. Generic patterns to extract the entities of interest were constructed by hand. Table 1 shows some of the creators and creation dates that are found for the "Mona Lisa" together with their frequency of occurrence. Simply counting the frequency of occurrence of each answer candidate gives good results for determining the creator in this example; the creation date however is more problematic. In fact there exist several opinions about when the "Mona Lisa" was painted, but most agree it must have been between 1503 and 1506. For each potential creator our algorithm tries to discover the date this person was born and the date this person died. Using this information $pos_C(x_w, x_b, x_d, x_p)$ and $neg_C(x_w, x_b, x_d, x_p)$ are calculated for each instantiation (x_w, x_b, x_d, x_p) of the variables X_{work}, X_{born}, X_{died} and X_{pers}. The answer tuples $\overline{x}$ (i.e. the instantiations of the variables) are ranked using the product of $pos_C(\overline{x})$ and $1 - neg_C(\overline{x})$; the results are shown in table 2. We omit answer tuples that are entailed by another answer tuple that is ranked higher.

Table 1. Frequency counts for the creator and creation date of the "Mona Lisa"

Creator	Frequency	Creation date	Frequency
Leonardo da Vinci	18	1506	6
Leonardo	8	1950	5
Slick Rick	6	1503	2
Everybody	6	between 1503 and 1506	2
Leonardo Da Vinci	6	early 1500s	1
Nick Pretzlik	2	between 1503 and 1507	1
Fernando Botero	2	1502	1

Table 2. Top candidates of our algorithm for the "Mona Lisa"

Creator	Creation date	Score
Leonardo da Vinci (1452 – 1519)	between 1503 and 1507	(0.038,0.460)
Leonardo (1452 – 1519)	between 1503 and 1507	(0.029,0.564)
Leonardo da Vinci (1452 – 1519)	early 1500s	(0.019,0.562)
Leonardo (1452 – 1519)	early 1500s	(0.014,0.607)

5   Conclusions

In this paper we have shown how the formalism of prioritized fuzzy constraints allows to unify and generalize three approaches to estimate the feasibility of an answer candidate: frequency counts (e.g. Eq. (8)), co-occurrence statistics (e.g. Eq. (9)) and asking additional questions (e.g. Eq. (5)). The usefulness of representing answer candidates by fuzzy sets was illustrated by considering the problem of searching the creation date of a work of art, which in practice is often stated by means of an interval or a fuzzy description instead of an exact date.

Acknowledgements

Steven Schockaert and Martine De Cock would like to thank the Fund for Scientific Research – Flanders for funding their research.

References

1. Atanassov, K.T.: Intuitionistic fuzzy sets. Fuzzy Sets and Systems **20** (1986) 87–96
2. Brill, E., Lin, J., Banko, M., Dumais, S., Ng, A.: Data-intensive question answering. Proc. of the 10th TREC Conf., "http://trec.nist.gov/pubs.html" (2001)
3. Clarke, C.L.A., Cormack, G.V., Lynam, T.R.: Exploiting redundancy in question answering. Proc. of the 24th annual int. ACM SIGIR conf. on Research and Development in Information Retrieval (2001) 358 – 365
4. Dubois, D., Fargier, H., Prade, H.: The calculus of fuzzy restrictions as a basis for flexible constraint satisfaction. Proc. of the 2nd IEEE Int. Conf. on Fuzzy Systems (1993) 1131-1136
5. Harabagiu, S., Moldovan, D., Paşca, M., Mihalcea, R., Surdeanu, M., Bunescu, R., Gîrju, R., Rus, V., Morărescu, P.: Falcon: boosting knowledge for answer engines. Proc. of 9th TREC Conf., "http://trec.nist.gov/pubs.html" (2000)
6. Kwok, C.C.T., Etzioni, O., Weld, D.S.: Scaling question answering to the web. Proc. of the 10th WWW Conf. (2001) 150–161
7. Luo, X., Lee, J.H-m., Leung, H-f., Jennings, N.R.: Prioritised fuzzy constraint satisfaction problems: axioms, instantiation and validation. Fuzzy Sets and Systems **136** (2003) 151–188

8. Novák, V., Perfilieva, I., Močkoř, J.: Mathematical Principles of Fuzzy Logic. Kluwer Academic Publishers (1999)
9. Prager, J., Chu-Carroll, J., Czuba, K.: Question answering using constraint satisfaction: QA-by-Dossier-with-Constraints. Proc. of the 42nd Annual Meeting of the ACL (2004) 574 – 581
10. Zadeh, L.A.: The concept of a linguistic variable and its application to approximate reasoning I. Information Sciences **8** (1975) 199–249

Mining Context Based Sequential Patterns

Jerzy Stefanowski and Radosław Ziembinski

Institute of Computing Science, Poznań University of Technology,
ul. Piotrowo 3A, 60–965 Poznań, Poland
{Jerzy.Stefanowski, Radoslaw.Ziembinski}@cs.put.poznan.pl

Abstract. Sequential pattern mining is an important task for Web usage mining. In this paper we generalize it to the problem of mining context based patterns, where context attributes may be introduced both for describing the complete sequence (e.g. characterizing user profiles) and for each element inside this sequence (describing circumstances for succeeding transactions). Such patterns provide information about circumstances associated with the discovered patterns what is not present in the traditional patterns. Their usefulness is illustrated by an example of analysing e-bank customer behaviour.

Keywords: Web Usage Mining, Web Log Analysis, Sequential Patterns.

1 Motivations

The enormous growth of the World Wide Web requires new methods for discovery and analysis of useful patterns from Web data repositories. *Web usage mining* can identify frequent users' behavior, identify groups of potential customers for electronic commerce, enhance the quality and delivery of various Internet services to the end user, building adaptive Web sites and improve Web server system performance [3, 5].

A Web usage pattern is usually a *sequential pattern* in a database of users' activities (Web server logs). The most popular methods for their discovery are based on the concept of mining sequential patterns, introduced by Agrawal and Sirkant [1]. It is following: given a *sequence database*, each sequence is a list of transactions ordered by transaction time and each transaction consists of a set of items, find all sequential patterns with a user-specified *minimum support*. The support is the number of data sequences that contain the pattern. For instance, let us analyse a behaviour of the Web music portal users, which are browsing some pages. An example of a sequential pattern is that 20% users/customers which access "*Jazz*" page, then go to "*Jazz trumpet players*", where they select "*Miles Davis discography*".

The first algorithms for mining sequential patterns were based on the modification of *Apriori* algorithm, originally introduced for association rules [1, 2]. Then, more efficient techniques were introduced, see e.g. PrefixSpan, SPADE, GSP algorithms. Moreover, the problem was generalized to include time constrains, time windows or user-defined taxonomy, for reviews see e.g. [3]. All these

P.S. Szczepaniak et al. (Eds.): AWIC 2005, LNAI 3528, pp. 401–407, 2005.

approaches recognize a pattern as a sequence of elements or so called *itemsets*, which are set of items (e.g. purchase goods or events from users during Web sessions). However, Web oriented problems may provide more information about user activities. For instance, registered users of Web portals are characterized by profiles containing personal information. Coming back to the example - having the users' description, one can get more general pattern saying that the frequent users moving from *"Jazz trumpet players"* to *"Miles Davis discography"* page and then buying *"Kind of Blue"* disc are *middle-aged men with at least medium income*. Moreover, it is possible to store other information characterizing a *context* of occurring each single transaction (e.g., location of users generating event, type of actions, used tools). Having such sets of context attribute characterizing both the sequence and its elements, it is possible to obtain richer knowledge on circumstances in which frequent patterns arise. According to our best knowledge the most related work to above postulates is [4], where the *multi-dimensional sequential patterns* were considered. However, the sequence was enhanced only by adding nominal attributes characterizing the customer.

Thus, the aim of this study is to discuss a problem of *Mining Context based Sequential Patterns*, where context attributes occurs both for the sequence and for each sequence element. That both kinds of attributes can be defined not only on nominal scales but also on ordinal and cardinal ones. This requires introduction of similarity functions for comparing values of context attributes while calculating a pattern support.

In the next section we present a simple example to clarify our approach. Then, in section 3, the problem of Mining Context based Sequential Patterns is introduced. The discussion of algorithms for mining these patterns and conclusions are given in the final section.

2   An Illustrative Example

Let us consider an e-bank which offers its services to users using Web portal and self service machines (e.g. modern WebATMs). We assume that the user can take the following actions (referring to items): deposit money into his account (denoted as SD), make a transfer money from his account to other payees (TM), withdraw part of money from his account (WM), block part of money on his running account by creating a time deposit (CD), cancel this deposit (RD). The user can perform a subset of these actions during one session with a bank service – this corresponds to the concept of a single transaction.

Transactions of each user are stored in the sequences database Each sequence from database contains the customer unique identifier and the list of customer transactions. In traditional approaches to pattern mining only the following data are collected: *customer id., transaction id.* and *itemset* as they are presented in the example in table 1.

Let us now consider our approach, where with each customer we associate a set of context attributes A (e.g. taken from the user profile collected while signing a contract with e-bank): *Monthly earnings* (abbreviated A_{ME}) – the customer

Table 1. A sequence database representing activities of e-bank customers

	Sequence		Transactions	
custo- mer id	sequence context $A_{ME}, A_{MS}, A_P, A_{AG}$	trans. id	transaction context C_{AS}, C_{DA}, C_F	itemset
1	(4200,married,high-tech,24)	1	(2,Monday,10)	{TM,CD}
		2	(4,Sunday,1)	{WM}
		3	(20,Saturday,2)	{RD,WM,TM}
2	(4000,married,high-tech,22)	1	(3,Tuesday,7)	{TM,CD,WM}
		2	(10,Sunday,8)	{WM,CD}
		3	(17,Sunday,1)	{WM,RD}
		4	(1,Tuesday,10)	{TM,CD}
3	(1500,single,retired,70)	1	(3,Monday,10)	{CD,TM,WM}
		2	(2,Monday,15)	{CD,TM,WM}
		3	(10,Sunday,1)	{WM}
4	(3800,married,teacher,32)	1	(1,Friday,3)	{CD,TM}
		2	(3,Sunday,1)	{WM}
		3	(20,Friday,2)	{WM,RD}
5	(1800,married,retired,60)	1	(1,Monday,34)	{CD,TM}
		2	(2,Sunday,1)	{CD,TM}
		3	(17,Saturday,2)	{WM,RD}

monthly wages defined on a ratio scale, *Marital status* (A_{MS}) – binary, *Profession* (A_P) – category of customer job (nominal multi-valued) and *Customer age* (A_{AG}) (ratio scale). Examples of customer contexts are given in the second column of table 1.

Let us now assume that each transaction stored in a database is described by another set of context attributes C, which characterize circumstances of customers' actions. This set has a following structure: *Number of days* from a last supply of money for the user account e.g. by transfer of his earnings (denoted as C_{AS}), *Day of the week* when the transaction has been done (C_{DA}), *Feast* - number of days till the nearest feast or holidays according to a calendar (C_F) - see an example of an extended database in table 1.

3   The Problem Statement

An introduction of the Context Based Sequential Pattern Mining problem will be followed by presenting some necessary notations and concepts originating from the basic version of the simple sequential pattern problem [1].

Let $L = \{i_1, i_2, \ldots, i_n\}$ be a set of items. An *itemset* X is a non-empty subset of items. A *sequence* is an ordered list of elements and is denoted as $s = < t_1, t_2, \ldots, t_m >$, where $t_i \subseteq L, i = 1, 2, \ldots, m$. An element t_i of sequence is an itemset and can be interpreted as transaction. An item can occur at multiple times in different elements of a sequence. The set of items is usually mapped by a set of integers. A sequence $\alpha = < \alpha_1, \alpha_2, \ldots, \alpha_r >$ is *contained* in another sequence $\beta = <\beta_1, \beta_2, \ldots, \beta_s>$ (what is denoted as $\alpha \sqsubseteq \beta$) if there exist integers $1 \leq j_1 < j_2 < \ldots < j_r \leq s$ such that $\alpha_1 \subseteq \beta_{j_1}, \alpha_2 \subseteq \beta_{j_2}, \ldots, \alpha_r \subseteq \beta_{j_r}$. In the set of sequences any sequence s is *maximal* if s is not contained in any other sequence from the same set.

All transactions of a customer can be viewed together as a sequence, where each transaction t_i corresponds to a set of items, and the list of transactions, ordered by increasing transaction-time (tid), corresponds to a sequence. These sequences are represented in a *sequence database DBS*, which contains a set of tuples $< sid, s >$, where sid is a sequence identifier and s is a sequence. A tuple $< sid, s >$ *contains* a sequence α, if $\alpha \sqsubseteq s$. In other words, a customer sequence s supports a sequence α. The *support* for a sequence α is a fraction of tuples in the database DBS containing (supporting) α. As presented in [1] the problem of mining sequential patterns is: given a sequences database, to find the maximal subsequences among all sequences that have a certain user-specified minimum support. Each such a maximal subsequence represents a *sequential pattern*.

Let us now generalize this concept to an extended sequences databases containing also *context attributes*. Here, the sequence is $((a_1, a_2, \ldots, a_p), es)$, where a_h are values of context attributes A_h (where $1 \leq h \leq p$) associated with a sequence. A value of the sequence context attribute $a_h \in (V_{a_h} \cup \{\star\})$, where V_{a_h} is a domain of an attribute A_h and "$\star$" denotes a universal value, which will be used in a pattern description for matching it against sequences while calculating its support. A sequence es is an ordered list of extended elements et_i having a form $((c_1, c_2, \ldots, c_r), X)$ where $X \subseteq L$ is again an itemset, and $c_1, c_2, \ldots, c_r$ are context attributes describing circumstances of each transaction. For any transaction values of context attributes $c_g \in (V_{c_g} \cup \{\star\})$, where V_{c_g} is a domain of an attribute C_g and "$\star$" denotes a universal value and as above it can be used only in a description of the pattern not a sequence. The choice of the set of transaction context attributes is the same for all elements of the sequence. However, each of the attribute values may be different among elements. As to domains of the both sets of context attributes, A and C, we assume that they can be defined on either nominal, ordinal or numerical scales.

A sequences database EDS contains tuples $< sid, a_1, a_2, \ldots, a_p, es >$. The essential concept of the sequence inclusion, $\alpha \sqsubseteq s$, should be now considered as a *similarity* between enriched sequence (being a candidate for a pattern) and tuples in EDS. It leads to calculating similarity between values of attributes, both for the sequence set A as well as for the transaction sets C. Thus, for each attribute a dedicated *similarity function* σ should be defined. For nominal attributes it can be based on a simply indiscernibility relation. However, for ordinal or numerical attributes more sophisticated functions should be used, e.g. based on distance measures or intervals comparisons. Such similarity functions have to be pre-defined for the sequence context attributes A (denoted as $\sigma_{a_1}, \sigma_{a_2}, \ldots, \sigma_{a_p}$) and transaction context attributes (denoted as $\sigma_{c_1}, \sigma_{c_2}, \ldots, \sigma_{c_r}$). While comparing the sequences α and β values of similarity functions computed for attributes in the compared contexts (either for sequence or for each element) can be aggregated into a single value. Let Θ_A and $\Theta_C^{t_i}$, $1 \leq i \leq m$, denote aggregated values resulting from comparing attribute vectors in α and β for the sequence context and transactions t_i contexts. Technically, the user should predefine threshold values (denoted as τ_A and τ_C, respectively) for establishing when similarity between compared sequences occurs.

An enriched sequence $\alpha = < a_1', a_2', \ldots, a_p', ep >$ is *supported* by a sequence s $< sid, a_1, a_2, \ldots, a_p, es >$ in database EDS iff they are similar, i.e. for itemsets in sequence elements $ep \sqsubseteq es$ hold and values of aggregated similarity functions satisfy $\Theta_A \geq \tau_A$ and $\forall_{t_i \in ep} \, \Theta_C^{t_i} \geq \tau_C$ for the set of sequence context attributes A and sets of transaction context attributes in each element of compared transactions t_i. The *support* for a sequence α is a fraction of tuples in the database EDS similar to α. Given a positive integer $min\_support$ as the *support threshold*, a sequence α is called a *context based sequential pattern* if it is similar to at least $min\_support$ tuples in EDS database. This pattern should be maximal sequence with respect to all frequent sequences.

The problem of Context Based Sequential Pattern Mining is defined as: given a database EDS, where sets of context attributes A, C with their similarity functions σ are defined, the task is to find all context based patterns among all sequences that are similar to at least $min\_support$ tuples in EDS.

Continuation of the example from section 2:
Let us define similarity functions as follows. For all nominal attributes the function returns 1.0 when two compared attribute values are equal and 0 otherwise. For all numerical the functions are usually constructed by using values comparisons, i.e. the difference measured between two attribute values is mapped to similarity value from range $\langle 0, 0; 1.0 \rangle$. For instance, let us consider the sequence attribute *Monthly earnings* A_{ME}. Let δ denotes the value of difference between two compared attribute values. If δ is less than 100 units, the similarity function σ_{A_ME} returns 1.0; If $100 \leq \delta < 1000$, $\sigma_{A\_ME} = 0.8$, if $1000 \leq \delta < 9000$, $\sigma_{A\_ME} = 0.4$, for larger δ, it is equal to 0.

Now, we will consider examples of different kinds of sequential patterns. Let us assume that the $min\_support$ is 2 tuples in EDS database, i.e. 40% customers. An example of the discovered traditional, simple sequence pattern is:

$$< \{TM, CD\}, \{WM\}, \{WM, RD\} >$$

which means that at least 40% customers after transferring money and creating a time deposit withdraw a sum of his money, and after some time perform again an operation of withdrawing money and canceling the deposit.

If we consider a *multi-dimensional point of view* [4], we should associate a set of context attributes A with customers. As only nominal attributes could be handled, the numerical ones have to be discretized, e.g. values of *Monthly earnings* A_{ME} are divided into three interval [0,1600] - small, (1600,2800) - average, ≥ 2800 high). Now the following sequential pattern could be discovered:

$$< (\text{high earnings}, \text{married}, *, *), \{TM, CD\}, \{WM\}, \{WM, RD\} >$$

which extend our knowledge about characteristics of frequent customers performing the above sequence of actions. Finally, for our new approach, the set of context attributes C describing transactions is also available:

$$(4000,\text{married},*,*),(3,*,*)\{TM,CD\},(*,\text{Sunday},*)\{WM\},(20,*,*)\{WM,RD\}$$

which provides more information about circumstances of each transaction. For instance, one can additionally notice that the first operation in this sequence is usually done around 3 days after the account is supplied by earnings, then part of this money is withdrawn on Sunday and the next operation of withdrawing money and canceling deposits occurs around 20 days from money supply.

4   Conclusion and Future Research

The problem of sequential pattern mining has been generalized into the context based version, where additional descriptions - context attributes may be introduced both for describing the complete sequence and for each element inside this sequence. Unlike the previous multi-dimensional mining proposal, the attributes may be defined not only on nominal scales but also on numerical or ordinal ones. Such context attributes provide information about circumstances associated with the discovered patterns what is not present in the traditional patterns. They could be useful for better identifying user categories referring to given sequences and to clarify that succeeding transactions are happening at different circumstances. The concept of similarity requires more cautious from the analyst, while selecting particular form of the similarity function, but it provides more flexibility for modeling richer relationships between attribute values than the equality relation previously considered, e.g. [4].

Our problem statement requires new algorithms for mining context patterns the allow us to calculate similarities between sequences, not only inclusion of their elements. We have built and tested a two step algorithm being an enhanced version of AprioriAll, where frequent non context patterns are discovered in the first step and used for finding context patterns in the second phase. As it is not sufficiently efficient, current research concern creating a new algorithm specific for mining larger sequence databases. Moreover, we will consider a specialized index data structure for fast searching in such databases.

Acknowledgement

The research was supported by KBN grant 3T11C 050 26.

References

1. Agrawal R., Sirkant R.: Mining sequential patterns. In: Proc. Int. Conf. Data Engineering, Taipei Taiwan, (March 1995) 3–14.
2. Agrawal R., Mannila H., Srikant R., Toivinen H., Verkamo I.: Fast discovery of association rules. In: Fayyad U.M. et al. (eds): Advances in Knowledge Discovery and Data Mining, AAAI Press (1996) 307–328.

3. Pei J., Han J. et al.: Mining access patterns efficiently from Web logs. In: Proc. of the 4th Pacific-Asia Conf, on Knowledge Discovery and Data Mining (2000) 396–407.
4. Pinto H., Han J., Pei J., et al.: Multidimensional Sequential Pattern Mining. In: Proc. 10th Conf. on Information and Knowledge Management (2001) 81–88.
5. Zhong N., Liu J., Yao Y. (eds): Web Intelligence. Springer 2003, chapter 9.

Can One Out-Link Change Your PageRank?

Marcin Sydow

Polish-Japanese Institute of Information Technology,
Koszykowa 86, 02-008 Warsaw, Poland
msyd@pjwstk.edu.pl

Abstract. We model potential behavior of a Web page creator trying
to change its PageRank ranking by changing out-links being under their
control. We demonstrate it on synthetic graphs of various sizes and properties (including the high quality *hybrid model*[9]) and on *topically unified* graph from real Web. Due to massive computations, we apply several
randomized algorithms including hill climbing and simulated annealing.
The experimental results presented here clearly show that it is possible
to significantly change Web documents PageRank score by changing its
outlinks properly[1]. This seems to shed new light on PageRank stability.

1 Introduction

A query passed by a user to a large scale Web search engine may easily result in
thousands or even millions of relevant[2] documents. Since a human user is able
to check only few tens of the retrieved documents[3], search engines present them
in non-increasing order of *authority* in order to allow the user seeing the most
authoritative of the relevant documents first. Link analysis of the Web graph[4]
turned out to be a very powerful tool for measuring authority of Web documents
in practice [5]. One of the most successful examples is PageRank algorithm [8]
applied in Google search engnine for ranking search results.

Motivation. Since ranking algorithms decide of the order of the documents
presented to a user of public search engines, the issue of analysing those algorithms or even manipulating them[5] became very attractive from the commercial
point of view, apart from the scientific one.

Previous Work. Despite the above, analysing how changing the link structure influences the induced authority ranking, is not richly represented in literature. Important work on stability of PageRank and other link-based ranking
algorithms under link graph perturbation was [7], where authors demonstrate

---

[1] As opposed to *inlinks*.
[2] Containing specified keywords.
[3] Usually not exceeding 20 documents.
[4] Web graph is obtained by treating each document as a node and each hyperlink as
a directed edge (see e.g. [4]).
[5] In order to artificially boost the authority.

P.S. Szczepaniak et al. (Eds.): AWIC 2005, LNAI 3528, pp. 408–414, 2005.

that PageRank is supreme to other algorithms in terms of stability. In [2] authors introduce and analyse several properties of link-based ranking algorithms and present experimental results. In [10] authors study a practical issue of approximate recomputing of PageRank after partial changes to the underlying graph.

PageRank Ranking Scheme. PageRank algorithm, on which we focus in this paper, takes into account only hyperlink structure of the Web. It assigns to each page p in the Web graph $G(V, E)$ non-negative authority score $A(d)$ satisfying the following equations:

$$\sum_{p \in V} A(p) = 1 \tag{1}$$

$$A(p) = d/|V| + (1 - d)[\sum_{i:(i,p) \in E} A(i)/outDeg(i)]^6 \tag{2}$$

where $outDeg(i)$ denotes the total number of links on page i, and d, called damping (or decay) factor, is introduced for practical and theoretical reasons (see [8, 3]) and is reportedly set to 0.15 in practice.

Due to the above, PageRank authority score of a document is defined roughly as the total authority of documents citing it (weighted by their out-degrees). Thus, it is regarded as one of the most immune to manipulation among publicly known ranking schemes [7], since the author of a Web page does not have control of the other authoritative documents that cite it.

1.1 Contribution of this Paper

What the author of a Web document has control of is pages to be *linked to*. The previous works mentioned above focus mostly on the *global* behavior of ranking schemes under graph changes. Meanwhile, from the point of view of individual documents authors it is interesting how *local* changes of link structure influence authority ranking of their *individual* documents.

In this paper we pose somewhat provoking[7] question: how does PageRank depend on pages *being cited* by a document? Even if the equations 1,2 do not give any explicit dependence between pages being linked to and PageRank score, we present experimental results that clearly show that changing out-links of a document may *significantly* change the resulting PageRank score. Up to the author's knowledge, such a result has not been reported before.

2   Experiments on Synthetic Graphs

We generated several random graphs of various sizes. We started with a simple *uniform* random graph model - where each node has random out-degree choosen

---

[6] In practice, there is also a third term present in this equation, which corresponds to redistirbuting the authority of pages without outlinks. We did not include it here for simplicity, but we take it into consideration in our computations.

[7] In the context of PageRank definition.

uniformly from interval $[l, h]$ and then links are assigned to nodes randomly according to uniform distribution over all nodes in the graph. We implemented the uniform generator in the way which avoids multiple links between pairs of nodes and self-loops[8]. In all those graphs we choose $l = 0$ and $h = 15$.

The idea of the experiment is as follows. Let us compute PageRank for each node in a graph. Then let us take any node of positive out-degree and change the original destination of one of its links to other destination. Lets now recompute the PageRank for the modified graph. Now let's compare the ranking position change of the node before and after the change.

At first, we generated 7 random graphs according to the *uniform model*. For each graph, we picked all[9] the nodes having only 1 out-link and changed its destination to *each* other node in the graph in turn, recomputing PageRank after each change. We recorded the minimal (best) and maximal (worst) *rank position* obtained for each node and expressed the observed position change range in percentiles (i.e. $100\% \cdot (max - min)/allNodesInGraph$). Then we computed the average range over all the tested nodes. We repeated this measurement for nodes of out-degree 2 and 7 as well[10] (always changing only 1 random outlink).

Table 1. Change of PageRank score after changing 1 out-link in uniform and hybrid random graphs. Columns marked "an", "mn" and "fn" represent average change range, maximal observed range and fraction of checked nodes (respectively), among all the nodes of out-degree n in the graph

name	nodes	a1(%)	m1	f1	a2(%)	m2	f2	a7(%)	m7	f7
uni1	1000	11.7	39%	all	5.28	13%	all	2.58	6.9%	all
uni2	1000	15.21	46%	all	6.45	15%	all	1.85	7%	all
uni3	500	12.25	26%	all	6.35	18%	all	1.92	8%	all
uni4	500	15.54	39%	all	7.35	18%	all	2.12	8%	all
uni5	500	12.78	44%	all	6.9	18%	all	1.96	7%	all
uni6	2500	12.1	27%	10/146	8.12	19%	17/166	2.4	6.6%	16/155
uni7	2500	12	34%	13/123	5.96	12.6%	16/154	1.85	4%	16/160
hyb1	874	4.94	12.7%	20/40	2.8	5.94%	25/50	1.06	3.54%	24/48
hyb2	962	6	20.79%	26/51	2.21	5.3%	22/43	1.15	3.32%	23/46
hyb3	1059	4.33	13.12%	22/44	2.25	7.36%	24/48	0.98	2.45%	29/57

Quite surprising, but we observe that changing a single out-link of a node may cause a *significant* change in this node's rank position (table 10). For out-degree 1, the average change range is astonishingly high, in the context of the definition of PageRank, where the rank of node depends on ranks of nodes linking *to it*. We can also see that changing one out-link causes higher changes when

---

[8] Edges of the form (i, i).

[9] For bigger graphs we picked random 10%, due to massive computations, without much loss of information, in our opinion.

[10] To observe average range change as a function of out-degree.

node's out-degree is lower (the highest changes for nodes with out-degree 1). This phenomenon is not very surprising, since the PageRank flowing through each out-link is divided by node's out-degree. Second important observation is that change range does not seem to depend very strongly on graph size.

We repeated the above experiment on much more sophisticated random graph model - the *hybrid model* ([9]) of our implementation. This model, despite having some imperfections, is regarded as one of the most realistic models of the Web and was especially designed for modeling Web graph evolution [9, 11].

Results gathered in table 10 show that changes observed on the hybrid-generated model are more moderate than on uniform-generated, in general, but they are still non-neglectable[11]. It also seems that rank change range depends much stronger on the graph strucutre[12] than on its size.

3   Experiments with Real Web

Encouraged by such promising results on synthetic graphs, we made similar experiments on the real subgraph of the Web. The graph was taken from publicly available J.Kleinberg's course page[1]. It is 9664-node graph obtained from extending 200-page "root" result set to the query "california" by adding pages linking to and linked by the "root" set (as in classic HITS algorithm [6]).

Table 2. Change of PageRank ranking position after modifying the unique link of one-outlink nodes in real Web subgraph *california*. Due to space limitations and massive computations we report only results for the first 10 one-outlink nodes in the graph

node	old	min	max	range	node	old	min	max	range
1	71	20	161	1.459%	20	255	64	444	3.93%
5	511	84	515	4.459%	21	740	509	749	2.48%
6	27	27	259	2.4%	23	478	78	484	4.2%
8	40	2	44	0.434%	31	138	60	142	0.84%
17	10	10	87	0.79%	42	693	179	699	5.38%

---

[11] It is important to note that the rank change quantities where divided by the *total number of nodes* in the graph. But it would be more appropriate to divide them by the *number of different rank positions* in the graph. Since PageRank is distributed as power-law on both uniform and hybrid graphs (see [11]), many nodes have very low rank score which, in practice, makes many nodes having *the same* ranking position. Thus, the number of rank positions is usually remarkably lower than number of nodes. Due to this, the change range values would have been even much *higher* than those actually present in the table. We decided not to divide by the number of different rank positions because it changes as graph's links change and computing the average would have been less natural in this case.

[12] More precisely: the random process that generated the graph.

In the next series of experiments, we measured rank change range for nodes of out-degree higher than 1. We arbitrarily chose out-degree of 7. There are $\binom{10000}{7}$ possible outlink combinations to be checked (in 10000-node graph), moreover, each implying PageRank recomputation (!). This is, undoubtedly, out of technical possibilities. To overcome this problem, we applied 4 different heuristical (under-optimal) randomized algorithms for searching this huge space for 7-outlink combination giving the best (lowest) PageRank position (table 14). Each algorithm was bounded to only 2000 trials. The algorithms were: simple random checking $(r1)$, kind of randomized greedy algorithm[13] $(r2)$, *hill climbing* $(r3)$ and a variant of *simulated annealing* $(r4)$. In the last two cases, the neighborhood of a given outlink combination in the solution space was defined as the set of all combinations having only 1 link destination different. The optimised (minimized) function was rank position of a node. In the simulated annealing algorithm, the rule of accepting a neighbor with worse rank was: $relDiff < probability$, where $relDiff = (rankNew - rankPrevious)/nodesInGraph$ and $probability = \frac{1}{200}e^{2.5/(\frac{LIMIT}{step}-1)}$ [14], where $step$ was the number of current step. Each algorithm was run a few times and its best result was recorded.

Table 3. The best (lowest) PageRank ranking in "california" graph for the first 10 nodes of out-degree 7 obtained by 4 heuristical algorithms r1-r4. We bold the old rank and the best rank obtained in each row

node	old rank	r1	r2	r3	r4	node	old rank	r1	r2	r3	r4
24	**357**	305	294	279	**253**	725	**1431**	1406	1406	**1382**	1429
54	**48**	48	35	**31**	35	735	**1418**	1370	1409	1370	**1370**
74	**43**	43	**35**	35	43	766	**2099**	2100	2099	2099	2099
110	**78**	57	50	30	**30**	810	**2099**	2100	2099	2099	2099
436	**2099**	2101	2099	2099	2099	817	**1609**	1491	1609	1609	1609

Note that it was almost always possible to improve PageRank position, sometimes significantly. Simulated annealing sometimes gave worse results than simpler algorithms, due to extremely tiny fraction of possible combinations checked.

4   Conclusion and Future Directions

The main conclusion is that changing *outlinks* of a Web page may significantly change the page's PageRank position in the graph. This seemingly paradoxical

---

[13] In this algorithm, for each of 7 outlinks (in order of randomly generated permutation) we made $LIMIT/degree$ (i.e. 2000/7) random checks and choose the link destination giving the best ranking, keeping other link destinations temporarily fixed.

[14] All the constants were tuned by experimentation.

(in the context of PageRank definition) phenomenon can be explained as follows. If Web page targets its outlinks to pages that link to it (not necessarily directly) its PageRank score increases. It is not very surprising. What is surprising, is the *extent* of possible changes (note, for example, a jump from 40th to the 2nd position in ranking by changing merely 1 outlink of node 8 in the table 10).

The author hopes, that techniques described here cannot be widely used to dishonestly manipulate Web pages' ranking, as they assume sophisticated algorithms and detailed knowledge of the Web graph. However, in the context of increasing commercial competition, increasingly sophisticated tools are supposed to be used in close future to manipulate rankings.

The results presented in this paper, despite being preliminary and purely experimental seem to shed new light on the stability of PageRank, usually regarded as being very stable link-based ranking algorithm among those publicly known [7] (and therefore rather *immune to manipulation*).

We observed (both on synthetic and the real graphs) that pages with very low PageRank score could not boost it by changing their outlinks. This is a direct consequence of the mechanism explained in the first paragraph of this section.

New directions of experiments and theoretical studies open here. More complex graph changes may be studied and other algorithms tested. The author plans to test also the RBS algorithm (PageRank enriched with back-button modeling [12]) in similar way. Due to extremely massive computations involved in this kind of experiments, PageRank computation acceleration (as in [10], for example) is necessary to be applied on larger graphs.

References

1. http://www.cs.cornell.edu/courses/cs685/2002fa/data/gr0.california.
2. J.S. Rosenthal A. Borodin, G.O. Roberts and P. Tsaparas. Finding authorities and hubs from link structures on the world wide web. In *In Tenth International World Wide Web Conference*, 2001.
3. C.D. Meyer. A.N. Langville. Deeper inside pagerank., 2003.
4. A. Broder, R.Kumar, F.Maghoul, P.Raghavan, S.Rajagopalan, R.Stata, A.Tomkins, and J.Wiener. Graph structure in the web. In *Proceedings of the 9th WWW Conference*, 2000.
5. M. Henzinger. Link analysis in web information retrieval. 23(3):3–8, 2000.
6. J. Kleinberg. Authoritative sources in a hyperlinked environment. In *Proceedings of the 9th ACM-SIAM Symposium on discrete algorithms*, 1998.
7. A. Ng, A.Zheng, and M.Jordan. Stable algorithms for link analysis. In *Proceedings of SIGIR'01*, 2001.
8. L. Page, S.Brin, R.Motwani, and T.Winograd. The pagerank citation ranking: Bringing order to the web. In *Stanford Digital Library Working Paper*, 1998.
9. G. Pandurangan, P.Raghavan, and E.Upfal. Using pagerank to characterize web structure. In *Proceedings of the 8th Annual International Computing and Combinatorics Conference*, 2002.

10. S. Kumar S. Chien, C. Dwork and D. Sivakumar. Towards exploiting link evolution. 2001.

11. M. Sydow. *Link Analysis of the Web Graph. Measurements, Models and Algorithms for Web Information Retrieval.* PhD dissertation, Polish Academy of Sciences, Institute of Computer Science, Warsaw, 2004.

12. M. Sydow. Random surfer with back step (poster). In *Proceedings of the 13th International WWW Conference, (Alternate Track. Papers and Posters)*, pages 352–353. ACM press, 2004.

Web Textual Documents Scoring Based on Discrete Transforms with Fuzzy Weighting

Piotr S. Szczepaniak[1,2] and Michał Pryczek[1]

[1] Institute of Computer Science, Technical University of Łódź, Wolczanska 215,
93-005, Lodz, Poland
[2] Systems Research Institute, Polish Academy of Sciences, Newelska 6,
01-447 Warsaw, Poland

Abstract. Recently, Fourier and cosine discrete transformations have been proposed for textual document ranking. The advantage of the methods is that rather than using only the count of a frequency term within document, the spatial information about presence of the term is considered. Here, further improvement of this novel approach is proposed. It is based on fuzzy evaluation of the position of words within the document.

Keywords: Information retrieval, text representation, word signal, discrete transforms, spatial information, fuzzy singletons.

1   Introduction

In the literature, the two main methods for text representation are reported: vector space models and string kernels.

The vector space model is, in a nutshell, representation of textual document by a vector [1, 2]. Within vector, the number of times each word appears in the document is given. Document vectors can then be easily compared to each other, or to query vectors.

String kernels operate on characters, they use a low level information [3, 4]. Features are extent to which all possible ordered sequences of characters are represented in the document. The modified idea of string kernels use has also been applied to sequences of words [5]. This considerably increases the number of symbols to process but on the other hand it causes the reduction of the average number of symbols per document; higher computing efficiency is reached. Moreover, strings of words carry more high level information than strings of characters. Further modifications of string kernels makes possible the soft-matching and cross-lingual document similarity [5].

Hypothesis that the information about the spatial location of words is an important factor which can improve the document search and ranking, has been recently confirmed in practice [6, 7]. The spatial information was preserved by application of Fourier and cosine discrete transformations what allows to store a term signal, and therefore to follow the spreading of the term throughout the

P.S. Szczepaniak et al. (Eds.): AWIC 2005, LNAI 3528, pp. 415–420, 2005.

document. The magnitude and phase are features used for comparison of query and document terms. The standard steps to be performed are:

- Preparation of word signals;
- Performing preweighting;
- Determination of the discrete transformation;
- Evaluating document relevance.

Within each of the steps different methods can be considered.

To make the presentation clear and complete, we briefly describe the two first steps following the mentioned works of Park et al. [6, 7], and then we introduce modification which reflects the importance of the word position within the document according to human user.

2   Word Vector and Word Signal

Let us explain the concept of word vector and word signal introduced in [6, 7]. The simplest word vector contain elements equal to the word count of the document. If the word w_i appears on the k-th position the value "1" is put on the corresponding position of the vector. For every position where this word does not appear the value "0" is set. To avoid the possible large vector dimension the grouping of words into bins is proposed [6]. Assuming T words (terms) and N bins within the considered document one obtains T/N words in each bin. The elements of word vectors are numbers representing the appearance of the selected word within the following bins of the document. Then for example, the first element of the word vector represents the number of times the considered word appears in the first bin of the length T/N.

$$[\sim\sim\sim t_1\sim t_1][\sim\sim\sim\sim\sim\sim][\sim\sim\sim\sim\sim\sim][\sim t_1\sim t_1\sim\sim][\sim\sim\sim\sim\sim\sim][\sim\sim\sim\sim\sim\sim][t_1\sim\sim\sim\sim\sim][\sim\sim\sim\sim\sim\sim]$$

$$[\sim\sim\sim\sim\sim t_2][\sim\sim\sim\sim\sim\sim][\sim\sim t_2\sim\sim\sim][\sim\sim t_2\sim t_2\sim][\sim\sim\sim\sim\sim\sim][\sim\sim\sim\sim\sim\sim][\sim t_2\sim\sim\sim\sim][\sim\sim\sim\sim\sim\sim]$$

Fig. 1. Grouping of words into bins ($N = 8$)

Consequently, elements of the vector representing text are integers; cf. Fig. 1 and Fig. 2 where the concept of signal representation on the example of the presence of two words t_1 and t_2 is shown. Here, for $N = 8$ one obtains two vectors:

$$t_1^T = [20020010]$$

$$t_2^T = [10120010]$$

For effective document retrieval one determines usually the significance of terms for document description (representation). There exist many ways for

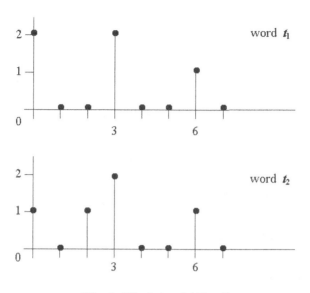

Fig. 2. Word signal ($N = 8$)

significance weighting; commonly accepted is the group of methods where two parameters are considered: frequency of the presence of the word within the document and inverse of the number of documents containing the given word.

Frequently, for a quick retrieval of word vectors an inverted index is created. The weighting of the document vectors may be performed in some ways, for example

$$w(n)_{t,d} = 1 + \log_e f(n)_{t,d} \cdot \left[\log_e\left(1 + \frac{N}{f_t}\right)\right] \tag{1}$$

or

$$w(n)_{t,d} = (1 + \log_e f_{t,d})\left(\frac{f(n)_{t,d}}{f_{t,d}}\right) \cdot \left[\log_e\left(1 + \frac{N}{f_t}\right)\right] \tag{2}$$

where $w(n)_{t,d}$ and $f(n)_{t,d}$ are the weight and count of term t in the spatial bin n of the document d, respectively, and $f_{t,d}$ – the count of term t in the document d; f_t — number of documents in which term t appears; N — number of documents.

The weights are then input signals for the chosen discrete transform, cosine or Fourier [6, 7].

Let for example the Fourier transform is applied:

$$F_{k,t,d} = \sum_{n=0}^{N-1} w(n)_{t,d} \exp\left(-\frac{j2\pi kn}{N}\right), \quad k = 0, \dots, N-1 \tag{3}$$

It transforms the input signal from the time or spatial domain to the frequency domain. As a result of it, instead considering the weight of the term t in the bin n of the document d, one consider the k-th frequency component $F_{k,t,d}$ in this document.

3   Fuzzy Weighting of Word Signals

Note that the word signal created according to the concept presented in the section 2 strongly depends on the division of the document into bins. Different number of bins causes diverse text partitions and consequently diverse vector signals. Moreover, the method in its original form does not consider the importance of the word location within the document. The latter imperfection can be improved when the following proposition is introduced. The idea is based on the rather obvious observation. The human user usually have knowledge about importance of words location for description of the document content. For example, in scientific papers title, abstract, first one hundred words of the document body, and summary are more important for the content identification than the rest of the text.

Taking this general statement as departure point, we can introduce for each given word t some function $\mu_t(k)$ with values in $[0,1]$ defined for the considered text (document); example is given in Fig. 3

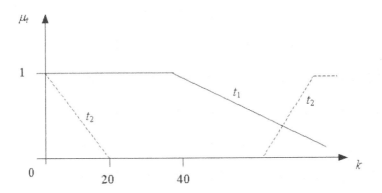

Fig. 3. Significance of words t_1 and t_2 depending on their location k within the document (example)

For each word t from a given set T of words, the function μ_t

$$\mu_t : K \rightarrow [0,1]$$

expresses the (subjective) degree of importance of word $t \in T$ for definition of the subject of the document when t is located on the position $k \in K$. The importance varies from $\mu_t(k) = 0$ for the complete unimportance to $\mu_t(k) = 1$ for the maximal significance. However, we should bear in mind that although in our example the function is evidently defined for the integer numbers ks only, it is depicted in a continuous form for clarity of presentation. Since all the sets of words are finite than the set K is finite as well, and the pairs $\{\mu_t(k), k\}$ in terms of the fuzzy sets theory are called fuzzy singletons, cf. [9, 10]. Using the notation common in the fuzzy sets theory, the fuzzy set K_t in K can be written as:

$$K_t = \{\mu_t(k), k\} = \sum_k \mu_t(k)/k$$

where $\sum$ denotes the set of ordered pairs, and it should not be confused with the standard algebraic summation.

Now, the degree of importance can simply be merged into the signal representation of documents. Instead of consideration of discrete $f(n)_{t,d}$, the values $f(n)_{t,d} = \sum_k \mu_t(k)$ become subject of processing. Let us remain that $f(n)_{t,d}$ denotes the count of term t in the spatial bin n of the document d. It may be used directly for discrete transformation (for example Fourier) or the usual weighting like (1), (2) may firstly be performed.

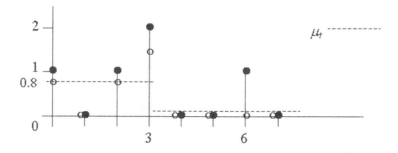

Fig. 4. Original $\{\bullet\}$ and modified $\{\circ\}$ word signals

The function determining the degree of importance may obviously be defined for bins and then expressions of the form $\mu_t(n) \cdot f(n)_{t,d}$ are in use. This more convenient way is shown in Fig. 4.

4   Summary

The Web is enormous, unlimited and dynamically changed source of useful and varied kinds of information. The aspiration to meet an obvious need for effective information retrieval by making improvements in the solutions offered by the popular indexing engines is observed. The improvement is expected in both, retrieval accuracy and speed. For accuracy the method of text representation and analysis is critical; for fastness apart from hardware, important is the processing method for the prepared textual data. The discrete transformations allow to use information about the spread of words throughout the documents. The proposed modification reflects human knowledge about term position and structure of the considered group of documents. Fortunately, it does not cause any substantially increase of computational complexity. Note, that some data formats are more convenient when incorporation of sophisticated methods is aspired, cf. [11]. For example, the RSS-supplied records always contain the same type of information (headlines, links, article summaries, etc.) what makes the application of importance weighting easier.

References

1. Baeza-Yates R., Ribeiro-Neto B.: *Modern Information Retrieval*, Addison Wesley, New York, 1999.
2. Witten I.H., Moffat A., Bell T.C.: *Managing gigabytes: compressing and indexing documents and images*, Morgan Kaufmann Publishers, 1999.
3. Lodhi H., Cristianini N., Shave-Taylor J., Watkins C.: *Text classification using string kernel*, In: Advances in Neural Information Processing Systems, 13, MIT Press, 2001.
4. Lodhi H., Saunders C., Shave-Taylor J., Cristianini N., Watkins C.: *Text classification using string kernels*, Journal of Machine Learning Research. 2, 419-444, 2002.
5. Cancedda N., Gaussier E., Gooutte C., Renders J.-M.: *Word-Sequence Kernels*, Journal of Machine Learning Research, 3, 1059-1082, 2003.
6. Park L.A.F., Ramamohanarao K., Palaniswami M.: *Fourier Domain Scoring: A Novel Document Ranking Method*,
Trans. on Knowledge and Data Engineering (submitted), 2002.
7. Park L.A.F., Ramamohanarao K., Palaniswami M.: *A Novel Web Text Mining Method Using the Discrete Cosine Transform*, In: T.Elomaa, H.Mannila, H.Toivonen (Eds.): Principles of Data Mining and Knowledge Discovery. (Proceedings of the 6th European Conference PKDD2002, Helsinki, Finland) LNCS, vol.2431, subseries LNAI, Springer-Verlag, Berlin, Heidelberg, 385-396, 2002.
8. Lebart L., Salem A., Berry L.: *Exploring Textual Data*. Kluwer Academic Publisher, 1998.
9. Kacprzyk J.: *Mulitistage Fuzzy Control*, John Wiley and Sons, Chichester, 1997.
10. Pedrycz W., Gominde F.: *An Introduction to Fuzzy Sets*, The MIT Press, Cambridge (MA), London, 1998.
11. Wegrzyn-Wolska K., Szczepaniak P.S.: *Classification of RSS-formatted Documents using Full Text Similarity Measures*, Proceedings of the 5th Int. Conference on Web Engineering, Sydney, Australia (submitted), 2005.

Recommendation System Using Multistrategy Inference and Learning

Bartłomiej Śnieżyński

AGH University of Science and Technology,
Institute of Computer Science, Kraków, Poland
sniezyn@agh.edu.pl

Abstract. This paper presents a new approach to build recommendation systems. Multistrategy Inference and Learning System based on the Logic of Plausible Reasoning (LPR) is proposed. Two groups of knowledge transmutations are defined: inference transmutations that are formalized as LPR proof rules, and complex ones that can use machine learning algorithms to generate intrinsically new knowledge. All operators are used by inference engine in a similar manner. In this paper necessary formalism and system architecture are described. Preliminary experimental results of application of the system conclude the work.

Keywords: Recommendation system, adaptive web sites, multistrategy learning, inferential theory of learning, logic of plausible reasoning.

1 Introduction

Developing adaptive web systems is a challenge for AI community for several years [1]. A broad range of soft computing methods is used in this domain: neural networks, fuzzy logic, genetic algorithms, clustering, fuzzy clustering, and neuro-fuzzy systems [2]. This paper presents a completely new approach: a knowledge representation and inference technique that is able to perform multi-type plausible inference and learning. It is used to build a model of recommendation system.

Multistrategy Inference and Learning System (MILS) proposed below is an attempt to implement the Inferential Theory of Learning [3]. In this approach, learning and inference can be presented as a goal-guided exploration of the knowledge space using operators called knowledge transmutations.

MILS combines many knowledge manipulation techniques to infer given goal. It is able to use a background knowledge or machine learning algorithms to produce information that is not contained in data. The Logic of Plausible Reasoning (LPR) [4] is used as a base for knowledge representation.

In the following sections LPR and MILS are presented. Next, preliminary results of experiments are described.

P.S. Szczepaniak et al. (Eds.): AWIC 2005, LNAI 3528, pp. 421–426, 2005.

2   Outline of the Logic of Plausible Reasoning

The core part of MILS is the Logic of Plausible Reasoning introduced by Collins and Michalski [4]. It can be defined as a labeled deductive system [5] in the following way.

Language consists of a finite set of constant symbols C, countable set of variable names X, five relational symbols and logical connectives: $\rightarrow$, $\wedge$. The relational symbols are: V, H, B, S, E. They are used to represent: statements (V), hierarchy (H, B), similarity (S) and dependency (E).

Statements are represented as object-attribute-value triples: $V(o, a, v)$, where $o, a, v \in C$. It is a representation of the fact that object o has an attribute a equal v. Value v should be a subtype of attribute a. If object o has several values of a, there should be several appropriate statements in a knowledge base. To represent vagueness of knowledge it is possible to extend this definition and allow to use composite value $[v_1, v_2, \ldots, v_n]$, list of elements of C. It can be interpreted that object o has an attribute a equal v_1 or v_2, ..., or v_n. If $n = 1$ notation $V(o, a, v_1)$ is used instead of $V(o, a, [v_1])$.

Relation $H(o_1, o, c)$, where $o_1, o, c \in C$, means that o_1 is a type of o in a context c. Context is used for specification of the range of inheritance. o_1 and o have the same value for all attributes which depend on attribute c of object o. To show that one object is below the other in any hierarchy, relation $B(o_1, o)$, where $o_1, o \in C$, should be used.

Relation $S(o_1, o_2, c)$ represents a fact, that o_1 is similar to o_2; $o_1, o_2, c \in C$. Context, as above, specifies the range of similarity. Only these attributes of o_1 and o_2 have the same value which depend on attribute c.

Dependency relation $E(o_1, a_1, o_2, a_2)$, where $o_1, a_1, o_2, a_2 \in C$, means that values of attribute a_1 of object o_1 depend on attribute a_2 of the second object.

Using relational symbols, *formula* of LPR can be defined. If $o, o_1, \ldots, o_n, a$, $a_1, \ldots, a_n, v, c \in C$, $v_1, \ldots, v_n$ are lists of elements of C, then $V(o, a, v)$, $H(o_1, o, c)$, $B(o_1, o)$, $S(o_1, o_2, o, a)$, $E(o_1, a_1, o_2, a_2)$, $V(o_1, a_1, v_1) \wedge \ldots \wedge V(o_n, a_n, v_n)$ $\rightarrow V(o, a, v)$ are formulas of LPR. To represent general rules, it is possible to use variables instead of constant symbols at object and value positions in implications.

To manage uncertainty the following *label algebra* is used:

$$\mathcal{A} = (A, \{f_{r_i}\}). \tag{1}$$

A is a set of labels which estimate uncertainty of formulas. A *labeled formula* is a pair $f : l$ where f is a formula and $l \in A$ is a label. A set of labeled formulas can be considered as a *knowledge base*.

LPR inference patterns are defined as classical *proof rules*. Every proof rule r_i has a sequence of premises (of length p_{r_i}) and a conclusion. $\{f_{r_i}\}$ is a set of functions which are used in proof rules to generate a label of a conclusion: for every proof rule r_i an appropriate function $f_{r_i} : A^{p_{r_i}} \rightarrow A$ should be defined. For rule r_i with premises $p_1 : l_1, \ldots, p_n : l_n$ the plausible label of its conclusion is equal $f_{r_i}(l_1, \ldots, l_n)$. Example of plausible algebra can be found in [6].

There are five main types of proof rules: GEN, $SPEC$, SIM, $TRAN$ and MP. They correspond to the following inference patterns: generalization, specialization, similarity transformation, transitivity of relations and modus ponens. Some transformations can be applied to different types of formulas, therefore indexes are used to distinguish different versions of rules. Formal definitions of these rules can be found in [4, 7].

3   Multistrategy Inference and Learning System

The core element of MILS is the inference engine. Its input is a LPR formula that is an inference goal. Algorithm builds the inference chain using knowledge transmutations to infer the goal. Two types of knowledge transmutations are defined in MILS: simple (LPR proof rules), and complex (using complex computations, e.g. rule induction algorithms or representation form changing procedures).

A knowledge transmutation can be represented as a triple: (p, c, a), where p is a (possibly empty) list of premises or preconditions, c is a consequence (pattern of formula(s) that can be generated) and a is an action (empty for simple transmutations) that should be executed to generate the consequence if premises are true according to the knowledge base.

Every transmutation has a cost assigned. The cost should represent transmutation's computational complexity and/or other important resources that are consumed. Usually, simple transmutations have low cost and complex ones have high cost.

MILS inference algorithm is a backward chaining that can be formalized as a tree searching. It is a strict adaptation of LPR proof algorithm [7], where proof rules are replaced by more general knowledge transmutations. It is based on the AUTOLOGIC system developed by Morgan [8]. To limit the number of nodes and to generate optimal inference chains, algorithm A* is used.

4   Preliminary Experimental Results

In experiments, model of a web version of a newspaper is considered. Its aim is to present articles to users. Users should register before they can read articles. During registration they fill preferences form, but they are not forced to answer all the questions. As a result, model of the user is not complete but the level of noise is low. Missing values can be inferred when they are necessary using machine learning algorithms.

Architecture of the system is presented in Fig. 1. Users' preferences and background knowledge are stored in KB. When user requests for an index page, all articles are evaluated using MILS to check if they are interesting to the user. If a new knowledge is learned using complex operators during this evaluation, it is stored in KB.

Knowledge generated by complex transmutations can be also used for other purposes. E.g. it can help to present appropriate advertisements for the current user.

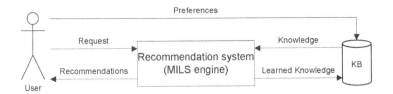

Fig. 1. System architecture

In the current version of software only one complex and several simple knowledge transmutations are implemented. Complex one is a rule generation transmutation based on Michalski's AQ algorithm [9]. All derived and stored formulas have uncertainty and other factors assigned. Label algebra used is very simple and because of the lack of space it is not presented here. Cost of MP transmutation is 0.2, cost of $SPEC_{o\rightarrow}$ is 0.3. The rest of simple transmutations have cost 0.1. The complex transmutation has the highest cost: 10.

Background knowledge consists of hierarchies used to describe articles (its topic, area, importance, and type) and users (gender, job industry, job title, primary responsibility, company size, area of interest, topic of interest), and several similarity formulas, e.g.

$$S(computerScience, telecommunication, topic). \tag{2}$$

There are also implications that are used to recommend articles. Three of them are presented below (U, A, R, T are variables):

$$V(U, article, A) \leftarrow V(A, importance, high), V(U, jobIndustry, finance) \tag{3}$$

$$V(U, article, A) \leftarrow V(U, jobIndustry, it), V(A, topic, computerScience) \tag{4}$$

$$V(U, article, A) \leftarrow V(A, area, R), V(U, area, R), V(A, topic, T), V(U, topic, T) \tag{5}$$

First rule can be interpreted as follows. User U is interested in article A if the article is important and the user job industry is finance. Second rule says that users working in IT are interested in articles about computer science. Third rule checks if article's topic and area are equal to user's topic and area of interest.

Data about twenty users and ten articles are stored in KB. Attributes of chosen three articles are presented in Table 1. Question mark means that the the value of attribute is not known and corresponding statement is not present in KB.

Table 1. Chosen Article Attributes

Article	Topic	Area	Importance	Type	Recommended
a_1	politics	?	high	news	yes
a_7	telecommunication	?	low	news	no
a_9	economy	USA	medium	report	yes

Let us trace reasoning of the system for user u_1 that is described by the following attributes: gender = female, job title = manager, job industry = banking, primary responsibility = human resources, area = North America. Other user preferences are unknown.

Status of article a_1 represented by a goal formula $V(u_1, article, a_1)$ is inferred using implication (3). First premise is matched to a statement $V(a_1, importance, high)$ from KB. Second premise, $V(u_1, jobIndustry, finance)$, is generated using value generalization transmutation (GEN_v), because banking is below finance in the hierarchy.

The article a_7 would be recommended if u_1 job was IT. In such case implication (4) would be used and a statement $V(a_7, topic, computerScience)$ would be derived from $V(a_7, topic, telecommunication)$ and similarity formula (2) using value similarity transmutation (SIM_v).

Proof for the third goal $V(u_1, article, a_9)$ is generated using implication (5). Article attributes are stored in KB. Statement $V(u_1, area, USA)$ is inferred using value specialization $(SPEC_v)$, because USA is below North America in the hierarchy. Derivation of $V(u_1, topic, economy)$ is more complicated. This statement is not supplied in user u_1 preferences, and it is not possible to derive it using simple transmutations. This is why complex transmutation AQ is used. It generates rules that allow to predict topic using other user attributes. One of rules generated is presented below:

$$V(user, topic, economy) \leftarrow V(user, jobIndustry, finance) \qquad (6)$$

It can be applied for user u_1 after specialization (application of $SPEC_{o\rightarrow}$) that replaces symbol $user$ with its descendant u_1. Its premise is inferred using GEN_v like above.

As we can see, system is able to infer plausible conclusions, automatically applying machine learning when necessary. Because system consists of on-line module only, the learning process can cause delays in responses to user requests. When such delays can not be accepted, inference engine should be modified to save information that some learning proces has to be performed and this process can be executed later.

5   Conclusions and Further Works

Multistrategy Inference and Learning System based on LPR can be used as a tool to build recommender systems. Such an approach has several advantages. Only one common knowledge representation and one KB is used to store user models, background knowledge, and user access history. All inference processes can be made using the same inference engine. This technique seems to be promising in adaptive web sites construction.

Further works will concern adding other simple and complex transmutations, such as other rule induction algorithms, and clustering methods that can be used to generate similarity formulas. On the other hand, simplification of the LPR formalizm is considered (e.g. dependency relation will be probably omitted). To extend system capabilities, user activity (attributes of read articles) will be used to build user models.

Current system is written in Prolog, what makes problems in debugging and further development. It will be rewritten in Java or C++. Next, it will be tested more intensively. Other applications in adaptive web domain will be examined.

References

1. Perkowitz, M., Etzioni, O.: Adaptive web sites: an AI challenge. In: Proceedings of IJCAI-97. (1997) 16–23
2. Frias-Martinez, E., Magoulas, G., Chen, S., Macredie, R.: Recent soft computing approaches to user modeling in adaptive hypermedia. In Bra, P.D., Nejdl, W., eds.: Adaptive Hypermedia and adaptive web-based systems, Proceedings of 3rd Int Conf Adaptive Hypermedia-AH 2004. Volume 3137 of Lecture Notes in Computer Science., Springer (2004) 104–113
3. Michalski, R.S.: Inferential theory of learning: Developing foundations for multistrategy learning. In Michalski, R.S., ed.: Machine Learning: A Multistrategy Approach, Volume IV. Morgan Kaufmann Publishers (1994)
4. Collins, A., Michalski, R.S.: The logic of plausible reasoning: A core theory. Cognitive Science **13** (1989) 1–49
5. Gabbay, D.M.: LDS – Labeled Deductive Systems. Oxford University Press (1991)
6. Śnieżyński, B.: Probabilistic label algebra for the logic of plausible reasoning. In Kłopotek, M., et al., eds.: Intelligent Information Systems 2002. Advances in Soft Computing, Physica-Verlag, Springer (2002)
7. Śnieżyński, B.: Proof searching algorithm for the logic of plausible reasoning. In Kłopotek, M., et al., eds.: Intelligent Information Processing and Web Mining. Advances in Soft Computing, Springer (2003) 393–398
8. Morgan, C.G.: Autologic. Logique et Analyse **28 (110-111)** (1985) 257–282
9. Michalski, R.S.: AQVAL/1 – computer implementation of a variable valued logic VL1 and examples of its application to pattern recognition. In: Proc. of the First International Joint Conference on Pattern Recognition. (1973)

User Activity Investigation of a Web CRM System Based on the Log Analysis

Bogdan Trawiński[1] and Marek Wróbel[1]

Wrocław University of Technology, Institute of Applied Informatics,
Wybrzeże S. Wyspiańskiego 27, 50-370 Wrocław, Poland
`trawinski@pwr.wroc.pl, m.wrobel@icentrum.pl`

Abstract. There are many tools for the analysis of Web system log files based on statistical or web mining methods. However they do not always provide information specific for a given system. In the paper special method for investigation of the activity of web CRM system users is presented. The method has been designed and implemented in the web CRM system at a debt vindication company. There was basic foundation, that analysis should be carried in three time groups, i.e. working days in hours of work, working days beyond hours of work and idle days. Besides, system should make it possible to perform analysis for a chosen employee, position, day, hour and CRM system file. The results of investigation allowed to reveal anomalies in staff activity, what was not possible using common web log analyzer.

1 Introduction

For years web logs have been the objects of numerous investigations which have provided valuable information used among others to assess quality of web site design, to trace user behaviour, to detect intrusions or adapt page content to user profiles [2,4,6,7,9]. To carry research many tools and methods have been developed. These tools are based on statistical web log analysis and the methods of web log mining [1,5]. One of the most popular and rich in functions web log analyzers is the AWStats [3]. It enables to explore the logs of WWW, ftp and mail servers. Using the AWStats to investigate staff activity of a debt vindication company on the basis of Web CRM system logs has proved to be unsatisfactory [8]. So that, in order to obtain information needed by the company management, a new analytical module for the CRM system has been designed and implemented. Specific method has been elaborated to make it possible to compare the activity of individual employee and individual position with the average activity within an hour, a day, a month. Detailed data of the system usage have been collected from the start of its operation. Firstly, the Apache web server maintains logs of all requests. Its monthly logs are saved in text files of the size of approximately 500 MB. Secondly, the PHP code contains an audit procedure which is executed before each script. This procedure writes its own log which holds information of a user, data he sent to forms, etc. Results of

P.S. Szczepaniak et al. (Eds.): AWIC 2005, LNAI 3528, pp. 427–432, 2005.

exploration of data from the period of the month of May 2004 contained in this log are discussed in the present paper.

2   Purpose and Method of the Analysis

Analysis of the behaviour of employees is very important, because it provides a big amount of information which can be used to assess and compare their work as well as to find irregularities in their work. An anomaly takes place in such period of time, when an employee works otherwise than his colleagues or than he worked earlier. May be something wrong happens, for example a salesman intends to quit work and collects data of company clients. Important is also to know how heavily the system is used, because then it may be possible to prevent the situation, when overloaded system disturbs staff to work efficiently. The usage of the CRM system was explored using the AWStats analyzer [3]. However information delivered by the AWStats proved to be insufficient to analyze behaviour of employees [8]. In order to obtain information needed by the company management, a special module of analysis has been designed and programmed. There was basic foundation, that analysis should be carried in three time groups, i.e.

– working days in hours of work,
– working days beyond hours of work,
– idle days.

In order to optimize the effectiveness of data processing, all data were aggregated for each hour of each day. Moreover, two fields were added to determine working days and working hours. In order to be able to compare data the measure of mean unit activity (MUA) was defined. The MUA is a number of file accesses within successive hour in a given day falling on one user operating this time. For example the MUA of 20 at sixteen o'clock on May 6th means that the average number of file accesses per one user within this hour was 20. The analysis was carried out for data for the period of May 2004. Within this month the Web system was loaded heavily mainly during working days and the number of users was between 50 and 60. Every day the server received from 25 to 30 thousand requests, what generated 200-300 MB of data transfer. It means that for a working days there was approximately 1 request per second and the loading about 10 KB. So the monthly data transfer reached 5 GB.

3   Results of the Investigation

3.1   The Analysis of Daily Activity

The purpose of first series of analysis was to show how the activity changed on a day-by-day basis within one month. Figures 1 and 2 show the distribution of activity (MUA) on working days in hours of work and working days beyond hours

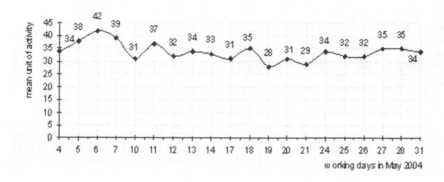

Fig. 1. Daily activity of whole staff during working days in hours of work in May 2004

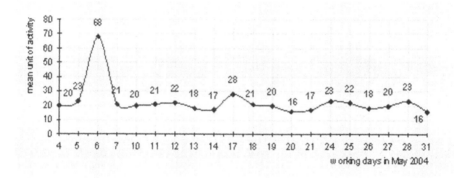

Fig. 2. Daily activity of whole staff during working days beyond hours of work

of work respectively. At first sight, it can be seen, that activity was unnatural big beyond hours of work on May 6th.

Further analyses of the activity of work postings enabled to detect the position of work and the employee responsible for this anomaly (Fig. 3). In Figure 3 the dashed line shows the activity of all postings while the continuous line presents the activity of the first posting only.

3.2   The Analysis of Hourly Activity

The analysis provides information of what is the distribution of staff activity on individual hours of a day. Figure 4 shows how the activity changed on a hour-by-hour basis during working days in May 2004. It can be easily noticed, that working day began at eight o'clock and ended at sixteen o'clock. The anomaly of greater activity at nineteen o'clock can also be noticed. But the Figure 5

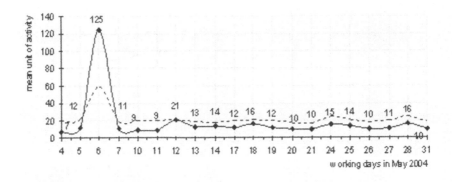

Fig. 3. Daily activity of the first posting in May 2004

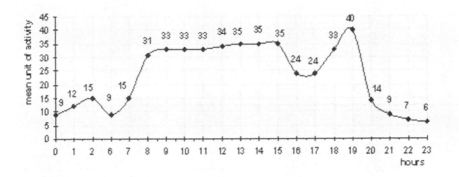

Fig. 4. Hourly activity of whole staff during work days in May 2004

presenting hourly activity on May 6th indicates the anomaly clearly. In the Figure 5 a continuous line shows the activity on a given day, while a dashed line presents an average activity within whole month. It can be seen that until seventeen o'clock daily activity was similar to monthly one, but later it started to increase.

3.3   The Analysis of the Activity of Position, Employee and File

The analysis of the activity of position revealed that the activity of first position (negotiators) did not conform to the average activity. It led to the conclusion that exactly the negotiators were responsible for the anomaly. The graphs representing the behaviour of individual employees allowed to determine which negotiator worked abnormally. In turn the graph in Figure 6 indicated which files were used heavily that day. It turned out later, that instead of performing his usual work, the negotiator was describing the content of fax documents.

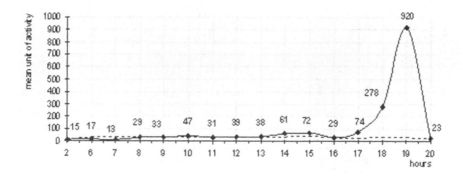

Fig. 5. Hourly activity of whole staff on May 6th

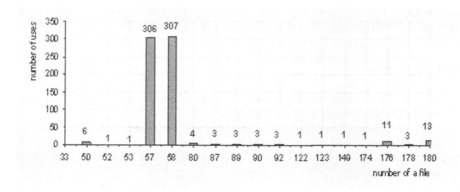

Fig. 6. File activity on May 6th beyond working hours

4   Conclusions and Future Works

All the tools and functions implemented to trace the behaviour of the company staff have proved to be useful. The anomalies could be detected and observed thoroughly. Due to the possibility to filter data and to compare individual data with average values, new information has been revealed. Such information was not available using common web log analyzer. The analysis carried separately for working days and idle days as well as for working hours has also turned out helpful. Using the measure of mean unit activity (MUA) has produced statistics on which anomalies were shown clearly. It is planned to develop new analytical functions of our tools, as the possibility to define the range of days, hours, groups of employees and files. In order to make our investigations closer to human perception of time new fuzzy time periods have been designed. They are night, dawn, morning, lunch time, afternoon and evening. The definitions of the fuzzy

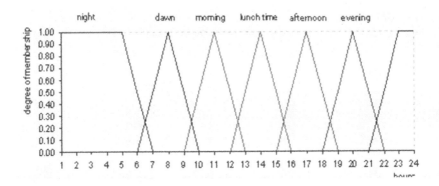

Fig. 7. Fuzzy definitions of time periods

time periods are shown in Figure 7. Besides, implementing of some intelligent mechanisms will enable us to detect anomalies automatically.

References

1. Ajith, A.: Business Intelligence from Web Usage Mining. Journal of Information & Knowledge Management **2** (2003) 375–390
2. Eirinaki M., Vazirgiannis M.: Web mining for web personalization. ACM Transactions on Internet Technology **3** (2003) 1–27
3. Free powerful and featureful tool that generates advanced web, ftp or mail server statistics, graphically (2004) http://www.awstats.org/
4. Kruegel, C., Vigna, G.: Anomaly detection of web-based attacks. In Proceedings of the 10th ACM Conference on Computer and Communications Security (2003)
5. Robertson, J.: The Value of Web Statistics (2001) http://www.intranetjournal.com /articles/ 200202/km_02_27_02a.html
6. Srivastava, J., Cooley, R., Deshpande, M., Tan, P-T.: Web Usage Mining: Discovery and Applications of Usage Patterns from Web Data. SIGKDD Explorations **1** (2000) 1–12
7. Wong, C., Shiu, S., Pal, S.: Mining Fuzzy Association Rules for web access case adaptation. In Proceedings of the Workshop Program at the Fourth International Conference on Case-Based Reasoning (2001)
8. Wróbel, M.: CRM Systems. Design and Implementation for a Chosen Company. M.Sc. Thesis (in Polish). Wrocław University of Technology (2004)
9. Zawitz, M. W.: Web statistics - Measuring user activity. Bureau of Justice Statistics (1998) http://www.ojp.usdoj.gov/bjs

Researching on Composition Framework of Web Components Based On Organization

Zhi-Jian Wang[1], Yu-Kui Fei[1,2], and Xiao-Feng Zhou[1]

[1] College of Computer and Information Engineering,
Hohai University, Nanjing 210098, P.R. China
zhjwang@hhu.edu.cn
http://cies.hhu.edu.cn.html
[2] College of Information Science & Engineering,
ShanDong Agricultural University TaiAn 271018, P.R. China

Abstract. In this paper, we present a composition framework of web components that can be used to specify and implement composition process of web components based on organization. We first , discuss the principle and process of web components in terms of organization/role. Then We present a conceptual framework for web components composition that incorporates the specification of global organizational characteristics with individual aims and capabilities .The framework consists of three interrelated models each describing different aspects of composition framework. The organizational model describes web component group with respect to roles, constraints and interactions rules. The social model populates the group with actual web components that realize the objectives of the group by enacting role(s) described in the organizational model. the interaction model describes the interaction commitments between those web components . Finally ,we make a comparison between this framework with others.

1   Introduction

As a new paradigm ,web components aims at developing services-oriented software systems[1]. Owing to its autonomy and intelligence(goal-directed , proactive etc.), it makes composition process of web components become practical and be easy to achieve. However, the autonomy of the web components also has a downside. If one creates a system with a number of autonomous web components it becomes unpredictable what the outcome of their interactions will be. This so-called emerging behavior can be interesting in settings where the composite web components is used to simulate a group of people and one tries to find out which factors influence the overall behavior of the system. E.g. some studies have been done in which groups of selfish web components are compared with cooperative web components. (In general the system with cooperative web components produces better results for the individual web components).However, in settings where the composite web components is used to implement a system with a

P.S. Szczepaniak et al. (Eds.): AWIC 2005, LNAI 3528, pp. 433–438, 2005.

specific goal one does not want this emergent behavior to diverge from the overall goal of the system.

In order to limit the autonomy of the web components in these situations and ensure a certain behavior of the overall system we need such an composition framework that can make allowable interactions between the web components under certain "norms". Of course it is important that we also define how the web components use these norms to govern their behavior. It is luck that organization theory can solve this problem . We can build a composition framework to describe the system composed by web components from an organizational perspective.

An organization can be defined as a specific solution created by more or less autonomous actors to achieve common goals. Social interaction emerges from a set of negotiated social norms and is regulated by mechanisms of social control.

n important element of organizations is the concept of *role*. A role is a description of an abstract behavior of web components. A role describes the constraints (obligations, requirements, skills) that an web components will have to satisfy to obtain a role, the benefits (abilities, authorization, profits) that an web components will receive in playing that role, and the responsibilities associated to that role. A role is also the placeholder for the description of patterns of interactions in which an web components playing that role will have to perform.

In this paper we will explore how to design a composition framework of web components based on organization.

The structure of this paper is as follows. First , we will introduce the role of web components composition framework (section 1). Then , we will discuss Principles of designing composition framework (section 2).In the following , we will give a concept model of web components composition framework (section 3) . Finally ,we make a comparison between this framework with others and conclude with a summary.

2   Principles of Designing Composition Framework

With organization and role, we can discuss how to build composition framework .First we will refer to what the advantages the method is . Then we will give some principles and designing process.

The main principles of designing composition framework is as follow:

Principle 1: The organizational level describes the "what" and not the "how". The organizational level imposes a structure into the pattern of web components' activities, but does not describe how web components behave.

Principle 2: No web components description and therefore no mental issues at the organizational level. The organizational level should not say anything about the way web components would interpret this level. Thus, reactive web components as well as intentional web components may act in an organization.

Principle 3: An organization provides a way for partitioning a system, each partition (or groups) constitutes a context of interaction for web components.

This design method has many advantages First, it defines a clean separation between the web components and the organization in which the web components works, which in turn simplifies each design. Secondly, separating the organization from the web components allows the developer to build a separate organizational structure that can enforce the organizational rules. This is especially critical in open systems where we do not know the intent of the web components working within the system.

The process of organizational design comprises four related activities:

(1) *Task specification and decomposition:* the overall task of an enterprise is divided into elementary subtasks. A subtask is called elementary if and only if it can be solved by processing one single function.
(2) *Selecting and integrating subtasks:* Next, subtasks exhibiting similar characteristics (e.g., operating on the same object, requiring the same type of skill, etc.) are grouped together in order to create coherent bundles of subtasks that can be mapped to individual actors or to circumscribed actor teams. Each of these bundles provides a base to formally define an organizational position.
(3) *Selecting and clustering positions (organizational units):* Organizational positions exhibiting similar characteristics (e.g., operating on the same object, requiring the same type of activity, etc.) or having close interdependencies are grouped together in order to create organizational units. Typical options are grouping by product and by function. This process repeats until positions and organizational units are integrated into an organizational structure, which may be a hierarchy.
(4) *Linking actors to positions:* Finally, each position needs to be filled with an actor exhibiting an individual profile of skills which matches with the task profile represented by the position.

3   A Concept Model of Composition Framework of Web Components

This model describes an composition framework in three levels.

1. Organizational model (OM): it describes the desired or intended behavior and overall structure of the society from the perspective of the organization in terms of roles, interaction scripts and social norms.
2. Social model (SM): it populates the organizational model with web components that are mapped to roles through a social contract. Social contracts describe the agreed behavior for an web components within the society in terms of externally observable events. Web components enacting a role are called actors.
3. Interaction model (IM): it speci⁻es interaction agreements between actors and describes the actual behavior of the society.

The relation between these models is depicted in[2] In general, roles interact with each other in different interaction scenes. For the sake of simplicity, in this paper we assume that an organizational model consists of only one interaction scene. That is, the society structure is completely defined by a set of roles. In the rest of this section, we will informally describe the concepts of role and web components as used in the Web components Society Model and introduce the working example which will be used in the rest of the paper.

Roles

Roles are one of the basic components of an organizational model. A role is the abstract representation of a policy, service or function. Role descriptions in the organizational model identify activities and services necessary to achieve society goals and enable us to abstract from the individuals that eventually will enact the role. Furthermore, roles must describe the necessary capabilities that must be performed by any web components enacting that role. Roles are organized into a role-relationship network.

In our model, roles can be seen as place-holders for web components and represent the behavior expected from web components by the society design. Roles are specified by goals, norms, and interaction rules. The goals of a role describe the results that the role enacting web components must seek to obtain. They are equal to what in other approaches such as[3] are called the responsibilities of the role. Norms of a role specify the obligations and prohibitions of the role enacting web components. Interaction rules describe the interaction between roles and specify how role enacting web components should interact with each other.

Web Components

In our model, web components are active entities that are able to enact roles described in the Organizational Model. Web components join a society by adopting some of its roles. In order to be able to take up a role in the society, it is necessary for an web components to alter (extend, modify or limit) its own behavior such that it will react within the society in ways that are in accordance to the expectations of the role.

3.1   Organizational Model

The organizational model specifies the structure of an web components society in terms of externally observed behavior and components. We define an organizational model as a tuple OM = (R, CF, I, N), where R is the set of role descriptions, CF is the communicative framework, I is the set of scripts for interaction scene and N is the set of society norms or rules. The elements of OM can be referred to by:

$roles(OM) = R$
$communication\_framework(OM) = CF$
$interactions(OM) = I$
$norms(OM) = N$

3.2   Social Model

The interaction structure as specified in the organizational model indicates the interaction possibilities for web components at each stage and the consequences of their choices. However, further representation of commitments between web components is necessary in order to verify the 'run-time' behavior of the society. Commitments enable actors to know how to proceed if the norm is violated but first of all indicate to the web components what behavior they can expect from the other web components. In this way, coordination can become possible. Therefore, a formal language for specification of commitments is needed in order to be able to evaluate and verify web components interaction. We define a social model as a tuple:

SM = (OM, WC, M), where OM is an organizational model of an web components society, WC is a set of web components and M is the set of social contracts mapping web components in WC to roles. M represents the accepted agreements for role-playing or contracts between web components and the society as of their presence in the society.

A social contract SC: $A \times goles(OM)^* \rightarrow g$ describes the conditions and rules applying to an web components enacting role(s) in the society. C is the set of contract clauses, defined as a tuple (P, N, V, S, T) where P is the set of preconditions, N is a logical expression defining a deontic-modality describing the role to be played by the web components, V is a time expression defining the validity of the clause, S defines the possible states of the contract clause, and T gives the transition rules between states.

Informally, social contracts must determine the operational roles and social norms applicable to an web components that is going to play a role in the society. Social contracts must describe:

Role(s) to be played by web components
Rules and interaction structures involved
Time period
Price and/or Conditions for web components action as enactor of role

3.3   Interaction Model

We define the interaction model of an web components society as a tuple IM = (SM, IC), where SM is a social model and IC the set of interaction contracts between web components in SM. An interaction contract IC: *web components*(SM)* $\rightarrow$C describes the conditions and rules applying to interaction between web components in the web components society. C is the set of contract clauses as above. In the some way social contracts describe the roles and norms applicable to an web components as enactor of a role in the society, interaction contracts describe the operational roles and social norms applicable to the interaction between web components. Interaction contracts have two or more contractors and must describe:

Description of the agreement(s)
Rules and interaction structures involved
Time period
Price and/or Conditions for action of each web components.

4 Conclusions

Research on web components(web services) composition has become a hot topic now. Mostly they are focus on how to compose web services , for example, Web Services Modeling Framework (WSMF)[4], DAML-S [5], BPEL4WS [6] and BPML [7]. The common point of them is centered on business logic and regarded web services static entity with explicit interface. Pires, P considered web components as a package mechanism and presented a concept of composition logic accomplished by XML[8]but without referred to dynamic of services. From view of organization , we present an composition framework of web components in this paper. It can easily balance between global behavior of organization and local behavior of web components, and can make use of the autonomy and intelligence of web components. It is useful in process of developing services-oriented software systems.

References

1. Fei Y. K. Wang Z. J. A concept model of web components. *Proc. of IEEE International Conference on Services Computing*, Sep. 2004.
2. H. Weigand V. Dignum J.J. Meyer and F. Dignum. An organizational-oriented model for agent societies.
3. M. Wooldridge N. Jennings and D. Kinny. The gaia methodology for agent-oriented analysis and design. *Autonomous Agents and Multi-Agent Systems*, 3(3):285, 2000.
4. D. Fensel C. Bussler. The web service modeling framework wsmf. *Electronic Commerce Research and Applications*, 1(2), 2002.
5. The DAML services coalition. Daml-s: Semantic markup for web services. *available at http://www.daml.org/services/daml-s/0.9/daml-s.pdf*, 2003.
6. BPEL. Business process execution language for web services. 2003.
7. BPML. Business process modeling language. *HTTP://www.bpmi.org*.
8. M Pires P. F. Benevides R. F. M. Mattoso. Webtransact: A framework for specifying and coordinating reliable web service compositions. *echnical Report ES-578/02 PESC/Coppe Federal University of Rio de Janeiro*, 2002.

Carrot²: Design of a Flexible and Efficient Web Information Retrieval Framework

Stanisław Osiński and Dawid Weiss

Institute of Computing Science, Poznań University of Technology,
ul. Piotrowo 3A, 60–965 Poznań, Poland
Dawid.Weiss@cs.put.poznan.pl

Abstract. In this paper we present the design goals and implementation outline of Carrot², an open source framework for rapid development of applications dealing with Web Information Retrieval and Web Mining. The framework has been written from scratch keeping in mind flexibility and efficiency of processing. We show two software architectures that meet the requirements of these two aspects and provide evidence of their use in clustering of search results.

We also discuss the importance and advantages of contributing and integrating the results of scientific projects with the open source community.

Keywords: Information Retrieval, Clustering, Systems Design.

1 Introduction

With a few notable exceptions, software projects rooting from academia are often perceived as useful prototypes, *spike-solutions* to use a software engineering term, that provide proofs for novel ideas but turn out to be unusable in production systems. In Carrot² we made an attempt to provide a useful, flexible and research-wise interesting system that can be efficient enough to satisfy real-life demands of commercial deployments. Two different software architectures coexist in the system: the XML-driven architecture is aimed at flexibility and ease of use, the local-interfaces architecture, developed later, targets the efficiency of processing.

Carrot² is mostly known for its Web search results clustering components, which successfully compete with commercial clustering solutions, such as Vivisimo or iBoogie (Carrot² was written at the same time Vivisimo was first released). The goal of this paper is to provide some insight into the internal architecture of Carrot² and to show that the applications of the framework are not limited to search results clustering only.

2 Goals, Design Assumptions and Requirements

The primary goal of Carrot² was to enable rapid research experiments with novel text/web mining techniques. To minimize the effort involved in implementation

P.S. Szczepaniak et al. (Eds.): AWIC 2005, LNAI 3528, pp. 439–444, 2005.

and evaluation of a new algorithm, Carrot^2 provides ready-to-use implementations of the most common text processing tasks, such as:

- an efficient JFlex-based (http://jflex.de/) text tokenizer,
- tigram-based language identification [1]
- stopword filtering, stemming for 7 languages,
- search engine interfaces (HTML scraping, API access),
- access to test collections, e.g. Open Directory Project data (http://dmoz.org),
- presentation of results (HTML rendering) and automatic quality measurements.

Additionally, Carrot^2 contains implementations of a number of search results clustering algorithms, including classic agglomerative techniques (AHC), K-means, fuzzy clustering [2], biology-inspired clustering [3], Suffix Tree Clustering (STC) [4] and Lingo [5].

To be truly useful in both research and production settings, Carrot^2 had to meet a number of requirements:

Component Architecture. The project should be a library; a set of *components* with clearly established communication interfaces and all the infrastructure needed to combine them into useful applications. Some of these applications should be provided as demonstration and proof-of-concept.

Flexibility. Components should be relatively autonomous and easy to reconfigure and customize. That is, components can be taken out of the project and put into other software easily.

Language and OS Independence. It should be possible to reuse components for systems written in any language and working on any operating system.

High Performance. The infrastructure in which the components cooperate should impose as little additional overhead as possible. In other words: efficient components combined together should produce an efficient system.

Permissive Licensing Options. Certain open source licenses impose rigorous restrictions on derivative works. The framework and any third party libraries it includes, should be covered by a permissive license that lets everyone use the framework, or its subcomponents in other software (commercial or open source).

3   Overview of the Design and Implementation

3.1   Framework's Fundamental Elements: Components

Central to the architecture of Carrot^2 is the notion of a *component*. The task of an *input component* is to acquire, or generate data for further processing based on some query (usually typed by a human). Examples of input components include search engine wrappers, test collections or even components returning random data. *Filter components* transform the data in some way. Examples include text segmentation, stemming, feature extraction, clustering or classification. *Output components* are responsible for consuming the result of previous components. Output components usually present the

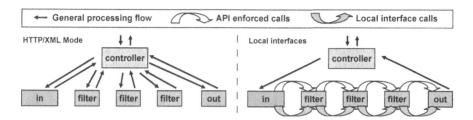

Fig. 1. Query processing in XML-based and local interfaces communication schemes

result to the human user, but may also process the result automatically as in bench-marking applications or tuning. A *controller component* combines other components into a *processing chain*: an ordered list of components where data obtained by an input component passes through a number of filtering components and is finally consumed by an output component.

3.2 Two Architectures for Component Communication Layers

Flexibility is usually achieved at the cost of performance and performance rarely goes along with flexibility. The mutually exclusive requirements are reflected in the frame-work's two different component communication layers: one design was aimed at language independence, component distribution and flexibility (*XML-based architecture*) the other was targeted at efficiency of processing (*local interfaces architecture*).

XML-Based Architecture. In the XML-based architecture, components communicate solely using HTTP POST requests, exchanging custom XML messages (an approach similar to XML-RPC protocol). The communication is mediated by the controller component that knows the order of components to invoke from the current processing chain (see Figure 1). This communication scheme is characterized by the following features:

– components can be easily distributed – the controller component takes care of remote components' invocations, regardless of their physical location;
– components can be written in virtually any programming language that supports rudimentary elements of XML parsing and HTTP protocol;
– data-centric processing; components may not know how or where the data is produced. The only required information is the format of the input and output XML files;
– configuration and order of components in a processing chain takes place at the level of the controller component. This makes load balancing and component failover quite trivial to achieve.

Local Interfaces Architecture. The XML-based architecture provides a great deal of flexibility with implementation and configuration of components. Alas, it also involves much cost in parsing/ serialization of XML files and network transfers. For production systems, an alternative solution had to be found.

We designed *local interfaces architecture* that stands for a very general concept of combining components using local method calls rather than network APIs. Note that from the viewpoint of the framework, nothing is known about these method calls – their signatures are not available for the framework until the components are assembled in a processing chain at runtime – this poses a very interesting design challenge. We have identified the following key criteria driving the local interfaces design:

Local Method Calls. Local method calls are the key to achieving high performance. Data must not be passed via bounded buffers, but directly from component to component.

Memory/Object Reuse. Intense memory allocation/ garbage collection slows down any application by a factor of magnitude. The design must provide means to reuse intermediate component data from request to request.

Incremental Pipelines. Components may not need all of their successors' data at one time. Data should be passed between components as soon as possible.

Flexible Data Types. Components should be able to exchange any data they need (using local method calls). The framework should provide means for this to happen with no extra overhead.

We separated the communication between components into *system* and *application-related* method calls. System-related calls are defined at the core Carrot[2] level. They include component lifecycle management methods and request-lifecycle methods; all components must implement these. Application-related method calls are unspecified, the components must perform an initial 'handshake' to establish their compatible methods.

At runtime, each processing chain is assembled dynamically by the controller component in the following way: each component knows its direct successor in the processing chain and itself expects data from its predecessor. Each component also declares its *capabilities* and capabilities it requires from the predecessor and successor component. A processing chain is successfully assembled only if capabilities of all components are pairwise compatible.

Capabilities are usually used to denote data-specific interfaces (with arbitrary method signatures) to perform a narrowing cast from an abstract component to a specific required type that lets the components communicate directly. For example, a component declaring `RawDocumentConsumer` capability may also declare a Java method `void nextDocument(RawDocument document)` that would accept a new document from its predecessor. The predecessor component, knowing its successor must be a raw document consumer, will simply cast the successor's object reference to a known interface and invoke the data-specific method `nextDocument` repeatedly for each new incoming document. This 'custom' communication between components is depicted as gray arrows in Fig. 1.

Each processing chain is assembled only once for all queries, so the casting and verification of capabilities overhead is minimal. After that, everything is already known and configured – almost no overhead at all is imposed by the framework at runtime. This makes local method calls extremely fast.

4   Examples of Practical Deployment and Use

We developed Carrot[2] to be a generic framework, but we also provided several implementations of components serving for clustering of search results: clustering algorithms, input (search engine wrappers) and output (XML/XSLT generators) components. Shortly after publishing the framework, we received a great deal of positive

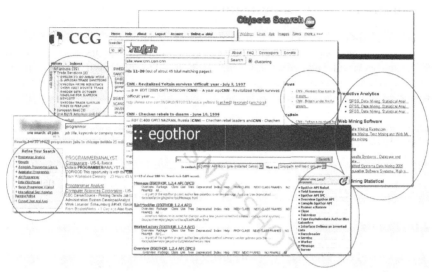

Fig. 2. Screenshots from commercial and open source software using Carrot^2 clustering and linguistic components (marked with red circles)

feedback from the research community. New research projects and papers were based on the foundation of the Carrot^2 architecture: an ant-colony document clustering algorithm [3] or a rough set approach to clustering documents from the Web [2]. Applications reusing certain components of the system were presented [6]. The framework was used as a testbed for cross-comparison of existing algorithms [7].

We were equally pleased to observe substantial commercial interest in Carrot^2 and its selected components (see Figure 2 for screenshots of systems that somehow integrated Carrot^2 components). The project's clustering components (with local controller components) were also swiftly integrated in other open source projects: Lucene (http://jakarta.apache.org/lucene), Nutch (http://www.nutch.org) and Egothor (http://www.egothor.org).

5   'Open Sourcing' Academic Software

From the very beginning, development of Carrot^2 followed the principles of open source software. The project is licensed under very permissive BSD license and hosted at SourceForge (http://carrot2.sourceforge.net). Communication among the developers and support for users community is provided through a mailing list. Public CVS access to source code and continuous integration facility (nightly builds and a demo) are also provided (http://carrot.cs.put.poznan.pl).

Our experience with Open Sourcing the software has been very positive. We especially appreciate broad interest and support from the user community – both academic and commercial. Releasing academic software as open source helps to confront it with real requirements and expectations of Web users. It also helps to make the software last longer and gain a wider audience by integration with other Open Source products – something the community is more than willing to undertake if there are evident gains from such fusions.

6   Summary and Conclusions

We have presented requirements and two different architectures for an efficient and flexible component-based software framework for simplifying the development of Web information retrieval and data mining applications. The presented ideas have been implemented and published as an open source project that spawned other research and commercial projects.

Acknowledgement

The authors would like to thank to all the committers, supporters and users of the Carrot[2] project. This research has been supported by grant KBN 3 T11C 050 26.

References

1. Grefenstette, G.: Comparing two language identification schemes. In: Proceedings of the 3rd International Conference on Statistical Analysis of Textual Data. (1995)
2. Lang, H.C.: A tolerance rough set approach to clustering web search results. Faculty of Mathematics, Informatics and Mechanics, Warsaw University (2004)
3. Schockaert, S.: Het clusteren van zoekresultaten met behulp van vaagmieren (clustering of search results using fuzzy ants). Master thesis, University of Ghent (2004)
4. Zamir, O.: Clustering Web Documents: A Phrase-Based Method for Grouping Search Engine Results. PhD thesis, University of Washington (1999)
5. Osiński, S., Stefanowski, J., Weiss, D.: Lingo: Search results clustering algorithm based on Singular Value Decomposition. In Kłopotek, M.A., Wierzchoń, S.T., Trojanowski, K., eds.: Proceedings of the International IIS: Intelligent Information Processing and Web Mining Conference. Advances in Soft Computing, Zakopane, Poland, Springer (2004) 359–368
6. Jensen, L.R.: A reuse repository with automated synonym support and cluster generation. Department of Computer Science at the Faculty of Science, University of Aarhus, Denmark (2004)
7. Osiński, S.: Dimensionality reduction techniques for search results clustering. MSc thesis, University of Sheffield, UK (2004)

Using Semantic Matching, Research on Semantic Web Services Composition*

Yu Xing, Yingjie Li, and Xueli Yu

Department of computer science and tech, Taiyuan University of Tech,
Taiyuan, Shanxi 030024, P.R. China
{youyangxy, lyj_613}@hotmail.com

Abstract. The traditional composition of web services is lack of semantic, the semantic web services composition makes use of semantic, but in the various research done here and abroad, the sequential and parallel compositions of services are seldom touched upon in terms of semantic matching. In order to address this deficiency, this paper proposes a service composition mechanism based on multi-dimensional user model. It realizes the sequential and parallel service composition. Employing this mechanism of service matching is beneficial to the realization of the service composition on the semantic web.

1 Introduction

Service composition is a key challenge to manage collaboration among web services[1]. It is an exciting area which has received a significant amount of interest. Recently, some work tries to solve the service composition problem by using planning techniques based on theorem proving(e.g. SWORD[2]), but these approaches assume that the relevant services description are initially loaded into the reasoning engine and that no discovery is performed during composition. Referring to the mentioned existed problems, this paper refers to semantic matching algorithm of semantic web service based on heuristic[3], emphasizes the two basic models of service composition. In the rest of this paper, we will give a summary about Description Logic and OWL-S, the main content of services composition and the next step of the future work.

2 Description Logic and Semantic Web Services Language

Description logic is objects-based formalization of knowledge representation. Because one of the most important applications of DL is to determine whether there is composition relation among existed conceptions. Therefore, the hierarchy of conception can be constructed.

---

* **Sponsored by** the Natural Science Foundation of China (No. 60472093).

P.S. Szczepaniak et al. (Eds.): AWIC 2005, LNAI 3528, pp. 445–450, 2005.

OWL-S is a semantic web services description language that enriches web services descriptions with semantic information, which is organized in three modules: ServiceProfile, ServiceModel and ServiceGrounding. OWL-S realizes the explicit formalized expression of web service properties and functions.

3   Semantic Composition

Three parts realize this process: designing the user's model, constructing the service ontology, realizing the service composition based on the matching algorithm.

3.1   Designing of the User's Model

The details of the user model are as following: $M =< D, V, W >$. In this model, $D =< D_0, D_1, ..., D_n >$ denotes a multi-dimension set of the user, D_i describes some aspect of the user. $V =< V_1, V_2, ..., V_n >$, V_i denotes the proper set of values corresponding to the D_i in M, $V_i = \{v|v = E(D_i)\}$ in which $E(D_i)$ denotes the admitted values of the D_i dimension. $W =< W_1, W_2, ..., W_n >$ denotes the weight value corresponding to the D_i in M, which reflect the importance of this dimension. $W_i = F(x_i, y_i)$ (i=1,...,n). $F(x, y)$ is a function used for returning the weight value of the D_i.

In addition, to every user, we also need to set up a requirement profile P based on the user models M to monitor the users' behavior. As follows: $P = \{E_1(D_1), E_2(D_2), ..., E_n(D_n)\}.E_i(D_i) \subseteq E(D_i)$. This profile can evolve through monitoring the users' behaviors. This process is: Give a user U_1 , and regard every service composition as a session, then in session K, user U_1's behavior $H_{1,K}$ is: $H_{1,K} = (h_1, h_2, ..., h_n).h_1 \in E_1(D_1), h_2 \in E_2(D_2), ... h_n \in E_n(D_n)$.

The behavior of user U_1 after q-steps sessions is $H_{l,k+q} = \{h_{1+q}, ..., h_{n+q}\}$. We introduce the variable $\Delta_{1,K \to K+q}$ show the changes of behavior of user U_1 after q-step sessions: $\Delta_{1,K \to K+q} = H_{1,K+q} - H_{1,K}$. We ascertain whether the profile of user U_1 make changes by $\Delta_{1,K \to K+q}$, if $\Delta_{1,K \to K+q} = \phi || (\Delta_{1,K \to K+q} + P) \subseteq P$, the profile doesn't change, otherwise user's profile will change, and new user's requirement profile will be created: P'. As shown above, profile's evolution can be achieved.

3.2   Construction of Service Ontology

In this paper, we need to construct three kinds of ontology. They are as follows:

Initial service ontology: The initial service ontology is constructed based on the initial information of the users and the users' model.

Service ontology: They are registered web services including atomic and composite services.

Object service ontology: According to users' model M and users' needs, construct object service ontology. The input and output attributes of the object service should be defined.

The construction of initial ontology and object ontology can adopt the WordNet technology [4].

3.3   Service Composition Mechanism

Definition 1. *In the same service procedure, a service is carried out after finishing another service, and calls such composition way as sequential composition.*

Definition 2. *In the same service procedure, the branch divided into a lot of service units that carried out side-by-side after a certain service node, this kind of composition is called parallel composition.*

Based on these two basic composition models, more complex models can be constructed, such as loop, select and nesting etc.

First of all, the effective space of matching for service composition should be determined, which can be accomplished by semantically annotating the already-registered service ontology, then the effective space of matching for service composition can be constructed heuristically by using those semantic meta-data. Secondly, the input of the initial service ontology should be matched against the input of the atomic service in the effective space. If the matching satisfies the judging requirement (as follows), then proceed to match the output of the atomic service ontology against the output of the object service ontology, if matched, then, the atomic service ontology which satisfy user's requirement will be found, otherwise, the user's requirement need to be decomposed into sub-requirement, and try to find the atomic or composite service which satisfies the sub-requirement. The process will be the same as before, if the registered service meeting the user's requirement or sub-requirement cannot be found, then service composition is needed.

The node describe the service ,the odd border describe the matching relations.

Fig. 1. Sequential Model

(1) *Sequential Model.* Figure 1 describes the sequential model of the service composition. Firstly, the multi-dimensional model M will be constructed. Secondly, construct the initial and the object service ontology.

The matching degree between services will be expressed by Match_Degree (class a, class b), the value range is $[0,1]$. Parameter 'class a' and 'class b' is the output/input of service S1 and S2.The model of composition will be decided according to the interval.

$$\theta_1 < Match\_Degree(out\_S1, in\_S2) \leq 1$$

If the matching degree is satisfied with formula (1), the sequential composition is chosen,$\theta_1 \in (0.5, 1]$. Since the matching degree is required stricter in sequential model, the prepositional value of θ_1 is 0.7. Assume the initial service ontology as a_1', the object service ontology as a_n' and the atomic service as a_i :(i=1,2,..n). First of all , service registry should be searched, so the input of atomic service ontology in effective space would be matched against the input of initial service ontology ,using the algorithm presented in section 3.4 to compute the matching degree. As to atomic service a_i , if the matching degree satisfies formula (1): $\theta_1 < Match\_Degree(in\_a'_1, in\_a_i) \leq 1$,the result shows that service(a_i) is matched against the initial information of initial service ontology(a_1').Because the matching degree of sequential composition is higher, we select the sequential model. If matching degree of service a_j and a_l' satisfy the formula: $\theta_2 < Match\_Degree(in\_a'_1, in\_a_j) \leq \theta_1.\theta_2 \in [0.5, \theta_1]$, the prepositional value of $\theta_2$is 0.5,then service a_j is considered partially satisfy the initial information of initial service ontology, then parallel model will be considered. If matching degree satisfies the formula:$0 < Match\_Degree(in\_a'_1, in\_a_i) \leq \theta_2$, the two services will be considered not matched. According to above, let's assume the atomic service ontology a_1 which matches the initial service ontology, then matching the output of a_1 against the output of object service ontology, if the matching degree between them satisfies formula (1), as below ($\theta_1 = 0.7, \theta_2 = 0.5$):$0.7 < Match\_Degree(out\_a_1, out\_a'_n) \leq 1$. The output of atomic service a_1 and object ontology a_n' is assumed to be matched, which shows the output of atomic service a_1 can satisfy user's requirement. We use DL to describe the matching between service a_i and service a_j. $a_i, a_j \in (a_1, a_2, ... a_n).\forall out\_x \in out(a_i), \exists in\_y_i \in (a_j)$, $i, j = 1, ..., n$. $out(a_i) \subseteq in(a_j)$.Describing the sequential model of service composition in figure 1 with DL as following:$a'_1 \subseteq a_1 \subseteq a_2 \subseteq ... \subseteq a_n \subseteq a'_n$.

(2) *Parallel Model.* Figure 2 show the structure of parallel composition model.:

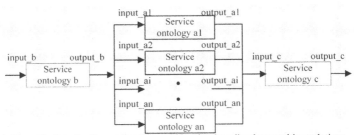

The node describe the service ;The odd border describe the matching relations.

Fig. 2. Parallel model

In the effective space, the sequential composition is the first choice. If the sequential model is not proper, the parallel composition model should be considered.

Assume three atomic services ontology: a1, a2, a3. At the same time, assume the matching degree between the output of atomic service ontology a1, a2 and the input of atomic service ontology a3 satisfies the formulas ($\theta_1 = 0.7, \theta_2 = 0.5$): $0.5 < Match\_Degree(out\_a1, in\_a3) \leq 0.7$; $0.5 < Match\_Degree(out\_a2, in\_a3) \leq 0.7$. According to these formulas, the input of atomic service ontology a1, a2 can only satisfy the input of a3 partially, now, we need to combine the output of a1,a2 with the input of a3 with parallelism. $0.7 < Match\_Degree((out\_a1) \cup (out\_a2), in\_a3) \leq 1$ Describing the process in DL: $\forall out\_x \in out(a1), out\_y \in out(a2), \exists in\_z_i \in (a3), i \in N. (out\_a1) \cup (out\_a2) \subseteq in\_a3$. Describing the parallel mode of service composition in figure 2 with DL: $b \subseteq (a1 \cup a2 \cup ... \cup an) \subseteq c$.

We need to emphasize that: during every steps of the service sequential or parallel composition, The output of service composition chain need to be match against the output of the object service ontology in order to determine whether the service composition chain that satisfy the user's requirement has been created. At the same time, sequential and parallel composition can combine with each other, so the two simple service composition models can create more complex service composition.

3.4   Semantic Algorithm of Service Matching

According to the matching relation between input and output[3] ,the matching relations among services can be classified into three categories: *Exact, Fuzzy, Fail*.

Exact(strong service matching):It means that the matching relation between out_S1 and in_S2 is exact.($out\_S1 = in\_S2$) or(out_S1 is subclass of in_S2).It is the best matching.

Fuzzy (weak service matching): out_S1 *subsume* in_S2.It means in_S2 is the part of out_S1.

Fail (non-matching): All the other matching results except those shown above are considered as failure.

4   Application Scenario

This paper takes 'Changing foreign currency' for instance to illustrate the two basic services composition mechanism involving the sequential and parallel composition. The composite service consists of several atomic services: Identity validation (S1), Kinds of exchange (S2), Credit verification (S3), Inquire exchange rate (S4), Currency exchange (S5). In these services, S3 and S4 cooperate together to achieve service S5. The sequential and parallel mechanism is adopted in this process. Table 1 Matching degree calculation table

At last, we can get the final service composition chain ($S1' \rightarrow S1 \rightarrow S2 \rightarrow (S3 \cup S4) \rightarrow S5 \rightarrow S5'$). S1' and S5' mean the initial and object service ontology. The user-supervising agent monitors the users' behavior and checks the minus set of the profile. In this instance, the profile doesn't change. Describing the process in DL as:$S1' \subseteq S1 = S2 = (S3 \cup S4) \subseteq S5 = S5'$. The matching degree of each step of this service composition is shown by table1.

Table 1. Matching degree calculation table

Match Degree	Value
Match_Degree(in_S1',in_S1)	1
Match_Degree(out_S1,in_S2)	1
Match_Degree(out_S2,in_S3)	0.688211
Match_Degree(out_S2,in_S4)	0.579420
Match_Degree(out_S2,(in_S3∪in_S4)	0.810276
Match_Degree((out_S3∪out_S4),in_S5)	0.729601
Match_Degree(out_S5,out_S5')	1

5   Conclusion

This paper mainly presents a kind of service composition mechanism based on multi-dimensional user model. This kind of mechanism realizes the sequential and parallel composition and we give some preliminary implementation of the algorithm of service matching. But how to refine the service matching space in the effective space has not been fully addressed, which will be our research emphasis in future.

References

1. Chakraborty,D.and JOSHI,A.(2001):Dynamic service Composition:State-of-Art and Research Directions,Technical Report TR-CS-01-19,Departmanet of Computer Science and Electrical Engineering.University of Maryland,Baltimore County,Baltimore,USA.
2. S.R.Ponnekanti and A.Fox.Sword:A devoloper toolkit for web sevice composition.In11th World Wide Web Conference(Web Engineering Track),2002.
3. Li Wang, Yingjie Li. The Semantic Matching of Semantic Web Services.In Proc.of KGGI,2004
4. D.11.Widyantror,T,R.logerger,and J.Yen,"an Adaptive Algorithm for Learning Changes in User Interests",proc.of the 8th CIKM,Kansas City,MS,USA,November 1999,pp.405-412.
5. B.Benatallah,M.Hacid,C.Rey,andF.Toumani:"Rwquest Rewriting-Based Web Service Discovery ", In Proc. of 2nd International Semantic Web Conference (ISWC 2003) pp. 242-257, 2003.

Ontology-Based Searching Over Multiple Networked Data Sources

Liang Xue and Boqin Feng

School of Electronic & Information Engineering,
Xi'an Jiaotong University, Xi'an 710049, China
feixuelian@yahoo.com.cn

Abstract. In this paper we propose an ontology model to describe the domain of searching over multiple data sources (SND). The ultimate goal of the model is to bridge the heterogeneity and to solve the distribution of the multiple networked data sources. Based on the model a query reconstruction algorithm is proposed to translate the initial query into different local queries suitable for individual data sources. And the result processing module defines grammar rules to extract the useful data returned by the individual data source, consolidates the retrieved data into one unified result, and presents the results in the web browser. In the ontology model two constraint rules are defined to evaluate the performance of SND and experiment results show that the federated retrieval offers a reliable and efficient reproduction with the retrieved results from the independent data sources. Moreover, the figures indicate the time comparisons among multiple data sources and give the contribution of each data source by the returned searching results based on the same query set.

1 Introduction

The digital libraries have bought many academic data sources [1], which provides retrieval functionalities by those noticeable website such as IEEE Society [2]. These data sources are autonomous and independent. Each has its own web user interface, mostly comprised of HTML forms, uses web applications and back-end databases to handle basic or advanced searching functionalities, and results in dynamic HTML pages with its own organization of the searched documents. It's time-consuming to access and retrieve data from each data source one by one, so the searching over multiple networked data sources (SND), a federated searching platform, is provided to implement an integrated retrieval of the independent data sources.

There are several papers in literature describing processes, methodologies and tools related to the development of an information-integrated system [3] [4] [5]. Notice that the above papers are mostly focused on the integration of relational databases. The networked data source which has its own user interface of web forms and returns results of its own organization in HTML format, is almost always disregarded. However, those aspects are extremely important relevant for the data source integration in digital library.

P.S. Szczepaniak et al. (Eds.): AWIC 2005, LNAI 3528, pp. 451–457, 2005.
© Springer-Verlag Berlin Heidelberg 2005

Our contribution is geared toward an integrated interface and the federated retrieval of multiple networked data sources. We propose an ontology-based model for SND whose goal is to bridge the heterogeneity and to solve the distribution of the multiple data sources. Based on the model a query reconstruction approach is used to generate new query suitable for each data source. The extracting grammars are defined to facilitate the extraction of the result from HTML pages and to consolidate them into a new XML document. As a consequence, the user is not really tied to a specific data source and new queries can be formulated, thus they can transparently access the multiple data sources.

The remainder of the paper is organized as follows: an ontology model describing the SND is proposed in section 2, then the query formulation approach is presented in section 3 and the result processing is discribed in section 4. The experiment results are discussed in Sections 5. Finally, the conclusions are given in section 6.

2   An Ontology-Based Model for SND

Ontology consists of concepts, the relationships among these concepts and predicates. It gives the user an unified semantic view of the whole system and provides a high level of abstraction of the domain. From these concepts and the relationships we can get the more clarified system view. It can be described in many formats: UML and recently XML, which makes a domain machine-readable and program-understandable.

An ontology-based model for SND has to specify abstractions representing the application, its components, the relations between components, and the constraints in the application. Therefore, we define SND model from three aspects as of concepts, relationships and constraints. The important concepts for SND include Initial Query, Web-Form (web user interface of each data source), Consolidated Results and so forth. The relationships among all the concepts are classified into several types including inheritance relation, aggregation relation, and request-response relation. The model defines two constraints as the time consistency and the space consistency. They are given as follows:

Definition 1. A model for searching over multiple networked data sources $SNDM = (V, E)$ is a directed graph, where

$V = V_s \cup V_q \cup V_f \cup V_r$ is a set of nodes representing the concepts in the SND, where V_s specifies the set of multiple data sources, V_q is the set of global queries, V_f corresponds to the set of web forms, and V_r is the set of returned HTML results.

$E = E_i \cup E_{ag} \cup E_{rr}$ is a set of edges specifying the relationships between objects and is defined in definition 5 to 8.

Definition 2. We define the process of SND as $Y = f(D, Q)$, where D is the finite set of data sources, Q specifies the initial query, Y corresponds to the returned results.

Definition 3. We define Global Query as $Q = (C, SD, P)$ where $C \in 2^{V_q}$ is the finite subset of concepts, $SD = 2^D$, is the subset of data sources; P is a finite set of predicates in the form of $P = \{(c \oplus v)\}$, $\oplus \in \{=, \varepsilon, \theta\}$, $c \in C$, $v \in M$, M specifies the value domain.

Definition 4. We define form as $F = (a, m, H_{Set}, E_{Set}, s)$, where a specifies the form element Action, which is the form handler in the server part the request should be submitted to; m is the submit method in HTTP protocol, which has two values with GET and POST; H_{Set} is the finite set of hidden attributes; E_{Set} is the finite set of explicit attributes; s is the submit button. When it is clicked on, the form elements paired with its values are submitted to the address specified by element a using the m method.

Definition 5. The results returned by the SND is a 3-tuple $R = (D, T, L)$, where D is the finite set of data sources, T is the finite set of the retrieved titles, L is the finite set of the retrieved links. For each $t \in T$, there is a $l \in L$, and $(t, l) \in 2^D$.

Definition 6. $E_{ih} \in V \times V$ is the directed edges specifying the inheritance relation between the concepts. For any two concepts $v_1, v_2 \in V$, then $(v_1, v_2) \in E_i$ indicates that v_2 is derived from concept v_1.

Definition 7. $E_{ag} \in V \times V$ is the directed edges specifying the aggregation relation between the concepts. For any two concepts $v_1, v_2 \in V$, then $(v_1, v_2) \in E_{ag}$ indicates v_1 contains one or more v_2 in one of the following two ways:
    Concept v_2 is defined as a sub concept in the concept v_1.
    Concept v_2 is included into concept v_1 as a part of concept v_1.
    For example, form element is a sub concept of form, whereas, concept of the Initial Query is a part of concept SND.

Definition 8. $E_{rr} \in V \times V$ is the set of directed edges specifying the HTTP request and response relation between client and the server part. For a client request $v_1 \in V$ and a response page $v_2 \in V$, then $(v_1, v_2) \in E_{rr}$ indicates that v_1 submits a request to the corresponding server data source and gets the returned page v_2 from the server.

Definition 9. Time consistency C_{time} specifies that for any local query q to the independent data source d with the retrieval time t, there has the time t' from the SND with the corresponding initial query. The t' and t has the relationship $|t' - t| < \sigma$, where σ is the time latency, the smaller the performance better.

Definition 10. Spatial consistency $C_{spatial}$ specifies that for any local query q to the independent data source d with the returned result sets r, there has the returned result sets r' from the federated user interface of the SND with the corresponding initial query. The r' and r has the relationship $r' = r$, which specifies r' is the same as r.

3   Query Formulation

The goal of query formulation is to reconstruct the initial query into different local queries suitable for individual data source. Combined with the selected data sources, the initial user query is first collected into a global query. For example, an instance of an initial query is described as retrieving the articles with the title as Java, publishing time between 2002 and 2003, and the result ranking by relevance. The selected data sources include IEEE Xplore, ACM and EI, thus based on the ontology model the global query is described as follows:

({G.qwords, G.scope, G.yearf, G.yeart, G.order},
{Dieee, Dacm, Dei},
{qwords = Java; scope = TI; yearf = 2002; yeart = 2003; order = relevance}).

Then to retrieve the forms associated with the selected data sources from the ontology model. They are annotated as XML-formatted documents in the model.

Next to map the concept names of the global query to those in the web form of the designated data source. For example, $Map(D_{ieee}) = \{$(qwords $\rightarrow$ query1), (Scope $\rightarrow$ scope1), (yearf $\rightarrow$ py1), (yeart $\rightarrow$ py2), (order $\rightarrow$ SortField)$\}$.

Finally to generate the name and value assignment pairs of the concept in the local query. Based on the three rules defined in our earlier work [6] the local query for the data source D_{ieee} is generated as:

q_{ieee} = ({query1, scope1, py1, py2, SortField},
{D_{ieee}},
{query1= Java; scope1=TI; py1= 2002; py2=2003; SortField =score; session = "21135"}).

Repeat the above steps until the local query sets for the data source D_{acm} and D_{ei} are generated too.

4   Result Processing

Result processing consists of three parts including HTML-Extraction, XML-Consolidation, and Data Presentation.

R_LIST ← <TABLE>(<TR>R</TR>)*</TABLE>
R ← <TD>N</TD><TD>C<TD><TD>B</TD>
B ← TU
<FONT>S</FONT>
T ← TEXT
U ← <A>TEXT</A>
S ← <A>ABSTRACT</A>

Fig. 1. The grammar for HTML-Extraction of EI

Combined with lexical analysis and syntactic analysis, using the predefined grammars the process of extraction is implemented automatically in HTML-

Extraction. Lexical analysis is to recognize the useful tokens including the HTML tags and the user defined metadata, and feed it into the syntactic analysis, which can get the right content information based on the grammar rules and the bottom-up parsing method. Finally, the parsed contents including the title of the result record and the link to it are stored in XML-formatted document. For example, Figure 1 shows the grammar for the HTML-Extraction from the EI data source.

In XML-consolidation, firstly, a new XML document with a root node is created; then for each result set an indentification is assigned to denote the heterogeneous data source uniquely, and finally, they are built up as an subtree of the new XML document.

In Data Presentation XSLT [7] rules are introduced to help rendering the data in the web browser.

5   Prototype and Experiment Results

The SNDM proposed in the paper offers an integrated retrieval over multiple data sources with a high-level transparency. During implementation the searching platform integrates part of the autonomous networked data sources [1] bought by the school library. The accessing user interface, which is "Least Common Denominators" [8], consists of five basic searching elements and a set of optional data sources. The searching result pages show the returned results consolidated together from several data sources. When clicked on, the link is navigated to the original data source articles.

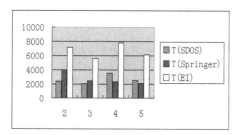
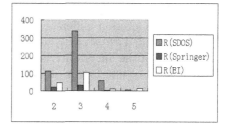

Fig. 2. The time consumed by each data source of SND

Fig. 3. The results retrived by each data source of SND

Three data sources are selected to collect the experiment results including EI CompendexWeb(EI), Elsevier ScienceDirect OnSite(SDOS), and Springer Link(Springer). The time of independent retrieval from the data source is about 5, 1, and 2 seconds respectively by average. Figure 2 shows the retrieval time(ms) of the three data sources in SND in relation to the number of the query words given the certain criteria. Based on C_{time} the σ for EI is 1.661s, for SDOS is 1.629s, and for Springer is 1.237s. Figure 3 shows the number of the retrieved results of three data sources of SND in relation to the number of the query words. Compared with the independent retrieval, it is found that the $C_{spatial}$ is satisfied perfectly.

From Figure 2 we get a comparison among the time consumed by each data source based on the same query set generated randomly. Also the contribution of each data source can be seen from Figure 3. These can help the SNDM to consider the data sources with priority for the users in different domains.

6   Conclusions

The diversity of the web query interfaces and the variance of the result organizations of the networked data sources make it difficult for the integration of SND. To settle the problem we propose an ontology model for the SND to provide a high-level abstraction of the multiple networked data sources to bridge the heterogeneity. In the model the concepts, the relationships, and the constraints are given to describe the domain of SND. Based on the model the initial query is easily transformed into local queries and data extraction is performed by the grammar rules associated with the original data sources.

Traditionally, The Precise and Recall rates are used to measure the performance of the searching system. However, there are no established guidelines to assess the adequacy of integrated retrieval. We propose two criteria including spatial consistency and time consistency to test the performance of the SND model and the experiment results show that both of the spatial consistency and the time consistency are satisfied well. Moreover, from the experiment results we can get the time comparisons among the data sources and the different contributions of the diverse data sources, which can help for considering the priorities of the data sources in different domain.

Networked data sources are steadily increasing. It is very likely that the complexity of the query criteria or result organization will increase too. In other words, the user interface is doing difficult to facilitate the transparent retrieval. However, ontology is becoming a de-facto standard in semantic web. For this reason we believe that it may be convenient to represent individual data source by means of ontology extensions.

The model has been applied into the platform of searching over multiple networked data sources in Xi'an Jiaotong University Library.

References

1. Networked data sources. http://202.117.24.24/html/xjtu/info/netdata.htm
2. IEEE Society. http://ieeexplore.ieee.org/xpls/VSearch.jsp
3. Wang H. Z., Li J. Z., and He Z. Y.: An effective wrapper architecture to heterogeneous data source. AINA (2003) 565–568
4. Zbigniew W. R., Agnieszka D.: Ontology-based distributed autonomous knowledge systems. Information Systems 29 (2004) 47–58

5. Ngamnij Arch-intPeraphon Sophatsathit.: Ontology-based Metadata Dictionary for Integrating Heterogeneous Information Sources on the WWW. Journal of Research and Practice in Information Technology, Vol. 35, No. 4, November (2003) 285–302
6. Xue L., Guan T., and Feng B. Q.: XML-based Meta-Retrieval of Networked Data Sources. WI'04 (2004) 437–441
7. XSL Transformations (XSLT)Version 1.0. http://www.w3.org/TR/xslt
8. Huang L., Ulrich T., Hemmje M., et al.: Adaptively Constructing the Query Interface for Meta-Search Engines. IUI'01 (2001) 97–100

Studying on the Awareness Model in Ontological Knowledge Community*

Xueli Yu, Jingyu Sun, Baolu Gao, Ying Wang, Meiyu Pang, and Libin An

Dept. of computer science and tech., Taiyuan Univ. of Tech.,
Taiyuan, Shanxi 030024, P.R. China
Phone (86) 351-6010071
xueli13287@263.net

Abstract. The efficiency of obtaining accurate knowledge in the WWW
is becoming more important than ever. It is therefore a critical issue for
the Web to precisely understand the semantic meaning of the words or
phrases chosen by users as well as to accurately locate the user's requirements. This article focuses on two approaches, CCAA and LCAA,
which can help the user acquire knowledge in ontological knowledge community of Semantic Web. It describes concepts and definitions about
context-awareness as well as content-awareness, and then brings forward
an awareness model in ontological knowledge routing. A proper instance
running in this tentative model is also provided in this article.

1   Introduction

This article aims to help users query knowledge in the ontological knowledge
community of Semantic Web. In the current Web, there is abundant information, which can be understood by humans, but "Most of these sites do not yet
make their data available in a machine understandable form"[1]. Formal ontology
is a kind of knowledge which can be understood by both humans and computers. With the widespread use and maturity of ontological knowledge bases (such
as CYC, TOVE and NKI), we need a concept of knowledge routing, which is
built on the application layer of the OSI model, to quickly and effectively access
the ontological knowledge base. Here, the ontological knowledge routing means
that we need to design a router for knowledge delivery. Mark A. Sheldon made
a content routing program using a content labels to permit the user to learn
about available resources[2]. We ever brought forward a tentative plan in the paper "A Kind of Ontological Knowledge Routing in the Communities of Semantic
Web"(has submitted to ICITA05 Conference). In this paper we also provided an
Ontological Knowledge Routing Model (OKRM, see part 3), the basic idea of
which is that the ontological knowledge bases can be organized into some virtual communities on Semantic Web according to different domains of knowledge;
hence it is possible for the user query some knowledge through knowledge router

---

* **Sponsored by** National Science Foundation of China (No. 60472093).

P.S. Szczepaniak et al. (Eds.): AWIC 2005, LNAI 3528, pp. 458–463, 2005.

and find the ontological knowledge nodes (OKN) they need. In other words, the model must accurately locate the user's requirements. Moreover ontology communities are those ontology groups, which share common conceptualization terminology. So it is much easier for people of an ontology community with similar background to communicate with each other in most domains of knowledge; the OKN is in fact a representation of ontological knowledge, and is also the destination of our ontological knowledge routing.

2   Related Work

The simplest definition of context-awareness is "acquiring and applying context." Applying context includes "adapting to context" [3] and "using context" [4]. In this paper, we present a Computable Context-Awareness Approach (CCAA) to enable the system to understand the user's backgrounds in community management, so user can gain knowledge in the corresponding ontology communities.

"content" in this article refers to representation of human in natural language, and it contains the three aspects: content-awareness through semi-automatic interaction, information acquisition of the user's personal taste, and the factor of transforming among different levels of knowledge. We call this model the Labeled Content-Awareness Approach (LCAA), which means that both the content of semi-automatic interaction and the user's personality could be used as knowledge labels to assist content-awareness system to comprehend the user's intention [5]. The Semantic network for traditional knowledge representation can be shown by a labeled directed graph. Also the data on the Semantic Web can be modeled in a directed labeled graph, wherein each node corresponds to a resource and each arc is labeled with a property type (also a resource)[1]. Thus, LCAA is a primary but effective method to capture the deeper meaning of the user.

Our contribution is that we can determine the rough scope of dynamic community by making use of Context-awareness, and thus locate the meaning of fine granularity knowledge (like OKN)by making use of Content-awareness .

3   Awareness Model in Ontological Knowledge Routing

The awareness model consists of 4 layers from the bottom to the top: knowledge layer, analysis layer, management layer and user interface layer, as shown in Fig.1. Here we focus on the shadowed parts: Login (receiving of login of the user's name etc), Input (receiving the user's inputs about keywords or interested knowledge), User's management (managing user's profile and login file), Community management (combining user's profile, logins and inputs to locate relative community) and Content awareness analysis module (analyzing inputs using content-awareness and mapping them to OKN).

There are ten definitions and two algorithms to elaborate the functions of five modules mainly in context-awareness and content-awareness.

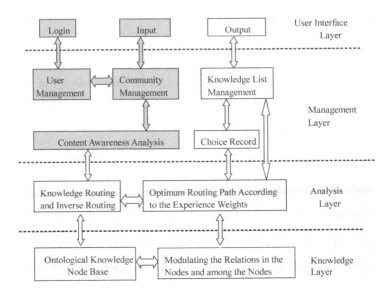

Fig. 1. An ontological knowledge routing model

3.1   Context-Awareness

The basic design train of thought: While user logs in, he or she can input or select the most *interested knowledge domain (*IKD), then the Role List of Communities(RLC) can be formed though the process of context-awareness on the basis of *users' profiles* and the IKD input newly. Thus, user can choose one community, which is usually the first one in the RLC list logged in the system.

Definition 1. *User Profile:"The system maintains a user profile, a record of the user's interests in specific items."*[5] *Here, it includes Basic Profile (BP), represented as a set BP* $\{b_1,b_2,b_3,\ldots,b_n\}$*, and Character Profile (CP), represented as CP* $\{p_1,p_2,\ldots,p_m\}$*.*

Definition 2. *Interested Knowledge Domain (IKD): the user's inputs which are his or her most interested domain knowledge, represents as IKD* $\{d_1,d_2,\ldots d_h\}$*.*

Definition 3. *Role List of Communities (RLC): a list of Communities in a descending order formed by interest degree of users.*

Definition 4. *Community (C): a virtual ontological knowledge base, represented as a set C* $\{c_1,c_2,\ldots,c_u\}$*.*

Definition 5. *Employing Frequency (EF): depending on the situation of obtaining knowledge and selecting community roles for users, system can designate* $b_i \in BP(or\ p_v \in CP,ord_w \in IKD)$ *as a value f, called employing frequency, and provide the value, which is 1 in default. Users can also specify a proper value according to interest degree.*

Definition 6. *Synonym Transforming Table (STT): this is used to transform non-normalized words into normalized words as shown in Table 1.*

Table 1. A Segment of Synonym Transforming Table

Key	Normalized words	Non-normalized Words
1	OS	Operation system
2	Windows	Win98
		Win2000
3	Unix	Linux
		Saloris
...	...	...

Definition 7. *Context-Awareness (CA) matrix: a procedure to confirm RLC through BP, CP, IKD and Community.*

Algorithm1: the target of CCAA is to narrow down the scopes of knowledge routing greatly; the whole execution of CCAA includes 3 steps:

1) Mapping rule through STT:

The community selection is implemented by mapping from BP, CP and IKD using STT.

2) Constructing CA matrix:

First, u communities are expressed as u columns in CA matrix, the j column is corresponding to c_j. . Then m elements b_i in BP are described as m rows. And the value of a_{ij} for corresponding element in the i row and the j column of CA matrix is confirmed as:

if $R : b_i \rightarrow c_j, a_{ij} =$ *numerical value f of EF;* otherwise $a_{ij=0}$.

Finally, m elements in CP as m rows and h elements in IKD as h rows are represented, the concrete constructing method is similar to the third step.

When there are no elements in IKD, system is able to only adopt BP and CP to construct CA matrix; and while there are indeed some elements in IKD, the order of users' input is assumed according to the input of IKD, it represents the interest degree to IKD, then system can fetch value according to formula:

Value of f $=f_{max}$ +h-w +1, so that the most interesting community role can be known. Here, f_{max} ={f|f= Max(a_{ij});i=1,...n+m;j=1,...,u}. Max ( ) is a function to get maximal value.

3) Computing the sequence of community role according to CA matrix

After summing up the value of each column, placing the sum in $c_1, c_2, \dots, c_u$, separately, then arranging them in descending order, we can get the order of community roles.

3.2   Content-Awareness Analysis Model:

The basic design train of thought: if there are too many choices for ontological knowledge classification then system must be able to analyze the essential meaning of the knowledge through the OKN mapping.

Definition 8. *Input Knowledge (IK): the concrete knowledge inputted by users after entering their communities, represented as IK* $\{k_1, k_2, \ldots, k_s\}$;

Definition 9. *Words (W): the word sets partitioning from IK set, represented as* $W\{w_1, w_2, \ldots, w_q\}$;

Definition 10. *Ontology Knowledge Node (OKN): This describes ontologies and instance data containing a hierarchical description of important concepts in a domain (classes), and denotes ontological knowledge; it consists of a 6-tuple set, which has domain semantic labels* [6]. *Individuals of OKN in the domain are instances of these classes, and properties (slots) of each class describe various features and attributes of the concept. The system can convert* $W\{w_1, w_2, \ldots, w_q\}$ *into an OKN set , and represented as OKN* $\{o_1, o_2, \ldots, o_t\}$.

Algorithm2:

The course of content awareness analysis, which reflects the implementation of LCAA, can be stated as follows:

First, users input knowledge IK $\{k_1, k_2, \ldots, k_s\}$. Then system deals with IK by the natural language processing method (i.e. Words segmentation), and gets a set of W $\{w_1, w_2, \ldots, w_q\}$. System can abstract the noun (subject or object) and verb from knowledge k_i of the IK set, to form main vocabulary sets, and then integrate function words into other vocabulary set. Taking users' habit of knowledge acquisition into consideration, the system can exchange synonyms in terms of STT, transforming the users' essential meaning to some existing domain vocabulary of the community, namely mapping the OKN, getting t OKN(ontological knowledge nodes) $\{o_1, o_2, \ldots, o_t\}$. Finally, these OKN having been converted can be the input to the lower layer, then ontology knowledge routing continues.

4   Application Instance

To demonstrate how the model works, we will take a concrete example to facilitate understanding. To simplify the situation we choose 14 communities in our system. These communities can be organized as a hierarchical tree, and a set C of communities is determined by the method mentioned in part 3: C (Education,Music,Movie,Computer,Software,Database,Oracle,SQL2000,OS,DOS, Windows, Unix, Internet, Management). For example, Mr. White has successfully registered and his profile has been produced. When he logs in the system, and inputs "OS" and "Windows" as his interested knowledge domain, then the system will analyze automatically and get BP, CP and IKD sets.

Finally, obtaining community roles list: $c_{11} c_1$ c_2 c_3 c_4 c_5 c_6 c_7 c_8 c_9 c_{10} c_{12} c_{13} c_{14}. This list can be converted follows:

Windows, Education, Music, Movie, Computer, Software, Database, Oracle, QL2000, OS, DOS, Unix, Internet, Management

Now, Mr.White can choose the "Windows" community role to log in to the system, and use knowledge about "windows" under the "Computer and OS" backgrounds.

A short time after he logs into the system, he may find that there is too much knowledge about Microsoft Windows, such as Windows 3.11,Windows NT 4.0,Windows 95,Windows 98, Windows ME, Windows 2000, Windows XP and so on. However, the user Mr.White only want to know "Apple Computer Windows' OS " .So he can input such a sentence as "I want to find apple's Windows' OS." to get his most interesting knowledge,

Mr.White inputs his words, and the system process them according to Part 3.2.

Now, the system inputs OKN {Apple, Windows, OS} to the lower layer, and carries on with ontology knowledge routing. The system lists knowledge as follows:

[1] Mac Rumors: Apple's Windows . . . .
[2] Apple Macintosh . . . .
[3] . . .

5   Conclusion

The Computable Context-Awareness Approach (CCAA) and the Labeled Content-Awareness Approach (LCAA) are the core parts of the awareness model. In a multi-object system, it is much more efficient to quantitatively calculate each factor than to qualitatively describe it. The model is an effective method to add content of query according to the information typed by the user. Therefore, the ideas of CCAA and LCAA are very useful, but there are still many problems which need further study. For example, how can we get as much information as possible from the least amount of input in the user profile? What can we do if the user makes mistakes or changes his mind? If the number of the user's increases, will the response time still can be acceptable? We will do our best effort to improve the OKRM model and awareness model.

References

1. R. Guha, R. McCool, and E. Miller. Semantic search. In WWW2003 — Proc.of the 12th international conference on World Wide Web, ACM Press, 2003, pp 700–709
2. Mark A. Sheldon, Andrzej Duda, Ron Weiss, A content Routing Systems for Distributed Information Severs, MIT/LCS/TR-578,6,1993
3. Abowd, Dey, Brown, Davies,Smith and Steggles, "Towards a better understanding of context and context-awareness", (panel statements), Handheld and Ubiquitous Computing, (H.-W. Gellersen, Ed.), Springer, Berlin, 1999, pp 304-307
4. Ward A, Jones A, Hopper A (1997) A new location technique for the active office. IEEE Pers Commun 4(5):42–47
5. Upendra Shardanand and Pattie Maes, Social Information Filtering: Algorithms for Automating "Word of Mouth", MIT Media-Lab, Proceedings of ACM CHI'95 Conference on Human Factors in Computing Systems, 1995, pp 210—217
6. Xueli Yu, Jingyu Sun, Baolu Gao, Xinqi Wang, A Kind of Ontological Knowledge Routing in the Communities of Semantic Web, International Conference on Information Technology and Applications Sydney, $4^{th} \sim 7^{th}$ July,2005(ICITA'2005), http://attend.it.uts.edu.au/icita05/

1st International Workshop on Knowledge and Data Mining Grid

Pilar Herrero, María S. Pérez, and Víctor Robles

Facultad de Informática, Universidad Politécnica de Madrid,
Campus de Montegancedo S/N, 28660 Boadilla del Monte,
Madrid, Spain
{pherrero, mperez, vrobles}@fi.upm.es

We wish to extend a warm welcome to the readers of the First International Workshop on Knowledge and Data Mining Grid (KDMG'05) proceedings. This workshop was held in June 2005, in conjunction with the 3rd Atlantic Web Intelligence Conference 2005 (AWIC'05). In the last decade, Grid computing has become one of the most important topics to appear and one of the most widely developed fields. Research into Grid computing is making rapid progress, owing to the increasing necessity of computation resources in the resolution of complex applications. Knowledge is playing an important role in current grid applications, allowing researchers to investigate aspects related to services discovery, service composition and service brokering. KDMG'05 aimed to provide a forum for novel topics related to Knowledge and Data Mining Grid, providing an opportunity for researchers to discuss and identify key aspects of this important area. The set of technical papers presented in this volume comprises the KDMG'05 selected papers. We can say that this selection was the result of a difficult and thorough review process. The KDMG'05 workshop received 22 submissions of high quality from which the 8 papers making up the technical program were selected. The number of submissions and the quality and diversity of the resulting program are testimony to the interest in this up-and-coming area.

This publication could not have taken place without considerable enthusiasm and encouragement as well as sheer hard work. Many people have earned the thanks of those who attended and organized KDMG'05. In particular, we would like to thank:

- The many supporters of AWIC'05 for their contributions to the conference. Many of these people have been involved with the AWIC conferences for several years.
- The members of the Workshop Program Committee who gave their time and energy to ensure that the conference maintained its high technical quality and ran smoothly. The many individuals we owe our thanks to are listed in this volume.
- All those who submitted to the workshop. The standard set was higher than our expectations and reflected well on the research work in the community.

P.S. Szczepaniak et al. (Eds.): AWIC 2005, LNAI 3528, pp. 464–465, 2005.

We would also like to acknowledge the organizers of the AWIC'05 conferences, as well as Piotr Szczepaniak for the support and encouragement they extended to this publication. This volume is the result of a close cooperation and hopefully will allow us to contribute to the growth of this research community.

Intelligent Database Distribution on a Grid Using Clustering

Valérie Fiolet[1,2] and Bernard Toursel[1]

[1] Laboratoire d'Informatique Fondamentale de Lille (Upresa CNRS 8022),
University of Lille 1, Cité Scientifique, 59655 Villeneuve D'ascq Cedex, France
{Fiolet, Toursel}@lifl.fr
[2] Service Informatique, University of Mons-Hainault 6, Avenue du Champs de Mars,
7000 Mons, Belgium
Valerie.Fiolet@umh.ac.be

Abstract. The increasing availability of clusters and grids of workstations allows to bring cheap and powerful ressources for distributed datamining. This paper deals with high performance search of association rules. It proposes to built an "intelligent" database fragmentation and distribution by using a prealable clustering step, a new method called Incremental clustering allows to execute this clustering step in an efficient distributed way.

Keywords: Grid parallel and distributed computing, Data Mining, clustering.

1   Introduction

Knowledge discovery in databases is an increasing valuable engineering tool that consists in extracting useful information from database. The huge amount of data available goes increasing more and more. Then the computation of this data need high computing capacities. To assure high performance computing, having resort to parallel and distributed approaches appears to be a solution to the problem . Thus **DisDaMin project**, context of this work, treats the problem of association rules (see Agrawal [A93] and Agrawal [A94]) by distributed considerations. In a parallel and distributed context, such as a grid or a cluster, constraints over the execution platform must be taken into account: the nonexistence of a common memory imposes to distribute the database in fragments; the high cost of communications suggests that parallel treatments must be as independent as possible. Since the problem of association rules needs to compare all data together, it is necessary to find **an intelligent data fragmentation** to distribute the computation (independent fragments). For the association rules problem this fragmentation is related to data similarity in a fragment according to the number of similar columns (attributes). This fragmentation could then be produced by a clustering treatment from which database fragments for distributed treatments will be identified. Clustering methods will be describe before introducing **Incremental Clustering** for execution on grid.

P.S. Szczepaniak et al. (Eds.): AWIC 2005, LNAI 3528, pp. 466–472, 2005.

2   Clustering

Clustering is the process of grouping data into classes so that objects within a class have high similarity in comparison to each other, but are very dissimilar to objects in other clusters. Similarity is based on the attribute values describing the objects. Distinct methods exist to solve the clustering problem. Two well-known are: KMeans (see McQueen [M67], Forgy [F65]): that furnishes approximate results but has an acceptable complexity; and Agglomerative methods (see Sokal [S63]): that furnishes exact results, but are limited with regard to the number of data to consider.

Principle of Kmeans. KMeans is an iterative algorithm that constructs an initial k-partition of data, and iterates by moving data from one class to another one. This iterative relocation technique attempts to improve the partitioning until an acceptable solution is obtained.

Principle of Agglomerative clustering. Hierarchical agglomerative clustering consists in a bottom-up approach of the problem that considers all data separately as classes and merge two nearest classes at each iteration until a termination condition. This method uses a similarity measure matrix that makes the method unsuitable to a huge number of data to compute.

Parallel algorithms. Parallel methods exist for KMeans (see for example Forman et Zhang [F00]) and agglomerative clustering (see Johnson [J99]) on vertical and horizontal data distribution (by attribute or by record instance), but need number of communications what brings performance problems in a Grid context. Those methods are adapted to supercomputers as CC-NUMA or SMP, using a common memory and with fast internal interconnexion network (Parallel Data Miner for IBM-SP3 for example).

Then it appears that classical methods need to be revisited taking under account constraints of a grid architecture. The Incremental Clustering method presented in the next section is based on those constraints.

3   Incremental Clustering

Taking under consideration distributed constraints, the proposition of the Incremental Clustering method is inspired from a sequential clustering algorithm called CLIQUE (see Agrawal [A98]). CLIQUE algorithm consists in clustering data by projections in each dimension, and by identifying thick classes. Incremental clustering works with back from CLIQUE, in a bottom up approach. It starts from one-dimension clustering results and builds multidimensional results by crossing unidimensional clusterings results. Thus first one-dimension clusterings are computed by independant distributed treatments, and crossing of results also takes benefits from distributed execution. The next paragraph explains the method of Incremental clustering with two-dimensional data. Three steps could be identified: initial clustering step, crossing step and merging step.

The **Initial Clustering step.** consists in computing each attribute of the database independently from others by one of the classical clustering algorithms (see Section 2). This step brings to a discretization of data which is an important information even outside the algorithm. Assuming that method is computed on two-dimensionnal data over attributes X and Y (see Figure 3 A). The inital clustering step over attribute X has fulfill 3 clusters over X: x1, x2, x3, respectively 2 clusters y1 and y2 over Y (see Figure 3 A). For each cluster, center, minimal and maximal values are known as well as associated records. Those unidimensional clustering treatments are computed in distributed context according to attribute fragmentation in the multibase.

Using initial clustering results, **the Crossing step** aims to fulfill candidates clusters. Thus, the first stage consists in "crossing" under-dimensionnal results of clustering (see Figure 3 B). The second stage consists in pruning potentials clusters by pruning empty two-dimensional clusters (see Figure 3 C). In the example, six potentials clusters and three final non-empty clusters are identified (Figure 3 B and C). This crossing step is computed taking advantages of the distributed execution (see Grid specifities paragraph for more details about the distributed execution).

Merging step. Crossing under-dimensionnal identified clusters will furnish "candidates" clusters and could bring to a big number of clusters with regard to the use that is intended for the results (database distribution). Adding other dimensions in an incremental way brings to get a number of records clusters unsuited to the problem to be treated, as obtained clusters will be in large number (increasing the complexity with the number of considered dimensions) and will represent a too thin distribution of records. Thus if the number of clusters after the crossing step is too big (according to the intended use), clusters are then considered as data for clustering algorithms to obtain a reasonable number of resulting groups. A third step is added to the incremental clustering consisting in grouping candidates clusters.

Grid specifities. As the previous method could be iterated, by incorporating unidimensional or multidimensional results, existing multidimensional methods

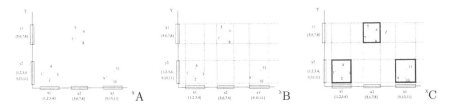

Fig. 1. Incremental Clustering Steps (over two-dimensional data)

could be used in treatment for which data are available on a common site (multi-base repartition - see next paragraph) and crossing and merging step could be used between sites (see Incremental Way paragraph).

Macro-Iterative vision. To test impact of distributed executions, solutions using unidimensional clustering for the initial step and solutions using multidimensional clustering for this initial step were compared. Those multidimensional clusterings could be computed on each site instead of computing several unidimensional clusterings on the site. This will be called macro iterative vision in the results presented in the Section 4.

Incremental way. The way "under-clustering" results are incorporated (order, integration of unidimensional or incremental clustering results) may have an impact on results. Two incremental ways of integrating clustering results are considered, a binary tree inspired way (see Figure 2 A) and a way dealing with results one at a time (see Figure 2 B). The second way is oriented towards a crossing as soon as available (from asynchronous execution on Grid). Testing distincts ways of incorporation will permit to assure that the integration order (depending on execution on the Grid) and Macro-Iterative improvements (to exploit distribution on the Grid) don't affect results.

Fig. 2. Incremental Scenarii (Ci: represent clustering results - unidimensionnal or macro-iterative, Cij, Cijk...: intermediary Incremental Clustering results)

Position of Incremental Clustering in the Association Rules problem. It is looked for an intelligent database fragmentation for the problem of Association Rules. Then the Incremental Clustering takes place as a distribution step of data in a general distributed schema for the association rules problem (see Fiolet [F02]). The general method starts with a distributed database in a vertical split, results of Incremental Clustering permit to deduce an horizontal split. Obtained groups of data records respect clustering properties: most similar data instances in a same group; less similar data instances in distincts groups. Groups could then be treated independently for the problem of association rules.

4   Experiments and Results

Experiments for the incremental clustering were realized over data from 2 to 25 dimensions, synthetized in such a way that groups exist (initial groups are known). According to the complexity of the agglomerative method, number of records was limited under 1000. Results from distinct scenarii were compared with clusters in initial data (known), and with global multidimensional KMeans and Agglomerative results.

Combination Principles Used. Clustering methods appear as initial and as crossing clustering (see Section 3). For those two stages, KMeans as well as Agglomerative methods could be considered. MA and MK represent respectively multidimensional Agglomerative and KMeans clustering. UXCYZ represent incremental clustering scenarii with: X, initial clustering (A-gglomerative or K-means); Y, cross clustering (A or K); Z incremental way (see Figure 2: B-inary or O-ne by one). MUXCYZ represent macro-iterative visions (see Section 3).

Generated Clusters. Of course referential groups (in synthetized data) are identified by multidimensional agglomerative as well as multidimensional KMeans clustering. Incremental scenarii using agglomerative clustering brings to false results: when used for initial step (UACYZ, MUACYZ), resulting clusters represent a mix of initial groups; when used for cross step (UKCAZ, MUKCAZ), the method converge until a 'huge' cluster and "unitary" ones. Scenarii using KMeans for initial step (UKCYZ and MUKCYZ) produce clusters similar to initial groups with some agglomeration of neighboor groups (10% of existing groups don't appear as independent resulting group but are included to a neighboor group). Instead, those incremental scenarii (UKCYZ and MUKCYZ) could be considered as good heuristical methods.

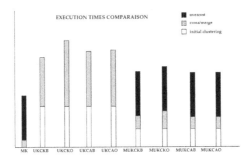

Fig. 3. Computation time comparison for scenarii including KMeans

Time Considerations. Tests permit to confirm that the use of agglomerative method brings to most expansive computation for time considerations, as those versions do not produce 'right' clusters, details about time's consideration for those methods are not given. Figure 3 represents computation times for KMeans based versions of incremental clustering (MK, UKCYZ et MUKCYZ).UKCYZ versions have computation's time 15 time greater to a MK multidimensional clustering, but offer high parallelisation capabilities. MUKCYZ versions have

Table 1. Balances

	Balance from using Agglomerative or KMeans clustering				Balance over incremental clustering and classical clustering			
Version	UACA	UKCA	UACK	UKCK	MA	MK	UKCKZ	MUKCKZ
Time	——	+	——	++	—-	+++++	++	++++
Quality of clusters	—	—-	—-	+++	+++	+++	+++	+++
Possible parallelisations					0	0	+++	+++

computation's time 6 time greater to a MK multidimensional clustering, but also offer high parallelisation capabilities (see Table 1). Then macro iterative scenarii furnish 'right' clusters, but also good computation time (even including a necessary overcost for the association rules problem, black zones on Figure 3). Macro Iterative vision also contains parallelisation capabilities at several steps (pluridimensional initial step as well as unidimensional, crossing..., see Table 1). Then those MUKCKZ scenarii hold attention for futur works.

Balance Sheets. Table 1 presents balance from clustering methods (Agglomerative or KMeans) as initial clustering and merging clustering (see Section 3) for execution time, quality of results and parallel capabilities, and balance from using multidimensional clustering or incremental clustering.

5   Conclusions and Perspectives

Conclusions. Incremental clustering results appears acceptable relatively to the possibility offered to distribute the algorithm in a suited way on a Grid. The incremental way (binary tree or individual based from which the clustering is done appears not to have a great influence on results since those results are similar for each way, but could be used to take advantages of distributed computing specificities and from the initial repartition of the multibase.

Perspectives. As the problem of incremental clustering has been studied to solve the problem of an intelligent fragmentation of data for the association rules problem (see Section 1), actual works consist in using this method as fragmentation in the general DisDaMin schema. Distributed considerations for incremental way are then inspired from the initial repartition of the multibase and global pipeline considerations are applied in relation with those incremental ways.

References

[A93]   R. Agrawal, T. Imielinski, and A. Swami. Database mining : A performance perspective. In *Special issue on learning and discovery in knowledge-based databases*, 5(6):914-925 IEEE (December 1993).

[A94]   R. Agrawal and R. Srikant. Fast algorithms for mining associations rules in large databases. In *Proc. of VLDB'94*, pages 478-499 (September 1994).

[A98] R. Agrawal, J. Gehrke, D. Gunopulos and P. Raghavan. Automatic subspace clustering of high dimensional data for data mining application. In *Proc. of the ACM Conf. on Management of Data*, 94-105.(1998).

[F02] V. Fiolet and B. Toursel. Distributed Data Mining. In *Proc. of the ISPDC'02*, pages 349-365(July 2002).

[F65] E. Forgy. Cluster analysis of multivariate data: Efficiency vs. interpretability of classifications. *Biometrics*, 21:768, (1965).

[F00] G. Forman and B. Zhang. Distributed data clustering can be efficient and exact. In *SIGKDD explorations*, volume 2(2000).

[J99] E. Johnson and H. Kargupta. Collective, hierarchical clustering from distributed, heterogenous data. In *LNCS*, volume 1759, pages 221-244 Springer-Verlag(1999).

[M67] J. McQueen. Some methods for classification and analysis of multivariate observations. In *Proc. of the Fifth Berkeley Symposium on Mathematical Statistics and Probability*, pp. 281-297, (1967).

[S63] R. Sokal and P. Sneath. Numerical Taxonomy. San Francisco: Freeman(1963).

A Semantically-Rich Management System Based on CIM for the OGSA Security Services[*]

Félix J. García Clemente, Gregorio Martínez Pérez,
and Antonio F. Gómez Skarmeta

Departamento de Ingeniería de la Información y las Comunicaciones,
University of Murcia, Spain
{fgarcia, gregorio, skarmeta}@dif.um.es

Abstract. The lack of explicit semantics in the current security management solutions for OGSA (Open Grid Services Architecture) makes them not suitable for large distributed systems as data mining grids. Management representations based on the concept of ontology are being used to incorporate semantic expressiveness and reasoning capabilities. This paper proposes the adoption of a semantically-rich CIM (Common Information Model)-based policy management system for the OGSA Security Architecture, in which the security policy development is based on the use of OWL (Web Ontology Language) and OWL-S (OWL-based Web Service Ontology).

1 Introduction and Rationale

During the past years, Grid Computing and Web Services have started to merge and to benefit from the synergy of both paradigms. The Global Grid Forum (GGF) [6] presented the Open Grid Services Architecture (OGSA) as the fusion between Grid Computing and Web Services.

Grids, as any computing environment, require some degree of system management, and especially security management. It is a potentially complex task that requires sophisticated services or applications. The immaturity of the current management solutions along with the limited scope and total absence of explicit semantics in the management representations make them less than ideal candidates, mainly in highly-distributed environments such as data mining grids.

To address this issue management representations based on ontological languages such as OWL (Web Ontology Language) [9] are being used to incorporate semantic expressiveness into the management information specifications and some reasoning capabilities which definitely will help in handling the security management tasks.

This paper proposes the adoption of a semantically-rich policy-based approach for the management system of the OGSA Security Architecture [8], in

---

[*] This work has been partially funded by the EU POSITIF (Policy-based Security Tools and Framework) IST project (IST-2002-002314).

P.S. Szczepaniak et al. (Eds.): AWIC 2005, LNAI 3528, pp. 473–479, 2005.

which the security policy development is based on the use of OWL and OWL-S [2]. Our proposal makes use of the policy-based management framework proposed by the IETF [7] and the Common Information Model (CIM) by the DMTF [3]. It is also based on previous research works [4] [5].

This document is structured as follows. Section 2 provides an overview of the security model and the management architecture in OGSA. Section 3 presents our CIM-based semantically-rich management representation oriented to Web services, which will be used in section 4 to describe our proposed semantic policy management system for OGSA grid. Then, section 5 shows a case of study for the authorization security service. Finally, we conclude the paper with our remarks.

2   OGSA Management Architecture Overview

The management in OGSA [1] can be layered in three levels, each level defining a particular management interface. At the resource level, resources are managed directly through their native management interfaces (e.g., SNMP, CIM/WBEM, or proprietary interfaces), while the infrastructure level determines the base management behaviour of resources, providing the basic management functionality that is common to the OGSA capabilities. Finally, the OGSA functions level provides the specific management interface for each particular OGSA capability (e.g. authorization).

At the OGSA functions level there are two types of management interfaces. The functional interface exposes the OGSA capabilities (e.g., create or remove an authorization privilege for a given grid service), whereas the manageability interface provides the management of the particular capability (e.g., to start or to stop the service). The clear separation between these interfaces is necessary, since different software agents with different roles and access permissions can make use of them, as we will see later in this paper.

Then, services such as security services need a functional management (i.e. specialized functional interfaces), and also need specialized manageability interfaces. However, there is a lack from GGF, and other standardization and research bodies regarding the definition of management models at this level, being the Common Information Model (CIM) the only proposal referenced as a possible candidate for such models, but without further work in this area. One of the advantages of using CIM at this level is that it can be used to define an interoperable management ontology providing semantics and reasoning to the management of grid systems.

3   Semantically-Rich Representation Oriented to the Management of Web Services

The Common Information Model (CIM) is an approach from the DMTF that applies the basic structuring and conceptualization techniques of the object-oriented paradigm to provide a common definition of management-related information for systems, networks, users, and services.

The CIM model is independent of any implementation or repository. However, for an information model to be useful, it has to be mapped into some implementation. As Figure 1 shows, CIM can be mapped to (or represented as) several structured specifications.

Thus, CIM could be mapped to structured specifications such as XML and WSDL [5], which could then be used to define management resources and management interfaces for web services. However, XML and WSDL do not provide formal semantics. A machine can validate the syntax of a XML document, but it cannot perform useful reasoning tasks.

We propose the mapping of CIM to OWL for describing the CIM objects (i.e. classes, associations, properties, references and instances), while OWL-S is used to describe the management services.

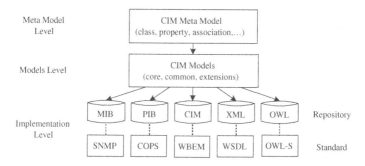

Fig. 1. CIM modelling levels

OWL is an ontology language, whereas OWL-based Web Service Ontology (OWL-S) is used to describe the properties and capabilities of Web services in unambiguous, computer-interpretable form.

The ontology for service has three main parts: the service profile for advertising and discovering services; the process model, which gives a detailed description of a service operation; and the grounding, which provides details on how to interoperate with a service, via messages.

Also note that the mapping of CIM to a valid representation for semantic web services is beneficial, since it permits to model a semantic web service using the DMTF methodology and hence obtain a standard representation of it. According to our approach, and regarding the mapping of CIM into OWL, the main principles identified as part of this mapping process were:

- Every CIM class generates a new OWL class using the tag <owl:Class>.
- Every CIM generation (inheritance) is expressed using the tag <rdfs:subClassOf>.
- Every CIM class attribute is specified using the tag <owl:DatatypeProperty> for literal values or <owl:ObjectProperty> as references to class instances.

– Every CIM association is expressed as an OWL class with two <owl:ObjectProperty> elements; this is the most suitable general-purpose mechanism currently available according to our research.

Our research also identified that the mapping of CIM operations can also be directly done taking the CIM specification and transforming it into OWL-S. Every CIM service generates a service profile, service model and service grounding. An example of the output of these transformations for the specific case of the authorization service is presented and explained in section 5.

4   A Semantic Policy-Based Management System

Our proposal defines the policy-based management of the OGSA security services as depicted in Figure 2. This architecture was designed as an evolution of the IETF approach to policies, but providing some new features, as the complete use of XML/OWL related technologies and tools in the policy life cycle. Moreover, the proposed architecture is independent of any particular security service.

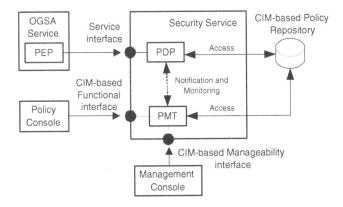

Fig. 2. CIM-based policy management interfaces and architecture

Policy Management Tool (PMT) allows software agents to develop OGSA security policies making use of the functional interface, and to monitor the status of the security service by means of the manageability interface.

Regarding the policy representation, the use of a semantically-rich language as OWL reduces human errors, simplifies policy analysis and conflict resolution tasks, and facilitates interoperability in largely distributed environments like data mining grids. Moreover, regarding the management interfaces for OGSA security services, the use of OWL-S facilitates the integration of the service in advanced web services, i.e. semantic web.

The CIM classes used to model the OGSA security services are the class SecurityService and its subclasses (i.e. AuthenticationService, AuthorizationService and AccountManagementService) each one representing a different security service. It is also important to note that these classes can be extended in the future to model other security services not supported yet (e.g., PrivacyService).

5   Case Study: The OGSA Authorization Security Service

CIM defines the classes depicted in Figure 3 to represent the management concepts that are related to the authorization security service. Privilege is the base class for all types of activities, which are granted or denied to a subject by a target. Authorized-Privilege is the specific subclass for the authorization activity.

Whether an individual Privilege is granted or denied is defined using the PrivilegeGranted boolean. The association of subjects to AuhorizedPrivileges is accomplished explicitly via the association AuthorizedSubject. The entities that are protected (targets) can be similarly defined via the association AuthorizedTarget. Note that AuthorizedPrivilege and its AuthorizedSubject/Target associations provide a static mechanism to represent authorization policies.

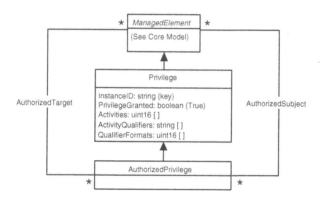

Fig. 3. UML diagram of User-Authentication classes

The mapping of these CIM objects to OWL defines the internal representation of the authorization policies. For this case of study, the following example shows a fragment of the mapping into OWL of the Privilege class defined in CIM (which follows the general steps explained in section 3).

```
<owl:Class rdf:ID=''CIM_Privilege''>
 <rdfs:subClassOf rdf:resource=''CIM_ManagedElement''/> </owl:Class>
<rdf:Property rdf:ID=''PrivilegeGranted''>
 <rdfs:domain rdf:resource=''CIM_Privilege''/>
 <rdfs:range rdf:resource=''Boolean''/> </rdf:Property>
<rdf:Property rdf:ID=''Activities''>
 <rdfs:domain rdf:resource=''CIM_Privilege''/>
 <rdfs:range rdf:resource=''Uint16''/> </rdf:Property>
```

Regarding CIM methods, the service PrivilegeManagementService is responsible of creating, deleting, and associating AuthorizedPrivilege instances. PrivilegeManagementService has the method AssignAccess that updates the specified Subject rights to the Target, and the method RemoveAccess that revokes a specific AuthorizedPrivilege for a particular target, subject, or subject/target pair. The method RemoveAccess is defined in CIM as follows:

```
RemoveAccess(
  [IN] Subject: ref ManagedElement,
  [IN] Privilege: ref AuthorizedPrivilege,
  [IN] Target: ref ManagedElment): uint32 {enum}
```

The mapping of this CIM service to OWL-S defines the functional interface for the service management. This is a simplified fraction of the OWL-S process model derived from the CIM methods:

```
<process:AtomicProcess rdf:ID=''RemoveAccess''>
<process:hasInput> <process:Input rdf:ID=''Subject''>
   <process:parameterType rdf:resource=''#ManagedElement''/>
</process:Input> </process:hasInput>
<process:hasInput> <process:Input rdf:ID=''Privilege''>
   <process:parameterType rdf:resource=''#AuthorizedPrivilege''/>
</process:Input> </process:hasInput>
<process:hasInput> <process:Input rdf:ID=''Target''>
   <process:parameterType rdf:resource=''#ManagedElement''/>
</process:Input> </process:hasInput>
<process:hasOutput> <process:UnConditionalOutput rdf:ID=''output''>
   <parameterType rdf:resource=''Uint32'' />
</process:UnConditionalOutput> </process:hasOutput>
</process:AtomicProcess>
```

The manageability interface is defined by the mapping of the CIM operations of the Service class to OWL-S. The method StartService places the service in the started state and the method StopService places it in the stopped state. Current research work is extending these two classes to add new methods that can model service-specific manageability requirements.

6   Conclusions

This paper contributes to the definition of a management system for the security services in OGSA (Open Grid Services Architecture) aligned with the Semantic Web model. It is based on the DMTF standardization initiative, thus providing a common definition of management information in the global standardization effort currently undertaken by the Grid community.

CIM is used to define the management interfaces and the policy internal representation of security services. Furthermore, the mapping of CIM to a valid representation for semantic web services is beneficial, since it permits to model the management interfaces using the DMTF methodology and hence obtain its standard representation. Moreover, the combination of CIM model and IETF policy-based management architecture facilitates the implementation of the management service.

References

1. F. Buchholz. *Resource Management in OGSA*. Global Grid Forum, June 2004.
2. OWL Services Coalition. *OWL-S: Semantic Markup for Web Services*, november 2003. http://www.daml.org/services/owl-s/1.0/.
3. DMTF. *Common Information Model (CIM) Standards*, 2004. http://www.dmtf.org/standards/cim.
4. G. Martínez F.J. García, O. Cánovas and A.F. Gómez-Skarmeta. Self-configuration of grid nodes using a policy-based management architecture. In *ICCS '04: Proceedings of the 2004 International Conference on Computational Science*, June 2004.
5. O. Cánovas F.J. García, G. Martínez and A.F. Gómez-Skarmeta. A proposal of a cim-based policy management model for the ogsa security architecture. In *GADA '04: Proceedings of 1st International Workshop on Grid computing and its Aplication to Data Analysis on the move federated conferences 2004*, Octuber 2004.
6. GGF. *The Global Grid Forum*, 2004. http://www.gridforum.org.
7. IETF. *Policy Framework (policy) Working Group*, 2004. http://www.ietf.org/html.charters/policy-charter.html.
8. N. Nagaratnam. *The Security Architecture for Open Grid Services*. Global Grid Forum, 2003.
9. W3C. *OWL Scheme*, 2004. http://www.w3.org/2004/OWL.

A Flexible Grid Infrastructure for Data Analysis

Hanna Kozankiewicz[1], Krzysztof Stencel[2], and Kazimierz Subieta[1,3]

[1] Institute of Computer Sciences of the Polish Academy of Sciences, Warsaw, Poland
[2] Institute of Informatics, Warsaw University, Warsaw, Poland
[3] Polish-Japanese Institute of Information Technology, Warsaw, Poland

Abstract. In this paper we present a novel infrastructure for data analysis based on the mechanism of updatable views. The views are used in two ways: as wrappers of local servers, which allow one to adopt local schemata to warehousing requirements, and as a facility for data integration and transformation to a federated canonical data model. Such updatable views present virtual data to the clients, but they themselves are also objects that can have methods and other features. The advantage of our approach is a simple architecture and a user-friendly query language for definition of views and for writing applications. Thus our approach can compete with Web Services, CORBA and other middleware technologies in terms of universality, flexibility and maintainability. This approach is based on the Stack-Based Approach to query languages, in which the query language is treated as a kind of programming languages.

1   Introduction

Grid computing is a technology dealing with integrating many computers into one big virtual computer which combines resources of particular computers (processing power, storages, data, services, etc.) In this paper we focus on data-intensive applications of grid where distribution of data implies distributed and parallel computation. Data mining and knowledge discovery apparently are among such data-intensive applications. In order to discover any hidden rules and/or trends the data must be well integrated and there must exist means to process them in a distributed environment.

The paradigm of distributed/federated databases as the basis for the grid technology is materialized in Oracle10g [1]. Technologies and applications based on CORBA [2] also follow this paradigm. It is based on data-centric (or object-centric) view, in which the designers start from developing a canonical federated data/object model and a data/object schema. In case of object-oriented models objects are associated with behavior. The next phase is development of applications acting on such federated (global) data/object resources.

In majority of cases of distributed/federated databases the design assumes the bottom-up approach, where existing heterogeneous distributed data and services are to be integrated into the virtual whole that follows some canonical or federated data/object model. This is just the idea of CORBA, which assumes the

P.S. Szczepaniak et al. (Eds.): AWIC 2005, LNAI 3528, pp. 480–485, 2005.

definition of a canonical model via IDL and skeletons/wrappers/adaptors that transform local server resources to the form required by the canonical model.

In this paper present a new infrastructure for data analysis, to handle problems with integration of data. In the approach we assume autonomy of local databases. Autonomy means that in order to be connected to the grid the service providers need not to change their current information systems (or change only a little). Data and services of a particular server are made visible for global applications through a wrapper that virtually maps the data/services to some assumed canonical object model. Then, all contributing services are integrated into the virtual whole by means of a updatable views. This way all data are seen through a canonical federated schema.

Although the idea of using views for integration of distributed data is not new (e.g. [3, 4]), the problem is still challenging due to updatability and practical universality of view definitions. In [5] we described how one can deal with virtual updatable object-oriented database views. In this paper we propose a novel approach to grid based on this approach. The approach allows one to reduce the time required for development of analysis framework. The proposed approach is based on the Stack-Based Approach (SBA) to query languages and the idea of updatable views defined within this approach.

The presented approach can be used as an integration framework for distributed and heterogeneous data/service resources. A view definition can handle not only passive data but also methods (operations). A view delivers to the clients virtual objects associated with operations. Such views offer similar facilities as Web Services and CORBA-based middleware. They also cover the functionality of federated databases and the CORBA Persistent State Service. The advantage of the approach is that it is much more flexible, universal and user-friendly than the mentioned technologies.

The rest of the paper is structured as follows. In Section 2 we describe Stack-Based Approach to query languages. In Section 3 we sketch approach to updatable views that is a core of the presented infrastructure for data analysis. In Section 4 we explain ideas of the infrastructure. In Section 5 we illustrate this approach by giving an example. Section 6 concludes.

2 Stack-Based Approach

In SBA [6] a query language is considered a special kind of a programming language. Thus, the semantics of queries is based on mechanisms well known from programming languages like the environment stack. SBA extends this concept for the case of query operators, such as selection, projection/navigation, join, quantifiers and others. Using SBA one is able to determine precisely the operational semantics (abstract implementation) of query languages, including relationships with object-oriented concepts, embedding queries into imperative constructs, and embedding queries into programming abstractions: procedures, functional procedures, views, methods, modules, etc.

SBA respects the naming-scoping-binding principle, which means that each name occurring in a query is bound to the appropriate run-time entity (an object, an attribute, a method a parameter, etc.) according to the name scope. The principle is supported by means of the environment stack, extended (in comparison to programming languages) to cover database collections and all typical query operators occurring e.g. in SQL and OQL. Due to stack-based semantics we achieve full orthogonality and compositionality of query operators. The stack also supports recursion and parameters.

SBA and its query language SBQL have several implementations: for the LOQIS system, for XML DOM model, for the European project ICONS, for Objectivity/DB and for the currently developed object-oriented platform ODRA.

3   Views in SBA

Views are mappings of stored data into virtual ones. The main feature of views is transparency, which assures that that the programmers should not distinguish virtual and stored data by any syntactic options. Transparency of views is easy to achieve for retrieval (see SQL), but it is an extremely hard issue for updating of virtual data. The problem of updatable database views has been known for decades. There are a lot of theoretical proposals, but the practical impact is very low, especially for object-oriented and XML-oriented databases. Some (very limited) view updating capabilities are offered by Oracle. In the case of relational databases (Oracle, MS SQL Server) the "instead of" triggers are the only sufficiently robust solution. Our approach goes exactly in this direction, but it is not based on triggers, it is more flexible and universal.

The SBA approach to updatable views is presented e.g. in [5]. The idea is to augment the definition of a view with the information on users' intents with respect to updating operations. The first part of the definition of a view is the function, which maps stored objects into virtual ones (similarly to SQL), while the second part contains redefinitions of generic operations on virtual objects. The definition of a view usually contains definitions of subviews, which are defined on the same principle. Because a view definition is a regular complex object, it may also contain other elements, such as procedures, functions, state objects, etc.

4   Infrastructure for Data Analysis

In this section we present our infrastructure for data analysis (see Fig. 1). The heart of it is the global virtual object and service store (or global virtual store). Global clients are applications that send requests and queries to the global virtual store. The global schema is a collection of definitions of data and services provided by the global virtual store. The infrastructure offers services and data of local servers to these global clients. The local schema defines data and services inside a local server.

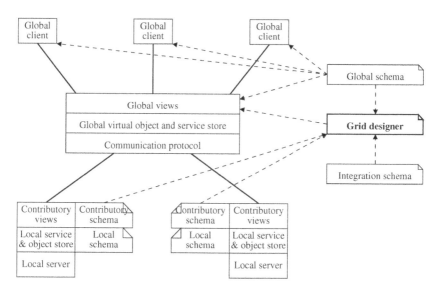

Fig. 1. The architecture of the grid

The first step of the integration of a local server into the grid is done by the administrator of this local server. He/she has to define the contributory schema which must conform to the global schema. It is the description of the data and services contributed by the local server to the grid. The local server's administrator also defines contributory views that constitute the mapping of the data to the form digestible to the grid.

The second step of the integration of local servers into the grid is the creation of global views. These views are stored inside the global virtual store. The interface of them is defined by the global schema. They map the data and services provided by the local servers to the data and services available to the global clients.

The communication protocol is the collection of routines used in the definition of the global views. It contains the functions to check e.g. the state (up or down) of a local server and the access time to a local server.

Global views are defined by the grid designer, which is a person, a team or software that generates these views upon the contributory schemata, the global schema and the integration schema. The integration schema contains additional information how the data and services of local servers are to be integrated into the grid. The integration schema holds only the items that cannot be included in the contributory schemata.

In the figure solid lines represent run-time relationships i.e., queries, requests, and answers. Global users ask global view for resources and the global view request resources from local servers. In the figure dashed arrows illustrate association that are used during development of the grid software. The programmers of global applications (global clients) use the global schema. The global views conform to the global schema. The grid designer uses the contributory schemata, the global schema and the integration schema in order to develop a global view.

5   An Example Application

We present a simple example of a data analysis application. It integrates resources stored at multiple locations. We assume that we deal with multiple stores located in Cracow, Warsaw and Radom. The application facilitates checking rules. A global schema and contributory schemata are the same, Fig. 2. Contributory views are the same.

Fig. 2. Schema of example database

In the integration schema we have only the information that global database is a union of all three databases. The example global view that integrates these distributed resources might look as follows:

create view mySaleDef {
  virtual objects mySale {
    return ((Radom.Sale) ∪ (Cracow.Sale) ∪ (Warsaw.Sale)) **as** s; }
  on_retrieve do {
    return s.(deref(customer) as cust, deref(date) as date, items as items); }
}

In this example we implicitly use some routine of the communication protocol, i.e., navigation ("."). These routines are called as if they were performed locally, although in fact they are performed on data from remote servers. Inside the global virtual store these operations are to be implemented as communication protocol features.

With this view in hand one can define procedures which check rules. These procedures can be defined by global clients themselves or be provided by the global virtual store. The following procedure uses the above view and checks the support for rules of form: for $s \in mySale$ holds $p_1 \in s.items.Item.product \rightarrow p_2 \in s.items.Item.product$.

proc support(p1, p2) {
  create local (count(mySale **where**
    exists (items.Item **where** product = p1 **and** product = p2))) **as** a;
  create local (count(mySale)) **as** b;
  return a / b;
}

Find pairs of products satisfying the rule with the support higher than 90

$$(\textbf{unique}(\text{mySale.items.Item.product}) \textbf{ group as } \text{p}).(\text{p as p1, p as p2})$$
$$\textbf{where } \text{p1} \neq \text{p2 and support(p1, p2)} > 0.9$$

This is a very simple application showing only location transparency available for the programmer due to the mySale view. The space limit does not allow us to present more complex examples, where we can cope with heterogeneity of local servers, replications, redundancies in source data and various forms of fragmentation of objects and their collections. Views in this approach are complex objects which can have any content, including local objects and procedures. This makes it possible to create stateful views, which could e.g. store rules to be tested, discovered rules, etc. Global users could use such views as a data analysis framework that integrates data sources, stores the rules and performs verification and applications of the rules.

6   Summary

We have presented a novel approach based on updatable views to implementing data analysis frameworks. The approach fulfills requirements for database integrating applications, such as transparency and interoperability. In the approach we integrate data sources using the query language SBQL and updatable views which ensure a high abstraction level. The advantage is shortened time of developing new applications and adapting existing application to changing requirements. The presented view mechanism is flexible and allows one to describe any mappings from a local database schema to any canonical federated database schema. Furthermore, our views can have methods, thus our architecture offers the same facilities as CORBA and Web Services.

Currently we are implementing this approach in the prototype platform ODRA which is an object (or XML)-oriented database management system based on SBA and SBQL.

References

1. Oracle 10g: Infrastructure for Grid Computing, Oracle White Paper, Sept. 2003.
2. OMG: OMG CORBA^{TM}/IIOP^{TM} Specifications. http://www.omg.org/technology-/documents/corbaspeccatalog.htm, 2002.
3. Halevy, A. Y.: Answering queries using views: A survey. VLDB J. **10**(4): 270-294 (2001).
4. Bellahsene, Z.: Extending a View Mechanism to Support Schema Evolution in Federated Database Systems. Proc. of DEXA 1997, 573-582.
5. Kozankiewicz, H., Leszczyłowski, J., Subieta, K.: Updatable XML Views. Proc. of ADBIS, Springer LNCS 2798, pp. 385-399, Dresden, Germany, 2003.
6. Subieta, K., Kambayashi, Y., Leszczyłowski, J.: Procedures in Object-Oriented Query Languages. Proc. of 21-st VLDB Conf., 1995, 182-193.

SoPhIA: A Unified Architecture for Knowledge Discovery

Dimitrios K. Korentzelos, Huaglory Tianfield, and Tom Buggy

School of Computing and Mathematical Sciences, Glasgow Caledonian University, 70
Cowcaddens Road, Glasgow G4 0BA, UK
{D.Korentzelos, H.Tianfield, T.Buggy}@gcal.ac.uk

Abstract. This paper presents a novel architecture Soph.I.A (Sophisticated Intelligent Architecture), which integrates Knowledge Management and Data Mining into a unified Knowledge Discovery Process. Within SophIA Data Mining is driven by knowledge captured from domain experts. Knowledge Grid is briefly reviewed to envision the implementation of the proposed framework.

Keywords: Data Mining, Knowledge Discovery Process, Knowledge Grid, Knowledge Management, Ontology.

1 Introduction

Data Mining (DM) is basically about knowledge discovery ([1] [5] [17]). Another field on knowledge discovery is Knowledge Management [15]. The adherence of DM with KM could be seen in Knowledge Mining. For instance, Knowledge-Based Systems can be used to discover knowledge on Knowledge Repositories [manipulating experts' knowledge], Data Warehouses and OLAP systems.

"Knowledge Discovery is the Process based on an intelligent and sophisticated mechanism, which works for the collection and process of data, information, and knowledge. This leads towards the discovery of expedient facts or relationships between them" [12]. The main characteristic of the Knowledge Discovery Process is that it has no compulsory tasks.

The use of *Domain Knowledge* could significantly improve the efficiency of Knowledge Discovery Process (KDP), if it is integrated within the process ([10] [18]). The domain expert can prevent the data miner from researching or being misguided within the database. It has to be noticed that during KDP, many potentially interesting patterns can be found but few of them contain nuggets interesting for the creation of new knowledge on the domain. Piatetsky-Shapiro [16] did a further analysis on objective rule interestingness. Obviously, there is a link between interestingness measures and domain knowledge. One of the challenges is how to capture the domain knowledge from the domain expert so to integrate it within the KDP mechanism.

Knowledge Management can have an important role during the KDP, in supporting the assimilation and capture of essential knowledge from the domain

P.S. Szczepaniak et al. (Eds.): AWIC 2005, LNAI 3528, pp. 486–491, 2005.

expert. For successful Knowledge Management, it is essential to have an effective collection, documentation, refinement, dissemination and utilisation of knowledge. Frank and Hampe [4] stress that Knowledge Management Systems (KMS) provide a collection of views, which are illustrated from user's perspective and conclude by sustaining that KMS can contribute towards overcoming the gap between business and technology. This gap is one of the factors that can block the effective use of computers and communications [11].

Another interesting perspective for processing human knowledge, so as to be generally accessible (e.g. in an organizational environment), is to implement Knowledge Management by the use of Ontologies. Gruber [7], defined 'Ontology', as the formal explicit specification of shared conceptualisation. Guarino [8] denoted that the problem of the above definition is the vagueness of the term 'conceptualisation'. After analysing several definitions, Guarino defined 'Ontology' as: "... a logical theory that constraints the indented models of a logical language" [8]. The construction of a knowledge base can be based on ontology and ontological theory. Guarino and Giaretta [9] gave three possible technical senses to the word 'Ontology': a)'ontological theory'; b)'Ontology' is a synonym of 'specification of an ontological commitment'; and c)'Ontology'is a synonym of 'conceptualisation'.

Ontologies can help Knowledge Management to form knowledge in a way so to be easily reusable. "Next generation knowledge management systems will likely rely on conceptual models in the form of ontologies to precisely define the meaning of various symbols" [14].

2   SophIA: An Architecture for Knowledge Discovery Process

This paper presents SophIA. SophIA's Knowledge Discovery Process is divided into four steps i.e. Domain Knowledge Assimilation, Data Preparation, Data Mining, and Knowledge Dispersion. Defining the boundaries, between different fields such as Data Mining and Knowledge Management, is helpful for the identification of malfunctions in KDP. Usually, several malfunctions happen during the transition from one step to another, especially when these steps belong to different disciplines. For example, the transition from 'Assimilation of Domain Knowledge' step (which involves how to manage knowledge) to 'Data Preparation' step (that has to do with managing data). For a smooth transition from one step to the other, the use of linkage steps (such as Data Understanding) is considered more than essential. SophIA's design supports the use of an object oriented design, a common sense language/rules (either for business people or for data miners) so to be able to translate/understand the messages from one discipline to another, an integrated user interface system and finally an easily comprehensible functionality.

SophIA's Design Rationale is characterised by the following attributes: a higher level of automation in KDP, higher level of abstraction, an effective User Interface, utilisation of Domain Knowledge (in order to reduce both the time that is needed for Knowledge Discovery, the amount of data that has to be processed during the KDP), and finally a unique repository of expert's knowledge, which can be fortified as intellectual capital.

Figure 1 presents the SophIA's Framework for the Knowledge Discovery Process. SophIA's kernel is the *Core Repository* (CR). CR holds information generated by both DM and KM, which has the potential to be transformed into new knowledge. The *Sophisticated Mechanism*, (see Figure 1) is responsible for managing knowledge that comes from a domain expert. Its basic parts are as follows: The *Domain Knowledge Worker Repository* (D-KnoWR), where the knowledge provided by the domain expert (with the help of a user interface) is stored, an Ontology responsible to translate the above knowledge, and the *Knowledge Repository* (KnoWR) where the translated domain knowledge from the Ontology is transformed into information. The KnoWR is also responsible to find new information, which could be considered as potential new knowledge (and so send them to the CR). The *Intelligent Mechanism*, is responsible for managing the data stored on a Data Warehouse. The results of mining, the Data Warehouse are also stored on CR. The information stored on CR, is processed so to give the new domain knowledge. With the help of a user interface, SophIA disseminates the new knowledge. The user interface is also used to answer any queries related to the new information.

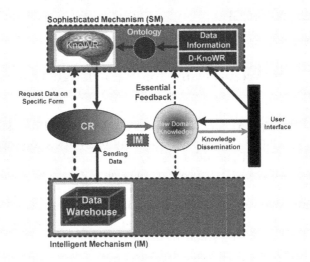

Fig. 1. Framework of SophIA

The Functionality steps of SophIA include: domain knowledge acquisition, data preparation, data mining, and knowledge dispersion.

Assimilation of Domain Knowledge. In general, the contribution of the business analyst is crucial, in guiding the data miner, for designing the DM project. Further assistance is essential for the data miner so to identify basic relationships or patterns, which the business analyst already knows. It would be easier for the data miner to extract information from a database, instead of trying to take advantage of the expert's knowledge instantly. Another significant reason for codifying business analyst's knowledge is that the human brain has capacity limitations and aging, comparing to computer databases, which are able to store, transfer, and manipulate petabytes. This step is an effort in the direction of the best possible way to codify domain knowledge. The main purpose is to enable the codified knowledge to be easily and comprehensibly accessible for the data miner. Figure 1 depicts SophIA's sophisticated mechanism for codifying domain knowledge: The business analyst, with the help of a user interface, passes his/her knowledge on to D-KnoWR. By the use of text mining techniques, several keywords are mined from D-KnoWR so to formulate an ontology. An object oriented schema, can be used to identify data, which has the potential to be interesting for the data miner. Finally, the data described from the ontology, is passed on to KnowR. Consequently, the data miner searches KnoWR for finding knowledge relative with the project's needs.

Data Preparation, in SophIA, involves the following steps: Transform the data from KnowR to the CR, enrich the CR with data from the DW and finally, prepare the data stored in CR for mining. This is feasible by organizing the data from knowR (used as metadata) and the data from the DW, in a structured model.

Data Mining. After the data is ready for mining, a specific type of algorithm (e.g. a back-propagation Neural Network algorithm) can be implemented. The type of algorithm depends on the type and the volume of the data. For instance, a clustering algorithm can be used to describe data that resides on the CR database. The purpose is to discover patterns with the potential to be characterised as new knowledge.

Knowledge Dispersion is the step where the results are expressed by the help of a user interface in a comprehensible way for the business analyst. The success of the whole process is measured primarily by checking if criteria as in manager's initial questionnaire have been answered, and secondly by investigating the optimisation of the new patterns that came up from SophIA.

3   The Advent of Knowledge Grid

The astonishing evolution of the World Wide Web has proved the power of global networking. The global use of the Web has created massive volume of data, information, and knowledge, which resides on servers in the form of HTML, XML documents and their derivatives. The superinduction of Ontologies, RDF and OWL languages, have transformed the Web into Semantic Web. In chorus, Grid technologies make an effort to take advantage of the data [data, information, and knowledge] that resides on Semantic Web.

Knowledge Grid is a relatively new concept regarding Grid terminology and definitions [2]. It can be said that Knowledge Grid is the evolution of merging Semantic Web with Grid Technology. Its effort is to collect and distribute Knowledge using the power of a Grid. Zhuge et al defined 'Knowledge Grid' as "...a mechanism that shares and manages the distributed heterogeneous re-

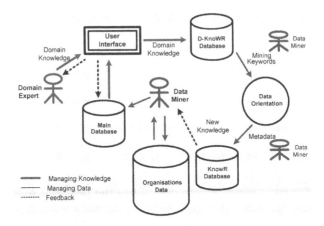

Fig. 2. Acquisition of Domain Knowlegde

sources spread across the Internet in a uniform way [19]. It has been advocated that Grid Architectures should be compliant with Open Grid Services Architecture (OGSA) [13] and Web Services Conceptual Architecture (WSCA) [3]. In an extended report for Semantic Web, Grid Computing and Cognitive/Knowledge/ Semantic Grid, Geldof [6] describes the benefits, the applications, the current status, critical issues and the challenges of Knowledge Grid.

4   Outlook

SophIA has been designed to take into consideration the use of domain expertise for the best possible implementation of a Knowledge Discovery Process. SophIA, is intended to manipulate knowledge that resides on the Knowledge Grid so to utilise it for more efficient guidance of Data Mining algorithms. Therefore, SophIA integrates an Unstructured Knowledge-Base and a Meta-Knowledge-Base, using Ontology as an interface. Currently, SophIA is in the stage of evaluating possible tools and platforms particularly from Knowledge Grid research for its implementation.

Acknowledgements

We are grateful to Professor Julian Newman for comments on an earlier version of this paper.

References

1. Fayyad, U., Piatetsky-Shapiro, G., Smyth, P.: The KDD Process for Extracting Useful Knowledge from Volumes of Data. Communicatios of the ACM. **39**(11) (1996) 27–34

2. Foster, I.: What is Grid? A Three Point Checklist. Argonne National Laboratory and University of Chicago. (2002)
3. Foster, I., Kesselman, C., Nick, J.M., Tuecke, S: An Open Grid Services Architecture. A Unified Framework for Distributed Systems Integration. Technical Report. Globus Project Technical Report. [Online: http://www.globus.org/research/papers/ogsa.pdf]. (2002)
4. Frank, U., Hampe, J. F.: An Object-Oriented Architecture for Knowledge Management Systems. Report Nr.16. Arbeitsberichte des Institus fur Wirtschaftsinformatic IWI. (1999)
5. Frawley, W.J., Piatetsky-Shapiro, G., Matheus, C.J.: Knowledge Discovery in Databases: An Overview. AI Magazine. **13**(3). (1992) 57–70
6. Geldof, M.: The Semantic Grid: Will the Semantic Web and Grid go Hand in Hand?. European commission DG Information Society Unit "Grid Technologies". (2004)
7. Gruber, T. R.: A Translation Approach to Portable Ontology Specifications. Knowledge Acquisition. **5**(2). (1995) 199–220
8. Guarino, N.: Understanding, Building, and Using Ontologies. LADSEB-CNR. National Research Council. Padova. Italy.
[http://ksi.cpsc.ucalgary.ca/KAW/KAW96/guarino/guarino.html]. (1996)
9. Guarino, N., Giaretta, P.: Ontologies and Knowledge Bases: Towards a Terminological Clarification. In Mars, N. (eds) (1995). Towards Very Large Knowledge Bases: Knowledge Building and Knowledge Sharing. IOS Press. Amsterdam. (1995) 25–32
10. Hsu, W. H., Welge, M., Redman, T., Clutter, D.: High Performance Commercial Data Mining: A Multi-strategy Machine Learning Application. Proceedings of the Data Mining and Knowledge Discovery. Kluwer Academic Publishers. **6**. (2001) 361–391
11. Keen, P.W.: Shaping the Future. Business Design through Information Technology. Harvard Business School. Press Boston. Massachusetts. (1991)
12. Korentzelos, D.: SophIA: A Mechanism for Knowledge Discovery. PhD Transfer Report CMS/COM/2004/9. Glasgow Caledonian University. Glasgow. UK. (2004)
13. Kreger, H.: Shaping the Future. Web Services Conceptual Architecture. Technical Report WSCA 1.0. IBM Software Group. (2001)
14. Maedche, A., Motik, B., Stojanovic, L., Studer, R., Volz, R.: Ontologies for Enterprise Knowledge Management. IEEE Computer Society. (2003) 26–33
15. Newman, B.: An Open Discussion of Knowledge Management. [Online: http://www.km-forum.org/]. (1991)
16. Piatetsky-Shapiro, G.: Discovery, analysis, and presentation of strong rules. In Piatetsky-Shapiro, G., Frawley, W. (eds). In Knowledge Discovery in Databases. AAAI/MIT Press. Menlo Park.CA. (1991) 229–248
17. Simoudis, E., Cabena, P., Haddjimian, P., Standler, R., Varhees, J., Zanasi, A.: Discovering Data Mining, From Concept to Implementation. Prentice Hall PTR. (1997)
18. Yoon, S. C., Henschen, L. J., Park, E. K., Makki, S.: Using Domain Knowledge in Knowledge Discovery. Proceedings of the 4th International Conference on Information and Knowledge Management (CIKM'99). ACM Press. (1999) 243–250
19. Zhuge, H., Liu, J.: A Fuzzy Collaborative Assessment Aproach for Knowledge Grid. Future Computer Systems 20. (2004) 101–111

Adapting the Weka Data Mining Toolkit to a Grid Based Environment

María S. Pérez, Alberto Sánchez, Pilar Herrero, Víctor Robles,
and José M. Peña

Facultad de Informática, Universidad Politécnica de Madrid, Madrid, Spain

Abstract. Data Mining is playing a key role in most enterprises, which have to analyse great amounts of data in order to achieve higher profits. Nevertheless, due to the large datasets involved in this process, the data mining field must face some technological challenges. Grid Computing takes advantage of the low-load periods of all the computers connected to a network, making possible resource and data sharing. Providing Grid services constitute a flexible manner of tackling the data mining needs. This paper shows the adaptation of Weka, a widely used Data Mining tool, to a grid infrastructure.

Keywords: *Data Mining, Data Mining Grid, Grid Services, Weka Tool.*

1 Introduction

Data mining is a complex problem, mainly because of the difficulty of its tasks and the huge volume of data involved in it. Roughly, the data mining tasks can be classified as preprocessing, specific data mining tasks (e.g, rule induction) and postprocessing tasks.

Several initiatives have tried to eliminate this complexity. In this sense, one of the most important trend is the development of high performance data mining systems [8].

Nevertheless, traditional and homogeneous distributed systems do not solve the challenging issues related to data mining. Grid computing has emerged as a new technology, whose main challenge is the complete integration of heterogeneous computing systems and data resources with the aim of providing a global computing space [4]. We propose the use of the grid technology as a new framework in which data mining applications can be sucessfully deployed.

On the other hand, Weka [11] is a widely used Data Mining tool, written in Java. This paper describes a generic architecture for making data mining grid-aware services. It also addresses WekaG, an implementation of this architecture, which uses Weka.

This paper is organized as follows. Section 2 shows how the grid technology allows data mining tasks to be performed in a flexible way. Section 3 describes WekaG, an adaptation of Weka to a grid environment. Furthermore, a generic architecture for making data mining libraries grid-aware is shown. This architecture is referred to as DMGA (Data Mining Grid Architecture). Section 4 analyses a sample data mining algorithm, the Apriori algorithm, deployed in a grid environment. Section 5 talks about works related to our proposal. Finally, we conclude with some remarks and the ongoing and future work.

P.S. Szczepaniak et al. (Eds.): AWIC 2005, LNAI 3528, pp. 492–497, 2005.

2   Data Mining Grid

Data mining applications demand new alternatives in the field of discovery, data place-
ment, scheduling, resource management, and transactional systems, among others. This
is due in part to the following reasons:

- It is required to access to multiple databases and data holders, in general, because
  no single database is able to hold all data required by an application.
- In a generic scenario, multiple databases do not belong to the same institution and
  are not situated at the same location, but geographically distributed.
- For increasing the performance of some steps of the data mining process, it is possible to use local copies of the whole dataset or subsets.
- Business databases or datasets may be updated frequently, which implies replication and coherency problems.

Several architectures have been proposed. In [3], Cannataro et al. define the *Knowledge Grid* as an architecture built on top of a computational grid. This architecture
extends the basic grid services with services of knowledge discovery on geographically
distributed infrastructures.

Another different architecture has been proposed by Giannadakis et al. in [6], named
InfoGrid. InfoGrid is mainly focused on the data integration. This infrastructure includes a layer of Information Integration Services, which enables heterogeneous information resources to be queried effectively.

In [10], we introduce a generic and vertical architecture (DMGA) based on the
main data mining phases: pre-processing, data mining and post-processing. Within this
framework, the main phases are deployed by means of grid services. WekaG, explained
in the following section, is an implementation of this architecture.

3   WekaG: A Data Mining Tool for Grids

Weka is a collection of machine learning algorithms for data mining tasks developed
at the University of Waikato in New Zealand [11]. Weka contains tools for all the data
mining phases: data pre-processing, data mining tasks (e.g. classification, regression,
clustering, association rules), and data post-processing. One important feature of this
toolkit is the flexibility of this tool for developing new machine learning schemes.

WekaG is thought as an extension of Weka for grid environments. WekaG is based
on a client/server architecture. The server side is the responsible of the creation of instances of grid services by using a factory pattern. These grid services implement the
functionality of the different algorithms and phases of the data mining process.

We have also developed a WekaG client, which is responsible for communicating
with the grid service and offering the interface to users. In this way, Weka is not modified. We only add a new input in the Graphical User Interface for providing this new
capability.

The main purpose of adapting Weka to a grid environment is to define an infrastructure for data mining that includes at least the following components and features:

- Coupling data sources, which can be dynamically installed and configured. This characteristic makes easier data movement and replication. Data filtering, data replication and use of local datasets help to enhance the efficiency of data mining applications on grid infrastructures.
- Authorized access to data resources, providing a controlled sharing of data within a virtual organization [5]. This implies the use of authentication and access control mechanisms, in the form of access policies, by using GSI (Grid Security Infrastructure).
- Data discovery based on metadata attributes.
- Planning and scheduling resources to the data mining tasks.
- Based on the application, and maybe on other parameters provided by the user, we can identify the available and appropriate resources to use within the grid. This task could be carried out by a broker function. In this case, if we have several equal or different grid services in different locations, we can use a trading protocol for deciding at run time which one can provide the features which fit most to the client requirements.

Although WekaG constitutes a useful tool for data mining, our main purpose is to extend this functionality for several libraries and new algorithms. In this sense, WekaG is a particular implementation of a more general architecture, whose name is DMGA (Data Mining Grid Architecture). DMGA is shown in Figure 1.

As we can see in this figure, we have chosen the use of Globus Toolkit 3 (GT3 in the figure). This release of Globus is stable.

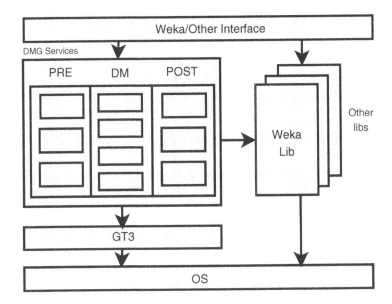

Fig. 1. DMGA Overview

DMGA can be thought as a flexible way of making services grid aware. Our services offer a client and an user interface, hiding all the problematic related to the management of GT3, which is tackled by the appropriate grid service.

4   AprioriG: A WekaG Case Study

We have built a first prototype, which demonstrates the feasibility of our design. Our first prototype only includes a sample data mining service, but we will intend to create several grid services, which can be composed in order to create dynamic workflows, which improve the Weka functionality. This prototype implements the capabilities of the Apriori algorithm [1] in a grid environment. The Apriori service (`buildAsso-ciation`), which produces association rules from a dataset, is specified by means of WSDL (Web Services Description Language).

For the development of this functionality, we have used the object serialization, in order to store and retrieve the state of the required objects. This feature allows Weka to be extensible to support marshaling and unmarshaling and thus, to access to

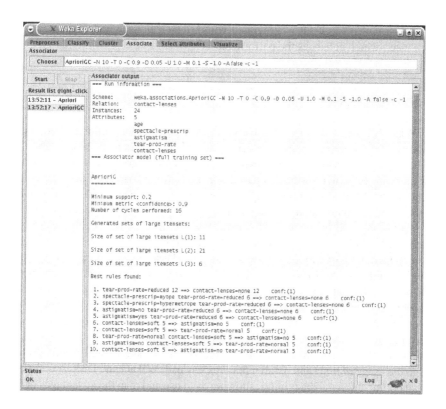

Fig. 2. AprioriG demonstration

remote objects. Most of the Weka classes are serializable, and specifically the Apriori class:

```
public class Apriori extends Associator implements
                        OptionHandler, CARuleMiner {
    /* Apriori class extends the abstrac class
       Associator */
}


public abstract class Associator implements
                        Cloneable, Serializable {
    /* Associator class implements the interface
       Serializable */
}
```

Figure 2 shows an example of execution of the Apriori algorithm over a sample dataset. The algorithm is performed by the AprioriG service, whose results are sent back to the client graphical user interface.

For the deployment of the files to the Grid services nodes, we use GridFTP [2]. The main reason is that GridFTP is integrated within the Grid stack and supports parallel data transfer, which enhances the performance.

5   Related Work

Grid Weka [7] is being developed in University College Dublin. In this system, the execution of all the tasks are distributed across several computers in an ad-hoc Grid. This proposal does not constitute a real adaptation of Weka to a grid environment, because the framework in which this tool is based is closed. Weka Grid provides load balancing and allow Weka to use idle computing resources. However, it does not provide a "flexible, secure, coordinated resource sharing among dynamic collections of individuals, institutions, and resources". Moreover, Weka Grid does not use an OGSA-style service, unlike WekaG, whose services are OGSA-compliant. Finally, WekaG is a specific implementation of a more general architecture (DMGA). Our purpose is to extend the functionality of DMGA with different libraries and algorithms, providing a flexible set of services for data mining, which can be used by different virtual organizations, transcending geographical boundaries.

On the other hand, the authors of this paper have developed earlier other tools for performing the Apriori algorithm in a parallel fashion. In [9], an optimization of this algorithm is shown. This work adapts the underlying storage system to this problem through the usage of hints and parallel features. Instead, WekaG and DMGA constitutes a global optimization to data mining, allowing us to use and reap the advantages of Grid computing in this heavy process.

6   Conclusions and Ongoing Work

This paper describes a generic architecture for making data mining grid-aware services. As an implementation of this architecture, WekaG provides all the functionality of Weka in a grid environment. We have developed a prototype of WekaG, porting the logic of the Apriori algorithm to this new framework.

The advantages of this proposal include the possibility of offering different data mining services in a combined and flexible way, making use of trading and negotiation protocols for selecting the most appropriate service.

As ongoing and future work, we are extending our prototype for building a complete WekaG tool, which includes all the algorithms. Our future work will also include the composition of grid services with the aim of providing suitable data mining services. Additionally, we will evaluate the performance of WekaG in a grid environment composed of different virtual organizations.

References

1. Rakesh Agrawal, Tomasz Imielinski, and Arun Swami. Mining association rules between sets of items in large databases. In *The 1993 ACM SIGMOD International Conference on Management of Data*, 1993.
2. W. Allcock, J. Bester, A. Bresnahan, A. Chervenak, L. Liming, and S. Tuecke. GridFTP: Protocol extensions to FTP for the Grid. *Global Grid Forum Draft*, 2001.
3. Mario Cannataro and Domenico Talia. The knowledge grid. *Commun. ACM*, 46(1):89–93, 2003.
4. I. Foster and C. Kesselman, editors. *The Grid: Blueprint for a New Computing Infrastructure*. Morgan Kaufmann, 1999.
5. Ian Foster. The anatomy of the Grid: Enabling scalable virtual organizations. *Lecture Notes in Computer Science*, 2150, 2001.
6. N. Giannadakis, A. Rowe, M. Ghanem, and Y. Guo. InfoGrid: providing information integration for knowledge discovery. *Information Sciences. Special Issue: Knowledge Discovery from Distributed Information Sources*, 155(3–4):199–226, October 2003.
7. Rinat Khoussainov, Xin Zuo, and Nicholas Kushmerick. Grid-enabled Weka: A toolkit for machine learning on the grid. *ERCIM News*, 59, October 2004.
8. William A. Maniatty and Mohammed J. Zaki. A requirements analysis for parallel kdd systems. In Jose Rolim et al., editor, *3rd IPDPS Workshop on High Performance Data Mining*, pages 358–265, May 2000.
9. María S. Pérez, Ramón A. Pons, Félix García, Jesús Carretero, and María L. Córdoba. An optimization of Apriori algorithm through the usage of parallel I/O and hints. *Rough Sets and Current Trends in Computing (LNAI 2475)*, October 2002.
10. Alberto Sánchez, José M. Peña Sánchez, María S. Pérez, Victor Robles, and Pilar Herrero. Improving distributed data mining techniques by means of a grid infrastructure. In Robert Meersman, Zahir Tari, and Angelo Corsaro, editors, *OTM Workshops*, volume 3292 of *Lecture Notes in Computer Science*, pages 111–122. Springer, 2004.
11. H. Witten and Eibe Frank. *Data Mining: Practical machine learning tools with Java implementations*. Morgan Kaufmann, San Francisco, 2000.

DCP-Grid
A Framework for Concurrent Distributed Transactions on Grid Environments

Manuel Salvadores[1], Pilar Herrero[2], Maria S.Pérez[2], and Víctor Robles[2]

[1] IMCS, Imbert Management Consulting Solutions IMCS,
C/ Fray Juan Gil 7, 28002 Madrid , Spain
[2] Facultad de Informática - Universidad Politécnica de Madrid,
Campus de Montegancedo S/N, 28660 Boadilla del Monte, Madrid, Spain

Abstract. This paper presents a Framework for Concurrent Distribute Transaction processing over Grid Environment, called DCP-Grid. DCP-Grid complements Web Services with some OGSI functionalities to implement the Two Phase Commit (2-PC) protocol to manage Distribute Transactions properly in this kind of environment. Although DCP-Grid is still under development at the Universidad Politécnica de Madrid, in this paper, we present the design and the general characteristics associated to the implementation of our proposed Framework.

1   Introduction

The introduction of Services Oriented Architectures (SOA) [1] [2], in the last few years, has increased the use of new distributed technologies based on Web Services (WS) [3]. In fact, e-science and e-business processes have adopted this technology to improve the integration of some applications. The coordination of this type of processes, based on WS, needs the transactional capability to ensure the consistency of those data that are being handled by this kind of applications.

A transaction could be defined as the sequence of actions to be executed in an atomic way. This means that all the actions should finish - correctly or incorrectly- at the same time as if they were an unique action.

The four key properties associated to the transactions processing are known as the ACID properties - Atomicity, Consistency, Isolation, and Durability [4]. The aim of our proposal is to build a Framework, based on grid technologies, to coordinate distributed transactions that are handling operations deployed as Web Services.

The Grid Technology, which was born at the beginning of the 90s , is based on providing an infrastructure to share and coordinate the resources through the dynamic organizations which are virtually distributed [5] [6].

In order to make possible the development of DCP-Grid we will take into account the Grid Web Services (GWS) characteristics. The GWS, defined in the Open Grid Service Infraestructure (OGSI) [7], could be considered as an

P.S. Szczepaniak et al. (Eds.): AWIC 2005, LNAI 3528, pp. 498–503, 2005.

extensin of the WS. The GWS introduce some improvement on WS, which are necessary to the construction of standard, heterogeneous and open Grid Systems. The OGSI characteristics on which DCP-Grid has being designed and built are: Stateful and potentially transient services; Service Data; Notifications; portType extensin; Grid Service Handle (GSH) and Grid Service Referente (GSR).

OGSI is just an specification, not a software platform, and therefore, we need a middleware platform, supporting this specification, in order to deploy the DCP-Grid Framework. From all the possible patforms to be used, we have decided to use the Globus Toolkit [8] platform for this Project because in the most extended nowadays. More specifically, we have being working with GT3 (version 3.2) for DCP-Grid due to its stability.

In this paper we will start describing the state of the art in the dealing area as well as their contributions to the DCP-Grid design, subsequently we will move to the architectural design of our proposal and we will give some details related to the framework implementation to finish with some conclusions, ongoing directions and future work.

2   Related Work

The standard distributed transaccional processing model more extended is the X/Open [14] model, which defines three rolls (Resource Manager RM,Transaction Processing Manager TPM and Aplication Program AP) [9] [14]. Conceptually, the three rolls interact as described in the following figure: Based on the Web Service technology two specifications to standardize the handling of transactions through open environments have arisen. These specifications are WS-

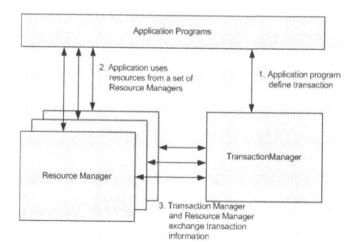

Fig. 1. X/Open Model Roles Interaction

Coordination [10] and WS-Transaction [13], developed by IBM, Bea and Microsoft. In them, the way to group multiple Web Services as a transaction is exposed, but the form of coordination of the transactions is not specified. On the other hand, the Business Transaction Protocol specification (BTP) [13], proposed by OASIS, defines a transaccional coordination based on workflows. This specification is complex to handle and integrate [12]. Based on GT3 [8] we try to construct a simple proposal for the implementation of a transaccional manager adopting the X/Open model show in Fig. 1. In the proposed design, the analogies are visible.

3   DCP-Grid Design

The architectural design for DCP-Grid, based on the X/Open model [14], raise the RM and TPM roles as Grid WS taking advantage of the OGSI characteristics [7]. The AP layer is defined as a Grid client to handle the transaction.

In the following sub-sections, we will describe the design of each of these components.

3.1   Resource Manager (RM) Design

In DCP-Grid, the interface associated to the RM component is imbibed in the TransactionSupportService Grid WS and therefore each transactional service before interacting with the TPM should extend from this service. Our design takes advantage of the OGSI PortType Extensin characteristic. Due to this characteristic, it is possible to extend the WS functionality with some inheritance relations.

The RM's operations defined in the TransactionSupportService interface are:

TransactionSupporService		
commit()	commitAtomicOperation()	readyToCommit()
rollback()	rollbackAtomicOperation()	

Fig. 2. TransactionSupport interface

The commit, rollback and readyToCommitOperation operations will allow to exchange information to coordinate the transaction in between the TPM and the RM (Fig. 1, step 3). Any service could be part of a transaction coordinated by DCP-Grid. This is the reason why the commit and rollback processes of each of these services are delegated in the service development.

This is the reason why the commitAtomicOperation and rollbackAtomicOperation operations are abstracts and must be implemented by their respective services extending from the TransactionSupportService service. For example, if the service is an access to a RDBMS, then the commitAtomicOperation and rollbackAtomicOperation operations will carry on a commit/rollback of the connexion established with the RDBMS.

Moreover, the TransactionSupportService has associated a Service Data Element SDE [7], named statusOperation, to keep the transactional state. These estates are defined as PROCESS, READY_TO_COMMIT, ROLLBACK and COMMITED. When the extended service request, the logic implemented in TransactionSupportService change the value of the operation's state as:

```
exampleService() {
try {
//Process service
// i.e. RDBMS Transaction
} catch (Exception e) {
rollback();
throw new RemoteException(e.getMessage());
}
readyToCommit();
}
```

The operation readyToCommit changes the SDE value and notify the changes to the TPM:

```
readyToCommit() {
operationInfoType.setStatus(READY_TO_COMMIT);
operationInfoSDE.notifyChange();
}
```

As for the rollback operation, the sequence would be similar, but taking into account that the rollbackAtomicOperation service knows that the transaction has already failed.

3.2   Transaction Processing Manager (TPM) Design

The TPM is based on the subscription to the value changes of the SDE statusOperation. Grid WS has this property when they are working in a listener mode [7]. Once the service has processed the business logia, the operation will change the value of the SDE and will notify the change to all the SDE subscriptions.

In DCP-Grid, the TPM is the Grid WS TXCoordinationService. This service keeps the structure of the information associated to those services that comprise the transaction. The addAtomicOperation(GSH) [7] operation will build this structure, and once all the Grid Services Handle (GSH) has been added to this structure, the beginTransaction() method will start the TPM process initialising all the subscriptions to each of these Grid WS.

Every time that each of these atomics operations change the SDE statusOperation value, and notify this change (see section 3.2), the TPM will detect if the state's change, updating the information. In this change, the algorithm to handle the transaction will be processed with the new value obtained in the SDE statusOperation.

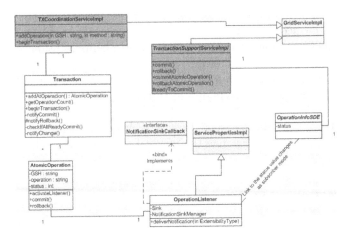

Fig. 3. Global design of DCP-Grid

*if (value == ROLLBACK) notifyRollback(); //Sends a ROLLBACK message
to all GSH less to the ROLLBACK sender.
if (value == READY_TO_COMMIT) {
updateInformation();
if (checkIfAllReadyCommit()) notifyCommit(); // Send a commit message (par-
allelly) to each GSH.*

To provide a concurrent access, we have decided to deploy the TXCoordinationService as Transient Service [7]. In this way, if there is not problems with
the concurrency while accessing to the instanced date associated to a statefull
Grid WS. In the following diagram (Fig. 3) it is possible to appreciate the blocks
previously described.

3.3   Aplication Program (AP) Design

The applicational layer is reduced to a logic in which the client will interact with
the TPM, through the TXCoordinationService. The sequence of steps that the
grid client has to follow to carry on a transaction will be:

1. Instance to the transient TXCoordinationService Grid WS
2. Add all the GSH that are comprising the transaction through the addAtomi-
   cOperation operation
3. Invoke to the beginTransaction() method
4. Invoke to all the GSH comprising the transaction

4   Conclusions, Ongoing and Future Work

In this paper we have presented our approach to implement an architecture supporting transactional Grid WS execution. This approach is based on some of

the main properties of OGSI specification [7]. As ongoing work, currently we are developing a similar framework for conversational distributed transactions on grid environments which will be presented in the Workshop on Grid Computing Security and Resource Management (GSRM'05). So many future research lines has been opened for DCP-Grid but maybe the most interesting would be the building of an environment to support transactions on distributed and heterogeneous databases based on the concepts and ideas that we have presented in this paper.

References

1. Douglas K. Barry. Web Services and Service-Oriented Architecture: The Savvy Manager's Guide. Morgan Kaufmann Publishers 2003
2. Mark Endrei, Jenny Ang, Ali Arsanjani, Sook Chua, Philippe Comte, Pal Krogdahl, Min Luo, Tony Newling. Patterns. Service Oriented Architecture. IBM RedBook SG24-6303-00
3. Web Services Main Page at W3C. http://www.w3.org/2002/ws/, Worl Wide Web Consortium.
4. Bernstein. New Comer Principles of Transaction Processing, Kaufman 1997
5. I. Foster, C. Kesselman. The Physiology of the Grid: An Open Grid Services Arquitecture for Distributed System Integration. 2002. http://www.globus.org/research/papers/ogsa.pdf
6. Miguel L. Bote-Lorenzo, Yannis A. Dimitriadis, Eduardo Gmez-Snchez. Grid Characteristics and Uses: A Grid Definition, LNCS 2970, 291-298
7. S. Tuecke, K. Czajkowski, I. Foster. Grid Service Specification. Technical Report. Jun 2003. http://www.globus.org/research/papers.html
8. Globus Toolkit Project, The Globus Alliance, http://www.globus.org
9. I. C. Jeong, Y. C. Lew. DCE "Distributed Computing Environment" based DTP Distributed Transaction Processing Information Networking (ICOIN-12) Jan. 1998
10. F. Cabrera et al., Web Services Coordination (WS-Coordination) Aug. 2002, ww.ibm.com/developerworks/library/ws-coor/
11. F. Cabrera et al., Web Services Transaction (WS-Transaction) Aug. 2002, www.ibm.com/developerworks/library/ws-transpec/.
12. Feilong Tang, Minglu Li, Jian Cao, Qianni Deng, Coordination Business Transaction for Grid Service. LNCS3032 pag. 108-114 (Related Work Section)
13. OASIS BTP Committee Specification 1.0, 3 June 2002, Business Transaction Protocol,
http://www.choreology.com/downloads/2002-06-03.BTP.Committee.spec.1.0.pdf
14. X/Open Specification, 1988, 1989, February 1992, Commands and Utilities, Issue 3 (ISBN: 1-872630-36-7, C211); this specification was formerly X/Open Portability Guide, Volume 1, January 1989 XSI Commands and Utilities. ISBN: 0-13-685835-X, XO/XPG/89/002.

A Roadmap to the Grid e-Workspace

Michalis Vafopoulos

Department of Business Administration,
University of the Aegean, Greece

Abstract. The GRID e-workspace provides a web-based integrated and collaborative hardware and software resources for an individual or an enterprise. Concentrates all services in a single domain for all citizens and companies in a specific geographical region in a collaborative working environment where it is possible to produce, post, search and exchange structured information. The GRID e-workspace is defined to have four interconnected aspects (a) digital storage, (b) network traffic, (c) processing power and (d) web services. Implementation issues involve organizational, social, economical and technological aspects. General principles driving our analysis could be summarized in the following: Co-operation culture and technological level characterizing societies under consideration determine: (i) business model (public-private funding mixture) and (ii) technology (centrality of entities).

1 Introduction

According to [11] "The HyperClustering framework, is a general operational web-based structure for a local economy which semantically analyses, clusters, integrates and boosts personal and social activities". Institutions (government, NGOs and private companies) and citizens are the two building blocks of the HyperClustering framework (Fig. 2). For example, a freelancer uses software (citizens back - office function) to produce a service, gets help in development from a company (shared workspace) and adopts standards introduced by government authorities (shared workspace). A small part of this process could be public in order to i.e. attract potential customers and employees (public view). Section 2 describes the GRID e-workspace as an envelope practice and a knowledge-based development mechanism. Section 3 introduces a decision matrix for real conditions identification and describes the adoption of Synchronization Point model as an information and security management component.

2 The GRID e-Workspace: An Envelope Practice and a Knowledge-Based Development Mechanism

The GRID e-workspace is defined to have four interconnected aspects:

1. Digital Storage (bytes)
2. Network Traffic (bits per second)

P.S. Szczepaniak et al. (Eds.): AWIC 2005, LNAI 3528, pp. 504–509, 2005.

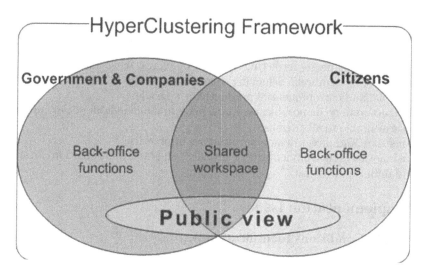

Fig. 1. The HyperClustering framework methodology

3. Processing Power (hertz)
4. Web Services (one-stop service provision model [10])

The first three factors are related to technological infrastructure investments. One-stop web services is the fundamental factor for ICT exploitation. In this context, HyperClustering is introducing an innovative, complete and direct method to employ ICT for local development by offering a creative and functional environment which encourages, structures and diffuses personal and social knowledge instauration. At the first stage, we develop synergies among human activities by mapping implementation paths for the most popular of them. Based on this structured information standard, a web-based Virtual Organization is constructed which integrates all the major activities of a local economy. The added value of Hyper-Clustering focuses on upgrading business environment by creating and organizing workflows between community members and exploiting the network externalities and spillovers ICT offer. Our research focuses on less favored regions at E.U., where there is locality awareness and substantial digital divide. We argue that access to structured information and computing power has to be public good in order to boost regional development. The final stage of HyperClustering constitutes the creation of GRID [9] e-workspace for every citizen and company. HyperClustering is defined to be top-level clustering of all fields in business life. Concepts of intra-regional learning networks [12], virtual communities of practice [4, 5, 6] online communities [7] and super-networks [8] are subsets of the proposed framework. Concurrently, operates on a semantic web portal basis as the *unique electronic gate* for a specific geographical region promoting:

1. Established web services like e-mail, yellow pages, maps, tour guides.
2. Innovative web services including semantic e-commerce and auctioning services for local goods, human resources, raw materials.
3. Advantageous mega-marketing features by aggregating marketing expenses under a single umbrella achieving economies of scale.
4. Personal and entrepreneurial productivity upgrade.
5. A structured, no disposable, comprehensive and expandable social knowledge base available to all citizens.
6. eInclusion and direct democracy schemes in practice.
7. An innovative environment where new ideas and individual creation can emerge and diffuse in less cost.

3   Implementation Issues

3.1   Real Conditions Identification

Implementation issues involve organizational, social, economical and technological aspects. General principles driving our analysis could be summarized in the following: *Co-operation culture* (which includes business culture) and *technological level* characterizing societies under consideration determine:

1. Business model (public-private funding mixture) and
2. Technology (centrality of entities).

In this context a decision matrix is introduced (Fig. 3.1). The fundamental idea is that in a society with low cooperation culture and low technological level (square 1) governmental action, education and more "centralized" technology is needed. On the contrary, for developed societies (square 4) is proposed a highly flexible private organizational scheme coupled by a powerful public-owned security and personal privacy unit. At the technological level, open and decentralized GRID services based on user's content contribution complete the development path. In the middle case at square 2 political decisions for technological investments are required since people "demand" effective means of cooperation. At square 3, technology is present but dissemination of its benefits to collaborative working environment is needed.

3.2   Building a Collaborative Working Environment

In HyperClustering framework [11] in order to tackle the complex challenges of building comprehensive user-centric model, a life-event approach was introduced. The human life-cycle model proposed, is based on the socioeconomic needs during different phases of a human being's life. Consequently, time paths and interdependencies between e-applications (Fig. 3.2) identified with the human life-cycle model are modeled and described in machine-readable language based on Topic Maps (www.topicmaps.org) and XML schemas. In this context, major role is assigned to an administrative unit consisting of three basic components: (1) *Information management and workflow* component, (2) *Security and personal data* component and (3) *Standardization* component. For components (1) and (2) modeling, the Synchronization Point (SP) methodology [12] is followed. "SP starts when

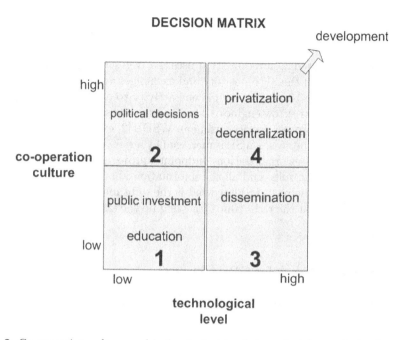

Fig. 2. Co-operation culture and technological level characterizing societies determine business and technological model for GRID e-workspace to be implemented

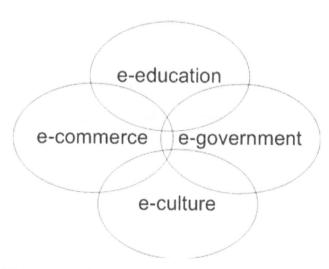

Fig. 3. Building synergies between e-applications is a key factor to integrated web services

partners decide to start a cooperative activity in order to ful?ll a given objective. Each partner only describes its activities, and contracts are established to express conditions and terms of data exchange and share. ..The current implementation is based on a distributed architecture that uses the Web services technology. Each partner hosts a part of the SP repository and exchanges are done using SOAP [1] messages..We use late binding to couple one activity to respectively an application, a participant, a work?ow engine or a back-end process. The only requirement is the description of process services using an WSDL [2] extended version for describing processes properties. An SP is managed by a tier (which can be viewed as a broker). The tier stores organizations endpoints, projects, abstract descriptions of processes, contracts, roles and all the information about SPs. A contract is a XML document that helps us to filter what is the right information to provide to the right participant at the right time by setting up the exchange between two or more partners."

3.3   Basic Framework for GRID Services

Web services originated in order to help and replace services occur in the traditional physical space. Due to heterogeneity and evolving nature characterizing human needs, combined to scarce resources available, emphasis must be given to knowledge management of web services. Namely, an ex ante topic mapping for web services interactions and interconnections could be crucial in comprehensive one-stop services development (Fig. 4). Despite the fact that popular standards for web services interoperability, information retrieval and knowledge discovery technologies analyze methods applied in existing and new datasets, have never being used explicitly and systematically in motivating novel knowledge creation. The final fundamental stage of HyperClustering is designed to be the introduction of the GRID e-workspace. The GRID e-workspace provides a web-based integrated and collaborative hardware and software resources for an individual or an enterprise. Concentrates all services in a single domain for all citizens and companies in a specific geographical region in a collaborative working environment where it is possible to produce, post, search and exchange structured information based on Open Grid Services Infrastructure 1.0 specification [3] which integrates WS-Resource Framework with GRID infrastructure. The HyperClustering framework offers a creative and functional environment which encourages, structures and diffuses personal and social knowledge instauration.

4   Further Research

Since the current paper is an introduction to the interdisciplinary analysis of the GRID e-workspace many issues remain unsolved needed further research. Knowledge representation techniques, XML schemas binding, GRID technologies for many users and random demand, economical, political and social implications of the GRID e-workspace, form an indicative list of issues for further investigation.

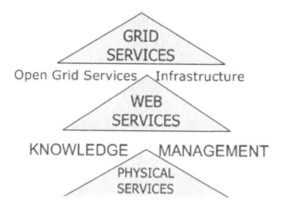

Fig. 4. From physical to GRID e-workspace

References

[1] Simple Object Access Protocol (SOAP) 1.1. W3C, May 2000
[2] Web Services Description Language (WSDL) 1.1. W3C, March 2001
[3] From Open Grid Services Infrastructure to WSResource Framework: Refactoring & Evolution; GLOBUS. http://www.globus.org/wsrf/specs/ogsi_to_wsrf_1.0.pdf
[4] Cronin, B. (Ed.): Annual review of information science and technology. Medford, NJ: Information Today (2002)
[5] Rheingold, H.: The virtual community: Finding connection in a competitive world. London: Secker and Warburg (1994)
[6] Wenger, E., Snyder, W.: Communities of practice: The organizational frontier. Harvard Business Review (January/February) (2000) 139-145
[7] Hall, H., Graham, D.: Creation and recreation: motivating knowledge capital in online communities. International Journal of Information Management (2004)
[8] Nagurney, A., Dong, J.: Supernetworks: Decision-Making for the Information Age. Edward Elgar Publishers Cheltenham England (2002)
[9] Foster, I., Kesselman, S., Tuecke, S.: The anatomy of the GRID: Enabling scalable virtual organizations. International Journal of Super Computer Applications **15** **(3)**, 2001
[10] Gouscos, D., Laskaridis, G., Lioulias, D., Mentzas, M., Georgiadis, P.: An approach to Offering One-Stop e-Government Services: Available Technologies and Architectural Issues. Proc. of the EGOV 2002 Conf. eds. R.Traunmuller & K. Lenk Springer-Verlag Berlin Heidelberg (2002) 264 - 271
[11] Vafopoulos, M., Aggelis, V., Platis, A.: HyperClustering: from digital divide to the GRID e-workspace. Proc. of the Data Mining 2005 conf. forthcoming
[12] Davenport, T., Prusak, L.: Working Knowledge: How Organizations Manage What They Know. Harvard Business School Press (1998)

Author Index

Lecture Notes in Artificial Intelligence (LNAI)